Taiv

a travel survival kit

Robert Storey

Taiwan – a travel survival kit

3rd edition

Published by
   Lonely Planet Publications
   Head Office: PO Box 617, Hawthorn, Vic 3122, Australia
   Branches: 155 Filbert St, Suite 251, Oakland, CA 94607, USA
                  10 Barley Mow Passage, Chiswick, London W4 4PH, UK
                  71 bis rue du Cardinal Lemoine, 75005 Paris, France

Printed by
   Singapore National Printers Ltd, Singapore

Photographs by
   Martin Moos (MM)
   Robert Storey (RS)
   Robert Strauss (R Strauss)
   Chris Taylor (CT)

   Front cover: Nankunshen Temple Mural, Taiwan (Steve Satushek), The Image Bank

First Published
   November 1987

This Edition
   July 1994

Although the author and publisher have tried to make the information as accurate as possible, they accept no responsibility for any loss, injury or inconvenience sustained by any person using this book.

National Library of Australia Cataloguing in Publication Data

Storey, Robert
   Taiwan – a travel survival kit.

   3rd ed.
   Includes index.
   ISBN 0 86442 228 8.

   1. Taiwan – Guide-books.
   I. Title. (Series: Lonely Planet travel survival kit).

915.1249045

text © Robert Storey 1994
maps © Lonely Planet 1994
photos © photographers as indicated 1994
climate charts compiled from information supplied by Patrick J Tyson, © Patrick J Tyson, 1994

Robert Storey

A refugee from the Third World (New York city), Robert climbed out of poverty and has since had a number of distinguished careers, including monkeykeeper at a zoo and slot-machine repairman in a Las Vegas casino. After graduating from the University of Nevada in Las Vegas with a worthless liberal arts degree, he then went on-the-road. In Taiwan, he ran out of funds and started a new career as an English teacher. Robert then diligently learned Chinese, wrote a textbook for teaching English *(Creative Conversation)*, went to work for Lonely Planet and became a respectable citizen and a pillar of the community. In an attempt to improve his own memory before senility sets in, Robert is currently writing a textbook for foreigners called *Memorising Chinese Characters*.

From the Author

I'd like to express my gratitude to a number of travellers and foreign residents of Taiwan, including Mark DeForge (USA), Eddy Butler (France), Bryan L Smith (USA), Krista Calhoun (USA), Suzie Tombs (UK), Peter Lines (UK) and Patricia Naccarato (Italy). Also thanks to computer expert Carlos McEvilly (USA), author of the programme 'Bamboo Helper'; and to Richard Flasher (USA), whitewater rafter extraordinaire.

There are many Chinese residents of Taiwan whose contributions to this book helped enormously. Special thanks to longtime friends George Lu of Kaohsiung and Chen Longchen of Tainan. Also thanks to Coco Lee of Taitung for superb hospitality; Liao Yuanxuan of Taichung for help with Chinese calligraphy; and Hsieh Yuhsia, Chiayi County's leading mountaineer and guide.

From the Publisher

This third edition of *Taiwan – a travel survival kit* was edited by Robert Flynn with help from Ian Foletta. Valerie Tellini drew the maps and designed the book. The cover was designed by Tamsin Wilson, and the cartoons were drawn by Peter Morris and Mike Woolson. The Chinese script was produced by Robert Storey and Lonely Planet.

Rachel Black helped with the art. Thanks to Sharon Wertheim for indexing, and Dan Levin for the Pinyin fonts. Last but not least, thanks to those travellers who took the time to write to us. Their names are listed on Page 352.

Warning & Request

A travel writer's job is never done. Before the ink is dry on a new book, things change. At Lonely Planet we get a steady stream of mail from travellers and it all helps – whether it's a few lines scribbled on the back of a used paper plate or a stack of neat typewritten pages spewing forth from our fax machine.

Prices go up, new hotels open, old ones degenerate, bus routes change, bridges collapse and recommended travel agents are indicted for fraud. This book is a guide, not the oracle – since things keep changing we can't tell you exactly what to expect all the time. Hopefully this book will point you in the right direction and save you some time and money.

If you find that Taiwan is not identical to the way it's described here, you can write to our hard-working readers' letters team. Your input will help make the next edition even better. The writers of the most useful letters will score a free copy of the next edition, or another Lonely Planet guide if you prefer. We give away lots of books, but unfortunately, not every letter receives one.

Map Legend

BOUNDARIES

— · — · — · —	........International Boundary
— · — · — · —	................Internal Boundary
++++++++++	....National Park or Reserve
— — — — — —	........................The Equator
·················	........................The Tropics

SYMBOLS

◉	NATIONAL	........................National Capital
●	PROVINCIAL	........Provincial or State Capital
●	Major	...............................Major Town
●	Minor	...............................Minor Town
■		...........................Places to Stay
▼		............................Places to Eat
⊠		...............................Post Office
✈		....................................Airport
i		....................Tourist Information
⊖		............Bus Station or Terminal
66		...........Highway Route Number
☿ ✝ 🕌 ✝		......Mosque, Church, Cathedral
∴		.........................Temple or Ruin
✚		....................................Hospital
※		....................................Lookout
⚑		.... Camping Area
⊓		...............................Picnic Area
⌂		.............................Hut or Chalet
▲		........................Mountain or Hill
⊢•••⊣		.... Railway Station
══		................................Road Bridge
⊢⊢⊢		..............................Railway Bridge
⇒ ⇐		.............................Road Tunnel
→) (←		.........................Railway Tunnel
⌢⌢⌢		....................Escarpment or Cliff
⌣		....Pass
⊓⊔⊓		............Ancient or Historic Wall

ROUTES

————————	.......Major Road or Highway
– – – – – – – –	.... Unsealed Major Road
———————	.... Sealed Road
– – – – – – –	..... Unsealed Road or Track
════════	.... City Street
++++++++++++	....................................Railway
▬▬◉▬▬	....................................Subway
– – – – – – –	........................Walking Track
– – – – – – –	.... Ferry Route
++++++++++	.... Cable Car or Chair Lift

HYDROGRAPHIC FEATURES

	.... River or Creek
	..............Intermittent Stream
	........Lake, Intermittent Lake
	.... Coast Line
	.....................................Spring
	...............................Waterfall
	.................................Swamp
	.... Salt Lake or Reef
	...................................Glacier

OTHER FEATURES

	Park, Garden or National Park
	.... Built Up Area
	... Market or Pedestrian Mall
	.... Plaza or Town Square
	...............................Cemetery

Note: not all symbols displayed above appear in this book

Contents

Introduction

On the world map, Taiwan looks very small when compared to the neighbouring giant landmass of Asia, the world's largest continent. With Hong Kong, mainland China and Japan drawing most of the tourists to the region, Taiwan tends to be forgotten. But that 'small island' – 395 km long with a population of 21 million – offers a great deal to those who take the time to visit.

Taiwan has one of the world's most dynamic export-oriented economies and is a familiar destination for many business travellers. Just a few decades ago, Taiwan produced only low-technology goods like clothes and cheap toys. Today, Taiwan manufactures high-quality TV sets, cameras and computers. No longer considered in the Third World, economists refer to Taiwan – along with South Korea, Singapore and Hong Kong – as one of Asia's four 'Little Dragons' or 'Little Tigers'.

Taiwan presents two faces to visitors: one is the factories, container ships and crowded cities; but there's also the other, lesser-known side of Taiwan – exotic Chinese culture, Taoist temples, wonderful food, friendly people, beaches, bamboo forests and spectacular mountain scenery. The early Portuguese sailors called Taiwan 'Ihla Formosa', which means 'Beautiful Island' – if you leave the urban areas behind, you'll discover why.

Taiwan is a fast-changing, complex society that defies simple generalisations. Due to rapid advances in health care and an increase in the average life expectancy, Taiwan has one of the highest population densities in the world; but the standard of living and level of education have also improved. Western pop music and clothing are in vogue, yet students still study traditional Chinese painting and calligraphy. Hamburgers, discos and Western videos are popular, but so are chopsticks and Chinese shadow-boxing. Taiwan today is a society in transition: despite the effects of Westernisation, Chinese culture flourishes.

When the Chinese travel abroad, it's usually with a tour group. A solo traveller far away from home is a real oddity, and people will be curious about you. Above all, the Chinese fear loneliness and will go out of their way to make sure you are not lonely. Wherever you go, you will discover that the Chinese are among the most hospitable people in the world – and this, perhaps, is the greatest pleasure of travelling in Taiwan.

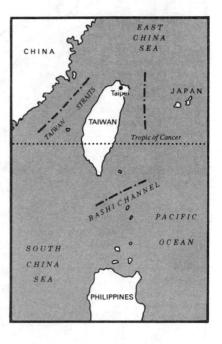

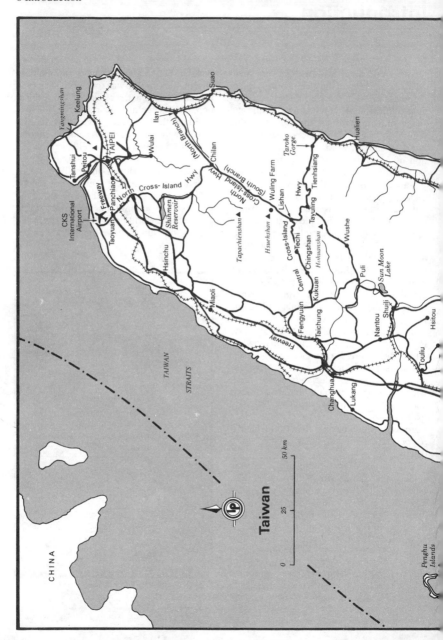

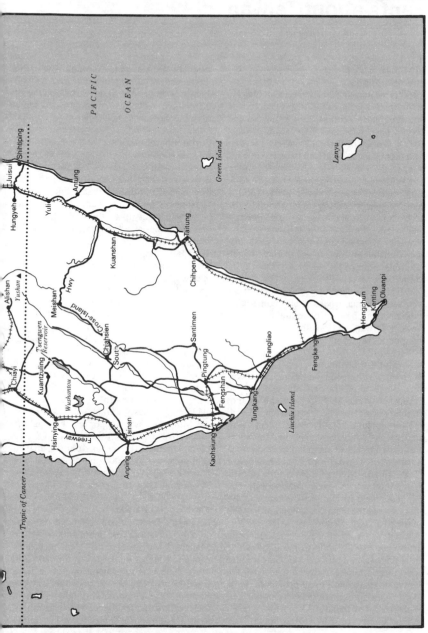

Facts about Taiwan

HISTORY

The Aborigines

Little is known of Taiwan's earliest history, but with the results of radiocarbon dating of primitive utensils it has been estimated that people have inhabited Taiwan for at least 10,000 years. The first inhabitants of Taiwan were not Chinese at all – Taiwan has always been on the periphery of the Chinese Empire and, although Chinese history dates back more than 3000 years, there was no significant Chinese migration to Taiwan until the 15th century. Taiwan's earliest inhabitants – these days simply known as 'aborigines' – probably migrated from the Pacific islands, as evidenced by their racial features which resemble those of the peoples of the nearby Philippines.

When the Chinese arrived in Taiwan, there were two distinct groups of aborigines. One lived on the rich plains of central and south-western Taiwan, and the other group lived in the mountains.

Arrival of the Chinese

Beginning in the 1400s and increasing thereafter, large numbers of Chinese from the Fujian province migrated to the island. Fujian is just across the straits from Taiwan, and the Fujian dialect is almost identical to modern-day Taiwanese. As their numbers grew, the Fujianese occupied the land most suitable for agriculture (Taiwan's west coastal plain), driving the aborigines into the mountains and the rocky east coast. The Fujianese have always been the keenest travellers among the Chinese, and today they can be found all over South-East Asia.

Along with the Fujianese came a small but steady stream of ethnic Chinese known as the Hakka. Coming from the Henan province in northern China, the Hakka first moved to the Guangdong and Fujian provinces in the south to escape severe persecution in their homelands. The name Hakka means 'guests' and as guests in search of a home, they gradually trickled into Taiwan. Today, the Hakka are an almost invisible minority in Taiwan – only their dialect (which many of them have forgotten) distinguishes them from the Taiwanese majority.

European Imperialism

In 1517 the first Europeans – Portuguese sailors – landed on Taiwan's shores and were so impressed by the beautiful scenery that they named it Ihla Formosa, which means 'Beautiful Island'. The name Formosa has been used right up to the present, though nowadays the island is better known by its Chinese name, Taiwan, which means 'Terraced Bay'.

Following the tradition of imperialism that was popular at the time, the Dutch decided to invade Taiwan in 1624. The Dutch established the first capital on Taiwan at what is now the city of Tainan in the south-west part of the island. Two years later the Spanish grabbed control of north Taiwan, but were expelled by the Dutch in 1641.

Taiwan had no real army to resist the Dutch, but events on the Chinese mainland soon changed all that. Blood was flowing in China as the up-and-coming Ching (Manchu) Dynasty armies were destroying the Ming Dynasty supporters. Fleeing the victorious Manchu armies, Cheng Chengkung, also known as Koxinga, arrived in Taiwan with 35,000 troops in 400 war junks. In 1661 he successfully expelled the Dutch from their stronghold in Tainan.

The Manchu Period

Koxinga's forces hoped to launch an invasion to recapture the mainland from the Manchus, but instead the Manchu armies captured Taiwan in 1682. For the next 200 years there was substantial migration from the Fujian province across the Taiwan Straits. These immigrants brought with them their culture and language, which are still in evidence today. Taiwan remained a county of the Fujian province from 1684 until 1887, when with a population of more than 2½ million it became a province of China.

Japanese Imperialism

In 1895 a dispute over Korea led to the Sino-Japanese War. China was defeated and Japan went on to occupy Korea. Being a somewhat remote place, Taiwan had managed to avoid most of the dislocations of the wars which took place on the mainland, but in 1895 Taiwan was ceded to Japan as one of the spoils of the Sino-Japanese War.

Although the Japanese brought law and order, they also brought harsh rule. Many of Taiwan's residents objected and rebelled, proclaiming an independent republic. The republic, the first in Asia, was short-lived as the Japanese quickly and brutally crushed it. For the next 50 years Taiwan remained part of Japan. The Japanese influence was quite extensive and even today many of the older people speak Japanese.

Although the Japanese ruled with an iron fist, they were efficient and contributed substantially to Taiwan's economic and educational development. During their rule Taiwan became more developed than mainland China. The Japanese built roads, railroads, schools, hospitals and also improved agricultural techniques. However, WW II created a great demand for men and raw materials to feed Japan's war machine. The Japanese drafted tens of thousands of Taiwanese into the Japanese army, and many were killed or wounded. The Western allies also bombed Japanese military installations, though the island mercifully escaped the carpet bombing that was used on Japan itself. By the time the war ended, Taiwan's economy, along with that of mainland China and Japan, was in ruins.

The Kuomintang Era

Events in mainland China were destined to affect Taiwan's future greatly. China's last dynasty – the Ching Dynasty – collapsed in 1911 following a nationwide rebellion led by Dr Sun Yatsen (1866-1925), who became the first president of the Republic of China (ROC). Dr Sun did not lust for power, but instead stepped down in favour of Yuan Shihkai. Unfortunately, Yuan did not share Dr Sun's vision of a democratic China and he attempted to install himself as a new emperor. He was unsuccessful and died in 1916.

A period of civil war ensued while various rival warlords and factions struggled for power. Unity was eventually restored when the Nationalist army, led by Generalissimo Chiang Kaishek (1886-1975), took power. However, the Nationalist Party (Kuomintang or KMT) soon found itself beleaguered by Japan's growing militancy and the Communist rebellion. In 1931, Japanese forces occupied Manchuria. In 1937, the Japanese invaded the Chinese heartland.

Under the Yalta Agreement, China regained sovereignty over Taiwan after Japan's defeat in WW II. At first the Taiwan-

Chiang Kaishek

ese were happy to be rid of the Japanese military and welcomed the Kuomintang, but their joy soon faded when Chiang Kaishek sent the corrupt and incompetent General Chen Yi to be Taiwan's governor. Chen Yi's misrule came to a head on 27 February 1947, when anti-Kuomintang riots broke out and were brutally repressed – somewhere between 10,000 and 30,000 civilians were killed. The incident, now known as '2-28' (for the date when it occurred), remained a forbidden topic of discussion in Taiwan until the lifting of martial law in 1987.

In 1949, the Communists wrested control of the Chinese mainland, and the Kuomintang, still led by Chiang Kaishek, fled to Taiwan. About 1½ million Chinese, including 600,000 soldiers, moved to Taiwan after the Communists captured the mainland. As a result, the island's population grew from around 6 million in 1946 to 7½ million in 1950. In 1950, disgraced former governor Chen Yi was executed by the Kuomintang.

As they fled, Kuomintang troops were able to hold onto three small islands just off the Chinese mainland – Kinmen (Quemoy), Matsu and Wuchiu – which still remain under the control of Taiwan. An invasion of Taiwan was fully expected, but the Communist army became bogged down in the Korean War, and the USA sent its 7th Fleet into the Taiwan Straits to thwart any invasion plans.

The Kuomintang maintained from the beginning that their stay in Taiwan was temporary – that they would retake mainland China from the Communists 'very soon', and that, in the meantime, no political opposition could be permitted. Such policies did not necessarily endear the KMT to the native Taiwanese. Nevertheless, the KMT proved itself capable of repairing Taiwan's war-torn economy. An excellent land-reform programme was introduced in the 1950s which resulted in a far more equitable income distribution than is found in most Asian countries. Rapid industrialisation in the 1960s made Taiwan one of the wealthiest places in Asia.

In October 1971 the Kuomintang lost the China United Nations seat. A further blow came in January 1979, when the USA withdrew recognition of the ROC and recognised the Communist regime on the mainland. Most countries have now withdrawn diplomatic recognition of the Republic of China. In spite of this, most of the non-socialist world maintains very strong unofficial economic ties with Taiwan.

Chiang Kaishek died from a heart attack in 1975, at the age of 87. His son, Chiang Chingkuo, became president of the Republic of China in 1978 after an election was held. He was re-elected in 1984 and served a second term.

Throughout the 1980s and up to the present, mainland China has kept relentless pressure on other countries not to sell military hardware to Taiwan. This has caused some serious rows, most often with the USA. China says arms sales to Taiwan are 'interference in the internal affairs of China'. China has also tried to get other countries to break economic links with Taiwan, but few have done so. Taiwan has consistently denounced these policies, which are referred to as 'Chinese-Communist united-front tactics'.

In 1986 a political upheaval occurred, with the formation of the Democratic Progressive Party (DPP). The DPP was formed in spite of a government ban on new political parties. After much debate, the KMT – under the specific orders of President Chiang Chingkuo – decided not to interfere with the DPP. A large number of DPP candidates were elected in 1986 and were permitted to take their seats in the legislature, thus creating Taiwan's first true opposition party.

In 1987, 38 years of martial law ended. It was one of the last acts of Chiang Chingkuo, who died in January 1988. He was succeeded by Lee Tenghui, the first native Taiwanese to hold the post of president.

One of the thornier political dilemmas for the Kuomintang was what to do with the 'ageing deputies' – legislators who were elected on the mainland before the Communist takeover. Unable to stand for re-election, they were frozen in office for over 40 years, absurdly claiming to represent their constituents on the mainland. In December 1991 those still living (over 460) were finally forced to retire, and the first really free election to the National Assembly was held.

With the ageing deputies gone, Taiwan soon accepted reality and has given up its position that it will 'retake the mainland'. However, Taiwan officially remains a part of China and has not declared independence, though a movement for independence (led by the DPP) certainly exists. The 'Taiwan question' still remains one of Asia's unsettled disputes.

GEOGRAPHY

Shaped roughly like a leaf, Taiwan is an island just a mere 160 km across the Taiwan Straits from the Fujian province of mainland China.

The maximum length of the island is 395 km and its maximum width is 144 km; the total area is 35,563 square km. In spite of its small size, the mountains are extremely high, reaching 3952 metres at Yushan (Jade Mountain). Yushan is higher than Japan's famous Mt Fuji. Indeed, apart from the Himalayan region, Yushan is the highest peak in North-East Asia.

The mountains rise straight out of the sea on Taiwan's east coast, but the west side of the island is a flat and fertile plain, much more hospitable to human habitation, and over 90% of Taiwan's population resides there. However, the mountainous eastern side of the island is far more scenic.

In addition to the island of Taiwan itself, there are a number of smaller offshore islands which can be visited by tourists. These include the Penghu Islands (64 including islets), Lanyu, Green Island, and Hsiao Liuchiu. Within eyeshot of mainland China are three islands controlled by the ROC – Kinmen, Matsu and Wuchiu – which serve as 'front-line' military bases.

Taiwan, like mainland China, lays claim to 53 rocks, shoals and reefs in the South China Sea known as the Spratly Islands. The Spratlys are also claimed by Malaysia, Brunei, the Philippines and Vietnam. The claims wouldn't be taken too seriously except that there is *possibly* oil under these islands, which has led to the area becoming heavily fortified. The largest islet in the Spratly chain is occupied by Taiwan's military.

Taipei, at the very northern end of the Taiwan, is the largest city and seat of the national government. Other large cities include Kaohsiung, Taichung and Tainan – all on the west side of the island.

CLIMATE

Taiwan is a subtropical island with two – rather than four – seasons. For such a small place, there are considerable variations in climate. There are basically three climatic regions: the north and east coastal region, the south-west coastal region, and the mountains.

In the north and east coastal region, which includes Taipei, there is really no dry season. Winter is cool, occasionally chilly, and characterised by heavy cloud cover and frequent drizzle. Statistically, more rain falls during summer but, ironically, the skies tend to be sunny most of the time. Summer rain comes in short, torrential thundershowers mostly during the afternoon. Summers are sticky and very hot.

The south-west has two distinct seasons. Summer is hot and humid, with frequent afternoon thundershowers. Winter is very dry and sunny, with pleasantly cool days.

The mountains get the most rain of all, especially during summer. The summer rain tends to come in short-lived afternoon thundershowers, starting around 2 pm and often ending by 4 pm. At higher altitudes there is often an afternoon fog. During winter the weather tends to be drier on the west side of the mountains than on the east side. Temperatures get very cold above 2000 metres, and winter snow is common above 3000 metres.

A striking feature of winter is the monsoonal wind (*hánliú*) from Central Asia, which can send the temperature plummeting

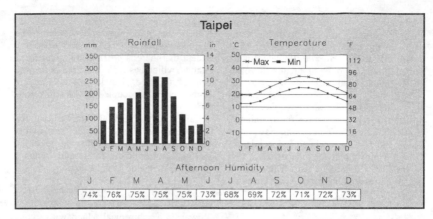

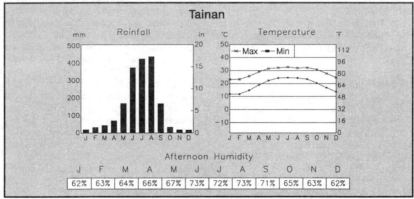

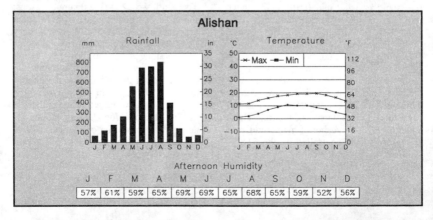

10°C or more in just a few hours. You might be comfortably wearing a T-shirt and shorts in the morning, but by noon you'll have to put on long trousers and a coat. At such times it can snow in the mountains.

Spring is warm and mild but there are frequent rains throughout the island, known as the 'plum rain'. The rains can continue through to August, but the wettest month is usually June.

Summer is the typhoon season. The brief autumn season (October and November) is the most delightful time to visit the island, though typhoons are possible in October. Autumn temperatures are ideal, and it is the driest time of year, especially in the southwest.

FLORA & FAUNA

Taiwan's wildlife has not fared well – the industrial revolution, rapid population growth, agricultural and urban development have all taken their toll. Development along the west coast has ruined the wetlands which once provided a habitat for Taiwan's numerous birds. During WW II the Japanese heavily logged Taiwan's forests for the war effort, with devastating consequences for plants and wildlife.

The good news is that Taiwan's mountainous interior has largely been reforested, providing a much improved habitat for animals. However, mammals like the Formosan brown bear, sambar (a species of deer), Reeve's muntjac (a very small deer) and Formosan serow (a type of wild goat) are still very rare. The birds have been the chief beneficiary of the reforestation programme – they can now be seen in abundance.

Taiwan's flora is in much better shape, at least in the mountain areas and along the east coast. However, many native species have been pushed aside by exotic imports. The high mountain forests are predominantly cypress. Camphor trees, which at one time provided the base material for Taiwan's thriving camphor industry, have nearly disappeared. In the past, camphor was Taiwan's leading export – obviously, this is no longer the case.

Typhoons

A typhoon is nothing more than a large tropical storm – just a lot of wind and rain. Typhoons occur mostly in the summer; in some years Taiwan gets no typhoons at all, but in other years there may be five or more. Outside the western Pacific Ocean region, typhoons are generally known as hurricanes or cyclones.

You should not be overly concerned about typhoons, but a few words of warning are in order. Some typhoons are weak and not much worse than a thunderstorm, but others are 'super-typhoons' which can level trees and houses. Typhoons are tricky – they can change course suddenly, wreaking havoc on the weather forecast. I've often cancelled a weekend trip due to the threat of a typhoon, only to have the storm change direction and move away from Taiwan. In Taiwan, the east coast gets the worst typhoons because they come in from the Pacific Ocean – the west coast is better protected by the mountains.

If a typhoon alert is issued while you are in Taiwan, be equipped to stay indoors for at least a day, maybe two. Going outside can be dangerous – most injuries or deaths are caused when people go outdoors and get hit by wind-driven debris. Have some books and magazines, candles and matches, a torch (flashlight), food (canned and dried goods) and water. Lastly, don't worry – a typhoon is just a bad storm and the worst that is likely to happen is that you'll get bored waiting for it to end. ∎

The visitor centres of Taiwan's various national parks can provide English-language pamphlets giving a rundown on the local plant and animal species.

National Parks

It was only in the 1980's that Taiwan began to think about preserving its natural treasures. As awareness of the issue grew, six national parks were established in rapid succession. The first was Kenting National Park, established on 1 January 1984. This was followed by Yushan, Yangmingshan, Taroko, Lanyu and Hsuehpa national parks.

Taiwan's national parks are not true wilderness areas. You will find houses, hotels, telephones, roads and other intrusions of modern civilisation in these areas. However, new developments are strictly controlled – houses cannot be built, for example, without permits which are extremely difficult to obtain. Hopefully, this will stop the recent trend of Taiwan's *nouveaux riches* to build villas in scenic spots purely for real-estate speculation. Although one very controversial road was built in Yushan National Park after it was established, the emphasis now is on constructing hiking trails.

The mountainous east coast of Taiwan is now at least semi-protected as the East Coast National Scenic Area – there are plans to construct a bicycle path in some as-yet-undetermined spot. Off the west coast are the Penghu Islands, now designated the Penghu National Scenic Area.

GOVERNMENT
Power

Power is distributed among five major branches of government which are called Yuan – the Legislative (National Assembly), Executive, Judicial, Examination and Control Yuan. The first three are largely self-explanatory.

The Examination Yuan oversees Taiwan's formidable system of exams, which determines one's access to education, jobs, business licences, the civil service, etc. The Control Yuan is a watchdog agency which tries to keep things honest.

The president is chosen by the legislature, though there is much debate now on changing the constitution to allow direct election of the president. The president appoints the premier, and the premier wields considerable power because he or she appoints the heads of Taiwan's many ministries, which oversee the ubiquitous bureaucracy. Important ministries include Economic Affairs, Education, Finance, Foreign Affairs, Interior, Justice, National Defence, and Transportation & Communications. The ministries themselves are multi-tiered bureaucracies, with numerous agencies, bureaus, commissions and directorates, some of which seem to perform no useful function whatsoever (what exactly

does the Mongolian & Tibetan Affairs Commission do?).

It shouldn't be forgotten that Taiwan is officially a province of China. Thus, there is a largely forgotten provincial government with its capital at Chunghsing Village in Taichung County. Just what the provincial government does is anybody's guess. In late 1993 a serious proposal was advanced by legislators to simply do away with the provincial government 'to improve efficiency'.

Politics

Many claim that Taiwan is the first Chinese democracy. This point can be debated, but there are few countries in Asia which have a more open political process than Taiwan. This is a very recent change – Taiwan was essentially a dictatorship until martial law was lifted in 1987. The Kuomintang is still in control, but the current president, Lee Tenghui, has shown himself to be a political moderate. He performs a delicate balancing act between the hardline conservatives, who still chant the slogan 'retake mainland China', and the younger generation who are more interested in Taiwan's political and economic development.

The Democratic Progressive Party (DPP) has emerged as the chief opposition party. Not interested in retaking the mainland, they have instead promised to 'retake Taipei'. Although the DPP contains many sincere and talented people, the party's image has been frequently tarnished by political buffoonery. Party leaders have become well known for throwing things and getting into fistfights with Kuomintang legislators while the TV cameras record the events for their constituents. There were particularly violent battles in July 1993 when the DPP launched an anti-nuclear protest on the floor of the National Assembly – some legislators went to the hospital with concussion. Although the DPP could hardly be called a green party, some DPP leaders have claimed that they will shut down all of Taiwan's nuclear-power plants if they gain power. Since this would be tantamount to shutting down Taiwan's industry, many of Taiwan's business people have shunned the DPP.

Although the DPP challenges the KMT on almost every issue, few people consider this to be more than political grandstanding. The chief ideological difference distinguishing the DPP from the KMT is the issue of Taiwanese independence. The DPP wants to establish an independent 'Republic of Taiwan' while the KMT insists that Taiwan will always remain 'The Rock' (ROC), a province a China. For its part, the Chinese Communist Party on the mainland is staunchly opposed to the DPP platform and has repeatedly warned that if Taiwan declares independence, it will have to 'face the consequences'.

Unofficially, things are a little less clear. Many young KMT legislators are less than enthusiastic about reunification with the mainland, preferring the status quo. The fast-growing two-way trade between Taiwan and the mainland dampens enthusiasm (even among DPP legislators) for rocking the economic boat by declaring independence. For now, most Taiwanese prefer to waffle on the issue, saying that independence is a good idea but the time 'isn't right yet'.

The DPP turned the 1992 National Assembly election into a referendum on Taiwanese independence. This provoked the wrath of Kuomintang hardliners, who called this tactic 'sedition'. Meanwhile, back in Beijing, the Chinese Communist Party was not amused and threatened a possible military invasion if Taiwan 'seceded'. The majority of voters decided that independence was too risky and that the Kuomintang – for all its faults – had delivered the economic goodies, while the DPP programme was basically nationalism and a new flag. Nevertheless, the DPP made a very good showing, capturing 36% of the vote against the KMT's 61%. This was a considerable gain from the previous election when the DPP captured less than 25% of the vote.

The DPP's gains are less likely to be a vote for independence than a protest vote against

---

The PRC, the ROC & Dr Sun

Mainland China's Communist Party and the KMT agree on little, but one thing they do agree on is that Taiwan is still a province of China, not an independent country. Both the KMT and the Communist Party claim to be the sole legitimate government of China. Reunification of China remains a national goal, even though the two sides are far apart in their ideologies. Foreign visitors should not make the mistake of calling Taiwan a country. Taiwan is a province of China and the people are Chinese. The term 'Taiwanese' is acceptable, but it refers to those Chinese born in the 'province' of Taiwan. It may all change someday, but for now this is the politically correct terminology.

All over Taiwan you can see statues and monuments honouring Chiang Kaishek and also Dr Sun Yatsen, the founding father of the Republic of China. Their pictures appear on all ROC-issued coins and paper currency, and they are officially regarded as national heroes. However, in recent years, some Taiwanese students have been exposed to the Western version of history, which gives a much less flattering account of Chiang Kaishek's rule, and have begun to question the official line on his 'great achievements'.

Those wishing to understand the political doctrine of the ruling Kuomintang might want to read Dr Sun Yatsen's *The Three Principles of the People*. Be forewarned that the book is both boring and vague. The Three Principles – Nationalism, Livelihood and Civil Rights – are constantly promoted by the government. The book is required reading for all students in Taiwan. To get a government job, one must pass an exam in the three principles. The national anthem is entitled 'Three Principles of the People'. Every city in Taiwan has a Mintsu (Nationalism) Rd, a Minsheng (Livelihood) Rd and a Minchuan (Civil Rights) Rd, as well as a Chungshan (Sun Yatsen) and a Chungcheng (Chiang Kaishek) Rd. Students are force-fed a steady diet of classes on the Three Principles from elementary school right through university – it is even possible to obtain a master's degree in the Three Principles. ■

the KMT's bureaucracy, infighting and big-money politics. Voters fed up with both KMT inefficiency and DPP antics have been given a ray of hope with the formation of the Chinese New Party (CNP). Originally the CNP was a reformist faction of the Kuomintang, known as the KMT New Alliance. In August 1993 it broke away to become a separate party. The CNP adheres to the major KMT policies – pro-business and lukewarm support for reunification with mainland China. The sharpest ideological difference between the parties is that the CNP denounces corrupt money politics, a big issue since many KMT legislators seem to have a great deal of unexplained wealth. Closely modelled on Japan's Renewal Party, the CNP includes some of Taiwan's most popular political figures. It's possible the CNP will put a sizeable dent in both the KMT's and DPP's support. For the moment, the CNP is Taiwan's political wild card – the next national assembly election will be the big test.

Besides the KMT, DPP and CNP, there are a few independent legislators, the so-called 'non-partisans'. There are also some insignificant parties. The Social Democratic Party was formed in 1990 as a breakaway faction of the DPP, but it has not proved popular. In the December 1992 National Assembly election, the Social Democratic Party received just 1.3% of the vote. The party was headed by colourful legislator Ju Gau-jeng (chairman) better known as 'Rambo', but he resigned as party chairman as a result of poor showing in polls. In 1993, the Social Democratic Party merged with the Chinese New Party.

Best known of the minor parties is the tiny Labor Party, famous for its unforgettable candidate Hsu Hsiaotan, a young dancer with a propensity for stripping in public. Ms Hsu's flamboyant campaign was unsuccessful, but she came within 107 votes of being elected to the National Assembly. Part of the reason for her good showing at the polls had less to do with her personal popularity than with public sympathy generated because the authorities put her in prison for three months for making a porno movie. Her imprisonment was seen as a political move that backfired against the ruling KMT.

ECONOMY

The business of Taiwan is business. Starting from an economy shattered by WW II, the island has experienced rapid economic growth. Taiwan is classified as a 'newly industrialised economy' (NIE). It was formerly known as a 'newly industrialised country' (NIC) until mainland China threw a tantrum, pointing out that Taiwan and Hong Kong are not countries, but part of China.

Annual per-capita income has risen to over US$10,000 and is increasing rapidly. The engine behind this economic success story is largely foreign trade. Not long ago, the label 'Made in Taiwan' was associated with cheap plastic toys that broke easily, but these days Taiwanese manufacturers have moved up-market into high-quality electronics and computers. Taiwan's exports in 1992 were valued at over US$83 billion, exceeding those of mainland China by US$5 billion.

Indeed, one of Taiwan's biggest headaches is trying to find a solution to the foreign trade imbalance, which is heavily weighted in Taiwan's favour. It's a problem, but a problem that many other countries wish they had. Taiwan now has the world's largest reserves of foreign currency, having surpassed Japan. So much foreign currency is piling up in Taiwan's banks that it is causing inflationary pressure. With too much money and too little investment, a lot of 'hot money' has poured into bloated real-estate speculation and the stock market, the latter often derided as a 'gambling casino'. This paper-asset boom could prove detrimental to Taiwan's long-term economic health – the stock market has already crashed once (losing over 60% of its value), wiping out the life savings of many unsophisticated punters. A lot of financial analysts predict that the real-estate market is getting ready to take a fall, too.

Mainland China has attempted to isolate Taiwan both politically and economically.

As a result of pressure from China, Taiwan has not yet been able to join the General Agreement on Tariffs & Trade (GATT). Even more ridiculous, China is also trying to prevent Taiwan from becoming a signatory to the Montreal Protocol, the international agreement to control emissions of ozone-destroying CFC gases. Their logic seems to be that as a non-signatory, Taiwan would face a possible international boycott of its exports, and China seems determined to slow down Taiwan's economic progress because it's such an embarrassment.

Although many foreigners assume that Taiwan has a thoroughly capitalist, free-market economy like Hong Kong's, it is in fact regulated by a number of cumbersome bureaucratic controls and more social programmes than most foreigners realise. The state heavily subsidises education, transportation and health care. A lot of government money has gone into public health, family planning, agriculture and reforestation. Government workers, of which there are far too many, enjoy generous benefits and pensions. It's true that there are no welfare schemes of the type found in Western Europe, but no one in Taiwan appears to be starving. Indeed, except for some rural backwaters like Lanyu (Orchid Island), Taiwan seems to have almost no poverty at all.

Another role the government plays in the economy is seen in the many large government-owned monopolies controlling such industries as tobacco, liquor, sugar, salt, telephones, rail transportation, and banking. In this sense, Taiwan's economy is more socialist than most people think. All banks were government-operated until 1993, when some new private banks were permitted to open. Unfortunately, new bureaucratic controls arbitrarily slapped on the upstart banks are enough to make Adam Smith turn in his grave. Nevertheless, private business somehow flourishes, often by violating laws. Furthermore, the economy is undergoing a cautious (some would say 'snail's pace') process of deregulation.

In addition to the legitimate economy, there is an enormous black economy. The chief culprit is the licensing and tax bureaucracy. Complying with the law is so arduous that many businesses prefer to operate illegally. In most cases penalties are lenient or even nonexistent, and becoming legally licensed is often impossible for small businesses. For example, it's next to impossible to get a licence to operate a youth hostel (even though the government operates youth hostels), so almost every private hostel is illegal. The requirements for opening up a private language school are so absurd (classrooms have to be the size of aircraft hangars) that half the schools are illegal. Those schools which are legal first rent aircraft-hangar-sized buildings, obtain the licence, then illegally subdivide the rooms using often dangerous flammable buildings materials (in violation of fire codes, now a source of concern after some recent spectacular disasters). Ditto for many restaurants, karaoke bars, and so on. Every now and then (like after 20 patrons get fried in a karaoke fire), the authorities 'crack down' and arbitrarily shut down a bunch of illegal businesses to demonstrate to the public how efficient they are. After a while, the illegal businesses open again.

Another major reason why businesses remain illegal is to avoid taxes. Taiwan's tax system bears little relation to Western models – taxes may be assessed arbitrarily according to the amount of office space used and the number of employees hired, rather than profits. Tax evasion is a time-honoured tradition in Taiwan, even among licensed businesses. Accounting standards are low and tax avoidance schemes are common – 'double-bookkeeping', employing workers off the books, using residences as office space, etc.

Taiwan is basically a cash economy and cheques are seldom used, which makes it even more difficult for the tax office to keep track of business transactions. No one knows for sure, but some sources estimate that up to 40% of Taiwan's economy operates outside the law and therefore doesn't show up in official statistics. In 1991, a police spot-check in the fashionable Dinghao neighbourhood along Chunghsiao E Rd of Taipei found that 67% of the businesses were operating without a licence. Closing these businesses down all at once would do severe damage to the economy. All this means that Taiwan's per-capita income is considerably higher than is officially recognised, and that the government is considerably poorer than it could be.

Small business has always been Taiwan's biggest employer and the foundation of the economy, but the government is constantly crying about the need to develop big business. The newspapers seem to support this theme, often pointing to South Korea as a good example of how big business should be the backbone of the economy. Ironically, the newspaper editorials in South Korea always point to Taiwan as an example of why small business should be the backbone of the economy.

Taiwan's economy is a lot more open to foreign investors that it used to be, but there are still many restrictions on service industries such as banking, insurance and telecommunications. The government has been under much pressure from its trading partners (particularly the USA) to open up. And it is happening gradually, but it often seems that Taiwan is being dragged kicking and screaming into a more open economy.

POPULATION

A combination of the postwar baby boom and an increase in the average life expectancy – largely due to better health conditions – has pushed the population of Taiwan close to 21 million. Thanks to government-instituted family planning and increased financial security, the population growth rate has slowed to about 1.4% annually and is still falling, but Taiwan has a population density of 573 persons per square km, making it one of the most crowded places in the world.

PEOPLE

Until recently, about 70% of the population were considered Taiwanese. For definition purposes, Taiwanese means someone of more or less Chinese background whose family was in Taiwan before the Kuomintang arrived en masse after WW II. Those who came after WW II are simply called 'mainlanders', but their numbers are diminishing due to natural attrition and because of intermarriage with the native Taiwanese. The Hakka, who originally comprised perhaps 5% to 10% of the population, have also intermarried to such an extent that they are no longer a visible minority.

Today, Taiwan's 325,000 aborigines represent about 1.5% of the population. Intermarriage between the aborigines and the Chinese majority occurs, but is far less common than marriages between Taiwanese and Westerners. The aborigines stand out because they have darker skin and rounder eyes than the Chinese, and the vast majority have converted to Christianity. There are 10 tribes – the Ami, Atayal, Bunun, Paiwan, Puyuma, Rukai, Shao, Saisiat, Tsou and Yami – each of which has its own language. Like elsewhere, the aborigines have been the victims of ridicule and scorn, but in recent years it has become very trendy to collect aboriginal art and to attend aboriginal song and dance shows.

EDUCATION

Literacy in Taiwan is over 90%, and most of the illiterate are elderly people who missed their chance at education due to WW II.

The Chinese are obsessed with higher education, and success at gaining admission to a university is determined by life-or-death exams. To pass these exams, a whole industry of private cram schools has emerged, a boon to foreigners wanting to teach English. Pity the poor students who have to spend all their evenings, weekends and holidays attending these schools. Higher education in Taiwan has a definite emphasis on science and technology – about 35% of Taiwan's 500,000 university students are enrolled in engineering programs.

Foreigners who have a reasonably good level of proficiency in Chinese can be admitted to a university in Taiwan and receive a degree after completing a course of study.

However, with such keen competition for university places, only a small percentage is allotted to foreigners, mostly overseas Chinese who are exempted from the formidable examinations. On the other hand, it's very easy for foreigners to enrol in private academy Chinese-language classes (see Language section).

Universities in Taiwan

If formal study in Taiwan interests you, write directly to the university you wish to attend or contact the Bureau of International Cultural & Educational Relations, Ministry of Education (☎ 02-3513111), 5 Chungshan S Rd, Taipei.

Chinese Cultural University
    (zhōngguó wénhuà dàxué) 55 Huakang Rd, Yangmingshan, Taipei (☎ 02-8610511)
Chungyuan (Christian) University
    (zhōngyuán dàxué) Chungli, Taoyuan County (☎ 03-4563171)
Fengchia University
    (féngjiǎ dàxué) 100 Wenhua Rd, Hsitun District, Taichung (☎ 04-2522250)
Fujen (Catholic) University
    (fǔrén dàxué) 510 Chungcheng Rd, Hsinchuang, Taipei County (☎ 02-9031111)
National Central University
    (zhōngyāng dàxué) Chungli, Taoyuan County (☎ 03-4427151)
National Chengchih University
    (zhèngzhì dàxué) 64 Chihnan Rd, Section 2, Wenshan District, Taipei (☎ 02-9393091)
National Chengkung University
    (chénggōng dàxué) Tahsueh Rd, Tainan (☎ 06-2361111)
National Chiaotung University
    (jiāotōng dàxué) 1001 Tahsueh Rd, Hsinchu (☎ 035-712121)
National Chungcheng University
    (zhōngzhèng dàxué) 160 Sanhsing Tsun, Minhsiung, Chiayi County (☎ 05-2720411)
National Chunghsing University
    (zhōngxīng dàxué) 250 Kuokuang Rd, Taichung (☎ 04-2873181)
National Kaohsiung Normal University
    (gāoxióng shīfàn dàxué) 116 Hoping-1 Rd (☎ 07-7517161)
National Open University
    (kōngzhōng dàxué) 172 Chungcheng Rd, Luchou, Taipei County (☎ 02-2829355)
National Sun Yatsen University
    (zhōngshān dàxué) Hsitszwan, Kaohsiung (☎ 07-5316171)

National Taiwan Normal University
    (shīfàn dàxué) 62 Hoping E Rd, Section 1, Taipei (☎ 02-3625101)
National Taiwan Ocean University
    (táiwān hǎiyyáng dàxué) 2 Peining Rd, Keelung (☎ 02-4622192)
National Taiwan University
    (táiwān dàxué) 1 Roosevelt Rd, Section 4, Taipei (☎ 02-3630231)
National Tsing Hua University
    (qīnghuá dàxué) 101 Kuangfu Rd, Section 2, Hsinchu (☎ 035-715131)
Providence Women's University
    (jingyí dàxué) 200 Chungchi Rd, Shalu, Taichung County (☎ 04-6311150)
Soochow University
    (dōngwǔ dàxué) Waishuanghsi, Shihlin District, Taipei (☎ 02-8819471)
Tamkang University
    (dànjiāng dàxué) 151 Yingchuang Rd, Tanshui, Taipei County (☎ 02-6215656)
Tunghai University
    (dōnghǎi dàxué) 181 Taichung Kang Rd, Section 3, Taichung (☎ 04-3590216)

Schools for Expatriate Children

Many expatriate business people come to Taiwan with children. Although some parents want their kids to attend a Chinese school, others prefer that their children have a Western-style education in the English language. There are also schools catering to speakers of French, German, Japanese and Korean. Most of these private academies offer education up to the 12th grade, some only to the 7th grade. The Morrison Christian Academy has branch schools in Taipei, Taichung and Kaohsiung. Both the Kaohsiung American School and Taipei American School are more expensive, but have good reputations. For more information, contact these schools directly:

Ecole Francaise
    731 Wenlin Rd, Taipei (☎ 02-8345221)
Kaohsiung American School
    123-3 Tapei Rd, Niaosung Hsiang, Kaohsiung (☎ 07-7315565)
Morrison Christian Academy
    136-1 Shuinan Rd, Taichung
    (PO Box 27-24, Taichung) (☎ 04-2921171)
    97 Tingchow Rd, Section 3, Taipei
    (☎ 02-3659691)
    400 Hsinhsing Lane (☎ 07-3718043)

Taipei American School
    800 Chungshan N Rd, Section 6, Taipei (☎ 02-8739900)
Taipei German School
    731 Wenlin Rd, Taipei (☎ 02-8326538)

ARTS

Traditional Chinese arts and culture have been well preserved in Taiwan – indeed, far more so than in mainland China.

Chinese Opera

(píngjù) 平劇

The traditional Chinese opera, and the closely related Taiwanese opera, are an integral part of Chinese culture that every visitor to Taiwan should see at least once. The dialogue is all in Mandarin Chinese, or Taiwanese for Taiwanese opera. The acting, colourful costumes, music and the entire atmosphere is thrilling even if you can't understand what is being said. In a few operas staged for foreigners, an English translation of the dialogue is flashed on a screen near the stage. But in most cases, no translation is available.

These operas are beautiful and well worth photographing. It is advisable to use a high-speed film, at least ASA 400, as the operas are often at night and you may have to watch from a distance. A telephoto or zoom lens would also be helpful.

Chinese opera is used to preach virtue. The operas are now shown on TV and this is gradually displacing the live performances. The opera is usually played near a temple to entertain the gods. Sometimes men play female roles and women play male ones, but the make-up is so good that it's hard to tell. Old people particularly love the opera, but young people are increasingly becoming more interested in other things like disco music and home video games.

Taijiquan

(tàijíquán) 太極拳

Taijiquan, or slow-motion shadow-boxing, has in recent years become quite trendy in Western countries. It has been popular in China for centuries. It is basically a form of

Taijiquan symbol

exercise, but it's also an art and is a form of Chinese martial arts. Kungfu *(gōngfū)* differs from taijiquan in that the former is performed at much higher speed and with the intention of doing bodily harm. Kungfu also often employs weapons. Taijiquan is not a form of self-defence but the movements are similar to kungfu. There are different styles of taijiquan, such as *chen* and *yang*.

Taijiquan is very popular among old people, and also with young women who believe it will help keep their bodies beautiful. The movements are supposed to develop the breathing muscles, promote digestion and improve muscle tone.

A modern innovation is to perform taijiquan movements to the thump of disco music. Westerners find it remarkable to see a large group performing their slow-motion movements in the park at dawn to the steady beat of disco music supplied by a portable cassette-tape player.

Taijiquan, dancing in the park and all manner of exercises are customarily done just as the sun rises, which means that if you want to see or participate in them, you have to get up early. In Taipei the best places to see taijiquan are the Chiang Kaishek Memorial Hall, the Sun Yatsen Memorial Hall, Taipei New Park, the hills around the Grand Hotel, and Yangmingshan Park and the Sungshan Nature Reserve. Some people, for lack of a better place, just perform their taijiquan on the footpath or on the roof of their homes. There are organised taiji classes and Westerners are usually welcome to participate in these activities.

Martial Arts
(wǔshù) 武術

While kungfu is the only martial art that is truly Chinese, you can find several imported varieties in Taiwan, borrowed from Japan and Korea. The different forms include aikido *(héqìdào)*, judo *(róudào)*, karate *(kōngshǒudào)* and taekwondo *(táiquándào)*. There are a number of schools in Taiwan – ask the Tourism Bureau to help you locate one.

Qigong
(qìgōng) 氣功

As much an art form as a traditional Chinese medical treatment, *qigong* cannot easily be described in Western terms, but it's rather like faith healing. *Qi* represents life's vital energy, and *gong* comes from kungfu – Chinese martial arts. Qigong can be thought of as energy management and healing. Practitioners try to project their chi to heal others.

It's interesting to see qigong practitioners at work. Typically, they place their hands above or next to the patient's body without actually making physical contact. To many foreigners this looks like a circus act, and indeed even many Chinese suspect that it's nothing but quackery. However, there are many who claim that they have been cured of serious illness without any treatment other than qigong, even after more conventional doctors have told them that their condition is hopeless.

Qigong is not extremely popular in Taiwan, although it has experienced a recent revival in mainland China. During the Cultural Revolution, it was denounced by rampaging Red Guards as yet another superstitious link to the bourgeois past, and qigong

and its practitioners were nearly obliterated. In Taiwan, you are most likely to see qigong in the ever-popular kungfu movies, where mortally wounded heroes are miraculously revived with a few waves of the hands.

Does qigong work? It isn't easy to say, but there is a theory in medicine that all doctors can cure a third of their patients regardless of what method is used. So perhaps qigong also gets its 33% cure rate.

Traditional Music
These days, people in Taiwan are more into disco and rock videos than traditional Chinese music. Nevertheless, traditional musical instruments are still studied in Taiwan. Courses are normally taught in the Chinese departments of various universities around the island, and a number of the students are foreigners. Probably the best place to study traditional Chinese music is at the Chinese Cultural University at Yangmingshan in Taipei. Most of the instruments are string and flute-like instruments that have a melodious sound. However, the instruments you are most likely to encounter while travelling are the awful-sounding gongs and trumpets used at temple worship ceremonies and funerals.

The most common traditional instruments include the following:

two-stringed fiddle	*èrhú*
three-stringed fiddle	*sānxuán*
four-stringed banjo	*yuèqín*
two-stringed viola	*húqín*
flute (vertical)	*dòngxiāo*
flute (horizontal)	*dízi*
piccolo	*bāngdí*
four-stringed lute	*pípá*
zither	*gǔzhēng*
trumpet (for ceremonies)	*suǒnà*
gongs (for ceremonies)	*dàluó*

CULTURE
Traditional Lifestyle
The Chinese have an intricate and fascinating culture which dates back at least 3000 years, making it one of the world's oldest surviving societies.

There are some important traditional customs or rules of social behaviour that you should be aware of:

Face Having 'big face' is synonymous with prestige, and prestige is important in Asia. All families, even poor ones, are expected to have big wedding parties and throw money around like water, in order to gain face. The fact that this causes bankruptcy for the young couple is far less important than losing face.

Much of the Chinese obsession with materialism is really to do with gaining face, not material wealth. Owning nice clothes, a big car (even if you can't drive), a piano (even if you can't play it), imported cigarettes and liquor (even if you don't smoke or drink), will all cause one to gain face. Therefore, when taking a gift to a Chinese friend, try to give something with snob appeal such as a bottle of imported liquor, perfume, cigarettes or chocolate. This will please your host and help win you points in the face game.

The whole concept of face may seem very childish to Westerners who never learn to understand it, but it is important in Asia.

Flattery Flatter your host and guests. Give them big face. Words of praise like 'You're so intelligent and humorous (or beautiful, etc)' will go down well. If you speak three words of Chinese someone will surely say, 'You speak Chinese very well'. The proper response should be self-deprecating: 'Oh no, my Chinese is very bad' (probably true). Boasting is a real faux pas. Remaining humble is very much a part of the Confucian tradition. The Chinese are famous for their humility. 'Oh, I'm so ugly and stupid!' is the kind of self-deprecating comment one often hears in Taiwan. Be sure you don't agree with such comments, even to be funny.

Flowery Rhetoric Form is more important than content. It has been said that the Chinese speak in circles, and there is some truth to this. Rather than saying exactly what is meant, a speaker or writer may beat around the bush with polite greetings, praise for your past deeds, hopes for more in the future, wishes for good health, enquiries about your family, and various other digressions, redundancies and superfluities.

One examination given to prospective employees involves taking a single meaningful sentence and rewriting it into a two-page essay with no increase in content. Many people also talk this way.

Chinese literature contains many examples of flowery rhetoric. One classic Chinese novel available in English translation, *The Red Chamber Dream*, is such a complex riot of plots, characters and digressions that diagrams are included to prevent the reader from getting lost.

Name Cards The Chinese love name cards. Get some printed before or immediately after you arrive in Taiwan. Throw them around like confetti. Every professional needs a name card and never mind if you are a professional dishwasher. Your name card can say that you are a sanitary engineer.

In Taiwan, name cards can be printed cheaply with one side in English and the other side in Chinese characters. If you get name cards or anything else printed in Taiwan, check the English carefully after it's typeset because misspellings are common.

Don't be caught without name cards if you are doing any business in Taiwan. You will almost certainly lose face if you mumble something about having run out of cards. Keep them in your wallet all the time.

Renao It's hard to translate *rènào* into English. It means something like 'lively', 'festive', 'happy' and 'noisy' – especially 'noisy'. Many Chinese seem immune to noise. You'll notice that in restaurants and department stores, the background music is often kept up at around 100 decibels. This is done to attract customers, whereas in Western countries it would surely drive them away. Lighting firecrackers is also very renao.

Many people in Taiwan have asked me why Americans like to live in the suburbs and commute to the city for work. 'The city is so much more exciting (renao),' they say, 'so why would anyone want to live out in the lonely countryside?' I have met a number of people in Taiwan who must work in the country, but they live in the city where housing is much more expensive and commute every day to the country. 'Why?' I ask. 'Because,' they say, 'the city is a good place to raise children.'

Guanxi The closest English word to *guanxi* would be 'relationship'. However, guanxi has a stronger meaning, similar to the English expression 'You scratch my back and I'll scratch yours'. To build up good guanxi, you have to do things for people, give them gifts, take them to dinner, grant favours, etc.

Once this is done, an unspoken obligation exists. It is perhaps because of this unspoken debt that people automatically try to refuse gifts. They may not wish to establish guanxi with someone, because sooner or later they may have to repay the obligation. Even after it is 'repaid', guanxi is rarely terminated. It is a continuing process of mutual gift-giving, back-scratching and favouritism that may last a lifetime.

I don't mean to make it sound all bad either. Knowing the right people can often dispense with a lot of red tape and can be mutually beneficial to all the parties involved – very important in traditional Chinese society, where stifling bureaucracy can make it difficult to accomplish anything.

Of course guanxi exists everywhere, and it's stronger on the Chinese mainland than in Taiwan, but you are likely to encounter it eventually. Those doing business with local people should pay particular attention to this.

Your Age Do you know how old you are? Many Chinese say you are already one year old on the day you are born. And they don't necessarily think that your second birthday comes a year later. You gain another year when the lunar New Year begins. So a child born a week before the New Year is already two years old when Westerners would say that he or she was only a week old.

Left-Handedness Conformity is valued over individualism in much of Asia and being left-handed makes one 'odd'. Children who are naturally left-handed are discouraged from using their left hand. If you are left-handed, you may draw comments when you sign your name or write a letter. However, the left hand is not unclean as in many parts of Asia so it is OK to touch people with it.

Family & Children The family is the basic foundation of Chinese society and children are highly prized. If you travel with children in Taiwan, everywhere you go someone will want to play with your kids. Avoid punishing your kids in public. If you spank your child publicly you will quickly draw a crowd of indignant onlookers. If you need to discipline a child, do it in private.

Chinese parents are very indulgent with their children and tend to baby them right into adulthood. It is not unusual to meet people in their late 20s still living at home. Chinese parents are appalled that Westerners leave teenage children at home while the parents go away for the weekend or that Western children can move out of the family home at the age of 18. The Chinese are also shocked that Western teenagers in high school and college often work part-time and use the money to pay for their education, rent an apartment or buy a car.

Chinese teenagers never baby-sit their younger brothers and sisters because a teenager is still considered a child. Chinese children are sheltered from most adult responsibilities until after they finish school. Perhaps as a result, most Chinese are overly dependent on their parents by Western standards.

The parent-child relationship is very strong in Taiwan throughout a person's lifetime and trouble within the family is never discussed publicly. When the parents get old and can no longer care for themselves, they usually live with their children rather than being packed off to rest-homes as in many Western countries. In my opinion, the strong family ties are one of the best characteristics of Chinese society.

Taiwan is a patriarchal society, in line with Confucian tradition. When a woman marries, her ties with her family are partially severed and she joins her husband's family – though, interestingly, she doesn't usually give up her maiden name. If the couple still live at home after marriage, it will be with the husband's family, never the wife's family. If they get divorced, the father gets custody of the children if he wants them.

A divorce is considered the ultimate catastrophe. Never tell people in Taiwan that you are divorced. It would be a major social blunder. You would be better off saying that your former spouse died.

Weddings If you spend any length of time in Taiwan, you're likely to be invited to a wedding. The wedding invitation is invariably red – a happy colour – and it usually brings with it the obligation to present money to the newlyweds. Therefore, it is often referred to as a 'red bomb'.

Should you receive a red bomb from a Chinese friend, you'll be happy to know that the money you are expected to give is really to pay for the fabulous 10-course meal that will be served at the wedding party. You needn't bring any other gifts, just the money. The money should be cash – not a cheque – and *must* be placed in a red envelope. It must be red because a white envelope is a death sign. Never give NT$400 or NT$4000 as the number four is also taboo. The typical amount expected these days is about NT$600 to NT$1000 per person. It's OK to bring an uninvited friend with you, but put an extra NT$600 in the envelope for each guest and let the host know in advance so enough food will be ordered. Be sure to write your name on the envelope so they know who it's from. Red envelopes should be used any time you give money to somebody, such as for a birthday, a gift or if you just owe money to somebody.

Wedding parties do not last very long, usually just a little more than an hour. Everyone just tends to eat and run, and there's very little time for talking and socialising. Guests are permitted to take home extra food in plastic bags which the restaurant will provide.

Funerals Hopefully, you won't be attending many of these. However, if someone you know dies, there are certain formalities that must be observed. If you receive a card informing you of the death of a friend or business associate, you are expected to send money, just as if you had received a wedding invitation. About NT$1000 is typical. Of course you don't have to, but if you value the relationship with the deceased's family you'd better pay up. In return, you will probably receive a cheap gift. I once received a towel (worth about NT$50) for my NT$1000.

You aren't expected to attend funerals unless specifically invited, and if you just send money, you can be excused. If you do go, you'll find it very different from a funeral in the West. The dearly departed can only be buried on an auspicious day, which could be a couple of months after death. During this time, the family sets up some sort of altar, usually in the street next to the house. Stacks of flowers and various gifts donated by friends (tinned food, beer and boxes of MSG are the usual items) surround the altar.

When the day for the funeral arrives, all invited guests must bring an envelope stuffed with cash – it *must* be a white envelope. If you're attending, dress neatly and be ready for anything – I say that because there are different types of funerals. A conservative, traditional Chinese funeral is a solemn affair, just as a funeral is in the West. However, the ceremony is very different. Children draped in white robes and with white hoods over their heads surround the casket. They also hold a white rope to keep out any bad spirits.

However, some people prefer a more festive occasion. They may employ the services of an 'electric organ flower car' *(diànzǐqín huāchē)*, which is a very brightly decorated truck containing an organ in the back. Beautiful young women clad in the scantiest bikinis will sing songs, and sometimes they strip off the bikinis. This is supposed to entertain the spirits. To remind everyone that this is indeed a funeral, people may be employed to cry. After the chanting, singing and stripping ceremonies, there's normally a little parade through the streets followed by a big feast.

It is perfectly acceptable to bring flowers to a funeral. Again, bring white flowers, not red.

Eating Orgies Rather than greeting someone by saying 'How are you?', many Chinese open a conversation by asking, 'Have you eaten yet?'. That might seem like a strange question to ask someone at 10 am, but food plays a big role in the formidable Chinese hospitality.

Proper hosts *must* feed their guests. If the guests aren't hungry, that is too bad – they will be force-fed. A proper guest, to avoid appearing greedy, *must* refuse. The host must do everything short of putting a funnel into your mouth and shoving the food in. One of the most amusing scenes you'll encounter in Taiwan goes something like this:

Host – Here, have something to eat.
Guest – Oh, no thank you, I just ate.
Host – Oh, but you must, I insist. Have some cake, some fruit.
Guest – No, no, I'm on a diet.
Host – But you must. Don't be shy. Have something.
Guest – Really, it's not necessary...(ad infinitum).

The best solution to this dilemma is to visit people when you are hungry. Such formidable hospitality not only means that you must eat with the appetite of a normal person but your host will see to it that you eat, eat and eat until you reach bursting point and then insist that you have some more. A phrase you'll soon learn to dread is *duō chī yīdiǎn* (eat some more).

Taboos
Showing Anger Venting your rage in public is bad form. Screaming and yelling will draw an instant crowd and some may regard you as being uncivilised. Rather than solving your problem, you may create more trouble for yourself. Smile. A lot of Westerners really blow it on this point. Maybe you want to say 'This food isn't what I ordered!' but if you need to complain about something, then do so in a polite, almost apologetic tone.

The Chinese are very successful at controlling their emotions in public. Even when greatly distressed, they try to look cheerful. Harmonious social relations are greatly stressed in Taiwan. Even when people disagree with what you are saying, they often pretend to agree or just smile rather than confronting you.

Westerners, on the other hand, tend to be argumentative and quick to complain when things don't go right. In the eyes of many Asians, this behaviour is rough-mannered or rude. Try to envision a scenario with a Western tourist in a hotel, screaming and yelling with much righteous indignation at the hotel clerk because the bed wasn't made and the hot water isn't turned on. The clerk just smiles and politely agrees, even though he thinks the tourist is a lunatic.

Speaking too Frankly In Asia, people don't always say what they mean. They often say what they think the other person wants to hear – it is always necessary to preserve face. Getting straight to the point and being blunt is not appreciated in Taiwan. If a local asks you, 'Do you like my new car?' be sure to say you love it, even if it's a piece of junk.

If you are asked, 'Are you married?' never say 'I just got divorced last month'. Divorce is a taboo topic, a deep, dark secret. If a Chinese friend asks for something of yours as a souvenir of your friendship, let him down easily if you don't want to give it to him. Don't simply say 'No'. You could say something like, 'Sorry, this book belongs to my brother and I borrowed it from him so I must return it. But if you give me your address, I'll send you another one from home when I get back'. Whether or not you send another one from home is not the point; you have helped preserve his face and yours by not bluntly saying 'No!'.

Avoid direct criticisms of people. The

Chinese stress polite manners and smooth social relations. It's better to make up a story or avoid the topic rather than confront someone with unpleasant facts that will cause embarrassment.

Red Ink Don't write a note in red ink. If you want to give someone your address or telephone number, write in any colour but red. Red ink conveys a message of unfriendliness. If you're teaching in Taiwan it's OK to use red ink to correct students' papers, but if you write extensive comments or suggestions on the back of the paper, use some other colour besides red.

Bad Omens Certain things are considered to be bad omens. Many Chinese are afraid to receive a clock as a gift, a sure sign that someone will die soon. The Chinese are very sensitive to death signs, so don't talk about accidents and death as if they might really occur. For example, never say to anyone, 'Be careful on that ladder or you'll break your neck'. That implies it will happen. Chinese people almost never leave a will, because to write a will indicates the person will die soon. If you write a will, it would be virtually impossible to find a local to witness your signature for you. They will not want anything to do with it.

In Chinese, the number 'four' sounds just like the word for death. As a result, hospitals never put patients on the 4th floor and you never give anyone a gift of NT$400 or NT$4000. If you give someone flowers, you always give red flowers, not white. In Chinese symbolism, white – not black – is the colour associated with death. The Chinese are really into longevity and death is a taboo topic. Sellers of life insurance have had an uphill battle in the Taiwan market.

The belief in omens probably explains why Chinese geographical names always mean something wonderful like 'Paradise Valley', 'Heaven's Gateway' or 'Happiness Rd'. There is one national park in America the Chinese never visit – Death Valley.

The Chinese (lunar) New Year has its special taboos and omens which are associated with your fortune in the coming year. You shouldn't wash clothes on this day or you will have to work hard in the coming year. On New Year's Day, don't sweep dirt out of the house or you will sweep your wealth away. Be sure you don't argue during the New Year, or you will face a year of bickering.

Young people are far less likely to pay heed to taboos and omens than the older generation. Similarly, urban residents care less about these things than rural people.

Avoiding Offence

Opening a Conversation Chinese people will often strike up a conversation with a total stranger by asking questions such as: 'Are you married?', 'How many children do you have?', 'How much money do you make?', 'May I know your name, address and telephone number?' or 'What is your blood-type?'. To be asked such questions in the West would be most unsettling, but it is quite normal in Taiwan. Asking personal questions is considered friendly.

How do you respond if you don't wish to reveal your blood type, how much money you make or your personal family history to a complete stranger? Simply make up whatever answer you feel comfortable with. No need to say how much money you make, just make up a figure. But don't blow up and yell, 'None of your business!'. That would be a major faux pas on your part. The person asking the question was only being friendly, not nosy.

Asking Favours The longer you stay in Taiwan, the more you will encounter people asking favours. Of course this happens everywhere, but in Taiwan it can reach irritating proportions. For example, having established guanxi by bribing you with a gift of Chinese moon cakes, you may then be asked to do some translating work – again and again. If you speak fluent English, you may soon find yourself in great demand to give lectures to English clubs, judge speech contests, correct term papers, proofread business faxes and write letters of recommendation for students who want to study abroad. All of this would be fine if anyone wanted to pay for these services, but that usually isn't the case.

What to do? First, try not to lose your temper, but politely make excuses. If that doesn't work, the last resort is to say you'll try to do it and then fail to complete the job. You will not be asked again.

Gift-Giving This is a very complex and important part of Chinese culture. When visiting people it is important to bring a gift, perhaps a tin of biscuits, flowers, a cake or chocolate. As a visiting foreigner, people will want to give you gifts. While sitting in a restaurant or just walking on the street, I've had total strangers come up to me and hand me candy, cigarettes and chewing gum. The first time it happened to me, I thought the guy was just a pushy door-to-door salesman so I handed the goods back to him and said abruptly 'I don't want to buy it'. I'm afraid I insulted the poor gentleman – a good example of cultural misunderstanding.

The most fascinating part of gift-giving is when you visit somebody's home. You are expected to bring a gift for your host. Your host will invariably refuse it. You are expected to insist. The verbal volleyball can continue for quite some time. If the host accepts too readily, then he or she is considered to be too greedy. They must first refuse and you must insist.

You – Here's a little gift I bought for you.
Host – No, no, it's not necessary.
You – Oh please, I want you to have it.
Host – No, you shouldn't waste your money on me.
You – Never mind, I've already bought it. It's my honour to give it to you.
Host – No, you should keep it for yourself.
You – Oh, but I insist that you take it.
Host – But I am not worthy of such a gift...ad infinitum, ad nauseam, ad exhaustium.

When receiving a gift, never open it in front of the person who gave it to you. That makes you look greedy. Express your deep thanks, then put it aside and open it later.

Removing Shoes One thing that the Chinese detest is a dirty floor. Never mind that the outside of their homes might look like a toxic waste dump, the inside must be spotlessly clean, especially the floor. Chinese people usually mop the floor daily, maybe even twice a day, and they won't appreciate you tramping dirt all over it. There are usually slippers by the entrance door, and if so, remove your shoes and wear the slippers. Your hosts may say, 'Never mind, just wear your shoes inside', but they aren't speaking frankly, they're being polite. You should take your shoes off.

When using the bathroom, there is usually another set of slippers especially for bathroom use because the floor is often wet. Most foreigners don't seem to mind this custom because it feels good to take your shoes off on a hot day. Unfortunately, the slippers provided are often too small for Western feet.

Dust Besides a dirty floor, another thing the Chinese detest is dust. You will often see motorcyclists and bicyclists wearing surgical masks to protect themselves from dust, even though they don't usually care about chemical pollutants from motor-vehicle exhaust. Students will often not want to sit in the front of the classroom because they fear the dust from the blackboard – as well as being afraid of the teacher.

Smiling A smile in Asia doesn't always mean the person is happy. Smiling is a proper response in an embarrassing situation. The waitress who smiles at you after pouring tea all over your lap isn't laughing at you. The smile is offered as an apology. If you get angry, she may smile more. I can assure you she doesn't think it's funny. If you jump up and yell, 'What are you smiling at, you idiot! Do you think it's funny?', then you have committed a major social error. Losing your temper is a big no-no. Smile.

Handing Paper to Somebody Always hand a piece of paper to somebody using both hands. This shows respect. This is especially true if that person is somebody important, like a public official, your landlord or a business associate. If you only use one hand, you will be considered rude.

Sport

Table tennis (ping-pong) is a traditional sport among the Chinese. These days, badminton and tennis are all the rage.

Western spectator sports have become prominent. Baseball, basketball and soccer games are occasionally broadcast on public television. During the soccer World Cup, Taiwanese viewers are glued to their TV screens.

Culture Shock

Perhaps you've never thought of this, but what Westerners see as so exotic in Asia is in fact very ordinary to Asians. They consider Westerners to be very exotic, and Western culture is fascinating to Asian peoples. Just as Westerners have guidebooks to explain Asian travel, art, architecture, music, religion, literature, fashion and languages, so the Asians have guidebooks to explain the exotic life in the USA, Europe and Australia.

When travelling abroad, the physical differences can be a source of endless delight. The exotic language, the interesting food, the strange but charming social customs, all make foreign travel fascinating and exciting.

But not everything you encounter overseas will be so charming. Many travellers come prepared to deal with such minor hazards as jet lag, diarrhoea and athlete's foot, but few recognise the problem of culture shock.

Tourists who only go abroad for a few days or weeks have little to fear, but those who are abroad for months or years are certain to suffer from some culture shock. Culture shock has been extensively studied by numerous psychologists, sociologists, anthropologists and various government organisations. The symptoms and stages of culture shock are well documented and predictable. Culture shock can be serious, in some cases leading to severe depression.

Some people are more susceptible to culture shock than others, and much depends on which countries you are visiting. As a general rule, the more alike two cultures are, the less problem there will be in adapting from one to the other.

If you stay in Asia for a long time, you can expect to encounter the first two (and possibly the third) stages of culture shock. Ironically, you may experience reverse culture shock when returning to your home country after a long stay overseas. The three stages of culture shock are:

Enrapture On arrival, most people are totally dazzled with the charming, exotic surroundings. 'Wow, I'm in Taiwan!' (or India or wherever) is a common reaction. Everything is new, interesting and exciting. Just riding an ordinary city bus is an experience. Eating dinner can be a real adventure and there is so much to see and do. It's all so much fun. You've discovered a new paradise, and many newcomers will even say things like: 'This country is more civilised than mine. There's a lot we can learn from this country.' Which may or may not be true, but it's doubtful that you really understand the country and its problems after just a few days or weeks. If you stay for a long time though, you will almost certainly reach stage two, which is:

Disillusionment Paradise lost. This feeling can come suddenly, gradually, very soon or very late, but it will come. The happiness bubble bursts. If you travel to a very poor country, disillusionment is liable to come sooner than if you visit a clean, prosperous, well-managed country. Yet even in a prosperous country, things will irritate you – maybe the food, language, climate, or people's ideas and attitudes.

Travellers will often get annoyed and start complaining about some minor cultural difference. How many times have people had rotten things to say about 'those Americans' and 'those British' and 'those French'. Yet, in spite of all the whining and complaining you may hear from travellers in Europe and the USA over petty issues, the cultural differences between these countries are trivial compared to what you will encounter in an Asian country.

In Asia, everything is different. Many things are 'illogical' according to Western ways. If you visit some of the poorest countries of Asia, Latin America and Africa, you are really going to have to tolerate a lot – an army of beggars, thieves, traveller's diarrhoea, amoebic dysentery, corrupt and brutal police, unbelievably dirty restaurants, etc.

Of course, conditions are much better than that in Taiwan, but you will get plenty of opportunities to experience culture shock. 'Why don't they Romanise the street signs?', 'The taxi drivers are crazy', 'How can anyone eat disgusting seaweed and watery rice for breakfast?', and 'Why do the little kids stare at me, yell *waiguoren* (foreigner) and pull the hair on my arms?' 'Why do people smile when they have an accident?'. Finally, 'Why are these people so illogical?'.

All the petty but irritating hassles pile up until the visitor ends up wishing for nothing but a plane ticket home, back to a 'sensible country'. Many do indeed leave, reducing the length of their intended stay. Others, both tourists and foreign residents, withdraw from the local culture entirely and seek out the refuge of their fellow expatriates. I should point out that Chinese living abroad also do this, which is why there are Chinatowns in many Western cities. The tendency is to look for something familiar in a foreign land. Expatriates in Asia often choose to live in 'foreigners' ghettos', eat familiar Western foods, and fail to learn the local language.

People who are suffering from the second stage of culture shock tend to complain a great deal. Many develop a 'superiority complex' ('We are superior to these natives'). They constantly write letters 'home' and always seem to be checking their mailbox. They search relentlessly for magazines and newspapers from their home country, and have no interest in local news. Some just bottle themselves up indoors with books or music tapes, or simply sleep all day, afraid to go out of the door. Instead of getting out and enjoying the experience of living in

a foreign country, expatriates working in Taiwan often fall into a rut, a boring daily routine of working, eating, sleeping and complaining. Chronic fatigue, a bad temper and frequent complaining are all signs of emotional depression. And that is the ultimate result of culture shock...depression.

The traveller can simply go home or at least to another country. An expatriate working overseas on a contract may not have this option. Married couples 'stuck overseas' are likely to take out their frustration on each other, and divorce is sometimes the result. The best solution, of course, is to try to reach the third stage:

Adaptation Asian people often ask a foreigner, 'So, how do you like my country?'. And the reply that they often get is, 'First of all, it's too hot, secondly I can't understand what people are saying, thirdly it's chaotic and no one obeys the traffic rules and...'

Face it. You cannot change Taiwan, you must adapt to it. It's hard to say how long it takes to adapt. Maybe three months, maybe six months, maybe a year, maybe never. Casual travellers of course don't have time to reach this stage. They must simply accept whatever comes and move on to a new country if the local culture becomes too frustrating. Foreign residents, on the other hand, must adapt or else suffer the consequences of isolation from the society they live in.

One suggestion I like to give to foreigners living in Taiwan – don't bottle yourself up; get out and explore. Even within the city limits of Taipei, there are opportunities for hiking (Yangmingshan, Sungshan Nature Reserve, etc). There are special-interest clubs (bungy jumping, computers, rock climbing, swimming, bowling, martial arts, Toastmasters, Hash House Harriers, etc). Taiwan also has very active nightlife – take advantage of it. Gluing yourself to a TV set or sitting around a hostel whingeing will only make you feel worse.

An important factor in adapting to a new culture is learning the local language. Communication is everything when it comes to social relations. Unfortunately, Chinese is not an easy language to learn for most Westerners. It takes several years of persistent effort to master the language, but you can get by with it in two years or so. I have known some foreigners to live in Taiwan for 30 years and never learn more than a couple of dozen words. Since Chinese is such a difficult language to write, it's probably best to concentrate on the spoken language at first and not worry about reading and writing until later. It takes a good five years to master the written language, but learning to speak Chinese can take less than half that amount of time. The opportunity to learn Chinese is one of the prime benefits of living in Taiwan.

Study everything you can about the country you are visiting or living in. There are many books written about Chinese culture and they apply as well to Taiwan as they do to the rest of China. Mix with the people and be sure to eat the local food. It may take some getting used to, but it's good. Don't head straight for McDonald's, Kentucky Fried Chicken or Pizza Hut every day. Try to avoid those 'foreigners' ghettos', where everything is 'just like home'.

This advice sounds easy to follow, but actually it's not. Only a small number of Westerners ever gain a true understanding of Asia. For most, a trip to Asia is a love-hate experience. But there are some who adapt very well.

There is also the opposite danger. Some foreigners are heavily influenced by the local culture, 'going native' in a sense. This is not necessarily a good adaptation. If it reaches the point of thoroughly rejecting your native culture and disparaging your home country to the point that you don't want anything to do with your country or its people, then you are suffering from another form of culture shock. For lack of a better term, I'll call it the 'rejection syndrome'. It's not a healthy sign at all.

The rejection syndrome is a common ailment among wandering Westerners who are drifting through Asia 'in search of themselves' and who think they've discovered 'true enlightenment' by adopting Eastern cult religions and rejecting all things

Western. Indeed, they come to believe that they now possess some exclusive wisdom that makes them superior to other Westerners. To put it more simply, they suffer from an inflated ego. What these 'enlightened' individuals fail to see is that Western culture, for all its faults, has many strong points, which is why it's so pervasive in the world today. While many Westerners go to China and India seeking knowledge and enlightenment, so do many Asians go to the West seeking the same thing. Just as the Chinese have contributed to the world's knowledge of science, literature, music, fashion and philosophy, so has the West. Living abroad for many years has made me recognise the strengths of Western culture, as well as its weaknesses. My advice would be to borrow the strong points of all the cultures you encounter and adapt them to your own needs. Very few manage to do so.

If you find yourself with the traveller's blues, be aware that you are in good company. Even Marco Polo had traveller's diarrhoea. Travel may not always be fun and games, but it is an enriching experience. To my mind, Asia is still the world's most fascinating continent.

RELIGION
China harbours many religions, and all the major ones have carried over to Taiwan. One outstanding fact of Chinese history is that the Chinese have never engaged in religious wars. The big three religions of China are Buddhism, Taoism and Confucianism.

Buddhism
(fó jiào) 佛教
One of the world's great religions, Buddhism originally developed in India from where it spread all over East and South-East Asia. With this spread of influence, the form and concepts of Buddhism have been changed significantly. Buddhism today has developed into numerous sects or schools of thought, but these sects are not mutually exclusive or antagonistic towards one another.

Buddhism was founded in India in the 6th

century BC by Siddhartha Gautama partly as a reaction against Brahmanism. Born as a prince, Siddhartha lived from 563 BC to 483 BC. In his early years, he lived a life of luxury, but became disillusioned with the world when he was confronted with the sights of old age, sickness and death. He despaired of finding fulfilment on the physical level, since the body was inescapably subject to these weaknesses. Dissatisfied with the cruel realities of life, he left his home at the age of 29 and became an ascetic in search of a solution. At the age of 35, Siddhartha sat under a banyan tree, and in a deep state of meditation, attained enlightenment. He thus became a 'Buddha', meaning 'Enlightened One'. It was claimed that Gautama Buddha was not the first Buddha, but the fourth, and is not expected to be the last.

The central theme of Buddhist philosophy is the belief that all life is suffering. All people are subject to the traumas of birth, sickness, feebleness and death; to what they most dread (incurable illness or personal weakness), as well as separation from what they love. The cause of suffering is desire – specifically the desires of the body and the desire for personal fulfilment. Happiness can only be achieved if these desires are overcome, and this requires following the 'eight-fold path'. By following this path the Buddhist aims to attain *nirvana*. Volumes have been written in attempts to define nirvana; the *sutras* (the Buddha's discourses) simply say that it's a state of complete freedom from greed, anger, ignorance and the various other chains of human existence.

The first branch of the eightfold path is 'right understanding': the recognition that life is suffering, that suffering is caused by desire for personal gratification and that suffering can be overcome. The second branch is 'right mindedness' – cultivating a mind free from sensuous desire, ill will and cruelty. The remaining branches require that one refrain from abuse and deceit; that one show kindness and avoid self-seeking in all actions; that one develop virtues and curb passions; and that one practise meditation.

Many Westerners misunderstand certain key aspects of Buddhism. First of all, it should be understood that the Buddha is not a god but a human being who claims no divine powers. In Buddhist philosophy, human beings are considered their own master and gods are irrelevant. There has been more than one Buddha, and there will be more in the future.

Reincarnation is also widely misunderstood. It is not considered desirable in Buddhism to be reborn into the world. Since all life (existence) is suffering, one does not wish to return to this world. One hopes to escape the endless cycle of rebirths by reaching nirvana.

Buddhism had reached its height in India by the 3rd century BC, when it was declared the state religion of India by the emperor Ashoka. It declined sharply after that due to factionalism and persecution by the Brahmans.

Numerous sects of Buddhism have evolved in different parts of the world. Classical Buddhists will not kill any creature and are therefore strict vegetarians. They further believe that attempting to escape from life's sufferings by committing suicide will only generate more bad karma and force one to be reborn at a lower level. Yet there are other Buddhist sects that hold opposite views – during the 1960s, Vietnamese Buddhists made world headlines by publicly burning themselves to death to protest against the war. Somehow, the various sects of Buddhism manage not to clash with each other.

Buddhism in China Buddhism reached China around the 1st century AD and became prominent by the 3rd century. Ironically, while Buddhism expanded rapidly throughout East Asia, it declined in India.

Buddhism in China mixed with other Chinese philosophies such as Confucianism and Taoism. The Chinese in particular had a hard time accepting the fact that they should not wish to return to this life as they believe in longevity. As many as 13 schools of Buddhist thought evolved in China, the most famous, perhaps, being Chan, which is usually known in the West by its Japanese name, Zen.

Taoism
(dào jiào) 道教

Unlike Buddhism, which was imported from India, Taoism is indigenous to China and second only to Confucianism in its influence on Chinese culture. The philosophy of Taoism is believed to have originated with Laozi, whose name is variously spelled Laotze, Laotzu or Laotse. Laozi literally means 'The Old One', a fitting description since he lived in the 6th century BC. Relatively little is known about Laozi, and many question whether or not he really existed. He is believed to have been the custodian of the imperial archives for the Chinese government and Confucius is supposed to have consulted him.

Understanding Taoism is not simple. The word *tao* (pronounced 'dào') means 'the Way'. It's considered indescribable, but signifies something like the essence of which all things are made.

A major principle of Taoism is the concept of *wuwei* or 'doing nothing'. A quote attributed to Laozi, 'Do nothing, and nothing will not be done', emphasises this principle. The idea is to remain humble, passive, nonassertive and nonaggressive.

Chien Szuma, a Chinese historian who lived from 145 BC to 90 BC, warned 'Do not take the lead in planning affairs, or you may be held responsible'. Nonintervention, or live and let live, is the keystone of the Tao. Harmony and patience are needed, action is obtained through inaction. Taoists like to note that water, the softest substance, will wear away stone, the hardest substance. Thus, eternal patience and tolerance will eventually produce the desired result.

Westerners have a hard time accepting this. The Western notion of getting things done quickly conflicts with this aspect of the Tao. Westerners note that the Chinese are like spectators, afraid to get involved. The Chinese say that Westerners like to complain and are impatient. Taoists are baffled at the willingness of Westerners to fight and die for abstract causes, such as a religious ideal.

It's doubtful that Laozi ever intended his philosophy to become a religion. Chang Ling is said to have formally established the religion in 143 BC. Zhuangzi (formerly spelled Chuangtzu or Chuangtse) is regarded as the greatest of all Taoist writers.

Taoism later split into two divisions, the 'Cult of the Immortals' and 'The Way of the Heavenly Teacher'. The Cult of the Immortals offered immortality through meditation, exercise, alchemy and various other techniques. The Way of the Heavenly Teacher had many gods, ceremonies, saints, special diets to prolong life and offerings to the ghosts. As time passed, Taoism increasingly became wrapped up in the supernatural, self-mutilation, witchcraft, exorcism, fortune telling, magic and ritualism.

Confucianism
(rújiā sīxiǎng) 儒家思想

Confucius is regarded as China's greatest philosopher and teacher. The philosophy of Confucius has been borrowed by Japan, Korea, Vietnam and other countries neighbouring China. Confucius never claimed to be a religious leader, prophet or god, but his influence has been so great in China that Confucianism has come to be regarded as a religion by many.

Confucius (551-479 BC) lived through a time of great chaos and feudal rivalry known as the Warring States Period. He emphasised devotion to parents and family, loyalty to friends, justice, peace, education, reform and humanitarianism. He also emphasised respect and deference to those in positions of authority, a philosophy later heavily exploited by emperors and warlords. However, not everything said by Confucius has been universally praised – it seems that he was a male chauvinist who firmly believed that men are superior to women.

Confucius preached the virtues of good government, but his philosophy helped create China's horrifying bureaucracy which exists to this day. On a more positive note, his ideas led to the system of civil service and university entrance examinations, where one gained position through ability and merit, rather than from noble birth and connections. Confucius preached against practices such as corruption, war, torture and excessive taxation. He was the first teacher to open his school to all students on the basis of their eagerness to learn rather than their noble birth and ability to pay for tuition.

The philosophy of Confucius is most easily found in the *Lunyu* or the *Analects of Confucius*. Many quotes have been taken from these works, the most famous perhaps being the Golden Rule. Westerners have translated this rule as 'Do unto others as you would have them do unto you'. Actually, it was written in the negative – 'Do not do unto others what you would not have them do unto you'.

No matter what his virtues, Confucius received little recognition during his lifetime. It was only after his death that he was canonised. Emperors, warlords and mandarins found it convenient to preach the Confucian ethic, particularly the part about deference to those in authority. Thus, with official support, Confucianism gained in influence as a philosophy and has attained almost religious status. Mengzi (formerly spelled Mencius; 372-289 BC) is regarded as the first great Confucian philosopher. He developed many of the ideas of Confucianism as they were later understood.

Although Confucius died some 2500 years ago, his influence lives on. The Chinese remain solidly loyal to friends, family and teachers. The bureaucracy and examination systems still thrive, and it is also true that a son is almost universally favoured over a daughter. It can be said that much of Confucian thought has blended into Chinese culture as we see it today.

Today's Religions

Depending on who's counting, about 2% to 5% of Taiwan's population is Christian. The vast majority of the people in Taiwan today consider themselves Buddhist or Taoist with Confucian influence. Most Chinese make no sharp distinction between Buddhism and Taoism in Taiwan, and the majority practise a hybrid of these two religions.

Confucianism is not truly regarded as a religion by most Chinese, although you may see statues of Confucius in Buddhist and Taoist temples next to the other major deities. However, in Confucian temples there are no statues or images of the gods. Confucian temples are simple and quiet. There are no monks or nuns in residence, just a temple caretaker.

Confucian temples hold only one ceremony per year and that is to celebrate the birthday of Confucius on 28 September. This ceremony begins about 4 am and lasts for two hours. It's a solemn affair with many dignitaries in attendance. An ox, goat or pig is sacrificed and those in attendance always hope to acquire some of the animal's fur, since it's believed to impart wisdom. Incense is never burnt in Confucian temples nor do they let off firecrackers.

Far more elaborate than the Confucian temples are the Buddhist and Taoist temples. The Buddhist temples are the quieter of the two. The most common deities you will see in a Buddhist temple are Kuanyin *(guānyīn)*, the goddess of mercy, and Shihchia *(shìjiā)*, from the Indian Sakyamuni, who represents the Buddha, Siddhartha Gautama (Siddhartha was his given name, Gautama his surname and Sakya the name of the clan to which his family belonged). One can often see large, fierce-looking statues of warriors brandishing swords placed near the temple doors. These are the temple guards, not deities. In Buddhist temples there are normally nuns and monks in residence; they are strict vegetarians and pass their time working in well-tended gardens.

Taoist temples are colourful, with lots of activity, burning of incense, parades, firecrackers, crashing of cymbals, ceremonies, exorcisms and offerings to the ghosts. Of all the Chinese religions, Taoism is the most steeped in mysticism and ritual. Among the better known Taoist deities are Matsu, goddess of the sea, and the red-faced Kuankung *(guāngōng)*, also known as Kuanti and Kuanyu. Fishermen often pray to Matsu for a safe journey, while Kuankung is believed to offer protection against war. Kuankung is based on an historical figure, a soldier of the 3rd century. You can read more about him in the Chinese classic *The Romance of the Three Kingdoms*.

Although Confucian temples are readily distinguished from other types, Taoist and Buddhist temples have partially merged, with the deities of both religions prominently displayed side by side in the same temple. Sometimes a statue of Confucius is displayed as well.

There are a few temples in Taiwan which are not Buddhist, Taoist or Confucian, but were simply built to honour a great hero. Many Chinese also worship their ancestors, building elaborate altars and tombs for their departed relatives.

Christian missionaries are active in Taiwan; there are representatives of nearly every denomination: Baptists, Catholics, Presbyterians, Mormons, Jehovah's Witnesses and Seventh Day Adventists, to name a few. Muslims are also represented in Taiwan and have built a mosque in Taipei. In addition, there are a very small number of people who practise what might be termed folk religions – the 'Duck-Egg Religion' is practised in the Kaohsiung area by one such group.

Temples

All over Taiwan you can find interesting and colourful temples ranging in size from a back-alley hut to a monumental, multi-storeyed structure that would dwarf some of the cathedrals of Europe.

One great thing about visiting temples in Taiwan is that they are free. Although they certainly welcome contributions, nobody in Taiwan will hustle you to pay. It's a sharp contrast to Japan, where at nearly every temple you are greeted by a monk selling admission tickets.

You are free to photograph inside temples, but be respectful of people praying. If you must photograph worshippers, do so from a distance with a long telephoto lens and no flash. Monks and nuns are usually camera-shy, so respect their wishes. Inside temples, avoid loud talk and romantic displays like kissing and hugging. Dress neatly, and be quiet and respectful so that travellers who come after you will continue to be welcomed. I have seen foreigners do some quite outrageous things in temples, such as ridiculing the deities, taking 'souvenirs', or climbing up onto a Buddha's lap to have a photograph taken. I know of at least one place where foreigners carved their initials into a wooden temple image.

In most temples you do not have to take off your shoes unless the floor is carpeted, but look to see what others do. If everyone piles their shoes outside the door, you should follow their lead.

Religious Ceremonies

Many forms of worship exist in Taiwan. Some worship takes place at home. Many people have altars in their homes and you can frequently see people performing a worship ceremony *(bàibài)* in front of their homes. A worship ceremony can take many forms as they're performed for different reasons. Most often, you will see somebody burning pieces of paper, which in fact represent money. If the money has a silver square in the middle it's 'ghost money'; if it has a gold square it's 'god money'. The money is usually burned to satisfy a 'hungry ghost' from the underworld (hell) so that it will not bother you or members of your family. The money could also be for a departed relative who needs some cash in heaven. Truck drivers often throw ghost money out of the window of their vehicles to appease the 'road ghosts', so that they don't have an accident. Some people place the ashes of ghost money in water and drink the resulting mixture as a cure for disease.

Another custom is for people to burn paper models of cars and motorcycles so the dearly departed may have a means of transport in heaven. Incense is frequently burned, often placed on a table with some delicious-looking food which is meant for the ghosts. However, after the ghost has had a few nibbles, the living will sit down to a feast of the leftovers. It's also possible for people to rent or borrow carved images of the deities to take home from the temple for home worship ceremonies.

If you visit a temple in Taiwan, you will probably encounter some strange objects that you may not have seen before. One such object is a box full of wooden rods *(qiān)*. Before praying for something you desire, such as health, wealth or a good spouse, select a rod. Then pick up two kidney-shaped objects called *shimbui* ('shimbui' is a Taiwanese word, not a Mandarin one). Drop them on the ground three times. If two out of three times they land with one round surface up and one flat surface up, then your wish may be granted. If both flat sides are down, then your wish might not be granted. If both flat sides are up, god is laughing at you.

Many festivals are held throughout the year in accordance with the lunar calendar. Some festivals only occur every 12 years at the end of every cycle of the 12 lunar animals, which are the rat, ox, tiger, rabbit, dragon, snake, horse, goat (sheep), monkey, rooster, dog and pig. Some festivals occur only once in 60 years. This is because each of the 12 animals is associated with five elements: metal, wood, earth, water and fire. The full cycle takes 60 years (5 x 12) and at the end of this time there is a 'super-worship' festival, which may involve tens of thousands of participants.

You can frequently see a Taoist street parade in Taiwan, complete with crashing cymbals and firecrackers. The purpose is usually to celebrate a god's birthday.

Look closely at the temples in Taiwan and you will see some Chinese characters inscribed on every stone, engraving, painting and statue. These characters are not those of the artist, but rather the names of the people who have donated money to purchase that particular temple ornament. Should you donate some money to a temple, you may also have your name engraved in stone.

Other than monks and nuns, practically nobody in Taiwan receives any formal religious education. Therefore, the majority of the population understands little of the history and philosophy behind Buddhism and Taoism.

Geomancy
(fēngshuǐ) 風水

The Chinese word *fēngshuǐ* means 'wind-water', but it has little to do with the climate. To be in correct geomancy is to be in proper physical harmony with the universe. This not only includes the living, but the spiritual world as well. If a Chinese person finds that their business is failing, a geomancer might be consulted. Sometimes the solution will be to move the door of the business establishment, at other times the solution may be to relocate an ancestor's grave.

Many Chinese worship their departed ancestors and build elaborate tombs for them. A geomancer should be consulted when this is done. If this wasn't done and misfortune strikes, then a geomancer may be called and the tomb moved. There is even a holiday in Taiwan known as Tomb Sweep Day, when you must clean the grave site of your ancestors.

Chinese Zodiac
(huángdàodài) 黃道帶

As in the Western system of astrology, there are 12 signs in the Chinese zodiac. Unlike the Western system, your sign is based on which year rather than which month you were born, though the exact day and time of your birth are also carefully considered in charting your astrological path.

Fortune tellers are common in Taiwan. Making use of astrology, palm reading and face reading, fortune tellers claim they can accurately predict the future. If you are so inclined, you can try out this service, though you are almost certain to need an interpreter since few fortune tellers in Taiwan can speak English.

If you want to know your sign in the Chinese zodiac, look up your year of birth in the following chart (future years given so you know what's coming). However, it's a little more complicated than this because Chinese astrology goes by the lunar calendar. The Chinese lunar New Year usually falls in late January or early February, so the first month will be included in the year before.

It's said that the animal year chart originated when Buddha commanded all the beasts of the earth to assemble before him. Only 12 animals came and they were rewarded by having their names given to a specific year. Buddha also decided to name each year in the order in which the animals arrived – the first was the rat, then the ox, tiger, rabbit and so on.

Lunar Calendar
(yuèlì) 月曆

There are two calendars in use in Taiwan. One is the Gregorian (solar) calendar which Westerners are familiar with, while the other is the Chinese lunar calendar. The two calendars do not correspond with each other because a lunar month is slightly shorter than a solar month. To keep the two calendars from becoming totally out of harmony, the Chinese add an extra month every 30 months to the lunar calendar, essentially creating a lunar leap year. Thus, the Chinese lunar New Year – the most important holiday – can fall anywhere between 21 January and 28 February on the Gregorian calendar.

You can easily buy calendars in Taiwan showing all the holidays for the current year. These calendars look just like the ones Westerners are familiar with, but the lunar dates are shown in smaller numbers.

LANGUAGE

Mandarin Chinese is the official language of Taiwan; it's spoken on TV and radio and taught in the schools. However, more than half the population speak Taiwanese at home, especially in the south and in the countryside. Taiwanese is nearly identical to the Fujian dialect spoken on the Chinese mainland. Taiwanese and Mandarin are similar in some respects, but they are still two different languages and not mutually intelligible. Taiwanese has no written script and therefore no literature, unless you count a Romanised version of the Bible used by missionaries. While virtually all the young people can speak Mandarin, many of the older people don't speak it at all. However, many older people know Japanese as a result of the 50-year occupation of Taiwan by Japan.

The study of English is required in Taiwan from junior high school on, but actually few students learn to speak it at all. They generally read and write English much better than they can speak it, so if you need to communicate in English, try writing your message down. The reason for this is that students

The Chinese Zodiac						
Rat	1924	1936	1948	1960	1972	1984	1996
Ox/Cow	1925	1937	1949	1961	1973	1985	1997
Tiger	1926	1938	1950	1962	1974	1986	1998
Rabbit	1927	1939	1951	1963	1975	1987	1999
Dragon	1928	1940	1952	1964	1976	1988	2000
Snake	1929	1941	1953	1965	1977	1989	2001
Horse	1930	1942	1954	1966	1978	1990	2002
Goat	1931	1943	1955	1967	1979	1991	2003
Monkey	1932	1944	1956	1968	1980	1992	2004
Rooster	1933	1945	1957	1969	1981	1993	2005
Dog	1934	1946	1958	1970	1982	1994	2006
Pig	1935	1947	1959	1971	1983	1995	2007

learn English by rote memory of textbooks, without any opportunity for conversation.

Another dialect found in Taiwan is Hakka, but its use is on the wane.

Taiwan's 10 aboriginal tribes each have their own language. These languages are not at all related to Chinese, and are generally regarded as Malayo-Polynesian in origin.

Mandarin Chinese, Taiwanese and Hakka are all tonal languages – by changing the tone of a word the meaning is completely changed. Mandarin has four tones, while other dialects can have as many as nine. For example, in Mandarin Chinese the word *ma* can have four distinct meanings depending on which tone is used:

high tone	*mā*	'mother'
rising tone	*má*	'hemp' or 'numb'
falling-rising tone	*mǎ*	'horse'
falling tone	*mà*	'scold' or 'swear'

In some words, the tone is not important. This so-called neutral tone is usually not indicated at all. Mastering tones is tricky for the untrained Western ear, but with practice it can be done.

A subtle difference in pronunciation can radically alter the meaning of a word. For example, the verbs *wèn* (to ask) and *wén* (to kiss) are only differentiated by the tone. I can only guess how many times I have said to my Chinese teacher 'I want to kiss you', when I meant to say 'I want to ask you'. Similarly, it's easy to forget the difference between *pifu* (skin) and *pigu* (buttocks). After a long day at the beach, I meant to tell one of my friends that his skin was red, but instead I told him...well, you get the idea.

So, try to be understanding when the Chinese err in their attempts to speak English. I met a nice gentleman on the train who told me that he was an 'executor' in Taipei. After further discussion, I determined that he meant 'executive'. My neighbour claimed he was a 'taxi diver'. On the bus, I sat next to a charming Chinese woman who asked me 'What is your obsession?'. I almost told her, but she probably meant 'profession'. Then there was the now famous case of a Taiwanese manufacturer who tried to market towel racks that attach to the bathroom wall with suction-cup feet. The name of his product was Suck-All. Another manufacturer tried his luck at exporting paint mixers that mix the paint by shaking and vibrating the container – his Jiggling Vibrators were an instant hit. Sissy-Boy Sportswear is probably doomed as an export item. Ditto for Boring Pie. Many Chinese seem to be confused about the difference between the bathroom and the toilet – which explains why one of my English students told me that he washed his hair in the toilet. And even after many years in Taiwan, it still brings a grin to my face when I check into a hotel and there is a sign on the front desk proclaiming 'We are happy to service you'.

Characters

Unlike most Western languages, written Chinese does not employ an alphabet. Instead, a system of 'idea-pictures' or characters is used – each character representing a different word or syllable. Scholars claim that about 50,000 Chinese characters exist, but most are variations of the same words and have long since become archaic. About 5000 are still in use today. Of these, only 2000 are very commonly used, and this would be considered the minimum needed to read a newspaper.

To twist a Chinese proverb, it can take a lifetime and a little bit more to learn how to read and write Chinese. Ironically, the spoken language is not very difficult to master, apart from the problems with tones. From my experience, it only takes about a month to learn to read and write 200 characters, but it's also very easy to forget them quickly if you don't practise constantly. In mainland China, a system of simplified characters was introduced to improve literacy. There is little doubt that the simplified characters are easier to learn and about twice as fast to write. However, traditions die hard – in Taiwan, Hong Kong and in most Chinese communities outside mainland China, the older complex characters are still used. In this book we will stick with the older characters, since these are the only kind you will encounter in Taiwan.

It is often said that Chinese is a monosyllabic language – that is, every word is claimed to be just one syllable long. Although I have seen this claim made in some academic texts, I dispute it. It's true that each character represents a single syllable and it's true that each character has a meaning of its own, but most modern Chinese words require more than one character to be written. The Chinese word for 'east' is composed of a single character *(dōng)*, but must be combined with the character for 'west' *(xī)* to form the word for 'thing' *(dōngxī)*. It's as if we took the English word 'carpet' and claimed it was two separate words, 'car' and 'pet'. We could then write English using the Chinese characters for 'car' and 'pet', but this would radically alter our perceptions of the English language. Perhaps we can say that Chinese has a monosyllabic writing system. Almost any language could be written with characters – Japanese, a language noted for very long words, uses a slightly modified version of Chinese characters. The Koreans and Vietnamese also used to write with Chinese characters, but abandoned them in favour of an alphabet.

Romanisation Systems

Chinese can be written in Romanised (alphabetical) form. Unfortunately, there are three competing Romanisation systems in common use, which causes great confusion. These are Yale, Pinyin and Wade-Giles. The three systems are similar, especially for vowels, but there are some significant differences in the way Chinese consonants are represented.

Yale is the easiest system for untrained Westerners to learn. It was developed by Yale University some years ago as a teaching aid, and at one time most Chinese textbooks for foreigners used it. Nowadays, Yale University has dropped this system in favour of Pinyin.

Pinyin takes more time to learn than Yale.

A number of Pinyin letters are confusing, as they are not pronounced the same as in English. On the other hand, Pinyin is the most accurate system of Romanisation yet devised for Chinese. Unfortunately, Pinyin is not used in Taiwan, except in some Chinese textbooks written for foreigners. It is used much more extensively in mainland China.

Wade-Giles is the oldest of the three systems, dating back to the early days of European contact with China. In Taiwan, Wade-Giles is still the official system used for street signs, maps, books, newspapers and name cards. The system is accurate if written correctly. Unfortunately, Romanisation is not taught in Taiwan's schools. Therefore most locals are unfamiliar with it and misspellings are common. For example, one street in Taipei alternately appears on maps as Tehui St and Tehhwei St; in Kaohsiung, Jeouru Rd and Chiuju Rd are the same place; a fashionable neighbourhood in east Taipei is variously spelled Dinghao, Dinghow and Tinghao.

A more serious problem with the Wade-Giles system is its use of the apostrophe. For example, the city of Taipei should be written with an apostrophe: T'aipei. Without the apostrophe, the initial **t** would be pronounced as a **d** – Daipei. But the apostrophes are almost always omitted, thus undermining the accuracy of the Wade-Giles system. As a result, the letter **ch'** is confused with **j**; **k'** with **g**; **p'** with **b** and so on. Without the apostrophe, the pronunciation radically changes, and the result is most confusing even for native speakers.

The presence of various conflicting systems of Romanisation poses a dilemma. Since maps, street signs and all official publications in Taiwan use the Wade-Giles system, I have decided to stick with convention and use the Wade-Giles system for all official geographical names and names of persons. Also in line with accepted practice in Taiwan, this book will ignore the apostrophes used in the Wade-Giles system. So we will write Taipei and Taiwan, not T'aipei and T'aiwan.

However, with the need for an accurate and easily learnt Romanisation scheme to assist foreign visitors in pronouncing Chinese words, the Wade-Giles name will be followed with the Pinyin Romanisation in italics and parentheses wherever necessary for clarification. For example, 'the second-largest city in Taiwan is Kaohsiung (*gāoxióng*)'. Whenever Pinyin is used in this text, it will always be in italics with tones shown. Other Romanised words will be written using the Wade-Giles system. Note that no tone marks will be shown with Romanised names on maps.

In line with the theory that Chinese is not a monosyllabic language, Romanisation shows multicharacter words as multisyllable words. Thus, the four character expression for 'messy' is written *luànqībāzāo* rather than *luàn qī bā zāo*.

Pronunciation

The following is a description of the sounds produced in spoken Mandarin Chinese. The letter **v** is not used in Chinese. The trickiest sounds in Pinyin are **c, q** and **x**. Most letters are pronounced as in English, except for the following:

Vowels

a	like the 'a' in 'father'
ai	like the 'i' in 'I'
ao	like the 'ow' in 'cow'
e	like the 'u' in 'blur'
ei	like the 'ei' in 'weigh'
i	like the 'ee' in 'meet' or like the 'oo' in 'book'*
ian	like in 'yen'
ie	like the English word 'yeah'
o	like the 'o' in 'or'
ou	like the 'oa' in 'boat'
u	like the 'u' in 'flute'
ui	like 'way'
uo	like 'w' followed by 'o' like in 'or'
yu	like German 'ü' – round your lips and try saying 'ee'
ü	like German 'ü'

*The letter 'i' is pronounced like the 'oo' in 'book' only when it occurs after c, ch, r, s, sh, z or zh.

Consonants

c	like the 'ts' in 'bits'
ch	like in English, but with the tongue curled back
h	like in English, but articulated from the throat
q	like the 'ch' in 'cheese'
r	like the 's' in 'pleasure'
sh	like in English, but with the tongue curled back
x	like the 'sh' in 'ship'
z	like the 'ds' in 'suds'
zh	like the 'j' in 'judge' but with the tongue curled back

Consonants can never appear at the end of a syllable except for n, ng, and r.

In Pinyin, apostrophes are occasionally used to separate syllables. So, you can write *(ping'an)* to prevent the word being pronounced as *(pin'gan)*.

The major differences between Pinyin and Wade-Giles are as follows:

Pinyin	Wade-Giles
b	p
c	ts'
c	ch'
d	t
g	k
p	p'
q	ch'
r	j
t	t'
x	hs
z	ts, tz
zh	ch

Pronouns

I
   wǒ 我
you
   nǐ 你

he, she, it
  tā 他
we, us
  wǒmen 我們
you (plural)
  nǐmen 你們
they, them
  tāmen 他們

Greetings & Civilities
hello
  nǐ hǎo 你好
goodbye
  zàijiàn 再見
thank you
  xièxie 謝謝
you're welcome
  búkèqì 不客氣
I'm sorry/excuse me
  duìbùqǐ 對不起

Useful Expressions
I want...
  wǒ yào... 我要
I want to buy...
  wǒ yào mǎi... 我要買...
No, I don't want it.
  búyào 不要
yes, have
  yǒu 有
no, don't have
  méiyǒu 沒有
How much does it cost?
  duōshǎo qián? 多少錢
too expensive
  tài guì 太貴
I don't understand.
  wǒ tīng bùdǒng 我聽不懂
I do understand.
  wǒ tīngde dǒng 我聽得懂
Do you understand?
  dǒng bùdǒng? 懂不懂
Wait a moment.
  děng yī xià 等一下

Necessities
toilet (restroom)
  cèsuǒ 廁所
toilet paper
  wèishēng zhǐ 衛生紙

tissue paper
  miàn zhǐ 面紙
bathroom (washroom)
  xǐshǒujiān 洗手間
tampons
  wèishēng mián tiáo 衛生棉條
sanitary pads (Kotex)
  wèishēng mián 衛生棉
sunscreen (UV) lotion
  fáng shài yóu 防曬油
mosquito incense coils
  wénxiāng 蚊香
vape mats (mosquito pads)
  diàn wénxiāng 電蚊香
laundrette (laundry service)
  xǐyī zhōngxīn 洗衣中心

Getting Around
airport
  fēijīchǎng 飛機場
reserve a seat
  dìng wèizǐ 定位子
cancel
  qǔxiāo 取消
ticket
  piào 票
refund a ticket
  tuìpiào 退票
reconfirm air ticket
  quèrèn 確認
boarding pass
  dēngjì kǎ 登記卡
motorcycle hire
  jīchē chūzū 機車出租
train
  huǒchē 火車
railway station
  huǒchē zhàn 火車站
bus station
  gōngchē zhàn 公車站
taxi
  jìchéngchē 計程車
local bus
  gōnggòng qìchē 公共汽車
highway bus
  bāshì 巴士
motorcycle
  jīchē 機車
car
  qìchē 汽車

petrol station
jiā yóu zhàn 加油站
fill it up
jiā mǎn 加滿
I want to get off (bus/taxi)
xià chē 下車
Which platform?
dì jǐ yuètái? 第幾月台
upgrade ticket (on train)
bǔ piào 補票
luggage
xínglǐ 行李
left-luggage room
xínglǐ shì 行李室
bonded baggage
cúnzhàn xínglǐ 存棧行李
lockers
bǎoxiǎn xiāng 保險箱

Directions
I'm lost.
wǒ mí lù 我迷路
Where is the...?
...zài nǎlǐ? 在那裡
Turn right.
yòu zhuǎn 右轉
Turn left.
zuǒ zhuǎn 左轉
Go straight.
yìzhí zǒu 一直走
Turn around.
zhuǎn gewān 轉個彎
alley
nòng 弄
lane
xiàng 巷
road
lù 路
section
duàn 段
street
jiē 街
No 21
21 hào 21號

Accommodation
hotel name card
míngpiàn 名片
hotel (all kinds)
lǚguǎn 旅館

cheap guesthouse
lǚshè 旅社
big hotel
dà fàndiàn 大飯店
mountain hostel
shān zhuāng 山莊
room
fángjiān 房間
dormitory
tuántǐfáng, duōrénfáng 團體房/多人房
private room
gerén fáng 個人房
tatami
tātāmǐ 榻榻米
room with shared bath
pǔtōngfáng 普通房
small room with private bath
tàofáng 套房
suite
gāojífáng 高級房
reserve a room
dìng fángjiān 定房間
deposit
yājīn 押金
check-in (register)
dēngjì 登記

Post & Telecommunications
telephone
diànhuà 電話
phonecard
diànhuà kǎ 電話卡
telephone company office
diànxìn jú 電信局
reverse-charge call
duìfāng fùqián 對方付錢
direct dial
zhí bō diànhuà 直撥電話
international call
guójì diànhuà 國際電話
post office
yóujú 郵局
poste restante
cún jú hòu lǐng 存局候領
GPO
zǒng yóujú 總郵局
stamp
yóupiào 郵票
aerogramme
yóujiǎn 郵簡

fax
  chuánzhēn　傳眞
telex
  diànchuán　電傳
telegram
  diànbào　電報
international express mail (EMS)
  kuàijié　國際快捷
domestic express mail
  kuài dì　快遞
registered mail
  guà hào　掛號
airmail
  hángkōng yùn　航空運
surface mail
  hǎi yùn　海運

Visas & Documents
passport
  hùzhào　護照
visa
  qiānzhèng　簽証
visa extension
  yánqī qiānzhèng　延期簽証
alien residence certificate (ARC)
  jū liú zhèng　居留証
household registration report
  jūzhù zhèngmíng　居住証明
driving licence
  jiàzhào　駕照

vehicle registration certificate
  xíngchē zhízhào　行車執照

Emergencies
I'm sick.
  wǒ shēng bìng　我生病
I'm injured.
  wǒ shòushāng　我受傷
hospital
  yīyuàn　醫院
police
  jǐngchá　警察
foreign affairs police
  wàishì jǐngchá　外事警察
Fire!
  huǒ zāi!　火災
Help!
  jiùmìng a!　救命啊
Thief!
  xiǎo tōu!　小偷
pickpocket
  páshǒu　扒手
rapist
  qiángjiānzhě　強姦者

Numbers

0	*líng*	零
1	*yī*	一
2	*èr*	二, 兩
3	*sān*	三
4	*sì*	四
5	*wǔ*	五

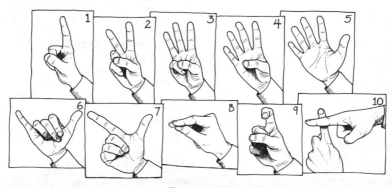

Finger counting

6	*liù*	六
7	*qī*	七
8	*bā*	八
9	*jiǔ*	九
10	*shí*	十
11	*shíyī*	十一
12	*shí'èr*	十二
20	*èrshí*	二十
21	*èrshíyī*	二十一
100	*yìbǎi*	一百
200	*liǎngbǎi*	兩百
1000	*yìqiān*	一千
2000	*liǎngqiān*	兩千
10,000	*yíwàn*	一萬
20,000	*liǎngwàn*	兩萬
100,000	*shíwàn*	十萬
200,000	*èrshíwàn*	二十萬

Time

What is the time?
  jǐ diǎn? 幾點
hour
  diǎn 點

minute
  fēn 分
now
  xiànzài 現在
today
  jīntiān 今天
tomorrow
  míngtiān 明天
yesterday
  zuótiān 昨天

Body Language

One of the most important things to learn is how to beckon to someone. This is done with the hand waved, palm down and it looks remarkably like the Western body sign to 'go away'. This same body sign is used throughout most of Asia. The typical Western form of beckoning, with the index finger hooked up, will draw a blank stare from an Asian.

The number 10 is indicated by using the index fingers on both hands to form a cross (see illustration of Chinese finger counting).

If you hold up all 10 fingers to indicate 10, no one will understand what you're doing.

Studying Chinese

There are a number of centres in Taipei and other cities where you can study Chinese, and some private schools teach Taiwanese as well. There are both government and privately run centres. The government places are good but tend to be advanced, inflexible and will really push you. The private ones will allow you to progress at a more leisurely pace and offer a good deal of flexibility in choice of teachers, curriculum, textbooks and scheduling.

You can get foreign-university degree credit through the Stanford Centre, but application must be made six months in advance for terms beginning in September – the other schools make it much easier to gain admission. Following is a list of language centres teaching Chinese to visitors to Taiwan:

Cathay Language Centre
　　2nd floor, 8 Lane 190, Chungshan N Rd, Section 7, Tienmu, Taipei (☎ 02-8729165)
China Language Institute
　　4 Lane 90, Anho Rd, Section 1, Taipei (☎ 02-7087157)

Tienmu Centre, 2nd floor, 51 Tienmu N Rd, Shihlin District (☎ 02-8726991)
Chinese Cultural University
　　Mandarin Learning Centre, 6th floor, 9 Roosevelt Rd, Section 2 (☎ 02-3567356)
Language Testing & Training Centre
　　170 Hsinhai Rd, Section 2, Taipei (☎ 02-3216385)
Mandarin Daily News
　　100 Fuchou St, Taipei (☎ 02-3915134)
My Language School
　　2nd floor, 126-8 Hsinsheng S Rd, Section 1, Taipei (☎ 02-3945400)
Perfect Language Institute
　　3rd floor, 55 Chungching S Rd, Section 1, Taipei (☎ 02-3120632)
Pioneer Language Institute
　　3rd floor, 59 Hoping E Rd, Section 1, Taipei (☎ 02-3410111)
Stanford Centre
　　Inter-University Programme, c/o National Taiwan University, 1 Roosevelt Rd, Taipei, PO Box 13-204, Taipei (☎ 02-3639123)
Taipei Language Institute (TLI)
　　7th floor, 104 Hsinyi Rd, Section 2, Taipei (☎ 02-3410022, 3938805)
　　Shihlin Branch, 2nd floor, 684 Chungshan N Rd, Section 5, Shihlin, Taipei (☎ 02-8360480/1)
　　Taichung Centre (☎ 04-2318842)
　　Kaohsiung Centre (☎ 07-2152965)
Taiwan Normal University
　　Mandarin Training Centre, 129 Hoping E Rd, Section 1, Taipei (☎ 02-3639123)
Tamkang University Language Centre
　　18 Lishui St (next to Taiwan Normal University), Ta'an District, Taipei (☎ 3567356)

Facts for the Visitor

As the Chinese say, 'A journey of 1000 miles begins with a single step'. If you're planning to visit Taiwan, the first step will be getting a visa.

VISAS & EMBASSIES

Taiwan has recently introduced a 'visa-free stay' period for the citizens of the following twelve countries: Australia, Belgium, Canada, France, Germany, Italy, Japan, Luxembourg, Netherlands, New Zealand, UK and USA. At the time of writing the Foreign Affairs Ministry was considering adding Sweden to the list. Visa-free entry allows you to remain in Taiwan for up to 120 hours (five days) only. You must have an onward or return ticket and your passport must have at least six-months validity remaining. Visa-free entry is available at any one of Taiwan's international entry points: the airports at Taoyuan and Kaohsiung and the seaports of Keelung and Kaohsiung.

If you wish to stay in Taiwan longer than five days or the conditions for a visa-free stay don't apply to you, then you need a visa. The problem is that visas for Taiwan are becoming increasingly difficult to get, in order to prevent people from coming to Taiwan to work illegally. In general, most Westerners will receive a single-entry visa valid for one to two months, and not extendable.

The visa regulations are inconsistent – it seems that visa offices have wide latitude to decide who gets what. At the time of writing, the Taiwan visa-issuing office in Bangkok was notorious for rejecting people, but Hong Kong was easing up after a long spell of xenophobia. This could change tomorrow – it all seems to depend on whoever is in charge, and staff changes are frequent.

To apply for a visa, you need your passport and three photos. Sometimes you need to show your plane ticket to prove that you have booked an onward flight from Taiwan. Any destination will do – it needn't be a return ticket to your home country. Often, no one will bother asking to see it at the visa office, but at the airport check-in counter it might be required. A visa can normally be issued in one day.

Most travellers from Europe will not usually be given a visa when they apply for one, but will be issued a letter which can be exchanged for a visa in the airport on arrival in Taiwan.

There are two kinds of visas, 'visitor' and 'entry' (resident). The vast majority of travellers will be issued visitor visas, of which there are two types, single-entry and multiple-entry. These usually permit a stay for 60 days, though recently 30 days has become the norm for Bangkok-issued visas. Under some circumstances it is possible to extend a visitor visa twice for a total stay of 180 days.

Single-entry visitor visas are easily obtained, but a multiple-entry visitor visa is usually only issued in your native country and is very hard to get while travelling in nearby Asian countries such as Hong Kong, Singapore or South Korea. Sometimes it is possible to exchange a single-entry visa for a multiple-entry visa after arrival in Taipei. See the Changing a Visa section further on in this chapter.

Entry visas, otherwise known as resident visas, are difficult to come by. They are usually issued only to people coming to Taiwan to work for a foreign company, to full-time students at a university, to spouses of ROC citizens, and to certain missionaries, researchers and big-time investors. To get this kind of visa, supporting documentation is required.

Visa-Issuing Offices

Visas are usually obtained from the embassy of the country you wish to visit, but in the case of Taiwan there are only a few countries which maintain diplomatic relations with the Republic of China. As there are so few ROC embassies in the world, Taiwan's government gets around this by maintaining a number of 'nongovernmental offices' in many countries. Besides issuing visas, these offices are important links in Taiwan's vital international trade. You can get a visa for Taiwan at any of the following offices:

Australia
Taipei Economic & Cultural Office, Unit 8, Tourism House, 40 Blackall St, Barton, ACT 2600 (☎ 06-2733344)
D401, International House (PO Box 148), World Trade Centre, Flinders & Spencer Sts, Melbourne (☎ 03-6112988)
Suite 1902, 9th floor, MLC Centre, King St, Sydney (☎ 02-2233207)

Austria
Institute of Chinese Culture, Stubenring, 4/III/18, A-1010, Vienna (☎ 512468)

Belgium
Office Economique et Culturel de Taipei, Avenue des Arts 41, B-1040 Brussels (☎ 02-5110687)

Canada
Taipei Economic & Cultural Office, Island Park Drive, Ottawa, Ontario (☎ 613-7226960)
Suite 1202, 151 Yonge St, Toronto, Ontario M5C 2W7 (☎ 416-3699030)
No 2008, Cathedral Place, 925 W Georgia St, Vancouver, BC V6C 3L2 (☎ 604-6894111)

Czech Republic
Taipei Economic & Cultural Office, Revolucni 13 7 P, 110 00, Prague 1 (☎ 2863257)

Denmark
Taipei Economic & Cultural Office, Falkoner Alle 53, 5 Sal 2000 Copenhagen F (☎ 31-197511)

Finland
Buleardi 1A 22, 00100, Helsinki (☎ 6801216)

France
ASPECT, 75 Rue d'Anjou, 75008, Paris (☎ 4470-7000)

Germany
Taipei Wirtschafts und Kulturburo, Dahlmannstr 23, 1000 Berlin 12 (☎ 030-3236010)
Villichgasse 17, IV, OG, 5300 Bonn 2 (☎ 364014)
Mittelweg 144, 2000 Hamburg 13 (☎ 040-447788)
Grassistrasse 12, 0-7010 Leipzig (☎ 041-7170563)
Tengstrasse 38, 8000 Munich 40 (☎ 089-2716061)

Greece
Taipei Economic & Cultural Office, 4th floor, 54 Queen Sophia Ave, GR 115 28, Athens (☎ 7224613)

Hong Kong
Chung Hwa Travel Service, 4th floor, Lippo Centre, No 89, Queensway, Hong Kong Island (☎ 5258315)

Hungary
1088 Budapest VIII, Rakoczi ut 1-3/III em (☎ 266884)

Indonesia
Taipei Economic & Trade Office, 7th floor, Wisma Dharmala, Sakti, Jalan Jend Sudirman 32, Jakarta 10220 (☎ 5703047)

Ireland
1st floor, South Leinster St, Dublin 2 (☎ 785580)

Italy
Instituto Culturale ed Economico di Taipei, Via Sardegna 50, II P Int 12, 00187, Rome (☎ 4741613)

Japan
Taipei Economic & Cultural Representative, 20-2 Shironganedai 5-Chome, Minato-Ku, Tokyo 108 (☎ 3280-7811)
3rd floor, Sun Life Building III, 5-19, 2-Chome, Hakataeki, Higashi Hakata-Ku, Fukuoka (☎ 092-4736655)

Macau
Taipei Trade & Tourism Office (information only), Edificio Commercial Central, 150 Andar Avenida Infante D Henrique, 60-64 (☎ 306282)

Malaysia
Taipei Economic & Cultural Centre, 9th floor, Amoda Building, 22 Jalan Imbi 55100, Kuala Lumpur (☎ 2410015, 2425549)

Netherlands
Taipei Economic & Cultural Office, Javastraat 46-48, 2585 AR, The Hague (☎ 070-3469438)

New Zealand
Taipei Economic & Cultural Office, Level 21, Marac House,105-109 The Terrace, Wellington (☎ 04-4736474)
4th floor, Norwich Union Building, cnr Durhan & Queen Sts, Auckland (☎ 09-3033903)

Norway
Taipei Economic & Cultural Office, POB 5613 Briskeby, Riddervolds Gate 3, 0209 Oslo 2 (☎ 555471)

Philippines
Taipei Economic & Cultural Office, 28th floor, Pacific Star Building, Sen Gil J Puyat Ave (PO Box 1097), Makati Central Post Office, Corner Makati Ave, Makati, Metro Manila (☎ 881381)

Portugal
Taipei Economic & Cultural Centre, Rua Castilho, 65-1 Andar Direito, 1200 Lisbon (☎ 3860617)

Singapore
Taipei Trade Representative, 460 Alexandra Rd, 23-00 PSA Building, Singapore 0511 (☎ 2786511)

South Africa
Embassy of the ROC, 1147 Schoeman St, Hatfield, Pretoria 0083 (☎ 012-437946)

Spain
  Centro Cultural y Economico de Taipei, Paseo de
  la Habana 12-4, 28036 Madrid (☎ 4113711)
Sweden
  Taipei Trade, Tourism & Information Office,
  Wenner-Gren Centre, 4tr, Sveavagen 166, S-113
  46, Stockholm (☎ 08-7288513)
Switzerland
  Delegation Culturelle et Economique de Taipei,
  Stampfenbachstrasse 56, 8006 Zürich
  (☎ 01 3634242)
  54 Ave de Bethusy, 1012 Lausanne
  (☎ 21-6535005)
Thailand
  Taipei Economic & Trade Office, 10th floor,
  Kian Gwan Building, 140 Wit Thayu Rd,
  Bangkok (☎ 2519274, 2519393)
UK
  Taipei Representative Office, South Grosvenor
  Gardens, London, SW1W 0EB (☎ 071-3969152,
  fax 3969151)
USA
  Coordination Council for North America Affairs
  (CCNAA), Head Office, 4201 Wisconsin Ave
  NW, Washington, DC 20016-2137
  (☎ 202-8951800)
  Suite 1290, 2 Midtown Plaza, 1349 W Peachtree
  St NE, Atlanta, GA 30309 (☎ 404-8720123)
  Suite 801, 99 Summer St, Boston, MA 02110
  (☎ 617-7372050)
  57th floor, 2 Prudential Plaza, 180 N Stetson Ave,
  Chicago IL 60601 (☎ 312-6160100)
  Suite 505, Bank of Guam Building, 111 Chalan
  Santo Papa (PO Box 3416), Agana, Guam 96910
  (☎ 671-4725865)
  2746 Pali Highway, Honolulu, HI 96827
  (☎ 808-5956347)
  Suite 2006, 11 Green Way Plaza, Houston, TX
  77046 (☎ 713-6267445)
  Suite 1001, 3100 Broadway, Kansas City, MO
  64111 (☎ 816-5131298)
  Suite 700, 3731 Wilshire Blvd, Los Angeles, CA
  90010 (☎ 213-3891215)
  The Colonnade, 2333 Ponce de Leon Blvd, Suite
  610, Coral Gables, FL 33134 (☎ 305-4438917)
  9th floor, 801 Second Ave, New York, NY 10017
  (☎ 212-6971250)
  Suite 501, 555 Montgomery St, San Francisco,
  CA 94111 (☎ 415-3627680)
  Suite 2410, Westin Building, 2001 6th Ave,
  Seattle, WA 98121 (☎ 206-4414586)
Vietnam
  Taipei Economic & Cultural Office, Building No
  2D, Khu Ngoai Giao, Doan Van Phue, Badinh
  District, Hanoi (GPO Box 104) (☎ 4-234403)
  No 68 Tran Quoc Thao St, District 3, Ho Chi
  Minh City (☎ 8-299343)

Visa Extensions

A visitor visa is normally valid for 60 days
and can be extended for another 60 days with
some hassle. Two-week visitor visas cannot
be extended. The first extension is easier to
get than the second. If you're lucky, you'll
be able to get a first extension simply by
showing that you've spent sufficient funds in
Taiwan (save the receipts from cashed
travellers' cheques). You also need to fill out
a Household Registration Report and get
your landlord (or hostel owner) to stamp it
with his or her chop. Some of the private
language schools in Taipei offer 'visa
services'. For a fee, they will handle the
paperwork for you. Usually this only works
for the first visa extension. I can't swear by
the reliability of such services, so you'll have
to make your own enquiries at the schools or
ask other travellers if it's worked for them.
These visa services are advertised in the local
newspapers, the *China Post* and *China
News*.

Warning Many privately run language schools
claim that they are government-approved and therefore can get you visa extensions. Don't take their word
for it! Once you hand over the tuition fee, don't expect
a refund even if it turns out that the school is not
government-approved. Some travellers have been
ripped off this way. To be sure, always first ask at the
Foreign Affairs Police if a certain school is government-approved and if enrolling at it will guarantee
you a visa extension.

The authorities take a dim view of second
extensions – sightseeing is not considered to
be a valid reason for extending beyond 120
days. You need a good excuse for the second
extension. Among the excuses considered
valid are study at a government-approved
language school, visiting close relatives,
medical treatment, doing business, or technical assistance. Supporting documentation
is required. Even then, you might be
requested to get a tax clearance from the tax
office before the extension is granted. To get
the clearance, you either have to pay taxes or
show you've received sufficient funds from
abroad to subsidise your stay.

When applying for an extension, you must

go to the Foreign Affairs Police. There are a total of 21 Foreign Affairs Police offices in Taiwan, one in each county seat and one in each of the five special municipalities – Taipei, Keelung, Taichung, Tainan and Kaohsiung. You need to bring your passport of course, but no photos. Don't go during or near the lunch hour (hours!) – about 11.30 am to 2 pm.

The Foreign Affairs Police wields god-like powers – be nice to them or reap the whirlwind. See the section on Useful Organisations for the locations and telephone numbers of all Foreign Affairs Police offices.

Changing a Visa Under some circumstances it is possible to exchange one type of visa for another kind after arrival in Taiwan. For example, it is possible to exchange a single-entry visitor visa for a multiple-entry visitor or entry (resident) visa. However, it isn't easy. You will need a good reason for requesting such a change and supporting documentation is required.

Enrolment at a government-approved school will usually get you a multiple-entry visitor visa, or a one-year entry visa if the school is a university. It is possible to get a resident visa by teaching English in one of Taiwan's numerous private 'cram schools', but only if the school is legally licensed (many are not) and only if you are paying taxes. You can also usually obtain an entry visa by becoming a missionary, investing a few million dollars in the local economy, or stealing a military jet from mainland China and flying it to Taiwan (the latter method may net you a substantial cash payment as well). Marrying an ROC national easily gets you a resident visa if you're female, but does not necessarily get you the right to work – in Taiwan, women are expected to stay at home and care for the children. For men who marry Taiwanese women, gaining residence is possible only if the husband remits sufficient foreign funds into Taiwan to pay all the living expenses for the family.

The only city in Taiwan where you can change your visa is Taipei. It is possible to do it by post, though this requires mailing your passport to Taipei, which means you have to trust the post office not to lose it. Use registered mail, which is very reliable in Taiwan. If your application is approved, it will still take several months to complete the procedure.

To change your visa contact the Ministry of Foreign Affairs (☎ 02-3897711) *(wàijiāo bù)*, 1 Kueiyang St, Taipei. For information about visas (how to obtain a resident visa, etc), contact the Department of Consular Affairs (☎ 02-3119292), Ministry of Foreign Affairs, 2 Chiehshou Rd, Taipei.

Overstaying a Visa If you overstay your visa by even one day you won't be able to leave the country until you clear up the matter. If you overstay by only a few days, you won't get into any serious trouble if you can give a valid reason, such as illness or missing your flight. If this happens to you, report as soon as possible to the Foreign Affairs Police at the main police station in whatever city you are in. You will have to pay a fine of around NT$600 – the exact amount will be determined by such factors as how long you overstayed and the reason why. The amount of paperwork you'll have to do is more of a punishment than the fine, so try to avoid overstaying. Overstaying can jeopardise your chance of getting a new visa later on, so if the Foreign Affairs Police puts a bunch of nasty stamps in your passport, you might have to get a new passport if you're determined to re-enter Taiwan.

Re-Entry Visas
Alien residents must apply for an exit and re-entry visa in advance every time they wish to leave the country. Failure to do this will result in loss of resident status. In order to get the re-entry visa, you have to get tax clearance – to do this, you must pay your estimated tax for the entire period up to time of departure. Those with visitor visas do not have to worry about this, but tax clearance may be required if you've extended your visa numerous times.

DOCUMENTS
Passport

A passport is essential, and if yours is within a few months of expiration, get a new one now – Taiwan and many other countries will not issue a visa if your passport has less than six-months validity remaining. Also, be sure it has plenty of space for visas and stamps.

Losing your passport is very bad news – getting a new one means a trip to your embassy or consulate and usually a long wait while they send faxes or telexes (at your expense) to confirm that you exist. Since there are so few consulates in Taiwan, you'll have to try to work through some of the 'trade offices' (see Pseudo-Embassies in the Taipei chapter) which will probably send the paperwork to the nearest consulate in Hong Kong. This process can take several weeks. If you're going to be in Taiwan for a long period of time, it might be wise to register your passport at your national consulate in Hong Kong, which will expedite matters should you need a replacement.

Driving Licence

If you plan to be driving abroad, get an International Driving Permit from your local automobile association. These are valid for one year only so there's no sense getting one far in advance of departure. Make sure that your permit states that it is valid for motorcycles if you plan to be driving a motorcycle over 50 cc in Taiwan.

Health Certificate

Useful (though not essential) is an International Health Certificate to record any vaccinations you've had. These can also be issued in Taiwan at any health department.

Student ID Card

Full-time students coming from the USA, Australia and Europe can often get some good discounts on tickets with the help of an International Student Identity Card (ISIC). This card entitles the holder to a number of discounts on airfares, trains, museums, etc. To get this card, enquire at your campus. ISIC cards can be issued in Taiwan at *Youth*

Travel International (☎ 7211978, fax 7212784) *(guójì xuéshēng qīngnián lüyóu)*, Suite 502, 142 Chunghsiao E Rd, Section 4, Taipei – a student ID card or a university letter of acceptance is required.

In Australia, STA Travel issues STA Youth Cards to persons aged 13 to 26 years. These can also be obtained in Taiwan from Youth Travel International.

ISIC cards are of very limited use in Taiwan. The airlines in Taiwan have it very good – high prices and often full seats, so they are not keen to give student discounts. Within Taiwan, you will need some sort of Chinese student ID to get discounts. You may be able to get such an ID card if you study Chinese at a Taiwan university, but don't count on it. They aren't happy about giving these cards to part-time students. I have seen some fake student IDs, but quality varies. Moreover, in Taiwan it's a serious offence to possess a fake ID – the official designation is 'document forgery' and penalties are severe.

Alien Resident Certificate

Those with resident visas are required to apply for an alien resident certificate (ARC) after arrival in Taiwan. This permits you to live and work in Taiwan for a specified period. The certificate must be renewed each year at a cost of NT$1000.

Mountain Permit

If you hike or travel in certain remote mountain areas of Taiwan, a permit might be required. At times, this can be a real nuisance. Fortunately, they are not required in all mountain areas; on the other hand, they are required for some of Taiwan's most spectacular peaks such as Yushan and Tapachienshan.

There are two types of mountain permit, one which is easy to obtain and another which is difficult. The difficult one is called a class A pass *(jiǎzhǒng rùshānzhèng)* and the easy one is a class B pass *(yǐzhǒng rùshānzhèng)*.

Class B permits can usually be obtained in a few minutes, right at the roadside entrance or trail head, after you've filled out a simple form. It's no hassle to get a class B pass, and if you can't read Chinese the police will probably fill out the form for you.

To apply for a class B mountain permit, you need some sort of ID. Your passport will do, but Chinese ID cards are preferred. Acceptable Chinese ID includes a driving licence or alien resident certificate. The processing fee is NT$10. The pass will be issued on the spot.

Class A mountain permits must be applied for in advance and are not easy to get. For most travellers, there are only two ways to obtain such a pass: join a mountain club and go on one of their regularly scheduled trips, or hire a government-licensed guide.

If you go with a mountain club, they will need photocopies of your passport and alien resident certificate (if you have one) at least a week in advance. The club will apply for the permit and make all the arrangements. The best club for arranging this is the ROC Alpine Association (02-5911498, 5942108) *(zhōnghuá shānyuè xiéhuì)*, 10th floor, 185 Chungshan N Rd, Section 2, Taipei; another is the Mountaineering and Hiking Association (☎ 02-7510938) 50-A, Lungchiang Rd, Taipei. If you choose to hire a licensed mountain guide, the Alpine Association can also arrange this. You need at least four people in your climbing party (including the guide), and you must submit the following documents to the Association: itinerary (one copy); member list (five copies); photocopies of members' passports (one copy). The climbing party is expected to pay the guide's expenses including food, accommodation and transportation. You must obtain suitable climbing gear, which you can buy, rent or borrow. In other words, don't expect to climb Yushan in thongs and a T-shirt.

If you want to climb solo, there are only two ways in which to obtain a class A pass. You must be a genuine missionary (with credentials to prove it) or a scientific researcher. Supporting documentation is definitely required – for example, a letter from a university saying you are studying botany, meteorology or archaeology. In addi-

tion, a letter from a consulate or the American Institute in Taiwan (AIT) endorsing your travel plans would be useful. Even with all this, it is by no means certain that the permit will be granted.

The place to apply for a mountain permit is at the Foreign Affairs Office, Taiwan Provincial Police Administration, 7 Chunghsiao E Rd, Section 1, Taipei – directly across the street from the Lai Lai Sheraton Hotel.

If you are not in Taipei, you can still apply for a class A pass at any office of the Foreign Affairs Police or at the main police station in any major city or county seat. However, they must send all the paperwork to Taipei, which delays the process by several days.

Remember, only some areas of Taiwan require these permits. If you don't want to bother with these passes, hike in the places where they are not necessary.

Notarised Documents

In Taiwan, it's not customary to notarise documents. Consequently, public notaries are few and far between, but they can be found in the county or city courthouse. Most foreigners will probably prefer the notary service offered by the American Institute in Taiwan (AIT), at both the Taipei and Kaohsiung offices.

Other Documents

If you're travelling with your spouse, a photocopy of your marriage licence just might come in handy should you become involved with the law, hospitals or other bureaucratic authorities.

If you're planning on working or studying in Taiwan, it could be helpful to have copies of transcripts, diplomas, letters of reference and other professional qualifications.

CUSTOMS

In the past, entering Taiwan was a trauma – customs agents gleefully ripped everything apart just to make sure you weren't smuggling in an extra Rolex or bottle of fancy perfume. These days, things are much easier and your bags might not even be opened.

Reasonable quantities of items for personal use can be brought in duty-free with no trouble. If you're taking a dutiable item out of Taiwan, register it with customs before you depart if you intend to bring it back in duty-free at some future date.

Arriving travellers are permitted a duty-free allowance of US$5000 worth of goods. The limit for children is half that of adults. These limits are not applicable to gold, liquor and cigarettes.

Customs rules regarding gold, silver and foreign currency are strict. Any amount of foreign currency can be brought in but must be declared on arrival. Otherwise, only US$5000 in cash or the equivalent amount in another foreign currency can be taken out on departure. No more than NT$40,000 can be brought in or taken out. Travellers' cheques and personal cheques are not considered cash and do not have to be declared.

Any gold or silver brought in must be declared on arrival or else it can be confiscated. You cannot bring in more than US$5000 worth without an import permit. However, if you arrive in Taiwan carrying gold or silver you may place it in storage under the custody of customs and a receipt will be issued – don't lose it. On departure the gold or silver will be returned on presentation of the receipt. Of course, you must depart from the same place where you arrived.

If you are carrying taxable items but only intend to stay 45 days or less, you can place your goods in bonded baggage and take them out again on departure. If you do this you won't be required to pay duty. If you want or need the dutiable item for use during your stay in Taiwan, it is possible to pay the duty and have the money returned to you on departure. This is a hassle, but some people do it.

Anyone aged 20 or over can bring in a litre of liquor and either 200 cigarettes, 25 cigars or 500 grams of tobacco duty-free.

Any literature deemed pro-Communist or subversive may be confiscated. You aren't supposed to bring in anything made in mainland China – virtually everyone breaks this rule, but remove obvious labels to avoid trouble. Pornography is prohibited (competes with the locally produced stuff). You can't bring in toy guns even though they are a major export and available from any toy store in Taiwan.

Needless to say, real guns, ammunition and narcotic drugs are prohibited items – these are the three things that can get you into big trouble fast. Most backpackers don't carry guns and ammunition, but narcotics have landed more than a few travellers in prison. In 1993, two foreigners received life sentences for smuggling heroin – it was probably only their foreign nationality that prevented them from being executed. Just one month earlier, three foreigners were given 14 years in prison for smuggling hashish. Don't let this happen to you.

MONEY
Currency
The official unit of currency is the New Taiwan dollar (NT$), which totals 100 cents. Coins in circulation come in denominations of 50 cents (very rare!), NT$1, NT$5, NT$10 and NT$50; notes come in denominations of NT$50, NT$100, NT$500 and NT$1000.

US$ and other major currencies are *not* widely accepted in shops and hotels. Though some people may exchange them for you, it's illegal to do so. The NT$ is a controlled currency – not a hard (freely traded) currency, so you will have difficulty exchanging it outside Taiwan. An exception is Hong Kong, where it can be easily exchanged, but at a slightly lower rate than in Taiwan.

Exchange Rates
Exchange rates in early 1994 included:

A$1	=	NT$18.00
C$1	=	NT$20.60
HK$1	=	NT$3.50
NZ$1	=	NT$16.20
UK£1	=	NT$40.30
US$1	=	NT$26.60
Y100	=	NT$24.60

Changing Money Foreign currency and travellers' cheques can be changed at the two international airports and at large banks. Some major international hotels will cash travellers' cheques, but they usually only do so if you're staying there. It can be difficult or even impossible to cash travellers' cheques in rural areas, so take care of this in the cities.

Many banks will change US$ cash, but other currencies can be a problem. Ditto for travellers' cheques – if they're not denominated in US$, cashing them could be problematic, especially outside of Taipei.

Only major banks will cash travellers' cheques, and only if they have a licence to do so issued by Taiwan's Central Bank. Banks so-licensed include the Bank of Taiwan, International Commercial Bank of China (ICBC), City Bank of Taipei (also called Taipei Bank), Changhua Commercial Bank, Hua Nan Commercial Bank and First Commercial Bank. ICBC is probably the best because all branches change foreign currency – with the other banks, it's uncertain. City Bank of Taipei gives good service, but it currently has no branches outside of Taipei (that's expected to change).

Many banks charge a fee for each cheque cashed, but it varies. The Bank of Taiwan only charges NT$10 per transaction in Taipei, but the Bank of Taiwan in Touliu asks NT$160! Some banks charge you a commission on each cheque, so those with small denomination cheques get burned. On the other hand, some banks set a limit of not cashing over US$300 at a time, so those with US$500 denominated travellers' cheques will have a problem in those places. The best practice is to change money in large cities, not in small backwaters. All banks, including the one at the airport, give the same exchange rate.

Taiwan does not have private moneychangers like you find in Hong Kong – the Central Bank prohibits this.

Normal banking hours are from 9 am to 3.30 pm Monday to Friday and from 9 am to noon on Saturday. The bank at CKS Airport is supposed to remain open whenever there

are international flights departing or arriving. The bank at Kaohsiung International Airport follows the same policy but seems to be somewhat unreliable. On departure from either airport, you must change money before heading through immigration – there is no moneychanger beyond this checkpoint.

When you change money, it is supposedly essential to save your receipts if you wish to reconvert your excess NT$ when you depart. To reconvert your NT$ into US$ on departure, you must take the receipts to the bank at the airport, *not* the city bank. If you stay in Taiwan for more than six months you cannot reconvert excess NT$ on departure. This is all according to the official rules – in practice, the airport bank will convert small amounts (up to NT$3000) without the receipts.

Black Market It is also possible to change money at some jewellery stores – you have to make enquiries to find out which stores will do it. Since this is illegal, they don't advertise. They only handle cash, not travellers' cheques, and they only deal in major currencies like US$ or Japanese yen. There are abundant rumours of counterfeit bills. You won't make money from Taiwan's black market – indeed, you'll be charged a small commission of around 2% which is included in the quoted exchange rate. There is little reason for visitors to use the black market – foreigners working illegally in Taiwan often seek out the black market to get US$ to take out of the country, but even this isn't really necessary since NT$ can be readily exchanged in Hong Kong.

Bank Accounts Silly as it may seem, the Central Bank has deemed that foreigners are not permitted to open NT$ bank accounts in Taiwan unless they have alien resident certificates. Since many foreigners living, studying, and doing business in Taiwan do not have resident status, this is a major inconvenience. This restriction was slapped on in 1987 to prevent 'currency speculation by foreigners'.

Foreigners can open US$ bank accounts,

though the money deposited is supposed to come in the form of travellers' cheques, bank drafts, telegraphic transfers or other types of inward remittance rather than cash. This is supposedly to thwart attempts to exchange NT$ on the black market and then deposit the US$ in a foreign currency account. If you need a place to stash NT$ while in Taiwan, non-resident foreigners are still permitted to have safe-deposit boxes.

Taiwan's Central Bank, which oversees banking policy, still believes that Taiwan is a Third World country that must carefully guard its foreign reserves. In reality, Taiwan is a First World country with a Third World banking system. There is a good deal of irony in this, because Taiwan has the world's largest foreign reserves, which means the NT$ is actually the world's strongest currency. However, it's untradeable on the foreign exchange markets – except on the black market. At the same time, the Central Bank has announced that it wants Taipei to replace Hong Kong as East Asia's financial centre – since the NT$ is not hard currency and foreigners can't have bank accounts, this is little more than a slogan.

Credit Cards Major international credit cards like American Express, Diners Club, MasterCard, Visa and others can be used at big hotels, some fancy restaurants and at major car-rental agencies. There is also a domestic credit card which residents can apply for. Overall, credit cards are not very popular, so don't expect to use them at the local noodle shop. You can get cash advances from American Express and some other credit card issuers.

The ATM machines in Taiwan will not accept either credit cards or foreign ATM cards.

Visa customers (Visa cards and travellers' cheques) can dial a toll-free emergency assistance number in Taiwan (☎ 0080-651019).

Telegraphic Transfers Having money wired to you seems to work OK, but it's a bit slow. Figure on at least a week, though some-times the banks will surprise you and have it in two days. It appears that banks have to go through many layers of bureaucracy when handling any foreign exchange.

If you have legal resident status, it is possible to get permission to exchange NT$ to foreign currency and send it out of Taiwan after filling out a zillion papers. If you don't have legal resident status, the only money you can wire out is foreign exchange. This includes travellers' cheques or money which was sent into Taiwan within the past six months (you must have receipts to prove it).

Costs
As Taiwan's standard of living has increased, so have prices. The cost of most goods and services has reached the level of many European countries, but Taiwan is still much cheaper than Japan...for now.

How much does it cost to visit Taiwan? Excluding airfare, you can probably manage on NT$500 per day if you stay in youth hostels, buy food from noodle vendors or cheap cafeterias, take buses rather than taxis and resist the urge to go shopping. If you require a higher standard of living, it could easily cost several thousand NT$ daily. Taipei has the highest rents by far in Taiwan, but even the countryside is no longer really cheap.

Tipping
Good news for the budget-minded: tipping is not customary in restaurants, taxis or in most other places in Taiwan. The Chinese almost never tip. The only time when you must definitely tip is when you are helped by a hotel bellhop or a porter at the airport. The usual tip is NT$25 per bag. Most of the bigger hotels or restaurants will automatically add a 10% service charge to your bill, plus a 5% value-added tax (VAT) – smaller places almost never do that.

Bargaining
Some good-natured bargaining is permissible in street markets, and sometimes in small shops (but don't count on it). Ironically, you

can sometimes negotiate a slight discount in a large department store simply by asking for it. In Taiwan, most department stores lease space to smaller vendors rather than trying to run the whole store under one management. If you speak to the manager of the particular department you may get a discount, but usually only if you are making an expensive purchase like a suit, TV set or some furniture. The most discount you can expect anywhere is around 10%.

Consumer Taxes
Taiwan's value-added tax, otherwise known as a sales tax, affects the prices of many everyday consumer goods. The tax is built into the retail price – you don't have to calculate it separately (as in the USA). Some countries (eg Japan) permit foreigners to obtain a refund of this tax if the goods are taken out of the country, but Taiwan has no such system.

The tax can work to your advantage in one way – you can participate in the 'tax lottery'. Every cash register receipt you receive when you buy something has a unique lottery number. Winning lottery numbers are announced in the newspapers monthly – if the number on your receipt matches, the cash prize is yours. The purpose of this system is to make customers insist on receiving a receipt, thus forcing stores to ring everything up on the cash register. This way, the government knows how much value-added tax to charge the store. As crazy as it sounds, this system of 'customer enforcement' of the tax laws actually works amazingly well.

WHEN TO GO
Anytime is OK for travelling in Taiwan, but summer is the peak season, which means higher airfares, not to mention the hot and humid weather. A time to *avoid* is the Chinese (lunar) New Year when all transport is packed to overflowing, stores and restaurants are closed and hotels double their prices. Other major holidays can cause transport bottlenecks. October has almost ideal weather, but there are three public holidays during this month bringing dramatic but short-lived chaos. November is a good time to visit, when the weather is still mild and tourists are relatively scarce. Some foreigners like Ghost Month (late August or early September) when the temples are active and the Chinese are afraid to travel.

WHAT TO BRING
Bring as little as possible. Many travellers try to bring everything and the kitchen sink. Keep in mind that you can and will buy things as you travel, so don't burden yourself down with a lot of unnecessary junk. Drill holes in the handle of your toothbrush if you have to – anything to keep the weight down.

That advice having been given, there are some things you will want to bring from home. But the first thing to consider is what kind of bag you will use to carry everything. If looks aren't important, then nothing is more convenient to carry than the trusty old backpack. A frameless backpack has the advantage of being very easy to load on and off luggage racks. A framed model is easier on your back if you are walking long distances. Travel packs with shoulder straps that zip away into a hidden compartment and internal frames are a modern innovation; they're halfway between the regular backpack and a shoulder bag.

I prefer an inexpensive, medium-sized, internal-frame backpack. Why spend a fortune on an expedition backpack when it might get lost, stolen or damaged? If that does happen to you, a reasonably cheap replacement can be bought in Taiwan.

If you're a business traveller and want to look the part, a shoulder bag makes sense – forget suitcases.

The following is a checklist of everyday travel items. Most are readily available in Taiwan. You don't necessarily need to bring all these but the list is here for you to consider while you are packing your bag: shorts, T-shirt, trousers/skirts and shirts, pullover, rain gear, underwear, socks, sunhat, toilet paper, razor, nail clipper, comb, towel, water bottle, small knife, sewing kit, daypack, wristwatch, swimsuit, name cards, small torch (flashlight), some paperback books, passport, air ticket, money and moneybelt.

Clothes

From May to October the lightest summer clothes will do, except in the mountains, where it can get quite cold at night any time of the year. A good quality rainsuit or poncho will come in handy.

'Face' is important. The Chinese tend to judge people by their clothing far more than Westerners do. If you saunter around the cities in a dirty T-shirt, shorts and floppy sandals, you may attract some rude stares. The rule to follow is to look neat and clean, even if dressed in shorts and sandals. This is especially important when visiting people, eating in restaurants, or going to discos and nightclubs – you may be refused entrance if your outfit isn't up to standard.

A sandal with a strap across the back of the ankle is considered more appropriate than thongs. Thongs are for indoor wear. True, you will see people wearing thongs outdoors, but some restaurants, theatres and other establishments may refuse you admission unless your feet are properly 'strapped in'.

Bikinis are rare but becoming more popular. As far as public nudity goes, forget it. True, the Chinese are great consumers of porno videos, and nude-dancing shows are more common than anyone likes to admit, but nudity at a public beach is just not on.

Sunbathing is a peculiarly Western custom that the Chinese don't understand at all. The Chinese, along with most Asians, feel that white skin is much more beautiful than suntanned skin; 'proper' Chinese women always carry a sun umbrella. A suntan is associated with labourers and farm workers, which are low-class positions according to the Chinese. On a hot, sunny day in Taiwan, when the Western expatriates head to the beach or swimming pool to bask in the sun, the Chinese stay indoors. They're likely to go to the swimming pool at night, when there is no risk of getting a tan.

Business travellers need to be spruced up – ties, jackets and white shirts for men, fashionable dresses for women.

TOURIST OFFICES

The ROC Tourism Bureau publishes all sorts of helpful maps, booklets and brochures which are available free to tourists. The most convenient place to pick up these free goodies is at the information desk at the airport when you arrive.

Local Tourist Offices

Taipei You can visit the Tourism Bureau at its main office near the Sun Yatsen Memorial. It's not too hard to find, but there is no sign outside the building. From the central area you get there on bus No 27, 212, 240, 259, 261, 281 or 504.

Places in Taipei where you can find tourist information include:

Tourism Bureau
    9th floor, 280 Chunghsiao E Rd, Section 4
    (☎ 02-7218541)
Tourist Information Hot Line
    daily from 8 am to 8 pm (☎ 02-7173737, or
    toll-free 080-211734)
Government Information Office ROC
    3 Chunghsiao E Rd, Section 1 (☎ 02-3419211)
Taiwan Visitors' Association
    5th floor, 111 Minchuan E Rd (☎ 02-5943261)
Travel Information Service Centre
    Sungshan Domestic Airport (☎ 02-7121212,
    extension 471)

Branch Offices The Tourism Bureau maintains branch offices in Taoyuan, Hsinchu, Taichung, Changhua, Tainan and Kaohsiung. A few smaller cities, such as Taitung, maintain local tourist information offices. They can provide you with some information about local attractions, but don't expect too much from them. The level of spoken English is close to zero, so unless you're fluent in Chinese you'll probably find these services close to worthless. The addresses of these branch offices is included in the relevant chapters.

Overseas Reps

Taiwan's overseas tourist bureaus are incorporated into the various 'trade offices' that Taiwan maintains around the world. See the section on Visa-Issuing Offices for the relevant addresses.

USEFUL ORGANISATIONS

The Consumers' Foundation of the ROC (☎ 02-7001234), 11th floor, 28 Jenai Rd, Section 3, Taipei, can advise you about places to shop, do business and places to avoid. If you believe you've been swindled, this is the best organisation to contact for advice.

CETRA, or the China External Trade Development Council, assists people coming to Taiwan on business. CETRA maintains good international business libraries in Taipei in Kaohsiung. See the Information section of those cities for addresses.

All Foreign Affairs Police can speak English and can provide assistance to travellers in emergencies. They also do visa extensions. The telephone numbers of all the Foreign Affairs Police offices follow:

Changhua
    Changhua County (☎ 04-7222101)
Chiayi
    Chiayi County (☎ 05-2274454)
Fengshan
    Kaohsiung County (☎ 07-7460105)
Fengyuan
    Taichung County (☎ 04-5263304)
Hsinchu
    Hsinchu County (☎ 035-513438)
Hsinying
    Tainan County (☎ 06-2229704)
Hualien
    Hualien County (☎ 038-224023)
Ilan
    Ilan County (☎ 039-325147)
Kaohsiung City
    (☎ 07-2154342)
Keelung City
    (☎ 02-4241991)
Makung
    Penghu County (☎ 06-9272105)
Miaoli
    Miaoli County (☎ 037-211302)
Nantou
    Nantou County (☎ 049-222111)
Panchiao
    Taipei County (☎ 02-9614809)
Pingtung
    Pingtung County (☎ 08-7336283)
Taichung City
    (☎ 04-2203032)
Tainan City
    (☎ 06-2229704)
Taipei City
    (☎ 02-3817475, 3818341)
Taitung
    Taitung County (☎ 089-322034)
Taoyuan
    Taoyuan County (☎ 03-3335107)
Touliu
    Yunlin County (☎ 05-5322042)

BUSINESS HOURS & HOLIDAYS

Business hours in Taiwan are almost the same as in Western countries – weekdays from 8 or 8.30 am to 5 or 5.30 pm. On Saturday, most people work until noon.

Chinese people take lunch very seriously. Most businesses and all government offices close for the 'Chinese siesta' from about noon to 1.30 pm. Don't expect to get anything done during this time. If you walk into an office during the lunch break, don't be surprised to find the whole staff asleep. Not being aware of this, on my second day in Taiwan I walked into a travel agency at 1 pm, only to find all the office workers slumped over their desks. My first thought was that there must be a gas leak! I was in a near state of panic until somebody woke up and asked me why I was there during the siesta.

Many small shops keep long hours, typically from 6 am to 11 pm. This is especially true of small, family-owned restaurants. You'll have no trouble in Taiwan getting something to eat at first light or at midnight. The Chinese like nightlife and normally stay up very late, so there is always some store or restaurant open late at night. They make up for the lack of sleep with the siesta.

Department stores don't open until around 10 to 11 am, and they close about 10 pm. The hours are the same seven days a week, and most are open on all holidays except Chinese New Year. Banks are open from 9 am to 3.30 pm Monday to Friday and from 9 am to noon on Saturday.

The majority of workers have a holiday on Sunday, but plenty of small businesses are still open.

Solar Calendar Holidays

Founding Day (*yuándàn*) The founding day of the Republic of China falls on 1 January of the Gregorian calendar. Many businesses and schools remain closed on 2 January as well.

Youth Day *(qīngnián jié)* Youth Day falls on 29 March of the Gregorian calendar. Of course, all schools are closed on this day.

Tomb Sweep Day *(qīng míng jié)* A day for worshipping ancestors; people visit the graves of their departed relatives and clean the site. They often place flowers on the tomb and burn ghost money for the departed. It falls on 5 April in the Gregorian calendar in most years, 4 April in leap years.

Teacher's Day *(jiàoshī jié)* The birthday of Confucius is celebrated as Teacher's Day. It occurs on 28 September of the Gregorian calendar. There is a very interesting ceremony held at every Confucius Temple in Taiwan on this day, beginning at about 4 am. However, tickets are needed to attend this ceremony and they are not sold at the temple gate. The tickets can sometimes be purchased from universities, hotels or tour agencies, but generally are not easy to obtain.

National Day *(shuāngshí jié)* As it falls on 10 October – the 10th day of the 10th month – National Day is usually called 'Double 10th Day'. Big military parades are held in Taipei near the Presidential Building. There is a huge fireworks display at night by the Tanshui River. It's one of the more interesting times to visit Taipei.

Retrocession Day *(guāngfù jié)* Taiwan Retrocession Day celebrates Taiwan's return to the Republic of China after 50 years of Japanese occupation. It is celebrated on 25 October.

Chiang Kaishek's Birthday *(jiǎnggōng dànchén jìniàn rì)* Chiang Kaishek's birthday falls on 31 October. Because it coincides with an American festival (Halloween), it's a good time for US expat parties in Taipei.

Sun Yatsen's Birthday *(guófù dànchén jìniàn rì)* Sun Yatsen is regarded as the father of his country. His birthday is celebrated on 12 November.

Constitution Day *(xíngxiàn jìniàn rì)* Most Westerners and many Chinese consider this to be a Christmas *(shèngdàn jié)* holiday since it falls on 25 December, but this isn't a Christian nation and the official designation is Constitution Day.

Lunar Calendar Holidays
There are only three lunar public holidays: the Chinese New Year, the Dragon Boat Festival, and the Mid-Autumn Festival, but many festivals are also held according to the lunar calendar (see the Cultural Events section).

Chinese (Lunar) New Year *(chūn jié)* The Chinese celebrate New Year on the first day of the first moon. Actually, the holiday lasts three days and many people take a full week off from work. It is very difficult to book tickets during this time and all forms of transport and hotels are filled to capacity – not a good time to travel. Workers demand double wages during the New Year and hotel rooms triple in price.

Dragon Boat Festival *(duānwǔ jié)* On the fifth day of the fifth moon, colourful dragon boat races are held in Taipei and in a few other cities – they're shown on TV. It's the traditional day to eat steamed rice dumplings *(zòngzi)*.

Mid-Autumn Festival *(zhōngqiū jié)* Also known as the Moon Festival, this takes place on the 15th day of the eighth moon. Gazing at the moon and lighting fireworks are very popular at this time. This is the time to eat tasty moon cakes, which are available from every bakery. Of course, you can buy moon cakes much more cheaply on sale the next day.

The solar calendar dates for these festivals, for the next few years, are as follows:

Lunar New Year
    first day of the first moon: 31 January 1995; 19 February 1996; 7 February 1997; 28 January 1998; 16 February 1999
Dragon Boat Festival
    fifth day of the fifth moon: 13 June 1994; 2 June 1995; 19 June 1996; 9 June 1997; 28 June 1998; 18 June 1999
Mid-Autumn Festival
    15th day of the eighth moon: 20 September 1994; 9 October 1995; 26 September 1996; 16 September 1997; 5 October 1998; 24 September 1999

CULTURAL EVENTS

In all major cities, there are various cultural events staged at the municipal cultural centres. Visit the cultural centres in individual cities (see the relevant city sections) and pick up a schedule of the current programme. Major bookshops also have this information.

Taiwan's festivals are held according to the lunar calendar. The most important festivals include:

Lantern Festival *(yuánxiāo jié)* Also known as Tourism Day, this is not a public holiday, but it's very colourful. It falls on the 15th day of the first moon. Hundreds of thousands of people use this time to descend on the towns of Yenshui, Luerhmen and Peikang to ignite fireworks – making them good places to visit or to avoid, depending on how you feel about fireworks and crowds.

Kuanyin's Birthday *(guānshìyīn shēngrì)* The birthday of Kuanyin, the goddess of mercy, is on the 19th day of the second moon and is a good time for seeing temple worship festivals.

Matsu's Birthday *(māzǔ shēngrì)* Matsu, goddess of the sea, is the friend of all fishermen. Her birthday is widely celebrated at temples throughout Taiwan. Matsu's birthday is on the 23rd day of the third moon.

Ghost Month *(guǐ yuè)* The Ghost Month is the seventh lunar month. The devout believe that during this time the ghosts from hell walk the earth and it is a dangerous time to travel, go swimming, get married or move to a new house. If someone dies during this month, the body will be preserved and the funeral and burial will be performed the following month. As Chinese people tend not to travel during this time, it is very convenient for foreign tourists to travel around the island and avoid crowds. It is also a good time to see temple worship. On the first and 15th day of the Ghost Month, people will be burning both ghost money and incense and will also place offerings of food on tables outside their homes; the 15th day is usually the most exciting. Definitely try to get to a Taoist temple during Ghost Month.

Lovers' Day *(qíngrén jié)* Somewhat ironically, the Chinese equivalent of St Valentine's Day falls during the Ghost Month. Lovers' Day is the seventh day of the seventh moon. Valentine cards, chocolate candies and the like are only starting to catch on, but the thing to do is go out for the evening. Classy restaurants, pubs, discos and theatres do a raging business on this night. Later in the evening, the parks are totally packed with young lovers trying to 'get away from it all'.

POST & TELECOMMUNICATIONS

Taiwan's postal service is fast and efficient. For domestic letters, you can count on delivery within two days to almost any place on the island. International mail is also fast – about seven days to the USA or Europe, fewer to Hong Kong or Japan.

Post offices are open from 8 am to 5 pm Monday to Saturday; they're closed on Sunday and holidays.

Postal Rates

Domestic express letters arrive within 24 hours. Rates are NT$5 for letters, and NT$10 for 'prompt delivery' *(xiànshí zhuān sòng)*. There is also a super-express mail *(kuài dì)* – very expensive, but your letter will be delivered in just a few hours. International Express Mail Service (EMS) is available –

Postal Rates from Taiwan

Destination	Airmail	Aerogram	Postcard
Hong Kong, Macau & China	NT$9	NT$8	NT$6
Asia & Australia	NT$13	NT$11	NT$10
South America	NT$17	NT$14	NT$12
Europe & Africa	NT$17	NT$14	NT$12
USA & Canada	NT$15	NT$12	NT$11

count on NT$350 minimum. Another service you might use is registered mail *(guà hào)*, available for both domestic and international mail for NT$24.

The rates on aerograms and international letters varies according to destination (refer to table).

Printed matter, including photographs, can be sent at a much cheaper rate than letters. If you want to send some photos home it will be much cheaper to send them in a separate envelope stamped 'printed matter'. Be sure to write 'airmail' on the envelope as well. You cannot seal the envelope with glue but it can be stapled closed. This is so the postal inspectors can open it and check that you didn't slip a letter inside. If you do hide a letter inside, it will be returned or sent by surface mail, and will probably take several months to arrive.

Sending Mail

When mailing a letter overseas from Taiwan, use the red mailboxes. The left slot on the box is for international airmail and the right slot is for domestic express. Green mailboxes are for domestic surface mail; the left slot is for 'out of town', and the right slot is for local letters. Should you mistakenly put the letter in the wrong box or slot, don't panic. It will be delivered but may be delayed a couple of days at the most.

Most large post offices offer a very convenient packing service if you want to send a parcel. They'll box it up and seal it for a nominal charge, saving you the time and trouble of hunting for a cardboard box. Unfortunately, they don't keep any padding at the post office, so bring some old newspaper with you if your goods are fragile. If you

pack your own, you can seal the box with tape but it must also have a heavy string around it – the post office will not accept parcels that are not well tied. Stationery, grocery and hardware stores sell a very strong plastic string for just this purpose.

Receiving Mail

You can receive letters poste restante (general delivery) at any post office. Addresses not in Chinese characters must use the Wade-Giles Romanisation system rather than Pinyin or Yale – the post office knows where Kaohsiung is but they've never heard of Gaoxiong.

Private Carriers If you're shipping something too large or heavy to be handled by the post office, you need the services of a freight forwarder. There are many, and they usually

advertise in the pages of *This Month in Taiwan*. One that I recommend is Jacky Maeder (☎ 02-5624225), 4th floor, 21-1 Lane 45, Chungshan N Rd, Taipei. They handle both sea and air freight.

You may also want to contact United Parcel Service (☎ 02-5975998 or 8833868, fax 5971002), 124 Mintsu W Rd, Taipei, or the Kaohsiung office (☎ 07-3920109) at 250 Ying'an St, San Min district.

Rapid service is offered by Federal Express (☎ 02-7883535, 8839898), 778 Pate Rd, Section 4. They also have a representative at CKS International Airport (☎ 03-3982463) and a toll-free number (☎ 080-251080). Federal Express also has an office in Kaohsiung (☎ 07-3361066) at 75 Hsingchung-2 Rd.

Telephone

Taiwan's government-owned monopoly is known by two names, the International Telecommunications Administration (ITA) or the Directorate General of Telecommunications (DGT). Whatever it's called, service is just about what you'd expect from a government-owned monopoly – expensive. Quality of service is decidedly mediocre, though it has improved in recent years.

First the good news – lines are generally clear, and you can almost always get connected straight away. Compared to some countries where calling across the street can take half a day, Taiwan's phone system seems to be highly functional.

Calls from public payphones usually work OK, though there are a few which can only be used for local calls. These are usually pulse dial (as opposed to touchtone), and if you get this type of phone you'll be cut off after three minutes – feeding more coins in will not buy you more time. Fortunately, these old phones are becoming rare.

The newer payphones have a digital display meter that tells you how much money you have put into the phone. You can clearly see how much money remains. When the meter reads zero, you get disconnected but you can always feed in more coins to continue talking.

Best of all are the phones which use a phonecard *(diànhuà kǎ)*, which you insert into a slot when you want to make a call. Phonecards cost NT$100 and can be bought in some grocery stores, bakeries, major railway stations or other locations where you see the phones that accept these cards. Most 7-Eleven and Family Mart stores sell phonecards, and you can always buy them from any telephone company branch office. Some of the card phones permit you to make international calls – this is clearly indicated on the phone in English and Chinese. Of course, NT$100 doesn't give you much time to talk on an international call, but you can change cards without breaking the conversation by pushing the button to the left of the keypad and inserting a new card. At least, you can in theory – sometimes it doesn't work and you get cut off when the card expires.

If you have your own phone, there are a few useful auxiliary services that can be ordered. These include call forwarding (redirect calls to another number when you're not at home), call waiting (answer a second call when you're already on the phone) and a wake-up service.

Now that you've heard all the good points, here is the bad news. Frustration with the phone company really piles up if you decide to live in Taiwan for a while and want to get a phone installed. In some cities it takes 10 days to get a phone line – in other places, three months. The phone company requires that you buy the line rather than simply rent it – the cost for buying a phone line varies by region but it's currently about NT$6500. The rate has fallen considerably – I can remember when it was NT$15,000, or NT$25,000 on the black market. The reason for the black market (second-hand phone lines) is because it's usually much faster to buy an existing line than to apply for a new one through the phone company. Just how fast you can get a phone line depends on just where in Taiwan you live. It also depends on when you apply – when the new stock exchange opened in Taipei, there was a huge surge in demand for phone lines and new customers had to wait six months to have one installed.

Buying a black-market line is somewhat risky unless you know the former owner well. Even after the line is transferred to your name, you are still responsible for the previous owner's phone bill for the first month! Whether your line is new or second-hand, you can easily wind up with a 'bad line' – one which is noisy or almost always out-of-order. The phone company seems incapable of fixing these problems, and the only cure is to apply for a new one.

The phone company also has an annoying habit of changing your phone number every few years without warning, and the recorded message advising people of the change is only valid for one month. The phone company also has problems with their billing procedures – hang on to your receipts because they occasionally say you didn't pay your bill when in fact you did.

Then there is the very messy situation with cellular phones. Not only is it expensive (typically around NT$5000 per month minimum), but the exchanges are so overworked that it's almost impossible to get through to anybody. Using a cellular phone from a moving vehicle also doesn't seem to work in Taiwan – the connection is terrible and you usually get cut off in mid-conversation.

In general, overseas calls are easy to make from major cities like Taipei and Kaohsiung, but making an international call from rural areas can be a frustrating experience. Line quality also varies according to destination – lines to the USA are *usually* as clear as calling the house next door, but connections to Europe can be plagued with noise.

Rates More bad news – telephone rates are high in Taiwan, a fact which has generated considerable criticism from politicians, the newspapers and irate customers. The phone company's 'solution' has been to launch a slick public relations campaign to convince everybody that phone calls are cheaper in Taiwan than in other countries (the USA is the usual basis for comparison). The campaign seems to have been a success – most Taiwanese are now convinced that they pay half of what Americans pay for the same service, even though the opposite is true. However, most people are still pretty unhappy when the phone bill arrives. The situation is unlikely to improve unless privatisation and real competition is permitted.

Local calls all cost NT$1 for three minutes. Domestic long-distance rates are as follows: full rate – 7 am to 7 pm; 50% discount – weekdays 7 to 11 pm, Saturday 1 to 11 pm, Sunday and holidays 7 am to 11 pm; 70% discount – every day from 11 pm to 7 am. A call from Taipei to Kaohsiung costs NT$10 per minute at the full rate, or NT$3 per minute at the cheapest night-time rate.

Due to special agreements (and heavy lobbying by US trade reps), calls to the USA are somewhat cheaper than for other countries, even cheaper than calling nearby Hong Kong. Discount rates apply for all calls to the USA from 4 to 9 pm, but the cheapest rate is from midnight to 7 am – the cheapest call to the USA would cost NT$60 for the first minute, and NT$20 per minute thereafter. Reduced rates are in effect for all calls to Hong Kong from 9 pm to 7 am on weekdays and for 24 hours on Sunday. For all other countries, reduced rates are in effect from midnight to 7 am.

Dialling To make an overseas call from a private phone, first dial 100 to reach the overseas operator. Anytime you use the overseas operator it's going to cost you big money, but person to person calls cost even more. Direct dialling is *much* cheaper. Direct dialling overseas is possible from private phones and from ISD (international subscriber dialling) phones. You can find ISD phones at the telephone company, some railway stations, bus stations and sometimes even the local 7-Eleven store.

To dial direct, the international prefix is 002, followed by the country code, area code and the number you want to dial. If you don't know the country code, contact ITA (☎ 02-3212535). International direct dialling is available in all major cities, but in many rural parts of Taiwan you will have to go through the operator – more expensive and time consuming, and the line quality is often poor.

To call Taiwan from abroad, the country code is 886. All Taiwanese area codes begin with zero – eg, Taipei is 02. However, when calling from abroad you must omit the zero.

Privately owned red or green payphones found in some hotels (especially youth hostels) are tricky to use. You must pick up the receiver *before* inserting the coin or else you will lose it – furthermore, when you are connected, you must push a button on the phone so the money goes down. If you fail to push the button, you will be able to hear the other party but they will not be able to hear you.

Numbers starting with the prefix 080 are toll-free numbers. There are very few of these in Taiwan, but some large companies have them. Even rarer are 008 prefixes, which are international toll-free numbers.

Many hotels charge a large fee to make a reverse-charge call on top of the fee that the phone company charges, so you're better off calling from a public payphone.

An easy way to make reverse-charge calls or bill to a credit card is to use a service called International Operator Direct Connection (IODC). This service is only offered to a few countries. One way to make an IODC call is to use a special telephone on which you simply push a button to be immediately connected to an operator in that country – these special phones are found in airports and a few major hotels. You can also make an IODC call on an ordinary telephone by dialling the IODC operator.

Calling reverse-charge or with a credit card offers no savings at all. Calling the USA with Sprint, for example, would cost US$3.42 for the first minute and US$1.44 for additional minutes, and the rates are consistent 24 hours a day, seven days a week.

Area Codes Taiwan's area codes all start with a '0'. Each county has its own telephone area code (refer to map opposite).

Finding Phone Numbers There is a telephone book for Taipei published in English, available free from ITA on request if you have your own phone. The book is not very complete – only companies are listed, not individuals.

There is a privately produced phone book for the whole of Taiwan, which costs a hefty US$45 and is also restricted to companies. Check the magazine *This Month in Taiwan* for ordering information.

Some useful phone numbers are as follows:

English directory assistance	02-3116796
Chinese local directory assistance	104
Chinese long-distance directory assistance	105
Overseas operator	100
Overseas dialling information	02-3212535
Fire (Chinese-speaking)	119
Police (Chinese-speaking)	110
Reverse-charges	108
Taipei Foreign Affairs Police	02-3818341
Telephone repair	112
Time	117
Weather	166

IODC Operators

Calls to	Operator No
Australia	(☎ 008-061-0061)
Canada	(☎ 008-012-0012)
Guam	(☎ 008-067-0671)
Hawaii (HTC)	(☎ 008-011-0011)
Hong Kong	(☎ 008-085-2111)
Indonesia	(☎ 008-062-0062)
Italy	(☎ 008-039-0039)
Japan	(☎ 008-081-0051)
Macau	(☎ 008-087-0853)
Malaysia	(☎ 008-060-0060)
Netherlands	(☎ 008-031-0031)
New Zealand	(☎ 008-064-0064)
Philippines	(☎ 008-063-0063)
Portugal	(☎ 008-035-0351)
Singapore	(☎ 008-065-6565)
South Korea	(☎ 008-082-0082)
Thailand	(☎ 008-066-0066)
UK	(☎ 008-044-0044)
USA (AT&T)	(☎ 008-010-2880)
USA (MCI)	(☎ 008-013-4567)
USA (Sprint)	(☎ 008-014-0877)

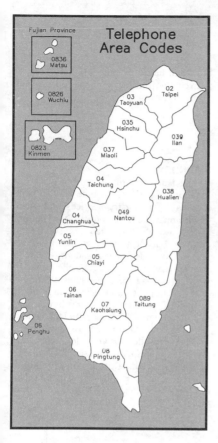

Telephone Area Codes

Fujian Province
0836 Matsu
0826 Wuchiu
0823 Kinmen

02 Taipei
03 Taoyuan
035 Hsinchu
039 Ilan
037 Miaoli
04 Taichung
038 Hualien
04 Changhua
049 Nantou
05 Yunlin
05 Chiayi
06 Tainan
089 Taitung
07 Kaohsiung
06 Penghu
08 Pingtung

operator. All pager numbers begin with 060 or 070, followed by six digits. To page someone, first dial the pager number (no area code, just the pager number), wait until you hear the beep, then press # followed by your phone number and end the message with another #, after which you'll hear more beeping. You can then hang up. The important point to remember is that you *begin and end* your message with #. So if your hotel's phone number is 8888888, dial the pager number, wait for the beep, and dial #8888888#. It's wise to include your area code, which in Taipei is 02, so in this example you'd dial #028888888#. If you fail to add the initial or final #, the message will not go through.

The question arises about how to deal with extension phones. The answer is to add a *0 after the phone number, and then the extension. So if you're staying in room 777 of a hotel, dial #028888888*0777#. The *0 will add a dash to your message and the result will be 028888888-777. I know it sounds complicated, but it's not – everyone in Taiwan knows the system, so get a local person to show you how to do it.

One warning – the phone systems in some hotels make it impossible to page from your room. This is because it's been programmed to prevent anyone from dialling over nine digits so you can't make international phone calls. In this case, you'll have to dial from a public payphone or ask the hotel operator to page for you.

If you want to get your own pager, apply at any telephone company office. The cost is NT$600 per month plus a refundable NT$2400 deposit.

Fax, Telex & Telegraph

A fax service is available from the ITA main office in major cities. The cost is NT$50 per page within Taiwan, and NT$200 per page for international faxes. Major hotels also offer this service but charge outrageous prices. You can also send telexes and cables (telegraph) from the ITA main office.

Pagers

Many people in Taiwan have pagers. Unlike in most Western countries, the system is fully automated – you can page someone from any touchtone phone without speaking to an

Electronic Mail (E-Mail)

The following information is for the real computer freaks. Taiwan Telecommunications Network (TTN) is a private company offering direct connections to two foreign networks, CompuServe and Japan's Nifty-Serve, which in turn provide gateways to other E-mail services like MCIMail, AT&TMail and Internet. Connect time to CompuServe costs about NT$14 per minute and reverse charging is possible, which means short-term visitors can gain access. For complete information, contact TTN (☎ 02-6516899 or 7881588 ext 236), 13 Lane 50, Nankang Rd, Section 3, Nankang District, Taipei. If you already have E-mail, you can also contact TTN on CompuServe 75300,314 or Internet 75300.314@compuserve.com.

The other (and more versatile way) to connect a computer to the phone is to use a packet-switching network. Taiwan's is called PACNET. To do this, you must have your own phone in Taiwan for billing purposes, so it's not an option for short-term visitors. The place to contact is the Data Communications Institute (DCI), a branch of the Ministry of Communications (☎ 02-3442791, 3210111).

TIME

Taiwan is eight hours ahead of GMT/UTC. Daylight-saving time is not observed.

When it's noon in Taiwan, it's also noon in Singapore, Hong Kong and Perth; 2 pm in Sydney; 8 pm the previous day in Los Angeles; 11 pm the previous day in New York; and 4 am in London.

Calendar

Year zero for the Kuomintang is 1911 – the year when the Republic of China was founded. All official documents in Taiwan use 1911 as a reference point in establishing the date. Thus the year 1994 is 83 (1994 minus 1911) – ie, the 83rd year since the founding of the republic.

In Taiwan the date is written in the order: year, month, day. So 20 October 1994 would be written 83/10/20.

ELECTRICITY

Taiwan uses the same standards for electric power as the USA and Canada – 110 V, 60 Hz AC. If you bring appliances from Europe, Australia or South-East Asia, you'll need a transformer.

However, 220 V is available in Taiwan in many buildings solely for the use of air-conditioners. Most new houses and apartments have at least one 220 V outlet, usually next to a window or hole in the wall where you'd expect to mount an air-conditioner. A few of my friends have managed to blow up their TVs and radios by plugging into these. To prevent this from happening to you, take note of the following diagram:

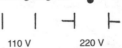

LAUNDRY

Doing laundry is often a big headache for travellers in Taiwan. Some of the youth hostels offer laundry services and others have a machine (often broken) for your use. There are plenty of laundry services in Taiwan, but most are slow, expensive and geared towards ironing and dry-cleaning. Fortunately, there are fast and cheap laundry services around the universities catering to the student population. They charge by the weight of the clothes and some have a four-kg minimum. Of course, student laundry services don't do ironing or dry cleaning.

Many travellers wind up doing their own laundry in the sink – a hassle, but it's better than smelling bad. If you're going to take this approach, light and thin stretch nylon is best for underwear and socks because it dries quickly. Wash everything as soon as you check into a hotel room so it has time to dry before you depart.

WEIGHTS & MEASURES

Officially Taiwan subscribes to the international metric system. However, ancient Chinese weights and measures still persist. The most likely ones that tourists will encounter are the 'tael' *(liǎng)* and the 'catty' *(jīn)*.

One catty is 0.6 kg (1.32 pounds). There are 16 taels to the catty, so one tael is 37.5 grams (1.32 ounces). Most fruits and vegetables in Taiwan are sold by the catty, while tea and herbal medicine are sold by the tael.

The other unit of measure that you might encounter is the 'ping'. Pings are used to measure area, and one ping is approximately

1.82 metres square (5.97 feet square). When you buy cloth or carpet, the price will be determined by the number of pings. Ditto for renting an apartment or buying land.

BOOKS & MAPS
Books dealing exclusively with Taiwan are scarce. Most people with an interest in this part of the world want to read about China. Taiwan, being only one small province of China (at least officially), hardly merits a footnote as far as most authors are concerned.

People & Society
The Island of Formosa, Past And Present by James W Davidson is a monumental work first published in 1903. It's now available for sale at some Taiwan bookshops (try Caves Books) or from SMC Publishing Co (☎ 3620190), PO Box 13-342, Taipei 10764.

Arts & Culture in Taiwan by B Kaulbach & B Proksch (Southern Materials Centre) is a more recent work.

Guides
A good coffee-table book is *Images of Taiwan* by Daniel Reid & Dan Rocovits (Hong Kong Publishing Co Ltd), available in Taiwan for NT$400.

One of the most beautiful coffee-table books is *Taiwan with a View* by the Independence Evening Post, Taipei, which sells for NT$500.

Taipei, a Times edition, has good photos, an interesting text and historical information.

Insight Guides' *Taiwan* (APA Productions, Singapore) has some practical but very out-of-date tour information. The cultural stuff is interesting, and the illustrations and photographs are excellent.

It doesn't require much explanation to understand the main topic of *The 100 Best Bars in Taipei* by Jim Ehrhart and Anthony Watts. The authors rate bars with from two to five stars – those meriting only one star were not considered worth including. This guide is available from all the major English-language bookshops in Taipei.

The *Directory of Taiwan* is published annually by the China News, one of Taiwan's two English-language daily papers. The book is basically a laundry list of names, addresses and phone numbers of organisations and businesses in Taiwan. There's a good deal of useful information in there (like dial-a-taxi phone numbers, addresses of hospitals and government agencies, etc) but most travellers probably won't be ringing up the Taipei Beancurd Trade Association or the Taiwan Coal Miners.

Maps
Every bookshop in Taiwan sells maps and atlases, but most are exclusively in Chinese characters. The Tourism Bureau has a collection of maps, which all have the great advantage of being free.

If you're willing to fork out NT$120, there is an excellent bilingual map of Taiwan available from some of the English-language bookshops. It's simply called 'Taiwan Map', published by International Travel Press (☎ 02-7139235, fax 7127255). If you can't find it in the stores, you could ring the publishers or drop in to their office in room 4, 7th floor, 181 Fuhsing N Rd, Taipei.

MEDIA
Newspapers & Magazines
Taiwan produces two English-language newspapers, the *China Post* and the *China News*. They're available from many hotels, bookshops or by subscription from the post office. In Taipei, you can also subscribe by telephone to the *China Post* (☎ 02-5969971) and the *China News* (☎ 02-3210882). At NT$12 for 12 pages, they rate as two of the most expensive newspapers in the world, and it doesn't take very long to read the 12 pages since about half the space is advertising. The *China News* is marginally better thanks to its fine weekend-entertainment guide published every Friday.

Sinorama Magazine (guānghuá) is a bilingual monthly magazine, available in either Chinese-English or Chinese-Spanish editions. It's certainly one of the more intelligent magazines published in Taiwan, and just about the only one for foreigners which discusses sensitive topics like social and political problems. The Chinese-English edition is available from better bookshops in Taiwan and even some shops in Hong Kong, but the Chinese-Spanish edition is only available by subscription. You can subscribe to either edition by contacting Sinorama (☎ 02-3922256, fax 3970655), PO Box 8-398, Taipei 100. One-year subscription rates for surface mail are NT$1200 in Taiwan, Hong Kong, Macau and North America. Elsewhere it costs NT$1300 by surface mail. For international airmail it costs NT$1600.

The *International Herald-Tribune* is produced jointly by the *New York Times* and the *Washington Post* for distribution outside the USA. It's rather expensive, but it's comprehensive. It can be purchased in Taiwan at major hotels, bookshops or by subscription from the Taiwan English Press. The *Asian Wall Street Journal* is also widely available.

Travel in Taiwan is a reasonably good magazine that gives a good rundown on sights around the island. It costs NT$100 per issue, but free copies are often available from the Tourism Bureau.

The *AIT Media Summary* is published daily by the American Institute in Taiwan, Cultural and Information Section. It gives perhaps the best news summary of events concerning Taiwan, but it's available by subscription only and isn't cheap. The printed version costs NT$24,000 per year, or if you have a computer and modem, you can receive it electronically for NT$20,000 per year. Business people and journalists may well find it worth the cost. For information, call AIT (☎ 02-7155625) or stop by their information office on the 6th floor, 365 Fuhsing N Rd, Taipei.

Radio & TV

Taiwan has one English-language radio station, ICRT, which stands for International Community Radio Taipei. ICRT broadcasts 24 hours a day on AM at 576 MHz, and FM at 100 MHz. There's a request line for FM (☎ 02-8615555) and for AM (☎ 02-8616161).

There are three broadcast TV stations in Taiwan – CTS, CTV and TTV. Most shows are in Chinese; even foreign shows are dubbed. English-language programmes are sometimes shown late at night, usually starting from 10 pm. Unfortunately, all three stations tend to broadcast their English programmes at the same time. Check the local English-language newspapers such as the *China Post* and the *China News* for the schedule.

Much of Taiwan TV is directed towards children, especially the advertising, with adult shows focused on kungfu and soap operas. Expatriates living in Taiwan will tell you there's nothing more mindless than Taiwanese TV (apparently they haven't seen North Korean TV), but the situation has vastly improved with the introduction of cable TV. Usually referred to as 'channel 4', cable TV includes local programmes and foreign broadcasts via satellite – you can enjoy the latest CNN reports of terrorism and air crashes in English. Just how many additional stations you get to see with a cable hookup varies by location and how much you pay, but count on 10 stations or more with at least half in English. Some of the best shows come from Hong Kong's Star TV and Japan's NHK.

If you have access to a video-cassette player there are plenty of English-language movies available for rent cheaply on video cassette from numerous shops in any major city in Taiwan.

Unfortunately, the world has many incompatible video standards. A 'video standard' refers to the many little dots that appear on the screen that make up the picture. This is no problem if you're renting a videotape in Taiwan and playing it on a Taiwanese TV – it does become a problem if you hook up your own video camera to play back on a local TV set or want to see a videotape mailed from home. Taiwan uses the NTSC standard, as does Canada, the USA and Japan. NTSC differs from the PAL standard used in Australia, Hong Kong and the UK, and the SECAM standard of France. Expatriates take note – bringing a TV set or video player from home can still create problems because Taiwan's broadcast frequencies are different. The video-tape player and TV must run at the same frequency to work together – even if both are NTSC. Frequency can be adjusted by a technician, for a cost. There is no problem playing an American or Japanese video tape on a Taiwan TV or vice versa, but European tapes won't work.

If you wonder why Chinese characters are displayed on the TV screen during a Chinese dialogue, it is because many older Chinese from the mainland can read and write characters but cannot speak Mandarin. Also, having the characters displayed helps children learn how to read.

FILM & PHOTOGRAPHY

Major brands of colour print film such as Kodak, Fuji, Konica and Sakura are available at reasonable prices in Taiwan. Colour photo-processing stores are abundant and many offer one-hour service. The quality varies between different establishments but is about the same standard as in Western countries. I've personally found the Kodak colour prints to be superior in colour rendition, but others might disagree.

Slide film is available, mostly Ektachrome and Fujichrome. A slide photo-processing service is available from most stores that sell slide film. Agfachrome is hard to come by, and Kodachrome is not available at all and cannot be processed in Taiwan. Prints made from slides often do not turn out very well – it's better to have this done elsewhere than Taiwan.

B&W film is available in Taiwan at reasonable prices. The quality of B&W photo-processing varies considerably, but it's done by hand and I've found it mostly to be poor. If you need B&W film processed in Taiwan, you might want to do it yourself.

US travellers should note that, for some reason, most stores in the USA will only process Kodak B&W film. So unless you do your own processing, you'd best use Kodak film if you want it machine-processed back home.

Taking photos around the airports, harbours and many coastal areas in Taiwan is illegal. It's also prohibited to take photos out of the window of a plane, though the rules are very loosely enforced. Chinese people feel much the same about being photographed as Westerners do – they'll pose for photos if they know you but they don't like being photographed by strangers. If you want candid photos of people doing their everyday tasks, it would be best to take them from afar, using a telephoto lens, so as not to upset anyone. Photography at temples is mostly OK.

Chinese (and Japanese) people have a near obsession with collecting photos of themselves posing in front of something. Thus, virtually everyone in Taiwan has hundreds or thousands of photos of themselves usually posed in the same rigid position, hands at the sides, etc. They can't understand why Westerners take pictures of scenery with no people posing – such photos are considered 'boring'.

HEALTH

In general, health conditions in Taiwan are good. Nevertheless, there are a few special health conditions and precautions worth noting.

Predeparture Preparations

Vaccinations No special vaccinations are required for Taiwan. However, that doesn't mean you shouldn't get any. For Taiwan, the most useful vaccinations are for hepatitis B, tetanus and influenza (during winter).

Health Insurance Although not absolutely necessary, it is a good idea to take out travellers' health insurance. The policies are usually available from travel agents, including student travel services. Some policies specifically exclude 'dangerous activities', which may include motorcycling, scuba diving and even hiking. Obviously, you'll want a policy that covers you in all the circumstances you're likely to find yourself.

Hopefully you won't need medical care, but do keep in mind that any health insurance

What's up Doc?

Medical facilities in Taiwan are well-advanced, but foreigners often encounter some unpleasant surprises, the first being the language barrier. Most doctors in Taiwan can read and write English because they must study foreign medical texts, but the level of spoken English varies from excellent to none at all. You may have to do some shopping around to find a doctor with whom you can effectively communicate.

Diagnosis and treatment is often handled differently than in the West. Medical tests are only performed for those deemed seriously ill – most patients are simply questioned by the doctor and then told they have *ganmao* (a cold). Treatment is a standardised bag of brightly coloured pills, a relatively benign mixture of antihistamines, aspirin, vitamins and antacids. For those who complain that they feel particularly lousy, a shot will be administered, usually a mixture of vitamin C and sterilised water.

Those who show signs of some serious illness will probably be sent over to a hospital for a battery of tests, x-rays and the like. Unless you question the doctor, it's not likely you'll be told what dread disease you have or what medicines are being prescribed. Many Taiwanese just dutifully swallow the pills, capsules and syrups given to them without knowing whether they're being treated for diabetes, epilepsy, cancer or just a cold.

All this might sound like doctors in Taiwan don't know what they're doing, but in fact most are well-trained and competent. The problem is simply cultural – although Westernisation is starting to bring a change in attitudes, most Chinese don't want to hear the gruesome details of their illnesses. Furthermore, most people in Taiwan are only happy when they have their own personal pharmacy – a doctor who doesn't give the patient a load of (mostly useless) pills and potions is considered 'no good'. ■

policy you have at home may not be valid outside your country. The usual procedure with travellers' health insurance is that you pay in cash first for services rendered and then later present the receipts to the insurance company for reimbursement after you return home. Other policies stipulate that you call reverse-charge to a centre in your home country, where an immediate assessment of your problem is made.

If you are unfortunate enough to get very ill while travelling in Taiwan, at least you can be grateful for one thing – medical care is much cheaper in Taiwan than in most Western countries.

Medical Kit You can buy almost any medication across the counter in Taiwan. Pharmacies (*yàojú*) are everywhere in the cities, but can be hard to find in some rural areas. If you're going to be spending time in the mountains, a basic medical kit would be handy. It should include paracetamol or aspirin for pain and fever, a pin and tweezers for removing splinters, plaster for blisters, Band-Aids, an antiseptic, insect repellent, sunscreen and chapstick.

If you wear glasses, bring an extra pair of spectacles and/or a copy of your lens prescription with you. Sunglasses come in useful, and a hat will help protect you from getting burned.

Basic Rules

Food and water is seldom a problem in Taiwan. If you suffer health problems, it's most likely to be because of difficulty adapting to the hot summer climate. If you're sweating profusely, you're going to lose a lot of salt and that can lead to fatigue and muscle cramps for some people. If necessary, you can replace lost salt by putting a little extra in your food (a teaspoon a day is plenty), but don't increase your salt intake unless you also increase your water intake. Soy sauce will also do the trick.

Medical Problems & Treatments

Some common and exotic ailments worth knowing about include:

Skin Problems (*pífū bìng*) Sunburn can be more than just uncomfortable. Among the undesirable effects of frying your hide are premature skin ageing and possible skin cancer in later years. Bring sunscreen lotion (fáng shài yóu) and wear a hat.

Sunburn is not the only hazard to your skin. Indeed, the most common summertime afflictions that visitors to Taiwan suffer from are skin diseases. This is because of the hot, humid climate. The most common varieties are 'jock itch' (a fungal infection around the groin), athlete's foot (known to the Chinese as 'Hong Kong feet'), contact dermatitis (caused by a necklace or watchband rubbing the skin) and prickly heat (caused by excessive sweating). Prevention and treatment of these skin ailments is often a matter of good hygiene.

For fungal infections, bathe twice daily and thoroughly dry yourself before getting dressed. Standing in front of an electric fan is a good way to get thoroughly dry. An antifungal ointment or powder should be applied to the affected area. It's more effective to use both an ointment and a powder in combination. Some popular fungicides available in Western countries include Desenex, Tinactin and Mycota. Some inexpensive brands available in Taiwan include Fundex and Nysco UU ointment. Whatever ointment and/or powder you use, it should include the ingredients undecylenic acid and zinc undecylenate. Wear light cotton underwear or very thin nylon that breathes. Wear the lightest outer clothing possible when the weather is really hot and humid. For athlete's foot, wearing open-toed sandals will often solve the problem without further treatment. It also helps to clean between the toes with warm soapy water and an old toothbrush.

Treat contact dermatitis by removing the offending necklace, bracelet or wristwatch. Avoid anything that chafes the skin, such as tight clothing, especially elastic.

If your skin develops painful red 'pin pricks', you probably have prickly heat. This is the result of excessive sweating which blocks the sweat ducts, causing inflammation. The treatment is the same as for fungal infections: drying and cooling the skin. Bathe often, soak and scrub with hot soapy water to get the skin pores open and dust yourself with talcum powder after drying off. Sleeping in a room that has air-con will help. If all else fails, a trip to Taiwan's high, cool mountains will do wonders for your itching skin.

Diarrhoea (lā dùzi) Tap water is not too bad in Taiwan, but the government does recommend that it be boiled before drinking. Most Chinese do boil their water anyway out of habit, even when it is not necessary. There has been a scandal in recent years when it was discovered that much of the expensive, bottled water sold in Taiwan's supermarkets was just plain, unboiled tap water.

I drink unboiled water in Taiwan often without any ill effect, but I have seen others rapidly develop that well-known ailment, 'travellers' diarrhoea'. Should it happen to you, first try a simple cure by switching to a light, roughage-free diet for a few days. White rice, bananas, pudding and boiled eggs will usually see you through. Further relief can be obtained by chewing tablets of activated charcoal, though these are expensive in Taiwan.

More serious cases can be treated with prescription drugs such as Lomotil and Imodium. These drugs only treat the symptoms, not the underlying disease. Use such drugs with caution because they can cause serious side effects. Only take the minimum dose needed to control the diarrhoea. Don't take so much that you become plugged up, as the diarrhoea serves a function – your body is trying to expel unwanted bacteria. If you continue to suffer, you may have a serious infection that requires antibiotics. Although prescription drugs are available across the counter in Taiwan, you would be wise to see a competent medical authority if you get to this stage. In this case, it's best to visit a hospital with a medical laboratory rather than a private doctor, otherwise you may just be told that you have a cold and given a bag of pills.

Hepatitis (gān yán) Infectious hepatitis also continues to pose a minor health hazard to

Chinese Herbal Medicine

(zhōngyào) 中藥

In virtually every town and nearly every street of the main cities of Taiwan, one can find shops peddling traditional 'herbal medicine'. Although there are now plenty of doctors and an abundance of modern clinics, many people like to back up Western medicine with a few herbs 'just in case'.

Some herbs are taken to cure disease while others are taken as preventive measures to ward off colds and flu. Some herbs serve as aphrodisiacs while others are longevity treatments. Many herbs are specific to a particular organ – one herb for good eyesight and another for a healthy liver, etc. No matter what your ailment or other motive, a Chinese herbal medicine dealer is certain to have some remedy for your condition.

Many Westerners will be surprised when they learn the ingredients of some herbal medicines. Many are spices like ginger, cinnamon, anise, nutmeg and the dried skins of particular fruits. Other ingredients are more exotic: powdered deer antlers, rhinoceros horn, cockroach droppings, dead bees and snake bile. Some ingredients, such as ginseng and rosehips, are well known in the West.

Adherents of herbal medicine claim that you don't use a single herb but rather a combination of herbs to produce the desired result. The herbs, when properly mixed, are believed to have a synergistic effect. That is, the whole is greater than the sum of its parts.

Another important property of herbal medicine is that the effects are supposed to be gradual, not sudden or dramatic. That is, you start taking herbs at the first sign of illness, such as a scratchy throat, or even before you get sick as a preventive measure. So in the cold and flu season you might start taking herbs before you even have your first cough or sniffle, so that you can build up resistance.

When reading about the theory behind Chinese medicine, the word 'holistic' appears often. Basically, this means that Chinese medicine seeks to treat the whole body rather than focusing on a particular organ or disease. Using appendicitis as an example, a Chinese doctor may try to fight the infection using the body's whole defences, whereas a Western doctor would simply cut out the appendix. While the holistic method sounds great in theory, in practice the Western technique of attacking the problem directly often works better. In the case of appendicitis, surgery is very effective. On the other hand, in the case of migraine headaches, asthma or chronic stomachache, herbs may well be more effective in the long run.

Understanding Chinese medicine involves a knowledge of the Yin and Yang theory. Stated briefly, all things in the universe have two aspects, a Yin aspect and a Yang aspect. Examples would include female and male, cold and hot, night and day, down and up, passive and active, and so on. In terms of illness, Chinese often speak of 'too much fire' which is very Yang, or of being cold which is Yin. Weakness is Yin, hypertension is Yang. The trick is to keep these two forces in balance.

Many Chinese practise *jìnbǔ*, the consumption of tonic food as well as herbs, in order to build strength, and in some cases to increase their sexual potency. It is a widely held belief in Taiwan that sex wears down the body and that frequent sex will result in a short life. To counter the wear and tear of sexual activity you should eat snake, since snakes are long and strong. Poisonous snakes are considered the most effective. An elixir made from deer antlers (also long and strong) is a good medicine for men whose virility is on the wane. However, bamboo shoots and sugar cane apparently are not effective. Another treatment requires drowning bees in a strong alcoholic drink. Drinking the resulting potion will bring out the machismo in any man. The flesh of a tiger will also really give your hormones a recharge, but it's very expensive, especially the sex organs.

To fight off those coughs and colds in winter, goat and dog meat are just what you need. Black goats and black dogs are the best. Eat liver to fight off hepatitis, and eat brains to increase your knowledge. The more expensive the tonic, the greater its reputation. Apples, once very expensive in Taiwan, were widely sought after as a medical treatment. Now that the price of apples has fallen drastically due to cheap imports, few people still believe in their medicinal value.

Does herbal medicine really work? In my opinion, the answer is both yes and no. I say yes because it is true that herbalists have made some important medical discoveries. And I say no because many people, even in the West, expect too much from herbs. If herbs could effect miracle cures for cancer, heart disease and pneumonia, then all Chinese should have a life expectancy of at least 100 years or more. Herbs are useful, as long as one doesn't catch the California Syndrome of trying to cure cancer and heart disease holistically with herbs, wheat germ, vitamin C and yoghurt made from unpasteurised goats' milk.

Herbs are not candy, and reckless consumption of these and any other medicines can be harmful. One friend of mine experienced serious allergic reactions and broke out in boils after taking a herbal medicine. He went on taking the medicine for several months and his condition only got worse. It cleared up miraculously when he stopped taking the herb. Many Chinese take herbs for years hoping to build up their bodies, and wind up destroying their liver because many herbs are partially toxic. Liver disease is a major cause of death in Taiwan.

On the other hand, there are some successful herbal treatments. One example of a dramatic herbal cure is the bark of the cinchona tree, which is used to make the antimalarial drug quinine. This particular herb was not discovered by the Chinese, but herbal medicine has a long history in many countries. The Chinese did discover Qing Haosu (Artemesinine), another malaria treatment which has recently generated much interest in medical circles. The dried seed of papaya has proved effective in battling dysentery. Deficiency diseases have long been successfully treated with herbs. For example, scurvy, caused by vitamin C deficiency, can be cured with rosehips, while other vitamin-rich herbs can cure beriberi, night blindness, pellagra and rickets.

My own experience with herbs is that they can be useful for relieving some symptoms and discomforts, but should not be considered a cure-all or replacement for surgery and antibiotics. For example, ginger root, placed in soup, seems to be helpful as a mild decongestant for colds. Other herbs such as mint and menthol soothe a sore throat, while liniment relieves sore muscles. Some herbs work well for an upset stomach. The oil of cloves is used worldwide to numb an aching tooth.

I'll recommend a couple of herbs, not unique to China, that I sometimes use. The most common is angelica *(dāngguī)*, which is placed in Chinese winter stew *(huǒguō)*. It's supposed to offer protection from colds and other illnesses. Visit any hospital ward in Taiwan during lunchtime and you will easily catch the scent of angelica in the air – the patients' relatives bring it in, sometimes over the protests of doctors.

I have achieved very good results with a herbal medicine called Ganoderma *(língzhī)*. Made from a rare mushroom, it's very expensive and therefore not something you take regularly. It might also be toxic in the long run. I used it when I was suffering from a serious intestinal disorder, and it was the *only* thing that helped when Western medicine had failed. It's widely available in Taiwan but care must be taken against fake or bad quality Ganoderma.

The Chinese make regular use of various liniments which are rubbed into the body where pain is felt. These liniments are claimed to cure just about anything, including headaches, stomachaches, backaches and nappy rash. I have tried many of these liniments and I can report that some of them really seem to work, at least for temporary relief of symptoms. Again, don't use liniments as if they were perfume – they may be harmful if overused and definitely should not be swallowed or put in the nose. Typical ingredients include eucalyptus oil and turpentine, both of which are toxic. They are available everywhere in Taiwan, as well as in Hong Kong and Singapore. My favourite one is called White Flower Oil *(bái huā yóu)*.

Before shopping for herbs, keep in mind that in Western medicine doctors talk about broad-spectrum antibiotics such as penicillin, which are good for treating a wide range of infections. But for many illnesses, a specific antibiotic might be better for a specific type of infection. The same is true in Chinese medicine. A broad-spectrum remedy such as snake gall bladder may be good for treating colds, but there are many different types of colds. The best way to treat a cold with herbal medicine is to see a Chinese doctor and get a specific prescription. Otherwise, the herbs you take may not be the most appropriate for your condition.

If you visit a Chinese doctor, you might be surprised by what he or she discovers about your body. For example, the doctor will almost certainly take your pulse and then may tell you that you have a slippery pulse or perhaps a thready pulse. Chinese doctors have identified more than 30 different kinds of pulses. A pulse could be empty, prison, leisurely, bowstring, irregular or even regularly irregular. The doctor may then examine your tongue to see if it is slippery, dry, pale, greasy, has a thick coating or maybe no coating at all. The doctor, having discovered that you have wet heat, as evidenced by a slippery pulse and a red greasy tongue, will prescribe the proper herbs for your condition.

Those interested in studying herbal medicine more thoroughly can find a number of reference books on the subject. For a good introduction to Chinese medicine, about the most clearly written introductory text is *The Web That Has No Weaver: Understanding Chinese Medicine* by Ted J Kaptchuk (Congdon & Weed, New York). A more advanced text, sprinkled with Latin terms and much more difficult to comprehend, is *The Theoretical Foundations of Chinese Medicine* by Manfred Porkert (MIT Press, Cambridge). Finally, there is *Treasures of Chinese Medicine (běn cǎo gāng mù)*, a classic published in the 16th century by Chinese doctor Li Shinchen. Although it has been over 400 years since it was written, it still remains the best reference in Chinese herbal medicine. An even older reference is the *Yellow Emperor's Classic of Internal Medicine (huángdì nèijīng sūwén)* – written, it's claimed, by the mythical Huang Ti around 2600 BC. ■

those visiting Taiwan. Hepatitis is a viral disease which affects the liver. There are two kinds of hepatitis: infectious (A) and serum (B).

Hepatitis A is spread if food, water or cooking and eating utensils have been contaminated. A simple preventive measure is to use the disposable chopsticks freely available in most restaurants in Taiwan.

A vaccine exists for hepatitis A, but is expensive and not widely available. There is also gamma-globulin – an antibody made from human blood which is effective for just a few months. Most people don't consider vaccination worthwhile for Taiwan, where hepatitis A is only a small risk. The best preventive measures are to eat food that is clean and well cooked, and to use disposable chopsticks.

Hepatitis B is usually transmitted in the same ways that HIV spreads: sexual intercourse, contaminated needles, blood transfusion or an infant contracting the disease from its infected mother.

For uncertain reasons, infection rates in Taiwan are among the highest in the world – it's probably a case of being passed down from mother to child and then spread sexually.

In recent years, hepatitis has also been spreading rapidly in developed countries due to casual sex and drug use. The innocent use of needles – ear piercing, tattooing and acupuncture – can spread the disease.

Fortunately, a vaccine exists against hepatitis B, but it must be given before you've had any exposure whatsoever. Once you've got the virus, you've got it for life. Therefore, you need a blood test before the vaccine can be given to determine if you've been exposed. The vaccine requires three injections, each given a month apart.

Unfortunately, the vaccine is expensive, but it's cheaper in Taiwan than it is in the West.

Hepatitis Non-A Non-B is a blanket term formerly used for several different strains of hepatitis which have now been separately identified. Hepatitis C through E have now been added to the medical alphabet soup. Travellers shouldn't be too paranoid about this apparent proliferation of hepatitis strains; they are fairly rare (so far) and following the same precautions as for A and B should be all that's necessary to avoid them.

For all kinds of hepatitis, the usual symptoms are fever, loss of appetite, nausea, depression, total lack of energy, and pain near the bottom of the rib cage where the liver is. The skin and whites of the eyes become yellow and urine turns a deep orange colour. There is no curative drug, but rest and good food are vital. Also stay clear of alcohol and tobacco for a full six months – the liver needs a long time to recover. Hepatitis A makes you very sick but complete recovery is the norm. You can also recover from hepatitis B but the disease can lead to liver cancer many years later – the vaccination is indeed worthwhile.

Dengue Fever *(tōnggǔrè)* This disease was once eradicated in Taiwan, but there have been outbreaks during the summer months in recent years. This is probably because more and more Taiwanese travel abroad, bringing the disease back with them. Dengue fever is transmitted between humans by biting mosquitoes. Also known as breakbone fever ('pain bone heat' in Chinese), the disease causes a sensation of extreme aching in the legs and joints at the onset of the illness. This gives way to high fever, sweating, headaches and a rash which spreads over the body. Although the patient feels very ill, the symptoms rapidly subside after about three or four days, then suddenly return. It may take up to three weeks to recover fully. There is no effective medication, but aspirin, paracetamol or codeine (15 to 60 mg every four hours) can help reduce the headache. Bed rest is important.

Although the disease is not dangerous in adults, it often has fatal complications in children under 10, especially infants. There is no vaccine, so the best prevention is to avoid mosquito bites. If you are taking care of a dengue fever patient, keep him or her under a mosquito net and use insect repellent or mosquito incense to prevent a mosquito transmitting the disease to you too. Having the disease produces immunity that lasts for about a year.

Tetanus *(pò shāng fēng)* There do seem to be quite a few motor accidents in Taiwan and although there is no vaccination that can protect you from getting run over by a bus, it would be prudent to get a tetanus shot before your arrival in Taiwan if you haven't had one for a few years.

Eye Problems Sunglasses not only give you that fashionable 'Hollywood look' but will protect your eyes. Ensure you buy sunglasses which filter out harmful UV radiation.

Conjunctivitis is a common eye infection which is easily spread by contaminated towels which are handed out by restaurants and even airlines. The best advice about wiping your face is to use disposable tissue paper or moist towelettes ('Wet Ones' or similar brands). If you think you have conjunctivitis, you need to see a doctor – the disease can damage your vision if untreated. Conjunctivitis is normally treated with antibiotic eye ointments for about four to six weeks. Be careful about diagnosing yourself – simple allergies can produce symptoms similar to eye infections, and in this case antibiotics can do more harm than good.

Sexually Transmitted Diseases *(xìng bìng)* The sexual revolution has reached Taiwan, along with the diseases that go with it. While abstinence is the only 100% preventive, using condoms is also effective. Gonorrhoea and syphilis are the most common of these diseases; sores, blisters or rashes around the genitals, discharges or pain when urinating are common symptoms. Symptoms may be less marked or not observed at all in women. Syphilis symptoms eventually disappear completely but the disease continues and can cause severe problems in later years. The treatment of gonorrhoea and syphilis is by antibiotics.

There are many other sexually transmitted diseases, for most of which effective treatment is available. However, there is no cure for herpes *(pàozhèn)* and there is currently no cure for HIV-AIDS *(àisì bìng)*. Using condoms is the most effective preventive.

HIV-AIDS can be spread through infected blood transfusions and dirty needles – vaccinations, acupuncture and tattooing can potentially be as dangerous as intravenous drug use if the equipment is not clean.

Illogical as it may seem, if you want to stay in Taiwan for a while, you'd better not get tested for HIV there. Foreigners who test positive for HIV are deported.

Bites & Stings
Snakes *(shé)* Thanks to American cowboy movies, people often associate snakes with

Acupuncture

(zhēnjiū) 針灸

Can you cure people by sticking needles into them? The Chinese think so and they've been doing it for thousands of years. Now the technique of acupuncture is gaining adherents in the West. In recent years, many Westerners have made the pilgrimage to China either to seek treatment or to study acupuncture. While acupuncture is also employed in Taiwan, it is by no means as common as on the Chinese mainland.

Getting stuck with needles might not sound pleasant, but if done properly it doesn't hurt. Knowing just where to insert the needle is crucial. Acupuncturists have identified more than 2000 insertion points, but only about 150 are commonly used.

The exact mechanism by which acupuncture works is not fully understood. The Chinese talk of energy channels or meridians which connect the needle insertion point to the particular organ, gland or joint being treated. The acupuncture point is sometimes quite far from the area of the body being treated. Acupuncture is even used to treat impotency, but I've never wanted to ask just where the needle is inserted.

Among acupuncturists there are different schools of thought. The most common school in China is called the Eight Principles School. Another is the Five Elements School.

As with herbal medicine, the fundamental question asked by potential acupuncture patients is: 'Does it work?' The answer has to be: 'That depends.' It depends on the skill of the acupuncturist and the condition being treated. Like herbal medicine, acupuncture tends to be more useful for those who suffer from long-term conditions (like chronic headaches) rather than sudden emergencies (like an acute appendicitis).

However, there are times when acupuncture can be used for an immediate condition. For example, some major surgical operations have been performed using acupuncture as the only anaesthetic (this works best on the head). In this case, a small electric current (from batteries) is passed through the needles. This is a good example of how Western medicine and Chinese medicine can be usefully combined.

While some satisfied patients give glowing testimonials about the prowess of acupuncture, others are less impressed. The only way to really find out is to try it.

Loosely related to acupuncture is massage (ànmó). The Chinese variety is somewhat different from the popular do-it-yourself techniques practised by people in the West. One traditional Chinese technique employs suction cups made of bamboo, placed on the patient's skin. A burning piece of alcohol-soaked cotton is briefly put inside the cup to drive out the air before it is applied. As the cup cools, a partial vacuum is produced, leaving a nasty-looking but harmless red circular mark on the skin. The mark goes away in a few days. Other methods include bloodletting and scraping the skin with coins or porcelain soup spoons.

A related technique is called moxibustion. Various types of herbs, rolled into what looks like a ball of fluffy cotton, are held just near the skin and ignited. A slight variation of this method is to place the herb on a slice of ginger and then ignite it. The idea is to apply the maximum amount of heat possible without burning the patient. This heat treatment is supposed to be good for such diseases as arthritis. ■

the desert, but they are in fact most common in damp, forested areas where they have plenty to eat. Taiwan's subtropical weather is just perfect for them – the island has a thorough assortment of deadly, poisonous snakes. The ones I've seen have mostly been the small but venomous bamboo snake. They are green and camouflage themselves in the bushes and trees, and are not necessarily limited to bamboo trees. Another interesting snake is the '100 pacer', so called because if it bites, you can expect to walk about 100 paces before dropping dead. There are also cobras, though I've yet to see one in Taiwan, except on a dinner plate in Taipei's exotic night market. Other common poisonous serpents include the banded krait, Taiwan habu and Russell's viper. Less common, but no less poisonous, are coral snakes, the Oshima's habu and Chinese mountain pit viper. All sea snakes are poisonous and are readily identified by their flat tails.

Now that I've got you thoroughly paranoid, let me add the following: almost all species of snakes are timid and will flee from humans. Even those which are not timid are unlikely to attack a big creature like a human unless you inadvertently step on one of them. Remember, snakes eat insects, birds and rodents, not people. They only bite humans when they feel threatened. Wearing boots rather than running shoes will help protect you from a bite on the leg should you step on a snake. There is such a thing as snakeproof trousers, though I haven't seen them for sale in Taiwan.

Don't be a fool and attack a snake with a stick – that's the most likely way to get bitten. Whenever I see a snake by the trail, I try to make some noise to scare it off before it can be attacked by a vicious hiker. Some Chinese hikers attach a small bell to their pack to scare off snakes – not a bad idea if you can tolerate all that damn noise.

If by some chance you do get bitten, the important thing to remember is to remain calm and not run around. Authorities differ widely on how to treat a snake bite in emergencies without a specific antivenin, but the conventional wisdom is to rest and allow the poison to be absorbed slowly. A constricting band (tourniquet) can be useful for slowing down the poison, but it's also very dangerous – if too tight, a tourniquet can cut off circulation and cause gangrene, a possibly fatal complication. If a tourniquet is applied, be sure you *do not* use a narrow band like a shoelace. Use something wide and soft, like strips of cloth or a T-shirt. Furthermore, be sure that you can feel the pulse below the tourniquet – if you've cut off the pulse, it's too tight! Keep the affected limb below the heart level.

The old 'boy scout' method of treating snake bite – cutting the skin and sucking out the poison – has also been widely discredited. It theoretically can help if done properly, but most people do not know how to do it and the result is often a deep cut, loss of blood (sending the patient into shock) and an infection. Even if done by an expert, only about 20% of the poison can be removed this way. Immersion in cold water is also considered useless.

Treatment in a hospital with an antivenin would be ideal. However, getting the victim to a hospital is only half the battle – you will also need to identify the snake. In this particular case, it might be worthwhile to kill the snake and take its body along, but don't attempt that if it means getting bitten again. Try to transport the victim on a makeshift stretcher which you can fashion from two bamboo poles and an overcoat.

Although I hate to say it, there isn't a whole lot you can do for a snake-bite victim if you are far from civilisation. Fortunately, the vast majority of snake-bite victims survive even without medical treatment. However, prevention is still the best medicine.

Insects Wasps (*hŭtóufēng*), which are common in the tropics, are a more serious hazard than snakes because they are more aggressive and will chase humans when stirred up. If you see a wasp nest, the best advice is to move away quietly. They won't attack unless they feel threatened, so don't do anything foolish like seeing how close you can get to their nest.

Every year, several people in Taiwan are killed or injured by swarms of angry wasps; the victims are most often children who throw rocks at the nests. Should you be so unfortunate as to be attacked by wasps, the only sensible thing to do is run like hell.

It would take perhaps 100 wasp or bee stings to kill a normal adult, but a single sting can be fatal to someone who is allergic to the venom. In fact, death from wasp and bee stings is more common than death from snakebite. People who are allergic to wasp and bee stings are also allergic to bites by red ants. If you happen to have this sort of allergy, you'd be wise to throw an antihistamine and epinephrine into your first-aid kit. Epinephrine is most effective when injected, but taking it in pill form is better than nothing.

Spiders (*zhīzhū*) are not something you need to worry much about, but you might encounter a large spider which looks very much like a tarantula. They reside in trees and I've occasionally bumped right into them. Fortunately, they are neither poisonous nor aggressive and will flee from humans.

Taiwan is also the habitat of the vinegaroon, or whip scorpion. The stinger points straight up like a needle rather than being curved and segmented as in the common scorpion. As nasty as they look, they are not venomous and therefore you needn't fear them. Still, I wouldn't want to pick one up and play with it – when confronted by a human, they assume an aggressive posture with claws and stinger bristling. Although it's debatable how capable they are of inflicting a wound on a human, they do spray a smelly solution of acetic acid which can irritate the skin, and which is how they got the name vinegaroon.

Mosquitos (wénzi) are a year-round annoyance almost anywhere in Taiwan, especially at night when you're trying to sleep. Electric mosquito zappers are useful, but are too heavy for travelling. A portable innovation is 'electric mosquito incense' (diàn wénxiāng), known in Taiwan as 'vape mats' or 'mosquito mats'. Vape mats and the vape mat electric heater (diàn wénxiāng zuò) are sold in grocery stores and supermarkets all over Taiwan – every 7-Eleven store stocks it. The vape mats do emit a poison – breathing it over the long-term may have unknown health effects, though all the manufacturers of this stuff insist that it's safe.

Mosquito incense coils (wénxiāng) accomplish the same thing as the vape mats and require no electricity, but the smoke is nasty. Mosquito repellent is somewhat less effective than incense, but is probably less toxic and gives protection outdoors where incense is impractical. Look for brands that contain 'deet' (diethyl toluamide). Some effective brands include Autan and Off!. Sleeping under an electric fan all night (not recommended during winter) will also keep the mosquitos away.

Poisonous Plants A minor but painful hazard is caused by a particular type of sting-ing nettle, a plant called 'bite people cat' (yǎorénmāo). I have touched this plant and can report it's much worse than a cat's bite. It took three days for the swelling to go away. It's a rather ugly plant with splotches on the leaves and is common at around 1500 metres elevation. Should you accidentally touch it, you'll never forget what it looks like.

'Bite People Cat' nettle

Public Toilets
(cèsuǒ) 廁所
Toilet paper is seldom provided in the toilets at bus and railway stations or in other public buildings. You'd be wise to keep a stash of your own with you at all times. In some places, women must pay NT$3 to NT$5 to use the toilet, while for men it is free. Women should keep some change handy for this. In a few resort areas, men may be charged to use the toilet, but this is rare. To avoid embarrassment, try to remember:

男　　女

Men　　　　Women

The issue of what to do with used toilet paper can be confusing. As one traveller wrote:

We are still not sure about the Chinese toilet paper...in two hotels they have been angry with us for flushing down the paper in the toilet. In other places it seems quite OK though.

In general, if you see a wastebasket with a plastic-bag liner next to the toilet, that is where you should throw the toilet paper. But don't throw used toilet paper in the basket if it is not lined with a plastic bag. The problem is that in many hotels, the sewerage system cannot handle toilet paper. This is especially true in old hotels where the antiquated plumbing system was designed in the pre-toilet-paper era. Also, in rural areas there is no sewage treatment plant – the waste empties into an underground septic tank and toilet paper will really create a mess in there. For the sake of international relations, be considerate and throw the paper in the wastebasket.

And while we're on the subject of toilets, in most Asian countries, including ultramodern Japan, you will encounter squat toilets. For the uninitiated who don't know what I'm talking about, a squat toilet has no seat for you to sit on while reading the morning newspaper...in other words, it is a hole in the floor, but it does flush. While it takes some practice to get proficient at balancing yourself over a squat toilet, at least you don't need to worry if the toilet seat is clean. Furthermore, experts who study such things claim that the squatting position is better for your bowels.

While most people in Taiwan now have Western-style toilets in their homes, many public restrooms still have the squat variety. While you are balancing yourself over one of these devices, take care that your comb, wallet, keys and the other valuables in your pockets don't fall into the abyss.

Women's Health

Gynaecological Problems Poor diet, lowered resistance due to the use of antibiotics for stomach upsets, and even contraceptive pills can lead to vaginal infections when travelling in hot climates. Keeping the genital area clean, and wearing skirts or loose-fitting trousers and cotton underwear will help to prevent infections.

Yeast infections, characterised by a rash, itch and discharge, can be treated with a vinegar or even lemon-juice douche or with yoghurt. Nystatin suppositories are the usual medical prescription. Trichomonas is a more serious infection; symptoms are a discharge and a burning sensation when urinating. Sexual partners must also be treated, and if a vinegar-water douche is not effective medical attention should be sought. Flagyl is the prescribed drug.

Pregnancy Most miscarriages occur during the first three months of pregnancy, so this is the most risky time to travel. The last three months should also be spent within reasonable distance of good medical care, as quite serious problems can develop at this time. Pregnant women should avoid all unnecessary medication, but vaccinations should still be taken where possible. Additional care should be taken to prevent illness and particular attention should be paid to diet and nutrition.

WOMEN TRAVELLERS

There are periodic reports of young, unescorted females who have been raped and/or robbed by a taxi driver, usually at night. Most of the victims are Chinese, but there have been a few attacks on foreign women as well. Most taxi drivers are OK, but there are enough bad ones to make you pause. Unfortunately, a large number of ex-convicts drive taxis in Taiwan because it's the only job they can get.

There is no way to be 100% safe, but a few precautions can help. Most importantly, a woman shouldn't take a taxi alone at night, unless absolutely necessary.

Perhaps the safest thing you can do is call a radio-dispatch taxi. There is an English-speaking dispatcher in Taipei (☎ 02-282 1166).

Another common precaution is to have a friend write down the taxi's licence-plate number before you enter the vehicle and note the time and location. It should be made clear to the driver that this is being done. This has become a common practice and drivers are used to it, so don't feel inhibited about doing it. The licence-plate number is displayed on the rear window and should be highly visible. Never get into a taxi if the licence-plate number appears to have been obscured, since potential rapists often deliberately try to hide the number.

Note that there are two designs for taxis, sedans and hatchbacks, and that hatchbacks pose an extra danger: in one common type of assault, an accomplice hides in the rear storage area and enters the passenger compartment by pushing forward the rear seat. Thus, the woman is faced with two attackers at once. This cannot happen with a sedan since the boot (trunk) is separated from the rear seat by a metal wall, although the metal wall can be cut. To be safe, learn to recognise sedans and also give one hard pull on the rear-seat back cushion as you're getting in – if it falls out of place, immediately get out of the taxi. Also make sure the window can be rolled down. Rapists have been known to remove the inside door and window handles so the victim cannot escape or yell for help.

Finally, don't be overly paranoid. These attacks do happen, but not so frequently that you need to bottle yourself up indoors. Nevertheless, a little bit of caution never hurt.

DANGERS & ANNOYANCES
Crime
If you believe the newspapers, Taiwan is a hotbed of criminal activity. Although it is no doubt less safe than it used to be, Taiwan is one of the safer places in Asia in terms of street crime. Pickpockets do exist, so you should keep your cash in a money belt or a small pouch under your clothes, but in general there is little to fear. Travellers' cheques are safer than cash, but be sure to have a receipt and/or written record of the serial numbers. Many of the better hotels have a safe where you can deposit your valuables rather than carrying them around

with you. If you're staying for a long time, you can rent a safe-deposit box.

Although street muggings are exceedingly rare, there is a serious problem with residential burglaries in the cities. Youth hostels are not immune, especially since they tend to leave the door unlocked. Also, it's sad but true that some of your fellow travellers may take a liking to your camera or Walkman, so never leave valuables lying around the dormitory.

The kidnapping of children has become a growth industry – at least if the parents are rich. While the victims tend to be mainly wealthy Taiwanese families, a few foreigners (mostly Japanese corporate executives) have had their children held for ransom. None of this need concern the average backpacker, but if you're bringing your whole family to Taiwan for a long stay, the best advice is to look poor. Young adult foreigners rarely seem to be the target of crime, especially since they usually have less money than the locals.

WORK
English Teachers
Word has spread far and wide through the travellers' grapevine that big bucks can be made teaching English in Taiwan. Some years ago when I first came to Taiwan, foreigners were such a rare commodity that I was practically kidnapped by eager students shortly after my arrival at the airport. Recruiters from the various language schools came knocking on my door so often I almost had to beat them off with a stick.

That was then and this is now. There are thousands of foreigners teaching English in Taiwan, so students aren't going to come and break down your door. However, it is still eminently possible to find work if you go out and look for it. The pay is still pretty good (starting at NT$350 per hour), but if you've got to make frequent trips to Hong Kong or sign up for unwanted Chinese lessons to keep Immigration off your back, it cuts into your profits. Your biggest problem is likely to be the immigration and tax authorities. At one time the authorities bent over backwards

Dogs

There is a disturbingly large number of half-starved stray dogs, many of which have lost most of their hair and are obviously afflicted with disease, wandering the streets of Taiwan's cities. There seems to be no attempt whatsoever by the authorities to round up the strays and put them in an animal shelter or put them down. These dogs are in such bad shape that even the restaurants serving dog meat won't touch them. These animals suffer constantly and therefore have grown quite mean, and they seem to have a particular antipathy for foreigners wearing shorts. Just why they should be xenophobic I'm not sure, but they seem to find the sight of a hairy foreigner's leg is as mouth-watering as smoked sausage. You needn't excessively fear these dogs, but they *can* be dangerous. Most are easily scared off if you menacingly shake an umbrella or stick at them, and long trousers is another preventive measure.

Where do these animals come from? The problem stems from the fact that many Taiwanese find cute and fluffy little puppies to be irresistible pets. Unfortunately, when Fido grows up and becomes decidedly less cute and fluffy, the dog winds up being unceremoniously dumped in the nearest alley. There is no animal shelter or humane society which takes responsibility for strays – most of these animals spend their short lives digging through rubbish bins looking for food scraps before eventually starving to death. No matter how much you love dogs, I don't suggest you try to pet these animals. A bullet through the brain would probably be the kindest thing you could do for them, though Taiwan has strict gun control laws so that isn't a legal option.

Dogs are also the bane of cyclists all over the world, and from my experience, they enjoy biting motorcyclists too. If you do much two-wheeled riding in Taiwan, you'll probably have an unpleasant encounter with Fido sooner or later. Motorcycles can easily outrun a dog, but bicyclists may not be so fortunate, especially when going uphill. Cyclists are divided on how to respond to a dog attack. Some people carry irritating chemical sprays to repel aggressive animals, while others are adept using a bicycle pump for the same purpose. Some cyclists say you should stop, dismount and keep the bicycle between yourself and the dog until it calms down and goes away. Still others suggest an air gun (not legal in Taiwan) or a crossbow (legal but awkward to carry). ■

to assist foreigners, but these days they have English-teacher fatigue.

Most of these English-teaching jobs are illegal. In the past, the authorities have turned a blind eye, but in recent years there has been a heavy crackdown on working illegally. Some of the private 'cram schools' (*bǔxíbān*) have been raided, and foreign teachers without working visas were arrested, fined and expelled from Taiwan. Many cram schools can, in fact, hire foreigners legally – this assumes the school itself is legally licensed, though many aren't.

However, if the school is legal and is willing to sponsor you for a resident visa, your visa problems will be solved. It takes about two months to process the visa application, and you are not supposed to work until the paperwork is finally completed. You need to go abroad to pick up the visa – Hong Kong is the nearest place offering this service.

If you clear all the visa hurdles, it's also worth noting that teaching English is not always as easy as it sounds. Getting the job is only half the battle; keeping it is the other. If you have ability and your students are good, it can be a pleasure. Unfortunately, it's quite likely that you'll get many students whose English is poor, especially if you teach children. In the case of children's classes, you may also get many students who are being forced to study by their parents and have little interest. By way of compensation, the pay for teaching children is often higher and such work is more readily available. Some people love teaching English, but many travellers say they find it plain boring.

Skilled Professionals

There are other jobs besides teaching, but you usually need some sort of high-tech skill to get these. The Foreign Affairs Ministry has a list of acceptable professions, not all of which are technical – 'corporate executive' or 'ambassador to Taiwan' are possibilities, though getting such plum jobs is not particularly easy.

Buskers & Musicians

Buskers were tolerated in Taipei for a while, but there has been a crackdown. If you want free accommodation (in prison), this is one way to get it. The police have even cracked down on foreigners playing in bands in nightclubs – only performances advertised 'benefit' are permitted to have foreign musicians.

Income Taxes

If you're working legally, you are required to file an income-tax return in February or March. The deadline is 31 March, but can be extended (after application) to 30 April. If you stay 183 days or more in a year, you are considered a resident for tax purposes. Note that this means calendar days – if you arrive in Taiwan after 2 July, you cannot qualify as a resident before the year finishes since 2 July through 31 December equals 183 days. Being a resident is an advantage – you are taxed at a much lower rate (6%) than nonresidents (20%).

ACTIVITIES
Hiking

(páshān) 爬山

With dozens of peaks over 3000 metres elevation, Taiwan offers some outstanding opportunities for walking and mountaineering.

Hiking Clubs There are many clubs in Taipei and in the other big cities. Some are non-profit clubs associated with universities, but most are commercial outfits. The clubs typically take a whole busload of hikers out for about NT$300 a head for day hikes, and considerably more for overnight trips. Most things are included: transport, meals, lodging and required mountain permits. The only bad thing I can say about these clubs is that at times their trips can be rather crowded. The Chinese like to do things in groups, so you may get 50 or 100 people or more hiking together. Fortunately, overnight trips are usually smaller, involving about 20 people or less.

To find these clubs, enquire at any shop which sells backpacking equipment. Many of these shops run their own trips, and several are listed in the Taipei chapter of this book. Additionally, all universities in Taiwan have hiking clubs, but usually these clubs only welcome students and faculty. Do bear in mind that most of these clubs are thoroughly Chinese and that few people will speak English.

Safety Issues The most immediate threat to hikers in Taiwan is the unpredictable mountain weather. It rains frequently, especially in the spring and summer months. It can be beautiful one minute, then the clouds and fog come out of nowhere and it starts pouring. This is not only unpleasant but dangerous. If you get soaking wet, you may die of exposure (hypothermia is the technical term). Therefore, adequate waterproof clothing is a must. Cheap plastic rain boots, widely available in Taiwan, are great for keeping the feet dry too.

The rain and steep mountains produce another hazard – landslides. In most cases, you won't have to worry about them if you stick to the trails, but be warned that trails and even roads get wiped out regularly in Taiwan by landslides, especially during the rainy season.

Hypothermia can occur in Taiwan's mountains even during summer if you're unprepared. It is surprisingly easy to progress from very cold to dangerously cold due to a combination of wind, wet clothing, fatigue and hunger, even if the air temperature is above freezing. It helps to dress in layers; silk, wool and some artificial fibres are all good insulating materials. A hat is important, as a lot of heat is lost through the head. A strong, waterproof outer layer is essential, as keeping dry is vital. Carry basic supplies, including food containing simple sugars to generate heat quickly and lots of fluid to drink.

Surfing
(chōnglàng) 衝浪
Being a subtropical island, you'd expect Taiwan to be a surfers' paradise. Actually, there are only a few spots on the island considered suitable for surfing. The west coast is a dead loss – the water in the Taiwan Straits is just too calm to generate sufficient waves (unless you want to try it during a typhoon!).

The east coast has far better waves, but it's also rocky and plagued by dangerous riptides. Still, there are a few sandy beaches in coves that have started to catch on with surfers. In particular, there are a couple in Taipei County, at least one each in Ilan and Taitung counties, and at Kenting National Park at the very southern tip of Taiwan. See the relevant chapters for details.

Windsurfing
(fēngfán) 風帆
Windsurfing is also starting to catch on. Unlike surfing, big waves are not a prerequisite, though wind is essential. Windsurfing equipment is available for rent at Kenting National Park and the beach resort at Chipei Island in the Penghu Archipelago.

Grass Skiing
(huá cǎo) 滑草
Taiwan is mountainous but doesn't get much snow; local skiers had to improvise, and grass-skiing was born. Grass-skis look like a cross between normal downhill-skis and the treads on army tanks. The sport is said to be somewhat dangerous – apparently, falling on grass is less forgiving than snow. I haven't heard of anyone trying grass-ski jumping yet – now that would be a challenge! Other variations on the theme include grass-toboggans and grass-sleds, providing additional work opportunities for acupuncturists and physical therapists.

The degree of danger depends largely on the steepness and length of the slope, as well as the skill of the participants. There are a number of venues to pursue the sport of sliding downhill without the benefit of snow. All are commercial resorts, but fees are not outrageous. If helmets, shoulder pads and other safety equipment are supplied, you're advised to wear them.

Paragliding
(huá xiáng yì) 滑翔翼
You can pursue this sport anywhere if you have the right equipment, but there are a few established spots with equipment rentals and instructors. You should make local enquiries, but one place to look is Sai Chia Paradise in Pingtung County (see the South-West Taiwan chapter).

Rafting
(fànzhōu) 泛舟
Taiwan's small size means few big rivers, but the presence of mountains and heavy rainfall adds up to a few interesting runs. The main venue for whitewater rafting trips is the Hsiukuluan River in Hualien County. The Laonung River in Kaohsiung has seen a few commercial river runners, but not many. A few hardy souls have taken off on their own and rafted the river running through Huisun Forest.

Bungy Jumping
(gāokōng tán tiào) 高空彈跳
First promoted by Oxford's Dangerous Sports Club in 1979, this craze has now come to Taiwan. There is a contact phone number for Taipei and Taichung – see those chapters for details.

HIGHLIGHTS

For the athletically inclined, climbing some of Taiwan's highest peaks such as Yushan, Hsuehshan, Tapachienshan and Kuanshan will certainly offer a delightful challenge. Other less strenuous hikes in the Alishan and Tungpu areas are very worthwhile.

For those who prefer to view their scenery from the road, a trip along the scenic east coast highway is one of Taiwan's highlights. Ditto for journeys along the Central Cross-Island and South Cross-Island highways. The road over Hohuanshan is Taiwan's highest, and offers incredible views (at least, when the weather cooperates).

Island lovers should check out Lanyu and Penghu. Lovers in general should visit Sun Moon Lake, a favourite honeymoon spot. Temple enthusiasts will want to explore Tainan. Just north of Taipei, the hot springs at Yangmingshan are worth visiting, but be sure to check out the better-appointed springs at Taroko Gorge, Hungyeh, Antung and Chihpen.

ACCOMMODATION

Prices have risen to the point where the only true budget accommodation left is dormitories.

The best way to save money on accommodation is to travel with a companion. Most hotels in Taiwan charge nothing extra for two people as long as you're willing to share a double bed. Hotels usually charge by the number of beds in the room, not by the number of people sleeping there. Most 'single rooms' in Taiwan are what Westerners usually call doubles. Twin rooms have two separate beds and cost considerably more.

The question you'll most likely be asked first at any reception desk is *Nǐ yào zěnme yàngde fángjiān?*, meaning 'What kind of room do you want?'. If you want 'the cheapest', then learn how to say *zuì piányide*. If the room you're shown is too dismal, you could ask for something 'a little better' *(hǎo yìdiǎnde)*. If you think the price they have quoted is high, tell them it is 'too expensive' *(tài guì)*. You can ask them to please give it

to you a little cheaper *(kěyǐ suàn piányì yìdiǎn ma)*.

Discounts are possible, especially off season, on weekends, when the place has a large number of vacancies, etc. However, there is no room for vociferous bargaining – Taiwan is not a Third World country. Hotel proprietors may knock off 10% or they may give you a cheaper room, but in general prices are not subject to haggling. If you bargain for more than a minute then you're really just arguing, which is a waste of time and likely to result in you being asked to leave. At the bottom end of the scale, reservations are usually not accepted and those planning to stay in youth hostels can usually find a bed. To save yourself some running around you can telephone ahead from the airport. The people at the information desk in the airport will do this for you for free. It's certainly better to call ahead than to scramble from place to place in search of a room.

Camping

Considering the shortage of beds in youth hostels, camping makes a good deal of sense if you'll be spending much time in rural areas. Many of the established camping grounds are in fact adjacent to youth hostels, providing a means of accommodating the masses when the hostels fill up. At the better hostels, tents are usually already set up so you needn't bring your own. Unfortunately, the trend of recent years has been to require campers to bring their own tents and other equipment. A camping fee of about NT$50 to NT$250 is charged and campers are permitted to use the hostel's showers and other amenities. Some of the hostels in mountain areas will allow you to set up your own tent next to the hostel for free, but always ask first.

In back country areas, there is usually no objection to setting up a tent just about anywhere.

You need to consider how much equipment you're willing to carry. Tents and sleeping bags are rather bulky and heavy items that most travellers would rather leave at home. You can get away without a sleeping bag in summer only at elevations below 1000 metres; above that, it gets cold at night. Above 2000 metres, the temperature can dip below freezing during winter. When it's cold, you not only need a good sleeping bag, but also a foam pad to put under it because the ground feels like a sheet of ice.

Give some thought as to what type of tent to bring. Afternoon and evening rain showers are a common feature in Taiwan, so you need something that's waterproof. At low elevations like beach areas, you also need something that's bugproof. You needn't worry about insects when the temperature is cold, so if you only plan to camp in high mountain areas, you might want to consider using a tube tent. This is a cylindrical sheet of plastic – it has no tent poles, and you keep it from falling down by stringing a nylon cord between two trees. A few well-placed rocks in each corner keeps it in place, but you won't want to use it on mountaintops exposed to high winds. The advantage of a tube tent is its light weight – less than ½ kg – but it offers no protection at all from insects because both ends of the 'tube' are open. I've seen tube tents for sale in the better back-packing shops in Taipei, and my experiments with them have been generally positive.

You need to keep your backpack and other equipment dry too. Plastic garbage bags will do the trick – these are available from any grocery store in Taiwan.

Youth Hostels

There are two types of youth hostels in Taipei – private and public. The private ones are definitely in the minority, currently found only in two cities, Taipei and Kaohsiung. These places offer both dormitory beds and sometimes small private rooms with a shared bath. Prices for a dorm bed are around NT$180 per night, with discounts if you rent by the week.

Taiwan's government-run youth hostels are operated by various branches of the bureaucracy. The majority are operated by the CYC, or China Youth Corps. This organisation is not connected with the International Youth Hostel Federation (IYHF)

and therefore you do not need an IYHF card. You also do not need a sleeping sheet and the hostels are open all day, unlike IYHF hostels which often kick you out during the daytime. Some of the urban hostels may lock their doors at midnight, but other than that there are no restrictions on your movements. Unlike IYHF places, these hostels do not provide kitchen facilities for your use, although they do have cheap cafeteria meals if you reserve them in advance.

In addition to CYC hostels, there are urban hostels in Keelung, Taipei, Tainan and Kaohsiung called Labourers' Recreation Centres – these are not associated with CYC. There are also Teachers' Hostels in some places – the ones in Hualien and Penghu are bargains at NT$150, but other Teachers' Hotels (like the one in Sun Moon Lake) are absurdly expensive, though there is a discount if you're a teacher (with valid ID issued in Taiwan).

Dormitory-style accommodation in the hostels costs between NT$150 and NT$300. Most of these places have private rooms available at usually ridiculous prices (NT$1000 to NT$4000). Reservations are advisable, especially during holidays – the CYC hotels in particular are often booked solid. There are also the so-called 'Public Hostels' *(guómín lüshè)* – these are nothing more than expensive government-owned hotels.

Call rural youth hostels first. They can be closed in winter or after landslides. If desperate, you can stay at schools for free or sometimes pay NT$50 and they might let you use the shower in the teachers' dormitory. Or ask the police – they might at least offer you a cup of tea. The desperate can sometimes sleep in temples too. People in Taiwan are eager to help lost-looking foreigners.

In the past, some remote mountain hostels (Yakou, for example) allowed travellers to 'camp out' on the dining room floor when all the beds were occupied. A small 'camping fee' of NT$30 was charged. Unfortunately, this practice seems to be on the way out.

All of the CYC hostels, Labourers' Recre-

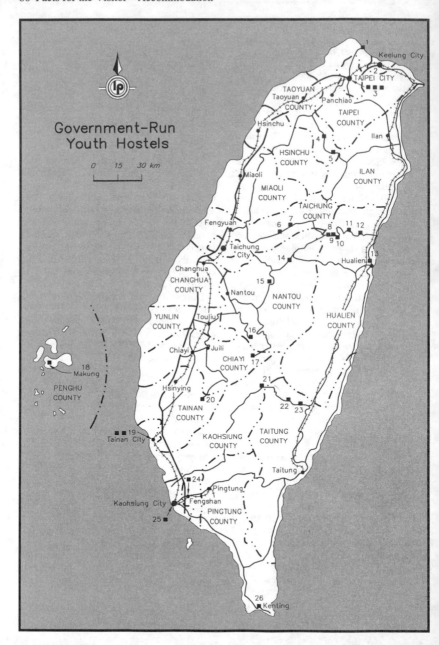

1 **Chinshan Youth Activity Centre**
(*jīnshān qīngnián huódòng zhōngxīn*),
Chinshan, Taipei County (☎ 02-4981191/3)

2 **Keelung Labourers' Recreation Centre**
(*láogōng péngyǒu huódòng zhōngxīn*), 22
Lane 370, Anyi Rd, Anle District, Keelung
(☎ 02-4286482)

3 **Chientan Youth Activity Centre**
(*jiàntán qīngnián huódòng zhōngxīn*), 16
Chungshan N Rd, Section 4, Taipei
(☎ 02-5962151)

Taipei International (TIYAC)
(*guójì qīngnián huódòng zhōngxīn*), 30
Hsinhai Rd, Section 3 (☎ 02-3621770), Taipei

Taipei Labourers' Recreation Centre
(*láoyǒu zhījiā zhōngxīn*), 2 Lane 101,
Hsinsheng N Rd, Section 2, Taipei
(☎ 02-5519300)

4 **Fuhsing Mountain Hostel**
(*fùxīng shān zhuāng*), North Cross-Island
Highway, Taoyuan County (☎ 03-3822276)

5 **Paling Mountain Hostel**
(*bālíng shān zhuāng*), North Cross-Island
Highway, Taoyuan County (☎ 03-3332153/4)

6 **Chingshan Mountain Hostel**
(*qīngshān shān zhuāng*), Central Cross-Island
Highway, Taichung County (☎ 04-5244103)

7 **Techi Mountain Hostel**
(*déjī shān zhuāng*), Central Cross-Island
Highway, Taichung County
(☎ 04-5981592; reservations ☎ 5244103)

8 **Tayuling Mountain Hostel**
(*dàyúlíng shān zhuāng*), Central Cross-Island
Highway, Hualien County
(enquire at Tienhsiang Hostel
☎ 04-5991009; reservations ☎ 038-691111)

9 **Kuanyun Mountain Hostel**
(*guānyún shān zhuāng*), dormitory costs
NT$200
(☎ 04-5991173; reservations ☎ 038-691111)

10 **Tzuen Mountain Hostel**
(*cíēn shān zhuāng*), Central Cross-Island
Highway, Hualien County (enquire at
Tienhsiang Hostel ☎ 038-691111/3)

11 **Loshao Mountain Hostel**
(*luòsháo shān zhuāng*), Central Cross-Island
Highway, Hualien County
(enquire at Tienhsiang Hostel
☎ 038-691111/3)

12 **Tienhsiang Youth Activity Centre**
(*tiānxiáng qīngnián huódòng zhōngxīn*),
Hualien County (☎ 038-691111/3)

13 **Hualien Student Hostel**
(*huālián xuéyuàn*), 40-11 Kungyuan Rd,
Hualien (☎ 038-324124)

Teachers' Hostel
(*huālián jiàoshī huìguǎn*), 10 Kungcheng St,
Hualien (☎ 038-325880)

14 **Wushe Mountain Hostel**
(*wùshè shān zhuāng*), Wushe, Nantou County
(☎ 049-223441)

15 **Sun Moon Lake Youth Activity Centre**
(*rì yuè tán qīngnián huódòng zhōngxīn*), Sun
Moon Lake, Nantou County (☎ 049-850070)

16 **Hsitou Youth Activity Centre**
(*xītóu qīngnián huódòng zhōngxīn*), Nantou
County (☎ 049-612161)

17 **Alishan Youth Activity Centre**
(*ālǐshān qīngnián huódòng zhōngxīn*),
Erwanping, Chiayi County (☎ 05-2679561)

18 **Penghu Youth Activity Centre**
(*pénghú qīngnián huódòng zhōngxīn*), 11
Chiehshou Rd, Makung, Penghu County
(☎ 06-9271124)

Teachers' Hostel
(*jiàoshī huìguǎn*), at 38 Shute Rd, Makung,
Penghu County (☎ 06-9273692)

19 **Tainan Student Hostel**
(*táinán xuéyuàn*), Lane 300, Funung St,
Section 1, Tainan (☎ 06-2670526/8, 2689018)

Tainan Labourers' Recreation Centre
(*láogōng xiūjià zhōngxīn*), 261 Nanmen Rd,
Tainan (☎ 06-2630174)

20 **Tsengwen Youth Activity Centre**
(*zēngwén qīngnián huódòng zhōngxīn*),
Tainan County (☎ 06-5752575, 5753164)

21 **Meishan Mountain Hostel**
(*méishān shān zhuāng*), Southern
Cross-Island Highway, Kaohsiung County
(☎ 07-7470134/5)

22 **Yakou Mountain Hostel**
(*yǎkǒu shān zhuāng*), Southern Cross-Island
Highway, Taitung County (☎ 089-329891)

23 **Litao Mountain Hostel**
(*lìdào shān zhuāng*), Southern Cross-Island
Highway, Taitung County (☎ 089-329891)

24 **Chengching Lake Youth Activity Centre**
(*chéng qīng hú qīngnián huódòng zhōngxīn*),
Kaohsiung County (☎ 07-3717181)

25 **Kaohsiung Labourers' Recreation Centre**
(*láogōng yùlè zhōngxīn*), 132 Chungshan 3rd
Rd, Kaohsiung (☎ 07-3328110)

26 **Kenting Youth Activity Centre**
(*kěndìng qīngnián huódòng zhōngxīn*),
Kenting Village, Hengchun, Pingtung County
(☎ 08-8861221/4)

ation Centres and the more useful Teachers' Hostels are shown on the Youth Hostels map. The English addresses aren't very useful for those hostels in rural areas, so outside the big cities use the Chinese address. The Taipei International will book a bed for you in other CYC hostels around the island. If booking by telephone, the hostels ask for a postal money order. These are very reliable, but you'll probably need a Chinese person to help you fill in the form.

Guesthouses

Guesthouses *(dà lüshè* or *lüshè)* are usually older hotels, a bit run down but not bad at all. Although it's no-frills, most are air-conditioned and have private bath. Starting prices can be as low as NT$300 in rural areas but more like NT$600 in Taipei.

Few guesthouses have English signs to identify themselves. You'll find it much easier to spot these places if you learn the Chinese characters for guesthouse (see opposite).

Hotels

Top end hotels can easily cost more than NT$3000 per night for a basic single; mid-range hotels cost from around NT$800 to NT$1500 for a double

Older hotels sometimes have very cheap Japanese-style *tatami* rooms, a legacy of the 50 years of Japanese occupation in Taiwan. A tatami room consists of straw mats or quilts laid out on the floor. Be sure to take your shoes off before entering these places! Even if you don't speak a word of Chinese, just say the word tatami *(tātāmǐ)*. They may say they have 'no tatami', in which case you could see if they have a dormitory *(tuántǐfáng)*. If they don't, then ask for a room with shared bath *(pǔtōngfáng)*. Rooms with private bath *(tàofáng)* are more expensive. All resort areas have discounts from Monday to Friday, excluding holidays. The usual discount is 20% but sometimes it's as much as 50%.

A dormitory *(tuántǐfáng)* is usually meant for large groups. In resort areas, the weekdays are slow and they will usually let you sleep in the dormitory, but on the weekends or holidays they will move other people into your room. If the hotel you are staying at is booked out by a tour group, you might be asked to move into another room which may be more expensive. If they have no room left, you might have to leave. The management isn't trying to be nasty or xenophobic, but if a large tour group arrives and you happen to be occupying a needed dormitory room, somebody has got to move. Most of these resort hotels only survive off the weekend traffic. On two occasions on a Saturday night, the hotel management asked me to leave. I hasten to add that on both occasions they were extremely apologetic and even found another room for me in a different hotel.

One traveller who stayed at the Tienhsiang Youth Activity Centre in east Taiwan wrote to Lonely Planet and said:

...the 2nd day we were asked to check out at 1.30 pm because Chinese people had arrived and wanted a room. This is normal procedure – Westerners must move out of rooms if Chinese people want to move in.

To which I must reply – not so! All hotels in Tienhsiang are heavily booked by tour groups – especially the Youth Activity Centre because it's cheap. So if you are asked to move, try to understand that demand exceeds supply and a busload of tourists with a prepaid deposit gets preference over a single budget traveller without a reservation.

It is very difficult to contact your Western friends in other hotels or even in the same hotel by giving their name. Best results are obtained by asking face to face rather than on the telephone. Having a room number greatly increases the chance of success. Knowing when your friend checked in is also helpful. The problem here is communication – most Chinese desk clerks have no idea how to deal with Western names. Rather than lose face by admitting this, the usual response to an enquiry will be: 'he checked out', even if 'he' is a 'she'.

One thing to keep in mind is that Chinese

people bathe in the evening rather than in the morning. In less-expensive hotels the hot water will not be turned on until the evening. Of course, you can bathe any time if you don't mind cold water. Although they expect madness from foreigners anyway, the management will probably be quite perplexed if you complain that there is no hot water for your morning shower.

Expensive hotels will often have a sign in English, but cheaper places usually will not. Probably the two most important Chinese characters that you can learn represent the word for 'cheap hotel' *(lüshè)*. You will save yourself a good deal of time and money by learning to recognise this. The best way to learn is by writing it many times.

Cheap hotel/Guesthouse *(lüshè)*

Hot Springs Hotels There are many hot springs in Taiwan and they tend to be commercialised. That is, the hot water is pumped into a pool or tub, rather than left in its natural condition. Hotels are built right next to the hot springs and water is pumped into private tubs in individual rooms. However, some of the better resorts have outdoor pools in beautiful natural settings.

You do not usually have to stay in a hotel to use the hot-spring facilities. If you want a private pool, most hotels will permit you to bathe in one for about half the price of a room. Outdoor public pools are much cheaper. They almost always rent out swimsuits for outdoor pools. To recognise a hotel that has hot-spring facilities, look for the hot springs symbol.

Rental

First the bad news – prices have been going up, so rentals aren't cheap. This is particularly true in big cities, especially Taipei.

The good news is that it's fairly easy to find a place to rent, and not difficult to find roommates if you need to split the cost. If you're going to work for someone, your employer might even assist you. Places where foreigners hang out (pubs, popular restaurants, etc) may have a noticeboard with people looking for roommates. Students should definitely check out the noticeboards around universities. Places for rent are usually advertised on red paper with black characters, fastened to any likely object in the neighbourhood such as a telephone pole. Finding an apartment through a newspaper advertisement is possible too. In most cases, you'll need the assistance of a Chinese speaker – ads are seldom in English.

Rents in Taipei are typically around NT$20,000 for a small three-bedroom apartment, but it's higher in classy neighbourhoods like Tienmu. In a rural area, the same-sized house could cost NT$4000, but there are few work or study opportunities in such places. Most landlords want one month's rent as a deposit and some ask for two months', but the whole amount is almost always refundable if you leave the apartment in one piece. Taiwan does not have the ridiculous custom of demanding 'key money' (extortionate non-refundable deposits) as in Japan and Korea, nor are there any restrictions on where you can live or who you can live with (as in mainland China).

As an alternative to renting an apartment, many travellers working in Taipei and Kaohsiung stay at the privately run youth hostels, most of which give discounts to long-term renters.

Hot springs symbol

FOOD

If Chinese food continues to receive rave reviews, it's for a good reason. Through the generations, the Chinese have perfected a unique style of cooking, which they regard as a fine art. As anyone who has been to Taiwan will tell you, the Taiwanese love to eat.

As always, the language barrier can be a hurdle, and the translations of menus into English is not an exact science (what exactly is 'complicated soup'?). Even packaged foods have mystifying labels: 'chocolate sand' turned out to be chocolate-sandwich cookies and 'hot spicy jerk' was spicy beef jerky. A popular soft drink made by a Japanese joint-venture is 'Pocari Sweat'. Advertisements help shed some light on the issue; one restaurant in Taipei innocently advertised its hamburgers as 'the best piece of meat between two buns'.

Don't chuckle too hard at other people's English blunders; foreigners manage to give the Taiwanese quite a laugh when ordering in Chinese. Once, when trying to explain to the waitress what vegetables I wanted, I asked if she had venereal disease *(cài huā)* instead of cauliflower *(huā cài)*.

Certain foods are sold at particular times of the day or year. Bread, fruit and smelly tofu are sold mostly at night. Soybean milk, steamed buns and clay-oven rolls *(shāobǐng)* are sold only in the morning. Spring rolls are sold mostly during April; moon cakes during the Mid-Autumn (or Moon) Festival; rice dumplings *(zòngzī)* are at their best during the Dragon Boat Festival. 'Red turtle cakes' are for birthdays and temple worship. Snake meat and snake blood are mostly served in the night markets.

It's true that some Chinese eat dog and it's for the same reason that they eat snake, tiger and other exotic animals – because it is believed to have medicinal value. As a medicine, it is expensive and therefore no one is going to sneak it into your soup, noodles or fried rice as a replacement for beef. If you want to eat dog, you have to seek out a restaurant that specialises in it. Such restaurants are not common because not many Chinese eat dog. Dog meat is most readily available in winter, since the Chinese believe it can prevent colds. If you prefer Fido with his tail wagging, try the medicinal (and very tasty) 'angelica chicken' *(dānggui jī)* or 'angelica duck' *(dānggui yā)*, which are served from street stalls or night markets.

Chinese cooks make liberal use of monosodium glutamate, or MSG. I personally have had no difficulty with this, but some Westerners complain that they are allergic to it. Heart patients in particular must avoid salt because of its sodium content, and MSG is loaded with sodium. If you are really worried about MSG, just tell the cook you don't want it by saying *(búyào wèijīng)*. Most cooks will readily comply.

Eating Etiquette

You'd better learn how to use chopsticks if you haven't already mastered this skill. People rarely use forks, and spoons are usually for soup. Eating with a knife is almost unheard of except in Western-style restaurants serving steak.

Proper etiquette demands that you hold your rice bowl close to your face rather than leaving it on the table – exactly the opposite

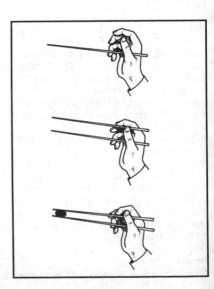

of what would be considered proper behaviour in Western countries. This only applies to bowls, not to plates.

It is also OK to spit out fish bones and pile them on the table next to your plate. When not eating, never leave your chopsticks sticking pointed-end down into the bowl. Always place them across the top of the bowl or on the table. To the Chinese, leaving chopsticks sticking vertically into the bowl looks like sticks of incense in a bowl of ashes, a clear death sign.

There is a proper etiquette to using a toothpick - you should use two hands, one to operate the pick and one to block the view of this process. Personally, I think using two hands makes the whole thing far more conspicuous, but local custom demands you do it this way. Just watch how the Chinese do it.

Places to Eat

Restaurants are anywhere and everywhere, and in cities you can find something to eat 24 hours a day with little effort. Pay careful attention to prices, especially with seafood. The Chinese try to impress each other by ordering exotic, high-priced fish which costs the earth. Don't just point to a fish that somebody else is eating and say you want that one, ask the price first. It could be NT$100 - or NT$3000, even if you buy it from what looks like a cheap foodstall in the night market.

Breakfast is the cheapest meal if you choose Chinese food. Western breakfasts are considerably more expensive. In resort areas all food can be pricey, so check out the grocery stores. Most hotels, bus and train stations have a machine providing hot and cold water. Buy cheap noodles in a styrofoam bowl for NT$20 and make a cheap, filling meal. You could also carry your own coffee or tea.

You can put together a cheap meal at any 7-Eleven store - check out the tea-eggs, instant rice and noodle dishes which can be heated in their microwave oven. I personally find 7-Eleven's steamed meat buns to be some of the best in Taiwan, especially the spicy ones (orange wrapper on bottom).

Cafeterias (zìzhù cān) offer cheap and usually good meals for lunch and dinner, but get there either just before noon or around 5.30 pm for the best selection. As soon as the crowd arrives, the good stuff disappears quickly - the leftovers sit around for hours stewing in the hot Taiwanese weather and you might get sick if you eat this stuff at 3 pm.

Western-style fast-food restaurants are ubiquitous in the cities though still hard to

---

The Last Supper

If you are invited to a feast – for instance, to a Chinese New Year celebration, a temple worship or a wedding – the meal will include at least 10 courses, so eat slowly and sparingly or you'll soon be filled to capacity with seven courses left to go. If you are a man, people will try to toast you. One of the best ways to avoid this is to choose a table with only women sitting around it. Alternatively, seat yourself between two women. Women rarely smoke or drink in Taiwan, at least not publicly. Bowls of delicious food will be put on the table and most of the guests will put their chopsticks right into them and help themselves. The idea of a serving spoon is only starting to catch on, mostly in high-class restaurants.

Comments like 'This food is delicious!' will be much appreciated. However, don't be surprised if your hosts apologise that the food was 'so poor', even though it was excellent. In accordance with the custom of Chinese humility, your hosts will often indicate that the service is inadequate and that the food is not enough. What they really mean is that nothing is too good for you, the honoured guest.

When it comes time to pay the bill be prepared for a rather amusing scene. If you are with a group of five people, don't be surprised if all five rush up to the cash register, each one insisting on paying for the entire group. It can turn into quite a battle as everybody pulls out their money and simultaneously tries to stuff it into the hands of the bewildered cashier. As a foreign guest, everyone will certainly insist that they pay for you. Keep smiling and insist at least a few times that you should pay. It's unlikely they will let you, but part of the ritual is that you pretend you really want to. ■

come by in rural areas. Fast food tends to be more expensive than Chinese food because it has considerable snob appeal to the face-conscious Taiwanese.

Main Dishes

There are many different styles of Chinese cooking, originating from the different regions of China. These regional variations are well represented in Taiwan as a result of immigration from the mainland.

There are four major styles of Chinese cuisine: Beijing-Shandong, Sichuan-Hunan, Shanghaiese and Cantonese-Chaozhou. There are also various off-shoots, of which Fujian-Taiwanese is one. In most cases, you probably won't know or care which style you're eating, but for the benefit of culinary connoisseurs, a brief rundown follows:

Beijing & Shandong Beijing and Shandong cuisine comes from the cold northland of China. Since this is China's wheat belt, steamed bread, dumplings and noodles figure prominently rather than rice.

The most famous speciality is Beijing duck, served with pancakes and plum sauce. Another northern speciality is Mongolian hotpot, composed of assorted meats and vegetables cooked in a burner right on the dining table – it's so good in Taiwan that it's hard to believe it can be so bad in Mongolia. Hotpot is usually eaten during winter. Bird's-nest soup is a speciality of Shandong cooking.

Not What it Seems

You may be surprised to see a restaurant displaying what appears to be a large swastika. In fact, it's not really a swastika at all, but the reverse image of one. This old Buddhist symbol is seen on many temples – when it appears on a restaurant, it indicates that the food is vegetarian. You may also find the symbol on packages of biscuits and noodles, indicating that the goods were made without lard or other animal products. ■

Shanghainese Of all Chinese cuisines, this one is my least favourite. Shanghainese cooking is noted for its use of seafood, but it's heavy and oily. Many Westerners say it's greasy, tasteless and disgusting, but liberal use of spices can make it almost palatable. Eels are popular, as is drunken chicken, cooked in wine. Other things to try are some of the cold-meat-and-sauce dishes, ham-and-melon soup, bean curd (tofu) and brown sauce, braised meat balls, deep-fried chicken, and pork ribs with salt and pepper.

Sichuan & Hunan Sichuan food is the hottest of the four major categories – it's great stuff if you like spicy food, but keep the drinking water handy! Specialities include frogs' legs and smoked duck. Other dishes to try are shrimps with salt and garlic; dried chilli beef; bean curd with chilli; bear paws braised in brown sauce; fish in spicy bean sauce and aubergines in garlic.

Hunan food is a variation, often hot and spicy like Sichuan cuisine. Duck, chicken and seafood are usually on the menu.

Cantonese & Chaozhou This is southern Chinese cooking – lots of steaming, boiling and stir-frying. Dim sum is a snack-like variation, usually served for lunch rather than dinner, and consisting of all sorts of little delicacies served from pushcarts wheeled around the restaurant floor. It's justifiably famous and highly addictive stuff.

The Cantonese are famous for making just about anything palatable; specialities are abalone, dried squid, 1000-year eggs (made by soaking eggs in horse's urine), shark's fin soup, snake soup and dog stew. Other culinary exotica include anteaters, pangolins (a sort of armadillo), cats, rats, owls, monkeys, turtles and frogs. One saying is that the Cantonese eat anything with four legs – except the table. Another Chinese joke is that the Cantonese are industrious people – capable of doing any job except zookeeper.

Despite the unusual ingredients, Cantonese food has long been a favourite of Westerners – Chinese restaurants around the world often include a rich selection of Cantonese dishes on the menu.

Taiwanese Being a subtropical island, Taiwan has a rich supply of rice, sugar and seafood, all basic staples in Taiwanese cooking. Some local specialties include simmered cuttlefish, oyster omelettes, fried dried fish with peanuts and squid balls.

Desserts

Fruit, rather than cake, ice cream or other sweets, is usually served at the end of the meal. This is not to say that Taiwan is suffering from any shortage of sweets. The Taiwanese produce some wonderful junkfood. The fruit with shaved ice and syrup *(bābǎo bīng)* is a personal favourite, especially during the hot, sticky summers. Some variations include tofu (bean curd) pudding with peanuts and ice *(huāshēng dòuhuā bīng)* or ice with red mung beans and milk *(hóngdòu niúnǎi bīng)*. The papaya milkshakes *(mùguā niúnǎi)* are superb. Sesame seed candy *(zhīmá táng)* is almost as ancient as China itself.

Be careful though, because looks can deceive. You may bite into what looks like a dreamy, creamy pastry, only to find the interior filled with salted pork and green beans. Then there are these things on a stick called *yāmǐxiě* which look like popsicles – in fact, they're made from sticky rice mixed with duck's blood!

Fruit

Taiwan's subtropical climate means you can expect year-round abundance of fruit. However, prices are generally high, a reflection of the fact that most young Taiwanese disdain farm life and there is a shortage of workers willing to grow and harvest the stuff. It's also a reflection of trade protectionism; the Taiwanese farm lobby is powerful and manages to keep out most cheaper imports. Imports do exist though, mostly cool-climate fruits like apples and pears which do not grow well in Taiwan. There are also some exotic tropical imports, like durians from Thailand and 'red dragon fruit' *(hóng lóng guǒ)* from Vietnam.

The Chinese almost never eat the skin on apples, pears and grapes. If you do, expect to draw a few amused stares and comments. They feel the same way about eating uncooked vegetables, like carrots. They figure only rabbits do that.

Many foreigners who have never eaten sugarcane before make complete fools of themselves the first time they try (much to the amusement of the Chinese). Do not eat the outer (purple coloured) skin of sugarcane – it must be removed with a peeling knife. Also, you do not actually eat sugarcane, you chew it to extract the sweet juices and then spit out the pulp. If you swallow the pulp, you'll practically choke (but the Chinese audience will have a giggling fit).

Ordering Food

You may find the following words and phrases useful when ordering food:

Food Restrictions

I'm a vegetarian.
　wǒ chī sù　我吃素
I don't eat meat.
　wǒ bù chī ròu　我不吃肉
I don't eat pork.
　wǒ bù chī zhū ròu　我不吃豬肉
I cannot eat spicy food.
　wǒ bù néng chī là　我不能吃辣
I cannot eat MSG.
　wǒ bù néng chī wèi jīng　我不能吃味精
I cannot eat salt.
　wǒ bù néng chī yán　我不能吃鹽
I cannot eat sugar.
　wǒ bù néng chī táng　我不能吃糖

Bread, Buns & Dumplings

boiled dumplings
　shuǐ jiǎo　水餃
clay oven rolls
　shāo bǐng　燒餅
fried bread stick
　yóu tiáo　油條
fried leek dumplings
　jiǔ cài hézi　韭菜盒子

fried meat dumplings
  guō tiē 鍋貼
fried roll
  yín sī juǎn 銀絲捲
fried vegetable dumplings
  shuǐ jiān bāo 水煎包
prawn cracker
  lóng xiā piàn 龍蝦片
rice-meat dumplings
  ròu yuán 肉圓
steamed buns
  mán tóu 饅頭
steamed dumplings (thick)
  xiǎo lóng bāo 小龍包
steamed dumplings (thin)
  zhēng jiǎo 蒸餃
steamed meat buns
  bāo zi 包子
steamed sandwich
  guǎ bāo, gē bāo 刈包
steamed vegetable buns
  cài bāo 菜包

Noodles
soupy noodles
  tāng miàn 湯麵
noodles (not soupy)
  gān miàn 乾麵
fried noodles
  chǎo miàn 炒麵
simple & cheap noodles
  yáng chūn miàn, yì miàn 陽春麵/意麵
sesame paste noodles
  má jiàng miàn 麻醬麵
bean & meat noodles
  zá jiàng miàn 雜醬麵
wonton & noodles
  hún dùn miàn 餛飩麵
seafood needles
  wū lóng miàn, guō shāo miàn
  烏龍麵/鍋燒麵
fried noodles with beef
  niú ròu chǎo miàn 牛肉炒麵
noodles with beef (soupy)
  niú ròu tāng miàn 牛肉湯麵
noodles with beef (no soup)
  niú ròu gān miàn 牛肉干麵
fried noodles with chicken
  jī sī chǎo miàn 雞絲炒麵

noodles with chicken
  jī sī tāng miàn 雞絲湯麵
duck with noodles
  yā ròu miàn 鴨肉麵
goose with noodles
  é ròu miàn 鵝肉麵
noodles, pork & mustard greens
  zhà cài ròu sī miàn 榨菜肉絲麵
fried noodles with shrimp
  xiā rén chǎo miàn 蝦仁炒麵
flat noodles
  bǎn tiáo, kē zǎi tiáo 板條/粿仔條
sliced noodles
  dāo shāo miàn 刀削麵
rice noodles
  mǐ fěn 米粉

Rice & Vegetable Dishes
plain white rice
  bái fàn 白飯
watery rice porridge
  xī fàn, zhōu 稀飯/粥
rice & vegetable roll
  fàn tuán 飯團
salty rice pudding
  wā guì 碗粿
sushi
  shòu sī 壽司
Chinese salad
  jiā cháng liáng cài 家常涼菜
assorted hors d'oeuvre
  shíjǐn pīn pán 什錦拼盤
assorted vegetarian food
  sù shí jǐn 素什錦
bean curd & mushrooms
  mó gū dòu fǔ 磨菇豆腐
bean curd casserole
  shā guō dòu fǔ 沙鍋豆腐
black fungus & mushroom
  mù ěr huá kǒu mó 木耳滑口磨
broiled mushroom
  sù chǎo xiān me 素炒鮮麼
dried tofu
  dòu fǔ gān 豆腐乾
fried bean curd in oyster sauce
  háo yóu dòu fǔ 蠔油豆腐
fried beansprouts
  sù chǎo dòu yá 素炒豆芽
fried cauliflower & tomato
  fān qié cài huā 炒蕃茄菜花

fried eggplant
sù shāo qié zi 素燒茄子
fried garlic
sù chǎo dà suàn 素炒大蒜
fried green beans
sù chǎo biǎn dòu 素炒扁豆
fried green vegetables
sù chǎo qīng cài 素炒青菜
fried noodles with vegetables
shū cài chǎo miàn 蔬菜炒麵
fried peanuts
yóu zhà huā shēng mǐ 油炸花生米
fried rape in oyster sauce
háo yóu pá cài dǎn 蠔油扒菜膽
fried rape with mushrooms
dōng gū pá cài dǎn 多菇扒菜膽
fried rice with vegetables
shū cài chǎo fàn 蔬菜炒飯
fried white radish patty
luó bo gāo 蘿卜糕
garlic & morning glory
dà suàn kōng xīn cài 大蒜空心菜
spiced cold vegetables
liáng bàn shí jǐn 涼拌什錦
spicy hot bean curd
má pó dòu fǔ 麻婆豆腐
spicy peanuts
wǔ xiāng huā shēng mǐ 五香花生米
stinky tofu
chòu dòu fǔ 臭豆腐

Beef Dishes

beef braised in soy sauce
hóng shāo niú ròu 紅燒牛肉
beef curry & noodles
gā lǐ niú ròu miàn 咖哩牛肉麵
beef curry & rice
gā lǐ niú ròu fàn 咖哩牛肉飯
beef steak platter
niú ròu tiě bǎn 牛肉鐵板
beef with green peppers
qīng jiāo niú ròu piàn 青椒牛肉片
beef with oyster sauce
háo yóu niú ròu 蚝油牛肉
beef with tomatoes
fān qié niú ròu piàn 蕃茄牛肉片
beef with white rice
niú ròu fàn 牛肉飯
fried rice with beef
niú ròu sī chǎo fàn 牛肉絲炒飯

Egg Dishes

1000-year egg
pí dàn 皮蛋
egg & flour omelette
dàn bǐng 蛋餅
fried rice with egg
jī dàn chǎo fàn 雞蛋炒飯
fried tomatoes & eggs
xī hóng shì chǎo jī dàn 西紅柿炒雞蛋

Chicken Dishes

angelica chicken
dāng guī jī 當歸雞
chicken braised in soy sauce
hóng shāo jī kuài 紅燒雞塊
chicken curry & noodles
gā lǐ jī ròu miàn 咖哩雞肉麵
chicken curry & rice
gā lǐ jī ròu fàn 咖哩雞肉飯
chicken curry
gā lǐ jī ròu 咖哩雞肉
chicken leg with white rice
jī tuǐ fàn 雞腿飯
chicken pieces in oyster sauce
háo yóu jī dīng 蠔油雞丁
chicken slices & tomato sauce
fān qié jī dīng 蕃茄雞丁
drunken chicken
suān jī 酸雞
fried noodles with chicken
jī sī chǎo miàn 雞絲炒麵
fried rice with chicken
jī sī chǎo fàn 雞絲炒飯
fruit kernel with chicken
guǒ wèi jī dīng 果味雞丁
mushrooms & chicken
cǎo mó jī dīng 草蘑雞丁
noodles with chicken (soupy)
jī sī tāng miàn 雞絲湯麵
roast chicken
shǒu pá jī 手扒雞
sautéed chicken with green peppers
jiàng bào jī dīng 醬爆雞丁
sautéed chicken with water chestnuts
nán jiè jī piàn 南芥雞片
sautéed spicy chicken pieces
là zi jī dīng 辣子雞丁
sliced chicken with crispy rice
jī piàn guō bā 雞片鍋巴

spicy hot chicken & peanuts
   gōng bào jī dīng   宮爆雞丁
sweet & sour chicken
   táng cù jī dīng   糖醋雞丁

Duck Dishes

angelica duck
   dāng guī yā   當歸鴨
duck with fried noodles
   yā ròu chǎo miàn   鴨肉炒麵
duck with noodles
   yā ròu miàn   鴨肉麵
duck with white rice
   yā ròu fàn   鴨肉飯
duck's blood & rice popsicle
   yā mǐ xiě   鴨米血
Beijing (Peking) duck
   běi píng kǎo yā   北平烤鴨

Pork Dishes

white rice & assorted meats
   sān bǎo fàn   三寶飯
boiled pork slices
   shuǐ zhǔ ròu piàn   水煮肉片
fried black pork pieces
   yuán bào lǐ jī   芫爆里肌
fried noodles with pork
   ròu sī chǎo miàn   肉絲炒麵
fried rice (assorted)
   shí jǐn chǎo fàn   什錦炒飯
fried rice Canton-style
   guǎng zhōu chǎo fàn   廣州炒飯
fried rice with pork
   ròu sī chǎo fàn   肉絲炒飯
golden pork slices
   jīn yín ròu sī   金銀肉絲
noodles, pork & mustard greens
   zhà cài ròu sī miàn   榨菜肉絲麵
pork & fried onions
   yáng cōng chǎo ròu piàn   洋蔥炒肉片
pork & mustard greens
   zhà cài ròu sī   榨菜肉絲
pork chop with white rice
   pái gǔ fàn   排骨飯
pork cubes & cucumber
   huáng guā ròu dīng   黃瓜肉丁
pork fillet with white sauce
   huá liū lǐ jī   滑溜里肌
pork with crispy rice
   ròu piàn guō bā   肉片鍋巴

pork with oyster sauce
   háo yóu ròu sī   蠔油肉絲
pork, eggs & black fungus
   mù xū ròu   木須肉
sautéed diced pork & soy sauce
   jiàng bào ròu dīng   醬爆肉丁
sautéed shredded pork
   qīng chǎo ròu sī   清炒肉絲
shredded pork & bamboo shoots
   dōng sǔn ròu sī   冬筍肉絲
shredded pork & green beans
   biǎn dòu ròu sī   扁豆肉絲
shredded pork & green peppers
   qīng jiāo ròu sī   青椒肉絲
shredded pork & hot sauce
   yú xiāng ròu sī   魚香肉絲
shredded pork fillet
   chǎo lǐ jī sī   炒里肌絲
soft pork fillet
   ruǎn zhá lǐ jī   軟炸里肌
spicy hot pork pieces
   gōng bào ròu dīng   宮爆肉丁
spicy pork cubes
   là zi ròu dīng   辣子肉丁
sweet & sour pork fillet
   táng cù lǐ jī   糖醋里肌
sweet & sour pork slices
   táng cù zhū ròu piàn   糖醋豬肉片

Seafood Dishes

fried rice & seafood
   shí jǐn chǎo fàn   什錦炒飯
braised sea cucumber
   hóng shāo hǎi shēn   紅燒海參
clams
   gé lì   蛤蜊
crab
   páng xiè   螃蟹
deep-fried shrimp
   zhà xiā rén   炸蝦仁
diced shrimp with peanuts
   gōng bào xiā rén   宮爆蝦仁
eel
   shàn yú   鱔魚
fish
   yú   魚
fish braised in soy sauce
   hóng shāo yú   紅燒魚
fried noodles with shrimp
   xiā rén chǎo miàn   蝦仁炒麵

Top: Jelly and fruit (CT)
Bottom: Teppanyaki stall (CT)

Top: Chinese bread (CT)
Left: Making sugar cane juice (CT)
Right: Tomatoes on sticks (a popular snack) (CT)

fried rice with shrimp
  xiā rén chǎo fàn 蝦仁炒飯
fried shrimp with mushroom
  xiān mó xiā rén 鮮蘑蝦仁
lobster
  lóng xiā 龍蝦
octopus
  zhāng yú 章魚
oyster
  mǔ lì 牡蠣
sautéed shrimp
  qīng chǎo xiā rén 清炒蝦仁
shrimp
  xiārén 蝦仁
squid with crispy rice
  yóu yú guō bā 魷魚鍋巴
squid
  yóu yú 魷魚
sweet & sour squid roll
  sūan là yóu yú juàn 酸辣魷魚卷
turtle
  hǎi guī 海龜

Soup
soup
  tāng 湯
soup, thick
  gēng 羹
bean curd & vegetable soup
  dòu fǔ cài tāng 豆腐菜湯
clear soup
  qīng tāng 清湯
corn & egg thick soup
  fèng huáng lì mǐ gēng 鳳凰栗米羹
cream of mushroom soup
  nǎi yóu xiān mó tāng 奶油鮮蘑湯
cream of tomato soup
  nǎi yóu fān qié tāng 奶油蕃茄湯
egg & vegetable soup
  dàn huā tāng 蛋花湯
fresh fish soup
  xiān yú tāng 鮮魚湯
mushroom & egg soup
  mó gu dàn huā tāng 蘑菇蛋花湯
pickled mustard green soup
  zhà cài tāng 榨菜湯
seaweed soup
  zǐ cài tāng 紫菜湯
squid soup
  yóu yú tāng 魷魚湯

sweet & sour soup
  suān là tāng 酸辣湯
three kinds seafood soup
  sān xiān tāng 三鮮湯
tomato & egg soup
  xī hóng shì dàn tāng 西紅柿蛋湯
vegetable soup
  shū cài tāng 蔬菜湯
wonton soup
  hún dùn tāng 餛飩湯

Miscellanea & Exotica
betel nut
  bīn láng 檳榔
cabbage roll
  gāo lì cài juǎn 高麗菜捲
deermeat (venison)
  lù ròu 鹿肉
dogmeat
  gǒu ròu 狗肉/香肉
frog
  qīng wā 青蛙
goat, mutton
  yáng ròu 羊肉
kebab
  ròu chuàn 肉串
Mongolian hotpot
  huǒ guō 火鍋
puffed rice (or popcorn)
  bào mǐ huā 爆米花
ratmeat
  lǎo shǔ ròu 老鼠肉
sandwich
  sān míng zhì 三明治
shaved ice & fruit
  bā bǎo bīng 八寶冰
snake
  shé ròu 蛇肉
spring roll (egg roll)
  chūn juǎn 春捲
tofu pudding
  dòu huā 豆花
vegetarian gelatin
  ài yù 愛玉

Condiments
black pepper
  hú jiāo 胡椒
butter
  huáng yóu 黃油

garlic
  dà suàn   大蒜
honey
  fēng mì   蜂蜜
hot pepper
  là jiāo   辣椒
hot sauce
  là jiāo jiàng   辣椒醬
jam
  guǒ jiàng   果醬
ketchup
  fān qié jiàng   蕃茄醬
MSG
  wèi jīng   味精
salt
  yán   鹽
sesame seed oil
  zhī má yóu   芝麻油
soy sauce
  jiàng yóu   醬油
sugar
  táng   糖
vinegar
  cù   醋

DRINKS
Tea

Tea is to China what coffee is to Brazil. Indeed, China is believed to be the first country where tea was cultivated and brewed as a beverage. Chinese tea is justifiably famous and Taiwan produces many top-grade varieties. This should not be surprising – tea seems to grow best in tropical to subtropical climates at high elevation with lots of moisture, and such conditions exist in most mountain areas of Taiwan.

What is there to know about tea? More than you think. There are many varieties and the price varies tremendously depending on what type you wish to buy.

Black tea, called 'red tea' by the Chinese, is the type most Westerners are familiar with. Black tea is fully fermented – that is, the tea is kept at around 27°C for several hours before being heated to 95°C to complete the drying process.

Green tea is not fermented at all. In order to kill the microbes the tea leaves are steamed immediately after the tea is picked, then the tea leaves are rolled, crushed and dried.

Oolong (literally 'black dragon') tea is a partially fermented tea and is considered prime quality. Some oolong teas fetch incredibly high prices, nearly worth their weight in gold. As oolong tea is so highly prized, there is a tendency among tea vendors to label teas 'oolong' which are in fact green tea. Different grades of oolong include *lóngjǐng* (dragon well), relatively mild stuff; *tiě guānyīn* ('iron goddess of mercy'), which is stronger; and *dōngfāng měirén* ('oriental beauty'), which is heavy on the caffeine.

Apart from these basic types of tea, there are other kinds produced by blending ingredients. For example, jasmine tea is a mixture of green tea and flowers. The possible combination of blends is endless.

Having good tea is only half the battle. To enjoy tea, one has to know how to prepare it. Most Chinese are dumbfounded by the Western custom of putting milk and sugar in tea. They drink it straight, and the more bitter the taste, the better.

There are several methods of preparing tea. The most popular way for a group to drink tea is 'old man style'. A tiny teapot is stuffed full of tea leaves and scalding hot water is poured inside. With very little time to steep, the tea is quickly poured into a small flask to cool, then served in very tiny cups which allows the tea to cool faster. More boiling water is poured into the teapot and a second brew is prepared. As the tea gets weaker, the time needed for steeping is progressively longer. Eventually, the leaves are discarded and the pot can be stuffed with fresh leaves again. In Taiwan, you can buy beautiful tea sets cheaply to make 'old man tea'.

The easiest way to prepare tea is to put the leaves directly into the cup or large teapot, pour boiling water into it, and then let it steep for no less than six minutes. The longer it steeps the more bitter it will become. Tea bags are also available, mostly familiar imported brands like Lipton.

The Chinese make health claims for drinking tea, and some Western research has backed this up. Tea is high in fluoride which benefits the teeth, and tea also contains polyphenol which *may* give some protection against cancer. Green tea contains more than twice the amount of fluoride and polyphenol as black tea.

On the other hand, Taiwanese tea is high in caffeine, and some of the more expensive oolong and green teas will make your head buzz. Caffeine is not particularly good for the stomach or intestines, and if you've got ulcers or colitis, you'd better keep away from the stuff. However, there are a few herbal teas available in Taiwan, though not nearly as many as most Westerners expect. Herbal teas are usually not sold in tea shops, but in grocery stores and supermarkets. Some common types are hibiscus tea (not bad), wheat tea (tastes a lot like coffee), chrysanthemum tea (awful stuff) and ginger tea (spicy but excellent). Also available is ginseng tea, but the price varies from reasonable to ridiculous (about NT$120 to NT$1400 for 50 small packets). The more absurd the health claims written on the box, the higher the price – one expensive brand of ginseng tea is claimed to cure 'chronic thirst'.

The last few years has seen a proliferation of teahouses in Taiwan. In Taipei, you pay around NT$130 to NT$360 for the tea and each person pays a cover charge of NT$100 (called a 'water fee'). However, you can sit for hours and chat or read, and refill the pot with hot water as often as you like.

Coffee

Taiwan does not produce any coffee. The coffee you buy in Taiwan is imported and usually grotesquely overpriced. Nevertheless, hanging out in a coffee shop with friends is a pleasant and popular pastime. The coffee itself comes in a tiny cup which costs as much as a whole dinner, at least NT$150 (if lucky, you might get one free refill), so if you're hungry order the dinner instead. Ironically, the dinner often includes a free cup of coffee, but usually iced coffee already flavoured with (too much) sugar and

milk. If you ask for hot coffee instead, you'll be charged an extra NT$150. Coffee shops usually have excellent ice-cream sundaes which are better value than the coffee. The atmosphere is comfortable and sometimes a band is provided, especially on Saturday night. Some places show video movies and serve 'old man tea' as well.

Soft Drinks

All the usual imported stuff (mostly now bottled in Taiwan) can be found. A popular local brand is Heysong (Black Pine) – try the sarsparilla. It's worth knowing that on large plastic bottles, there's a NT$2 refundable deposit.

Alcohol

Taiwanese beer is cheap and excellent and it's easy to remember the local brand, which is simply called Taiwan Beer. Apart from beer, Chinese booze doesn't attract much of a following among Westerners. Most liquors are rather harsh, although Taiwan produces a good sweet red grape wine and plum wine. There is also a white grape wine which some Westerners like.

Some of the liquors make a fairly good mixed drink, but the Chinese prefer it straight from the bottle. The strongest stuff, called Kaoliang, is made out of sorghum. It's 65% alcohol and makes a reasonably good substitute for rocket fuel. The most popular liquor is Shaoshing, distilled from rice with an alcohol content of 15%. Taiwanese rum mixes well with Coca-Cola.

If you attend a feast or dinner party, be careful of getting drawn into the 'finger game' *(huá jiǔ quán)*. It's a drinking game and the loser is obliged to empty the glass – lose too many times and you'll need to be carried out the door.

As a Westerner, you may find yourself being toasted. This only applies to men, as women aren't expected to drink. Someone will lift his glass and say *gān bēi*, which literally means 'dry glass'. If you accept the challenge, see the local herbal medicine shop for some hangover remedies. If you would rather not get wasted, just answer *suí yì*, or 'as you like'. You can then just take a sip.

You can purchase alcohol most cheaply from grocery stores and department stores. Restaurants, however, charge tax in addition to the list price. Any imported liquor and tobacco products carry an import tax, so bring the maximum if you need this stuff. You are permitted one litre of liquor and 200 cigarettes duty-free. There is no minimum age for purchasing liquor or for drinking it.

Ordering Drinks

The following words and phrases may be useful when ordering drinks:

ice cold
  bīngde 冰的
ice cubes
  bīng kuài 冰塊
hot
  rède 熱的

Cold Drinks

water
  kāi shuǐ 開水
mineral water
  kuàng quán shuǐ 礦泉水
fizzy drink (soda)
  qìshuǐ 汽水
Coca-Cola
  kěkǒu kělè 可口可樂
lemon soda
  níngméng qìshuǐ 檸檬氣水
carrot juice
  hóng luóbó zhī 紅蘿蔔汁
orange juice
  liǔchéng zhī 柳橙汁
passionfruit juice
  bǎixiāngguǒ zhī 百香果汁
soybean milk
  dòu jiāng 豆將
starfruit juice
  yángtáo zhī 楊桃汁
sugarcane juice
  gānzhè zhī 甘蔗汁
papaya milkshake
  mùguā niúnǎi 木瓜牛奶
pineapple milkshake
  fènglí niúnǎi 鳳梨牛奶

watermelon milkshake
  xīguā niúnǎi 西瓜牛奶
grass jelly
  xiàn cǎo 現草

Tea & Coffee

tea
  chá 茶
black tea
  hóng chá 紅茶
green tea
  lǜ chá 綠茶
jasmine tea
  mòlìhuā chá 茉莉花茶
oolong tea
  wūlóng chá 烏龍茶
hisbiscus (herb) tea
  luòshén chá 洛神茶
wheat tea
  mài chá 麥茶
coffee
  kāfēi 咖啡

Alcohol

beer
  píjiǔ 啤酒
Taiwan Beer
  táiwān píjiǔ 台灣啤酒
San Miguel
  shēnglì píjiǔ 生力啤酒
whisky
  wēishìjì jiǔ 威士忌酒
vodka
  fútèjiā jiǔ 伏特加酒
rum
  lánmǔ jiǔ 蘭姆酒
red grape wine
  hóng pútáo jiǔ 紅葡萄酒
white grape wine
  bái pútáo jiǔ 白葡萄酒
rice wine
  mǐ jiǔ 米酒

TOBACCO

You can find the usual imported products like Marlboro, Winston and 555, but Taiwan produces a few native brands. Most popular is the ironically named 'Long-Life Cigarettes'; another well-known brand is 'Prosperity Island'. Taiwan-produced cigars and pipe tobacco are available, but are not very common.

These days more and more young women are smoking and drinking, but overall these vices are still regarded as being suitable for men only. A women who smokes and drinks in public is referred to as a 'bad girl'. This is especially true in the conservative hinterland outside of big cities.

ENTERTAINMENT
MTV

Music & TV (MTV) clubs offer the chance to see movies on video tapes in either a large group room or in the privacy of your own little cubicle. It's not quite the same as what we think of as MTV in the West – the films may be full-length feature films. These clubs were extremely popular, but most have run afoul of the copyright law and have been shut down by the government. A few still exist – their legal status is questionable, but some clubs claim to have secured rights from the copyright owners.

KTV

(kǎlā OK) 卡拉OK

Derived from the Japanese word *karaoke* (empty music) and MTV, KTV is one big amateur singing contest to the accompaniment of a video tape. There have been some variations on the theme, such as DTV (dance TV) and HTV (hotel TV).

The Chinese love singing and if you visit a KTV you will certainly be asked to perform. No matter how badly you sing, you will undoubtedly receive polite applause. The Chinese love to hear foreigners sing even if they can't understand a word you say. However, if your singing is truly awful don't subject the audience to more than one song, for the sake of international relations.

Pubs & Discos

(píjiǔ wū) 啤酒屋

Pubs and discos have become increasingly popular in the large cities. Some places have taped music while others feature live bands. In a few places (mostly Taipei), there are pubs which cater to foreigners by offering English-language menus and Western food and playing Western rock music in the background. Prices in pubs and discos tend towards the high side.

Saunas

(sān wēn nuǎn) 三溫暖

It might sound strange, but Taiwan's saunas offer an acceptable alternative to hotels. For about NT$500, you can spend a full evening steaming, soaking, watching videos and sleeping in lounge chairs wearing a bathrobe (supplied free) or nothing at all. Saunas are segregated by sex, but are available for both men and women. Massage services are available for an extra fee, and in *most* cases this is legitimate massage, not simply a front for prostitution. Lockers are provided so you can safely secure your valuables. The facilities are plush and free tea and snacks are usually provided.

The big problem is finding these places. They go into and out of business with regularity, and some of the elegant ones deteriorate until they really do become fronts for prostitution. Furthermore, many of the saunas don't call themselves saunas at all (not even in Chinese) because of problems with the tax and licensing bureaucracies; the neon sign might say 'market' or 'restaurant'. For these reasons, I only include a few well-established ones in this book. Ask a local if you need help to find one of these places.

Barbershops

This is meant more as warning than a 'how to' guide. A trip to a barbershop in Taiwan can be a delightful experience. From among the services offered you can have a haircut, shampoo, blow-dry, manicure, and massage of the head, neck and shoulders. Men can have a shave, and for an extra fee you can have the wax cleaned out of your ears. Prices can be as low as NT$150, though you could spend as much as NT$1000 in a luxurious place for the same thing. It's a real treat and still a bargain if you choose the right place.

Barbershops *(lǐfǎ tīng)* are generally for men; for women, there are beauty parlours *(měiróng yuàn)*. But many places are unisex.

Alas, things are not always what they seem. In some 'barbershops' not a hair gets cut nor a whisker gets shaved – they are nothing but brothels! More than a few travellers have wandered into barbershops innocently looking for a haircut, and wound up making complete fools of themselves.

How to distinguish a real barbershop from a house of ill repute? Usually, you can judge from the outside appearance. Real barbershops have windows that you can look through so you know what's going on inside. The brothels have mirrored glass or no windows at all. The pimp standing outside is also a giveaway. Brothels have gaudy bright lights and sometimes a neon butterfly. To the Chinese, a butterfly symbolises a man who cheats on his wife, 'fluttering' from flower to flower.

THINGS TO BUY

Shopping is something of a national sport among the Chinese. When they travel abroad, the Chinese spend more time in the department stores than sightseeing. Prices in Taiwan may or may not be a big bargain, depending on what you buy.

Taiwan is no longer the bargain it used to be. Overall, Hong Kong is much better for shopping. There are still a few bargains to be had on toys, clothing, shoes, sporting goods, camping equipment, luggage, jade and coral jewellery and certain electrical appliances. Custom-made bicycles are a good buy, about half the price they would cost in the West.

Some good deals in Taiwan include hiking and camping equipment. Taiwan is a great place to buy motorcycle accessories, including special security locks, alarm systems and luggage racks. Check out hardware stores for all sorts of cheap miscellaneous items, including dishes, crockery, electric appliances and tools.

Keep in mind that clothing sizes are different in Taiwan. Most things, such as shoes, gloves, garments, even bicycles, are smaller than in the West. 'Extra large' in Taiwan is about equal to medium in the West. Don't believe the sales assistants when they say, 'It will stretch'. It won't. Also take a good look at the English slogans written on the T-shirts – misspelled words and broken grammar are common.

Top-quality rainsuits – meant for motorcycle riders but useful for hiking – are available from grocery stores, supermarkets and motorcycle-accessory shops. Quality varies by brand name and price – check carefully. Remember that a medium-sized Westerner will probably want size extralarge. The maroon-coloured suits are meant for women while blue ones are for men – if a man wears a maroon rainsuit, he'll be laughed at. A good rainsuit costs around NT$500.

With electronic goods and cameras, ask if there is a warranty. For 'grey-market' goods (imported by someone other than the authorised agent), there might be no warranty at all. This is especially a problem with goods imported from Japan and Hong Kong.

Chinese shopkeepers are shrewd and will try to soften up a customer with little gifts like soft drinks, cigarettes and chewing gum. That's all very nice, but don't feel obliged to buy unless you really want the goods. Better yet, refuse such gifts unless you really intend to buy something.

Shopkeepers may follow you all around the store, standing right on your heels. This is considered polite not pushy. However, many Chinese customers don't like it any more than Westerners do.

Beware of counterfeit merchandise. Taiwan used to be notorious for fake labels, but is now much less so since the government has cracked down. It probably doesn't matter so much when it comes to designer jeans, but it can be crucial when buying electronics. Many of those fake 'Rolex' watches don't work at all.

Name Chops

(yìnzhāng) 印章
The traditional Chinese name chop or seal has been used for thousands of years. It is quite likely that people began using name chops because Chinese characters are so complex and few people in ancient times were able to read and write. In addition,

chops date back to a time when there was no other form of identification such as fingerprinting, picture ID cards and computer files.

A chop served both as a form of identification and as a valid signature. All official documents in China needed a chop to be valid. Naturally, this made a chop quite valuable, for with another person's chop it was possible to sign contracts and other legal documents in their name.

Today, most Chinese are literate, but the tradition is still kept alive in Taiwan. In fact, without a chop it is difficult or impossible to enter into legally binding contracts in Taiwan. A chop is used for bank accounts, entrance to safe-deposit boxes and land sales. If you extend your visa in Taiwan, the official who grants the extension must use their chop to stamp your passport. Only red ink is used for a name chop.

If you spend any length of time in Taiwan, you will almost certainly need to have a chop made. If you're staying a short time, a chop makes a great souvenir. A chop can be made quickly, but first you will need to have your name translated into Chinese characters.

There are many different sizes and styles of chops. Inexpensive small chops can be carved from wood or plastic for about NT$150 or so. Chops costing several thousand NT$ can be carved from ivory, jade,

Author's name chop

marble or steel. Most Chinese people have many chops to confuse a possible thief, though they run the risk of confusing themselves as well. One chop might be used for their bank account, another for contracts and another for a safe-deposit box. Obviously, a chop is important and losing one can be a big hassle.

Most foreigners in Taiwan do not like to have access to their bank accounts or safe-deposit box with a chop. Fortunately, international banks recognise this fact and permit foreigners to use just a signature.

Since the people who carve chops don't check your ID, it might occur to you that obtaining a fake or forged chop would be very easy. Indeed, it is. It's also a very serious crime in Taiwan.

Computers

(diànnǎo) 電腦

Taiwan is one of the world's leading centres for manufacturing IBM-compatible personal computers. Of course, before you buy a computer in Taiwan you should check prices in your home country. You may find that Taiwan is not that much cheaper, and if you buy the computer in your home country you'll have the benefit of a local dealer who will readily honour the warranty.

Within Taiwan, the most popular computer brand names are Twinhead *(lúnfēi)*, Acer *(hóngjī)* and DTK *(xùqīng)*. All are good quality – my personal preference has been for Twinhead due to their excellent customer service. Twinhead is sold outside Taiwan and has gained a large share of the world's market for portable computers – guarantees are international. With other brand names, you'll have to check – an international guarantee is imperative if you want to take the machine outside Taiwan during the first year of use.

There are many 'generic' computers sold in Taiwan. These have no real brand name and are assembled from off-the-shelf components. Prices are a bit lower than the name brands, but quality varies. In general, I advise against buying a generic computer unless you know that the local dealer will service it. Beware of tiny fly-by-night shops selling no-name computers.

The Apple Macintosh is also available in Taiwan, but it's imported so it's not likely to be any cheaper than in most Western countries. However, some Macintosh accessories are made in Taiwan – modems are a particularly good buy. Good Chinese-language word-processing software is also available, one of the strongest selling points of the Macintosh.

Anyone interested in computers should visit the electronics show (October) and the computer show (June) at the Taipei World Trade Centre. It's sometimes possible to pick up electronic equipment for discount prices at these shows as 'samples', but test it before you leave Taiwan – even 'samples' can be defective.

Some Taiwan computer shops still sell pirated computer software, although the authorities have cracked down hard on this. Bear in mind that besides being illegal, pirated programs often contain computer viruses (one is called 'AIDS') and wearing a condom offers no protection whatsoever.

Other Souvenirs

Tea sets for serving 'old man's tea' are an attractive souvenir and can be purchased in supermarkets and tea shops. For the artistically inclined, calligraphy sets are worthwhile, but are not cheap – small brushes start at around NT$200. Lukang is considered a good place to shop for furniture, lacquerware and Buddhist artwork, but don't expect to walk away with a bargain.

Rip-Offs

Getting ripped off is seldom a problem in Taiwan. No matter what bad experiences you may have had in mainland China or Hong Kong, don't assume that Taiwan is the same – it's not. Foreigners occasionally get overcharged, especially by elderly people who haven't heard that WW II has ended. But as a general rule if the store says it's jade, it will be jade, not coloured glass. If they say it's a genuine Rolex watch, then it will be real, not a fake. If merchandise is sold with a warranty, it will generally be honoured. In all the years I've lived in Taiwan, I can't say that I've ever been cheated.

Nevertheless, not everyone is honest. If you think you've been ripped off, there are a few places you can take your complaint. First, try to obtain a refund or exchange from the store itself. In many cases that will work if you do it immediately. If you can't get any satisfaction that way, call the ROC Consumers' Foundation (☎ 02-7001234, fax 7060247) *(xiāofèizhě jījīn huì)*, 10th floor, 390 Fuhsing S Rd, Section 1. The Consumers' Foundation can't enforce the law, but they have publicised many cases of dishonesty and the manufacture of defective merchandise. Finally, in cases of outright fraud, file a complaint with the Foreign Affairs Police at the main police station in any large city.

Getting There & Away

AIR

Taipei is the principal gateway to the island, but there is an international airport in Kaohsiung with frequent flights to Hong Kong and a few other places.

Except during the busy times, like the summer vacation and Chinese New Year, there is no shortage of air services to Taiwan. Taipei lies right on the major air routes between Japan and Hong Kong, so there are numerous daily flights on many of the major airlines.

A number of major airlines do not fly to Taiwan. This is not because they don't want to, but because the government of mainland China has threatened them with retaliation (loss of landing rights in China) if they provide services to Taiwan. The policy of the regime in Beijing is that it alone has the right to negotiate aircraft landing rights for all of China, including Taiwan. To get around this, some airlines have simply created new subsidiaries just to serve the Taiwan market: Japan Airlines created Japan Asia Airways, for example. Most airlines have bowed to China's wishes, though a few – backed by their governments – have refused to yield to China's bullying tactics, warning China that its landing rights can also be revoked.

Taiwan is also forced to play the game. Taiwan's government-owned carrier, China Airlines, created a privatised subsidiary called Mandarin Airlines just for flying to those countries which want to pacify China. Taiwan's other major international carrier is the privately owned EVA Airways.

Buying a Plane Ticket

To get the best deal, it's useful to know what type of airfares are available and become familiar with airline ticketing jargon.

There are plenty of discount tickets which are valid for 12 months, allowing multiple stopovers with open dates. These tickets allow for a great deal of flexibility.

APEX (Advance Purchase Excursion) tickets are sold at a discount but will lock you into a rigid schedule. Such tickets must be purchased two or three weeks ahead of departure, do not permit stopovers and may have minimum and maximum stays as well as fixed departure and return dates. Unless you definitely must return at a certain time, it's best to purchase APEX tickets on a one-way basis only. There are stiff cancellation fees if you decide not to use your APEX ticket.

'Round-the-world' tickets are usually offered by an airline or combination of airlines, and let you take your time (six months to a year) moving from point to point on their routes for the price of one ticket. The main restriction is that you have to keep moving in the same direction. A drawback is that because you are usually booking individual flights as you go, and can't switch carriers, you can get caught out by flight availabilities and have to spend more or less time in a place than you want.

One thing to avoid is a 'back-to-front' ticket. These are best explained by example – if you want to fly from Taiwan (where tickets are relatively expensive) to the USA (where tickets are about 20% cheaper), you can pay by cheque or credit card and have a friend or travel agent in the USA mail the ticket to you. The problem is that the airlines have computers and will know that the ticket was issued in the USA rather than Taiwan, and they will refuse to honour it. Consumer groups have filed lawsuits over this practice with mixed results, but in most countries the law protects the airlines, not consumers. In short, the ticket is only valid starting from the country where it was issued.

If the ticket is issued in a third location (such as Hong Kong), the same rule applies. You cannot fly from Taiwan to the USA with a ticket mailed to you from Hong Kong – if you buy a ticket in Hong Kong, you can fly from there to Taiwan and then to the USA, but you can't start the journey from Taiwan.

'Frequent flyer' plans have proliferated in recent years and are now offered by most airlines, even some budget ones. Basically, these allow you a free ticket if you chalk up so many km with the same airline. The plans aren't always as good as they sound – some airlines require you to use all your frequent-flyer credits within one year or you lose the lot. Sometimes you find yourself flying on a particular airline just to get frequent-flyer credits using a ticket which is considerably more expensive than you might have gotten from a discount airline without a frequent-flyer bonus.

Many airlines have 'blackout' periods – peak times when you cannot use the free tickets you obtained under the frequent-flyer program. When you purchase the ticket be sure to give the ticket agent your frequent-flyer membership number, and again when you check-in for your flight.

A common complaint seems to be that airlines forget to record your frequent flyer credits when you fly with them. Save all your boarding passes and ticket receipts and be prepared to push if no bonus is forthcoming. In this regard I've personally had much trouble with United Airlines, and for this reason I no longer fly with them. Taiwan's China Airlines also has a frequent-flyer program, but it isn't too good – you must fly 160,000 km (100,000 miles) to qualify for a free ticket, which is equivalent to eight return flights between Los Angeles and Taipei. North-West Airlines have the most generous frequent-flyer programme, with a free ticket after you've flown 32,000 km (20,000 miles).

Some airlines offer discounts of up to 25% to student-card holders. In some countries, an official-looking letter from the school is also needed. You also must be aged 26 or younger. These discounts are generally only available on ordinary economy-class fares. You wouldn't get one, for instance, on an APEX or a round-the-world ticket since these are already discounted.

Courier flights can be a bargain if you're fortunate enough to find one. The way it works is that an airfreight company takes over your entire checked-baggage allowance. You are permitted a carry-on bag, but that's all. In return, you get a steeply discounted ticket. These arrangements usually have to be made a month or more in advance and are only available on certain routes. Such flights are occasionally advertised in the newspapers, or you can contact airfreight companies listed in the phone book.

Airlines usually carry infants up to two years of age at 10% of the relevant adult fare – a few may carry them free of charge. Reputable international airlines usually provide nappies (diapers), tissues, talcum and all the other paraphernalia needed to keep babies clean, dry and half-happy. For children between the ages of four and 12 the fare on international flights is usually 50% of the regular fare or 67% of a discounted fare. These days most fares are likely to be discounted.

Buying plane tickets from a travel agent is almost always cheaper than buying directly from the airline because airlines don't give discounts. It's a good idea to call the airline first and see what their cheapest ticket costs. Use that as your starting point when talking to travel agents.

Use common sense before handing over the cash and always get a receipt. Whenever possible, try to avoid handing over the cash until they hand over the ticket, or else pay only a deposit and be sure your receipt clearly states the total amount due.

It's important to realise that when you buy an air ticket from a travel agent, you must also go back to that agent if you want to obtain a refund – the airlines will not refund to you directly unless you purchased the ticket from the airline yourself. While this is no problem if you don't change your travel plans, it can be quite a hassle if you decide to change the route halfway through your trip. In that case, you'd have to return to the place where you originally purchased the ticket to get a refund on the unused portion of the journey. Of course, if you had a reliable friend who you could mail the ticket to, that person could possibly obtain the refund for you, but don't count on it. It's also true that some travel agents (and airlines) are extremely slow to issue refunds – I had one friend who waited a full year!

To/From Australia

Because China threw a fit, Qantas doesn't fly into Taiwan. To appease the People's Republic, Qantas created a new subsidiary, Australia Asia Airlines (AAA) just to serve the Taiwan route.

An alternative is to fly between Australia and Taiwan by changing airlines in Singapore, Bangkok or Hong Kong, with the bonus of a free stopover in one of these cities.

Australia is not a cheap place to fly out of, and air fares between Australia and Asia are absurdly expensive considering the distances flown. However, there are a few ways of cutting the costs.

Among the cheapest regular tickets available in Australia are APEX fares. The cost depends on your departure date from Australia. The year is divided into 'peak' (expensive), 'shoulder' (less expensive) and 'low' (relatively inexpensive) seasons; peak season is December to January.

It's possible to get reductions on the cost of APEX and other fares by going to the student travel offices and/or some of the travel agents in Australia that specialise in discounting.

The weekend travel sections of papers like the Melbourne *Age* or the *Sydney Morning Herald* are good sources of travel information. Also look at *Student Traveller*, a free newspaper published by STA Travel, the Australian-based student travel organisation which now has offices worldwide. STA has offices all around Australia (check your phone directory) and you definitely do not have to be a student to use them.

Also well worth trying is the Flight Shop (☎ (03) 670 0477), 386 Little Bourke St, Melbourne. They also have branches under the name of the Flight Centre in Sydney (☎ (02) 233 2296) and Brisbane (☎ (07) 229 9958).

To/From Canada

Getting discount tickets in Canada is much the same as in the USA – go to the travel agents and shop around until you find a good deal.

CUTS is Canada's national student bureau and has offices in a number of Canadian cities including Vancouver, Edmonton, Toronto and Ottawa – you don't necessarily have to be a student. There are a number of good agents in Vancouver for cheap tickets; CP-Air are particularly good for fares to Thailand.

To/From Mainland China

The mainland Chinese government has been pressuring Taiwan for years to establish direct air links. So far, Taiwan has adamantly refused, partly because of Beijing's previously mentioned policy of insisting that Taiwan has no legal right to make aircraft landing-rights agreements with other countries.

But things seem likely to change soon. On 1 July 1997 the British flag will be lowered over Hong Kong and stewardship of the colony will revert to China. Even before then – in 1995 – Taiwan's aircraft landing rights in Hong Kong will expire. Taiwan will be forced to cut some sort of deal with the Beijing government, or risk seeing all air service to Hong Kong severed. The most logical route between Taiwan and the mainland is Taipei-Xiamen, but Taipei-Shanghai is another possibility.

The big question is which airlines will be permitted to fly these routes when they're finally opened. If the experience in Hong Kong is any indication, the Chinese government will give all the lucrative landing rights to its own state-run airline, CAAC, and keep private carriers out.

To/From Europe

The Netherlands, Brussels and Antwerp are good places for buying discount air tickets. In Antwerp, WATS has been recommended. In Zürich, try SOF Travel and Sindbad. In Geneva, try Stohl Travel. In the Netherlands, NBBS is a reputable agency.

To/From Guam

Guam is just four hours by air from Taipei and has emerged as a popular honeymoon and vacation spot for the Taiwanese. Continental Airlines Micronesia and Northwest Airlines have regular flights between the two islands, though fares to Guam are nearly as high as those to California.

To/From Hong Kong

Hong Kong travel agents dish out some of the cheapest tickets to be found anywhere on Earth. Many of the airlines offer special promotional fares for a short time only, and not all of the travel agents are aware of these cut-rate fares, so ask around at a couple of places before buying. Also note that some of these super-cheap tickets have restrictions, like you can only fly on Tuesday and Thursday or you must complete your return itinerary within 60 days, and so on. Be sure you understand these restrictions when buying rock-bottom priced tickets.

Two agents that I've found to be cheap and reliable are Phoenix Services, Room B, 6th floor, Milton Mansion, 96 Nathan Rd, Tsimshatsui, Kowloon (☎ 7227378); and Traveller Services, Room 1012, Silvercord Tower 1, 30 Canton Rd, Tsimshatsui (☎ 3752222, fax 3752223).

Tickets from Taiwan to Hong Kong are overpriced, but some airlines offer special APEX fares, as low as NT$5200 return. Flights from Kaohsiung to Hong Kong are slightly cheaper.

To/From Japan

Japan is not a good place to buy cheap air tickets. In fact, I can't think of anything you can buy cheaply in Japan, not even rice. The cheapest way to get out of Japan is by ferry to either Taiwan or Korea. However, if you need a plane ticket, Council Travel (☎ 03-35817581) does have an office in Tokyo at the Sanno Grand Building, Room 102 14-2 Nagata-Cho, 2-Chome, Chiyoda-ku, Tokyo 100.

Flights from Taipei to Tokyo cost NT$6200/11,500 one-way/return.

To/From Korea

The best deals are available from the Korean International Student Exchange Society (KISES) (☎ 02-7339494), Room 505, YMCA building, Chongno 2-ga, Seoul.

To/From New Zealand

There's nothing direct to Taiwan, but it's easy enough to fly from Auckland to Hong Kong with Air New Zealand. In 'peak' season a return excursion ticket costs NZ$1828, and in 'low' season NZ$1550. You have to pay for your ticket at least 21 days in advance and spend a minimum of six days overseas.

Cathay Pacific also flies from Auckland to Hong Kong, using Air New Zealand carriers. In 'peak' season a one-way excursion ticket from Auckland to Hong Kong is NZ$1426. An APEX ticket is NZ$1828. As with the Air New Zealand excursion ticket, a minimum of six days must be spent overseas, not that this is likely to be a problem if you're going to Taiwan.

To/From the Philippines

Daily flights connect Taipei and Kaohsiung to Manila. There is also a Kaohsiung-Cebu flight. Flights to Manila cost NT$5900 one-way, NT$11,000 return.

Makung Airlines (a Taiwanese domestic carrier lobbying hard for international routes) is experimenting with daily 'charter' flights from Kaohsiung to Laoag in the northern Philippines. Tickets on this route are sold on a round-trip basis only (though you can fly free – with a hotel room included – if you're prepared to wager US$10,000 in the local casino!).

To/From the USA

There are some very good open tickets which remain valid for six months or one year (opt for the latter), but which don't lock you into any fixed date of departure and allow multiple stopovers. For example, there are cheap tickets between the US west coast and Taipei with stopovers in Japan and Korea and continuing on to Hong Kong for very little extra money – the departure date can be changed and you have one year to complete the journey. However, be careful during the peak season (Chinese New Year) because seats will be hard to come by unless reserved months in advance.

Usually, and not surprisingly, the cheapest fare to any country is offered by a 'bucket shop' (air-ticket dicounter) owned by someone of that particular ethnic origin. San Francisco is the bucket shop capital of America, though some good deals can be found in Los Angeles, New York and other cities. Bucket shops can be found through the Yellow Pages or the major daily newspapers. Those listed in both English and Chinese are invariably discounters. A more direct way to shop is to wander around San Francisco's Chinatown where most of the shops are – especially in the Clay St and Waverly Place area. Many of these are staffed by recent arrivals from Hong Kong and Taiwan who speak little English. Enquiries are best made in person. One place popular with budget travellers is Wahlock Travel in the Bank of America Building on Stockton St.

It's not advisable to send money (even cheques) through the mail unless the agent is very well established – some travellers have reported being ripped off by fly-by-night mail-order ticket agents. Nor is it wise to hand over the full amount to Shady Deal Travel Services unless they can give you the ticket straight away – most US travel agencies have computers that can spit out the ticket on the spot.

Council Travel is the largest student travel organisation, and, though you don't have to be a student to use them, they do have specially discounted student tickets. Council Travel has an extensive network in all major US cities and is listed in the telephone book. There are also Student Travel Network offices which are associated with STA.

One of the cheapest and most reliable travel agents on the west coast is Overseas Tours (☎ (800) 2225292), 475 El Camino Real, Room 206, Millbrae, CA 94030. Another good agent is Gateway Travel (☎ (214) 9602000, (800) 4411183), 4201 Spring Valley Rd, Suite 104, Dallas, TX

75244. Both of these places seem to be trustworthy for mail-order tickets.

To/From the UK

British Airways now flies direct to Taiwan, though like many other airlines they had to create a special subsidiary to appease the People's Republic. The new 'airline' is called British Asia Airways (BAA). Alternatively, you can travel to Hong Kong, change planes and be in Taiwan an hour later.

Air-ticket discounting is a long-running business in the UK and it's wide open. The various agents advertise their fares and there is nothing under-the-counter about it at all. To find out what's going, there are a number of magazines in Britain which have good information about flights and agents. These include *Trailfinder*, free from the Trailfinders Travel Centre in Earls Court, and *Time Out* or *City Limits*, London weekly entertainment guides widely available in the UK.

Discount tickets are almost exclusively available in London. You won't find your friendly travel agent out in the country offering cheap deals. The danger with discounted tickets in Britain is that some of the bucket shops are unsound. Sometimes the backstairs over-the-shop travel agents fold up and disappear after you've handed over the money and before you've received the tickets. Get the tickets before you hand over the cash.

Two reliable London bucket shops are Trailfinders in Earls Court, and the Student Travel Association, with several offices. Fares from London to Hong Kong are often far cheaper than to Bangkok, but check current prices.

Flights from London and Manchester to East Asian destinations are cheapest on Thai, Singapore Airlines, Malaysian (MAS) and Cathay Pacific. These airlines do not charge extra if passengers want to stop over en route, and in fact offer stopover packages which encourage it. There are also direct flights on Lufthansa and Air France – both are significantly more expensive than the Asian-based carriers.

To/From Vietnam

Taiwan's government has actively encouraged Taiwanese businesses to invest in Vietnam as an alternative to mainland China. Consequently, Taiwan has become Vietnam's No 1 foreign investor, with the result that business travel and tourism is booming. There are daily flights between Taipei and Saigon. Vietnam Airlines is slightly cheaper than Taiwan's Mandarin Airlines.

Discount 30-day APEX fares are the only way to get a cheap flight on this route, but fares are falling fast. For those who want to stay longer than 30 days, it's usually cheaper to fly via Hong Kong.

Leaving Taiwan

Plane tickets are not nearly as cheap in Taiwan as they are in Hong Kong, but they can still be bought at reasonable discounts below the airlines' list price. I've never heard of anybody getting ripped off by a travel agent in Taiwan, but should it happen to you, report it to the police. Travel agents are licensed by the government, and the licence can easily be revoked if the agent indulges in unscrupulous practices. If a foreigner is involved, the authorities will usually come down like a tonne of bricks on the offending company. On the other hand, don't make a complaint unless you really have something to complain about. I've used Jenny Su Travel Service and found it to be reliable (for recommended travel agents in Taipei and other cities, see the relevant Getting There & Away sections).

It is possible to get fares even lower than those quoted here if you buy a group ticket. While you do not need to be on a group tour, you must depart and return on the same flight as the group. The problem with group tickets is that the dates are fixed and cannot be changed. Also, you need to give the travel agent considerable advance notice to book such a ticket. Most of the dirt-cheap advertised fares that you find in the newspapers are in fact group fares.

From Kaohsiung Almost everyone arrives at and departs from Taiwan at the airport near Taipei, but there is a second, smaller international airport at the southern end of the island near the city of Kaohsiung.

Although there are far fewer flights available than from Taipei, some travellers might find it more convenient to fly from Kaohsiung. Flights go to Hong Kong, Japan, Korea, the Philippines and a few other destinations.

Airfares from Taipei

	One-Way	Return
Auckland	NT$19,200	NT$31,400
Bangkok	NT$4600	NT$9000
Frankfurt	NT$13,700	NT$21,500
Guam	NT$8200	NT$9700
Hanoi	NT$9400	NT$15,300
Ho Chi Minh City	NT$9400	NT$15,300
Hong Kong	NT$3500	NT$5500
Honolulu	NT$11,100	NT$17,000
Jakarta	NT$7500	NT$14,500
Laoag		NT$7000
London	NT$13,700	NT$21,500
Los Angeles	NT$11,500	NT$17,700
Manila	NT$5200	NT$9800
New York City	NT$15,200	NT$27,800
Okinawa	NT$3375	NT$6750
Seoul	NT$4300	NT$7600
Singapore	NT$7800	NT$10,700
Sydney	NT$15,200	NT$26,400
Tokyo	NT$5700	NT$8800
Vancouver	NT$13,900	NT$22,700

Airfares from Kaohsiung

	One-Way	Return
Cebu	NT$6900	NT$13,000
Hong Kong	NT$4500	NT$6500
Laoag		NT$6000
Manila	NT$5200	NT$9800
Tokyo	NT$6700	NT$9800

Departure Tax If you are leaving Taiwan by air, there's a departure tax of NT$300. It should be paid in local currency.

Duty-Free When you leave Taiwan, the duty-free shops at the airport offer the usual assortment of overpriced chocolate and perfume but reasonably priced cigarettes and booze.

SEA

Travelling to and from Taiwan by ship is possible and economically feasible from either Macau or Japan. From anywhere else forget it, unless you have friends in the sea-freight business. Taiwan does not seem to be on the international luxury cruise circuit.

To/From Macau

A passenger ferry runs between Macau and the port of Kaohsiung in southern Taiwan. The name of the ship is the *Macmosa*, a combination of Macau and Formosa.

This is one of the cheapest ways to leave Taiwan if you've arrived without an air ticket. (At the time of writing, service was temporarily suspended as the *Macmosa* underwent a refit. It should be back in service by the time you read this, but check with the Macau Government Tourist Office (☎ 3491500) to make certain.)

There is one boat weekly during the winter, but at least two weekly during the summer months. The journey takes 24 hours. In winter, departures from Macau are at 2 am on Tuesday. From Taiwan, the ship leaves Kaohsiung at 4 pm on Wednesday. Check departure times – they can change.

From Macau, a one-way 1st-class fare is M$1060; 2nd class is M$860. From Taiwan, one-way 1st-class tickets cost NT$3700, and 2nd class is NT$3000. Return fares are exactly double.

In Macau, tickets are most easily purchased at the ferry pier. In Hong Kong, you can buy tickets from Kwanghua Tour & Travel Service (☎ 5457071), Room 803, 317-321 Des Voeux Rd, Central, Hong Kong Island. In Taiwan, you can buy tickets at the pier in Kaohsiung or from Kuohua Travel Service in Taipei and Kaohsiung. The Taipei office (☎ 02-5310000, 5715669) is on the 11th floor, 82 Sungchiang Rd. The Kaohsiung ticket office (☎ 07-2821166) is on the 6th floor, 79 Chunghua-3 Rd. In Kaohsiung, the boat departs from Pier 1 on Penglai Rd – take bus No 1 to get there.

The ticket price entitles you to three free meals of reasonable quality. These are served only at set times, so don't be late or you'll have to catch your own dinner (bring a fishing line and hooks). Actually, there is another restaurant on board where you can buy meals, but it's not cheap. There is also a small shop on the ship selling a few snacks, but nothing outstanding.

If there is something you particularly crave (chocolate, fruit, biscuits, etc) bring your own. It's wise to bring books or magazines to help pass the time – the only entertainment on board is the karaoke cocktail lounge and the slot machines in the mini-casino.

The *Macmosa* doesn't stop in Hong Kong, but this is hardly a problem. Fast and cheap jetfoils, hydrofoils and hovercraft run between Hong Kong and Macau approximately every 30 minutes and the trip only takes about an hour.

To/From Japan

There is a weekly passenger ferry that operates between Taiwan and Naha on the Japanese island of Okinawa. From Naha,

Ferry Fares between Taiwan and Okinawa (Japan)

From	To	1st Class	2nd Class	3rd Class	Student
Naha	Keelung	Y21,900	Y18,600	Y15,600	Y12,480
Naha	Kaohsiung	Y24,300	Y21,000	Y18,000	Y14,400
Keelung	Naha	NT$3300	NT$2600	NT$2200	NT$1800
Kaohsiung	Naha	NT$3600	NT$2900	NT$2400	NT$2000

there are many passenger ferries to Japan's major port cities, Tokyo, Osaka, Fukuoka and Kagoshima.

Economy class on the ferry is cheaper than going by plane. The ferry departs Okinawa and arrives in Taiwan the next day. Sometimes it will make brief stops at the islands of Miyako and Ishigaki, but the schedule for this is irregular – if you really want to visit those islands you'll probably have to backtrack from Okinawa. Departing from Taiwan the ferry alternates between the ports of Keelung and Kaohsiung – twice monthly from each port. Departure from Okinawa is on Thursday or Friday; departure from Taiwan is usually on Monday.

You can buy tickets from some travel agents in the port cities from where the ferry departs, but it's usually as easy to go straight to the ferry company. Arimura Line has an office in Naha (☎ 098-8640087) and Osaka (☎ 06-5319269).

In Taiwan, you can buy tickets from Yeong An Maritime Company (☎ 02-771 5911), 11 Jenai Rd, Section 3, Taipei. You can also buy tickets in Kaohsiung (☎ 07-5510281) and Keelung (☎ 02-4248151).

Departure Tax If you are leaving Taiwan by ferry or ship, departure tax is NT$300.

TOURS

Many Western travel agencies are obsessed with tours to mainland China – those dealing with Taiwan are thin on the ground indeed. In most cases, you'll simply have to book your own air tickets in your home country, and contact a local Taiwanese travel agent by fax to meet you or your group on arrival.

For information on Taiwanese tour agents, see the Getting Around chapter.

However, there are a handful of tour agencies in the USA, Europe and some Asian countries which can make bookings for you. In the USA, you can try Southeast Travel Service (☎ 213-6232560), Suite 526, 530 W 6th St, Los Angeles, CA 90014. Southeast Travel (☎ 3689638) also has an office in Hong Kong on the 3rd floor, Tung Fai Building 27A Cameron Rd, Kowloon. In the UK, check out Regent Holidays (UK) Ltd (☎ 0272-211711, fax 254866, telex 444606), 15 John St, Bristol BS1 2HR.

One enterprising company in the USA has started doing adventure tours to Taiwan, including such activities as whitewater rafting, cycling, hiking, etc.

For information, contact Nonesuch Whitewater (☎ (707) 8236603; fax 8231954), 4004 Bones Rd, Sebastopol, CA 95472.

Top: Port, Suao (MM)
Bottom: East Gate, Chiang Kaishek's birthday, Taipei (MM)

Top: Guards marching in Martyrs' Shrine, Taipei (MM)
Left: Guard at the Martyrs' Shrine, Taipei (RS)
Right: Furnace for burning 'ghost money' (RS)

Getting Around

Inter-city buses, trains and planes are frequent, fast and dependable. There is almost nowhere on the island that is not served by some means of public transport. You should have no trouble getting to wherever you wish to go except on a Sunday or public holiday, when all means of transport can be very crowded.

If you travel by train or bus on a Sunday, you will probably have to stand during the trip unless you've bought a reserved-seat ticket in advance. If there is a shortage of seats, expect any queue to quickly deteriorate into a push-and-shove match when the bus arrives. However, the advantage of travelling on local buses and trains – as opposed to taxis or private cars – is that you will have plenty of opportunity to meet the local people. Some of them will be happy to practise their English with you, even though you may not necessarily welcome the practice. You can always use the opportunity to practise your Chinese.

I don't know why, but Chinese people seem to be unusually susceptible to motion sickness. It may be something in the diet, or the fact that the Chinese like to eat big meals while travelling, or maybe it's just a psychological fear of travelling – which is not surprising considering how they drive. Children are particularly susceptible. If the person sitting next to you looks very pale, change your seat or give them a plastic bag if you have one handy. Most highway buses in Taiwan are prepared for this and place a barf-bag by each seat, as in planes.

AIR

Due to Taiwan's small size there is little need to fly in most cases unless you are in a big hurry or plan to visit some of the smaller islands around Taiwan, like Penghu or Lanyu. If you do fly, carry your passport with you and arrive at the airport at least an hour before departure time. This is especially important during the holidays, when the airline could re-allocate your seat if you arrive late.

Taiwan has seen an explosion of domestic carriers in recent years. The current line-up includes China Airlines, Far Eastern Air Transport (FAT), Formosa, Great China, Makung, Taiwan Airlines and Trans-Asia. It is said that several of these airlines make no profits or even lose money, and only exist because they anticipate being given permission (some day) to fly to mainland China. In the meantime they operate domestic flights for the sole purpose of gaining experience running an airline.

It's usually best to buy domestic air tickets directly from the airlines. Travel agents give discounts only on international tickets, so prices on domestic air tickets are uniform. If you buy directly from the airline, it will be much easier to obtain a refund if your plans change or if the flight is cancelled. This happened to me once – my flight was cancelled due to bad weather and I obtained my refund right in the airport, but others who had purchased tickets from agents were told they had to go back to the agent and apply for a refund.

BUS

With the completion of the North-South Freeway, highway buses are able to compete with trains for comfort and speed. A trip from Taipei to Kaohsiung now typically takes 4½ hours by bus, which is faster than the train unless there is a big accident on the freeway (a frequent occurrence), in which case it could take six or ten hours. The buses make a 10-minute stop en route at a freeway rest area, where dried-out food from last week can be purchased at ridiculous prices.

In rural areas, the bus service has deteriorated sharply in recent years thanks to Taiwan's 'car revolution'. As more people buy cars, fewer take the bus, forcing the bus companies to reduce their services. Further-

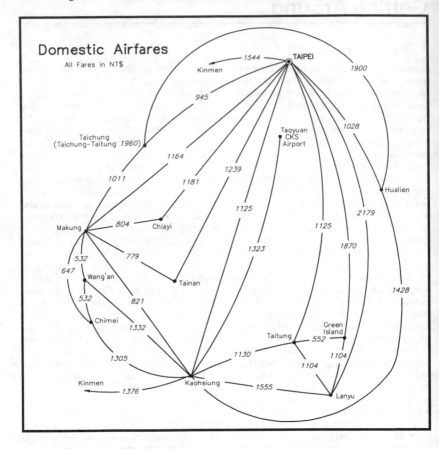

Domestic Airfares

All Fares in NT$

TAIPEI

Kinmen — 1544 —

1900

945

Taoyuan
CKS
Airport

1028

Taichung
(Taichung–Taitung 1960)

1164

1239

1011

1181

1125

Hualien

Makung — 804 — Chiayi

2179

1125

779

1323

1870

532

1428

647   Wang'an

532   821

Tainan

Chimei

1332

Green
Island

Taitung — 552 —

1305

1130

1104

Kinmen — 1376 —

Kaohsiung — 1555 —

1104

Lanyu

more, when Chinese go on holiday and decide to leave the car at home, they usually go by tour bus. The result is that many public and private bus companies have now gone bankrupt.

Ironically, in urban areas bus use is increasing, mainly because the parking problem is now so severe that many people don't dare to bring their car into the city. Unfortunately, the actual number of cars is increasing since everyone wants to own one whether they drive it or not, and virtually every road is plugged up with double-parked cars, slowing Taipei's traffic to a crawl. The

traffic slows down the buses and motorcycles too.

On all buses (except the airport bus) you must save your ticket stub. You should turn it in to the driver or conductor when you get off the bus or you will have to pay the full fare again.

Classes

There are two classes of bus, the Kuokuang (*guóguāng hào*) and the Chunghsing (*zhōngxīng hào*). The Chunghsing is the cheaper of the two, but some of the older model buses are in a rickety condition and give a rough ride on mountain roads. The Kuokuang has a toilet on board and gives you a smoother ride than the Chunghsing, but both cover the route in the same amount of time. The Kuokuang and Chunghsing are both air-conditioned in summer and winter and are often too cold. There is no way to turn off the air-conditioning. Rather than freezing for several hours, some travellers carry tape and tape up the vents – the bus company is not amused.

Reservations

Tickets can be purchased four days in advance. Normally this is not necessary unless you plan travel during a major public holiday when everything is chock-a-block.

Costs

Following are some sample bus fares from Taipei to destinations around the island:

Bus Fares from Taipei

Destination	Kuokuang	Chunghsing
Changhua	NT$222	NT$179
Chiayi	NT$314	
CKS Airport		NT$85
Hsinchu		NT$81
Hsinying	NT$342	NT$277
Kaohsiung	NT$442	NT$357
Keelung		NT$29
Kenting	NT$584	
Pingtung	NT$457	
Suao		NT$170
Sun Moon Lake		NT$258
Taichung	NT$207	NT$166
Tainan	NT$387	
Touliu	NT$282	NT$238

Wild-Chicken Bus Companies

Taiwan has semi-legal bus companies affectionately known as 'wild chickens' (yějī gōngchē). The wild chickens have been known to use all sorts of methods to attract customers, including videos to entertain passengers during a long journey. While these buses may not win points for safety or reliability, they are faster, cheaper and becoming more popular.

Most wild-chicken bus drivers allow passengers to smoke, supposedly against the rules. If smoking bothers you, you'd better avoid these buses because the air gets as thick as oyster sauce after a few hours. The government keeps declaring that they will put the wild-chicken bus companies out of business – instead, it appears that the wild chickens may soon put the government bus company out of business.

Many of the wild chickens are marginal operations and their bus terminals move frequently, so it's difficult to list their locations. An exception is Tonglien Bus Company, the most stable operator. In general, all wild-chicken buses set up operations close to the government bus terminal or else next to the freeway with a sign prominently displayed (in Chinese, of course).

TRAIN

The train services are frequent and generally good, though not quite up to the standards of Japan and Europe. There are two major lines, the west coast line, which is electrified, and the east coast line, which still uses diesel trains. There are several spur routes to places like Alishan and Shuili. Taiwanese trains are more expensive than the buses.

Food is available on trains. A few trains have dining cars, but most of the time you will have to settle for *biàndāng*, precooked rice, meat and vegetables in a cardboard box. There is little variety and the quality is so-so, but it beats starving. Food bought on the train and in or around the train and bus stations tends to be more expensive than elsewhere, but not outrageously so. However, there is free hot tea on the train and you can help yourself. If you're going to be spending a long time on a train, it's best to buy something to eat before you board.

Car Nos 1 and 10 are *usually* for smokers. To be sure, look for a 'No Smoking' symbol in the front of the car – if it's not there, smoking is OK. Unfortunately, the no-smoking rules are frequently broken when the conductor isn't around.

Save your ticket when you get off the train. You need to turn it in at the gate when you leave the railway station. If you lose it, you have to pay a big fine.

Timetables (shí kè biǎo) are available but they are written completely in Chinese. If you can read any Chinese, they are very handy. They cost NT$20 and can be purchased at the service counter in almost any railway station – the same place where you buy the platform tickets. The timetables cover the entire railway system and are updated every few months.

Toilets on the trains discharge the waste directly onto the tracks, so you are not allowed to use them while the train is in a station or in tunnels. The Railways Administration says that they plan to eventually install chemical toilets, as in the buses.

Every major railway station has a left-luggage room that charges NT$14 per day. An exception is Taipei's main railway station which only has lockers. It's possible that lockers will be introduced elsewhere.

Classes

Currently, there are four classes of train and it is fair to say that you get what you pay for. In descending order of comfort they are:

Tzuchiang
    (zìqiáng hào) a very fancy express with air-con; usually has a dining car

Chukuang
    (jǔguāng hào) has air-con but is slightly slower than Tzuchiang
Fuhsing
    (fùxīng hào) has air-con, but is slower and not as luxurious as Chukuang
Putong or 'common train'
    (pǔtōng chē) very slow with no reserved seats, but cheap and stops in many small towns – the best bargain for budget travellers with lots of time, though it could wind up costing you an extra night's accommodation; no air-con, but since the windows can be opened these trains are better for photography (there isn't much to photograph on the west coast line, but on parts of the east coast and spur lines there's good scenery); another advantage Putong has over the more luxurious trains is that no one likes to take this train – on a Sunday or holiday it's still easy to find a seat when the express trains are packed

Reservations

On the fast trains (Tzuchiang, Chukuang, and Fuhsing) it is often wise to buy your ticket a day or two in advance, especially on weekends and holidays. There is no need to buy advance tickets on the Putong trains as there are no reserved seats. If no seats are available, you are permitted to board any train but will have to stand.

Costs

You can receive a 15% discount on return tickets, but the ticket must be used within 15 days of purchase.

If you buy a return ticket from Taipei to

Train Fares from Taipei

West Coast

Destination	Tzuchiang	Chukuang	Fuhsing	Putong
Hsinchu	NT$150	NT$121	NT$101	NT$78
Taichung	NT$305	NT$245	NT$205	NT$158
Chiayi	NT$492	NT$396	NT$331	NT$255
Tainan	NT$609	NT$490	NT$409	NT$316
Kaohsiung	NT$696	NT$560	NT$468	NT$361

East Coast

Destination	Tzuchiang	Chukuang	Fuhsing	Putong
Fulung	NT$110	NT$89	NT$74	NT$57
Hsin Suao	NT$222	NT$178	NT$149	NT$115
Hualien	NT$371	NT$298	NT$249	NT$193
Taitung	NT$679	NT$546	NT$456	NT$352

Kaohsiung, for example, you reserve the return seat when you get to Kaohsiung. You cannot do this from Taipei as the booking system is not computerised. On any advance-ticket sales you cannot reserve a seat more than three days in advance. This includes the return portion of a round-trip ticket. If you don't use the return portion of a round-trip ticket, you can refund it (minus the 15% discount you previously received) within 15 days of purchase.

If you are rushing for the train, you can board without a regular ticket if you have bought a platform ticket for NT$4. You must then find the conductor and upgrade your ticket. The same applies if you buy a cheap ticket and then decide to get on a more expensive train. When you find the conductor, you must say 'upgrade ticket' *(bǔ piào)*. Of course, if you only have a platform ticket, you also have to tell him where you intend to get off.

TAXI

Like private buses, long-distance taxis are generally referred to as 'wild chickens'. These taxis are usually painted dark red or black, are bigger than city taxis and often have diesel engines. The reputation of the wild-chicken taxis is not a good one. The drivers hang around bus and railway stations chewing betel nut, gambling and gobbing on the footpath between trying to arm wrestle passengers into their cars.

If you speak Chinese, you may enjoy listening to their sales pitch as they solicit customers. They often approach people standing in line at a ticket window and say something like, 'The bus you want is out of order' or 'It has just left' or 'It drove off a cliff', or whatever. Most people ignore them and wait for the bus to arrive, on time, five minutes later.

Foreigners should be careful around resort areas. The drivers may approach you and yell out the name of the destination they think you want to go to and they'll usually quote a ridiculously low price. The price then gets raised once you are out in the middle of nowhere. If you refuse to pay more, you might get kicked out on a country road. In recent years this has been happening less as a result of a government crackdown, but before you get into a wild-chicken taxi, at least take the precaution of writing down the licence-plate number.

The most likely use you'll get out of wild chickens is either in remote corners where they are the only form of transport, or during holidays when buses become cattle cars. At these peak times, the wild-chicken drivers congregate right next to the bus or railway stations and try to solicit business. You can also expect to pay more at these times, but it is very likely that you'll be able to share the taxi with other passengers and split the cost. This is a common practice and fully expected by the drivers, and you can even tell the driver you'll only take the taxi if he can round up some more passengers.

CAR & MOTORCYCLE

You might ask yourself whether or not you really need a car. For well-heeled tourists or a group splitting the cost, a car could be useful for getting to some remote areas not easily accessible by public transport. In cities like Taipei or Kaohsiung, either renting or buying a car is an insane idea. Traffic barely moves, parking space is more difficult to find than the Holy Grail and the chance of getting a ticket or having an accident is exponentially greater than in rural areas. As for the Chinese, the main reason why many buy cars is for face. Foreign residents with fragile egos also drive cars for the same reason. In the cities you can save yourself a mountain of cash and aggravation by taking taxis.

A motorcycle can be very useful in Taiwan, but there are a few drawbacks. Chief among these is the possibility of getting killed. Also, motorcycles aren't all that comfortable in the often rainy weather. Motorcyclists are more likely than car owners to receive traffic fines because the police know that high-level government officials drive cars, but only small potatoes ride motorcycles. On the other hand, finding a place to park a motorcycle is far easier than for a car, and a bike can give you a lot of freedom, particularly in the countryside where public transport is poor or nonexistent.

Touring the island by bike is most enjoyable during the summer season when the warm breeze makes riding pleasant. It can be a real drag during a thunderstorm in the mountains when the temperature comes close to freezing. Since rainy weather is almost guaranteed sooner or later, equip yourself with a rainsuit and waterproof boots. A helmet with a faceshield will not only help keep your head in one piece, but will also keep the rain off your face. Don't forget your hands either – a pair of leather gloves (with Goretex or similar lining) is ideal in cold, wet conditions, but you may have to bring these with you as most Taiwanese riders prefer household rubber gloves.

Road Rules

Basically, there aren't any. When the Taiwanese get behind the wheel of a car or on the seat of a motorcycle, they smell blood. At least, that's the impression you'll have the first time you see Taipei's traffic. Actually, there are quite a few rules, it's just that nobody seems to know what they are.

The problem is that the police appear to be more interested in filling quotas than solving the traffic problem. Fines seem to be handed out at random for the most minor infractions (or even for no reason), while the most serious traffic violations continue to go unpunished. Some cities have experimented with giving the police a commission on every ticket written to encourage strict law enforcement – this has caused an explosion of random ticket writing with no visible improvement in safety.

Furthermore, every city seems to have its own rules, and the rules don't seem to make much sense. For example, in Taipei you can't ride a motorcycle in the car lane, though it seems to be OK for cars to ride or park in the motorcycle lane, thus blocking it completely. Motorcycles are *required* to park on the pedestrian footpaths, which means pedestrians usually have to walk in the motorcycle lane (I'm not making this up). The police frequently tow away motorcycles even when they're legally parked (chaining your bike to a pole helps prevent this).

Driving at night with no lights seems to be legal and is very popular because Chinese drivers believe (erroneously) that the headlights consume more petrol. Driving on the footpath also seems to be OK, but it appears that motorcycles aren't permitted to make left turns in Taipei, though it's allowed in other cities. Things are a lot simpler in Tainan – there are no rules and you can do whatever you like.

The vast majority of traffic tickets issued are for turning right on a red light. In most countries of the world (at least those where people drive on the right-hand side of the road), turning right against a traffic light is legal. In Taiwan, it's illegal. The police take particular delight in enforcing this moronic rule since everyone breaks it, thus making the job of filling ticket-writing quotas much easier. However, tickets for driving faster

---

Fights

The Taiwanese are among the most hospitable people in the world towards foreigners, but fights resulting in bloodshed sometimes occur. Most true knock-down fights between foreigners and Taiwanese usually have something to do with traffic. What typically happens is that a taxi comes within an inch of hitting a foreigner on a motorcycle. The foreigner doesn't much like that and catches up with the cabbie at the next traffic light, dismounts, and kicks the side of the taxi, putting a dent in the door. The driver doesn't much like that, gets out of the taxi with a tyre lever and puts a dent in the foreigner's head.

In such a case, most Taiwanese would clearly say that the foreigner was in the wrong. True, the taxi was speeding, ran through a red light and was driving on the wrong side of the road, but that's typical driving procedure in Taiwan. Attempts to enforce the law by foreigners is not appreciated. If you're going to drive in Taiwan, you need to learn that ancient Chinese virtue: tolerance. ∎

than the speed limit are *never* issued except on the freeways.

The most obnoxious policy is the use of hidden cameras to catch traffic violators. The citation will be charged against the owner of the vehicle, no matter who was driving at the time. It takes the slumbering bureaucracy many months to finally send the citation by mail, but if not paid promptly the fine will be automatically tripled! By this time, the driver of the vehicle may have long left Taiwan, leaving the unfortunate owner of the vehicle holding the bag – a big headache for the car rental agencies. Because of the time lag, if the vehicle is sold the new owner may inherit the tickets!

Officially, driving is on the right hand side of the road, though it appears to be optional.

There are over 10 million motorcycles in Taiwan, one for every two people. This rates as the world's highest per-capita motorcycle ownership, a fact which becomes immediately obvious from the moment you step off the airport bus. It's quite possible that Taiwan also boasts the world's highest accident rate. Should you contemplate riding on two wheels, be sure to wear a sturdy helmet and have your will updated. Few drivers in Taiwan carry liability insurance, so you'd be wise to have medical insurance, not to mention life insurance. Riding with your headlight on makes you more visible, but every time you stop at a traffic light people will remind you to turn off your lights to 'save petrol'.

An International Driving Permit is necessary for car or motorcycles (over 50 cc) unless you obtain a Taiwanese driving licence. If you intend to drive and will be travelling to other countries in the region, an international licence will save you much trouble. They are valid for a year.

If you remain in Taiwan for over two months, you are expected to obtain a Taiwanese licence. If you wish to obtain a Taiwanese driving licence be sure to bring along your own national licence – you can use it to get the Taiwanese licence without taking a written exam or driving test. You'll also need two B&W photos of yourself, approximately 3 x 2 cm in size. These can be obtained easily and cheaply in Taiwan from photo shops. Finally, you will need to go to the Foreign Affairs Police and obtain a Report of Alien Residence. The address you put on this report will also be put on your driving licence, so don't use a hotel address. Take these documents and photos to the Department of Motor Vehicles (*jiānlǐ suǒ*) and you can receive your licence in about an hour. You'll need to pass an eye exam, so if you normally wear glasses or contacts be sure to bring them. A Taiwanese driving licence is valid for six years. Separate licences are issued for cars and motorcycles. The Department of Motor Vehicles can also issue an International Driving Permit in case you need one for other countries that you'll be visiting.

Rental

If you've got the cash and want to hire a car, you'll find plenty of rental agencies ready, willing and able to put you in the driver's seat. When you rent a car, be sure that it's fully insured against accidents and theft, and that the rental company will cover repairs and towing costs. If you're renting for a long time, discounts should be available. Many companies now demand some sort of deposit to protect themselves against traffic fines that they may receive months after your departure thanks to the hidden cameras. Rather than cash, they may ask you to leave a blank, signed cheque or to run off an extra signed receipt from your credit card. How should you deal with this request? Don't ask me, I've yet to figure it out myself. Car rental agencies are listed in the relevant chapters (Taipei, etc) under the Getting Around sections.

In large cities like Taipei, motorcycle shops are very reluctant to rent bikes thanks to the hidden cameras mentioned previously. It's much easier to rent in rural areas, especially tourist resorts like Hualien, Penghu and Kenting. Rentals cost about NT$300 to NT$400 per day. To ride a motorcycle you must have a licence valid for motorcycles *unless* the bike's engine displacement is 50 cc or less, in which case no licence is required (but you must be at least 18 years of age). This glaring loophole in the law explains why you see so many little bikes on the highways being driven by people who appear to be suicidal or insane.

A car licence is not acceptable for hiring a motorcycle, though most motorcycle shops are not capable of reading an International Driving Permit written in English. They much prefer you to have a Taiwanese licence. You should always carry the ownership papers of the bike you're riding – the police do spot checks and dish out fines to violators.

Purchasing a Vehicle

Buying a motorcycle and reselling it a few months later used to be a popular option. Unfortunately, it's no longer feasible for the typical traveller. The big barrier is that you need a resident visa or you will not be able to register the bike. In the past, some motorcycle shops got around this by working out a deal where you bought a bike and sold it back to them later for NT$4000 less than you paid – the shop would keep the bike registered in its own name but you would have use of it for two months. Essentially, they were leasing it to you.

Sadly, this is no longer possible because of the already mentioned traffic ticket problem. Either you now need a resident visa or a Chinese friend willing to register the bike for you (and thus, take all the risk if you get any tickets).

If you do have a resident visa, or Chinese friends willing to trust you, then the best all-round touring bike you can (legally) buy in Taiwan is the Sanyang (Honda) or Kwangyang 125 or 150 cc. I highly recommend that you buy a model with a four-stroke engine – the two-stroke models sound like an overstressed lawn mower and generate as much toxic smoke as a small petrochemical plant. There has been much discussion for the past 10 or 15 years about banning two-stroke engines, and perhaps in another decade or two some legislation will be introduced to rid Taiwan of this scourge. In the

meantime, you can help out by not buying a two-stroke bike.

Bikes larger than 150 cc would be more comfortable for long distances, but these aren't legal although they are available on the black market at premium prices. The black-market bikes can't be registered, though people simply transfer the licence plates from a legal vehicle. The 125-cc four-stroke engines use very little petrol, are reliable, and repairs of any kind are very cheap. Motor scooters are a poor choice for long distances – the small wheels are dangerous on rough roads and will quickly vibrate your posterior into marshmallow. Even if you have to ride a 90-cc bike, try to get one with large wheels.

Motorcycles are not permitted on freeways, no matter how large the engine. You can transport a motorcycle by train – indeed, this is very common. The Taiwanese spend ages wrapping their bikes in cardboard and tape before giving it to the railway freight office – hardly seems worth the effort for the tiny scratch it might get.

One visitor actually seemed to enjoy the challenge of riding his bike in Taiwan:

The free-form traffic pattern is unnerving, what with disregard of traffic signals; disregard of life and limb; disregard of common sense; disregard of accepted (Western) vehicle maintenance practices, etc. But myself? Being a desert car and motorcycle racer who kind of thrives on running on the ragged edge, it's OK. Always a challenge. But for others it may not be their cup of oolong.

Anthony H Tellier

Buying a used vehicle from a private individual (as opposed to a car or motorcycle shop) presents some serious bureaucratic hurdles. The biggest is Taiwan's household registration system. Every citizen of the ROC is issued a registration certificate, called a *hukou*, at the time of birth – the certificate lists their city and county of residence. If they move to another city, they must wait six years before they can transfer the hukou to the new location, and doing so involves quite a bit of bureaucratic wrangling so most people don't bother. The hukou is like a stone around the neck – Taiwanese must return to their 'home' (the place where the hukou was issued) to perform various bureaucratic requirements – to vote, buy a house, register a motor vehicle, etc. So if you're in Taipei and you buy a motorcycle from someone whose hukou was issued in Kaohsiung, you have to return to Kaohsiung to process the paperwork.

BICYCLE

Taiwan is a major producer of 10-speed bicycles and mountain bikes, well-known brands being Giant and KHS. These are generally cheap, though the top-quality models carry premium price tags. However, the bikes that the shops keep in stock are usually the smaller frame sizes. If you need a larger frame they may have to order it for you; you'll probably get it within one or two days. If you decide to take the bike to another country, it can be taken on a plane for free as a piece of checked baggage if it's properly boxed.

Bicycle touring is most sensible on the east coast where traffic is relatively light. The West coast plains are relatively boring, hot, dusty and have an abundance of traffic – not ideal for cycling. However, if you do want to ride down the west coast, follow Highway 3 – it's mountainous, but scenic and not heavily used by motor vehicles. A few hardy travellers have tackled the mountains on the scenic cross-island highways – very rewarding if you're in good physical condition. Some mountain roads are still gravel, and for those places a mountain bike makes far more sense than a street-style 10-speed.

You can transport your bicycle around Taiwan on the trains. The cost for this is about half that of a passenger ticket. Your bike must ride in the freight carriage, and it will probably not go on the same train that you do. The freight office in the railway station can estimate when your bike will arrive, but take the estimate with a grain of salt – it's often several hours later.

As for city riding, you'll have to put up with insane traffic, noise and pollution. At least the police won't bother you – they are more interested in raising revenue by busting motorcyclists. Bicycle theft is a problem – keep yours securely chained to a pole or park it indoors if possible.

There is one thing positive I can say about riding a bicycle in Taipei – the death rate from traffic accidents seems to be declining. This is not because people drive more safely, but because there are fewer and fewer cyclists every year. Furthermore, the traffic

now moves so slowly that injuries are seldom serious.

HITCHING

Hitching is never entirely safe in any country in the world, and we don't recommend it. Travellers who decide to hitch should understand that they are taking a small but potentially serious risk. However, many people do choose to hitch, and the advice that follows should help to make their journeys as fast and safe as possible.

It is certainly possible to hitchhike in Taiwan. Indeed, you may have no other choice in remote areas now that the rural bus service has all but collapsed.

In urban areas it's a different story – the bus service is good and hitching is nearly impossible in the complicated grid of city roads. In cities, most people assume that you want to get to the bus station, and that's where they'll take you – you'll need a good command of Chinese to explain otherwise. And most Chinese will be shocked if they learn that you're only hitching to save money – the main reason they would pick you up in a city is because they'll assume you're lost.

Hitching can be problematic even in rural areas. Country people are friendly and will usually pick you up, though on a few occasions I've been asked for money. Communicating can be a problem since almost no one speaks English. If you can't speak Chinese, you and the driver will probably spend the whole journey grinning at each other.

Attacks on hitchhikers are almost unheard of, though this is probably because the Chinese never hitchhike. However, single women may prefer to travel with a companion rather than hitching solo.

The biggest danger to hitchhikers is getting picked up by drunks. It's happened to me a few times, and the last time was pretty exciting. A motorcycle pulled over. The driver was friendly enough – he even pulled a bottle of Kaoliang out of his coat pocket and offered it to me. The problem was that he kept zigzagging all over the twisting, precipitous mountain road we were travelling on. Worse still, he was speeding, turning

his head to talk to me, driving with one hand and holding the bottle of Kaoliang with the other. The brakes weren't working very well and music blasted us from a stereo he had built into his motorcycle. After five minutes of this, I was suffering from a severe case of sensory overload and finally had to get off.

BOAT

There are several ferry trips which can be made to the islands around Taiwan, and they are mentioned in the relevant sections of this book. Some destinations that can be reached by boat include the Penghu Islands, Liuchiu, Lanyu, and Green Island. You must take your passport with you on boat trips, although it might not be checked.

LOCAL TRANSPORT
To/From the Airport

About 99% of arriving travellers head directly to Taipei, which is east of CKS Airport. There is an express bus service from the airport to Taipei – see the Taipei chapter for details.

If you are heading to south or central Taiwan, there is no need to go to Taipei. If you want to head directly south, there are buses from the airport directly to the city of Taichung. There is also one bus daily in the afternoon direct to Tainan and Kaohsiung. There are numerous buses throughout the day to the city of Taoyuan – this is close to the airport and right on the main north-south railway line, where trains run about once every 30 minutes from 6 am until midnight.

However, except for the buses to Taipei, few of the airport buses run at night. If you arrive late you can take a taxi to Taoyuan, but the cost is around NT$400 – so it may be cheaper (though slower) to get a bus to Taipei unless you're sharing the cab with someone.

Buses from the airport to Taichung depart at 10.30 and 11.30 am, 12.30, 1.30, 2.30, 3.30, 4.30, 5.30, 6.30 and 8 pm. There are two buses daily from the airport to Kaohsiung at 1.50 and 4.50 pm. There is one to Tainan at 3 pm and one to Pingtung at 2.50 pm.

Bus

The city bus service is generally excellent in Taipei, workable in Taichung, almost workable in Kaohsiung, and dismal in Tainan. Elsewhere, it's pretty decrepit if it exists at all. The cost is NT$10 in Kaohsiung and Tainan, at least NT$12 elsewhere. See the Getting Around sections of individual cities for details.

Taxi

You won't have to look for a taxi in most large cities, they will be looking for you. Just stand on a street corner, raise your hand to scratch your nose, and three or four of them will stop. However, this does not apply during rush hour when competition for taxis is keen. This is usually only a problem in Taipei, not in other cities.

In Taipei, the taxi service is good but there are two negative points that you must deal with. Firstly, the drivers seldom speak a word of English and secondly, many of them wish to demonstrate their Grand Prix racing skills. The first difficulty can be overcome easily enough if you speak Chinese, have a Chinese person with you or if you have your destination written down in Chinese characters. Be sure to have the name of your hotel and its address written in Chinese for the return trip.

The second problem is a little more difficult to solve. To avoid getting into a demolition derby, I employ several tactics. The first is to look for an old driver, as they are usually wiser (how else did they survive so long?) than a young driver. I also prefer the simpler taxis to the ones with racing stripes, air scoops and Christmas lights. Finally, you can tell the driver to slow down by saying *kāi màn yìdiǎn, hǎo bù hǎo*. If that doesn't work, you can always ask to get out by saying *xià chē*.

The taxis in Taipei, Taichung, Tainan and Kaohsiung are required to have meters. In the big cities the metered fare is set by the government and there is no bargaining; just make sure they use the meter. However, with country taxis you should agree on the fare before you get in. The usual price is around NT$70 (NT$100 at night) for any place within the town or city, and the drivers usually won't bargain. When going out into the countryside, there are no set rates and bargaining with the driver is essential. Never get into an unmetered taxi until you've settled on the price. In general, country taxis cost more than urban taxis because the drivers can seldom get a return fare.

Meters charge for both time and distance. Fares are higher in Taipei city and Taipei county than elsewhere. The fare in Taipei at the time of writing was NT$50 at flagfall, which is good for the first 1.4 km. Each additional 350 metres will cost you NT$5. If the taxi gets stuck in traffic, there is an additional NT$5 waiting charge for every three minutes.

Outside of Taipei county the rates are lower. The first 1.5 km costs NT$35 and each additional 400 metres is NT$5. The waiting charge is NT$5 for five minutes. Just to add a little more confusion, fares are 20% higher during the rush hours as follows: Monday to Friday, from 7 to 9 am and from 5 to 7 pm; Saturday from 7 to 9 am and noon until 2 pm; and every night from 11 pm to 5 am.

During these hours the driver is supposed to press the button on the right (usually blue) to start the meter. During regular hours drivers should use the red light button on the left side of the meter.

If all that isn't complicated enough, it could cost more than what the meter says. The government periodically grants a fare increase and it takes about six months (sometimes much longer) to get the meters adjusted. After a fare increase was granted in 1991, it took three years to get the meters adjusted – just in time for the next fare increase!

Taxis waiting at railway stations and airports have a minimum charge because they must line up and wait for a long time, sometimes an hour. The minimum charge is around NT$250 or more, so don't get a taxi from the railway station if you're only making a short trip. For NT$250, you could go almost 10 km in a regular taxi. To get a regular taxi, walk a couple of blocks from the station or airport and hail a passing cab.

Tipping is not necessary and not expected. Most taxi drivers do quite well for themselves.

Never ask taxi drivers for directions, and don't believe anything that they tell you. As one traveller wrote:

Without our Chinese speaker, we would have been at the mercy of taxi 'hucksters' telling us that our map (your book) was wrong and that the bus station moved, must take taxi. Kept walking and asking questions – took only five minutes walk – found the station (obviously been there for years).

The Ministry of Communications has complaint hot lines for taxis in Taipei (☎ 02-729 1181, 7678217, 3949007, 6837869) and Kaohsiung (☎ 07-7614621, 3631040, 771 5349). Be sure you correctly write down the taxi's number displayed on the rear window or licence plate before making a complaint. Drivers can be fined for rude service or cheating on fares. If you're in a city with no complaint hot line, you can contact the Foreign Affairs Police. They are generally sensitive about complaints by foreigners and will try to assist you. However, be certain that you really have something to complain about – some cases of 'rudeness' and 'cheating' are due to bad communication.

TOURS

Most Chinese tourists prefer organised tours to individual travel. The tour guide wears a smart uniform, carries a brightly coloured flag and speaks through a megaphone. Those who take the tours get to wear bright yellow caps with visors and sing songs together. It's customary to dress formally (black suits and ties for the men) – you'd think they were attending a funeral rather than going on holiday. The tours are usually spending sprees with frequent 'rest stops' at shopping plazas. Many people claim that the tour companies get a commission from the vendors for bringing in customers – it certainly looks suspicious when more time is spent in souvenir shops than at sightseeing spots. A huge lunch at a fancy restaurant is a major feature of Chinese tours and is always included in the tour price. The actual sightseeing part of the tour tends to be rushed – most of the time is spent shopping, eating and posing for group photos.

It's only fair to add that a few tour operators are used to dealing with groups of Westerners and have customised their itineraries to suit Western tastes. The foregoing applies mainly to tour packages geared towards locals, overseas Chinese and Japanese.

Packaged tours take the work out of travelling. You won't get to experience the country in depth when you travel by tour coach, but at least you'll be comfortable. You'll also spend a good deal of money. If packaged tours interest you, these can easily be booked in Taipei and a few other cities. Some reputable tour agencies include:

Grayline
    China Express Transportation, 70 Chungshan N Rd, Section 2 (☎ 02-5416466, fax 5221960)
Golden Foundation Tours Corporation
    8th floor, 134 Chunghsiao E Rd, Section 4, Taipei (☎ 02-7733266, fax 7734994)
    Kaohsiung branch, 85 Chunghua-3 Rd (☎ 07-2166833, fax 2164233)
Huei-Fong Travel Service
    4th floor, 50 Nanking E Rd, Section 2, Taipei (☎ 02-5515805, fax 5611434)
Edison Travel Service
    4th floor, 190 Sungchiang Rd, Taipei (☎ 02-5635313, fax 5634803)
Southeast Travel Service
    60 Chungshan N Rd, Section 2, Taipei (☎ 02-5517111)
Taiwan Coach Tours
    Room 802, 27 Chungshan N Rd, Section 3, Taipei (☎ 02-5955321)

Costs

The following prices assume that you are starting out from Taipei:

Taipei & National Palace Museum
    half-day, NT$500
Wulai
    half-day, NT$750
North Coast
    half-day, NT$650
Window on China
    half-day, NT$800
Taipei night tour
    NT$750

Taroko Gorge
    one day, NT$3300
Alishan
    overnight, NT$3900
Sun Moon Lake
    overnight, NT$3500
Window on China, Sun Moon Lake, Kaohsiung
    three days & two nights, NT$7000
Sun Moon Lake & Taroko Gorge
    three days & two nights, NT$6800
Sun Moon Lake & Alishan
    three days & two nights, NT$7000
Round-the-island
    four to eight days, NT$8500 minimum

Youth Group Tours

Group tours can be arranged for rates as low as US$750 per day, including food, accommodation and transport around Taiwan. This is possible thanks to the government-owned youth hostels – the accommodation is either dormitory-style rooms or tatami mats. These tours are mainly aimed at overseas Chinese students and these groups tend to be large – *very* large.

One overseas Chinese student who attended told me the tour was nicknamed 'The Love Boat' (apparently teenage romance is a big attraction). If you are active with a youth group that might be interested, contact China Youth Corps (☎ 02-5435858) *(jiùguótuán)*, 219 Sungchiang Rd, Taipei, Taiwan.

The centres and hostels are heavily booked during the summer vacations and the Chinese New Year. All arrangements should be made well in advance.

Taipei 台北

Not long ago, the valley of the Tanshui River was home mainly to rice and vegetable farmers but today it's the site of Taipei, the bustling centre of commerce, government and culture in Taiwan. Almost without exception, Taipei is the first stop for Western visitors arriving in Taiwan; it is also home for most of the Western expatriates. As far as most people are concerned, this is the heart of Taiwan and the place where things happen.

The city proper has a population of 2.7 million, but surrounding Taipei County adds another 3 million to the total. It's easily the most densely populated place in Taiwan and the number of residents is growing rapidly. The population increase is due primarily to an influx of people from other parts of the island who are attracted to the city by the economic and educational opportunities. This has driven the cost of land to astronomical levels, making Taipei an expensive place to live and work. The high price of housing and office space is beginning to have an effect – many companies are relocating to other parts of the island to escape the sky-high rents. The government is also making an effort to locate industry and educational institutions in other parts of the island. Nevertheless, most people in Taiwan still see Taipei as the pot of gold at the end of the rainbow, and continue to flock there. As far as they're concerned, if you want to make it big, you must live in Taipei.

As a boom town, Taipei has its share of problems. Social problems such as crime and drug addiction have increased sharply. More noticeable to the visitor are environmental problems such as overcrowding, noise and incredible traffic jams. Unless the wind is blowing, the air is toxic. The skyrocketing price of real estate has made home ownership an impossible dream for the working class. In an attempt to deal with the onslaught of people, industry and automobiles, there is a tremendous amount of construction going on

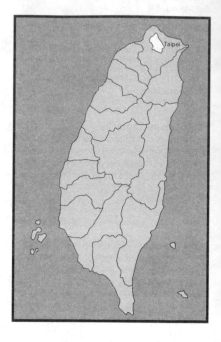

– half the streets seem to be torn up at any one time. A gigantic new subway system is being built, but many think it will be obsolete by the time it's completed.

Whether or not you like Taipei depends on how you feel about big, booming cities. Taipei is not known for its architectural excellence – many of the buildings are just plain ugly. At the same time, for such a large city it's a very friendly place, with adventure and discovery at every corner. Travellers often develop a love-hate relationship with Taipei – they hate it so much that they stay for months and never get out of the city at all. Even if you like Taipei, one thing is for sure – it's an expensive place to hang out unless you're working there.

Taipei is not blessed with congenial

weather. Winter is grey, drizzly and chilly. All those buildings, coupled with the thermal pollution from cars and air-conditioners turns the city into one big heat sink from June through to September. October is considered the best month, but the only thing about Taipei's weather that you can count on is that you can't count on it.

Although Taiwan's magnificent scenery lies beyond the city's glittering glass and concrete, Taipei should not be missed. It's the economic, cultural and trendsetting heart of the island, and if you haven't seen Taipei then you haven't seen Taiwan.

ORIENTATION

Taiwan's cities – and Taipei in particular – might at first seem like a confusing sprawl to the uninitiated. A good map helps, and it's also useful to carry a small pocket compass to keep yourself oriented.

Sprawling as Taipei might be, there is a logical system to locating addresses. In fact, it's more logical than the system normally used in Western countries. Naturally, it's easier if you can speak, read and write Chinese, but that isn't absolutely necessary. It's certainly helpful to have your destination written down in Chinese characters and, of course, you should always have the name card of your hotel so you can find your way back.

The city of Taipei (as opposed to Taipei County) is divided into twelve urban districts, and these districts appear on most postal addresses so they are worth knowing. The districts (qū) are Chungcheng, Chungshan, Hsinyi, Nankang, Neihu, Peitou, Shihlin, Sungshan, Ta'an, Tatung, Wanhua and Wenshan. Within these districts are neighbourhoods, well-known ones being Tienmu, Dinghao and Waishuanghsi.

The city is also divided into compass points. Chunghsiao Rd bisects the city into its north and south grids. All major roads that cross Chunghsiao Rd are labelled accordingly. Thus, we have Linsen N Rd and Linsen S Rd, Yenping N Rd and Yenping S Rd, etc.

Chungshan Rd bisects the city into east and west grids. Roads to the east of Chungshan Rd are labelled east and those to the west are labelled west. Thus, we have Nanking E Rd and Nanking W Rd.

Major roads, such as Chungshan N Rd, are divided into sections. In Taipei there is Chungshan N Rd, Section 1, Section 2, Section 3 and so on right up to Section 7. In some places, instead of writing 'Wufu Rd, Section 3', they might write 'Wufu-3 Rd', but the meaning is the same. A section is normally about three blocks long. When finding an address you really have to pay attention to which section you are in.

Then there are lanes. A lane, as the name implies, is a small side street – and they never have names, just numbers. A typical address might read like this: No 16, Lane 20, Chungshan N Rd, Section 2, Chungshan District. The No 16 is the house number, and Lane 20 is the name of the lane which intersects with Section 2 of Chungshan N Rd. That's not too difficult, but is there an easy way to locate Lane 20?

Fortunately, there is. As you walk along Chungshan N Rd, Section 2, keep your eye on the house numbers. Lane 20 should intersect with Chungshan N Rd just near a building bearing the street address number 20. Once you understand this system, it becomes very easy to find the lane you are looking for. It's even true that even-numbered lanes are on the same side of the street as even house numbers.

Occasionally, you'll have to find an alley. An alley is a lane which runs off a lane. Again, the same system is used. Alley 25 will intersect with a lane, and the house at the corner of this intersection should be number 25. A typical address could be 132 Alley 25, Lane 20, Chungshan N Rd, Section 2, Chungshan District, Taipei. It may look complicated, but it's very systematic.

Budget travellers, in particular, should learn this method of finding places, as many of the inexpensive hostels in Taipei are in these small lanes.

It's worthwhile spending your first day in Taipei exploring the city on foot – it's a bustling place with plenty to see. Chungshan N Rd is a good place to start, as it is full of shops, restaurants and tempting bakeries. If you are looking for a cheap meal, get off the main street and into the narrow lanes and alleys where you will find all sorts of tiny restaurants selling various inexpensive Chinese delicacies. The Dinghao neighbourhood in east Taipei and Kungguan near National Taiwan University are other good walking areas.

INFORMATION
Visa Extensions
Visas can be extended in Taipei at the Foreign Affairs Police (☎ 3818341) *(wàishì jǐngchá)*, 96 Yenping S Rd, close to Chunghua Rd.

Tourist Information
The ROC Tourism Bureau (☎ 3491500) *(guānguāng jú)*, 9th floor, 280 Chunghsiao E Rd, Section 4, is not far from the Sun Yatsen Memorial. It's a good place to pick up some free maps.

There is another small branch of the Tourism Bureau in the Taipei railway station, but this is largely Chinese-speaking and geared towards domestic tourists. However, they will try to help you if you're lost.

There is a Tourist Information Hot Line (☎ 7173737), which accepts calls from 8 am to 8 pm, every day of the year. The operators speak English and can provide useful information such as the schedule of cultural events, exhibitions, even current bus and train schedules. They also provide an emergency translation service if you need to summon the police or an ambulance. They will also forward your complaints to the relevant authorities.

Notice Boards
Apart from the notice boards at the youth hostels, there is a good notice board for travellers at Taiwan Normal University, Mandarin Training Centre, 6th & 7th floors, 129-1 Hoping E Rd, Section 1, Taipei.

Post & Telecommunications
The GPO in Taipei is on Chunghsiao W Rd,
close to the railway station, and is called the North Gate Post Office. There is a separate window for poste restante.

Taipei's telephone area code is 02. With a phonecard, you can make international direct-dial phone calls from the Taipei railway station.

At the government-owned telephone monopoly (ITA) you can make international phone calls and send fax messages, telegrams and telexes. The main office (☎ 3443781) is at 28 Hangchou S Rd, Section 1 – open 24 hours a day. Other ITA branch offices are at:

CKS International Airport
    7 am to 9 pm (☎ 03-3832790)
23 Chungshan N Rd, Section 2
    8 am to 10 pm (☎ 54174340)
118 Chunghsiao W Rd, Section 1
    8 am to 10 pm (☎ 3443785)
Sungshan Domestic Airport
    8 am to 9 pm (☎ 7126112)

Taxes
You need tax clearance before you can extend a visa. If you're working (legally) and want to leave Taiwan, you also need tax clearance before you can leave. This can be obtained from the National Tax Administration, Foreign Affairs Section (☎ 7633636 ext 240-245), 547 Chunghsiao E Rd, Section 4.

Pseudo-Embassies in Taiwan
Because Taiwan has diplomatic relations with only a handful of countries, the following offices in Taipei are not true embassies (South Africa is an exception). These 'unofficial organisations' can issue visas and replace lost passports, but the paperwork might be sent elsewhere, usually Hong Kong, which can cause delays of up to three weeks. However, that can vary – the Japan office can process a visa application in three days and some offices offer next-day service.

American Institute in Taiwan (AIT)
    (měiguó zài tái xiéhuì), 7 Lane 134, Hsinyi Rd, Section 3 (☎ 7092000)
Anglo-Taiwan Trade Committee
    (yīngguó màoyì cùjìn huì) 9th floor, 99 Jenai Rd, Section 2 (☎ 3224242)

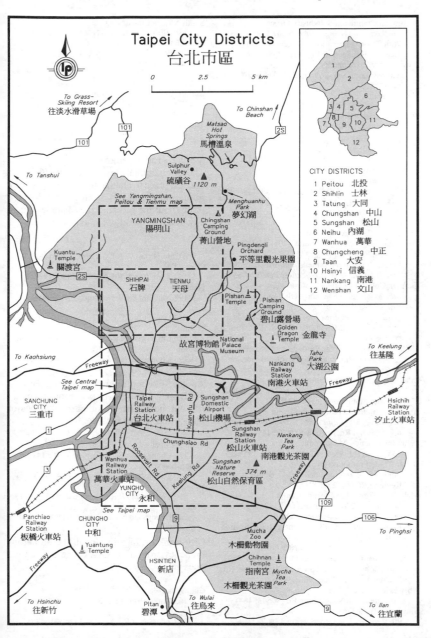

Taipei City Districts
台北市區

0   2.5   5 km

CITY DISTRICTS

1 Peitou 北投
2 Shihlin 士林
3 Tatung 大同
4 Chungshan 中山
5 Sungshan 松山
6 Neihu 內湖
7 Wanhua 萬華
8 Chungcheng 中正
9 Taan 大安
10 Hsinyi 信義
11 Nankang 南港
12 Wenshan 文山

To Grass-Skiing Resort 往淡水滑草場

To Tanshui 往淡水

To Chinshan Beach 往金山海水浴場

Matsao Hot Springs 馬槽溫泉

Sulphur Valley 硫磺谷

▲ 1120 m

Menghuanhu Park 夢幻湖

YANGMINGSHAN 陽明山

Chingshan Camping Ground 菁山營地

See Yangmingshan, Peitou & Tienmu map

Pingdengli Orchard 平等里觀光果園

Kuantu Temple 關渡宮

SHIHPAI 石牌

TIENMU 天母

Pishan Temple

Pishan Camping Ground 碧山露營場

Golden Dragon Temple 金龍寺

National Palace Museum 故宮博物館

To Kaohsiung 往高雄

Tahu Park 大湖公園

To Keelung 往基隆

See Central Taipei map

SANCHUNG CITY 三重市

Taipei Railway Station 台北火車站

Sungshan Domestic Airport 松山機場

Kuangfu Rd

Nankang Railway Station 南港火車站

Hsichih Railway Station 汐止火車站

Chunghsiao Rd

Sungshan Railway Station 松山火車站

Nankang Tea Park

Nankang Tea Park 南港觀光茶園

Roosevelt Rd

Keelung Rd

Wanhua Railway Station 萬華火車站

Sungshan Nature Reserve 松山自然保育區

▲ 374 m

YUNGHO CITY 永和

See Taipei map

Panchiao Railway Station 板橋火車站

CHUNGHO CITY 中和

Yuantung Temple 圓通寺

HSINTIEN 新店

Mucha Zoo 木柵動物園

Chihnan Temple 指南宮

Mucha Tea Park

木柵觀光茶園

To Pinghsi 往平溪

To Hsinchu 往新竹

Pitan 碧潭

To Wulai 往烏來

To Ilan 往宜蘭

Australian Commerce & Industry Office
(aòzhōu shānggōng bànshì chù) Room 2605, 26th floor, International Trade Building, 333 Keelung Rd, Section 1 (☎ 7202833, 7576544)

Austrian Trade Delegation
Suite 608, Bank Tower, 205 Tunhua N Rd (☎ 7155221)

Belgian Trade Association
Suite 901, 131 Minsheng E Rd (☎ 7151215)

Brazil Business Centre
Suite 702, 129 Minsheng E Rd, Section 3 (☎ 5149099)

Canadian Trade Office
(jiānádà màoyì bànshì chù) 13th floor, 365 Fuhsing N Rd (☎ 7137268)

Chilean Trade Office
7B06-07, TWTC Building, 5 Hsinyi Rd, Section 5 (☎ 7230329)

Danish Trade Organisation
4th floor, 12 Lane 21, Anho Rd (☎ 7213386)

France Asia Trade Association
(fǎyǎ màoyì cùjìn huì) Suite 1401, Bank Tower, 205 Tunhua N Rd (☎ 7133552)
French Institute in Taipei (fǎguó zài tái xiéhuì), 15th floor, 99 Jenai Rd, Section 2 (☎ 3940850)

German Cultural Centre
(déguó wénhuà zhōngxīn) 11th floor, 24 Hsinhai Rd, Section 1 (☎ 3657294)
German Trade Office (déguó jīngjì bànshì chù), 4th floor, 4 Minsheng E Rd, Section 3 (☎ 5069028)

Hellenic Organisation for Promotion of Exports
Room 2, 6th floor, 125 Roosevelt Rd, Section 3 (☎ 3635597)

Indonesian Chamber of Commerce
3rd floor, 46-1 Chungcheng Rd, Section 2, Tienmu, Shihlin district (☎ 8310451)

Ireland Institute of Trade & Investment
(aièrlán màoyì cùjìn huì) 7B-09, TWTC Building, 5 Hsinyi Rd, Section 5 (☎ 7251691)

Japan Interchange Association
43 Chinan Rd, Section 2 (☎ 3517250, 3943181)

Italian Trade Promotion Office
Suite 1807, International Trade Building, 333 Keelung Rd (☎ 7251542)

Malaysian Friendship & Trade Centre
8th floor, 102 Tunhua N Rd (☎ 7132626)

Netherlands Trade & Investment Office
Room B, 5th floor, 133 Minsheng E Rd, Section 3 (☎ 7135760)

New Zealand Commerce & Industry Office
(niǔxīlán shānggōng bànshì chù) Room 2501, 25th floor, CETRA Tower, 333 Keelung Rd, Section 1 (☎ 7577060)

Norwegian Trade Office
11th floor, 148 Sungchiang Rd (☎ 5435484)

Singapore Trade Office
9th floor, 85 Jenai Rd, Section 4 (☎ 7721940)

South African Embassy
13th floor, 205 Tunhua N Rd (☎ 7153250)

Spanish Chamber of Commerce
7th floor, 40 Tunhua S Rd (☎ 3256234)

Swedish Trade Council
Room 812, 8th floor, 333 Keelung Rd, Section 1 (☎ 7576573)

Swiss Industries Trade Office
Room 3101, 31st floor, 333 Keelung Rd, Section 1 (☎ 7201001)

Thai Airways International Ltd
6th floor, 150 Fuhsing N Rd (☎ 7121882)

Money – local banks

The International Bank of China (ICBC) is the best place to change money, as they have numerous branches strategically located throughout the city and they handle almost any brand of travellers' cheques.

Central Taipei
6 Chunghsiao W Rd, Section 1 (☎ 3118298)
Chungshan
15 Chungshan N Rd, Section 2 (☎ 5119231)
Nanking
198 Nanking E Rd, Section 3 (☎ 7516041)
Dinghao
233 Chunghsiao E Rd, Section 4 (☎ 7711877)
Shihlin
126 Chungshan N Rd, Section 6 (☎ 8345225)
Tienmu
193 Chungshan N Rd, Section 7 (☎ 8714125)

Another likely place to change money is at the Bank of Taiwan. Expect more forms to fill out here than at other banks. Major branches in Taipei include:

Central Taipei
120 Chungching S Rd, Section 1 (☎ 3147377)
Chungshan
150 Chungshan N Rd, Section 1 (☎ 5423434)
Dinghao
560 Chunghsiao E Rd, Section 4 (☎ 7073111)
Shihlin
248 Chungshan N Rd, Section 6 (☎ 8367080)

City Bank of Taipei chips in the numerous branches around the city. Some convenient ones are:

Chungshan
162 Chungshan N Rd, Section 2 (☎ 5963171)
Chang'an
36 Chang'an E Rd, Section 1 (☎ 5216437)

Nanking
   261 Nanking E Rd, Section 3 (☎ 7172803)
Tunhua
   201 Tunhua N Rd (☎ 7131660)

Money – foreign-owned banks

American Express only cashes American
Express travellers' cheques. Similarly Bank
of America, Citibank, etc will only change
travellers' cheques issued by their own
banks. Not all banks have this rule, so ask.

American Express
   (měiguó yùntōng yínháng), 2nd floor, 214
   Tunhua N Rd (☎ 7151581, fax 7130263)
ANZ Bank
   8th floor, 44 Chungshan N Rd, Section 2
   (☎ 5683353, fax 5111232)
Bangkok Bank
   121 Sungchiang Rd (☎ 5062800, 5064625)
Bank of America
   Bank Tower, 205 Tunhua N Rd (☎ 7154111, fax
   7132850)
   Sungshan Branch, 2nd floor, 62 Tunhua N Rd
   (☎ 7775533, fax 7773052)
Bankers Trust Company
   3rd floor, 51 Chungking S Rd, Section 2
   (☎ 3225555, fax 3225261)
Barclays Bank
   14th floor, 205 Tunhua N Rd (☎ 7185918, fax
   7132405)
Chase Manhattan Bank
   9th floor, 115 Minsheng E Rd, Section 3
   (☎ 5141234, fax 5141299)
Citibank
   (huāqí yínháng), 52 Minsheng E Rd, Section 4
   (☎ 7155931, fax 7127388)
Dai-Ichi Kangyo Bank
   167 Tunhua N Rd (☎ 7153911, fax 7153780)
Hollandsche Bank-Unie
   2nd floor, 49-51 Minsheng E Rd, Section 3
   (☎ 5037888, fax 5023017)
Hongkong & Shanghai Banking Corporation
   (huìfēng yínháng), 14th floor, 333 Keelung Rd,
   Section 1 (☎ 7230088, fax 7576388)
Metropolitan Bank & Trust
   107 Chunghsiao E Rd, Section 4 (☎ 7766355)
Société Générale
   7th floor, 109 Minsheng E Rd, Section 3
   (☎ 7155050, fax 7152781)
Standard Chartered Bank
   337 Fuhsing N Rd (☎ 7166261, fax 7164068)
Toronto Dominion Bank
   2nd floor, 337 Fuhsing N Rd (☎ 7162160, fax
   7134816)

Westpac Banking Corporation
   15th floor, 99 Fuhsing N Rd (☎ 7129133, fax
   7154207)

It's said that many gold shops on Yenping Rd
(north and south) are black-market money
exchange facilities. Rumours of counterfeit
bills abound.

Travel Agencies

The following are some discount travel
agencies in Taipei. Many other travel agencies advertise in the local English-language
newspaper, the *China Post*.

Country Club Travel
   5th floor, 152 Chunghsiao E Rd, Section 1
   (☎ 3567003)
David's Special
   8th floor, 216 Nanking E Rd, Section 2 (at
   Chienkuo N Rd (☎ 5099877, 5170183)
Evergrace Travel
   11th floor, 173 Chang'an E Rd, Section 2
   (☎ 7506757, fax 7721463)
Hawk Express
   3rd floor, 258 nanking E Rd, Section 3
   (☎ 7416663)
Jenny Su Travel
   10th floor, 27 Chungshan N Rd, Section 3
   (☎ 5947733, 5962263, fax 5920068)
Linda
   Room 303, 3rd floor, 328 Changchun Rd
   (☎ 5455160, fax 5149785)
Southeast Travel
   60 Chungshan N Rd, Section 2, Taipei
   (☎ 5713001)
Wing On Travel
   73-79 Jenai Rd, Section 4 (☎ 7722998)

Bookshops

The widest selection for English-language
titles in Taipei is Caves Books (☎ 5371666)
(dūnhuáng shūjú), 103 Chungshan N Rd,
Section 2. There is another Caves nearby at
81 Chungshan N Rd, Section 2, but this is for
Chinese books though there is a good stationery store upstairs. Perhaps more useful is
the Caves (☎ 8742199) in Tienmu at No 5,
Lane 38, Tienyu St. This store also stocks
major foreign newspapers, magazines,
music cassettes and tickets for concerts and
other cultural events.

New Schoolmate Bookstore (☎ 7007000)
(xīn xué yǒu shūjú) is at 259 Tunhua S Rd,

Section 1, on the south-east corner of the roundabout at the intersection with Jenai Rd. Some have called this the McDonald's of bookshops – it's a chain store with a large selection of English-language glossy-covered bestsellers, magazines and Chinese books. Like Caves, it's also a good place to pick up tickets for cultural events. Other branches in Taipei include the following:

Chunghsiao
    465 Chunghsiao E Rd, Section 6 (☎ 6518000)
Chungking
    235-4 Chungking N Rd, Section 2 (☎ 5572221)
Minsheng
    69 Minsheng E Rd, Section 4 (☎ 7191273)
Shihlin
    281 Wenlin Rd (☎ 8822002)
Tienmu
    36 Tienmu E Rd (near Taipei American School)
    (☎ 8735566)

Lucky Bookstore (☎ 3927111) (shídà shūyuàn), 129-1 Hoping E Rd, Section 1, is very popular with foreigners studying Chinese in Taipei due to it's location in the same building as the Mandarin Training Centre of Taiwan Normal University. Because of the student traffic, prices here are slightly discounted and selection is geared heavily towards students' tastes.

Nearby to Lucky is Crane Publishing Company (☎ 3934497, 3941791), 6th floor, 109 Hoping E Rd, Section 1. You can't see the shop from the street – take the lift to the 6th floor and you're there. This branch is open from 9 am to 6 pm. Crane operates another branch (☎ 3225437) at 59 Chung-ching S Rd, Section 2 (just south of Nanhai Rd) and is open from 10 am to 7 pm. Crane is heavily into publishing educational books – English teachers can get a 20% discount. Even for non-teachers, there's quite a good collection of classical English literature.

Lai Lai Book Company (☎ 3634265, 3929765) (láilái shūjú) 4th floor, 271 Roosevelt Rd, Section 3, is close to National Taiwan University. The emphasis is on text-books, but the selection is good.

Sung Kang Computer Book Company (☎ 7082125) (sōnggāng diànnǎo shūdiàn)

specialises in – you guessed it – computer books. Unlike most computer bookshops in Taipei, this place has computer manuals in English. The store is on the 3rd floor, 337 Tunhua S Rd, Section 1, near the intersection with Hsinyi Rd.

Bookman Books (☎ 3924715, 3928617) (shūlín shūdiàn), 5 Lane 62, Roosevelt Rd, Section 4 (near National Taiwan University), is a very small store but has a reasonable collection of English literature. There is another branch on the 2nd floor (just above McDonald's) at 88 Hsinsheng S Rd, Section 3.

For expensive arts & crafts coffee-table books, the best place in Taipei is Eslite (☎ 7755977) (chéngpǐn shūdiàn), 249 Tunhua S Rd, Section 1, on the north-east corner of Jenai Rd. There is another branch (☎ 3455577) in the basement (under Lotteria fast food restaurant) at 2 Hsinyi Rd, Section 5 (opposite the World Trade Centre).

Kingstone (☎ 7518202), 230 Chunghsiao E Rd, Section 4, is mostly Chinese books but has some English titles. This store is most useful for buying tickets for concerts. There is another Kingstone (☎ 3215447) at 782 Tingchow Rd.

Libraries

The American Cultural Centre (☎ 7155625), 365 Fuhsing N Rd (at Minchuan E Rd), is a library maintained by the American Institute in Taiwan (AIT). Library hours are from 10 am until 5 pm Monday to Friday.

The China External Trade Development Council (CETRA) maintains an international Trade Data Library in the high-rise building adjoining the World Trade Centre on the 4th floor, 333 Keelung Rd, Section 1, Hsinyi district. There is also a traders' hot line (☎ 7255960).

The American Institute in Taiwan has a Trade Unit Library in the same building as the CETRA Trade Data Library. This small library offers business, telephone, and other directories covering the USA. It also has materials on American import regulations.

The National Central Library (☎ 3619132), adjacent to the Chiang Kaishek Memorial Hall, at 20 Chungshan S

Rd, is Taiwan's largest. The facilities are stunning – even if you don't like libraries, just wander around and admire the architecture. Both Chinese and English periodicals are available. The 6th floor of the library has a complete set of highly detailed topographic quadrangle maps of Taiwan, produced by the government. These maps are not for sale to the public, but you can photocopy them within the library.

The Taipei Municipal Library's (☎ 7553029) fancy new building is at 125 Chienkuo S Rd, Section 2, between Hoping and Hsinyi Rds.

Academia Sinica (☎ 7899326), 128 Yen Chiu Yuan Rd, Section 2, Nankang district, has the most modern facilities for serious researchers. The library is in the far eastern part of Taipei. You can reach it from the centre on bus No 270.

The Information and Computing Library (☎ 7377737), Science & Technology Building *(kējì dàlóu)*, 13th floor, 106 Hoping E Rd, Section 2 has a collection of up-to-date computer books and magazines. Perhaps more useful is the shareware collection, which you are permitted to copy freely onto floppy disks sold at the library. On the 10th floor of the same building is the somewhat less-useful Institute for Information Industry Library (☎ 7377133).

Laundry

There are heaps of laundries in Taipei, though they tend to be in back alleys and have no English signs. If you can't spot one yourself, get a Chinese person to help you. Logical places to look for inexpensive laundry services are in the alleys around National Taiwan University *(táidà)* and Taiwan Normal University *(shīdà)*. One of many places is *shīdà zìzhù xǐyī* (☎ 3621047), 72 Lungchuan St. Lungchuan St is one block east of Shihta Rd and runs parallel to it.

Emergency

English-speaking police can be contacted at the central office by calling ☎ 3119940 or 3119816, ext 264; in the Chungshan area, call ☎ 5119564; in Tienmu, call ☎ 8714110

or 8714440. As elsewhere in Taiwan, the Chinese-speaking emergency numbers are ☎ 110 for police and ☎ 119 for fire.

For an ambulance call ☎ 7216315. If this doesn't work, call the Tourist Information Hot Line (☎ 7173737, or 080-211734).

The Adventist Hospital has English-speaking doctors and caters to foreigners, but is very expensive – if you have health insurance you might be covered. The other hospitals are government-run and cheap for the high standard of service provided, but public hospitals in Taipei can be very crowded.

From my personal experience, two of the less-crowded hospitals are Taipei Medical College and Mackay Memorial Hospital, but they don't handle every type of illness. If you require major surgery, you'll probably have to go elsewhere but they can refer you.

Adventist Hospital
   (tái ān yīyuàn) 424 Pate Rd, Section 2 (☎ 7718151)
Chang Gung Memorial Hospital
   (cháng gēng yīyuàn) 199 Tunhua N Rd (☎ 7135121)
Mackay Memorial Hospital
   (mǎjiē yīyuàn) Chungshan N Rd, Section 2 (☎ 5433535)
National Taiwan University Hospital
   (táidà yīyuàn) 7 Chungshan S Rd (☎ 3970800)
Taipei Medical College Hospital
   (táiběi yīxué yuàn) 252 Wuhsing St (☎ 7372181)
Tri-Service General Hospital
   (sānjūn zhǒng yīyuàn) 226 Tingchow St (☎ 3117001)
Veterans General Hospital
   (róngmín zhǒng yīyuàn) 201 Shihpai Rd, Section 2 (☎ 8712121, English extension 3530)

Dentist

Dr Luo Taihua is a good dentist who speaks excellent English and charges relatively low prices. You can drop by his Roosevelt Dental Clinic (☎ 3625760, 3923829) at 3 Lane 81, Roosevelt Rd, Section 2.

Mountain Permits

To get a mountain permit, visit the Foreign Affairs Office, Taiwan Provincial Police Administration, 7 Chunghsiao E Rd, Section

1, directly across the street from the Lai Lai Sheraton Hotel.

Left Luggage

The Taipei railway station does *not* have a left-luggage office. However, there are lockers in the basement. You don't pay by time, but for each time you open the locker. The small lockers cost NT$30 and the large ones are NT$60.

The Sungshan railway station in east Taipei has a left-luggage office for NT$14 per day per bag and you can get your luggage whenever you want it. The office is open daily from 7 am to 10 pm. A passport or some other identification is needed.

In most other large cities in Taiwan you can also find left-luggage offices at railway stations, but the hours will be shorter, around 8 am to 8 pm, and they will probably close during lunch time.

THINGS TO SEE & DO
National Palace Museum

(*gùgōng bówù yuàn*) 故宮博物館

Taipei's National Palace Museum (☎ 8812021), 221 Chihshan Rd, Section 2, in the Waishuanghsi neighbourhood of the Shihlin district, is the pride of Taiwan. It ranks as one of the four best museums in the world, in a class with the Louvre, British Museum and Metropolitan Museum of Art. The museum holds the world's largest collection of Chinese artefacts, around 700,000 items in all. Since the museum only has space to display around 15,000 pieces at any given time, the majority of the treasures are kept well protected in air-conditioned vaults buried deep in the mountainside. The displays are rotated once every three months, which means 60,000 pieces can be viewed in a year and it would take nearly 12 years to see them all. Real enthusiasts might find this a bit frustrating. Furthermore, the collection continues to grow through donations and purchases.

Some of the oldest artefacts in the collection are pieces of prehistoric pottery over 5000 years old, though these are obviously not in the best of condition. The vast majority of the art objects are from the private collection of China's emperors.

Included in the collection are artefacts made from jade, bronze, porcelain, lacquerware and enamel. There is also tapestry and embroidery, and many priceless documents and books containing excellent examples of ancient Chinese calligraphy.

There are good English tours of the museum twice daily at 10 am and 3 pm, starting from the information desk in the main lobby. The tours will run even if only one person shows up. In October, there are special showings of rare and fragile artefacts and this is the best time to visit.

The museum's gift shop near the main entrance is worth visiting. Items on sale include calligraphy brushes, T-shirts, books, postcards and scrolls. You can buy excellent reproductions of rare paintings for the low price of NT$50 each – probably the best buy in Taiwan. Photography is prohibited inside the museum and you are requested to check cameras at the entrance.

Just to the east of the museum steps is Chihshan Garden, which has fine Sung dynasty landscaping but costs NT$10 for admission. The museum has its own restaurant, which is not too expensive and much better than the not-too-good restaurants across the street. On the 4th floor is a coffee shop and teahouse.

The museum is open from 9 am to 5 pm every day of the year; admission is NT$40. It's too far to walk there from the centre of the city. Buses which go to the museum are Nos 213, 255 and 304, and minibus No 18. If you take No 304, you get off at the terminus, but for the other buses you have to ask for the museum. From the city centre you must pay double fare (NT$24), as it is a long way out.

Movie Studio

(*zhōngyāng diànyǐng wénhuà chéng*)
中央電影文化城

Also known by its more formal name, the Central Motion Picture Cultural Village (☎ 8812681), the Movie Studio is within walking distance of the National Palace Museum and therefore easy to visit. Basi-

The History of the National Palace Museum

It all started during the Song dynasty (960-1279) when Emperor Dai Cong decided he wanted to monopolise China's art treasures. He sent teams of servants into the countryside to search for, and ultimately confiscate, paintings, sculptures, pottery, calligraphy scrolls, books, wood carvings and everything else an emperor could want. The tradition continued right up to the Qing dynasty (1644-1911). The donations were shuttled back and forth numerous times between the various palaces of the emperors in Beijing and Nanjing, but finally came to rest in the 1400s when Emperor Yong Le established Beijing's Forbidden City. The art collection was to remain there for the next 500 years.

The Forbidden City was just that – forbidden to entry without an invitation. Anyone foolish enough to attempt an unauthorised visit could expect a decidedly unhospitable reception consisting of torture followed by execution. As far as the imperial art treasures were concerned, they remained for the exclusive viewing of emperors and empresses along with some of their consorts.

China's revolution of 1911 theoretically put emperors out of business and put the KMT in power, but it wasn't until 1924 that Emperor Puyi got his eviction notice and left the Forbidden City for good. In 1925, the gates of the Forbidden City were thrown open for the first time to ordinary Chinese citizens. The emperors' palace was thus transformed into the central showcase of China's new National Palace Museum.

Unfortunately, the museum only had a life span of about eight years. In September 1931 the Japanese occupied the potentially wealthy but underdeveloped area of Manchuria, setting up a puppet state with the last Chinese emperor, Puyi, as the symbolic head. Relations between China and Japan continued to go downhill, and in 1933 the KMT realised that war was increasingly likely. The possibility of having the entire collection of the National Palace Museum fall into Japanese hands was something the Chinese couldn't swallow, so the goods were packed up and hauled by train to Nanjing for safe-keeping. A month later they were transferred to a warehouse in Shanghai. In 1937, the collection was transferred back to Nanjing, just in time for the Japanese invasion of Beijing and Shanghai. These were the opening shots of China's entry into WW II.

Some 7000 crates of the collection were shipped by rail southwards to Changhsa, then to Guiyang and finally to the KMT's wartime capital of Chengdu. Even then, the crates were not safe – Japanese bombers pounded Chengdu frequently. The crates were moved to the remote village of Emei in 1939. Another 10,000 crates were spirited out of Nanjing on a boat just as the Japanese attacked that city. The boat remained moored in the Yangzi River near Chongqing until the war ended.

Despite all the bombings and land battles, virtually the entire collection survived intact. In 1947, everything was moved back to the KMT's capital of Nanjing and a public exhibition was held in December. If congratulations were in order, it wasn't for long. By January, 1949, the communists had all but defeated the KMT's army in the north and were driving south. Thousands of crates were shipped out to the Taiwanese port of Keelung. About 700 crates had to be left behind in Nanjing during the KMT's hasty withdrawal.

The KMT expected the retreat to Taiwan to be a temporary affair. Plans to retake the mainland were under way, and official policy was that the invasion would be launched within two years. Therefore, no plans were made to establish a museum in Taiwan and the national treasures were simply warehoused. However, as two years stretched to five, then a decade, some began to suggest displaying the artefacts to the public was wiser than leaving everything in crates. In 1965, the 'temporary' National Palace Museum opened its doors in Taipei. Miraculously, in the 32 years that the collection was shuttled from Beijing's National Palace Museum to Taipei's, not a single piece was broken.

Although physical fighting between the mainland and Taiwan had ceased, the war of words continued. The Communists harshly criticised the KMT for 'stealing' this priceless collection of Chinese treasures and demanded that it be returned. The KMT had an easy answer to that – it's doubtful that much would have survived China's Cultural Revolution of the 1960s, when rampaging Red Guards swept through the country destroying temples, antiques and all other reminders of China's 'bourgeois past'. The Communists had virtually extinguished China's cultural heritage, and the KMT felt justified in claiming the moral high ground. Thus, the artefacts remain in Taipei. The National Palace Museum that one sees today in Beijing also has art treasures, but many are re-creations or were gathered from other parts of China after the Cultural Revolution. ■

cally, it's a movie set where the buildings are all designed in the traditional style of ancient China. If you watch TV in Taiwan, you are sure to see some Chinese kungfu dramas – this is where they are filmed. The buildings are a good introduction to Chinese architecture and you may also have the chance to see some filming.

The movie set is open to the public daily from 8.30 am to 5.30 pm, but is closed during lunch hour (noon to 1 pm). There is an entrance fee of NT$80. There is also a wax museum – entrance fee NT$50 – which contains some realistic figures from Chinese history.

Overall, the Movie Studio doesn't have much to see unless you're fortunate to catch them filming a movie. Sensitive to the fact that many visitors give the place the thumbs down, the management has recently decided to add a new attraction – an 'ancient Chinese night market' *(zhōngguó gǔchéng yèshì)*. It wasn't yet functioning at the time of this writing, but should be by the time you read this. Unlike other night markets in Taipei, this one will exclude motorcycles and the vendors will dress in traditional Chinese clothes. Fortune tellers, story tellers, opera performances and kungfu exhibitions will add to the ancient Chinese atmosphere. Furthermore, everything you buy in the night market has to be paid for in 'ancient Chinese money' printed just for this purpose.

Since it wasn't yet in operation, I can't say much good or bad about the night market. If done well, it could prove interesting. The night market will operate daily from 6.30 pm to 11 pm, but presumably will reach its zenith of activity on warm summer weekends when the weather cooperates. Two types of admission tickets will be sold. The NT$350 ticket includes NT$150 worth of food plus NT$200 of 'ancient money'. For those with a ravenous appetite, there will be an NT$600 ticket which includes NT$400 of food and NT$200 of traditional cash.

Walk west for 10 minutes from the National Palace Museum and you'll find the Movie Studio on your left-hand side. The official address is 34 Chihshan Rd, Section 2, Shihlin, and a big sign in Chinese (no English) marks the spot. Right next to the Movie Studio is Soochow University *(dōngwú dàxué)*, but there isn't anything much to see there either.

Martyrs' Shrine
(zhōng liè cí) 忠烈祠

The Martyrs' Shrine is a fairly peaceful place with colourful buildings set against a backdrop of hills. It was built to honour those who died in various wars fighting for the ROC. There are two rifle-toting military police who stand guard at the gate in formal dress – absolutely rigid, not moving a muscle or blinking an eye – while tourists harass them. It's a wonder these guys don't run amok and bayonet a few of their camera-clicking tormentors.

The changing of the guards is quite a spectacle – too bad you can't ask the guards just what time this occurs. It seems to be about once every two hours and the whole elaborate ceremony takes about 15 minutes. You can march with the guards if you wish – at least some tourists do this, and none (so far) have been shot.

The Martyrs' Shrine is less than a 10-minute walk east along Peian Rd from the Grand Hotel. You can get there on bus No 213, 247, 267 or 287.

Lin Antai Old Homestead
(lín āntài gǔcuò jiǎnjiè) 林安泰古厝簡介

This fully-restored traditional Taiwanese homestead is remarkable for simply having survived amidst Taipei's urban building boom. Until recently, there were many such houses in Taiwan. While quite a few such buildings still exist in remote mountain areas, they are not easily accessible and many are in poor condition. Without preservation efforts, this style of architecture seems certain to disappear.

There are some temples which pre-date it, but the Lin Antai Homestead is the oldest residential building in Taipei. The original dwelling was built in 1783, and was gradually expanded over the generations as the family's size grew. It reached its present size in 1823. It was built with the principles of Chinese geomancy in mind – the entrance, for example, had to face south-west. Most of the building materials were imported from mainland China's Fujian province.

The structure was not always located at its present site. Originally, it was built in Taipei's Ta'an District several km to the south. It would have been demolished in 1978 when Tunhua S Rd was being widened, but officials were persuaded to preserve it. The preservation proved to be more difficult than anyone had imagined – the whole building had to be dismantled brick by brick in the reverse order of construction. The roof came down first, followed by the walls, floors and foundation. Every piece had to be numbered, blueprints had to be made, and everything had to be packed away and stored.

In 1984, it was decided to reconstruct the building in Pinchiang Park (bīnjiāng gōngyuán) in the Chungshan District, just east of Hsinsheng N Rd and north of Mintsu E Rd. The only unfortunate thing about this location is that it's right in the landing path of Sungshan Airport – aircraft come in so low it's a wonder they don't knock the roof ornaments off.

Buses which can take you to the homestead include Nos 33, 222, 279, 283 and 286. Bus No 222 is probably most convenient – you can catch it on Chungshan S Rd. If you're feeling energetic, you could walk from the Fine Arts Museum. Admission to the homestead is free.

Fine Arts Museum
(měi shù guǎn) 美術館

Exhibits at this museum are rotated every few months, and there are many works by foreign artists. Exhibits have included everything from Australian aboriginal art to rare artefacts by the now-extinct Mayan civilisation of Mexico. The museum's gift shop sells works by local artists, often reasonably priced – NT$1500 to NT$3000 is typical. The gift shop also sells calligraphy brushes, ink stones, ceramic tea cups and various unidentifiable objects made from metal scraps welded together.

The big problem with this museum is that virtually all explanations are in Chinese. Even the foreign exhibits are explained in Chinese only, and ditto for most of the books in the gift shop.

Photography is prohibited inside the museum, though the sign advising you of this is also written in Chinese only. There is a room where you can check your belongings, though this isn't required if you keep your camera out of sight. The security guards are under instructions to confiscate your film if you violate the ban on photography.

The Fine Arts Museum (☎ 5957656) is at 181 Chungshan N Rd, Section 3, just south of the Grand Hotel. It's open from 10 am to 6 pm daily, except Monday. Bus Nos 21, 40, 42, 47, 203, 208, 213, 216, 217, 218, 220, 224, 260, 269, 277, 287 and 308 pass by. Admission is NT$10.

Children's Recreation Centre
(értóng yùlè zhōngxīn) 兒童育樂中心

As the name implies, the Children's Recreation Centre is for kids. It's basically a park divided into two sections, the World of Yesterday and World of Tomorrow. The World of Yesterday has an ancient Chinese village, statues depicting the life of Taiwan's aborigines plus a kiddie entertainment area. The World of Tomorrow reminds me of an old TV show called 'Mr Wizard', in which general science was introduced. This place is built on what was the former Taipei Zoo – an opposition legislator once suggested that the National Assembly should be moved here.

The Children's Recreation Centre is opposite the Fine Arts Museum, so the bus transport is the same. Admission costs NT$20 for adults, NT$10 for children. The Space Theatre costs NT$100 for adults and NT$70 for children, and you must purchase the tickets before entering the main entrance to the compound.

Confucius Temple
(kǒngzǐ miào) 孔子廟

In sharp contrast to the Lungshan and Paoan temples, the Confucius Temple is a sedate place. There are no statues or deities and the

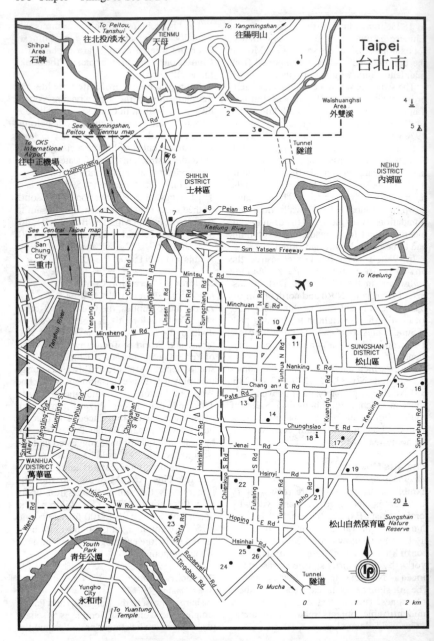

1 National Palace Museum
故宮博物館

2 Movie Studio
電影文化城

3 Soochow University
東吳大學

4 Pishan Temple
碧山寺/碧山巖開漳聖廟

5 Pishan Camping Ground
碧山露營場

6 Shihlin Night Market
士林夜市

7 Grand Hotel
圓山大飯店

8 Martyrs' Shrine
忠烈祠

9 Sungshan Domestic Airport
松山機場

10 American Express
美國運通銀行

11 Citibank
花旗銀行

12 Taipei Railway Station
台北車站

13 Chunglun Bus Station
中崙站

14 Dinghao Market
頂好市場

15 Jaoho Night Market
饒河街夜市

16 Sungshan Railway Station
松山火車站

17 Sun Yatsen Memorial
國父紀念館

18 Tourism Bureau
觀光局

19 World Trade Centre
世貿中心

20 Sheng'en Temple
聖恩宮

21 Tunghua Night Market
通化街夜市

22 AIT
美國在台協會

23 Taiwan Normal University
師大

24 National Taiwan University
台大

25 Language Training Centre
財團法人語信訓練測驗中心

26 TIYAC
國際青年活動中心

only time it comes to life is on 28 September, the birthday of Confucius (Teacher's Day), when there is an interesting festival held at dawn. Check with some of the tourist offices or your hotel to see if you can get a ticket if you are in Taiwan at this time. The temple is on Talung St, near Chiuchuan St and the Paoan Temple.

Paoan Temple
(bǎo'ān gōng) 保安寺
The lovely old Taoist Paoan Temple is a short walk from the Confucius Temple. The address is 16 Hami St, not far from the Grand Hotel. It's best to hit it on a day when a worship festival is on (any lunar holiday). At such times this can be one of the most interesting temples in Taipei. Take bus Nos 0-North, 2, 24, 41, 246 or 288.

Hsingtien Temple
(xíngtiān gōng) 行天宮
This is another Taoist temple worth visiting. It's at 261 Minchuan E Rd, at the intersection with Sungchiang Rd (north-east corner).

New Park
(xīn gōngyuán) 新公園
Taipei's New Park is a good place to take refuge from the urban chaos. The pleasant tree-shaded grounds contain a lake, pagoda and pavilions. On the north side of the park is the Taiwan Provincial Museum (☎ 3613925) *(shěnglì bówùguǎn)* at 2 Hsiangyang Rd. There are interesting displays of artefacts made by Taiwan's aborigines. Of special interest is an excellent, well-organised display of herbs on the main floor. The museum is open from 9 am to 5 pm daily except Monday.

It's fairly important to know that the park takes on a totally different character at night. After dark, it's taken over by transvestites and becomes 'gay park'. Taipei's gays are very much on the defensive, and there have been serious fights when tourists have showed up at night with their cameras. Unless you want to be part of the gay scene yourself, I'd recommend avoiding New Park at night.

The park is within walking distance of the Taipei railway station. Heaps of buses stop near the park including 0-West, 0-South, 3, 15, 18, 20, 48, 57, 65, 222, 236, 240, 241, 243, 244, 245, 247, 249, 251, 259, 263, 276, 287, 291, 504 and 605.

Chiang Kaishek Memorial

(zhōngzhèng jì niàn táng) 中正紀念堂

The Chiang Kaishek Memorial Hall is a fantastic piece of architecture and is surrounded by a magnificent garden, making it a popular place in the morning for joggers and practitioners of taijiquan (Chinese shadow boxing). These days it is more common to see people practising jazz dancing to the thump of disco music in the morning. There is a museum downstairs, inside the memorial.

Within the grounds of the Chiang Kaishek Memorial is the National Chiang Kaishek Cultural Centre (☎ 3925060), which consists of two buildings: the National Theatre (☎ 3925091) *(guójiā jùyuàn)* and National Concert Hall *(guójiā yīnyuè tīng)* (☎ 3924954). A schedule of events is published monthly and is available from the Tourism Bureau.

The Chiang Kaishek Memorial is on Hsinyi Rd, Section 1. The main hall is open from 9 am until 5 pm. Buses which pass nearby are Nos 0-East, 18, 20, 22, 70, 204, 209, 236, 237, 248, 249, 251, 252, 291, 294, 275 and Hsinyi Rd Line.

Chang Foundation Museum

(hóngxǐ měishùguǎn) 鴻禧美術館

The Chang Museum (☎ 3569575) is unusual in that it's privately owned. The emphasis is on ancient Chinese art with a rich assortment of ceramics dating back over 2000 years. While this collection can't compete with the National Palace Museum, it's worthwhile if you're an enthusiast. While some people object to private art collections, the Chang family deserves some credit for putting theirs on display to the public.

The museum is in the basement at 63 Jenai Rd, Section 2, between Hsingsheng S Rd and Chinshan S Rd. From the east entrance of the

Taipei Railway Station, you can catch bus No 36 or 37 to the museum. Other buses which pass close by include Nos 214, 254, 261, 263, 270, 280 and 311, or Chihnan bus Nos 1 and 5. Admission costs NT$100, and students are offered a 50% discount. Opening hours are from 10.30 am to 4.30 pm. The museum is closed on Monday and during the first two weeks of July.

Presidential Building

(zhǒngtǒng fǔ) 總統府

Very close to New Park is the Presidential Office Building. Normally, there is not much to see here, but on Double 10th Day (10 October or National Day) there are enormous rallies and military parades at this site. Should you be in Taipei at this time you may want to see these impressive parades. For several weeks after Double 10th, the area is lit up and presents an excellent opportunity for night photography.

Double Trouble

The military uses Double 10th Day to show off it's hardware, including rockets and tanks. Construction of the Taipei subway along Chunghsiao Rd created some problems a few years ago – the street was all dug up, turning it into one big ditch. Cars and buses had to drive on metal grates, and heavy trucks were prohibited. Since Taiwan's military planners realised tanks and rocket launchers would collapse the metal grates, a solution had to found if the parade was to go on as scheduled – rather than moving the parade route, the subway was filled in with dirt. After the festivities, it had to be dug up again. ■

One of the world's most dazzling displays of fireworks is held on the night of Double 10th over an island in the middle of the Tanshui River. You can watch the fireworks from Huanho S Rd near the Chunghsing Bridge. The fireworks start around 7.30 pm, but be there earlier to secure a good viewing place. The fireworks run for one hour.

Buses that go here include Nos 0-East,

0-West, 0-South, 3, 5, 18, 38, 204, 209, 227, 235, 236, 241, 244, 251, 270 and 604.

Botanical Gardens

(zhíwù yuán) 植物園

The Botanical Gardens, on Nanhai Rd, south of the central area, are a pleasant retreat from the noisy city. There is a beautiful lotus pond in the gardens; it's one of the ponds adjacent to the National Museum of History *(lìshǐ bówù guǎn)*, National Science Hall *(kēxué guǎn)* and National Arts Hall – all worth looking into.

Travellers give the National Museum of History high marks. It's sort of a scaled-down version of the National Palace Museum. It has a good pottery collection and is open daily from 9 am to 5 pm, NT$10 admission. You can get there on bus No 1, 204, 242 or 259.

Postal Museum

(yóuzhèng bówùguǎn) 郵政博物館

For stamp enthusiasts, the Postal Museum (☎ 3945185) is at 45 Chungking S Rd, Section 2. It's open daily except Monday.

For stamp collectors, the real action takes place not inside in the museum, but right in front of it. On weekends, private collectors and vendors stake out the front of the museum and form their own impromptu stamp market. If this isn't enough, there are seven stamp shops within two blocks of the Postal Museum.

Lungshan Temple

(lóngshān sì) 龍山寺

This is a superb example of a temple dedicated to Kuanyin, the goddess of Mercy.

Lungshan (Dragon Mountain) Temple was originally built in 1738 in a district that was then known as Mengchia (now renamed Wanhua). In 1815 an earthquake leveled Mengchia, including the temple, but the Kuanyin statue survived and a new temple was reconstructed. The temple was wrecked again by a typhoon in 1867 but was restored. In 1945, US bombers hit the temple when conducting a raid against Japanese troops.

The temple was rebuilt yet again, and remains one of the most popular in Taipei. It's extremely colourful and is packed with worshippers most of the time; the air is heavy with smoke from burning incense and 'ghost money'. Adjacent to the temple is an active market, and two blocks away is the touristy Snake Alley.

Lungshan Temple is at 211 Kuangchou St and is open from 5 am to 10 pm. You can get there on bus No 0-West, 25, 38, 49, 65, 231, 242, 264, 265, 310 or 601.

Snake Alley

(huáxī jiē) 華西街

Until it was discovered by tourists, Snake Alley was a truly fascinating place. I suppose it's still fascinating, but it's taken on a bit of a carnival atmosphere. The presence of busloads of Japanese tourists has also driven up the cost of snake products to Japanese nightclub levels.

What you get to see are skilled snake handlers playing with real live cobras as though they were wind-up toys. For a fee, you can sample snake soup or drink a cup of snake bile – not for the squeamish. This is also the place to stock up on snake-penis pills and powdered gall bladder. Because Chinese herbalists claim that snake meat acts as an aphrodisiac, Snake Alley has long been known for brothels. The brothels are not in Snake Alley itself, but in some adjacent side streets. The thug-like pimps used to not bother the tourists, but lately have become more aggressive. There have been problems with pimps grabbing male tourists by the arm and trying to pull them into a brothel; the tourists get mad and hit the pimp, the pimp retaliates and the end result means a trip to the hospital for one or more persons.

Even if you're not in the market for snake's gall bladder, Snake Alley is a decent night market. A particularly good buy are the cheap music cassettes, but it's mostly Chinese music. The market gets going around 7 pm and closes sometime after midnight. You can get there on bus No 0-West, 25, 38, 49, 65, 231, 242, 264, 265, 310 or 601.

Sun Yatsen Memorial
(guófù jì niàn guǎn) 國父紀念館

The Sun Yatsen Memorial is an interesting place for history buffs, as it is stocked with many photographs of mainland China taken during the early part of the 20th century. Dr Sun Yatsen is an important figure in China's history. He is highly regarded as a national hero and the father of his country for the key role he played in the 1911 revolution, which created the Republic of China. He is revered by both the Kuomintang and the Communist Party for his role in overthrowing China's last dynasty.

The Sun Yatsen Memorial contains an auditorium which is used for staging cultural events. The memorial is on Jenai Rd, Section 4, near the Tourism Bureau.

Buses which stop close to the Sun Yatsen Memorial are Nos 31, 70, 212, 232, 240, 254, 259, 263, 266, 270, 281, 282, 288, 299, 504 and Jenai Rd Line.

World Trade Centre
(shì mào zhōngxīn) 世貿中心

This huge exhibition complex is home to the product display shows of the China Export Trade Development Council (CETRA). The centre hosts several large trade shows every year and some are definitely worth seeing. The shows are not just for looking – you can often buy 'samples' directly from the manufacturer for bargain prices. Even if you don't buy, the shows can be a lot of fun. Some good ones to look for include the Sporting Goods Show (April), the Cycle Show (bikes and accessories – April), the Footwear & Leather Goods Show (May), Computex (computer show – June), the Jewellery & Timepiece Show (September), the Toy Show (September) and the Electronics Show (October). You can get a complete schedule of the shows from the Tourism Bureau or from CETRA (in the World Trade Centre). You may want to call to see what's on (☎ 7251111). It's worth noting that the Sungshan Airport Exhibition Centre *(sōngshān jīchǎng wàimào zhǎnlǎn guǎn)* often has better shows than the World Trade Centre.

The World Trade Centre has also played a role in politics. The Kuomintang held its 14th National Party Conference here, an event which set a new benchmark for intra-party squabbling. Frequent fistfights broke out during the debate over selecting a vice-chairperson for the KMT. However, it was military-branch representative Wang Kunsheng who stole the show; he was sent to the hospital with concussion after one of his colleagues broke a cellular telephone over his head.

Normally, it's not that exciting, but you may want to visit the World Trade Centre anyway. It's at 5 Hsinyi Rd, Section 5, in east Taipei near the Sun Yatsen Memorial. Operating hours are Monday to Friday from 8 am to 5.30 pm, and from 8.30 am to noon on Saturday. Children under 15 are not admitted.

Buses which stop in front of the World Trade Centre include Nos 1, 22, 37, 38, 207, 226, 258, 266, 284, 288, Hsinyi Rd Line and Jenai Rd Line.

Youth Park
(qīngnián gōngyuán) 青年公園

Youth Park is the largest park in the city. It's not special, but its facilities include swimming pools, tennis courts and a roller-skating rink. This park is in the south-west part of the city along the Tanshui River. Buses that go there include Nos 0-West, 12, 24, 30, 31, 223, 249, 250 and 253.

National Taiwan University
(táidà) 台大

National Taiwan University is Taiwan's largest and reputedly best institution of higher learning. The campus serves as an official park, and you can stroll, visit the bookshop and use the library. If you want to meet Chinese students, you will find that most of them are friendly and are anxious to practise their English.

National Taiwan University is in the Kungkuan neighbourhood. Buses that stop near the campus include Nos 0-South, 10, 30, 52, 60, 236, 251, 252, 253, 311 and 501.

Sungshan Nature Reserve

(sōngshān zìrán bǎoyù qū) 松山自然保育區
If you gaze to the south-east from the steps
of the World Trade Centre, you can see some
moderate-sized hills in the distance. While
this may not look like much from far away,
it's one of the loveliest spots in Taipei. The
Sungshan Nature Reserve is a huge, mountainous park laced with hiking trails. The
reserve is heavily forested and dotted with
temples.

Within the reserve are 'four animal
mountains' *(sì shòu shān)*, so called because
someone with a wide stretch of the imagination reckons that's what the peaks look like
from a distance. Two of the mountains have
adopted other non-animal names.

Elephant Mountain *(xiàngshān)* is the
smallest of the four mountains (strange that
an elephant should be smallest). Climbing
this easy peak is a good way to warm up the
muscles for the other more-strenuous hikes.
Along the hiking path are various exercise
machines – parallel bars, chin-up bars, sit-up
ramps and the like.

The next-highest peak is Governess
Finger Mountain *(mǔzhǐshān)* – not exactly
an animal, but so-named because it resembles a finger.

Tiger's Head Mountain *(hǔtóu shān)* is the
second-highest peak. The elevation at the
summit is 325 metres. Nine-Five Peak
(jiǔwǔfēng) is not named for Taipei's
working hours, but instead refers to a feat
accomplished by a gentleman named Yu Hui
who climbed the peak aged 95, auspiciously
on the fifth day of the ninth month in 1915.
This is the highest peak of the lot and the
summit is decorated with some fancy calligraphy commemorating Yu Hui's
accomplishment.

The nature reserve is spread out and there
are many approaches for entering it. Probably the easiest way to find it is to take a train
to the Sungshan railway station (in east
Taipei). This station is one stop past the
Taipei main railway station, going towards
Keelung. From Sungshan station, you need
to head south for one km along Sungshan Rd
to where it intersects with Hsinyi Rd, Section

6. You can walk, or take one of several buses
(Nos 279, 286 and many others) which run
south on Sungshan Rd. South of Hsinyi Rd,
Sungshan Rd changes from busy urban street
to winding mountain road, eventually termi-
nating at magnificent Sheng'en Temple
(shèng'ēn gōng). From the temple, you can
easily find numerous hiking trails heading up
into the hills.

Pishan Temple

(bì shān sì) 碧山寺/碧山巖開漳聖廟
Pishan (Green Mountain) Temple, also
known by a more formal name *(bì shān yán
kāi zhāng shèng miào)*, is one of the finest
sights in Taipei. Perched on the side of a
mountain with a breathtaking view of Taipei,
the temple gets surprisingly few visitors, at
least on weekdays. The scenery is great and
the area is laced with hiking trails. You can
stay overnight in the temple for a NT$500
'donation' but food costs extra.

Nearby is the Pishan Camping Ground *(bì
shān lùyíng chǎng)*. Even if you're not particularly interested in temples, coming up
here is a great way to escape the chaos of
Taipei.

The Pishan Temple is in the Neihu district
in north-east Taipei. The temple is on a long
loop road through the mountains, and buses
stop at both ends of the loop; one end is far
from the temple and one is near, so be sure
to get off at the correct end. It's best to take
a bus to the Golden Dragon Temple *(jīnlóng
sì)*, which is also on the loop road near Pishan
Temple. While Golden Dragon Temple is
worth looking at, don't mistake it for your
final destination which is higher up the
mountain. Buses which can get you to the
Golden Dragon Temple include Nos 240,
247, 267 and 604. Probably most useful is
No 247, which runs from the Hilton Hotel
area (Taipei railway station) to Golden
Dragon Temple. From Golden Dragon
Temple, you must walk uphill along a paved
road. There are minibuses (No 2) on the loop
road which go all the way to Pishan Temple.
A taxi from Neihu to Pishan Temple would
cost around NT$130.

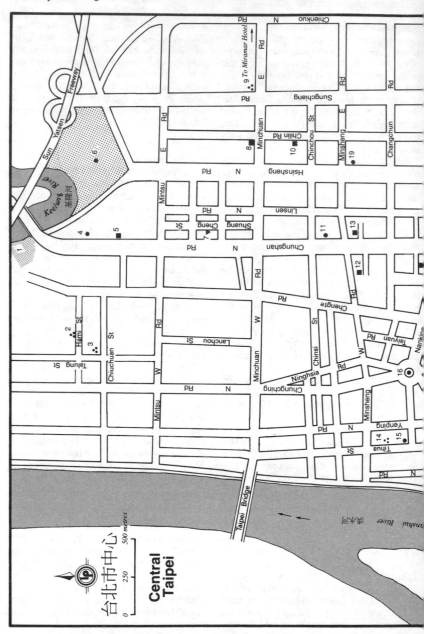

1 Children's Recreation Centre
兒童育樂中心

2 Pao'an Temple
保安寺

3 Confucius Temple
孔子廟

4 Fine Arts Museum
美術館

5 Rainbow Guest House
彩虹招待所

6 Lin Antai Old Homestead
林安泰古厝簡介

7 Pubs
啤酒屋

8 Ritz Hotel
亞都大飯店

9 Hsingtien Temple
行天宮

10 Amigo Hostel
吉林路286號3/4樓

11 Caves Books
敦煌書局

12 Formosa Hostel II
中山北路二段62巷5號2樓

13 Happy Family Hostel IV
中山北路二段77巷12-5號5樓

14 Chenghuang Temple
城隍廟

15 Tihua St Night Market
迪化街夜市

16 Food Circle
圓環

17 Formosa Hostel I
中山北路二段20巷16號3樓

18 ICBC
中國國際商業銀行

19 Taipei Labourer's Recreation Centre
新生北路二段101巷2號

20 Hotel 6F
銀寶賓館

21 Queen Hotel
皇后賓館

22 Senator Hotel
信州大飯店

23 Tonglien Bus Company
統聯客運

24 North Gate
北門

25 Buses to Tanshui
往淡水公車站

26 West Bus Station
台汽西站

27 East Bus Station
台汽東站

28 North Bus Station
台汽北站

29 Taipei Railway Station
台北車站

30 Happy Family Hostel II
中山北路一段56巷2號2/3樓

31 Happy Family Hostel I
北平西路16-1號4樓

32 Provincial Police (mountain permits)
警政署

33 Taipei Hostel
林森北路5段11號6樓

34 Kuanghua Computer Market
光華商場

35 Lai Lai Sheraton Hotel
來來大飯店

36 Buses to Wulai
往烏來公車站

37 Chinese Handicraft Centre
中華工藝館

38 Taiwan University Hospital
台大醫院

39 Taiwan Provincial Museum
台灣省博物館

40 YMCA
基督教青年會

41 Paradise Hotel
南國大飯店

42 Yon Hong & Chuan Chia Huam Hotels
懷寧街10號

43 New Mayflower Hotel
華美大飯店

44 GPO
郵政總局

45 Buses to Sanhsia
往三峽公車站

46 Foreign Affairs Police (Visa Extensions)
警察局外事課

47 Tower Records
淘兒唱片行

48 Bank of Taiwan
台灣銀行

49 Presidential Building
總統府

50 Foreign Affairs Ministry
外交部

Nankang Tea Park

(nángǎng guānguāng cháyuán) 南港觀光茶園
Similar to Mucha Tea Park, the tea park in the Nankang District is less developed but still very interesting. There are a number of hiking trails here winding through the forested hillsides, plus the area is dotted with small temples.

Bus No 6, operated by the Chihnan Bus Company, follows a scenic route from the Mucha Zoo to Golden Dragon Temple in Neihu, via the Nankang Tea Park.

Taipei-Mucha Zoo

(mùzhà dòngwù yuán) 木柵動物園
The zoo (☎ 9382300) is in the south-east section of Taipei. This area is officially called the Wenshan District, but it was formerly Mucha (Wooden Fence) and that's the name still usually applied to the zoo. It's Taiwan's best zoo by far, but isn't large by world standards. Limited space also limits the ability to create a very natural environment for the animals. For that you have to go to the Leofoo Safari Park. Bus Nos 236, 237, 258, 282, 294 and 295 go there. If the MRT ever gets finished, the brown line will terminate at the zoo. Opening hours are 8.30 am to 4.30 pm daily, and admission costs NT$40.

Chihnan Temple

(zhǐnán gōng) 指南宮
One of the largest temples in north Taiwan, the Chihnan Temple is 19 km south-east of the Taipei Railway Station in the Wenshan District. The temple is over 100 years old. Perched on a mountainside, there are outstanding views of Taipei when the weather is clear. When the weather isn't clear, it's even better – who wants to see Taipei anyway?

There are several approaches for getting there. You can take bus No 236 or 237 to Chengchih University in the Wenshan District, then walk uphill to the temple. Alternatively, you can get there from the city centre by taking a bus operated by the Chihnan (CN) Bus Company *(zhǐnán kèyùn)*. CN bus No 1 runs along Nanking E Rd, then Sungchiang Rd, Hsinsheng S Rd, Roosevelt Rd and on out to Mucha, ending at the Chihnan Temple. CN bus No 2 runs down Chunghua Rd, Aikuo Rd, Roosevelt Rd and finally terminates in the Wenshan District. Be sure to tell the driver your destination – some of the buses take a different route and terminate at the Mucha Zoo rather than the temple.

No matter which bus you take, from where the bus drops you off you cannot see the temple. Follow the steep steps up and up until you reach a small Taoist temple. The main temple is to your right; to the left are some picnic grounds – a good place to relax, except on weekends when it's crowded.

Kuantu Temple

(guāndù gōng) 關渡宮
The impressive Kuantu Temple is on the main road between Peitou and the suburb of Tanshui. The outside may not look like much, but the most striking feature is the 100-metre-plus tunnel carved through the mountainside displaying statues of various gods and demons. You can reach the Kuantu Temple on bus Nos 223 and 302.

Mucha Tea Park

(mùzhà guānguāng cháyuán) 木柵觀光茶園
This hilly park is a good area for walking. As the name implies, it's also known for tea

plantations and teahouses. At the present time, there are over 60 teahouses here, and the number keeps increasing. The teahouses serve not only tea, but also local specialities like 'tea gelatin' and chicken baked in tea leaves. There are several small temples in the park.

The tea park is in the Wenshan District, the very southernmost part of Taipei city. Minibus Nos 10 and 11 go to the park from Chengchih University – these buses only run about once every 30 minutes and do not run late in the evening. To reach the Chengchih University, you can take bus No 236 or 237.

Pitan
(bìtán) 碧潭

South of Taipei is Pitan (Green Lake), which is basically just a park on the edge of the city. The lake features rowing boats and swimming. Local daredevils impress their friends by diving off the 12-metre cliffs into the lake – there is a sign in Chinese saying that cliff-diving is prohibited.

The lake is adjacent to the town of Hsintien *(xīndiàn)*, which can be reached easily from Taipei. I don't recommend going out of your way just to visit this place, but if you are on your way to Wulai you can take in Pitan along the way.

Buses operated by the Hsintien Bus Company *(xīndiàn kèyùn)* depart every 10 minutes or so from Chingtao E Rd, one block east of Chungshan S Rd and one block south of Chunghsiao Rd.

Even more frequent are the unnumbered buses operated by the Hsintien Bus Company. These are marked (in Chinese, of course) 'Hsintien-Tanshui'. You can catch these along Chungshan Rd and Roosevelt Rd.

Yangmingshan
(yángmíngshān) 陽明山

Perhaps the most scenic place within the Taipei city limits, Yangmingshan park dominates the northern end of town. Yangmingshan is noted for its beautiful flowers, especially in spring (February to April) when the cherry blossoms are in bloom. The cherry trees are in Chungshan Park, which is part of the Yangmingshan National Park area.

Many wealthy Taiwanese and Westerners live on the lower slopes of Yangmingshan, preferring life in the cooler mountains above the smog to living down in the city. Real-estate developers have recently moved into the lower slopes and have erected some ultra-expensive US-style housing projects with names like 'Taipei California'. Fortunately, most of the mountain is protected by a national park and no further construction is allowed.

The park itself offers many opportunities for hiking and provides a welcome relief from Taipei's bustle. The only bad thing one can say about this place is that on Sundays it tends to be packed out with hordes of people trying to get away from it all, especially during the blossom season. Also, on rare occasions the higher slopes of Yangmingshan get dusted by snow. If this occurs on a weekend, you'll be able to witness the greatest pilgrimage of Chinese people since the Long March.

There is a restaurant in the park and also a large, impressive Chinese-style building called the **Chungshan Building** (zhōngshān lóu), the site of high-level Kuomintang meetings. You can admire the building from the outside, but getting inside requires connections.

Yangmingshan has hot-spring resorts similar to nearby Peitou. One of the roads that connects Yangmingshan to Peitou is called Shamaoshan Hudi Rd – this passes through the **Chiku Hot Springs** area *(qīkū wēnquán)*, which is lined with resorts. At No 7-1 Shamaoshan Hudi Rd is Huangtien Restaurant (☎ 8611135, 8616339) *(huángtián cānfíng)*, an excellent hot spring and restaurant complex. Bus No 230 (running from Peitou to Yangmingshan) passes by. The cost for using the hot springs here is NT$50. It's open late into the evening but don't go near the place on weekends. Further up the slopes of Yangmingshan is the **Matsao Hot Springs** area *(mǎcáo wēnquán)*, where there are yet more bathing resorts.

One of the more interesting thermal areas is **Sulphur Valley** *(liúhuáng gǔ)*. It's not for bathing, but a totally undeveloped spring with an eerie appearance. One traveller wrote 'it's one of the weirdest things this boy has ever seen'.

If you would like a moderately difficult hike, climb **Seven Star Mountain** *(qīxīngshān)*. At an elevation of 1120 metres, it's the highest peak within Taipei's city limits. From the summit, you can look down one side of the mountain and see Taipei – in the opposite direction the ocean is visible. Weather up here can be unpredictable – no matter how sunny and warm it is in the city, be prepared for rain, wind and cold.

Staying in Yangmingshan may not be as convenient as central Taipei, but offers something Taipei doesn't have – breathable air. Accommodation is not very expensive compared with Taipei, but then Taipei isn't cheap either. There are no dormitories for budget travellers; however, there are organised camping areas like the Chingshan Camping Ground *(jīngshān yíngdì)*, or you can camp out in the park for free and not see another soul.

The up-market *Hotel China, Yang-mingshan* (☎ 8616661, fax 8613885) *(yáng-míngshān zhōngguó dà fàndiàn)* at 237 Kochih Rd, Yangmingshan, has doubles and twins for NT$3000; facilities include a swimming pool and hot spring.

From Taipei you can get to Yangmingshan on bus No 301 or 260, which run along Chungshan N Rd. Minibus No 9 also goes to the park. From Peitou you can catch bus No 230. Stay on the bus to the very last stop at the top of the mountain. It's about a 10-minute walk to the park entrance – follow the footpath behind the bus terminal.

The most interesting way of all to see Yangmingshan is by bicycle or motorcycle, assuming you can beg, borrow or buy one. This is the only way you can really get into the backwaters, although reaching the high peaks requires walking. Equip yourself with a good Taipei city map, and also the free Yangmingshan map available from the Taiwan Tourism Bureau, and start exploring.

Peitou
(běitóu) 北投

A hot-spring resort area 13 km north-west of central Taipei, Peitou was at one time known as a red-light district. Nowadays, Peitou has been 'cleaned up' – the prostitutes are still there but maintain a very low profile so as not to tarnish the community's family image. Mostly they serve upper-class clientele including wealthy Taiwanese and visiting Japanese businessmen.

Peitou still has many nice inns and spas; they're a legacy of the Japanese occupation when Peitou was one of Taiwan's three big luxury hot-spring resorts. The other two were Kuantzuling and Szechunghsi, both of which have deteriorated markedly in recent years. However, all the hotels in Peitou tend to be up-market.

Peitou may have lost some of its former glory, but it still retains a certain charm. Wellington Heights is one of Peitou's affluent neighbourhoods which has a large number of well-to-do foreign residents. Even for the less well-to-do, there are a couple of unusual sights in the area which cost little or nothing to visit.

One of these is **Hell Valley** *(dìyù gǔ)*, an enormous spring with scalding hot water. This is no place to go bathing, but it certainly is interesting. The locals seem to get a kick out of boiling eggs here. It's to the north-east of Peitou Park, off Chungshan Rd.

Another place worth a visit if you are in the area is **Chaoming Temple** *(chǎomíng sì)*. Known at one time as the Lovers' Temple *(qíngrén miào)*, romantic couples flocked to the place to swear their undying love to each other. Then the building was sold to another Taoist order with no sense of humour, and it was renamed the Chaoming (Bright Tomorrow) Temple. The architecture is still exotic and the place is worth a look, but the romance is gone. You can reach Chaoming Temple on bus No 223, 224, 277 or 601.

Also in Peitou is the **Taiwan Folk Arts Museum** (☎ 8912318, 8931787) *(běitóu wénwù guǎn),* at 32 Yuya Rd, dedicated to traditional Taiwanese culture. Check out the teahouse and Mongolian barbecue restaurant

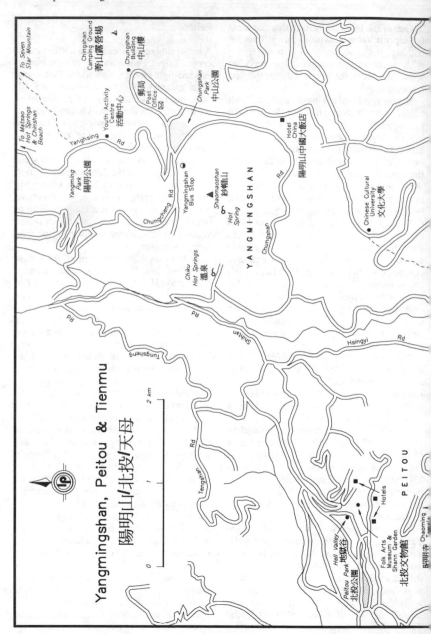

Yangmingshan, Peitou & Tienmu
陽明山/北投/天母

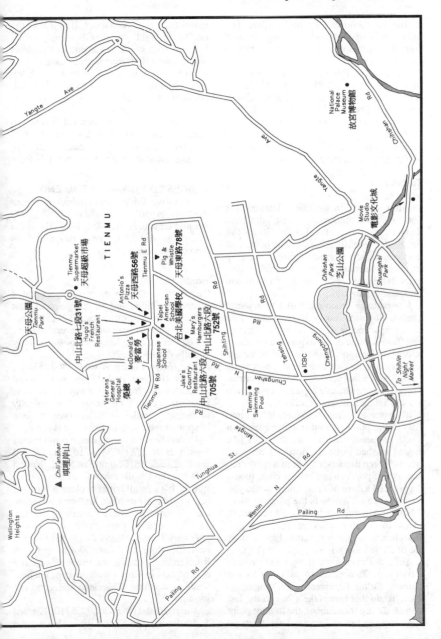

in the neighbouring Shann Garden. The museum is open Monday through Friday from 10 am to 8 pm, and on Sunday from 9 am to 10 pm.

From central Taipei, you can reach Peitou on bus No 216, 217, 218, 219, 223, 302 or 308. Whenever they finish the new subway line you will be able to use it to get to Peitou, but don't hold your breath for it.

From Yangmingshan, you can reach Peitou by bus No 230, which leaves from the bus terminal near the park.

Tienmu
(tiānmǔ) 天母

Tienmu (usually misspelled 'Tienmou'), is not exactly a renowned tourist attraction. Rather, you might think of it as the foreigners' ghetto in the Shihlin district of northern Taipei. Actually, Chinese make up the overwhelming majority of the inhabitants, but there are also many Western and Japanese expatriates.

It used to be much more of a foreigners' ghetto, but now many have moved into luxury apartments in the Hsinyi District of east Taipei. Most of the expats are representatives of foreign companies but some are missionaries, technicians and teachers at the Taipei American School (TAS) in Tienmu. There is a considerable Japanese contingent too, including a Japanese school.

It's worth exploring the stores in Tienmu. This is the place to find imported Western foods, especially treats from the USA like instant mashed potatoes, artificial whipped cream, frozen dinners, cheese in a spray can, microwave popcorn and other plastic foods. If you need a dose of these things while you are in Taiwan, Tienmu is the place to shop. When buying imported foods it's prudent to check the expiry dates on the packages, though most of these products have a shelf life of 25 years or so.

As far as I'm concerned, the most pleasant activity in Tienmu is to hike up to the Chinese Cultural University in Yangmingshan. To do this hike, take a bus to the last stop on the big roundabout, the highest point you can go by bus in Tienmu. Two streets go

uphill from the roundabout. If you take the one to the right, you'll walk steeply uphill but will soon come to the end of the street where you'll find stone steps leading up into the forest. It's signposted as being a 1.8 km hike. Head up the steps. After a while you'll come to a fork, but both paths will lead you uphill to the university.

Buses going from central Taipei to Tienmu include Nos 220, 224, 267, 268, 601 and 603. All these buses lead to the big roundabout at the top of Chungshan N Rd.

PLACES TO STAY – BOTTOM END

In expensive Taipei, for definition purposes the 'bottom end' is anything under NT$1000 per night. From NT$1000 to NT$2500 is the mid-range. Anything above that qualifies as 'top end' accommodation.

Hostels

There are a number of privately operated hostels in Taipei, and all charge nearly the same price. For dormitories, it's NT$180 per night or NT$1050 per week. Several of these hostels even have single rooms for only slightly more.

The *Happy Family Hostel I* (☎ 3753443) is on the 4th floor, 16-1 Peiping W Rd, about a stone's throw from the railway station – the location couldn't be better. The friendly management makes an effort to keep it clean in spite of the constant flow of travellers.

Under the same management is the *Happy Family Hostel II* (☎ 5810716), 2nd & 3rd floors, 2 Lane 56, Chungshan N Rd, Section 1; it's a short walk away from the railway station. It's a small but very clean hostel and has a washing machine, kitchen and video-tape player – the owner lives on the premises. Call first because it's often full.

Happy Family Hostel IV (☎ 5633341) is on the 5th floor, 12-5 Lane 77, Chungshan N Rd, Section 2. This is one of the newest and best hostels in Taipei with air-con, kitchen, washing machine, TV, video and good hot showers.

Amigo Hostel (☎ 5420292, 5710612), 3rd & 4th floors, 286 Chilin Rd is also a good deal. It's clean, has air-con and a video-tape player. From the railway station take bus No 502 and get off at the corner of Minchuan E Rd and Chilin Rd, opposite the Ritz Hotel *(yǎdū dà fàndiàn)*. Bus No 49 also stops nearby.

Better yet, if you're coming from the airport (and you've phoned ahead to reserve a bed), take the airport bus going to Sungshan Airport *(not* the railway station) and get off at the stop for the Miramar Hotel *(měilìhuá dà fàndiàn)*.The Miramar is on the corner of Minchuan E Rd and Chienkuo N Rd, two blocks east of the hostel.

Another excellent clean and well-managed hostel is *Formosa Hostel II* (☎ 5116744). The hostel is on the 2nd floor, 5 Lane 62, Chungshan N Rd, Section 2.

The nearby *Formosa Hostel I* (☎ 5622035), 3rd floor, 16 Lane 20, Section 2, Chungshan N Rd, is under the same management but is slightly more tattered than the Formosa II. Nevertheless, it's a fine place to stay and the location off Chungshan N Rd is convenient. Facilities include a kitchen and washing machine.

The *Taipei Hostel* (☎ 3952950), 6th floor, 11 Lane 5, Linsen N Rd, features enormous dorms. Double rooms are available here for NT$400 per night or NT$2450 per week. The location is very central near the Lai Lai Sheraton Hotel. They have a very good notice board for travellers, a laundry service, a TV and kitchen.

Government Hostels

The government operates a number of youth hostels which are intended for students and rarely have room for a traveller. Foreigners are welcome, but most short-term visitors are tour groups of overseas Chinese. Students are permitted to reside on a long-term basis – if you enrol in classes at National Taiwan University or Taiwan Normal University, you might consider staying at one of these government hostels. The facilities are salubrious – spotlessly clean and equipped with telephones & TVs in each room, air-con and plenty of hot water.

Chientan Youth Activity Centre
  (jiàntán huódòng zhōngxīn), 16 Chungshan N Rd, Section 4 (☎ 5962151, fax 5951861); dormitory/doubles NT$200/800
Taipei International Youth Activity Centre (TIYAC)
  (guójì huódòng zhōngxīn), 30 Hsinhai Rd, Section 3 (☎ 3621770, fax 3634104); dormitory/doubles NT$200/800.
Taipei Labourers' Recreation Centre
  (láoyǒu zhījiā zhōngxīn), 2 Lane 101, Hsinsheng N Rd, Section 2 (☎ 5519300); dorms NT$200
Taipei Student Hostel
  (táiběi xuéyuàn), 133 Tunhua N Rd (☎ 7130900, fax 7133371); dormitories NT$200

Hotels

Huaining St *(huáiníng jiē)* is just south of the railway station and is a happy hunting ground for relatively cheap hotels. One of the best bargains on this street is the *Paradise Hotel* (☎ 3313311) *(nánguó dà fàndiàn)*, 7 Huaining St, where doubles cost NT$600 to NT$700. Just across the street is the *Yon Hong Hotel* (☎ 3611906) *(yǒngfēng bīnguǎn)*, 10 Huaining St, where doubles are NT$650. Also nearby is the plush-looking *Chuan Chia Huam Hotel* (☎ 3814755) *(quánjiā huān bīnguǎn)*, 4th floor, 6 Huaining St, where doubles cost NT$900.

One block to the west is Chungking S Rd, which has a few places worth checking out. The *New Mayflower Hotel* (☎ 3617581) *(huáměi dà fàndiàn)*, 1 Chungching S Rd, Section 1, has singles and doubles for NT$800. Chang'an W Rd, one block north of the railway station, is another place to look for cheap hotels. An excellent bargain is the *Queen Hotel* (☎ 5590489) *(huánghòu bīnguǎn)* on the 2nd floor at No 226. Doubles are NT$500 to NT$600. There's no English sign, so look for the street number.

Also in the vicinity is the *Senator Hotel* (☎ 5586511) *(xìnzhōu dà fàndiàn)*, 839 Chang'an W Rd, where doubles cost NT$830 to NT$930. The same management runs the *Hotel 6F* (☎ 5551130) *(yínbǎo bīnguǎn)*, on the 6th floor at 251 Chang'an W Rd; doubles are NT$830 to NT$930.

PLACES TO STAY – MIDDLE

Some of the better known hotels in this price category are listed here.

China Hotel
   (zhōngguó dà fàndiàn; 155 rooms), 14 Kuanchien Rd (☎ 3319521, fax 3812349); doubles and twins NT$2300 to NT$2500, suites NT$3400 to NT$3800

Cosmos
   (tiānchéng dà fàndiàn; 300 rooms), 43 Chunghsiao W Rd, Section 3 (☎ 3617856, fax 311 8921); doubles NT$1800 to NT$2400, twins NT$2200 to NT$2800, suites NT$4000 to NT$4500

Empress
   (dìhòu dà fàndiàn; 100 rooms), 14 Tehuei St (☎ 5913261, fax 5922922); doubles/twins NT$2400/3000, suites NT$5000

First
   (dìyī dà fàndiàn; 200 rooms), 63 Nanking E Rd, Section 2 (☎ 5418234, fax 5512277); doubles NT$2000 to NT$2400, twins NT$2600 to NT$2800, suites NT$4200 to NT$6000

Flowers
   (huáhuá dà fàndiàn; 200 rooms), 19 & 36 Hankou St, Section 1 (☎ 3123811, fax 3123800); doubles NT$1250 to NT$3000, twins NT$1500 to NT$3000, suites NT$3500 to NT$5000

Gala
   (qìngtài dà fàndiàn; 200 rooms), 186 Sungchiang Rd (☎ 5415511, fax 5313831); doubles NT$3000, twins NT$3200, suites NT$4800

Golden Star
   (jīnxīng dà fàndiàn), 9 Lane 72, Chungshan N Rd, Section 2 (☎ 5519266, fax 5431322); doubles NT$1100 to NT$1400, twins NT$1400 to NT$1600, suites NT$1800 to NT$2000

Keyman's
   (huáiníng lüdiàn), 1 Huaining St (☎ 3114811, fax 3115212); singles/doubles NT$1460/1540

Kilin
   (qílín dà fàndiàn; 300 rooms), 103 Kangting Rd (☎ 3149222, fax 3318133); doubles NT$1800, twins NT$2000 to NT$2200, suites NT$3200 to NT$4000

King
   (dìwáng dà fàndiàn; 100 rooms), 135 Ta'an Rd, Section 1 (☎ 7760760, fax 7115575); doubles NT$2600-2900, suites NT$3500

Kodak
   (kēdá dà fàndiàn; 60 rooms) (☎ 5422221, fax 5435507); doubles NT$1200 to NT$1550, twins NT$1750 to NT$2250

Leofoo
   (lìùfú kèzhàn; 237 rooms), 168 Changchun Rd (☎ 5073211, fax 5082070); doubles NT$2400, twins NT$2640, triples NT$3060, suites NT$4800

Mengcheng
   (méngchéng dà fàndiàn; 54 rooms), 14 Lane 56, Hsinsheng N Rd Section 3 (☎ 5943901, fax 5959276); doubles NT$1200-1890

Merlin Court
   (huámào dà fàndiàn), 15 Lane 83, Section 1, Chungshan N Rd (☎ 5210222, fax 5510521); doubles/twins NT$1800/2000

New Asia
   (xīnyǎ dà fàndiàn; 120 rooms), 139 Chungshan N Rd, Section 2 (☎ 5117181, fax 5224204); doubles/twins NT$2200/2400, suites NT$3600 to NT$4600

Orient
   (dōngfāng dà fàndiàn; 120 rooms), 85 Hankou St, Section 1 (☎ 3317211, fax 3813068); doubles/twins NT$1700/2000, suites NT$3200

Paradise
   (yīlèyuán dà fàndiàn; 256 rooms), 24 Hsining S Rd (☎ 3142122, fax 3147873); doubles/twins NT$1900/2200, suites NT$4000 to NT$15,000

Rainbow Guest House
   (cǎihóng zhāodàisuǒ), 91 Chungshan N Rd, Section 3 (☎ 5965515); doubles NT$880 to NT$1760

Star
   (míngxīng dà fàndiàn), 11 Hoping W Rd, Section 1 (☎ 3943121, fax 3943129); doubles/twins NT$1500/1900

Unic
   (yōushì dà fàndiàn; 284 rooms), 108 Hsinsheng N Rd, Section 2 (☎ 5662135, fax 5812808); doubles NT$2200 to NT$2400, twins NT$2800, suites NT$4000 to NT$6000

YMCA
   (jīdūjiào qīngnián huì bīnguǎn), 19 Hsuchang St (☎ 3113201, fax 3113209); doubles NT$1300 to NT$1500, twins NT$1500 to NT$1700

PLACES TO STAY – TOP END

Many up-market hotels impose an additional 10% service charge and a 5% value-added tax (VAT) over their quoted prices. On the other hand, you may get prices lower than those quoted here because of discounts. The discounts are offered periodically to anybody who walks in simply because some of these hotels are now hurting for business due to excessive competition. A sampling of what's available includes:

Ambassador
   (guóbīn dà fàndiàn; 500 rooms), 63 Chungshan N Rd, Section 2 (☎ 5551111, fax 5617883); doubles NT$3900-5300, twins NT$4500-6500, suites NT$9900-58,000

Asiaworld Plaza
   (huányǎ dà fàndiàn; 1057 rooms), 100 Tunhua N

Rd (☎ 7150077, fax 7134148); doubles & twins NT$5200-7000, suites NT$9200-140,000

Brother
(xiōngdì dà fàndiàn; 268 rooms), 255 Nanking E Rd, Section 3 (☎ 7123456, fax 7173334); doubles NT$3200 to NT$4000, twins NT$4000, suites NT$7500

Emperor
(guówáng dà fàndiàn; 120 rooms), 118 Nanking E Rd, Section 1 (☎ 5811111, fax 5312586); doubles and twins NT$2800, suites NT$6200

Fortuna
(fùdū dà fàndiàn; 304 rooms), 122 Chungshan N Rd, Section 2 (☎ 5631111, fax 5619777); doubles NT$2750 to NT$3800, twins NT$3800 to NT$4200, suites NT$6500 to NT$23,100

Fortune Dragon
(lóngpǔ dà fàndiàn; 312 rooms), 172 Chunghsiao E Rd, Section 4 (☎ 7722121, fax 7210302); doubles and twins NT$3570 to NT$4620, suites NT$5250 to NT$6510

Gloria
(huátài dà fàndiàn; 250 rooms), 369 Linsen N Rd (☎ 5818111, fax 5815811); doubles NT$3500 to NT$4500, twins NT$4050 to NT$4500, suites NT$5600 to NT$7900

Golden China
(kānghuá dà fàndiàn; 280 rooms), 306 Sung-chiang Rd (☎ 5215151, fax 5312914); doubles NT$2900 to NT$3500, twins NT$3100 to NT$3500, suites NT$7000 to NT$10,000

Grand Hotel
(yuánshān dà fàndiàn; 530 rooms), 1 Chungshan N Rd, Section 4 (☎ 5965565, fax 5948243); doubles NT$3800 to NT$4600, twins NT$4200 to NT$5000, suites NT$5200 to NT$17,400

Grand Hyatt
(kǎiyuè dà fàndiàn; 872 rooms), 2 Sungshou Rd (☎ 7201200, fax 7201111); twins NT$5500-6100, suites NT$9500 to NT$42,000

Hilton
(xī ěrdùn dà fàndiàn; 394 rooms), 38 Chunghsiao W Rd, Section 1 (☎ 3115151, fax 3319944); doubles NT$5400-6800, twins NT$5900-7300, suites NT$6500 to NT$8400

Howard Plaza
(fúhuá dà fàndiàn; 606 rooms), 160 Jenai Rd, Section 3 (☎ 7002323, fax 7000729); doubles NT$4900-6200, twins NT$5200-6500, suites NT$7800-25,000

Imperial
(huáguó dà fàndiàn; 338 rooms), 600 Linsen N Rd (☎ 5965111, fax 5927506); doubles NT$3300-4500, twins NT$3700-4500, suites NT$5200-16,000

Lai Lai Sheraton *(láilái dà fàndiàn;* 705 rooms), 12 Chunghsiao E Rd, Section 1 (☎ 3215511, fax 3944240); doubles NT$5500, twins NT$5500-8500, suites NT$10,500-80,000

Magnolia
(zhōngtài bīnguǎn; 341 rooms), 166 Tunhua N Rd (☎ 7121201, fax 7122122); doubles and twins NT$4800, suites NT$8900 to NT$21,600

Miramar
(měilìhuá dà fàndiàn; 584 rooms), 420 Minchuan E Rd, Section 3 (☎ 5053456, fax 5072000); doubles/twins NT$3600/3800, suites NT$5600

President
(tǒngyī dà fàndiàn; 421 rooms), 9 Tehuei St (☎ 5951251, fax 5913677); doubles NT$3800 to NT$4200, twins NT$4600 to NT$5000, suites NT$6300 to NT$8500

Rebar Crown
(lìbà dà fàndiàn; 300 rooms), 32 Nanking E Rd Section 5 (☎ 7635656, fax 7679347); doubles/twins NT$4200/4500, suites NT$7000 to NT$8600

Regent *(lìjīng jiǔdiàn; 550 rooms),* 41 Chungshan N Rd Section 2 (☎ 5238000, fax 5232828); twins NT$5800 to NT$7000, suites NT$8000 to NT$32,000

Ritz
(yǎdū dà fàndiàn; 200 rooms), 41 Minchuan E Rd Section 2 (☎ 5971234, fax 5969222); twins NT$5600, suites NT$7000-32,000

Riverview
(háojǐng dàjiǔdiàn; 201 rooms), 77 Huanho S Rd, Section 1 (☎ 3113131, fax 3613737); doubles/twins NT$3500/4400, suites NT$8000

Royal
(lǎoyé dajiudian; 203 rooms), 37-1 Chungshan N Rd, Section 2 (☎ 5423266, fax 5434897); doubles NT$4000 to 4800, twins NT$5200 to NT$5500, suites NT$7000 to NT$21,000

Santos
(sāndé dà fàndiàn; 300 rooms), 49 Chengte Rd, Section 3 (☎ 5963111, fax 5963120); doubles NT$3400, twins NT$3400-5000, suites NT$6500-10,000

Sherwood
(xīhuá dà fàndiàn; 350 rooms) (☎ 7181188, fax 7130707); doubles NT$5800 to NT$6800, twins NT$6200 to NT$6800, suites NT$8400 to NT$40,000

United
(guólián dà fàndiàn; 328 rooms), 200 Kuangfu S Rd (☎ 7731515, fax 7412789); doubles NT$3000 to NT$3500, twins NT$3400 to NT$3600, suites NT$3900 to NT$10,200

PLACES TO EAT

Looking for places to eat in Taipei is like looking for leaves in a forest. Restaurants are everywhere and anywhere, and ever-changing. Keeping up to date with the literally thousands of restaurants is nearly impossible.

Budget Eats

Inexpensive Chinese food is ubiquitous. Many cheap foodstalls and restaurants can be found in the small lanes and alleys off the main streets. It is possible to enjoy a filling meal of noodles or dumplings for around NT$40. Keep your eyes open for cafeterias where you can just point to what you want. Restaurants on the main boulevards are, of course, more expensive – you're paying for the prime real estate.

The basements of department stores all have moderately priced foodstalls. This includes Sunrise, Ming Yao, Mitsukoshi, Sogo, Tonlin and others. See the Shopping section further on for the addresses of department stores.

Besides back-alley foodstalls, there is a large collection of cheap restaurants in a place called the Food Circle *(yuánhuán)*, at the intersection of Chungching N Rd and Nanking W Rd. In addition to the Food Circle itself, street vendors appear at night in all the side streets adjoining the circle.

Where you find students, you find cheap restaurants. About 400 metres south of the railway station is Wuchang St, the home of numerous 'cram schools' that train students to pass Taiwan's rigid university entrance exams. The high concentration of schools and students guarantees an infinite choice of cheap eating places in this area.

Cheap restaurants also surround Taiwan University and Taiwan Normal University. Don't forget the universities themselves – no student ID is needed to eat in the student cafeterias.

In the basement of the dormitory (on the south side of Hoping Rd) across the street from the Mandarin Training Centre (Taiwan Normal University) is a superb cafeteria – NT$35 for a mountain of rice and three dishes that would cost twice this much elsewhere. If you eat in the university cafeterias, you have to be on time – lunch from 11.30 am to 12.30 pm, and dinner from 5.30 pm to 6.30 pm.

A great place to sample Taiwan's famous dumplings *(shuǐjiǎo)* is at the row of restaurants on the north-west corner of Linsen N Rd and Nanking E Rd. These places charge NT$2 for each dumpling.

The best steamed dumplings in Taipei can be found at a restaurant with no English name, so learn how to pronounce *Dǐng Tài Fēng* (☎ 3218927). It's at 194 Hsinyi Lu Section 2. Prices are mid-range and it gets really crowded at dinner time. It's open from 8 am to 2 pm and from 5 pm to 8.30 pm, but closed on Monday.

The 2nd floor of the Taipei railway station has a collection of moderately priced restaurants.

Night markets are always great places to eat, and generally cheap if you lay off the seafood. See the Entertainment section in this chapter for the location of Taipei's biggest night markets.

Taiwanese Food

Traditional Taiwanese food largely consists of endless courses of exotic seafood, which is very expensive. One of Taipei's most notable Taiwanese restaurants is *Hai Pa Wang* (☎ 5626345) *(hǎi bà wáng)* 7 Hsining N Rd. There are several branch stores, including 59 Chungshan N Rd, Section 3 (☎ 5963141), and 169 Nanking W Rd, near the Food Circle (☎ 5377323).

Cantonese

In Hong Kong, Macau and mainland China, fabulous Cantonese *dim sum* is dirt cheap. In Taiwan, Cantonese food is regarded as an exotic delicacy and therefore is not cheap. If you can get out for NT$300, then you've done well, but it could easily cost twice that. In Hong Kong, dim sum gets served for breakfast and lunch, but never dinner. In Taipei, it's usually only for lunch and sometimes for dinner, only rarely for breakfast. Hotel restaurants are the main venue for dim sum. Places to try include:

Cantonese
    Ambassador Hotel, 2nd floor
Canton Palace
    Asiaworld Plaza, 1st floor
Imperial Chinese
    Imperial Hotel, 12th floor

Jade Garden
    Lai Lai Sheraton
Lotus Garden
    Rebar Crown
Mandarin Palace
    President Hotel
Ming Court
    Royal Hotel
Pearl River
    Howard Plaza Hotel, 2nd floor
Plum Blossom
    Brother Hotel, 2nd floor
Tsai Yi Lo
    Regent Hotel, 3rd floor

Fast Food

Expatriates living in Taipei call it the 'US Embassy', but most of us know it as *McDonald's*. There seem to be branches (consulates?) everywhere in the city.

The Dinghao neighbourhood of east Taipei is a haven for gourmets in search of fast-food cuisine. Among the many choices are *Wendy's* at 209 Chunghsiao E Rd, Section 4; and *Kentucky Fried Chicken (kěndéjī jiāxiāngjī)* at 71 Chunghsiao E Rd, Section 4.

Pizza Hut (bìshèngkè) has numerous branches; a convenient one is at 130 Chunghsiao E Rd, Section 4. Pizzas can be delivered to your home, dispatched by motorcycle.

Kiss Pizza International (☎ 3657792) doesn't seem to really be international, but serves delicious homemade pizzas and fried chicken. It's at 63-1 Yunho St which is one block south of Hoping E Rd, Section 1, off Shihta Rd. By Taipei standards, prices here are cheap.

Chicago Pizza (☎ 5118989) at 12 Nanking W Rd offers home delivery from 11 am until 9.30 pm. There is an NT$50 surcharge for the service.

The fast food isn't always fast but it's certainly good at *Round Table Steak & Pizza* (☎ 7037004) in the basement at 65 Anho Rd, Section 1, or at 60 Nanking E Rd, Section 2.

There is a *Swensen's (shuāngshèng xīcàn)* at 218 Tunhua N Rd; 109 Jenai Rd, Section 4; and at 685 Chungshan N Rd, Section 5, Shihlin. *Wendy's* has a branch at 116 Tunhua N Rd. *Lotteria* is a Korean-Japanese fast

food chain doing fried chicken and the like – there's one opposite the World Trade Centre on the corner of Keelung Rd and Hsinyi Rd. There are plenty of fast-food restaurants along Chungshan N Rd, such as...well, why go on? Just follow the familiar odours wafting down the street and you are sure to find what you're looking for.

Not really fast, but definitely American is *TGI Fridays* (☎ 7133579) *(xīng qī wǔ cān tīng)*, 150 Tunhua N Rd. If you can afford the ticket, check out all the up-market pubs and coffee shops just behind this place. TGI Fridays (Thank God It's Fridays) also has a branch (☎7113579) at 151 Chunghsiao E Rd, Section 4, and another in Tienmu at 34 Chungshan N Rd, Section 7.

Dan Ryan's Chicago Grill (☎ 7788800) at 8 Tunhua N Rd offers good American fare.

No matter what you think of fast food, the familiar Western chain restaurants are the cheapest places to buy coffee; a standard NT$25 at McDonald's as opposed to at least NT$100 in most coffee shops.

French

Fine French food isn't cheap; dinner for two – *sacré bleu* – is a cool NT$800 or more. A recommended French restaurant is *La Lune Vague* (☎ 8372214), 7 Alley 7, Lane 290, Chungshan N Rd, Section 6, Shihlin district. *Hugo's French Restaurant* (☎ 8719974, 8314363), 31 Chungshan N Rd, Section 7, Tienmu, Shihlin district, is a well-known place. Many pricey hotels have French restaurants, including the *Brother*, *Howard Plaza*, *Lai Lai Sheraton*, *Rebar Crown*, *Ritz*, *Riviera* and *Royal*. See the Places to Stay section for addresses.

Indian

An old favourite is *Dazzle Curry* (☎ 7069504), 84 Jenai Rd, Section 3. You can also get your hot curries at *Gaylord's*, 328 Sungchiang Rd, where set lunches are NT$300. Identical prices are found at *Taj Palace Restaurant* (☎ 5672976), 2nd floor, 270 Sungchiang Rd.

The outstanding buffet luncheon is also NT$300 at *Tandoor Indian Restaurant*

(☎ 5099853), 10 Lane 773, Hochiang St. It's between Minsheng E Rd and Minchuan E Rd, near Lungchiang Rd, behind the Saab dealership.

Indonesian

If satay and gado-gado are on your mind, you can try *Pulau Kelapa* (☎ 3684717), 86 Tinchou Rd, Section 3.

Italian

All the Italian restaurants in Taipei are good. Some to try include:

Antonio's Pizzeria
    2nd floor, 26 Chungshan N Rd, Section 7, Tienmu, Shihlin district (☎ 8731027)
Casa Mia
    Building B, 627 Linsen N Rd (☎ 5917478)
Galliano
    41 Alley 25, Lane 113, Minsheng E Rd, Section 3 (☎ 7188289)
L'Amico
    10 Lane 55, Section 4, Minsheng E Rd (☎ 7193688)
La Cucina
    8-2 Lane 198, Hsinyi Rd, Section 2 (☎ 3974176)
Papa Joe's
    41 Fuhsing S Rd, Section 2 (☎ 7081221)
Pasta West East
    7 Anho Rd, Section 1 (☎ 7765216)
Ruffino
    15, Lane 25, Shuang Cheng St (☎ 5923355)

Japanese

One of the less-expensive Japanese restaurants is *Natori* (☎ 7052288), 3 Lane 199, Hsinyi Rd, Section 4.

Unfortunately, that's an exception. In general, if you want Japanese food, you have to pay Japanese prices. One place where you can thin out your wallet is *Tsu Ten Kaku* (☎ 5117372), 8 Lane 53, Chungshan N Rd, Section 1. There are also Japanese restaurants in up-market hotels, including the *Asiaworld*, *Brother*, *Grand Hyatt*, *Howard Plaza* and *Royal*.

Korean

Korean food can be had for mid-range prices at the *Seoul Korean Barbecue* (☎ 5112326) (*hànchéng cāntīng*), 1 Lane 33, Chungshan N Rd, Section 1.

Kosher

If you thought it wasn't possible to find corned beef, cheese blintzes and Hebrew National salami in Taipei, guess again. *YY's Kitchen & Steak House* (☎ 5922868) at 49 Chungshan N Rd, Section 3, claims to be Taipei's only kosher restaurant. Eating gefilte fish with chopsticks can be tricky, but if you have trouble with the matzo balls (slippery little devils) then just use a single chopstick and spear them.

Mexican

Taiwan's first Mexican restaurant is *La Casita* (☎ 3223092), 23 Chunghsiao E Rd, Section 2, which has both meat and vegetarian dishes.

Tequila Sunrise (☎ 3627563), 42 Hsinsheng S Rd, Section 3, has no lunches but dishes up Mexican dinners and midnight snacks. It's open from 6 pm until 1 am.

Mongolian Barbecue

A Mongolian barbecue is so good in Taiwan it's hard to believe it can be so bad in Mongolia. Make sure you don't eat breakfast, because you'll want plenty of extra room in your stomach so you can gorge yourself.

One of the best deals in tasty barbecue is *Xibei Shitang* (☎ 3688938, 3655379) at 9 Lane 24, Roosevelt Rd, Section 4.

One of Taipei's most famous venues for this style of cooking is the *Ploughman Inn* (☎ 7733268), 8 Lane 232, Tunhua S Rd, Section 1. You can expect to pay around NT\$350 or so.

Another place to try is the *Tienmu Bar-B-Que Pit* (☎ 8714677), 766-768 Chungshan N Rd, Section 6, Tienmu, Shihlin district.

Sri Lankan

If you're up in the Tienmu area, check out *King Coconut Garden Restaurant* (☎ 8741909), 83 Lane 8, Shihlin district. It's just behind the Taipei American School.

Swiss & German

The place to go for German food is *Zum Fass* (☎ 5313815), 55 Lane 119, Linsen N Rd. You can guess what kind of food is served at

Chalet Swiss (☎ 7152051), 47 Nanking E Rd, Section 4, and at 2 Lane 82, Tienmu E Rd.

Teppanyaki

If you choose the restaurant carefully, eating Teppanyaki can be very cheap. The trick is to have two people, split the meat and vegetable dishes, and order an extra rice. *Nanhai Teppanyaki* at the corner of Nanhai Rd and Kuling St (two blocks from Roosevelt Rd and near Shihlin Night Market) is a good deal. Beef Teppanyaki dishes cost NT$120, and an extra order of rice is NT$10.

If you're willing to spend more, *Sun Chi* (☎ 7089273) does a lunch buffet for NT$320 and dinner buffet for NT$380. It's at 206 Hsinyi Rd, Section 4.

Thai

If this spicy, hot cuisine appeals to you, there are a number of venues to try, including:

Ban-Thai Restaurant
    8 Lane 78, Sungchiang Rd (☎ 5233362)
Chiang Mai
    153 Tunhua S Rd, Section 1 (☎ 7318809)
Golden Triangle
    11 Lane 49, Shihta Rd (☎ 3632281)
Pantip
    7 Lane 112, Jenai Rd, Section 4 (☎ 7084392)

Vegetarian

Taipei's vegetarian restaurants offer amazing variety and can produce dishes which look like meat – some even put fake chicken (made from soybeans) onto chicken bones! There is a budget vegetarian restaurant near Taiwan Normal University called *Yeang Sheng Jai* (☎ 3212830) at 4 Lane 59, Shihta Rd. Right next door at No 4 (☎ 3621762) is *Tianran Sushi* which offers similar fare. Actually, the whole area abounds in vegetarian restaurants. Another one in this neighbourhood is *Hoping Vegetarian Restaurant* (☎ 3412239) *(hépíng sùshí cāntīng)*, 3rd floor, 177 Hoping E Rd, Section 1.

Vietnamese

Some of the best Vietnamese food to be had outside of Vietnam itself is at *Madame Jill's* (☎ 3680254) *(cuìlín yuènán cāntīng)* at 11 Lane 24, Roosevelt Rd, Section 4.

Another in-vogue place is *Madame Nhung's* (☎ 3636400), 198 Hoping E Rd, Section 1. It's close to Taiwan Normal University and just opposite the Ta'an District post office.

Mei-Kung (☎ 7523051, 7814067), 157-3 Yenchi St (between Jenai and Chunghsiao E Rd), does both Vietnamese and Thai dishes. Ditto for the *Ho Chi Minh Restaurant* (☎ 5149552) at 9 Lane 113, Minsheng E Rd, Section 3 (next to Sherwood Hotel).

Other Speciality Restaurants

Grandma Nitti's (☎ 7330449) advertises 'home cookin' – just like Grandma used to make'. It's at 61 Lane 118, Hoping E Rd, Section 2 and is open from 7 am to 9 pm, but sometimes closed for siesta from 2 pm to 4.30 pm (except Sunday). It's become a popular venue for breakfast with the all-night disco crowd – some come here to drink coffee and nurse their hangovers. The waffles are outstanding.

Jake's Country Kitchen (☎ 8715289) serves such exotica as blueberry pancakes, tacos, pizza and cheesecake. The address is 705 Chungshan N Rd, Section 6, Tienmu, Shihlin district.

Mary's Hamburgers is another Tienmu institution. It's at 752 Chungshan N Rd, Section 6, Shihlin district.

ENTERTAINMENT

Taipei is a good city for nightlife, but it's not particularly cheap. Still, there are a few places that cater to the budget-minded, offering cheap beer and music. Most businesses close around 11 pm to midnight, but pubs and dance halls may stay open until dawn.

Night Markets

A trip to Taipei wouldn't be complete without a visit to one or more of the city's colourful night markets. These are great places to eat, drink, shop and get your pocket picked. Markets are most lively on weekends if the weather cooperates.

The most exotic night market is in the

Wanhua area between Chunghua Rd and the river (near the Lungshan Temple, in the oldest and most traditional part of Taipei). The centre of activities is Snake Alley *(huáxī jiē)*, which lately has become more of a tourist trap than a market.

One of the oldest and largest evening street markets is the Shihlin Night Market *(shìlín yèshì)*. It's to the north-west of the Grand Hotel, just to the west of Wenlin Rd and starting from the south side of Chungcheng Rd. This market is open in the daytime, but really comes alive around 7 pm and normally shuts down around 10 to 11 pm – even later on weekends. Besides food, there's heaps of other items on sale, everything from clothing to perfume and hand tools.

The Jaoho St Night Market *(ráohé jiē yèshì)* is in the Sungshan District at the northern end of Keelung Rd. This is one of the newest and largest markets in the city.

The Tunghua Night Market *(tōnghuà jiē yèshì)* is one block of Hsinyi Rd, Section 4, between Tunhua and Keelung Rds. This long alley is one big eating orgy in the evening.

The Kungguan Night Market *(gōngguǎn yèshì)* is on Roosevelt Rd, Section 4, near Hsinsheng S Rd and National Taiwan University – a popular venue with students. It's not so much an established night market as a collection of stores and sidewalk vendors – there are no permanent foodstalls. A similar student night market is found along Shihta Rd *(shīdà lù)* next to Taiwan Normal University.

The Tihua St Night Market *(díhuà jiē yèshì)* is just west of the Food Circle, at the intersection of Tihua St and Nanking W Rd. This is near the Chenghuang Temple in the old part of town. It's a great place for eating and shopping.

Chinese Opera

(píngjù) 平劇

There are not very many places in Taipei where you can see regularly scheduled operas. Operas are performed almost nightly at 7 pm in the Armed Forces Cultural Activity Centre (☎ 3114228) *(guó jūn wényì zhōngxīn)*, 69 Chunghua Rd, Section 1. However, performances here tend to be by amateur groups and are often not of high standard. Another place to see Chinese opera is at the Fuhsing Opera School *(fùxīng jùxiào)*. The school (☎ 7962666, fax 7941529) is at 177 Neihu Rd, Section 3. It's open three days a week to visitors.

The National Theatre *(guójiā jùyuàn)* – adjacent to the Chiang Kaishek Memorial Hall – publishes a monthly schedule of events which often includes Chinese opera performances. The schedule is available from the Tourism Bureau, Caves Books and New Schoolmate Book Company. Performances at the National Theatre tend to be professional but expensive.

Cinemas

The largest collection of movie theatres is on Wuchang St, Section 2, near the Lai Lai Department Store. See the English-language newspapers – *China News* and *China Post* – for the current movie selection. The *China News* gives a much more thorough listing than the *China Post*.

For some reason the newspapers don't have the addresses of the cinemas, so they are given in the following list:

Ambassador
  (guóbīn) 88 Chengtu Rd (☎ 3611222)
Capitol
  (shǒudū) or *Governor* 219 Chang'an E Rd, Section 2 (☎ 7415992)
Chang Chun
  (cháng chūn) 172 Changchun Rd (☎ 5074141)
China
  (zhōngguó) 127 Hsining S Rd (☎ 3318517)
Chunghsiao
  (zhōngxiào) 5th floor, 201 Chunghsiao E Rd, Section 4 (☎ 7515515)
Fuhsing
  (fùxīng) 337 Nanking E Rd, Section 3 (☎ 7153777)
Great Century
  (dà shìjì) 325 Roosevelt Rd, Section 3 (☎ 3629629)
Hoover
  (háo huá) 91 Wuchang St, Section 2 (☎ 3315097)

Majestic
    (*zhēn shàn měi*) 7th floor, 116 Hanchung St
    (☎ 3312270)
New Oscar
    (*aòsīkǎ*) 3rd floor, 115 Omei St (☎ 3611691)
New World
    (*xīn shìjiè*) 13 Chengtu Rd (☎ 3312752)
Oriental Pearl
    (*dōngfāng míngzhū*) Rebar Department Store,
    5th floor, 14 Nanking W Rd (☎ 5114771)
Oscar
    (*jīn xiàng jiǎng*) 3rd floor, 215 Chang'an E Rd,
    Section 2 (☎ 7118298)
Shin Shin
    (*xīn xīn*) 4th floor, 247 Linsen N Rd (☎ 5212211)
Sun
    (*rìxīn*) 87 Wuchang St, Section 2 (☎ 3315256)
Tashin
    (*dà xīn*) 87 Wuchang St, Section 2 (☎ 3319975)
Treasure Lion
    (*bǎoshī*) 88 Chengtu Rd (☎ 3142214)
Tung Nan Ya
    (*dōngnán yǎ*) 3 Lane 136, Roosevelt Rd, Section
    4 (☎ 3416839)

MTV

Most of Taipei's MTV houses have been forced to close due to stringent government regulations on fire safety and copyright infringement. One of the few to survive and prosper is Barcelona (☎ 7012174), 175 Hsinyin Rd, Section 4. This place is expanding – ring them for the location of other branches which should be opening up around the city.

Viewing a movie typically costs NT$160 (depending on the length of the film) if you have a VIP card, or NT$200 without the card. The VIP card costs NT$200, so it's a good investment long-term. On some evenings you get free popcorn with each drink purchased from the snack bar.

KTV

Karoake bars are everywhere – you'll be tripping over the KTV signs wherever you go so there's little need to make recommendations. Most of these places don't interest foreigners, but if you're desperate to find one, all the major tourist hostels can accommodate you.

Pubs & Discos

One of the longest-running popular pubs in Taipei is Roxy (☎ 3635967) at 22 Hoping E Rd, Section 1. There's an enormous selection of CDs and the DJ takes requests, but the volume is definitely *loud*. No cover charge, but minimum expenditure on food or drinks is NT$70. It's open from noon until 4 am. There is also a Roxy IV (☎ 3625273), 6-1 Hsinsheng S Rd, Section 3, but the cover charge is NT$200.

High recommendations go to the Pig & Whistle (☎ 8731380) 78 Tienmu E Rd. Congenial atmosphere, good pubgrub and fine live music. Take bus No 220 from anywhere on Chungshan N Rd. The same management also operates the very congenial Ploughman's Cottage (☎ 7124965), 305 Nanking E Rd, Section 3.

A place which continues to draw foreigners like a magnet is Spin (☎ 3569288), in the basement at 91 Hoping E Rd, Section 1. This place features dancing and loud music. The cover charge is NT$100.

Another place getting rave reviews from travellers is Whiskey A-Go-Go (☎ 737 5773, 7354715), 65 Hsinhai Rd, Section 3, near National Taiwan University. There's a large dance floor, flashing strobes, the whole lot. An unusual feature is the small pool at the back where you can take a dip.

Enjoy (☎ 3629257), 10 Lane 104, Hoping E Rd, Section 1, has drinks and decent food – the big sandwiches are especially recommended. The environment is European style, right down to French and British newspapers. Sometimes there are live bands. Also on Lane 104 is Fuba, a quiet but romantic place good for drinking, watching cable TV, chatting and playing draughts (checkers)– there are comics in the toilets!

Cheers Pub (☎ 3638194), in the basement at 128-1 Shihta Rd, is an excellent place. Or go up to the 4th floor of the same building to find Blue Note, a jazz bar with sometimes loud music.

Another favourite with foreigners is DV8 (☎ 3931726), at 223 Chinhua St. It's a little hard to find – Chinhua St is the lane just to the east of Lucky Bookstore (129-1 Hoping

E Rd, Section 1) and you should look for the Heineken sign. This place does good pizzas and sandwiches, and the DJ plays selections on request. You're free to play billiards on the tables downstairs, and it's permitted to write on the walls (and ceilings) in the basement!

Lane 86 (☎ 3671523) is at 7 Lane 86, Hsinsheng Rd, Section 3. This is a student district so it's not expensive. There's a DJ and a big selection of CDs. During the day it's a reasonably quiet Chinese coffee shop, but it really gets hopping at night. Food is mostly limited to almonds and drinks – if hungry, McDonald's is just next door.

Shuang Cheng St (*shuāng chéng jiē*) and adjacent alleys are where you'll find the densest concentration of pubs and Western restaurants in the city. Shuang Cheng St is sandwiched between Linsen N Rd and Chungshan N Rd and runs in a north-south direction. However, it's not a particularly cheap neighbourhood – geared more towards the business traveller than the backpacker. One place in this neighbourhood is The Farmhouse (☎ 5951764), 5 Lane 32, Shuang Cheng St, which features live music every night from 9.30 pm to 12.30 am. There is a second Farmhouse (☎ 7361998) on the 2nd floor at 164 Tunhua S Rd, Section 2, at the corner of Hoping E Rd.

Sam's Place (☎ 5942402), 2-2 Lane 32, Shuang Cheng St, is a pub and restaurant specialising in chilli, hamburgers, pizza and sandwiches.

The Sunset Lounge (☎ 7081221) of the Dynasty Hotel is a fashionable place for drinks, with a happy hour from 5 to 7 pm. Upstairs is a grill room dishing out steaks, seafood and pasta. The Dynasty Hotel is at 41 Fuhsing S Rd, Section 2.

WOWWOW (☎ 5163031), in the basement at 156 Chienkuo N Rd, Section 1, is a music pub with great tunes. There is no cover charge.

One of the most interesting places to visit in Taipei is Indian (☎ 7410550) (*yìndì'ān*), 196 Pate Rd, Section 2. It's hard to define what this place is – it's a pub, it's a restaurant, but with a difference. There is a skeleton of a dinosaur on the roof and the sides of the building. The interior decorating follows the same design scheme – dinosaur bones stick out of the walls, ceiling and floor. The waiters and waitresses wear dinosaur bone shirts. Beer is served from large wooden kegs. The place definitely has character and it's usually packed with customers, both foreign and Chinese. Indian has two other branches, one (☎ 7335977) at 195 Hsinhai Rd, Section 2 and another (☎ 7058866) at 47 Anho Rd, Section 2. It's open from 5.30 pm until 1.30 am.

If it's thumping music you're looking for, check out Gorgon Discoland (☎ 7534992) at 47 Kuangfu S Rd. This place has incredible décor – strobe lights, monsters hanging out of the walls and a moving Gorgon head. If you don't know your Greek mythology, the Gorgons were three sisters with live snakes for hair, so terrifying to look at that the beholder turned into stone – almost as scary as driving in Taipei's traffic. Gorgon Discoland is open from 8 pm until 3 am, and the cover charge is NT$100 Monday, Tuesday, Thursday and Friday. On Wednesday, women get in free (if dressed 'nicely') but men pay NT$250. It's NT$250 for everyone on weekends and holidays. If you spend a fair bit of money at the Indian, you can get a free pass for Gorgon.

Another large, slick disco is Kiss (☎ 7121201), in the Magnolia Hotel at 166 Tunhua N Rd. Admission is NT$350 from Monday to Thursday, but it rises to NT$500 on Friday and Saturday. It's extremely popular with the locals, but less so with foreigners.

Beer Houses

Anho Rd is east Taipei's beer-house alley. The most famous beer house in the city is Five Star Beer King (*wǔ kē xīng*) (☎ 701 7642), 95 Anho Rd. Nearby is Fandango Beer House (☎ 7017540), 136 Anho Rd; it has a good, cosy atmosphere. A very inexpensive beer house in the same neighbourhood is *yín jiā qiú zhǎng* (☎ 7075653), 133 Anho Rd.

An even bigger 'beer-house alley' is

Chungcheng Rd in Tienmu, though it's more for Chinese than foreigners.

Teahouses

There are plenty of teahouses in Taipei, though plagued with the usual problem of going out of business quickly. One which is reliable is on the fourth floor of the National Palace Museum and is called The Traditional Chinese Tearoom.

There is a mannequin decked out in scholar's garb in the middle of the tearoom. Small birds – real, not like the stuffed scholar – flit about in bamboo cages and provide light music; walls of windows provide a great view of the woods surrounding the museum. One can stay as long as one wishes, and there is even a collection of art books one can peruse while one's leaves steep; the books can be found on a wooden shelf on the far wall (copies of some are on sale in the gift shop downstairs). It's surprisingly inexpensive, considering the location and atmosphere; an afternoon splurge on myself and a friend did not cost more than approximately US$15, including pastries.

N Leavitt

You might also want to check out Shann Garden (☎ 8947185), 32 Youya Rd, Peitou district. Built in a former Japanese officers' club on a hill, it's included in the complex with the Taiwan Folk Arts Museum and a Mongolian barbecue restaurant.

Some other teahouses in Taipei include:

Lu Yu Tea Centre
  2nd floor, 62 Hengyang Rd (☎ 3316636)
Wisteria
  1 Lane 16, Hsinsheng S Rd, Section 3 (☎ 3637375)
Yuan-Yuan
  1st floor, 24 Alley 155, Lane 66, Tunhua N Rd (☎ 7135640)

Coffee Shops

There are plenty of coffee shops in Taipei, but most are expensive. One that is more reasonably priced is Doutor (luóduōlún kāfēi diàn) which has two branches: one at 63 Poai Rd (near Taipei railway station) and one at 77 Nanking E Rd, Section 2. If you're in the Shihlin district, check out Black Beans (☎ 8831125), 527 Chungshan N Rd, Section 5.

ACTIVITIES
Hiking Clubs

Some hiking clubs in the Taipei area include:

ROC Alpine Association
  (zhōnghuá shānyuè xiéhuì), 10th floor, 185 Chungshan N Rd, Section 2, Taipei (☎ 5911498, 5942108). Annual membership NT$300, non-members welcome. Members receive the club's newsletter every two months. This is Taiwan's largest mountain club.
Rain Road Mountain & Rafting Club
  2nd floor, 12 Chungshan N Rd, Section 1, Taipei (☎ 3811530, 3319093)
Shan Yuan Mountain Climbing Education Training Centre, 4th floor, Room 400, 2 Chungshan N Rd, Section 1, Taipei (☎ 3147271)
Chungho City Mountain Climbing Club
  (zhōnghé shì dēngshān huì), 4th floor, 4 Lane 26, Chunghsiao St, Yungho City, Taipei County (9291576)
Mountaineering & Hiking Association
  50-A, Lungchiang Rd, Taipei (☎ 7510938)

Exercise

If late-night carousing is making you feel run-down, you can get in shape at Clark Hatch Physical Fitness Centre (☎ 7416670), 86 Tunhua S Rd, Section 1. Clark's competition is Body-Talk (☎ 7713212), 11th floor, 235 Chunghsiao E Rd, Section 4 (side entrance).

Both of these centres have fine facilities but are pricey. A much cheaper alternative is the Centre's Gym in the basement at 89 Shita Rd – NT$4000 for the first three months, reducing to NT$2500 after nine months.

Another option is the Taipei Gym. An initial quarterly membership costs NT$4500, each subsequent quarter NT$3500. There is a gym (☎ 711145) at 306 Kuangfu S Rd (across from Sun Yatsen Memorial Hall). Another is at 58 Hsinsheng S Rd, Section 3 across from National Taiwan University Stadium. Of course, you could just run for free at the track inside the university campus. The Taipei Gym is open Monday to Saturday from 9 am to 11 pm, and on Sunday from 2 pm to 9 pm.

Sauna

(sān wēn nuǎn) 三溫暖
Having a sauna and soak in a hot tub is

appealing during Taipei's chilly, dreary winters. One place which accepts both male and female clients (in separate facilities) is Hangong Sanwennuan (☎ 5160191) at 400 Fuhsing N Rd (at the intersection with Minchuan E Rd). Just around the corner at 66 Minchuan E Rd, Section 3, is Rijing Sanwennuan (☎ 5156023). Both places charge about NT$500. The Hilton Hotel also operates a 24-hour sauna which costs NT$600.

Swimming

There is a swimming pool in Youth Park *(qīngnián gōngyuán)* in south-west Taipei. All outdoor pools are only open during the summer. Some of the big hotels have an arrangement where you pay a monthly fee which gains you access to their swimming pools, tennis courts, exercise rooms and other recreational facilities.

Ten-Pin Bowling

Among the foreign community, the most popular bowling venue is Yuanshan (☎ 8812277) *(yuánshān bǎolíng qiúguǎn)*, 3rd floor, 6 Chungshan N Rd, Section 5, Shihlin, near the Grand Hotel. This place also boasts a snack bar, rollerblades, rollerskate disco, pool, air hockey, video games and (brace yourself) karaoke.

Bungy Jumping

Bungee International (☎ 3325523) has an office on the 9th floor, Room 1, 180 Chungching S Rd, Section 3. The club does jumps wherever they find a convenient bridge or crane. The cost is NT$2000 the first time and NT$1000 thereafter. Bungee International is also expanding into water-skiing and 'skurfing' (surfing on a board pulled by a jetski). Call the club for full details.

Hash House Harriers

This is mainly for foreign residents of Taipei – if you're just passing through you might not be enthusiastically welcomed. Hash House Harriers is a loosely strung international club with branches all over the world. It appeals mainly to young people, or the young at heart. Activities typically include a weekend afternoon easy jogging session followed by a dinner and beer party which can extend until the wee hours of the morning.

Taipei's Hash is very informal – there is no club headquarters and no stable contact telephone or address. The best place to find the Hash is to look in the monthly magazine *This Month In Taiwan* under the heading 'Taipei Clubs and Lodges'.

That disclaimer given, there is usually a run every Sunday at noon, and every Saturday at 2 pm. The usual meeting place is the Post Home Restaurant (☎ 8356991), 32 Lane 35, Chungshan N Rd, Section 6. This is just behind Ricardo Lynn Furniture *(qiáodà jiājù)* at the corner of Fukuo Rd and Chungshan N Rd. Again, you should always call to check this – otherwise, you might be the only one to show up.

Computer Clubs

The Taipei User's Group (TUG) is the largest English-speaking club for computer users in Taiwan. There are meetings on the second Thursday of every month at 7.30 pm at the American Legion, No 31, Lane 35, Chungshan N Rd, Section 6, Taipei. TUG has a phone number listed in the magazine *This Month in Taiwan*.

TUG maintains a relationship with an electronic bulletin-board service (BBS) called World Data Exchange (WDE). Regular users must pay a small monthly fee, but you can get a single three-day trial at no cost. Plug in your modem and dial up (☎ 6952326). For information, you can call by voice phone (☎ 6952318). Since phone numbers can change, if the preceding doesn't work, call TUG.

ClubMac is, of course, for Macintosh users. The club meets every third Thursday from 7 to 9 pm in the Multimedia room, 16th floor, 1035 Tunhua S Rd (corner of Keelung Rd), Taipei. Call Wolfgang (☎ 8953452) for details.

Toastmasters

This is an informal club with meetings at various times all over Taipei. It's mainly a chance for the locals to practise their English by giving speeches on some topic of interest. It's a good way to socialise with the locals and the odd foreigner who shows up.

Look in the monthly magazine *This Month In Taiwan* under the heading 'Taipei Clubs and Lodges' for the meeting times and places.

THINGS TO BUY
Clothing
Taiwan is not a cheap place to buy clothing, but good deals on T-shirts and the like can be picked up in the nightmarkets. Otherwise, check out the Dinghao Market *(dǐnghǎo shìchǎng)* for clothing and shoes. The market is in the alleys just north of Chunghsiao E Rd and immediately east and west of Tunhua S Rd in the Ta'an district. A store to try in this area (east of Tunhua) is Longtai (☎ 721 9654), 48 Lane 390, Tunhua S Rd. Another in this neighbourhood (west of Tunhua) is See's (☎ 7711101) at 14 Lane 51, Ta'an Rd, Section 1. See's has another good branch in the Kungkuan neighbourhood at 166 Roosevelt Rd, Section 4.

Backpacking Gear
The place to go for backpacking gear is *(táiběi shānshuǐ)*, 12 Chungshan N Rd, Section 1, just to the north of the intersection with Chunghsiao Rd. Just a few doors up the street is another excellent shop, *(dēng shān yǒu)* (☎ 3116027), 18 Chungshan N Rd, Section 1. Both shops have a wide selection of gear for hiking, climbing and camping, but even if you don't indulge in such activities, they're good places to replace a worn-out backpack.

Bicycles
There's a KHS Bike Shop (☎ 7005572) at 15 Chienkuo S Rd, and a nearby Giant Bike Shop (☎ 7000788) at 102 Hsinyi Rd, Section 3. There are plenty of others scattered around the city.

Motorcycles
Assuming you have the necessary resident visa, you can purchase new motorcycles or good used ones with a full six-month warranty from Zhengcheng Motorcycle Shop (☎ 9323051, 9333834), 27 Roosevelt Rd, Section 5. The owner, Mr Chen, has a good reputation among foreigners for being impeccably honest.

Music Tapes & CDs
These are sold everywhere, but the widest selection by far is at Tower Records *(táoér chàngpiàn háng)*. The original and more spacious branch (☎ 3892025) is at 12 Chengtu Rd on the huge roundabout at the intersection of Chunghua Rd in the Hsimenting area. The newer branch (☎ 7414891) is on the 2nd floor 71 Chunghsiao E Rd, Section 4 between Fuhsing Rd and Tunhua Rd.

Holiday Flower Market
(jià rì huā shì) 假日花市
This incredible outdoor market is held on Saturday (when there are relatively few customers) but expands enormously on Sunday and holidays. The market is under an overpass on Chienkuo N Rd, between Jenai Rd and Hsinyi Rd. Buses which stop nearby include Nos 36, 37, 48, 65, 263, 270, 275, 298, Hsinyi Rd Line and Jenai Rd Line. Operating hours are roughly from 10 am until 8 pm.

The Holiday Jade Market *(jià rì yù shì)* is underneath the overpass at the intersection of Pate Rd and Hsinsheng S Rd. Even if you don't want to buy flowers or jade, it's interesting to come here and look.

Handicrafts
The Taiwan Handicraft Centre (☎ 3315701), 7th floor, 110 Yenping S Rd, is the place to go. Even if you don't buy, there are interesting displays here. It's open from 10 am until 6 pm, every day except Monday.

Cakes
Fancy cakes and biscuits are a favourite gift among the Chinese. The ones meant for gift-giving are in a special class by themselves, beautiful in appearance and wrapped in fancy (but not very ecologically sound) packaging. To get some idea of what's on

offer, check out Kuo Yuan Ye (☎ 3821759, 3314729) *(guō yuán yì)*, 12 Huaining St, just a few blocks south of the railway station. There is another Kuo Yuan Ye (☎ 5946756, 5965719) in the north-west part of the city, near the Confucius Temple at 32-2 Yenping N Rd, Section 3.

Cameras
Taipei's 'photography street' is Poai Rd, around the intersection with Kaifeng St. There are more than a dozen camera shops here and prices are about as low as you can find in Taiwan. The prices here are similar to those in Hong Kong, but Taiwanese-made camera accessories are cheaper.

Computers
Kuanghua Bazaar *(guānghuá shāngchǎng)* at Hsinsheng S Rd and Pate Rd has possibly the world's largest collection of computer and electronic stores. There are over 100 shops sprawled along the major streets and into the side alleys, and it's difficult to recommend one over another. On the south-west corner of Hsinsheng S Rd and Pate Rd is a shopping arcade with two basements – descend the stairs to find some of the best bargains in Taipei.

Macintosh dealers seem to come and go quickly in Taiwan. One of the longest surviving is Support & Solutions (☎ 8962866, fax 8949894) at 32 Chyuan Yuan Rd in Peitou. More centrally located are Machouse, 54-6 Hsinsheng S Rd, Section 3 and One & All, 32-1 Hsinyi Rd, Section 3.

Toys
Neighbourhood toy shops are everywhere, but if you're looking for that special something to keep the toddlers out of mischief, you might want to check out Toys R Us (☎ 5219025) at 28 Hsinsheng N Rd, Section 2.

Department Stores
Probably the most useful thing about Taipei's large department stores are the supermarkets in the basements. The line-up includes:

Asiaworld
  50 Chunghsiao W Rd, Section 1 (opposite Taipei railway station)
  337 Nanking E Rd, Section 3
Evergreen
  6 Nanking E Rd, Section 2
  246 Tunhua S Rd, Section 1
Far Eastern Department Store
  68 Jenai Rd, Section 4
  32 Paoching Rd (near Chunghua Rd)
Lai Lai
  77 Wuchang St, Section 2
Ming Yao Department Store
  200 Chunghsiao E Rd, Section 4
Mitsukoshi
  12 Nanking W Rd (near Chungshan N Rd)
Rebar
  14 Nanking W Rd
  110 Yenping S Rd
Shin Shin
  247 Linsen N Rd
Sincere
  1 Chingcheng St (cnr Fuhsing and Nanking Rds, behind Brother Hotel)
SOGO
  45 Chunghsiao E Rd, Section 4
Sunrise
  15 Fuhsing N Rd
Today's
  54 Omei St
Tonlin
  201 Chunghsiao E Rd, Section 4

GETTING THERE & AWAY
Air
Taipei is well served with international and domestic connections. You won't have trouble getting tickets on weekdays except during major holidays. Seats can sometimes be tight on weekends, too.

If you qualify as a student (studying Chinese at a Taiwanese university will do) or if you're under the age of 27, you can get a special discount on international air tickets from Youth Travel International (☎ 7211978, fax 7212784) *(guójì xuéshēng qīngnián lüyóu)*, Suite 502, 142 Chunghsiao E Rd, Section 4. With proper credentials (student ID card or acceptance letter from a university), you can purchase an ISIC card here for NT$150. You can also get an STA Youth Card for NT$250 if you're aged 13 to 26, even if you're not a student. This place also sells the International Youth Hostel Federation (IYHF) Guidebook.

Although travel agents are cheaper for buying international air tickets (see the Travel Agencies section in this chapter), the airline offices are where you must go for reconfirmations. International airlines in Taipei include the following:

Air New Zealand
(niŭ xīlán hángkōng), 6th floor, 98 Nanking E Rd, Section 2, Taipei (☎ 5313980)
Asiana
(hányă hángkōng), 5th floor, 65 Chienkuo N Rd, Section 2 (☎ 5081114)
Australia Asia
(aòyă hángkōng), 3rd floor, 101 Nanking E Rd, Section 2 (☎ 5221001)
CKS Airport (☎ 03-3982619)
British Asia Airways
(yīngyă), 5th floor, 98 Nanking E Rd, Section 2 (☎ 5418080)
Canadian International
(jiānádà guójì hángkōng), 4th floor, 90 Chienkuo N Rd, Section 2, Taipei (☎ 5034111)
CKS Airport (☎ 03-3982985)
Cathay Pacific
(guótài hángkōng), 12th floor, 129 Minsheng E Rd, Section 3, Taipei (☎ 7152333)
CKS Airport (☎ 03-3982502)
China Airlines
(zhōnghuá hángkōng), 131 Nanking E Rd, Section 3 (☎ 7151212 – 24 hours)
CKS Airport (☎ 03-3834106)
Continental
(dàlù hángkōng), 2nd floor, 150 Fuhsing N Rd, Taipei (☎ 7152766)
CKS Airport (☎ 03-3834131)
Delta Airlines
(dàměi hángkōng), 50 Nanking E Rd, Section 2, Taipei (☎ 5513656)
CKS Airport (☎ 03-3834500)
EVA Airways
(chángróng hángkōng), 166 Minsheng E Rd, Section 2, Taipei (☎ 5011999)
CKS Airport (☎ 03-3982968)
Garuda Indonesia
(yìnní guójiā hángkōng), 66 Sungchiang Rd, Taipei (☎ 5612311)
CKS Airport (☎ 03-3982977)
Japan Asia
(rìyă hángkōng), 2 Tunhua S Rd, Section 1 (☎ 7765151)
CKS Airport (☎ 03-3833761)
Taichung, 393 Taichung Kang Rd, Section 1 (☎ 04-3217700)
KLM
(hélán hángkōng), 1 Nanking E Rd, Section 4 (☎ 7171000)
CKS Airport (☎ 03-3833034)

Korean Air
(dàhán hángkōng), 53 Nanking E Rd, Section 2, Taipei (☎ 5214242)
CKS Airport (☎ 03-3833787)
Lauda Air
(wéiyěnà hángkōng), 7th floor, 18 Chang'an E Rd, Section 1 (☎ 5435083)
Malaysian Airlines
(măláixīyă hángkōng), 102 Tunhua N Rd, Taipei (☎ 7168384)
CKS Airport (☎ 03-3834855)
Mandarin
(huáxìn hángkōng), 13th floor, 134 Minsheng E Rd, Section 3 (☎ 7171230, 7171188)
Northwest
(xīběi hángkōng), 7th floor, 168-170 Tunhua N Rd (☎ 7161555)
CKS Airport (☎ 03-3982471)
Philippine Airlines
(fēilùbīn hángkōng), 2nd floor, 90 Chienkuo N Rd, Section 2 (☎ 5051255)
CKS Airport (☎ 03-3982419)
Royal Brunei
(huángjiā wènlái hángkōng), 11th floor, 9 Nanking E Rd, Section 3 (☎ 5312884)
CKS Airport (☎ 03-3834106)
Sempati
(sēnbādí hángkōng), 174 Chunghsiao E Rd, Section 1 (☎ 3966934, 3966910)
Singapore Airlines
(xīnjiāpō hángkōng), 148 Sungchiang Rd (☎ 5516655)
CKS Airport (☎ 03-3982247)
South African Airways
(nánfēi hángkōng), 12th floor, 205 Tunhua N Rd, Taipei (☎ 7136363)
CKS Airport (☎ 03-3834716)
Thai Airways
(tàiguó hángkōng), 2nd floor, 150 Fuhsing N Rd (☎ 7175299, 7175200)
CKS Airport (☎ 03-3834131)
United Airlines
(liánhé hángkōng), 12th floor, 2 Jenai Rd, Section 4 (☎ 3258868)
CKS Airport (☎ 03-3982781)

Every domestic carrier has an office in Taipei or a counter at Sungshan Airport. The domestic airlines are:

China Airlines
(zhōnghuá hángkōng), 131 Nanking E Rd, Section 3 (☎ 7151122)
Far Eastern Airlines
(yuăndōng hángkōng), 36 Kuanchien Rd (☎ 3615431)

Formosa Airlines
(yŏngxīng hángkōng), Sungshan Airport
(☎ 5149636)
Great China Airlines
(dàhuá hángkōng), 38 Jenai Rd, Section 1
(☎ 3568000)
Makung Airlines
(măgōng hángkōng), Sungshan Airport
(☎ 5148188)
Taiwan Airlines
(táiwān hángkōng), Sungshan Airport
(☎ 5142881)
Trans-Asia Airways
(fùxīng hángkōng), 8th floor, 139 Chengchou Rd
(☎ 5579000)

Train

There are three railway stations in the city, but the most important by far is the enormous Taipei Railway Station, a palatial multi-storey building that looks like a temple (from the outside at least). The ground floor is where you buy tickets; you catch your train in the basement, and upstairs are numerous restaurants and shops which you might want to visit if you have time to kill.

In the east part of Taipei is the Sungshan Station, and in the south-west part of town is Wanhua Station. If you want to ship or receive a bicycle or motorcycle, you have to do it from Sungshan or Wanhua station – the Taipei Railway Station is for passengers only.

Bus

There are four important bus terminals near the railway station and another about two km to the east. Probably most important is the West Bus Station, where you get govern-ment-operated (Taiwan Bus Company) highway buses to major west-coast cities, including Taichung, Chiayi, Tainan and Kaohsiung. There are also buses from here to a few major resorts areas like Kenting and Alishan. The West Bus Station is on Chunghsiao W Rd, a three-minute walk west of the railway station.

The East Bus Station is almost right in front of the railway station. From here you get buses to CKS Airport and to Keelung.

The North Bus Station is on the north side of the railway station. Here you can get buses to Changhua, Chiaohsi Hot Springs,

Chungli, Hsinchu, Hualien (transfer in Suao), Ilan, Keelung, Lotung, Lukang, Miaoli, Puli, Suao, Sun Moon Lake, and Taoyuan.

One block north of the North Bus Station at the north-east corner of Chengte and Chang'an Rds is the Tonglien Bus Station. This company is Taiwan's leading 'wild chicken' bus company. Departures for all major west-coast cities are frequent.

The Chunglun Bus Station is on the south-west corner of Pate Rd and Fuhsing Rd, over two km east of the railway station. You can get there from the Taipei Railway Station area (Chunghsiao E Rd in front of Asiaworld Department Store) by taking city buses Nos 57, 205 and 276. Important departures from Chunglun Station include buses to Chinshan Beach, Keelung, Yehliu, Fengyuan and Peikang.

For details of day trips from central Taipei to places of interest in the surrounding area, see the North Taiwan chapter.

GETTING AROUND
To/From CKS Airport

The vast majority of travellers will arrive in Taiwan at Chiang Kaishek (CKS) Interna-tional Airport, near the city of Taoyuan 40 km south-west of Taipei.

There are two classes of buses connecting the airport to Taipei: limousine buses (Chunghsing Line) for NT$85, which is fast, frequent and has a luggage compartment on the underside of the bus; and the local bus for NT$40, which makes many stops, runs less frequently, is more crowded and has scant luggage space. Unless you're really broke, the limousine buses are usually worth the extra money – the local buses are used mainly by airport workers and run only during commuting hours.

Limousine buses run every 15 to 20 minutes, beginning at 6.30 am and ending at 10.30 pm. There are two routes – one termi-nates at the Taipei Railway Station in the city centre, the other goes to Sungshan Domestic Airport. There is only one route for the local bus – it makes a few stops near the city centre and then terminates at Sungshan Domestic Airport. All the buses pass some major hotels and youth hostels along the way, so which one you should take depends on where you want to stay. If undecided, take the bus to the railway station and start your hotel search from there. You might save yourself some hassle by phoning ahead to the hotels – the visitor information desk in the airport can recommend places to stay and make free phone calls for you to Taipei. It's worth taking advantage of this service even if you're staying at a youth hostel.

The limousine bus drivers speak almost no English, but they are supposed to ask you where you will get off before you board the bus. The reason is because of your luggage. There are three bus stops en route, and three luggage compartments under the bus. Each compartment is designated for a particular bus stop – the compartments remain locked to prevent other passengers from walking off with your bag when they leave the bus. When heading to the airport from Taipei, you can catch the express bus from two locations: the East Bus Station at 173 Chunghsiao W Rd (in front of the Taipei Railway Station), or from the bus terminal at the western end of Sungshan Domestic Airport.

There are plenty of taxis lined up at the airport – the drivers generally have to wait an hour before they get a customer and are therefore permitted to charge 50% more than the meter reads, making the fare from the airport to central Taipei over NT$1000. However, going the other way, from Taipei to the airport, the drivers are only supposed to charge you the meter fare.

If you are staying at one of the better hotels in Taipei, they may have a limousine service from the airport directly to your hotel. However, if you want them to meet you at the airport you'd better fax, write or telephone ahead. Otherwise, you'll have to call them from CKS Airport and wait nearly an hour or more for them to arrive. If they know when you are coming, they will stand at the arrival gate just after you clear customs and hold up a sign with your name on it. It's hardly worth the trouble – limousine service is seldom free unless you're a VIP. They charge about NT$1000, the same as a taxi.

To/From Sungshan Airport

This is Taipei's domestic airport, although international charter flights can also fly from here. It's so close to the city centre that the planes have to manoeuvre between the skyscrapers. Thanks to the central location, you can probably afford to take a taxi. There is a regular bus service between CKS International Airport and Sungshan Airport from around 8 am until 10 pm. Bus No 502 connects Sungshan Airport to the Taipei Railway Station.

Bus

Taipei's bus system is run by a consortium of private companies which operate at a profit, and one government bus company which loses money. On most routes, buses are frequent and the service is good. There are a few problems for English-speaking foreigners, however, in that the bus drivers don't speak English and the destination is written on the bus in Chinese characters. Armed with a street map, your destination written in Chinese characters and maybe a compass, you should be able to manage.

If you've been studying Chinese characters for a while, you can take advantage of the bus-route guidebooks written in Chinese. These can be purchased from kiosks near the bus stops or from bookshops for NT$50. These guides have different names – just ask for a *táiběi gōngchē zhǐnán* or *táiběi gōngchē shǒucè*. Unfortunately, if you can't read Chinese, it's of little use. There is also a reasonably good English bus guide available from Caves Books and Lucky Bookstore for NT$100, but it's getting out of date.

If you do get lost, you can always bail out and take a taxi, but again, most of the drivers don't speak English. I certainly recommend having your hotel name and address written down in Chinese characters so that you can get back. Another tactic is to have the words for railway station written down, as it makes a good reference point when using a map.

The words for railway station are *huǒchē zhàn*.

The standard bus fare is NT$12, though on longer trips the fare can be double or even triple this amount, depending on the number of zones you travel through. By the time you read this, 'bus cards' will probably be in use – you pay NT$120 and get a card good for 12 rides. These cards will be sold from little kiosks near the bus stops (the same places that sell cigarettes, newspapers and betel nut).

Sometimes you pay when you board, but usually you pay when getting off. Sometimes you must pay both when you get on and when you get off, but only if you have crossed two zones. Sometimes the driver hands you a ticket with a number on it. Save it, you must return it when you get off. The ticket tells him which zone you were in when you got on the bus. The various systems seem unnecessarily confusing, but this reflects the fact that there are numerous companies operating these buses and each company has its own way of doing things.

Somewhere near the driver should be a sign in Chinese or a red light telling you to pay when you get on *(shàng)* 上 or when you get off *(xià)* 下. Figuring out when you are supposed to pay can be confusing even for the Chinese.

Most buses begin service at 6 am and end around 11.30 pm. Some buses return on the same route, others make a circular route. Routes change periodically, and the opening of the Metropolitan Rapid Transit will no doubt cause many buses to be rerouted and some services to cease operating.

MRT

The Metropolitan Rapid Transit, or MRT, has been a long time coming. First planned in 1975, construction was delayed until 1988 because of repeated design changes and bureaucratic wrangling. At US$16 billion, it's believed to be the world's most expensive mass-transit system. Plagued by cost overruns (more than 60% over budget so far), accusations of corruption, faulty design,

technical difficulties and numerous delays, it was not yet open at the time of writing.

However, there appears to be light at the end of the tunnel, and hopefully *something* will be running by the time you read this. Test runs have already been made – in two cases, the trains literally went up in smoke. Cracks have developed in the support pillars holding up the elevated tracks on Fuhsing Rd, raising the possibility that some of the system may have to be rebuilt.

Many experts have been scratching their head as to why the Fuhsing line has been designed with a unique 90° turn in its route. There's been lots of finger-pointing at the Ministry of Transportation, heads have rolled, lawsuits have been filed and a special committee is investigating. In a dispute over money, an arbitrator ordered DORTS (Department of Rapid Transit Systems) to pay MATRA (the French contractor) US$37 million for losses caused by delays. Lai Shyhsheng, the director of DORTS resigned in disgust in late 1993. Meanwhile, commuters just sigh and take the bus. As for why it's taking so long to build, I've talked to engineers who have worked on the project, and they seem unanimous about the cause – bureaucracy.

There are four lines which are scheduled to open sometime soon (this decade, at least). A map is included to help you navigate the system. Please be aware that this map is somewhat tentative – the stations may be renamed.

Taxi

English-speaking radio-dispatchers can summon a taxi for you if you call ☎ 5576611, but this doesn't mean that the driver will be able to speak English.

Car

There are a number of car-rental places with English-speaking staff, catering to the foreign market. Many are listed in the English-language newspapers, the *China Post* and *China News*. Besides its central

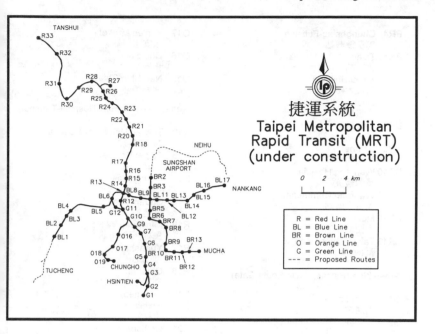

捷運系統
Taipei Metropolitan
Rapid Transit (MRT)
(under construction)

0   2   4 km

R   = Red Line
BL = Blue Line
BR = Brown Line
O   = Orange Line
G   = Green Line
--- = Proposed Routes

Blue Line (Panchiao-Nankang)

BL1 Panchiao
板橋站

BL2 Hansheng
漢生路站

BL3 Hsinpu
新埔站

BL4 Chiang Tzu Tsui
江子翠站

BL5 Lungshan Temple
龍山寺站

BL6 West Gate
西門站

BL7 Taipei Railway Station
台北車站

BL8 Shantao Temple
善導寺站

BL9 Chunghsiao-Hsinsheng
忠孝新生站

BL10 Chunghsiao-Fuhsing
忠孝復興站

BL11 Chunghsiao-Tunhua
忠孝敦化站

BL12 Sun Yatsen Memorial
國父紀念館站

BL13 City Hall
市政府站

BL14 Sungshan
松山站

BL15 Houshan Pi
後山埤站

BL16 Kunyang
昆陽站

BL17 Nankang
南港站

Brown Line (Neihu-Mucha Zoo)

BR1 (planned)

BR2 Chungshan Jr High School
中山國中站

BR3 Nanking E Rd
南京東路站

BR4 Chunghsiao-Fuhsing
忠孝復興站

BR5 Ta'an
大安站

BR6 Kochi Building
科技大樓站

BR7 Liuchangli
六張犁站

BR8 Linkuang
麟光站

BR9 Hsinhai
辛亥站

BR10 Wanfang Hospital
萬芳醫院站

BR11 Wanfang Community
萬芳社區站

BR12 Mucha
木柵站

BR13 Taipei-Mucha Zoo
動物園站

Green Line (Hsintien-Little South Gate)

G1 Hsintien
新店站

G2 Hsintien Government Office
新店公所站

G3 Chichang
七張站

G4 Tapinglin
大坪林站

G5 Chingmei
景美站

G6 Wanlung
萬隆站

G7 Kungkuan
公館站

G8 (planned)

G9 Taipower Building
台電大樓站

G10 Kuting
古亭站

G11 Chiang Kaishek Memorial
中正紀念堂站

G12 Little South Gate
小南門站

Orange Line (Roosevelt Rd-Chungho)

O16 Tinghsi
頂溪站

O17 Yun'an Market
永安市場站

O18 Ching'an
景安站

O19 Nan Shih Chiao
南勢角站

Red Line (University Hospital-Tanshui)

R12 Taiwan University Hospital
台大醫院站

R13 Taipei Railway Station
台北車站

R14 Chungshan
中山站

R15 Shuanglien
雙連站

R16 Minchuan W Rd
民權西路站

R17 Yuanshan
圓山站

R18 Chientan
劍潭站

R19 (planned)

R20 Shihlin
士林站

R21 Chihshan
芝山站

R22 Tienmu
天母站

R23 Shihpai
石牌站

R24 Chili An
唭哩岸站

R25 Chiyen
奇岩站

R26 Peitou
北投站

R27 New Peitou
新北投站

R28 Fuhsingkang
復興崗站

R29 Chungyi
忠義站

R30 Kuantu
關渡站

R31 Chuwei
竹圍站

R32 Hung Shulin
紅樹林

R33 Tanshui
淡水站

office in Taipei, Hertz also has branches in Taoyuan, Hsinchu, Taichung, Changhua, Tainan and Kaohsiung. Some agencies to try include:

Taipei Budget Rent-A-Car
   10 Wenchang Rd, Shihlin district
   (☎ 8312906, fax 8348916)

Central Auto Rental
   164 Chengte Rd, Section 4
   (☎ 8819545, 8821000, fax 8816534)
International Auto Service
   37 Tehsing E Rd, Shihlin district, Tienmu
   (☎ 8331225, 8341225)
VIP Car Rental
   148 Minchuan E Rd, Section 3
   (☎ 7131111)

North Taiwan 台灣北部

If you want to understand why the Portuguese called this island Formosa, you'll have to get out of Taipei. Unfortunately, too many foreigners seem to get stuck in the big city and never see the rest of the island – a pity.

Within a short distance from Taipei, you can forget all about the problems of urban life and find peace and relaxation visiting some of Taiwan's mountains, beaches and hot spring resorts. You can experience some of the pleasures of rural living, breathe air that you can't see, visit waterfalls and temples, and enjoy some of Taiwan's best food.

Taipei County 台北縣

WULAI
(wūlái) 烏來

It rains a lot in Taipei, and many have asked me if there's any good sightseeing places that can be done on a rainy day. The answer is Wulai, a mountain area 29 km (a one-hour bus ride) south of Taipei. Wulai has beautiful, though nowadays commercialised, mountain scenery. The star attraction is the magnificent waterfall – the harder it rains, the more dramatic the falls. As an added bonus, rain scares off the tourists. Wulai has the advantage of being a lot higher and therefore cooler than Taipei. Other features are a magnificent gorge and aboriginal villages.

Wulai can be wall-to-wall people on weekends and holidays. The Chinese describe this phenomenon as a 'people mountain, people sea' *(rén shān rén hǎi)*. Come on weekdays or you'll be sorry.

Wulai Hot Springs Village
(wūlái wēnquán qū) 烏來溫泉區

Perhaps this is more of a non-attraction. From where the bus lets you off, you walk across a short bridge and enter a small street which is a solid mass of souvenir shops

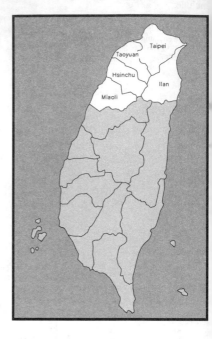

selling everything a tourist desires. So if you'd like to pick up an alligator with a light bulb in its mouth, or a Buddha with a clock in his stomach, this is the place to do it.

There are indeed hot springs here, but they are fully developed. The only way to gain access is to rent a room at one of the pricey hotels in the village.

Wulai Falls
(wūlái pùbù) 烏來瀑布

When you come to the end of the street in Wulai Hot Springs Village, there is another bridge going over the river. You have to pay an admission charge of NT$35 to cross. After crossing the bridge, you will encounter a congregation of persistent taxi drivers. Ignore them and walk up the steps. You'll

174

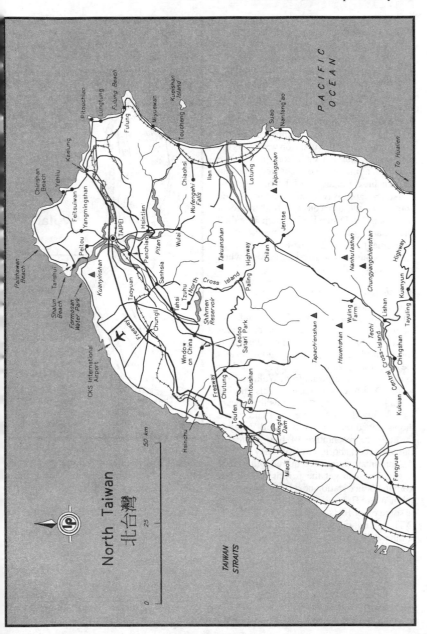

soon come to the electric minitrain. It's not expensive, so take the train and you'll be whisked away to the base of Wulai Falls. At the base of the falls, you will almost certainly see a couple of aboriginal girls in red miniskirts. They welcome you to take their picture posing by the waterfall, but you are expected to pay.

There's a collection of shops and restaurants here. 'Aboriginal culture' makes the cash register ring at Wulai – on weekends the local aborigines put on a song and dance show. An admission fee is charged. You can take a cable car to the top of the falls; the cost of a return ticket is NT$180 for adults. When you get to the top you will find the local equivalent of Disneyland, which is called Dreamland (yúnxiān lèyuán). In spite of the amusement park atmosphere, it's fun to go there – as long as you go on a weekday, when it's not crowded.

Doll Valley
(wáwa gǔ) 娃娃谷
Wulai Hot Springs Village, Dreamland, and the toy train and cable car are hardly representative of traditional aboriginal lifestyle. If you want to get away from the tourists and see a real aboriginal village, you can do a four-km (each way) walk from Wulai to Doll Valley. Don't expect to see the locals running around in loincloths and brandishing spears – they only do that in the song and dance shows staged for tourists. But Doll Valley is certainly representative of how many of Taiwan's rural aborigines live today.

A mountain permit is required, but is easy to get. You can get the permit for NT$10 from the police station next to the bus terminal in Wulai Hot Springs Village. A passport or some other ID is needed.

There's not much nightlife in Doll Valley, but the walk up there – through a gorge with a rushing river below – offers brilliant scenery. Avoid it on Sundays, when the place gets overrun by local hiking clubs. You can also take a taxi or hitch to Doll Valley, or drive your own vehicle if you have one. There's no bus service.

At the upper end of the gorge, it's possible

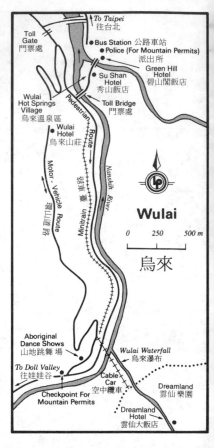

to reach the river and enjoy a cool swim. There are a number of outstanding hikes from Doll Valley along rugged trails. It's even possible to walk all the way to the east coast near Chiaohsi in Ilan County, but finding the way will require detailed directions, if not a guide.

Places to Stay
Even though most people prefer to do Wulai as a day trip, you can spend the night. There's no real budget accommodation, but discounts on weekdays are the norm. In Wulai Hot Springs Village, near the police station,

Top: Funeral hearse (RS)
Left: Wufengchi Waterfall, Chiaohsi Hot Springs (RS)
ight: Statue of Chiang Kaishek, Taipei (RS)

Top: Ceremony during Chinese New Year, Luerhmen (RS)
Left: Pagoda at Carp Mountain, Taitung (RS)
Right: Chingshui Cliff, East Coast (MM)

is the *Green Hill Hotel* (☎ 6616342) *(bìshāngé fàndiàn)* where good-looking rooms cost NT$1500. Close by is the *Su Shan Hotel* (☎ 6616789) *(xiùshān fàndiàn)* which charges an absurd NT$2500 for a double!

Across the bridge and up the hill (see map) is the friendly *Wulai Hotel* (☎ 6616204) *(wūlái shān zhuāng)* where doubles are NT$1500. It's a quiet and pleasant place to stay, but a long walk from the bus station if you don't have your own vehicle.

Ride the cable car up into the Dreamland Amusement Park to find the *Dreamland Hotel* (☎ 6616510, fax 6616710) *(yúnxiān dà fàndiàn)*. You might want to dream about lower prices – doubles cost NT$1000 to NT$1500, twins NT$1350 to NT$3500, but you get a free soak in the hot springs.

Getting There & Away

Buses operated by the Hsintien Bus Company *(xīndiàn kèyùn)* depart every 10 minutes or so from Chingtao E Rd in Taipei, one block east of Chungshan S Rd and one block south of Chunghsiao E Rd. The trip takes about an hour each way. There's also a bus to Wulai which departs from the east side of New Park.

TSUSHIH TEMPLE

(zǔshī miào) 祖師廟

Certainly one of the most magnificent temples in Taiwan, the Tsushih Temple has been fully renovated, a process which took 45 years (starting in 1947!). Of particular interest (and one of the reasons why restoration took so long) is the intricate temple art. Like most Taoist temples, Tsushih comes to life during festivals – Ghost Month is particularly good, as are the first and sixth days of the lunar month. This is a good temple for photography. Admission is free, but donations are welcomed.

Getting There & Away

The Tsushih Temple is a little inconvenient to get to. It's in the town of Sanhsia *(sānxiá)* about 30 km south-west of Taipei. There aren't any other tourist attractions along the

route, so it's an out-and-back trip unless you have your own vehicle and want to visit nearby Tzuhu. Sanhsia itself is an historical town with many ancient houses, some dating back to the Ming Dynasty. The departure point for buses from Taipei to Sanhsia is on the west side of Chunghua Rd, between Hankou and Wuchang Sts. Bus Nos 205 and 212 go to Sanhsia. There is also a bus to Sanhsia from the east side of New Park.

LIN GARDENS

(línjiā huāyuán) 林家花園

The Lin Gardens (☎ 9653061) are in the suburb of Panchiao *(bǎnqiáo)*, south-west of Taipei proper. These classical gardens were constructed in 1894 as part of the Lin family's home. In the succeeding years the gardens were allowed to deteriorate – until 1976, when they were donated to the government. After a financial outlay of NT$157 million, the gardens were finally restored in 1987 and opened to the public.

Covering an area of only 1.2 hectares, the gardens have been declared an historic site. The grounds have numerous pavilions, arches and ponds. However, it would be stretching things to say they're very scenic. Consider them a place to kill time on a rainy Taipei day.

The gardens are at 9 Hsimen St, a 15-minute walk (slightly under one km) north-west of the Panchiao railway station. You could take a train to Panchiao, and then take a taxi or walk to the gardens. Also, bus Nos 264, 307 and 310 from Taipei pass nearby. You can catch bus No 310 from directly in front of the Taipei railway station on Chunghsiao E Rd.

The gardens are open from 9 am to 5 pm every day, except Monday and the day after public holidays. Admission is NT$60.

YUANTUNG TEMPLE

(yuántōng sì) 圓通寺

This large Buddhist monastery is in the foothills of Chungho *(zhōnghé)*, a suburb to the south-west of Taipei. It's slightly up in the hills, giving it a bit of a view. However, it's considerably less attractive now that a new freeway was built next to the temple. Probably the best reason to come here is to eat at the temple's vegetarian restaurant.

From Taipei railway station, you can get there on bus No 243. It's entirely possible to take this in with a trip to the Lin Gardens – a taxi ride between the two places would cost around NT$100.

TANSHUI
(dànshuǐ) 淡水

Tanshui (frequently misspelled 'Tamsui') is 20 km north-west of Taipei, at the mouth of the Tanshui River. Though it was once the largest port on the island, Tanshui (which means 'Freshwater') is now a fishing village. Today the town boasts a fine university, a golf course, and a good beach; Taipei residents know it as a good place to eat seafood.

The notable historic site in Tanshui is **Fort San Domingo** *(hóng máo chéng)*, a legacy of the brief Spanish occupation of north Taiwan from 1626 to 1641 and one of the oldest buildings in Taiwan. The fort was built in 1629 and was occupied by the Dutch when they expelled the Spanish in 1641. The Dutch

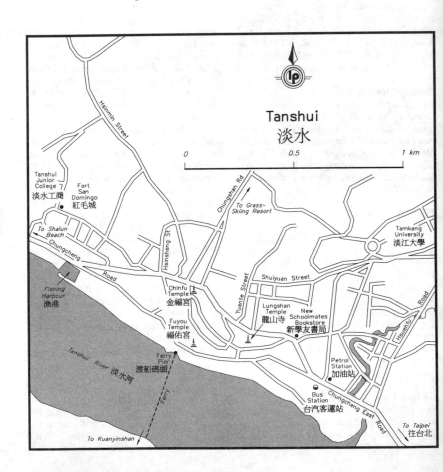

in turn were kicked out by the Chinese in 1661. In 1724, the fort was renovated and a wall with four gates was built around it. Three of the gates have disappeared, but the fourth gate remains.

The fort saw the return of the Europeans one more time. In 1867, the fort was lent to the British to establish their consulate in Taiwan. The British added considerable improvements, constructing the beautiful red brick consul's residence (which still stands) just next to the fort. The British would probably still be there were it not for the severing of relations with the ROC in 1972. The consulate was closed, but the entire structure has now been reopened as a museum.

From the Tanshui bus station, it's only a 15-minute walk or two-minute taxi ride to the fort. Admission is NT$20.

Where the Tanshui River meets the ocean is a beach known as **Shalun Beach** (*shālún hǎishuǐ yùchǎng*). This is one beach where surfing and windsurfing is possible. You can also go horse riding at the nearby Yuanye Chi Horse Riding Club (*yuányě qímǎ jùlèbù*).

In the hills above Tanshui is the Tanshui **Grass-Skiing Resort** (*dànshuǐ huácǎo chǎng*), one of the most convenient venues in Taiwan for pursuing this peculiar form of recreation.

Getting There & Away

Buses operated by the Chihnan Bus Company (*zhǐnán kèyùn*) go to Tanshui from Taipei. They depart from the North Gate area west of the railway station. Take bus No 2 or 5.

Hsintien Bus Company has lots of buses running all the way through the city from north to south, especially along Roosevelt and Chungshan roads, from Hsintien to Tanshui. These are more frequent than the numbered buses, but you'll need to be able to read the Chinese characters saying 'Hsintien-Tanshui'.

From Tanshui, you can continue on to see Chinshan Beach, Yehliu and Keelung, and then return to Taipei. This loop trip can be done in a day and in either direction.

KUANYINSHAN

(*guānyīnshān*) 觀音山

This mountain, named after Kuanyin the goddess of mercy, is a pleasant half-day hike in the Taipei area. The mountain is 612 metres high and is directly across the river from Tanshui. You can cross the river from Tanshui by taking a tiny ferry or a bus that crosses a bridge several km away, but it is quicker to reach Kuanyinshan directly from Taipei. In summer, try to head up in the morning to avoid the frequent afternoon thundershowers.

The Sanchung Bus Company (*sánchóng kèyùn*) offers a direct bus service from Taipei. The bus terminal is on Tacheng St (*tǎchéng jiē*), which is just north of the North Gate, by the GPO.

FORMOSAN WATER PARK

(*bāxiān lèyuán*) 八仙樂園

Where the slopes of Kuanyinshan meet the sea is the Formosan Water Park, or literally 'Eight Fairy Amusement Park' in Chinese. Although the name alone puts many foreigners off, it's not a bad place. The waterslides can be fun in summer, but needless to say, keep a safe distance from here on weekends.

Getting There & Away

A bus with no number, operated by the Sanchung Bus Company, leaves from a stop just by the North Gate (see West Taipei map). The bus is marked in Chinese *běimén-bālǐ* which means 'North Gate-Eight Village'.

PAISHAWAN BEACH

(*báishāwān hǎishuǐ yùchǎng*) 白沙灣海水浴場

A nice beach to the north of Tanshui, Paishawan has surfing, windsurfing and hang-gliding. Of course, it's only really enjoyable to go there during summer. There is a small entry fee but you get snack bars, lifeguards, changing facilities and someone to clean up the litter. From Tanshui, there are plenty of local buses making the north coast run.

CHINSHAN BEACH

(jīnshān hǎishuǐ yùchǎng) 金山海水浴場

Chinshan Beach is one of the best beaches close to Taipei. Of course, it does get crowded during summer weekends, but the rest of the time it's a relaxing change of pace.

If this is your first time at a beach in Taiwan, you'll notice an interesting fact – this may be an island, but few people can swim. An amazing number of people drown in Taiwan every year in small lakes, streams and the perfectly calm sea. What most Taiwanese call 'swimming' is what I'd call wading. Public swimming pools are usually no more than waist deep – some are only knee deep. At Chinshan Beach, if you get into neck-deep water you'll leave the crowd behind, but the lifeguards will frantically blow their whistles at you and perhaps launch a heroic rescue effort.

Admission to the beach costs NT$40. Admission to the swimming pool is NT$100. There are also hot spring baths.

Places to Stay

Most people treat Chinshan as a day trip from Taipei, but if you want to stay, there is the *Chinshan Youth Activity Centre* (☎ 498 1190) *(jīnshān huódòng zhōngxīn)*. It costs NT$250 to stay in the dormitory, NT$800 for a double and NT$2200 for a bungalow. The youth hostel is by the beach and crowded in summer, so try to make a reservation first.

Getting There & Away

You can reach Chinshan very easily from Taipei by first taking the bus or train to either Keelung or Tanshui (Keelung is closer), then transferring to a local bus. Chinshan is on the loop road that takes you through Tanshui, Chinshan, Yehliu, Keelung and back to Taipei, making a fine trip for a day or two.

A more direct approach from Taipei is the bus that goes over the mountains in Yangmingshan Park. You catch this bus from the Chunglun Station *(zhōnglún zhàn)* in Taipei. It's more appealing to take the coast road going there and the mountain road when returning.

YEHLIU

(yěliǔ) 野柳

About 10 km north of Keelung is Yehliu Park, known for its bizarre, jagged rock formations which have been moulded by the elements. The rocky coastline is indeed beautiful, but don't go too near the edge. A statue has been built in honour of a man who drowned while trying to save another drowning man at this spot. Unless you want to get your statue built here too, keep away from the cliffs.

After you've seen the main area of rock formations – frequently crawling with camera-clicking tourists – continue along a footpath that climbs steeply up and towards the end of the promontory. When you reach the top you'll see a lighthouse overlooking the coastline; the view is magnificent. Continue out to the end of the promontory and you'll discover nearly deserted little alcoves. The area is rarely crowded, since most of the tourists can't handle walking up the hill and prefer to hang out close to the parking lot.

Admission to the park is NT$50, but on weekdays you may well get in for free, especially if you show up during lunch break.

Yehliu restaurants have earned a bad reputation for overcharging foreign tourists. If you eat here, agree on the price in advance or bring along a suitcase full of money. Better yet, bring your own lunch and thumb your nose at the restaurant owners.

FEITSUIWAN

(fěicuì wān) 翡翠灣

Feitsuiwan (Green Bay) is a small stretch of sandy beach just east of Yehliu. It's distinguished by the fact that it's the closest spot to Taipei that offers good surfing possibilities.

Local buses from Keelung frequently run to this part of the coast. From Taipei, you can get a bus directly to Feitsuiwan from Taipei's Chunglun station.

KEELUNG

(jīlóng) 基隆

Keelung – which really should be spelled 'Chilung' – is better known as a container port than as a tourist attraction. It's the second largest port in Taiwan, the largest one being Kaohsiung. Taiwan's booming trade has turned Keelung into a very prosperous city, and as an international seaport, there are many foreigners passing through here.

Keelung has a pleasant atmosphere and is not that large – the population is around 350,000. The view from the green hills around the city is fine, though up close the harbour is much less attractive due to pollution. The water has the look of cola (including the bubbles), though I wouldn't recommend that you drink it.

During the winter months, this is one of the rainiest places in Taiwan – if you visit at that time, bring an umbrella or expect to buy one. Sunny skies are the norm during summer, though short thunderstorms in the afternoon are a common occurrence.

Information
The Bank of Taiwan (☎ 4283171) is at 16 Yi-1 Rd.

Statue of Liberty
(zìyóu nüshén) 自由女神
On the hill just behind McDonald's is a replica of New York's most famous woman. Actually, there are many such replicas in Taiwan – the Statue of Liberty and Mickey Mouse seem to be the two symbols of the USA that have really caught the imagination of the Taiwanese. While this may not be one of Keelung's most famous tourist attractions, it makes a great photograph – the golden arches of McDonald's, the Statue of Liberty and some Chinese billboards all together. You need to use a powerful telephoto lens for the best results.

Kuanyin Statue & Temple
(guānyīn miào) 觀音廟
The north-east skyline of Keelung is dominated by the huge, white statue of Kuanyin, the goddess of mercy. The statue is visible from many parts of the town, so you'll have no trouble finding it. You can climb the stairs inside the statue for a splendid view, particularly at night. Adjacent to Kuanyin is a large

temple built in her honour, and the whole area is surrounded by the greenery of Chungcheng Park. A series of smaller temples dot the ridgeline.

Sea Gate Barrier Fort
(hǎimén tiānxiǎn) 海門天險
Just a short walk north-east of the Kuanyin Temple are some old cannons and other remains of a fort said to have been built by the Dutch. Even if you have no particular interest in cannons, the views from the ridge are fine and you can continue walking for a long distance. You'll be rewarded with splendid views of the sea.

Temple 十方大覺禪寺
(shífāng dàjuéchán sì)
The Shihfang Tachuehchan temple commands a magnificent view from its hillside location among the trees. The temple is on the west side of town just off of An-1 Rd. You could walk up there from the centre of Keelung, but it's a bit far and the road is not especially attractive. Buses running from Keelung to Chinshan Beach stop nearby the temple.

Temple St Night Market
(miàokǒu yèshì) 廟口夜市
This is one of Taiwan's most renowned night markets. During the day, it's an ordinary street, but in the evening it's closed to traffic and becomes one big eating orgy. Seafood is the local speciality, though snake, dog, pangolin and other delicacies are available on demand. Ask the prices first – some of this stuff isn't cheap.

Places to Stay
You may find it convenient to spend a night in Keelung if you are entering or leaving Taiwan by ship, or if you are touring the east coast.

The cheapest place in town is the *Keelung Labourers' Recreation Centre (láogōng péngyǒu huódòng zhōngxīn)* (☎ 4286482), 22 Lane 370, Anyi Rd, Anle district. Rooms with private bath and air-conditioning cost NT$400. Unfortunately, it's too far from the

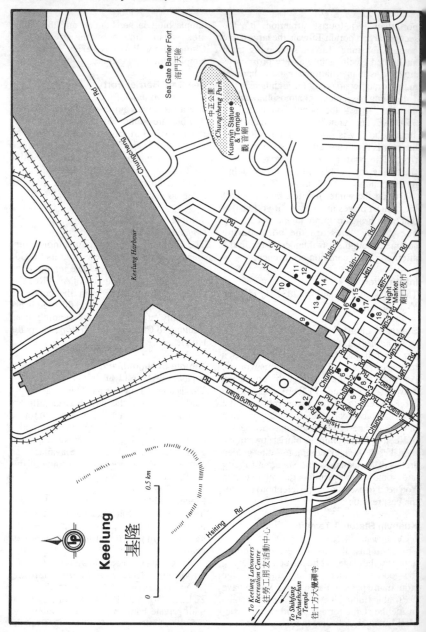

1	Bus Station
	車站
2	Police Station (Visa Extensions)
	警察局外事課
3	Longfa Hotel
	隆發旅社
4	Jindongxing Hotel
	金東興大飯店
5	Kentucky Fried Chicken
	肯德基家鄉雞
6	Huashuai Hotel
	華帥大飯店
7	Huaxing Hotel
	華星大飯店
8	Ching'an Temple
	慶安宮
9	Okinawa Ferry
	基港大樓東二碼頭
10	Hotel Kodak
	柯達大飯店
11	Dream Palace Hotel
	夢殿大飯店
12	Aloha Hotel
	阿樂哈大飯店
13	Cultural Centre
	文化中心
14	Bank of Taiwan
	台灣銀行
15	Telephone Company
	電信局
16	GPO
	郵政總局
17	Pizza Hut
	必勝客
18	McDonald's
	麥當勞

centre to walk, but the Chinshan Beach-Keelung bus can drop you off right in front of the place. The hostel is on a hillside with fine views of the harbour.

The *Longfa Hotel* (☎ 4224059) (*lóngfā lüshè*), 23 Hsiao-4 Rd, is the cheapest place in the city centre. Doubles cost NT$500.

The *Dream Palace Hotel* (☎ 4223939) (*mèngdiàn dà fàndiàn*), 22 Yi-1 Rd, is a good choice in the mid-range. Doubles are NT$780. The big sign only says 'hotel' in English, but it's easy to find – it's opposite

the Hotel Kodak and just above a 7-Eleven. The entrance is down a small alley.

Apart from these hotels, everything else is pricey. *Jindongxing Hotel* (☎ 4228206) (*jīndōngxīng dà fàndiàn*), 58 Chung-2 Rd, charges NT$1050 for a cushy double. Check out the circular beds.

The *Huashuai Hotel* (☎ 4223131) (*huáshuài dà fàndiàn*), 108 Hsiao-2 Rd, has normal rectangular-shaped beds but is still comfortable. Doubles are NT$1300.

The Huashuai is not to be confused with the similarly named *Huaxing Hotel* (☎ 4223166) (*huáxīng dàfàndiàn*), 54 Hsiao-1 Rd, where rooms cost NT$1050, NT$1200 and NT$1300.

Just opposite the Bank of Taiwan is the *Aloha Hotel* (☎ 4227322) (*ālèhā dà fàndiàn*), 292-11 Hsin-2 Rd, where doubles/twins cost NT$1080/1300.

One of the best hotels in town is the *Hotel Kodak* (☎ 4230111, fax 5435507) (*kēdá dà fàndiàn*), 7 Yi-1 Rd, where doubles are NT$1000 to NT$1200, twins NT$1450 to NT$1550.

Getting There & Away
Bus Buses depart for Keelung about once every five to 10 minutes from Taipei's East Bus Station and the fare is NT$28. The Suao to Taipei buses only stop near the ferry departure point rather than at the bus terminal near the railway station; make sure you get off at the ferry stop, or you could end up in Taipei!

Train Although this mode of transport helps you avoid the heavy traffic, most of the trains are slower than the buses. There are a few expresses, but most are local trains with infrequent departures and no air-conditioning. There also tends to be long lines at the ticket counter in Keelung station. In general, the bus is faster and cheaper.

Boat Keelung is the arrival and departure point for the international ferry to Okinawa (Japan). The ferry departs from pier No 2 on the east side of Keelung harbour. From Okinawa, you can change boats and reach the main islands of Japan. You can also catch this ferry in Kaohsiung, but the Keelung-Okinawa route is shorter and cheaper. See the Getting There & Away chapter for more details.

LUNGTUNG
(lóng dòng) 龍洞

Taiwan's most beautiful stretch of rocky coastline is between Lungtung (Dragon Hole), to the north-east of Taipei, and Pitouchiao *(bítóujiǎo)*. It's not a place for swimming, but the sheer cliffs have made this area Taiwan's prime spot for technical rock climbing. Westerners have started to come here also to test their skills on the cliffs. Even if rock climbing isn't your forte, the scenery is excellent.

To get there, first get yourself to Keelung. From Keelung, take a bus to Lungtung, about a 40-minute ride. The bus passes Pitouchiao and then enters a tunnel. After it leaves the tunnel it stops in the town of Lungtung, which consists of a few houses and small stores. From where the bus lets you off, walk back towards the tunnel. Just before you reach the tunnel, you will see a path dropping down to your right. Follow the path all the way down to the sea, about a 25-minute walk. When you hit the coast, turn left and continue walking until you see the rock-climbing area. As long as you go when the weather is fine, you should see climbers. During the wet winter months you probably won't see anybody.

FULUNG BEACH
(fúlóng hǎishuǐ yùchǎng) 福隆海水浴場

Fulung Beach is one of the best beaches in northern Taiwan. The east coast of Taiwan is mostly mountains and jagged rocks, but Fulung is one of the few places on the east coast with a broad, white-sand beach. It's also one of the few sandy beaches in Taiwan where the waves are good enough for surfing. It's also possible to go water-skiing here.

Fulung Beach is close enough to Taipei (57 km) to make a good day or weekend trip. During summer it becomes quite crowded on the weekends, but at other times you may have the scenic surroundings to yourself.

The town of Fulung is very small, pleasant and quiet. There is a NT$50 admission fee to the main beach area. The area east of the broad sandy beach is free and has good coral formations for snorkelling – plus you get away from the music that the management blasts for the customers' enjoyment. The east beach has no lifeguards.

Surfers from Taipei come here. The waves are said to be good, but the riptide can be dangerous.

Places to Stay

The *Fulung Public Hostel* (☎ 4991211, fax 4991501) *(fúlóng guómín lüshè)* is right on the beach. Actually, it doesn't seem so much like a hostel as a complex of beach cabins and a camping ground. Prices are NT$1000 for doubles, or a ridiculous NT$300 for camping (tent included) and NT$150 if you supply your own tent. The only other place to stay is *Xinli Hotel* (☎ 4991539) *(xīnlì dà fàndiàn)*, a small hotel next to the railway station. Doubles are NT$400 with shared bath, NT$700 with private bath, with substantial off-season (winter) discounts.

Getting There & Away

You can reach Fulung in less than an hour by train from Taipei's main station. Failing that, take a bus first to Keelung and then transfer to the local bus to Fulung.

Taoyuan County 桃園縣

TAOYUAN
(táoyuán) 桃園

West of Taipei is CKS International Airport, adjacent to the city of Taoyuan. There is little reason to visit unless you need to spend the night near the airport. If you're coming up from south Taiwan, you'll probably find it easier to take the train to Taoyuan and spend the night, rather than do a mad scramble in the morning. If you're coming from Taipei, it's relatively easy to reach the airport and

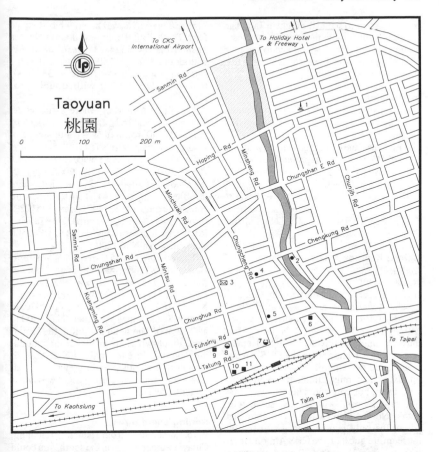

1 Pao'an Temple
  寶安寺
2 ICBC
  國際商業銀行
3 GPO
  郵政總局
4 Far Eastern Department Store
  遠東百貨
5 McDonald's & Bank of Taiwan
  麥當勞/台灣銀行
6 Hotel Today
  今日大飯店

7 Taoyuan Bus Company
  桃園客運
8 Taiwan Bus Company
  台灣客運
9 Taoyuan Plaza Hotel
  南華大飯店
10 Nestle Hotel
  雀巢大飯店
11 Hangong & Fushi hotels
  漢宮大旅社/富士大旅社

isn't necessary to spend the night in Taoyuan. It's important to note that the airport closes at night and you are *not* allowed to sleep on the sofas even if you have a ticket for the first flight out in the morning.

Information

The Tourism Bureau (☎ 3376611) maintains an office on the 2nd floor, 2 Chengkung Rd, Section 2.

You can easily change money at the airport. However, if you prefer to do it in the city, ICBC (☎ 3376611) has a branch at 2 Chengkung Rd, Section 2.

If you still haven't bought an air ticket to leave Taiwan, you can get one at Southeast Travel Service (☎ 3354677), 244 Fuhsing Rd.

Chiang Kaishek Aviation Museum

(zhōngzhèng hángkōng kēxué guǎn)

中正航空科學館

If you've been reading the pamphlets put out by the Tourism Bureau, you might have heard of the Chiang Kaishek Aviation Museum (☎ 3832677). It's not a bad museum, but most travellers will find it inaccessible. It is right next to the CKS Airport Hotel, a full two km from the airline terminal building. You might think that you could walk there, but you would have to walk on a freeway-like road with no pedestrian footpaths. Nor is there a regular shuttle bus. About the only people who get to see the museum are guests at the CKS Airport Hotel. It's open from 9 am to 4.30 pm daily except Mondays, and admission is NT$50.

Places to Stay

Not surprisingly, hotels are abundant in Taoyuan, though precious little qualifies as budget accommodation. As usual, you can find some of the best deals clustered around the railway station. If you really want a dirtcheap dormitory, Taipei is a better bet as there are no hostels in Taoyuan.

As you exit the railway station, the alley immediately to your left is Changshou ('long life') St. This place has a couple of cheap and cheapish hotels. *Hangong Hotel* (☎ 332 7189) *(hàngōng lǚshè)* at No 9 has doubles for NT$400/500. Right next door at No 7 is *Fushi Hotel* (☎ 3324161) *(fùshì dà lǚshè)* with doubles for NT$500. At No 5-1 is the better-appointed *Nestle Hotel* (☎ 3365800) *(quècháo dà fàndiàn)* with doubles for NT$860.

Moving up-market, there's the *Hotel Today* (☎ 3324162, fax 3337778) *(jīnrì fàndiàn*; 100 rooms) at 81 Fuhsing Rd. Doubles/twins go for NT$1100/1500.

Some more expensive places are: *Taoyuan Plaza Hotel* (☎ 3379222, fax 3379250) *(nánhuá dà fàndiàn)*, 151 Fuhsing Rd, where doubles/twins are NT$1500/1800; and *Holiday Hotel* (☎ 3254021, fax 3251222) *(jiàrì dà fàndiàn*; 391 rooms), 269 Tahsing Rd, where doubles/twins are NT$2100/2500 and suites cost NT$4200.

There is also the 511-room *CKS Airport Hotel* (☎ 3833666, fax 3833546) *(zhōngzhèng guójì jīchǎng lǚguǎn*, PO Box 66, CKS Airport, Taoyuan. Doubles are NT$2400, twins range from NT$2520 to NT$3020 and suites are a mere NT$5000 to NT$12,500. The hotel is right in the airport area, about two km from the terminal building, and not close to anything else. Most of the guests are either flight crews or transit passengers whose departing flight was unexpectedly delayed.

Getting There & Away

If you are coming from Hsinchu, Taichung, Chiayi or other places in the south, you could take a train or bus to Taoyuan. The train is usually more convenient because most highway buses bypass Taoyuan and head directly to Taipei. All north-south trains on the west coast stop in Taoyuan.

Getting Around

The airport *(zhōngzhèng jīchǎng)* can be reached during the day and in the early evening by buses run from the Taoyuan Bus Company terminal. Otherwise, there are plenty of taxis swarming around the railway station area. Negotiate the fare in advance and expect to pay around NT$400.

TZUHU
(cíhú) 慈湖

Tzuhu, which translates as 'Lake Kindness', is where the body of Chiang Kaishek is entombed. The site is regarded as temporary; it is intended that the body will be returned to the mainland after China is reunited. Most of the Chinese in Taiwan and many foreigners have visited this site.

Go into the main building and you'll find the security desk right near the snack bar. Let them see your passport and they'll fill out a form which you give to the guard at the entrance. You have to walk for about 10 minutes to reach the actual mausoleum. Along the way you'll pass the lake.

You can take photographs outside the mausoleum but not inside. You're allowed about a minute inside to view the granite case in which the body has been placed. It is customary to give a respectful bow.

It's OK to visit Tzuhu on Sundays, as it doesn't get overly crowded.

Getting There & Away
To reach Tzuhu from Taipei, first take a train to Taoyuan *(táoyuán)* or Chungli *(zhōnglì)*. From there you can get a bus directly to Tzuhu or else to the nearby town of Tahsi *(dàxī)*, from where you'll have to get another bus to Tzuhu. Buses from Tahsi to Tzuhu are not very frequent so you might have to take a taxi. Fortunately, it's not very far so it's not too expensive.

It is possible to combine a visit to Tzuhu with a trip to the Tsu Shih Temple and Shihmen Reservoir. However, there are no direct buses between these places even though they are very close to each other. You must first go back to Tahsi, which is out of the way, and either change buses or take a taxi. The most convenient way to get between these places is to drive yourself.

SHIHMEN RESERVOIR
(shímén shuǐkù) 石門水庫

Shihmen Reservoir forms the largest lake in northern Taiwan. The Shihmen Dam, on the Tanshui River, is nestled in the foothills south-west of Taipei. Construction of the dam began in 1955 and was completed in 1964. It's an attractive area, but becoming badly congested on weekends because of its proximity to Taipei.

If you arrive by bus, the driver will drop you off right by the dam, the No 1 touristy spot. From there you can join a boat tour or walk around. The road on the north shore of the lake is an attractive but very long hike – a motorcycle would be useful. Swimming is not permitted in the lake but fishing is allowed.

If you go far enough upstream on the north shore road, you'll reach Fuhsing Village *(fùxīng xiāng)*, an attractive place which has a youth hostel – the only cheap place to stay in the Shihmen area.

There is a beautiful trip starting from Shihmen Reservoir and continuing over the mountains, via the North Cross-Island Highway (Highway 7) to Chilan *(qīlán)*. Details about making this trip are given in the North Cross-Island section further on in this chapter.

Places to Stay
Shihmen Reservoir is really not the greatest place to stay – if you head further into the mountains you'll pay less and probably enjoy it more.

The *Sesame Hotel* (☎ 4712120) *(zhīmá dà fàndiàn)* sets a high standard but does not command a view of the lake, though it overlooks the river below. Doubles cost NT$1000. The *Yun Hsiao Hotel* (☎ 471 2111/2) *(yúnxiāo dà fàndiàn)* is on a hill right next to the dam. Doubles start from NT$800. The *Shihmen Lake Hotel* (☎ 4883883) *(húbīng dà fàndiàn)* is slowly turning into a carnival. Doubles are NT$1200.

Camping The *Grand Canyon Camping Ground* at the eastern end of the lake is one possibility. On the south shore of the lake is the *Pine Forest Camping Ground*.

Getting There & Away
To get to Shihmen Reservoir, first take a bus or train to Chungli *(zhōnglì)*, which is 36 km south-west of Taipei. Then transfer to a local

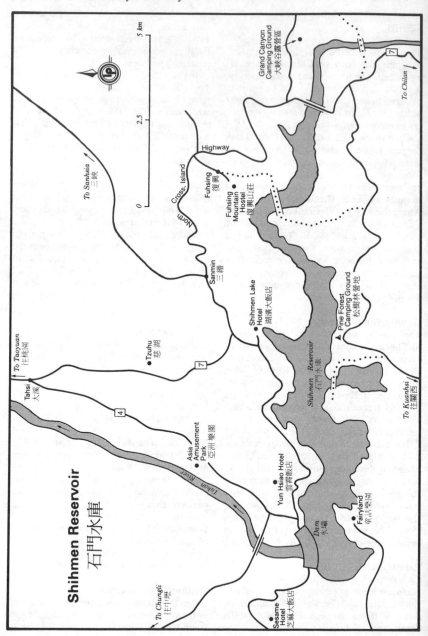

bus which will take you to Shimmen Reservoir. Buses to the reservoir are not very frequent. If you don't catch one right away, take a bus to Tahsi (dàxī) and then get a bus or taxi or hitchhike up to the reservoir.

NORTH CROSS-ISLAND HIGHWAY
(běibù héngguàn gōnglù) 北部橫貫公路

Highway 7, also called the North Cross-Island Highway, is a beautiful but little-travelled mountain road that starts from Taoyuan and then heads up into the hills above Shimmen Reservoir. Buses operated by the Taoyuan Bus Company (táoyuán kèyùn) use the highway. Cars are infrequent, so hitching is not easy except on weekends. It's a good route to drive along if you have your own vehicle.

The highway branches at Chilan (qílán): the north branch heads down to the east coast at Ilan (yílán) and the south branch heads still higher up into the mountains until it intersects with the Central Cross-Island Highway at Lishan. If you stay at the Paling Mountain Hostel, there is an interesting day hike that you can do. Just to the north of Paling is the mountain Takuanshan (dáguānshān) in the Lalashan Forest Reserve (lālāshān shéngmù qún), which can be reached by walking 13 km along the gravel road. You gain about 1000 metres in elevation, so you might consider hitching uphill and walking back, assuming that you see any cars. A mountain permit is needed, but it can easily be obtained along the way. The area is known for its giant cypress trees, some of which are more than 2500 years old. Takuanshan itself reaches 2030 metres above sea level.

Places to Stay

The choices are limited. The Fuhsing Mountain Hostel (☎ 3822276) (fùxīng shān zhuāng) is at the entrance to the highway, just above Shimmen Reservoir (see the Shimmen Reservoir map). They have doubles for NT$700 and dormitory beds for NT$200. The Paling Mountain Hostel (☎ 3332153) (bālíng shān zhuāng) is further up the mountains and costs the same. For the addresses of the youth hostels, refer to the Youth Hostels map in the Facts for the Visitor chapter. Camping is another possibility.

WINDOW ON CHINA
(xiǎo rén guó) 小人國

Many years ago I read a novel entitled Slapstick by Kurt Vonnegut. According to the story, the Chinese found that the only way they could feed their massive population was to make people smaller. Chinese scientists discovered a way to shrink people. So China closed its borders to the world and began the downsizing process. Several years later, the world was gripped by a massive killer plague. People were dying like flies. An American doctor discovered the reason why – the disease was caused by inhaling microscopic Chinese.

'Nonsense' you say? Then welcome to the Window on China. It's an outdoor park that contains exact models of many of China's famous architectural wonders such as the Great Wall and the Forbidden City. And yes, miniature people too. Some of Taiwan's notable building projects are also included, such as the Chiang Kaishek Memorial, the Sun Yatsen Freeway (with miniature cars) and CKS Airport (with miniature planes). Everything is reduced to 1/25 of normal size. The Tourism Bureau calls it a 'world class tourist attraction'. Who says the Taiwanese don't have a sense of humour? Admission is NT$190. The Window on China is open daily from 8.30 am to 5.30 pm.

Getting There & Away

To reach the Window on China from Taipei, take a train to Chungli (zhōnglì) and then a bus from the Hsinchu Bus Company (xīnchú kèyùn) terminal, which is near the railway station.

The Window on China is close to Leofoo Safari Park and it is possible to visit both places on the same day. You may also want to visit Tzuhu and Shimmen Reservoir in the same trip, especially if you have your own car or motorcycle.

Hsinchu County 新竹縣

LEOFOO SAFARI PARK
(liùfú cūn yě shēng dòngwù yuán)
六福村野生動物園

Leofoo Safari Park (☎ 872626) is an outdoor zoo where the animals wander around loose while you drive through in a car or tour bus. It's very touristy and most suited to families with children.

The park features a wide range of animals including deer, lions, tigers, baboons, giraffes and zebras. As in other tourist areas, it's best to visit it on weekdays, although this safari park doesn't get especially crowded. Admission is NT$185, and it's open from 9 am to 4.30 pm daily.

Getting There & Away
Certainly the most convenient way to get to the park is to take the bus operated by the Leofoo Hotel (☎ 02-5073211) *(liùfú kèzhàn)* at 168 Changchun Rd, Taipei. Buses depart daily at 9 am. The price of the ticket includes the return fare, admission and a tour around the park.

Should you decide to visit the Leofoo Safari Park on your own, you can reach it by taking a train to Chungli *(zhònglì)* and then catching a bus from the terminal across the street from the railway station.

HSINCHU
(xīnzhú) 新竹

Hsinchu is a moderate-size city and is known mainly for its windy winter weather and Science-Industrial Park. The Science-Industrial Park is where many of Taiwan's high-technology companies are located, but it's not a place for tourists. Likewise, the city itself is not of special interest to most travellers, other than as a transit point on the way to Shihtoushan or Tapachienshan.

Information
Tourist Office The Tourism Bureau (☎ 217171) has a branch on the 3rd floor, 115 Chungcheng Rd.

Money ICBC (☎ 217171) *(guójì shāngyè yínháng)* is at 129 Chungcheng Rd. The Bank of Taiwan (☎ 266161) *(táiwān yínháng)* is at 29 Linsen Rd. Citibank (☎ 23 6622) *(huāqí yínháng)* can offer cash advan-

1 ICBC
中國國際商業銀行
2 Telephone Company
電信局
3 City Hall
市正府
4 Police (Visa Extensions)
警察局外事課
5 Chinatrust Hotel
& Far Eastern Dept Store
中信大飯店/遠東百貨
6 Chenghuang Temple
城隍廟
7 GPO
郵政總局
8 McDonald's & Sunrise Dept Store
麥當勞/中興百貨
9 Bank of Taiwan
台灣銀行
10 Hotel Central
中央旅社
11 Wantai Hotel
萬太大飯店
12 Golden Swallow Hotel
金燕大飯店
13 Hsinchu Bus Company
新竹客運站
14 Bin-Chen Hotel
賓城大飯店
15 Yinchuan Hotel
銀川大旅社
16 Dongbin Hotel
東賓大旅社
17 Bus Station
台汽客運站
18 Kuanyin Temple
觀音廟
19 Confucius Temple
孔子廟
20 Zoo
動物園
21 Swimming Pool
游泳池

ces to Citibank card holders from the branch at 79 Tungmen St.

Things to See

The main attraction in Hsinchu is the **Hsinchu Zoo** *(xīnzhú dòngwù yuán)*. As zoos go, it's quite small. You can find it in Chungshan Park, behind the railway station, just near the Confucius Temple *(kǒngzǐ miào)*.

Also worth visiting is the **Chenghuang Temple** *(chénghuáng miào)*, near the intersection of Chungshan Rd and Tungmen St.

The temple contains lots of artwork and is especially active during Ghost Month and on the first and sixth days of the lunar month.

Just outside of town is **Grass Lake** *(qīngcǎo hú)*. The locals seem to think it's a very impressive sight. Personally, I just think it's a small lake with grass around it.

There are two national universities in Hsinchu, specialising in science and technology. You could check out the bookshops and perhaps meet some students. The two universities are Tsinghua University *(qīnghuá dàxué)*, 855 Kuangfu Rd, and Chiaotung University *(jiāotōng dàxué)*, 100 Tahsueh Rd.

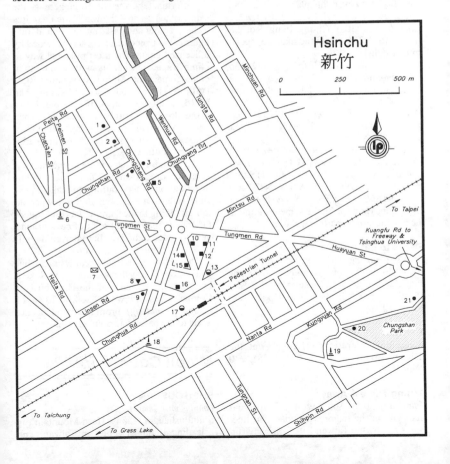

Hsinchu
新竹

Places to Stay

There is no need to look any further than the area near the railway station. I like the *Golden Swallow Hotel* (☎ 227151, fax 227511) *(jīnyàn dà fàndiàn)*, 13 Mintsu Rd. They even have waterbeds! At NT$550 for a double, it's good value, at least by Hsinchu standards.

Wantai Hotel (☎ 254117) *(wàntài dà fàndiàn)*, 17 Mintsu Rd, is almost next door to the Golden Swallow. Doubles are NT$550. The *Dongbin Hotel* (☎ 223162) *(dōngbīn dà lüshè)*, 14 Linsen Rd, has doubles for NT$400 and serves a good breakfast. However, this place is often full.

The *Hotel Central* (☎ 224126) *(zhōngyāng lüshè)*, 30-1 Chungcheng Rd, has singles for NT$500 and the manager speaks some English.

The *Yinchuan Hotel* (☎ 224135) *(yínchuān dà lüshè)*, 5 Chungcheng Rd, has friendly management and doubles cost NT$600 to NT$700.

The *Bin-Chen Hotel* (☎ 269255) *(bīnchéng dà fàndiàn)*, 15 Chungcheng Rd, has doubles for NT$650.

Top of the line is the *Chinatrust Hotel* (☎ 263181, fax 269244) *(zhōngxìn dà fàndiàn*; 132 rooms). Doubles are NT$2550 to NT$2650, twins NT$2900 to NT$3400, suites NT$6600 to NT$9900. The hotel is at 106 Chungyang Rd, in the same building as the Far Eastern Department Store.

Places to Eat

Jake's Country Kitchen (☎ 346028) is related to the Taipei restaurant of the same name, and offers fine Western food. It's at 450 Chingkuo Rd, Section 1. Open 7 am until 9.30 pm.

Activities

If bowling interests you, check out the Hsinchu Bowling Centre (☎ 224128), 240 Peimen St.

Getting There & Away

Hsinchu is 70 km south-west of Taipei and sits right on the major west-coast rail line. Buses run by the Taiwan Bus Company run frequently from Hsinchu to Taipei and Taichung. There are less frequent services to smaller cities such as Tainan and Chiayi.

EVA Airways (☎ 235467) *(chángróng hángkōng)*, maintains a representative office on the 7th floor, 141 Chungcheng Rd.

TAPACHIENSHAN

(dà bà jiān shān) 大霸尖山

Tapachienshan means 'Big Chief Pointed Mountain'. Whatever it's called, it's the most beautiful peak in Taiwan. At an elevation of 3505 metres, it's one of the jewels of Hsuehpa National Park.

Unfortunately, the situation here is the same as at Yushan – the whole area requires a class A mountain pass, and individual travellers cannot get one unless accompanied by a licensed guide. The most practical way to climb Tapachienshan is with a mountain club. Contact the Alpine Association ROC (☎ 02-5911498), 10th floor, 185 Chungshan N Rd, Section 2, Taipei. If possible, try to avoid doing the climb on weekends when you have to stand in line to get up the trail. Some clubs also make a quick run up nearby Hsiaopa (Little Chief).

The summit is shaped like a pyramid and is sheer on all sides. The government installed some metal railings to make it possible to reach the top, but after a few people fell off, going to the summit was prohibited. Of course, there aren't a lot of cops around here to enforce the law, but your guide will have something to say about it.

The peak is not actually near Hsinchu, but that's more or less the starting point. Take a bus from the terminal of the Hsinchu Bus Company *(xīnzhú kèyùn)* to the town of Chutung *(zhúdōng)*. From there you can get a bus to the base of Tapachienshan.

Miaoli County 苗栗縣

SHIHTOUSHAN

(shītóushān) 獅頭山

Shihtoushan, or 'Lion's Head Mountain', is a leading Buddhist centre in Taiwan. The name derives from the fact that the mountain vaguely resembles the head of a lion when viewed from a distance. For foreign visitors, the main attraction is the chance to visit temples and the opportunity to stay in a Buddhist monastery with beautiful natural surroundings.

The temples are not very old, and indeed there were some new ones under construction when I first visited, but they are all very nice.

Spending the night in one of the monasteries can be interesting, but this is not the place for nightlife. Shihtoushan is a very restful place and draws a steady stream of pilgrims from all over Taiwan. You can watch the morning services at the crack of dawn.

Monks and nuns lead a spartan lifestyle and follow a rigid daily routine. They go to bed early and get up early. In a monastery you must bathe daily, not in the morning but always in the evening or late afternoon when hot water is available; expect to bathe between 3 and 6 pm, which is early by Chinese standards. This is because the monks and nuns go to bed at 8 pm. You can stay up later if you like, so long as you don't disturb those who are sleeping.

Since the monks and nuns get up at dawn, you will have to as well. Expect breakfast to be served at about 5.30 am, lunch at noon and dinner at 5.30 pm. The food is good and vegetarian. Strict silence is observed while eating. Don't waste your rice! If you throw any away the monks are liable to get upset, as they believe in wasting nothing. If you need additional snacks, you can buy them from some of the vendors at the foot of the hill.

During the day, you are free to come and go as you like. You only need to be on your best behaviour in the temple grounds. The monks and nuns realise that Westerners have their own peculiar customs and they are reasonably tolerant, but when you're on their turf they also want you to be tolerant and respect their religion and lifestyle. After all, you're living in their temple.

Couples cannot sleep together, even if they're married. Kissing and caressing in public are also unacceptable. You may take photographs in the temple but don't disturb the worshippers. If the daily routine and social practices of a monastery are too confining for you, it's better not to stay there.

The Hsinchu area is very windy, especially in winter, so bring a jacket as it can be really chilly at night. From the bus stop there's an hour's hike up a steep incline to the top of the mountain, so try to keep luggage to a minimum. If your backpack is overloaded, you can put the heavy items in a box and stash it in the left-luggage room at the Hsinchu railway station for NT$14 per day.

Places to Stay

Staying at a monastery is a major attraction for many travellers. The more or less mandatory donation is NT$700 and this includes dinner and breakfast. It's another NT$50 if you stay for lunch. In keeping with Buddhist custom, all the meals are vegetarian. If you don't want to stay in a monastery, you can visit Shihtoushan as a day trip from Hsinchu.

The most popular monastery is the *Yuankuang Temple*. It's near the top of the mountain, offers the best scenery and there is a caretaker who can speak English. The other monasteries which offer accommodation are *Linghsia Cave (língxiá dòng)* and *Chuanhua Hall (quànhuà táng)*.

Getting There & Away

From Hsinchu, you cannot go directly to Shihtoushan – you must transfer buses. First take a bus to Chutung *(zhúdōng)*, which is a 25-minute trip. Buses run about once every 10 minutes from the terminal of the Hsinchu Bus Company *(xīnzhú kèyùn)*, which is on the traffic island in front of the Hsinchu railway station.

From Chutung there are buses to Shihtoushan, a 40-minute trip. They are not frequent. As always, the schedule is subject to change, but at the time of writing departures from Chutung were at 6.40 and 10.40 am, and at 1.55 and 5 pm. The first bus does not run on Sunday or holidays because it's

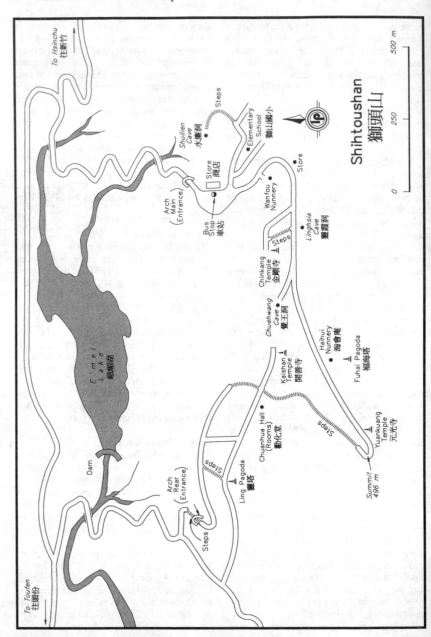

Shihtoushan 獅頭山

used primarily to shuttle schoolchildren. On weekends, there are additional buses at 8.30 and 9.15 am and at 3.30 pm. The bus lets you off at the last stop and from there you walk up, up, up.

Ilan County 宜蘭縣

MIYUEWAN
(mìyuèwān) 蜜月灣

Also known by its English name, Honeymoon Bay, Miyuewan is a small but beautiful black-sand beach at the northern end of Ilan County. This is also the home of the Honeymoon Bay Surfing Club and the Surfing Centre. Both places operate hostels with basic rooms for NT$250. Camping is also possible here. There are plenty of places to eat at this popular spot, at least during summer when the weather cooperates. Like at most east-coast beaches, rip tides can be a problem here.

You can reach Miyuewan by taking a train to Tahsi *(dàxī)* station. Only two express trains stop here daily – if you miss those, take a local train *(pǔtōng chē)* which takes about two hours from Taipei. The Chunghsing bus from Keelung and Taipei also stops here.

CHIAOHSI HOT SPRINGS
(jiāoxī wēnquán) 礁溪溫泉

Wufengchi Waterfall *(wǔfēngqí pùbù)* in the hills above the town is about the best reason for visiting Chiaohsi. Within walking distance of the waterfall is a luxury hotel complex. In winter, residents of Taipei who are weary of the city and cold come to Chiaohsi to soak in the hot springs. It's certainly much more relaxed than Peitou, though it should definitely be avoided on weekends. There is a horse-riding stable near the falls, but the staff prefers you ride around the car park in circles rather than on trails through the forest.

Places to Stay

There are dozens of hotels in the town of Chiaohsi itself, and most have signs in English so they're easy to find for the non-Chinese-speaking foreigner. However, I feel it's only worth spending the night in Chiaohsi if you stay by the waterfall area, which is much more beautiful than the town. Near the waterfall is a complex of several luxury hotels with their own restaurants, swimming pools and other amenities.

Sorry to say there is no place for budget travellers. Comfortable rooms are available at the *Wufengchi Hotel* (☎ 885211, fax 883050) *(wǔfēngqí dà fàndiàn)*, where doubles are NT$1200 to NT$1400 but there is a 40% discount on weekdays.

Next door is the *Happy Hotel* (☎ 881511, fax 882108) *(kuàilè shān zhuāng dà fàndiàn)*, with doubles from NT$1320. Discounts here are only 15% on weekdays.

Getting There & Away

Reaching Chiaohsi Hot Springs from Taipei is easy enough. Local trains heading down the east coast stop there, as do numerous buses plying the route between Taipei and Suao. Get off the bus or train in the town of Chiaohsi. From Chiaohsi to the waterfall it is about a 50 minute walk or a short taxi ride.

TAIPINGSHAN
(tàipíngshān) 太平山

Towering majestically over the scenic east coast is Taipingshan, one of the closest places to Taipei where you can experience Taiwan's rugged mountain wilderness. It's close enough to the city to spare you a long, tedious bus ride into the mountains. Yet Taipingshan is so clean, quiet and beautiful that visitors can easily forget Taipei lies only 50 km away. Perhaps this accounts for it's Chinese name, which means 'Peaceful Mountain'.

Hiking is a favourite pastime at Taipingshan. One place worth visiting is Tsuifeng Lake *(cuìfēng hú)*. The lake is very small but beautiful. If you have the time and the energy, you could follow the main road and walk back down the mountain to Jentse *(rénzé)*, known for its hot springs. It's an eight-hour hike, but at least it's downhill and you'll be rewarded with a nice soak in the hot springs. From Jentse, you can get a bus out the next day to return to Ilan.

If you're going to hike, pay attention to the weather. The best time of the year to visit is during the summer and autumn months. It's usually fine in the morning, although thunderstorms are a distinct possibility in the afternoon. In winter, the weather is similar to Taipei only colder, and snow is a possibility near the summit. Personally, I wouldn't recommend this trip in winter. All of north-east Taiwan is uniformly soggy from about December through to March. If it's raining in Taipei, head further to the south-west (near Lishan, for example) to find drier but equally cold mountain weather.

There is an NT$80 admission fee to enter the Taipingshan Forest Recreation Area.

Places to Stay

In Taipingshan itself there is only one place to stay: the *Taipingshan Mountain Hostel* (☎ 544052, 546055) *(tàipíngshān shān zhuāng)*, where rooms cost NT$700 to NT$1000. At 1930 metres above sea level, Taipingshan gets cold – so come prepared.

The *Jentse Mountain Hostel* (☎ 544052, 546055) *(rénzé shān zhuāng)*, Jentse Hot Springs *(rénzé wēnquán)*, is near the base of the mountain at an altitude of 650 metres. Prices here are exactly the same as the Taipingshan Mountain Hostel. The weather is warmer at Jentse and you can enjoy a nice long soak in the hot springs. In summer, I prefer the top of the mountain.

You may notice that both hotels have the same telephone number. In fact, both places use the phone of the Forest Service headquarters at Taipingshan. If you want to make a reservation you have to call this number during the day, which is the only time they are open.

Getting There & Away

Taipingshan is a remote area and getting there can be a headache. One major problem is that there is no public transport going all the way up the mountain. There used to be, but we can thank Taiwan's car revolution for the bus company's collapse. Fortunately,

there are daily buses as far as Jentse. From there you'll have to walk or hitch. Traffic to Taipingshan is rare on weekdays but usually plentiful on weekends. Since walking downhill is easier, probably your best bet is to hitchhike up on Sunday and walk down on Monday.

Buses depart only once a day for Jentse – from the town of Ilan at 7.50 am. Buses leave from the terminal of the Taiwan Bus Company (☎ 322067) *(táiqì kèyùn)*. All this poses another problem because getting to Ilan before the Jentse bus departs is no easy feat. The best thing to do is to stay in Ilan the night before to catch the morning bus. The returning bus from Jentse to Ilan departs at 1.30 pm – but check that, because the schedule can (and does) change.

In contrast to the scarce public buses, tour buses from Taipei descend on Taipingshan en masse during the peak (summer) season.

SUAO

(sū ào) 蘇澳

Although Suao itself is nothing to write home about, many travellers wind up staying there overnight so they can catch the early morning bus to Hualien (see East Coast chapter). Suao has a smattering of sights around the town which can keep you amused for the day.

Information

The Bank of Taiwan (☎ 962566) is at 97 Chungshan Rd.

Hsienkung Temple

(xiāngōng miào) 仙公廟

This classic Taoist temple is on Chungshan Rd. On most days it's slow, but it gets jumping for lunar festivals.

Nanfang'ao

(nánfāng'aò) 南方澳

Suao has a large harbour with an entrance surrounded by fences and a police checkpoint. This one isn't worth looking at – the real attraction is about two km to the southeast at Nanfang'ao. This is an attractive fishing harbour and it's possible to wander

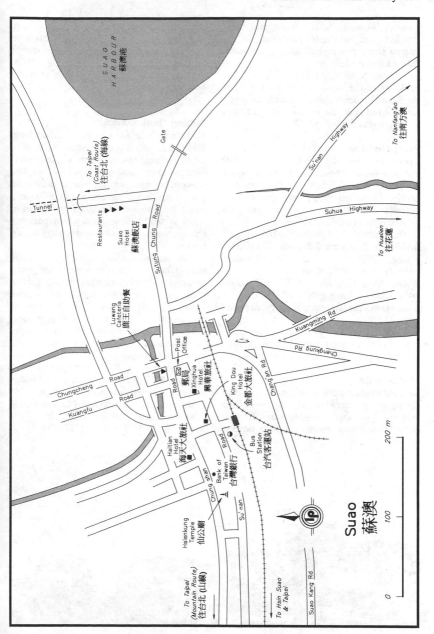

Suao
蘇澳

around. Wooden fishing boats and steel freighters are built here. Just south of the fishing harbour is a good, little-used beach (*nèipí hǎishuǐ yùchǎng*).

To reach Nanfang'ao, follow the road that leads out of the south side of town (part of the Suao-Hualien highway), which takes you up a big hill. Take the left fork which brings you right into the village.

Places to Stay

There are a few cheap hotels near the bus station. One of the best deals for the money is the *Xinghua Hotel* (☎ 962581) (*xīnghuá lüshè*), 13 Su'nan Rd, where doubles are NT$400 with shared bath, NT$500 with private bath and air-conditioning.

The *Haitian Hotel* (☎ 962576) (*hǎitiān dà lüshè*), 96 Chungshan Rd, costs NT$500 for a single, NT$600 for a double. All rooms have a private bath and are clean.

The *King Dou Hotel* (*jīndū dà lüshè*) (☎ 962586), 6 Taiping Rd, costs NT$500 for a double but the atmosphere is a bit depressing.

If money is no object, the *Suao Hotel* (☎ 965181) (*sū aò fàndiàn*), 7 Sutung Chung Rd, offers good, clean doubles for NT$800.

Places to Eat

Seafood is ubiquitous – the locals even dish up squid for breakfast. If you don't like seafood, you face possible starvation in Suao. Fortunately, there seems to be one place that serves up cheap but good rice, veggies and meat: *Luwang Cafeteria* (*lùwáng zìzhù cān*) on the north-west corner of Chungshan and Chungcheng roads. Luwang means 'deer king' – I didn't see any deer meat though.

Getting There & Away

There are three ways to get to Suao from Taipei. The fastest way is to take the train to Suao. The next-fastest option is to take a bus over the mountains from Taipei to Suao. The slowest, but most scenic route, is to take the coastal bus. Bus departures are from Taipei's North Bus Station. The fare from Taipei to Suao is NT$196 – there are departures throughout the day in both directions from 6 am until 8.30 pm.

Suao has two railway stations: the old one next to the bus station in central Suao and a new one several km out of town called 'Hsin Suao' (*xīn sū aò*). All express trains from Taipei stop only in Hsin Suao. The port of Suao itself is only served by the slow local trains. Therefore, if you arrive from Taipei by express train and want to switch to the Suao-Hualien bus, you have to take a bus from Hsin Suao to the Suao bus station (15 minutes, NT$10). Occasionally, local trains also run between Hsin Suao and Suao.

One bus daily departs Suao for Hualien at 2.30 pm. From Hualien, buses depart for Suao at 6.30 am. The fare is NT$137.

The East Coast 台灣東部

If you plan to travel around Taiwan, I recommend doing it clockwise, heading down the east coast and returning to Taipei by the west coast. The main reason is that the east coast presents such a startling change from Taipei's urban jungle, whereas the changes on the west coast are gradual.

Only 10% of Taiwan's population resides on the east side of the island. The reason for this is the terrain. The eastern part of the island presents a dramatic coastline of jagged rocks and towering cliffs, not the friendliest environment for agriculture and industrialisation. Furthermore, the east coast is prone to severe typhoons and some nasty earthquakes.

On the east coast it's easy to forget where you are. The sparsely inhabited rugged landscape could pass for the coast of New Zealand rather than crowded Taiwan. The scenery is stunning.

If you don't have the time to travel all the way around Taiwan, a good option is to head down the east coast to Hualien and then cut across the island over the mountains to Taichung. This is a very scenic route, although you will miss some of the major attractions in the south of the island.

The time needed to do any travelling in Taiwan is at least 10 days. As small as Taiwan is, there is a lot to see, and two to three weeks would be a much better length of time to spend travelling. To visit all the places in this book and do the hikes, figure on over a month, maybe two. If you are in a big hurry but have sufficient funds, you could save time by flying to a few scenic spots.

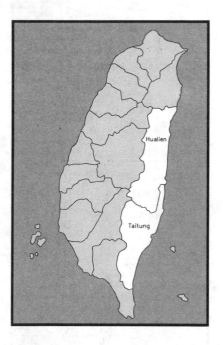

dramatic, especially a section called the Chingshui Cliff *(qīngshuǐ duànyaí)* where sheer walls drop straight into the sea from towering mountains over 1000 metres high. In the 1920s the Japanese, who then occupied Taiwan, managed to carve a narrow road through this section, but ever since it has been a continuous battle between road crews and landslides, rockfalls, typhoons and occasional earthquakes.

Given the fact that the transport system was poor on the east coast and had been a major impediment to economic development, the government gave priority to opening a reliable railway line. Incredible as it might seem, in 1980 the railway was finally completed between Suao and Hualien, ending the isolation of the east

Hualien County 花蓮縣

SUAO to HUALIEN
(sūhuā gōnglù) 蘇花公路
The east coast of Taiwan is lined with spectacular mountains and cliffs. The area between Suao and Hualien is particularly

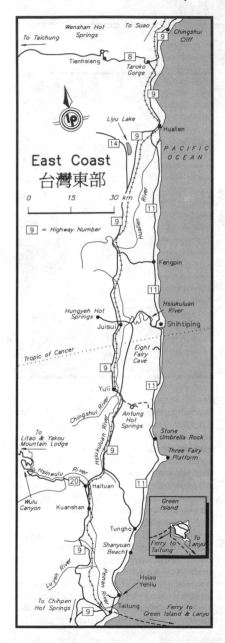

East Coast
台灣東部

0   15   30 km

9 = Highway Number

coast. It cost over US$200 million to construct (and those are 1980 dollars), as it passes through 15 tunnels and over 91 bridges. The railway line is one of the world's great engineering feats. Previously, the most reliable way to go between Taipei and Hualien was to take a ferry from Keelung Harbour. Since the railway opened, the ferry has gone out of business.

If you take the train you'll find it much faster and safer than the bus, but the bus trip is far more scenic. The train spends much of its time going through tunnels, whereas the bus climbs up and down the mountains, passing numerous valleys, beaches and incredible cliffs. This is one of the world's most scenic highways and if you miss it you've missed a lot. But nowadays, the majority of travellers take the train to Hualien.

Doing this trip by bicycle sounds appealing, but there is a hazardous tunnel 4.5 km long. Traffic is one-way, regulated by a traffic light. As one cyclist noted:

Along the Chingshui Cliff is a long, narrow and dark tunnel. The one-way traffic is regulated with lights. If you bicycle in Taiwan's mountains, you'll often meet dark tunnels, but this one is particularly dangerous. You absolutely need powerful rear and front lights, also available if you have to stop (battery powered) because you'll have to do so – the traffic light sequence won't allow you to get through in one pass. So you'll have to find a refuge when big trucks come toward you – at least you must be visible.

P Bruyere

I should add that there are the occasional idiots who get impatient and try to jump the traffic light, sometimes with spectacularly disastrous results.

HUALIEN

(huālián) 花蓮

The largest city on the east coast, Hualien is a pleasant place that sees a fair bit of tourist traffic. Besides the tourist dollar, the local economy is partly based on mining marble and limestone (for concrete) – there is a small international port to handle the marble exports.

Although Hualien is worth a look, most visitors use the city as a launching point for explorations in nearby Taroko Gorge, considered one of Taiwan's prime scenic attractions. Don't miss it! Hualien and Taroko Gorge are such a pleasant contrast to the hustle and bustle of Taipei that they are sure to give you a much more satisfying impression of the country.

Information

ICBC (☎ 350191) is at 26 Kungyuan Rd. The Bank of Taiwan (☎ 322151) is nearby at 3 Kungyuan Rd.

Ami Cultural Village

(àměi wénhuà cūn) 阿美文化村
If you arrive in Hualien in the early afternoon and plan to visit Taroko Gorge the next day, you'll have some time to take a look around. There are some Ami aboriginal song and dance shows put on for the tourists at the Ami Cultural Village (☎ 525231, 523571), which are worth seeing if you are in the area. Hotels and travel agents in Hualien can arrange a ticket for you. Admission is NT$150 if you get there by yourself; a taxi from Hualien will cost you NT$150. On a tour, expect to pay NT$250. The dance shows are at 2.20, 3.20, 4.20, 6, 7.20 and 8.20 pm every day, but the schedule can change. Most tours take in the 8.20 pm show.

East Hawaii Amusement Park

(dōngfāng xiàwēiyí lèyuán) 東方夏威夷樂園
Volcanoes and surfboards are notably absent, but 'Hawaii' is the motif of Hualien's latest theme park. Amusing amenities include dodgem (bumper) cars, dodgem boats, grass-skiing, a bobsled course and canoe rides. Perhaps most interesting are the water slides and swimming pools. When the crowds are sufficiently large (basically during weekends), you'll be entertained by hula dancers and Taiwanese-Hawaiian warriors. The restaurant is top-notch, though you won't find common Hawaiian cuisine like *poi* and Big Macs.

The amusement park is four km south of the Hualien railway station and only reachable by taxi or your own vehicle. Admission costs NT$250.

Liyu Lake

(lǐyú tán) 鯉魚潭
If you'd like to get out of town, a nice half-day excursion is to Liyu Lake, a small but very attractive lake near Hualien. The main activities there are boating, fishing and hiking. If you go there, take the time to walk around the lake. There is a road going all the way. You will also find several well-marked trails leading up from the road behind the lake. These trails lead to the summits of some nearby peaks, a very pleasant walk if you're up to it. Avoid Liyu Lake on weekends when the jet-ski gorillas take over the place.

There are buses approximately every two hours from the local bus station in Hualien. The journey takes around 40 minutes, and the last bus leaves after 6 pm.

Hsiukuluan River

(xiùgùluán xī) 秀姑巒溪
Besides the Taroko Gorge excursion, one of the most exciting things to do around Hualien is to take a rafting trip on the Hsiukuluan River. These trips run mostly during the summer. Most travel agents in Hualien can book the trip, which is good value at around NT$1000 with transport, equipment and lunch included. You can also book the trip from travel agents in Taipei. A brochure by one travel agent in Hualien warns that 'sicked person heart attack are not be allowed'. Departure time is around 7 am, and you return to town at about 5 pm. You'll get soaking wet, so bring some clothes to change into later.

My experience was that you have changing facilities at the beginning of the rafting trip, but once you change, everything you take along will probably get wet. So if you don't want those things to get soaked, leave them on the tour bus, which will meet you at the end of the trip.

Eugene Hirte

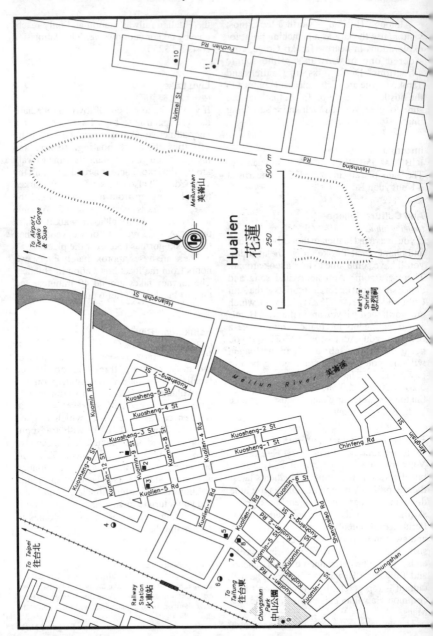

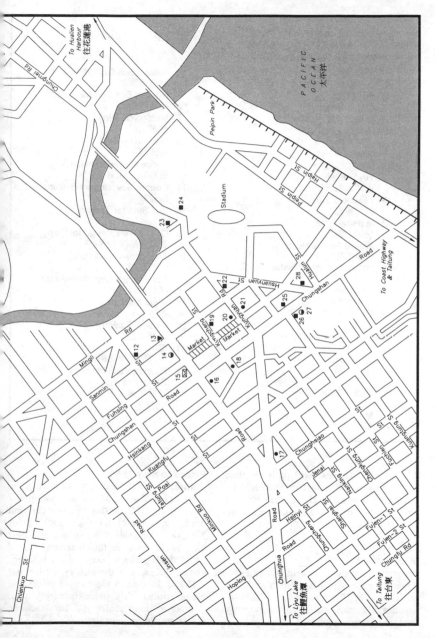

PLACES TO STAY

1 Hotel Royal
老爺賓館
2 Dongjing Hotel
東京賓館
3 Seaview Hotel
海賓大飯店
5 Qingye Hotel
青葉大飯店
8 Chan Tai Hotel
仟台大飯店
12 Toyo Hotel
東洋大飯店
19 Teachers' Hostel
教師會館
22 Marshal Hotel
統帥大飯店
23 Armed Forces Hostel
國軍英雄館
24 Hualien Student Hostel
花蓮學苑
25 Wuzhou Hotel
五洲大旅社
26 Daxin Hotel
大新大旅社
27 Hotel Golden Dragon

28 Jinri Hotel
今日大飯店

PLACES TO EAT

13 McDonald's
麥當勞

OTHER

4 Taiwan Bus Company Station
台汽客運站
6 Hualien Bus Company Station
花蓮客運站
7 Motorcycle Hire
機車出租
9 Swimming Pool
游泳池
10 Police (Visa Extensions)
警察局外事課
11 County Government Building
縣政府
14 Bus Stop for Taitung
往台東巴士
15 GPO & Telephone Company
郵政總局/電信局
16 Zhongyuan Bookstore
中原書局
17 Far Eastern Department Store
遠東百貨
18 Night Market
夜市
20 Bank of Taiwan
台灣銀行
21 ICBC
中國國際商業銀行
27 Hualien Bus Company
Central Station
花蓮客運市中心站

Although the Chinese will probably think you're crazy, cycling the road from Juisui to Shihtiping along the Hsiukuluan River is almost as much fun as rafting. The scenery is outstanding.

Beach
(hǎibiān) 海邊
For some quiet entertainment, you can stroll down to the beach. It's a pretty stretch of coastline, but like most of east Taiwan's beaches, it's stony and the surf is too rough for safe swimming.

Places to Stay
Central Area All the cheap hotels are in the central area of town, all within walking distance of the GPO. In this area you can find dormitories for NT$150 or doubles for NT$500. For budget travellers, the best bargain in town is the *Teachers' Hostel* (☎ 325880) *(jiàoshī huìguǎn)*, 10 Kung-cheng St, where dormitory beds cost NT$150. In spite of the bargain prices and clean rooms, this place is rarely full. Although theoretically just for teachers, others are welcome to stay.

Another cheap dormitory is the *Hualien Student Hostel* (☎ 324124) *(huālián xuéyuàn)*, 40-11 Kungyuan Rd. Beds are NT$150. Directly across the street is the *Armed Forces Hostel* (☎ 324161) *(guójūn yīngxióng guǎn)*, 60-1 Chunghsiao St, which is not so cheap at NT$800 for a four-person room.

The *Wuzhou Hotel* (☎ 324132) *(wǔzhōu dà lüshè)* prints name cards saying it's a youth hostel, but it's really just a cheap hotel at 84 Chungshan Rd. Singles/doubles cost NT$200/300 with shared bath, and NT$500 with private bath.

The *Daxin Hotel* (☎ 322125) *(dàxìn dà lüshè)*, 101 Chungshan Rd, is one of my favourites due to the extremely friendly management. Rooms are clean and air-conditioned. Doubles with private bath cost NT$500 to NT$600.

Right next to the downtown bus station is the *Hotel Golden Dragon* (☎ 323126) *(jīnlóng dà lüshè)* with doubles for NT$600.

The *Jinri Hotel* (☎ 325180) *(jīnrì dà fàndiàn)*, 8 Hsuanyuan St, charges NT$800 for a double.

Some top-end places in the downtown area include the following:

Astar Hotel
  (yàshìdū dà fàndiàn; 170 rooms), 6-1 Minchuan Rd (cnr Haibin Rd) (☎ 326111, fax 324604); doubles/twins NT$1800/2800, suites NT$4000 to NT$6500
Chinatrust Hotel
  (zhōngxìn dà fàndiàn; 237 rooms), 2 Yunghsing Rd (☎ 221171, fax 221185); doubles NT$2600, twins NT$2900 to NT$3800, suites NT$12,000
Marshal Hotel
  (tǒngshuài dà fàndiàn; 350 rooms), 36 Kungyuan Rd (☎ 326123, fax 326140); doubles/twins NT$2000/2600, suites NT$3500
Toyo Hotel
  (dōngyáng dà fàndiàn; 112 rooms), 50 Sanmin St (☎ 326151, fax 338076); doubles/twins NT$1800/2000

Railway Station Area There's a large collection of hotels near the railway station, but these are newer than those downtown. Prices start at NT$800 for a double and all these places are good. When I last visited, I noticed

some new hotels were being built behind the railway station and they may well be open by the time you get there. Some hotels fronting the railway station area include:

Chan Tai Hotel
  (qiāntái dà fàndiàn), 83-1 Kuolien-1 Rd (☎ 330121); doubles NT$800, twins NT$1000 to NT$1200
Dongjing Hotel
  (dōngjīng bīnguǎn), 212 Kuosheng-1 St (☎ 356151); doubles/twins NT$700/1200
Hotel Royal
  (lǎoyé bīnguǎn), 51 Kuomin-9 St (☎ 362952); doubles NT$1000/1200
Qingye Hotel
  (qīngyè dà fàndiàn), 83 Kuolien-1 Rd (☎ 330186); doubles NT$800
Seaview Hotel
  (hǎibīn dà fàndiàn), 192 Kuolien-5 Rd (☎ 342101); doubles/twins NT$800/1000

Places to Eat
Hualien has a great market on Fuhsing St, one block east of Chungshan Rd. Prices are low and everything is available from complete meals to snacks and milkshakes. There's plenty of seafood and traditional Taiwanese cuisine in this area. In the evening, check the night market on Kungcheng St just south of Chungshan Rd.

The eight-storey Far Eastern Department Store at the intersection of Chunghua and Chungcheng Rds is worth a visit. The first three floors are the usual high-fashion perfume, pantyhose and jewellery, but the 7th floor has a good collection of restaurants. The basement has the best supermarket in Hualien.

A busy Western restaurant is *East King* (☎ 336166) *(dōngwáng niúpái xīcān)*, 255 Chungshan Rd. Good Japanese food is available at *Heba Restaurant* (☎ 333826) *(hébā rìběn liàolǐ)*, 22 Fuhsing St.

Things to Buy
Marble is the main export of Hualien. It's not exactly lightweight stuff, but you'd be surprised what some people will fill their backpacks with.

Personally, considering all the environmental destruction being caused by the mining operations, I would prefer to see the marble left in the ground. The Hualien area also produces a lot of cement in case you need to stock up.

For those determined to contribute to the ecological ruin, finished marble items can be bought everywhere – you practically trip over marble tables, vases and statues as you walk around town. The biggest venue for marble sales is the factory operated by the Retired Servicemen's Engineering Agency (róngmín dàlǐshí gōngchǎng), 106 Huahsi Rd near the airport. Some travel agencies offer a stop at this factory with a trip to Taroko Gorge and the Ami Cultural Village.

There appears to be only one bookshop in Hualien offering English-language magazines (Newsweek, etc) and newspapers. Check out the Zhongyuan Bookstore (zhōngyuán shūjú) at 548 Chungcheng Rd (south-east corner of Chungcheng and Chungshan Rds). This place also has a good collection of maps (Chinese only), including Hualien and other cities in Taiwan.

Getting There & Away

Air For those with little time but a liberal budget, it is possible to fly to Hualien, take a bus tour of Taroko Gorge and fly back to Taipei the same evening. This can be done on an organised group tour if you don't mind playing Tommy Tourist (seven cities in three days), but I personally think it is essential to spend at least one night in this beautiful part of Taiwan.

Hualien has air connections to Kaohsiung, Taichung and Taipei. The following airlines are represented in Hualien:

Far Eastern Airlines
    (yuǎndōng hángkōng), 318 Chungshan Rd
    (☎ 326191)
Formosa Airlines
    (yǒngxīng hángkōng), Hualien Airport
    (☎ 263989)
Trans-Asia Airways
    (fùxīng hángkōng), 408-7 Chungshan Rd
    (☎ 321995)

Bus There are three bus stations in Hualien, and depending on where you're going (and

when) it makes a significant difference. See the following Getting Around section for details.

The bus schedules seem to change a lot in Hualien, so when reading what follows, consider the quoted times as approximations and make local enquiries.

There is no direct bus between Taipei and Hualien – first you must get to the town of Suao and then take the bus down the spectacular Suao-Hualien Highway. From Suao to Hualien there is only one bus daily at 2.30 pm. The trip takes three hours and costs NT$137. If you arrive in Suao too late to catch the Hualien bus, you can spend the night at one of several hotels near the bus station. Going the opposite direction, buses to Suao depart Hualien at 6.30 am. When going southwards to Hualien sit on the left (ocean side) for the most spectacular views. The best seat is right at the front. Of course, some will say this seat is the most dangerous, but I always think that if the bus plunges over a cliff, where you sit doesn't make any difference.

Buses to Taichung depart from the Taiwan Bus Company depot, about 100 metres north of the railway station, at 7.35, 9.35 and 11.05 am. The journey takes eight hours and tickets cost NT$459. There is another bus departing at 11.50 am which only goes as far as Lishan, halfway to Taichung along the same route. Coming the other way, buses depart Taichung at 7, 8 and 9.30 am. The route is spectacular – it's part of the Central Cross-Island Highway. This incredible road runs from Taroko Gorge on the east coast to Taichung in the west, twisting and climbing over Taiwan's awesome central mountain range.

Buses between Taitung and Hualien run in both directions about once every hour from 6.30 am until 7 pm. Buses departing Taitung at 7.30 am and 2.30 pm follow the coastal route. Going the opposite direction, buses departing Hualien at 8.10 am and 2.30 pm also follow the coastal road. The others all take the inland highway. In Hualien, you can catch the bus to Taitung at either the Taiwan Bus Co terminal (near the railway station) or from a bus stop next to the telephone-company office *(diànxìn jú)*.

There are four buses a day to Kaohsiung, which go via Taitung. You could almost as easily take a bus to Taitung and change to a Kaohsiung bus from there. The buses from Hualien to Kaohsiung depart Hualien at 8.35 and 10.35 am, and 1.35 and 5.45 pm. The journey takes eight hours.

For information on getting to and from Tienhsiang and Taroko Gorge, see the Tienhsiang section.

Train As the trip to Hualien is popular, it's best to book your train ticket a couple of days in advance, especially if you want a reserved seat. The fare of course depends on which class you travel in, but a fast train will cost about double the bus.

Avoid the old (cheap) trains which don't have air-conditioning. The trains spend a lot of time going through tunnels, which makes them very noisy and dirty when the windows are open.

Bicycle If you are athletically inclined, a bicycle trip down the east coast on a sturdy 10-speed offers an exciting journey. The only problem is that the stretch of highway between Suao and Hualien is so mountainous that you need to be in topnotch physical condition to challenge it. From Hualien to Taitung and to the southern tip of Taiwan is a much easier ride.

If you want to do this beautiful trip as a bicycle tour, consider taking the bicycle from Suao to Hualien on the train. It doesn't cost much to do this. You can ride down the coast to Taitung and then ship the bike back to Taipei, or continue on to Kenting at the southern tip of Taiwan and then up the west coast. The west coast is not as beautiful, so you can ship the bicycle back to Taipei from Fangliao, a small city south of Kaohsiung, if you want to.

Renting a 10-speed bicycle is not easy. Your best bet is to buy a new or second-hand model from a Taipei bicycle shop.

Getting Around

Hualien has three bus stations, and it's important to know which is which. The buses operated by the Hualien Bus Company *(huālián kèyùn)* provide local transport, both around the city and to nearby places like Taroko Gorge. This bus company has two terminals – one right in front of the railway station, and another downtown on Chungshan Rd near the southern end of Hsuanyuan St. All the buses operated by this company can be caught at either terminal.

Long-distance buses to places like Taitung, Suao and Taichung are operated by the Taiwan Bus Company *(táiqì kèyùn)*. These buses operate out of a terminal about 100 metres to the north of the railway station. As you exit the station, turn left, pass the 'rockpile' (a bunch of rocks supposed to look nice), and it's right there. You can't see it from the station entrance because of the rocks. Although these buses are long-distance, they do pass through Taroko Gorge and can be used for getting there.

To/From the Airport Transport is mainly by taxi – NT$150 and there is no bargaining. If you walk outside the airport, you can sometimes catch a taxi returning to the city – these drivers can be bargained with because otherwise they will return with no fare. The taxis which are lined up waiting for passengers are definitely in no mood to bargain.

On this same highway, you can also catch one of the buses connecting Hualien to Taroko. These are irregular and you might have to wait a while. It's easier getting the bus from Hualien to the airport because the Hualien bus station has a posted schedule so you can judge the time better.

Bus If you arrive by highway bus you can sometimes get off in the city centre, but most long-distance buses only stop at the railway station area. The rule is that those buses operated by Hualien Bus Company go to the city centre, but the buses operated by Taiwan Bus Company don't – with the exception of the bus from Taitung, which can drop you off by the phone-company main office *(diànxīn jú)*.

Bus No 105 connects the railway station to the city centre every 20 minutes – fare is NT$10. The bus from the railway station does not terminate at the central bus station, but continues on – be sure you get off in the city unless you want an impromptu tour.

Taxi Hualien taxi drivers do not use meters so you must agree on the fare before you get in. It should be around NT$70 in the daytime and NT$100 at night or at the crack of dawn. The price is more or less fixed and is not subject to bargaining. Many drivers will try to talk you into a chauffeur-driven tour of Taroko Gorge at NT$2000 or more, so just keep saying 'No' if they get pushy. If you find yourself heading out of town, stop the driver unless you want the tour.

Motorcycle Being a resort area, motorcycle rentals are easy to find in Hualien. Most of the rental shops are right by the railway station entrance on Kuolien-1 Rd. Rates are in the range of NT$400 daily for a 125-cc bike.

Organised Tours If you're interested in tours to Taroko Gorge, the Ami Cultural Village or rafting on the Hsiukuluan River, there are several agents in Hualien who would be happy to arrange them. One of the best known is Hualien Travel Service (☎ 325108) *(huālián lüxíngshè)*, 137 Chungshan Rd. Another efficient agency is Southeast Travel Service (☎ 338121) *(dōngnán lüxíngshè)*, 148 Chienkuo Rd. They also book tickets on international flights.

TAROKO GORGE
(tàilŭgé) 太魯閣
This fantastic canyon, 19 km long with a rushing white-water river surrounded by sheer cliffs, is considered Taiwan's top scenic attraction.

The highway running through the gorge is an engineering feat rivalling the construction of the nearby Suao to Hualien railway. The road was carved out of the sheer cliffs, at a cost of some US$11 million and 450 lives, and is part of the Central Cross-Island Highway which runs right over the mountains connecting the east and west coasts of Taiwan. The road is an important transportation link for the centre of the island.

During the construction of this highway huge marble deposits were discovered, setting off a mineral boom in the Hualien area. For a while there was considerable pressure by certain interests to mine Taroko Gorge itself. However, after much debate the government came down on the side of the conservationists and the area has now been designated a national park. Whether the legislators were motivated by genuine concern for the environment or tourist revenues is not known. An equally appalling plan to build a huge dam in Taroko Gorge was defeated, but a smaller, token dam was built just outside the prime scenic area.

At the entrance of the gorge you can see some mini-skirted aboriginal girls dressed in colourful costumes. Of course, they are there for a purpose – to pose for photos for a fee. They seem to do a thriving business. If you want to take their picture, negotiate the fee in advance.

A short distance above the entrance to the gorge is the Eternal Spring Shrine *(cháng chūn cí)*, which features a pavilion with a waterfall passing through it. The shrine is reached by hiking up a short hill from the highway and is well worth the walk. It was built in memory of those who lost their lives while constructing the highway – the names of the deceased are inscribed on stone tablets. Unfortunately, a series of recent landslides has made the walk dangerous – be careful unless you want your name inscribed on stone tablets too.

Information
There is an excellent Visitor Information Centre at the base of the gorge, where you can get the latest news on hikes, including places to avoid (washed out by landslides) and camping possibilities. Some of the staff speak good English.

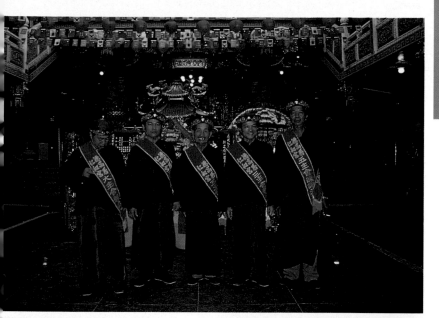

Top: Men in festival clothes inside temple, Tainan (MM)
Left: Mural in Kaiyuan Temple, Tainan (RS)
Right: Men with painted faces waiting for parade, Tainan (MM)

Top: View from Suao-Hualien Cliff Highway (RS)
Bottom: Aboriginal village, Lanyu (R Strauss)

Getting There & Away

For details of getting to Taroko Gorge, refer to the Getting There & Away section for Tienhsiang.

TIENHSIANG

(tiānxiáng) 天祥

At the top of the gorge, nestled in between the towering cliffs, is the lovely resort village of Tienhsiang. It's a beautiful, relaxing place, certainly more tranquil than Hualien. Of course it offers no nightlife, other than gazing at the moon and stars; the main attraction is the scenery, plus the peace and quiet.

There are a number of short hikes you can do around Tienhsiang. Apart from the gorge itself, there is a pagoda and temple just across the river on a hill; they're easily reached by crossing the suspension bridge.

Up at Tienhsiang, one of the nicer things we did was to just walk upstream along the river. After 100 metres we were completely alone with the beautiful landscape, since nobody else bothered to go this far...On a hot, sunny day, swimming in the cool, crystal-clear water was wonderful – it is not allowed in the centre of Tienhsiang.

Maria Ahlqvist & Staffan Jonsson

Tunnel Hike

If you walk exactly one km uphill from Tienhsiang on the main highway, on your left you will find a tunnel with a red gate. The gate is too small to permit motor vehicles to enter, but a hiker can easily squeeze through. This is your gateway to a really fun hike, but you'll need a torch (flashlight) and plastic bag to protect your camera because some of the tunnels 'rain' inside. Just follow the road – you can't get lost. Walking for 2.2 km will bring you to Paiyang Waterfall *(báiyáng pùbù)*, which slows to a trickle during the dry season but becomes a raging torrent after a storm. There's another waterfall further upstream, though during heavy rains you might need diving gear to reach it. The road continues for a total of six km with outstanding scenery along the way.

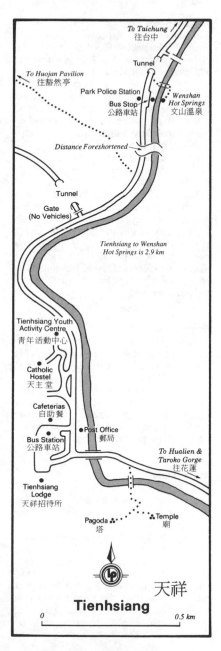

To Taichung 往台中

Tunnel

To Huojan Pavilion 往豁然亭

Park Police Station

Bus Stop 公路車站

Wenshan Hot Springs 文山溫泉

Distance Foreshortened

Tunnel

Gate (No Vehicles)

Tienhsiang to Wenshan Hot Springs is 2.9 km

Tienhsiang Youth Activity Centre 青年活動中心

Catholic Hostel 天主堂

Cafeterias 自助餐

Post Office 郵局

Bus Station 公路車站

To Hualien & Taroko Gorge 往花蓮

Tienhsiang Lodge 天祥招待所

Pagoda 塔

Temple 廟

天祥

Tienhsiang

0   0.5 km

Wenshan Hot Springs
(wénshān wēnquán) 文山溫泉

From Tienhsiang, it's 2.9 km up the main highway to Wenshan Hot Springs which is at 575 metres above sea level. You can reach the springs by taking a bus to the national park police station. From the police station you still must walk up the road for 400 metres. Before you enter the first tunnel up from Tienhsiang, there are some steps leading down to the river. Walk down, then cross the suspension bridge and go down a path on the other side to reach the hot springs.

Many hot springs in Taiwan have been ruined by the fact that the hot water has simply been diverted into the hotels to fill up the bathtubs so that the guests can have a private soak. This has been done because many of the locals are conservative and don't wish to be seen publicly in the nude. The Wenshan Hot Springs, however, are first rate and totally natural.

Huoran Pavilion
(huōrán tíng) 豁然亭

The hike up to Huoran Pavilion is short but steep. The length of the trail is only 1.9 km, but the elevation gain is 400 metres. By way of compensation, the views from the pavilion are stunning if the weather cooperates. When walking from Tienhsiang to Wenshan Hot Springs, you'll find the trailhead on your left about one km from the bus station.

Other Hikes

The National Park Service is busily constructing new trails in the hills surrounding the gorge. Unfortunately, typhoons and the subsequent landslides wipe out these trails periodically. To find out the current status of the footpaths and to obtain a free map, drop into Park Service Headquarters at Taroko. Until a typhoon turned the trail into rubble, one of my favourite walks was from Park Headquarters along the ridge to Wenshan Hot Springs. It's possible that this route will be resurrected soon.

Places to Stay

This resort is popular with honeymooners and tourists, so hotel space can be a problem at times and a reservation is advisable. On weekends or holidays, forget it.

At the downhill end of the Tienhsiang parking area is the *Tienhsiang Lodge* (☎ 691155/8) *(tiānxiáng zhāodàisuǒ)*. Doubles start from NT$1800. If you want to make a reservation from Taipei phone ☎ (02) 5515933.

A much cheaper place to stay and probably the best bargain in town is the *Catholic Hostel* (☎ 691122) *(tiānzhǔ táng)*, where it is NT$100 in the dormitory and NT$800 for a double. It sits on a hill just above the parking area.

Continuing up the same hill just a little further will bring you to a gleaming white building which is the *Tienhsiang Youth Activity Centre* (☎ 691111/3) *(tiānxiáng huódòng zhōngxìn)*, a government-run place that has dormitory beds. In spite of the fact that it has over 300 beds it's often full, so call ahead. Dormitory/doubles are NT$200/800.

Places to Eat

You don't have many choices. There are a couple of tiny cafeterias adjacent to the bus terminal. The prices are about double those in Hualien, but that's what the market will bear.

An alternative is to eat at the *Catholic Hostel* – breakfast is NT$50, lunch and dinner cost NT$100. It's advisable to purchase the breakfast ticket the night before. Meal times are fixed – breakfast is around 7 to 7.30 am.

It's also possible to eat at the *Youth Activity Centre* even if you're not staying there, but ask first because they tend to make only enough food for those who ordered in advance. Meals are served from 7 to 7.30 am, noon to 12.30 pm, and 6 to 6.30 pm.

The best meals are served at the *Tienhsiang Lodge*. The food is excellent but prices are higher than the cafeterias.

Getting There & Away
Tour Bus There are several tour buses from

Hualien going to the gorge, all of which start out in the morning. They stop often so you can admire the scenery while the Chinese tourists take pictures of each other standing in front of the bus. There is a lunch stop before the tour concludes and then they bring you back to Hualien. The total cost is NT$500, lunch included, often with an aboriginal song and dance show thrown in. For NT$300, you can book half the tour – you'll be taken up to the gorge but some tour companies will expect you to take public transport for the return portion of the trip. If you book half the trip, you don't get lunch or a song and dance show.

Public Bus The cheapest way by far to see the gorge is to take the local bus to Tienhsiang (NT$68) and then walk back down to the Eternal Spring Shrine at the bottom of the gorge. The walk takes about four hours and it's best to hike in the morning when rain is least likely. There are no stores in the gorge, so be prepared to be self-sufficient for four hours. It's best not to go on Sunday or holidays, since the number of cars on the road will be much greater at those times.

The bus schedule is a confused mess because there are two bus companies. The Hualien Bus Company officially only has buses to Tienhsiang at 6.50 and 11.45 am, and 1.15 pm. However, there are a number of long-distance buses operated by the Taiwan Bus Company which pass through Tienhsiang – an important one is the 4.30 pm bus, your only hope of getting to the gorge in late afternoon. The last bus returning to Hualien departs from Tienhsiang at 5 pm. The two bus companies won't tell you about each other's bus schedule, so you need to check for yourself at the different bus stations. See the Getting Around section for Hualien to find out where the respective bus stations are.

From Tienhsiang, as from Hualien, you can take a bus westward over the Central Cross-Island Highway all the way to Taichung (NT$379) on the west coast. More details of the journey over the Central Cross-Island Highway are provided in the West-Central Taiwan chapter.

Train You can't get to Tienhsiang itself by train, but there is a railway station in Taroko. The station's name is Hsincheng *(xīnchéng)*. Most travellers don't arrive this way, but some find it more convenient to depart from Hsincheng rather than backtracking to Hualien.

Taxi If you decide to go by taxi, it's essential that you agree on a price beforehand and don't pay until the tour is over. If you pay in advance, your driver may suddenly vanish while you are still photographing the scenery. Prices of NT$2000 are typical, but the drivers may demand more if you keep them waiting.

Motorcycle It's easy to hire a motorcycle in Hualien. See the Hualien section for details.

TAYULING
(dàyǔlǐng) 大禹嶺
Further west on the Central Cross-Island Highway is Tayuling, the highest point on this magnificent road. This is one of the staging points for hiking trips up Hohuanshan (Harmonious Happiness Mountain) at the westernmost edge of Taroko National Park. Nearby is Chilaishan, another well-known hiking area famous for its fatal accidents. For information about Hohuanshan and Chilaishan, see the Nantou County section of the West-Central Taiwan chapter.

Places to Stay
The *Tayuling Youth Hostel (dàyǔlǐng shān zhuāng)* is the best known, with dorm beds for NT$200. Like all these government-owned hostels in the mountains, it tends to pack out in summer and during holidays, but remains empty the rest of the time. Take the switchback trail up the hill to reach the hostel. Otherwise, you'll have to walk up a long dirt driveway. Reservations for this hostel are usually made from the Tienhsiang Youth Hostel (☎ 691111/3).

An alternative is the small and obscure

Luoyin Hostel (luòyīn shān zhuāng), slightly uphill from Tayuling on the road leading to Hohuanshan. Tatami singles cost NT$120.

Getting There & Away

Buses running on the Central Cross-Island between Hualien and Taichung or Hualien and Lishan all stop in Tayuling. There are four buses daily in each direction.

DOWN THE EAST COAST

There are two routes between Hualien and Taitung. One route follows the coastline and the other runs through a long, narrow inland valley. Both routes are nice, but the coast road wins the prize for being the more scenic. If you take the inland route, you have the option of going by either bus or train. The train is slightly faster and more comfortable, but costs more than the bus.

The best way to enjoy the east coast of Taiwan is undoubtedly on a motorcycle or 10-speed bicycle. If you can arrange this, it is worth the effort. One possibility is to rent a motorcycle in Hualien, ride to Taitung on the coast road and ride back through the inland valley. All along the mountainous east coast there are fine, nearly deserted beaches. Most are rocky, but there are a few broad, sandy beaches. If you have your own transport, you can stop and have a look any time you see something particularly interesting.

If you don't have your own transport, one thing you could consider doing is to take the local rather than express bus. You can get off the bus at several places along the way to have a look around, then catch the next local bus. This requires some patience, since east coast buses are not very frequent, but the scenery compensates for the lack of convenience. It's often hard to decide where to get off the bus as the whole coast is nice. An excellent place to visit is Shihtiping *(shítīpíng)*, which has great ocean scenery, a beautiful rocky coast and an interesting cemetery up on a hill. The cemetery probably explains why this area does not attract many Chinese tourists. Shihtiping is at the mouth of the Hsiukuluan River, Taiwan's No 1 venue for whitewater rafting.

On the inland valley route, the scenery is rolling farm country surrounded by mountains. There are two good hot springs along the way, Hungyeh and Antung, but they're only easily accessible if you are driving your own vehicle. The Chihpen Hot Springs in Taitung County feature outdoor pools and have a bus service, making them much more accessible to travellers than Hungyeh or Antung.

HUNGYEH HOT SPRINGS

(hóngyè wēnquán) 紅葉溫泉

If you're driving your own vehicle along the Hualien to Taitung highway (inland route), then these hot springs are well worth visiting. They are six km west of Juisui *(ruìsuì)*, which is on the main highway. If you're determined to visit these hot springs by public transport, take a train to Juisui and then get a taxi or hitch. Juisui is an out-of-the-way place and only local trains – not express – stop there.

There are no outdoor pools. The hot spring water is piped into bath houses which are part of a hotel complex. There is only one place to stay, the *Hungyeh Hot Springs Hotel* (☎ 872176) *(hóngyè wēnquán lüshè)*. If you don't want to spend the night, you can rent a room for a few hours and use the hot springs for NT$300. However, for NT$350 you can get a tatami room and stay overnight, using the hot springs for free. There are large tatami rooms for groups at NT$200 per person. A double room costs NT$600. The tatami rooms are really pleasant – a big hit with the Japanese tourists who occasionally come through here. The hotel's restaurant serves up delicious meals.

ANTUNG HOT SPRINGS

(āntōng wēnquán) 安通溫泉

Another hot spring resort just off the Hualien to Taitung inland highway, Antung is mainly for those who have their own transportation. There is only one hostel, the *Antung Hot Springs Hotel* (☎ 886108) *(āntōng wēnquán dà lüshè)*. Beautiful tatami rooms cost NT$300 for a single, NT$400 for a double and NT$450 for three people. If you prefer a bed, double rooms with private bath are NT$600, twins are NT$1000.

The hot springs are piped into private baths, not outdoor pools. Personally, I thought the bath houses at Hungyeh were better.

If you have your own vehicle, the hot springs are reached by first driving six km south of Yuli *(yùlǐ)*, then five km to the east on a narrow road. If you want to go to Antung by public transport, first take a train to Yuli (express trains *do* stop there) and then take a taxi (NT$200, 11 km) to Antung.

Taitung County 台東縣

On Sundays or holidays, tour buses from Taipei and Kaohsiung rumble up and down the east coast highway. The tour companies focus on three main attractions: Eight Fairy Cave *(bā xiān dòng)*, Stone Umbrella Rock *(shí yǔsǎn)* and Three Fairy Platform *(sān xiān tái)*. At the risk of being crude, I need to explain – the Eight Fairy Cave resembles the female sexual organs. Chinese men like to stand in front of it and get their pictures taken. The Stone Umbrella Rock is a gigantic phallic symbol. Chinese women like to stand in front of it and get their pictures taken (I'm not making this up). The Three Fairy Platform is just a fancy bridge connecting some offshore rocks to the mainland – I guess that one is for the children.

From Taitung City, you can easily visit all three places in one day on a rented motorcycle.

TAITUNG
(táidōng) 台東

In the south-east corner of Taiwan, Taitung is a somewhat remote city that has escaped the feverish growth and industrialisation that characterises the north and west of the island. Taitung means 'east Taiwan' and the slow pace of development is thanks to its location on the mountainous, typhoon-battered and earthquake-prone east coast. Taitung is likely to remain a relatively quiet backwater for a long time, though there are some

ominous signs – wealthy residents of Taipei and Kaohsiung have now started building villas along the east coast, causing Taitung's real-estate values to escalate dramatically. Improved air transport has brought in a rush of weekend tourists, along with five-star hotels catering to this market.

Nevertheless, Taitung is blissfully free of the traffic jams, noise and pollution which characterise Taiwan's big cities. Taitung County is overwhelmingly rural, a land of mountains and rugged coastline. Taitung city is the main departure point for many interesting trips, particularly to Lanyu and Chihpen Hot Springs.

Information
Tourist Office There is a local travel information office in the City Hall building on the corner of Chungshan Rd and Kungsheng Rd.

Money The Bank of Taiwan (☎ 324201) has a branch at 313 Chungshan Rd.

Dragon Phoenix Temple
(lóngfèng fógōng) 龍鳳佛宮
In Taitung itself, the main attraction is the Dragon Phoenix Temple, which is on a hill less than 10 minutes by foot from the long-distance bus station. Be sure to go up the stairs in the temple and climb the big pagoda. On a clear day you can easily see Green Island. As you face the main temple, on your left you'll see some stone stairs. Follow those to the top of the big hill for a magnificent view of Taitung and the surrounding coastline.

Tienhou Temple
(tiānhòu gōng) 天后宮
This temple is mostly of interest at night, thanks to the lively night market in front of the complex. This classic Taoist temple is also very active at appropriate times, such as the 1st and 16th day of each lunar month. The temple is on Chunghua Rd at the north end of town.

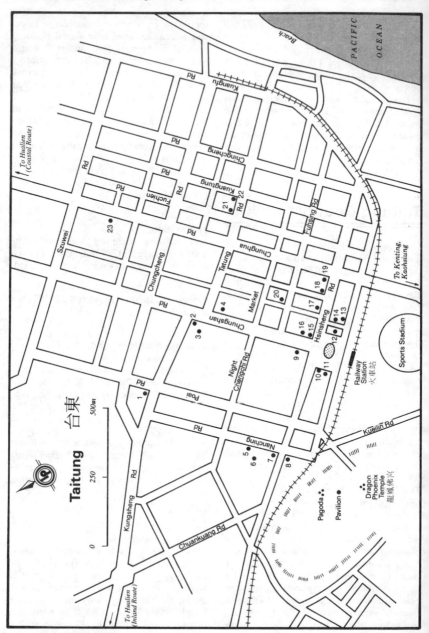

PLACES TO STAY

6 Teachers' Hostel
公教會館
7 Air Park Hotel & Makung Airlines
馬公航空
10 Hotel Zeus & Far Eastern Airlines
興東園大飯店
13 Lenya Hotel
聯亞大飯店
14 Renai Hotel
仁愛旅社
15 Hsin Hsin Hotel
新新大旅社
16 Hotel Hsin-Fu-Chih
新福治大旅社
17 Hotel Jin An & Taiwan Airlines
金安旅社
18 Quan Cheng Hotel
全成旅社
19 Dongbin Hotel
東賓旅社

OTHER

1 Lanyu Shipping Office
台東縣輪船管理處
2 Police (Visa Extensions)
警察局外事課
3 City Hall
市政府
4 Bank of Taiwan
台灣銀行
5 Swimming Pool
游泳池
8 Tungnung Supermarket
東農超級市場
9 Formosa Airlines
永興航空
11 Coastal Bus Station
鼎東客運海線總站
12 Long-Distance Bus Station
台汽客運站
20 Inland Bus Station
(to Chihpen Hot Springs)
鼎東客運山線總站
21 Telephone Company
電信局
22 GPO
郵政總局
23 Tienhou Temple
天后宮

Beaches

(hǎibiān) 海邊

About 10-minutes walk from the centre of Taitung is a beach at the end of Tatung Rd. It looks very enticing for swimming, but can be dangerous at times. The land seems to drop straight down here, making the water very deep just a few metres offshore. The surf is often rough and there are no lifeguards. Nevertheless, some people do swim at this beach – just be careful.

About 13 km north of Taitung is an excellent beach called Shanyuan *(shānyuán hǎishuǐ yùchǎng)*, which can be reached by bus or rented motorcycle. There is an NT$50 admission charge, though you can avoid it if you walk to the beach just to the north. This is one of Taiwan's few venues for surfing.

Hsiao Yehliu *(xiǎo yěliǔ)* is just north of Fukang Harbour, about eight km by road north of Taitung. The scenery is great, but it's rocky and the surf is too rough to allow safe swimming. Local residents from Taitung go there to fish off the rocks. There is now an NT$50 admission charge on holidays.

Swimming Pool

(yóuyǒng chí) 游泳池

If you are in the mood to go swimming, the Taitung Municipal Swimming Pool at 37 Nanching Rd is safer than the beach and not too bad as pools go.

Places to Stay

All the places listed here are within one block of the bus or railway station in central Taitung. Accommodation is usually no problem, except on Saturday night when the tour buses invade.

Bottom of the barrel is the *Renai Hotel* (☎ 322423) *(rén'ài lüshè)*, directly behind the bus station. All rooms are depressing boxes; singles are NT$180 with fan, or NT$500 with air-con. The latter is hardly worth the price.

The *Quan Cheng Hostel* (☎ 322611) *(quánchéng lüshè)*, 52 Hsinsheng Rd, is NT$300/400 for singles/doubles.

The *Dongbin Hotel* (☎ 322222) *(dōngbīn*

lüshè), at 536 Chunghua Rd, Section 1, has doubles for NT$400.

The *Jin An Hotel* (☎ 331168, 322368) *(jīn 'ān lüshè),* 96 Hsinsheng Rd, has doubles for NT$500.

The *Teachers' Hostel* (☎ 310142) *(gōngjiào huìguǎn),* 19 Nanching Rd, is clean and pleasant, but not very cheap unless you're a teacher or civil servant. Prices for singles/doubles start at NT$390/450 (with the right credentials), but it jumps to NT$660/830 if you don't have the proper ID cards.

Some moderately up-market hotels in Taitung include:

Hotel Hsin-Fu-Chih
    (xīnfúzhì dà lüshè), 417 Chungshan Rd
    (☎ 331101); NT$700 a double
Hotel Zeus
    (xīngdōng yuán dà fàndiàn), 402 Chungshan Rd
    (☎ 325101); clean double rooms NT$800
Hsin Hsin Hotel
    (xīnxīn dà lüshè), 429 Chungshan Rd
    (☎ 324185); doubles NT$800
Lenya Hotel
    (liányǎ dà fàndiàn), 296 Tiehua Rd (☎ 332135);
    doubles NT$800
Air Park Hotel
    (hángkōng huāyuán bīnguǎn), 268 Hsinsheng Rd
    (in Makung Airlines ticket office) (☎ 346422);
    doubles NT$1500

Places to Eat

Chunghua Rd is lined with numerous restaurants. Between Chunghua Rd and Chungshan Rd are many little alleys which become an active market at night – you can find almost anything imaginable to eat there. Fruit in this part of Taiwan is particularly excellent, and Chengchi Rd (between Chunghua Rd and Poai Rd) becomes a fruit market at night.

Self-catering should be no problem. If you need the widest selection, Tungnung Supermarket *(dōngnóng chāojí shìcháng),* opposite Makung Airlines, is Taitung's biggest.

Things to Buy

A local specialty available from the supermarkets in Taitung and the gift shops at nearby Chihpen Hot Springs is candied hibiscus flowers *(luò shén huā mì jiàn).* In Taiwan, hibiscus flowers are normally harvested to be dried and sold as herbal tea. Only in Taitung have I seen it candied and served as a dried fruit. Quality varies, but there are some excellent brands on the market and it's not expensive. I'm sorry to say that I've never seen any of this stuff labeled in English, but look for the brand sold in a purple box with a picture of the hibiscus flowers.

Getting There & Away

From Taitung it's possible to make the spectacular trip over the mountains on the Southern Cross-Island Highway. However, most prefer to make this trip from the opposite direction (Tainan to Taitung) because this gives you easier (mostly downhill) walking. See the South-West Taiwan chapter for details.

Air Taitung's remote location makes flying a reasonable idea if your time is limited. You'll almost certainly fly if you want to visit the offshore islands. Flights connect Taitung to Green Island, Kaohsiung, Lanyu, Taichung and Taipei. The airline booking offices are as follows:

Far Eastern Airlines
    (yuǎndōng hángkōng), 241 Hsinsheng Rd
    (☎ 326107)
Formosa Airlines
    (yǒngxīng hángkōng), 380 Chungshan Rd
    (☎ 326677)
Makung Airlines
    (mǎgōng hángkōng), 268 Hsinsheng Rd
    (☎ 346422)
Taiwan Airlines
    (táiwān hángkōng), 86 Hsingsheng Rd
    (☎ 327061)

Bus It takes about four hours by express bus along the coastal highway to get from Hualien to Taitung. Sit on the ocean side of the bus (left side) for the best views. If you are taking the bus from Taipei you must change buses in Hualien, from where there are frequent buses to Taitung.

There are plenty of buses connecting Taitung with Kaohsiung (NT$269) on the west coast, also a four-hour journey. This same bus also stops at Fengkang, where you can change buses to reach Kenting.

There are three bus stations in Taitung, and each serves different routes. Long-distance buses (Taipei, Hualien, Kaohsiung, etc) originate at the long-distance bus station *(táiqì kèyùn zhàn)*. If you're heading up the east coast, you need the coastal bus station *(dǐngdōng kèyùn hǎixiàn zǒngzhàn)*. The inland bus station *(dǐngdōng kèyùn shānxiàn zǒngzhàn)* serves the route to Chihpen Hot Springs and other mountain areas.

Train From Taipei there is a frequent train service direct to Taitung via Hualien. The fastest trains take over five hours.

The rail line between Taitung and Kaohsiung opened in 1992. The ride on the express trains takes as little as three hours. There are some spectacular vistas along the way, though part of the time in the mountains is spent in tunnels. A Taitung-Kaohsiung ticket costs NT$314 on the Tzuchiang express, or NT$253 on the Chukuang train.

Getting Around
To/From the Airport Besides taxis, the airlines all run their own free shuttle buses. You only need to show your air ticket to get on board.

Taxi Taxis do not use meters in Taitung – establish the fare in advance. There is a flat rate around town of NT$70, but considerably more for rural destinations.

Motorcycle Motorcycles can be rented all around the railway station area – there are signs everywhere (in Chinese). The cost is NT$350 to NT$400 per day for a 125-cc bike. If you really want a good look at the east coast, you could ride all the way up to Shihtiping, across to Juisui (following the Hsiukuluan River), and back to Taitung along the inland valley. This would take a full day.

CHIHPEN HOT SPRINGS
(zhīběn wēnquán) 知本溫泉
Just 30 minutes south-west of Taitung is Chihpen Hot Springs, one of the most pleasant hot spring resorts on the island. What

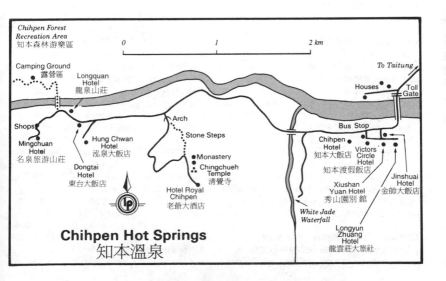

makes it so attractive are the opportunities for outdoor bathing, in both the hot springs and the river. Hiking is another possibility and there's an interesting Buddhist monastery.

All these attractions haven't gone unnoticed. The downside is that big hotels have sprouted on the hillsides among the trees and cliffs, and on weekends the place packs out. You can easily escape the crowd on weekdays, but if you visit on a holiday, you'll be sorry.

Hot Springs

(wēnquán) 溫泉

The best hot springs are the outdoor pools at the Chihpen Hotel *(zhībĕn dà fàndiàn)*. There are three pools, surrounded by swaying palm trees. One pool has cool water, one warm and the other scalding hot. I don't know what they use the super-hot pool for, maybe boiling eggs. The medium temperature pool is just right. Admission to the pool is NT$60 and you can hire swimsuits for NT$50 and a towel for NT$35. The swimsuits tend to be small for most Western bodies and the towels are so tiny that you need four of them to dry off. The pool is open from 7 am until 11 pm and is illuminated at night.

Chingchueh Temple

(qīngjué sì) 清覺寺

Back on the main road, continue walking upstream parallel to the river. Some 10 minutes of walking will bring you to a red steel archway to your left. Follow the road that goes through the archway – a short but steep climb uphill will bring you to a Buddhist monastery. The Chingchueh Temple is most unusual in Taiwan as it contains a large white-jade Buddha from Burma and a large golden Buddha from Thailand. There are some typically Chinese-looking deities off to either side. Remove your shoes if you go inside the temple.

Chihpen Forest Recreation Area

(zhībĕn sēnlín yóulè qū) 知本森林游樂區

Back on the main road, walking uphill again,

you will pass the luxurious and expensive Dongtair Hotel. Walk a little further and you will come to a foot suspension bridge across the river. It costs a ridiculous NT$50 to cross the bridge – the admission fee to enter the Chihpen Forest Recreation Area. If you don't mind wading across the river (easily done except during floods), you can enter for free.

Once inside the forest recreation area, there is a hiking trail that follows the north bank of the river, continuing upstream. You can walk in the river if you prefer. It's likely you won't see anybody in the park as cars and motorcycles cannot get in. The area near the suspension bridge is a great place to go swimming during summer. I've spent many an hour here, the rushing white water gently massaging my body – as good a place as any to reach nirvana.

Strangely, an amazing number of people have managed to drown here. I don't know how they manage to do it as the water is about 30 cm deep – rather like drowning in a bathtub. Admittedly, some of the victims (but not all) have been children – if you bring the kids, keep on eye on them. High-diving off the suspension bridge is also not recommended.

Places to Stay

The *Chihpen Hotel* (☎ 512220, fax 513067) *(zhībĕn dà fàndiàn*; 137 rooms) has the most congenial hot spring and, since the hot springs are the chief attraction, it's a logical place to stay. If you stay here, you can use the hot springs as many times as you like free of charge. However, the hotel is not cheap. Doubles are NT$1900 to NT$2400 and twins cost NT$2400 to NT$3000.

You can get off cheaper than this. Just to the east of the Chihpen Hotel is the *Xiushan Yuan Hotel* (☎ 512150) *(xiūshān yuán biéguǎn)*, where doubles are NT$700. The neighbouring *Jinshuai Hotel* (☎ 512508) *(jīnshuài dà fàndiàn)* is under the same management – doubles are NT$1000. Right next to that is the *Longyun Zhuang Hotel* (☎ 512627) *(lóngyún zhuāng dà lǚshè)*, where doubles cost NT$800.

Also next to the Chihpen Hotel is the

fancy *Victors Circle* (☎ 510510) *(zhǐběn dùjiā fàndiàn)*. All rooms here cost NT$2000.

Up on the western end of the road, just before the foot suspension bridge, is the *Dongtair Hotel* (☎ 512621) *(dōngtái dà fàndiàn)*, where doubles/twins go for NT$1600/2000. Fortunately, there is a 40% discount on weekdays. Nearby is the *Hung Chwan Hotel* (☎ 510150) *(hóngquán dà fàndiàn)*, which charges NT$1300/2000 for doubles/twins.

A short walk inland from the Dongtair is the *Longquan Hotel* (☎ 511311) *(lóngquán shān zhuāng)*, a small place offering doubles for NT$1200 to NT$1800. It seems overpriced for what you're getting.

The *Mingchuan Hotel* (☎ 513996) *(míngquán lǚyóu shān zhuāng)* is at the western end of the road, past the suspension bridge. It's up on a hill with a nice view, and they have cottages for rent. Doubles/twins cost NT$1040/1600 on weekdays, but the price escalates to NT$1300/2000 on weekends and holidays.

The *Hotel Royal Chihpen* (☎ 510666, fax 510678) *(lǎoyé dà jiǔdiàn*; 182 rooms) is a five-star hotel situated behind the Chingchueh Temple. Plush doubles are NT$3600 to NT$4000, twins begin at NT$4200 and suites start at NT$6600.

If you prefer to camp, cross the suspension bridge to the forest recreation area (at night, climb over the locked gate) and sleep under the stars. There is a camping spot, lighted restrooms and running water. A man in a small hut (a few minutes walk up the path and to the left) rents out tents for NT$150 and blankets (NT$25 per person).

Getting There & Away

From Taitung there is a bus about every 45 minutes between 6.20 am and 10 pm. There are several places where you can catch the bus – the starting point is the inland bus station *(dǐngdōng kèyùn shānxiàn zǒngzhàn)* at 184 Fuhsing Rd. Many people catch the bus from the stop in front of the Lanyu Travel Agency on Hsinsheng Rd. The fare is NT$35.

Returning to Taitung, the bus departs from the vendor's roadside stand next to the Chihpen Hotel, or further upstream from the Dongtair Hotel. You can purchase tickets on the bus.

By taxi, the fare between Taitung and Chihpen is NT$300 or so, subject to negotiation.

LANYU
(lányǔ) 蘭嶼

Some 62 km south-east of Taiwan proper is the island of Lanyu, which has been designated a national park. Lanyu means 'Orchid Island', but don't come here just to see orchids – the flowers are scarce, though the scenery is spectacular enough. The landscape resembles that of a volcanic Pacific island rather than Taiwan and the climate is more tropical.

The island is noted as a prime venue for minority-watching – it's inhabited by some 2000 aborigines belonging to the dwindling Yami tribe. The culture is closer to the nearby Philippines and the Pacific islands than to China. Many of the older islanders still wear loincloths and speak their own dialect, which is definitely not related to Chinese. They live by cultivating taro and sweet potato and also by raising pigs and catching fish. The women like to chew betel nut and, unlike Chinese women, they have no fear of getting a suntan.

The traditional homes of the Yami are built underground to offer refuge from the typhoons, which are severe in this region. There is no industry and most of the island is uninhabited.

If all this sounds like you are about to embark on a journey into the Stone Age, you may be disappointed. Lanyu is very different from Taiwan, but outside influences are definitely creeping in and the native culture is rapidly changing. Christian missionaries have done their job so well that now in each of the six villages on the island there are two churches, one Catholic and the other Presbyterian.

There are a few small Chinese businesses on the island, and taxis, TV, radio, beer and cigarettes are all having an impact on the

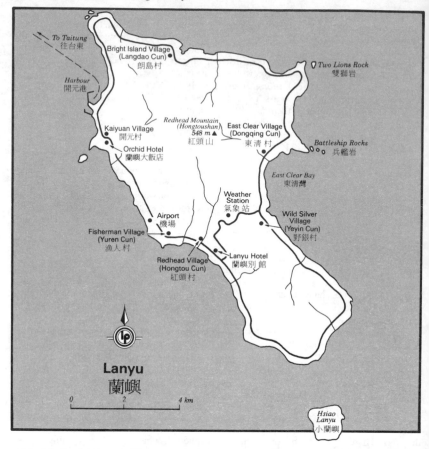

island culture. There are schools on Lanyu which provide education up to the junior high-school level, so all the young people can speak Mandarin Chinese. The elders may still wear their loincloths, but young people have discovered blue jeans and Walkmans. Many of the young people now go to work in Taiwan and the majority never return.

The tourist business has had quite an impact – if you snap a photo of anything (even just the landscape) don't be surprised if a local resident pops out of nowhere and asks for NT$500! The islanders are friendly enough, but most are still very poor and will incessantly try to peddle their souvenir models of Lanyu canoes. You'll often be asked for cigarettes and the children have learned to beg for candy. If you want to barter, it's advisable to carry a pack or two of cigarettes even if you don't smoke.

Lanyu offers excellent coastal scenery. As the island originated from volcanic eruptions, the coastline is of jagged black volcanic rock. It's certainly beautiful but makes swimming difficult. About the only beach where you can swim is south of the airport, near the Lanyu Hotel.

The main activity for tourists is to walk around the island, a distance of 37 km with no big hills. That's a very stiff one-day or a comfortable two-day hike.

Walking across the island near the weather station might not be all fun, because the trail is not well maintained. I nearly got impaled by a bull, who thought I was intruding, so people pitching their tent should have a good look around.

LM Kirsch

In winter bring a raincoat, as it rains lightly nearly every day and it's also windy. In summer, carry water as the island is very hot and suffers from drought. As poet Samuel Coleridge wrote, 'Water, water, everywhere, nor any drop to drink'. Don't attempt to go anywhere on Lanyu during a typhoon.

Chinese tourists bring in plenty of cash, but are not exactly loved by the local aboriginal population. If you visit on Sundays or holidays, you'll see why. Residents of Taipei catch the morning flight to Taitung, then fly over to Lanyu for a one-hour tour of the island. Men dressed in suits and ties, and women in high-heels, diamond rings and slit dresses come to Lanyu just to take pictures of each other standing in front of a Lanyu canoe; they point and giggle at the aborigines in their loincloths, eat lunch, take in a phoney aboriginal song and dance show, and return to Taitung to catch the afternoon flight back to Taipei. They can then proudly brag to their friends that they've 'done Lanyu' – after all, they have pictures to prove it.

Although you can buy film on Lanyu, it's cheaper in Taiwan so bring an adequate supply.

Places to Stay

The *Orchid Hotel* (☎ 325338, fax 325777) *(lányǔ dà fàndiàn)*, in Kaiyuan village, is operated by Taiwan Airlines. Dormitory accommodation costs NT$400 and doubles/twins are NT$1200/2000. It's also the closer of the two hotels to the harbour, should you arrive by boat. Kaiyuan village has the island's best 'nightlife', which con-sists of a couple of noodle shops with TV sets.

The *Lanyu Hotel* (☎ 732111, fax 732189) *(lányǔ biéguǎn)*, operated by Formosa Airlines, has dorm accommodation for NT$400, doubles/twins for NT$1800/3000. It's also adjacent to what is probably the best beach on the island.

If you want to save some cash, it's possible to camp out next to a schoolhouse. You should ask permission first, though this will nearly always be granted. Sometimes they'll let you stay inside the schoolhouse, if you can find the person with the key to open it, but nobody speaks English. It's also possible to sleep in a church, but again, ask first. Lanyu is a laid-back place and nobody will hassle you if you set up a tent just about anywhere. You won't need much equipment as it's never cold, but a waterproof tent would be wise. In winter, a blanket would be warm enough, and in summer it's so hot you won't be able to stay in the tent.

Places to Eat

Food in Lanyu is available at the two hotels – NT$100 for breakfast and NT$200 for lunch or dinner. There are a couple of reasonably priced noodle shops around the island and some closet-size grocery stores selling dried noodles and canned goods. If you're desperate, you could buy some taro roots and sweet potatoes from the locals.

Getting There & Away

Air Formosa Airlines and Taiwan Airlines fly small propeller-driven aircraft to Lanyu. There is no way a jet aircraft can land here as the airport runway is so short. From Taitung, the flight time is about 30 minutes.

Both airlines also operate flights between Kaohsiung and Lanyu once a day – flight time is 50 minutes. There are infrequent holiday flights between Lanyu and Taipei, but most visitors transit Taitung.

It appears that communication between the booking offices in Taitung and the airport is poor. At the airport check-in counter, if you attempt to buy a ticket on short notice you'll often be told the flights are all full. Meanwhile, back at the ticket office in Taitung, you'll be able to buy a ticket straight away for flights departing 30 minutes later.

Don't believe the printed timetables published by these airlines. They put on as many flights as they need. Especially on holidays and weekends, the schedule is ignored. When there are not enough customers to fill a plane, they won't fly at all. Except during holidays, you can usually get a flight for same day departure with no hassle.

One thing to keep in mind is that both airlines will offer you free transport to and from the airport from their offices in Taitung, a very welcome service. If you are waiting for a flight to Lanyu, you can store your baggage in the airline offices while you mess around in Taitung. If you have extra baggage that you don't want to take to Lanyu, you can leave it with the airlines, even for several days.

Boat It's possible to reach Lanyu by ship from Taitung via Green Island, but this is a slow trip and not very comfortable. I certainly wouldn't recommend it if the sea is rough. The ship is designed mainly to handle cargo, but they will take passengers. To buy a ticket, you must book it yourself at the Lanyu Shipping Office (☎ 310815) *(táidōng xiàn lún chuán guǎnlǐ chù)*, 306 Po'ai Rd.

The fare to Lanyu is NT$348 but the boat service is not reliable. If they don't get enough passengers and cargo, they don't sail. The ship is periodically taken out of service for maintenance. Departures are usually twice weekly, on Saturday and Tuesday, from Fukang at some indefinite time between 3 and 7 am. The ship takes five hours to reach Lanyu, four hours to return. You must buy the ticket in advance and be at the pier at the crack of dawn or earlier. There are buses to Fukang, but not at this early hour, so you must either get a taxi or find a place to stay in Fukang. You must have your passport for this boat trip.

You get a free stopoff along the way at Green Island because the boat needs to unload cargo. There will be taxi drivers at the pier to greet you and you can race around the

island by taxi if you like, but make sure you don't miss the boat. The taxi drivers will accommodate you with their Grand Prix driving skills. A rented motorcycle is another option.

Getting Around
To/From the Airport The two airlines which fly to the island also operate the two hotels, and both hotels offer a free shuttle service to and from the airport. Otherwise, transport is by rented motorcycle or foot.

Bus A bus goes around the island four times daily, twice in a clockwise direction and twice anticlockwise. The last bus makes a run between 3.30 and 4.30 pm, so don't miss it because there is practically no chance to hitchhike and there are very few telephones around to call a taxi from. These buses are rather expensive for the short distance they travel – it costs about NT$250 to go around the island.

The two hotels occasionally run a touring minibus around the island for NT$300 per person if they can get enough passengers.

Motorcycle Most visitors rent motorcycles, which are readily available from the two hotels and other rental shops. The cost is NT$500 per day.

Walking Walking is great for those who have the time and energy, but as the island really is large, many travellers opt for motorised transport.

GREEN ISLAND
(lüdǎo) 綠島
Relatively few foreign tourists make it to Green Island, even though it's closer to Taitung and cheaper to visit than Lanyu. There are several good reasons for this. Lanyu is larger, more beautiful and has a unique aboriginal culture, whereas Green Island is more typically Taiwanese, more developed and more densely populated. It certainly is not as developed as Taiwan, of course, but it offers few surprises for those already familiar with Taiwan. There is also a

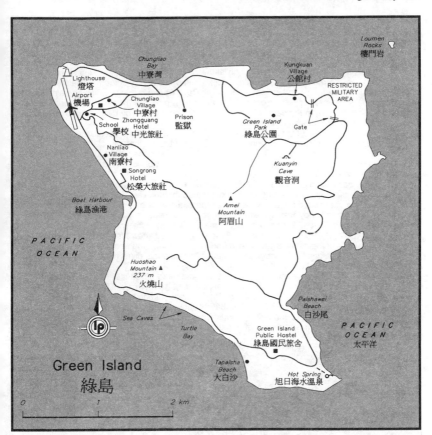

lot of military stuff and a prison on the island, neither of which do much to attract tourism.

On the other hand, Green Island does offer some interesting scenery, unspoilt beaches and a chance to get away from it all. Overall, I would say that the trip to Green Island is worth doing if you are in Taitung anyway with an extra day to spare and don't mind paying the additional airfare – just don't expect it to be another Hawaii. The island can be seen in a day if you catch the 7.30 am flight out there and return on the last flight at 4.30 pm. If you take the boat to Lanyu you get a free stopoff in Green Island, but it's uncertain how long the boat will stay there loading and unloading cargo.

Glass-Bottomed Boat
(hǎidǐ guānguāng chuán) 海底觀光船

When there are sufficient numbers of tourists, a glass-bottomed boat makes a cruise and gives impressive views of the coral reefs, as the passenger compartment is actually below the surface of the water. If you are romantically inclined, the captain is authorised to perform marriage ceremonies on board. The boat trip costs NT$300 per

Around Green Island

I suggest touring the island in a clockwise direction. If you're taking a taxi, make it clear to the driver that you want a chance to stop and see some of the sights along the way and don't simply want to race around at high speed.

You should take the taxi to the hot spring at the south end of the island. First stop off in the village of Kungkuan *(gōngguǎn)* and have a look around. It's a very colourfully painted village. Then head up the steep hill and stop at the Kuanyin Cave *(guānyīn dòng)*, which has a miniature temple inside. One stalagmite is dressed in a cape and represents the deity Kuanyin. There is always incense burning in the cave. It's placed there in the morning by pilgrims who come from both Green Island and Taiwan to worship.

After the cave, the road continues along the hills of the rugged and scenic east coast of the island. You finally come to the hot spring *(xù wēnquán)* at the southern tip of the island, right on the beach. It's not a very large spring but it's totally natural and the temperature is comfortable for bathing. Locals claim this is one of only two seawater hot springs in the world – the other is near Italy's Mt Vesuvius.

Although it looks like a great place for nude bathing, I don't recommend this in Taiwan. First of all, you could easily offend someone and make it tough on travellers who follow you. Secondly, the Chinese are unabashed starers. When I was there, a couple of foreigners decided to take a swim. No sooner had they taken their clothes off than four taxis pulled up carrying 20 very proper-looking, camera-clicking tourists. When the tourists saw what was going on, they quickly moved in for the best view. Then came the photo session. You know the Chinese – they always like to get a picture of themselves standing in front of something. And what could be a better prop than a few naked foreigners? Although these particular foreigners didn't mind being the centre of attention, all this was a little too much for them.

When you get to the hot spring, pay your driver and head off on foot after you've seen the spring. Soon you will come to a new youth hostel built at the southern tip of the island. Continuing around the island, you will come to a beach called Tapaisha *(dàbáishā)*, which means 'Big White Sands'. You have to wonder why they call it that, because there isn't any sand at all, just coral. Not a place for swimming, but snorkelling should be good here. Continuing along the road, you'll see three beautiful caves in succession. You can go inside two of them, but the third has too much water in it.

If you keep walking, you'll soon reach the boat harbour and then the airport. You can enjoy a good meal at one of the small restaurants in Chungliao while waiting for your flight out. ■

person. There's an additional fee for the marriage service.

Places to Stay

Camping near the hot springs at the southern end of the island is starting to become popular.

Alternatively, the only relatively cheap place to stay is *Zhongguang Hotel* (☎ 672516) *(zhōngguāng lüshè)* in the village of Chungliao *(zhōngliáo)*. It's certainly a no-frills hotel, but Green Island doesn't offer many choices. Prices start at NT$400.

Near the boat harbour is Nanliao *(nánliáo)*, where you can find the comfortable but expensive *Songrong Hotel* (☎ 672515) *(sōngróng dà lüshè)*. It's nice, clean and friendly, which it should be at NT$1800 for a double.

At the very southern tip of the island is the *Green Island Public Hostel* (☎ 672314, 672244) *(lüdǎo guómín lüshè)*. Doubles/twins are ridiculously priced at NT$1100/1800. It's a long way from the airport and just about everything else, except the hot springs and Tapaisha Beach.

Getting There & Away

Air The details of getting to Green Island are almost exactly the same as for Lanyu. Formosa Airlines and Taiwan Airlines have this market sewn up. There are periodic flights from Taipei, mostly on holidays. There is an even rarer flight between Green Island and Lanyu, but don't count on it.

Make sure you book your return flight as soon as you arrive in Green Island and make them write it on your ticket, as they have a habit of 'forgetting' and giving your seat to someone else.

Boat The unreliable ship to Lanyu has a two-hour stop at Green Island (depending on how much cargo they have to unload). Taitung to Green Island costs NT$135; Green Island to Lanyu is NT$284.

Getting Around

Bus There is supposed to be a bus service around the island but it seems to be very irregular. Groups visiting the island often charter the one bus available, thereby taking it out of circulation.

Taxi The drivers will be looking for you. Try to find a decent (safe) driver to take you at least halfway around the island – figure on NT$400 minimum. It's 17 km around the island; not far unless you must get back to catch your plane back to Taitung the same day. If you're staying overnight, it's no problem to walk the entire route.

Motorcycle This is the means of transport most preferred by visitors. Motorcycle rentals are available right at the airport for a daily rate of NT$400. You won't have to look hard for the bikes – people will approach you and make the offer.

South-West Taiwan 台灣西南部

This is Taiwan's banana belt. Flat and fertile, the region has the sunniest and warmest weather in Taiwan (and is stinking hot during the long summer). The climate is favourable to tropical agriculture, and the south-west was for centuries the most heavily populated and prosperous region in Taiwan. Those honours now go to Taipei, but the south-western port city of Kaohsiung is a close second.

The south-west coast has long been the cradle of Taiwanese culture – the old city of Tainan was the island's first capital – and much of the traditional Taiwanese way of life has been preserved. Most of the people in this part of the island prefer to speak Taiwanese.

Of course, modern influences have made their mark. New skyscrapers and factories sprout up on farms. The coast in particular has become heavily industrialised and, thanks to water pollution, Kaohsiung's Love River is lovely no longer. In spite of this, south-west Taiwan is one of the more interesting parts of the island. The rural areas are endless expanses of sugar cane, rice paddies and betel nut trees. Temples are pervasive in this region and it is in the south-west that you will find Taiwan's largest and most beautiful temples. It is not uncommon to see a huge Buddhist-Taoist festival or parade. Some 50 km to the west are the Penghu Islands – unspoilt, starkly beautiful and home to much of Taiwan's fishing fleet.

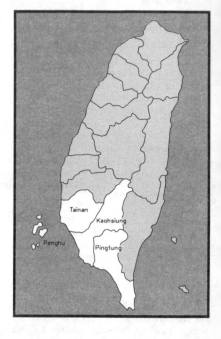

Pingtung County 屏東縣

KENTING
(kěndīng) 墾丁

Kenting is Taiwan's answer to Hawaii, the French Rivière and Australia's Gold Coast. More than anywhere else in Taiwan, Kenting lives or dies according to the weekend tourist trade. Situated on a bay just a few km from Taiwan's southernmost tip, Kenting has beautiful white sandy beaches, lush tropical forests and, not surprisingly, the warmest winter weather in Taiwan. People from Taipei and elsewhere will tell you that Kenting is horribly hot – in fact, Kenting's summer weather is cooler than Taipei's thanks to the afternoon (after 3 pm) sea breeze. Although there is a chilly wind in winter, it's just warm enough for year-round bathing.

Kenting is a beach playground. The main activities are swimming, sunbathing, surfing, windsurfing, snorkelling and scuba diving. You can swim and fry in the sun for free at all the beaches, except for the beach next to the Kenting House Beach Restaurant, where admission is charged. There is a small

226

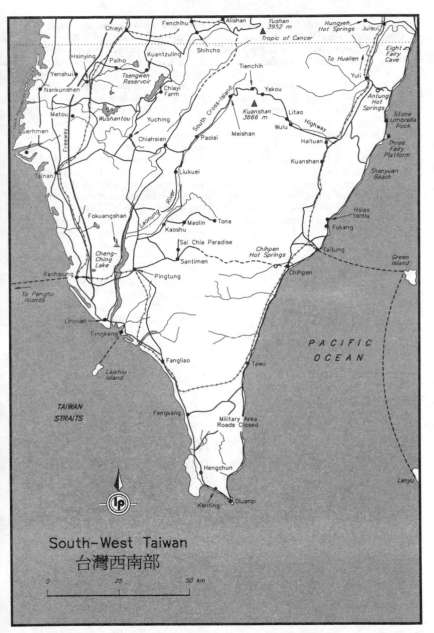

South-West Taiwan
台灣西南部

0   25   50 km

but pleasant beach at Little Bay, just opposite the Caesar Park Hotel. The beach next to the Kenting Youth Activity Centre is reputedly good for surfing when the weather cooperates.

The other water activities require equipment which can easily be hired. Everything from diving masks to sea scooters are available. Most of the sea toys are available from shops in central Kenting and at the beach. You won't have a hard time finding what you want; indeed, you'll be tripping over the stuff when you walk through town.

On 1 January, 1984, Taiwan's first national park was established at Kenting. Since then it has become a popular recreation area for both Chinese and expatriate workers from Taipei, Taichung and Kaohsiung. The seashore is relaxing enough on weekdays, but becomes a sea of humanity on weekends and holidays.

Information

There is a conspicuous Visitor Information Centre right at the park entrance. Some of the staff speak excellent English and can advise you about hikes, camping, etc. You can also pick up a good map here.

Livestock Research Station

(kěndīng mùchǎng) 墾丁牧場
Adjacent to the beach at Kenting is a Livestock Research Station. It's open to the public and you can have a look around. Be careful of the fences as some of them are electrified. The voltage is low and not dangerous, but enough to restrain a cow or give someone a thrill.

Frog Rock

(qīngwā shí) 青蛙石
All around the Kenting Youth Activity Centre are congenial walks that lead to the beach. Be sure to climb Frog Rock, the big rock adjacent to the hostel. There's a steep path leading to the top, but it's not a difficult climb.

Kenting Forest Recreation Area

(kěndīng sēnlín yóulèqū) 墾丁森林游樂區
After you've enjoyed the sun and surf in Kenting, head towards the Forest Recreation Area. The park is famous for its Botanical Gardens. Just inside the park is a tall, steep, pointed peak named Big Point Mountain *(dàjiān shān)*. Although only 318 metres high, you can't miss it – it dominates the skyline. At first it looks as if it would be impossible to climb, but in fact there are two routes, neither of which are terribly difficult so long as you are not afraid of heights. One route goes up the steep front face and the other safer, but longer, route is at the back. If you want to climb it, I suggest you use the steep front track to climb the mountain and descend using the gentler slope at the back.

To find the way up, first walk through the park entrance gate. A short walk will bring you to a dirt road on your left. Walk down the road a short distance until the mountain is directly in front of you. There are some cow pastures and a gate which you go through. Walk uphill through the pastures, following the fence, and eventually the path becomes obvious. The view from the top is fantastic.

Inside the park, high on a hill overlooking the area, is the Kenting House hotel and restaurant. There is an infrequent bus that goes into the park from the park entrance gate. One of the highlights of the park is the viewing tower, from where you can see the Pacific Ocean, Taiwan Straits and Bashi Channel (which separates Taiwan from the Philippines). It's claimed that on a clear day you can see Lanyu and the Bataan Islands in the Philippines. I've been able to spot Lanyu but not the Bataan Islands, which doesn't mean they aren't there. You can often see military patrol boats cruising the channel – a reminder that this is the prime smuggling route for Philippine-produced drugs and fire-arms.

Sheting Natural Park

(shèdīng gōngyuán) 社頂公園
Kenting National Park consists of two areas – the Kenting Forest Recreation Area, where

you pay an admission fee, and Sheting Natural Park. Sheting is free, relatively uncrowded, has good caves and some excellent walks, though slippery after rain. Sheting is two km from the entrance of the Forest Recreation Area, but you will have to look for it. To the south of Kenting village you will see the sign on your left pointing to Sheting Natural Park. Walk on until you come to a parking area where some vendors sell umbrellas and other junk – this is the main entrance.

Sail Rock

(chuánfán shí) 船帆石

You'll have to stretch your imagination a bit to think the rock looks like a sail. However, the main attraction here is not the rock, but the small bay with a sandy beach on the north end. There's a small collection of hotels, restaurants and places renting sea scooters and fishing gear. If you stay here, you'll find it noticeably quieter than Kenting itself.

Oluanpi

(éluánbí) 鵝鑾鼻

The southernmost tip of Taiwan is eight km south-east of Kenting. Oluanpi is known for its coral gardens and lighthouse. There is a small admission charge for the gardens, and heaps of vendors congregate near the gate to plug seashells, dried squid and other souvenirs.

As for beaches, there is a tiny stretch of sand just north of Oluanpi, but it doesn't look very attractive and I've never seen anyone swimming there.

There are a few hotels in Oluanpi, mostly luxurious and expensive. Overall, I can see little reason for wanting to stay here other than to get away from the noisy crowd at Kenting. For the Chinese, a big deal is getting up at 4 am to catch the sunrise from a scenic overlook just a few km north of Oluanpi.

Chialeshui

(jiālèshuǐ) 佳樂水

On the eastern shore north-east of Kenting is Chialeshui (beautiful happy water), so-named in the interests of promoting mass tourism. The drawcard here is the coastal rock formations, admittedly some of the best in Taiwan. There is also a big collection of souvenir shops near the entrance gate (where you pay admission), but inside the area has been mostly left unspoiled.

Just south of Chialeshui is a stretch of sandy beach at Fengchuisha which is said to have good surfing, but an often dangerous current.

Chialeshui can be reached by bus from Hengchun, but motorcycle or bicycle are the usual modes of transport.

Maopitou

(māobítóu) 貓鼻頭

Maopitou (cat's nose head) is the peninsula across the bay from Kenting, near the nuclear power plant. The rugged coastline with its twisted coral formations is the major attraction.

There is an excellent bicycle ride along the west coast (north of Maopitou). This route has much less traffic than the main highway between Kenting and Hengchun.

If you don't have your own or rented wheels, you can get there by bus if you go back to Hengchun and then catch a bus to Maopitou. The town of Maopitou occupies much of the peninsula, though it isn't very large.

Lungluan Marsh

(lóngluǎn tán) 龍鑾潭

If you're a bird-watcher, bring your binoculars and head for Lungluan Marsh just north of the nuke power plant. A large number of birds nest there – not because they are attracted to the warm glow of leaking radiation, but because this is a migratory route between the Asian mainland and the Philippines. The birds were once relentlessly hunted but are now under the protection of the Park Service. Autumn and spring are the best times for viewing migratory species.

South Bay

(nán wān) 南灣

A pleasant cove with a superb beach, South

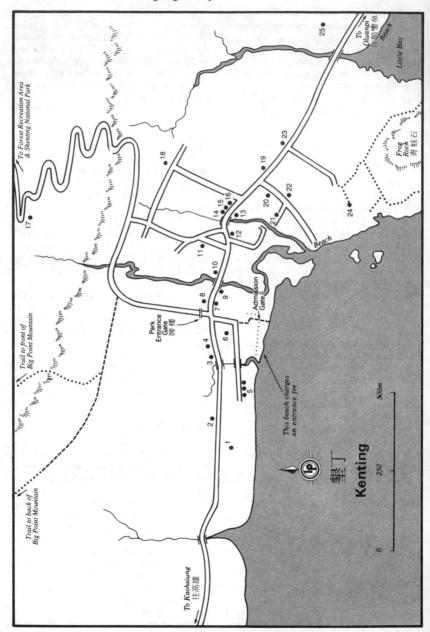

1 Kenting House Beach Annexe
墾丁賓館海濱部
2 Petrol Station
加油站
3 Guangdong Hotel
廣東大飯店
4 Xin Taofang Hotel
新陶芳大飯店
5 Beach Cottages
小房子
6 Kenting House Beach Restaurant
墾丁賓館海濱餐廳
7 Gau Shang Ching Hotel
高山青大飯店
8 Park Headquarters
& Visitor Information Centre
國家公園管理處
9 Motel
雅客之家
10 Golden Beach Bar
金海濱啤酒屋
11 Temple
廟
12 Open Bar
開方啤酒屋
13 Helong Restaurant
合隆餐廳
14 Hongbin Hotel
鴻賓旅社
15 Foremost & Meixie hotels
福樂別館/美協別館
16 Beiping Hotel
北平大飯店
17 Kenting House Hotel
墾丁賓館
18 Livestock Research Institute
墾丁牧場
19 Herng Chang Hotel
恒昌賓館
20 Catholic Hostel
天主教活動中心
21 Dawan Hotel
大灣山莊
22 Teachers' Hostel
教師會館
23 Sea View Park (Pizza Castle)
海根園
24 Kenting Youth Activity Centre
青年活動中心
25 Caesar Park Hotel
凱撒大飯店

Bay has become a mini-Kenting in its own right. Swimming and sea-scooter rentals are the big attraction here, but there is also surfing and windsurfing. Snorkelling might be a possibility – the neighbouring nuke power plant might give birth to some unusual sea life (killer sponges?).

Szechunghsi Hot Springs
(*sìchóngxī wēnquán*) 四重溪溫泉
During the Japanese occupation Szechunghsi was one of Taiwan's top three hot springs resorts, along with Peitou and Kuantzuling. These days, the springs are major tourist bait, attracting bus loads of weekend sightseers from Taipei who come here to get their picture taken in front of the Szechunghsi Guest House (proves they've been there), take a quick dip in the hotel hot springs, gorge themselves on 'famous mountain food' and throw it up on the bus heading home.

If you want to see tourists in their native habitat, come on Sunday or holidays. During the week, the place is dead – a preferable time to visit. It's 14 km from Hengchun and the main reason for going there is to enjoy the ride on a pretty tree-lined road. It's a good bicycle ride with little traffic, though there's nothing to see in Szechunghsi itself.

Hengchun
(*héngchūn*) 恒春
There's not much to see in this small but bustling town, but locals are proud of the four city gates which are still intact (unusual in Taiwan). For most visitors, Hengchun is an important transit point and little else. Relatively cheap accommodation and motorcycle rentals (adjacent to the bus station) are available.

Places to Stay
It's very easy to find accommodation in Kenting, except on weekends and holidays. Indeed, as soon as you get off the bus you'll likely be greeted by five or six people yelling *tàofáng!* (room with private bath). You can negotiate with them on the spot (remember to smile and keep it friendly), but you'll

possibly get something cheaper if you do your own exploring. If you arrive during the week you can book into a room, but be warned that some places will ask you to leave on Saturday because another group has booked and paid for all the rooms in advance. Weekend prices may be double, if you can get a room at all.

On weekends, you might be forced to stay in Hengchun, a less attractive town nine km to the north. Other possible places to stay include Oluanpi, Sail Rock, South Bay and Szechunghsi Hot Springs.

Places to Stay – Kenting The National Park Service can advise you about places to camp, but if you go back-country you aren't likely to be bothered. Private camping grounds near the beach want at least NT$200 for a tent!

The *Kenting Youth Activity Centre* (☎ 8861221) *(qīngnián huódòng zhōngxīn)* is a government-operated place that boasts a unique architecture designed to resemble an ancient Chinese village. On the negative side, it's expensive for a youth hostel with dormitory beds costing NT$300. It's also somewhat isolated from the centre of town, where you'll probably want to eat and stroll around at night.

The *Teachers' Hostel* (☎ 8861241) *(jiàoshī huìguǎn)* is a good deal, but to stay here you need some sort of Chinese student or teacher ID. Foreigners studying Chinese at a university are accepted. The dormitory costs NT$150 and doubles are NT$600. This place is often full during the school holidays.

There are three cheap hotels in a row in the central part of Kenting. One of these is the *Foremost Hotel* (☎ 8861007) *(fúlè biéguǎn)*, where singles/doubles cost NT$400/600, but there are more high-class rooms (with refrigerator!) for NT$600/800. As you face the Foremost, immediately to your right is the *Meixie Hotel* (☎ 8861176) *(měixié biéguǎn)* where prices are exactly the same. On the left side of the Foremost is the *Hongbin Hotel* (☎ 8861003) *(hóngbīn lüshè)* where singles/doubles cost NT$500/600 during weekdays.

Just a little to the east of these is the *Herng Chang Hotel* (☎ 8861531) *(héngchāng bīnguǎn)*, a modern-looking hotel with doubles for NT$600.

The *Catholic Hostel* (☎ 8861540) *(tiānzhǔjiào huódòng zhōngxīn)* costs NT$500 for double rooms. There are dormitories, but you need to supply your own group – they will not put you in with another group even if empty beds are available. I've found the staff here to be most unfriendly – it's not nearly as good as the Catholic Hostel in Tienhsiang or Alishan.

Almost behind the Catholic Hostel on an obscure side street is *Dawan Hotel* (☎ 886 1059) *(dàwān shān zhuāng)*, a lovely, clean place with doubles for NT$700. As yet, there is no English sign.

Just west of the park entrance gate is the *Xin Taofang Hotel* (☎ 8861021) *(xīn táofāng dà fàndiàn)* where single rooms cost NT$500. The *Guangdong Hotel* (☎ 886 1032) *(guǎngdōng dà fàndiàn)* is next door and has doubles for NT$800.

Motel (☎ 8861270) *(yǎkè zhījiā)* is close to Park Headquarters in the centre of Kenting. From the outside if looks like an up-market place (because it is), but there are a few pleasant tatami rooms where doubles are only NT$500, but the bath is down the hall. Fancier rooms with private bath go for NT$1200 and up.

The *Beiping Hotel* (☎ 8861027) *(běipíng dà fàndiàn)* boasts an enormous seafood restaurant, but doubles are a steep NT$2500.

Opposite the park entrance gate is the *Gau Shang Ching Hotel* (☎ 8861527) *(gāo shān qīng bīnguǎn)*, which has doubles for NT$2200.

Kenting House (☎ 8861370, fax 886 1377) *(kěndīng bīnguǎn)* is in the park itself, far from the beach but it's quiet and the views are grand. Doubles/twins cost NT$1200/1400. The same hotel operates the *Kenting House Beach Annexe (kěndīng bīnguǎn hǎibīn bù)* which is not such a good deal – cramped twins cost NT$1600. On the other hand, the beachfront cottages are wonderful, but not exactly budget travel at NT$4200 for four people.

The *Caesar Park Hotel* (☎ 8861888, fax 8861818) *(kǎisā dà fàndiàn)* is a five star place designed to attract international tourists. The facilities are magnificent but you pay for what you're getting – doubles start at NT$4500 and escalate to NT$38,000 for the 'Imperial Suite'. This place gets overrun with well-heeled Japanese visitors. The hotel operates a shuttle bus from Kaohsiung's railway station which also stops at Kaohsiung airport – it costs NT$320 one way. There is a money-changing service but only for the hotel's own guests.

Places to Stay – Sail Rock The *Jinhua Hotel* (☎ 8851340) *(jīnhuá biéguǎn)* is at the south end of the cove, almost directly opposite the big rock. Singles/doubles are NT$700/1000.

The *OK Hill Hotel* (☎ 8861601) *(ōukè shān zhuāng)* dominates the hillside behind sail rock. It's a pricey luxury resort with rooms starting at NT$3600.

Places to Stay – Oluanpi The *Oluanpi Recreation Centre* (☎ 8851210, fax 8851191) *(éluánbí huódòng zhōngxīn)* is in an isolated

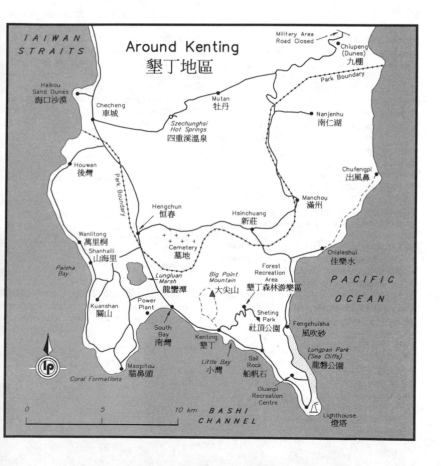

Around Kenting
墾丁地區

TAIWAN STRAITS

Military Area Road Closed

Chiupeng (Dunes) 九棚

Park Boundary

Haikou Sand Dunes 海口沙漠

Checheng 車城

Mutan 牡丹

Nanjenhu 南仁湖

Szechunghsi Hot Springs 四重溪溫泉

Houwan 後灣

Park Boundary

Chufengpi 出風鼻

Hengchun 恒春

Manchou 滿州

Hsinchuang 新莊

Wanlitong 萬里桐

Shanhaili 山海里

Cemetery 墓地

Paisha Bay

Lungluan Marsh 龍鑾潭

Big Point Mountain 大尖山

Forest Recreation Area 墾丁森林游樂區

Chialeshui 佳樂水

PACIFIC OCEAN

Kuanshan 關山

Power Plant

South Bay 南灣

Kenting 墾丁

Little Bay 小灣

Sheting Park 社頂公園

Fengchuisha 風吹砂

Maopitou 貓鼻頭

Coral Formations

Sail Rock 船帆石

Lungpan Park (Sea Cliffs) 龍磐公園

Oluanpi Recreation Centre

Lighthouse 燈塔

0   5   10 km

BASHI CHANNEL

location about three km north of Oluanpi on the Oluanpi to Chialeshui highway. They have relatively cheap rooms in their annexe at NT$330 for a single. Otherwise, it's pricey with suites for two people starting at NT$1650 and rising to NT$2970 for the best rooms. The hotel sits on a hill and has fine views but no beach.

In Oluanpi itself, the *Oluanpi Inn* (☎ 8851261) *(éluánbí xiūjià biéshù)* costs NT$1500 for a double – you can sometimes bargain a 20% discount on weekdays. Nearby is the luxurious *Nan Yang Hotel* (☎ 8851088) *(nán yáng dà fàndiàn)* where doubles start at NT$3000.

Places to Eat

There are so many seafood restaurants in Kenting that you'll be lucky not to trip over a lobster. In general, seafood is not cheap, so if you're minding the budget, look for places doing noodle and rice dishes. One such place is the *Helong Restaurant (hélong cāntīng)*, almost directly opposite the Hongbin Hotel. A pork chop and rice dinner *(páigǔ fàn)* or chicken leg with rice *(jītuǐ fàn)* costs NT$70 a plate.

For some reason, pizza restaurants are all the rage in Kenting. There are numerous places including *Dolce Vita* and *Pizza Castle* – the latter is attached to a seafood restaurant though I didn't see any 'squid pizzas' on the menu.

If money is no object, you can get your pickles and seaweed delights at the Japanese restaurant inside the *Caesar Park Hotel*.

The cheapest option for budget eats is to hit one of the numerous grocery stores and buy instant noodles for around NT$25.

Entertainment

One reason why Kenting remains so popular is that the town offers the sort of warm-weather beachside nightlife normally associated with places like Bali and Pattaya (Thailand), rather than Taiwan. OK, I know it's more tame than that, but you won't be stuck for something to do. Pubs, discos and karaoke bars have sprung up, and judging from the pace of change, maybe this place really will catch up with Pattaya.

The liveliest (and most expensive) disco in town is in the Caesar Park Hotel. Outdoor pubs broadcasting heavy rock music are conspicuous, examples being the Open Bar and Golden Beach Bar. As for karaoke, the KTV signs are everywhere.

Getting There & Away

Some buses go directly to Kenting, but if you can't catch one of these, then go to Hengchun, nine km north of Kenting. In Hengchun, the bus station is on the street immediately to the left of the police station (as you face the building). Shuttle buses connecting Hengchun with Kenting run about every 40 minutes between 8 am and 6 pm and cost NT$18. You will encounter all sorts of aggressive taxi drivers yelling 'Kenting' or 'Kaohsiung' as you walk around Hengchun – you can simply ignore them unless you want to pay NT$200 or more for their services.

To/From Taitung Fengkang *(fēnggǎng)* is the crucial bus-transfer point. All buses on the Kaohsiung-Taitung and Kaohsiung-Hengchun routes stop in Fengkang.

If you look at a map, it appears that there is a road running directly between Taitung and Kenting. Unfortunately, that road is closed to the public because of the military base in the area. You must go by way of Fengkang.

To/From Kaohsiung There are frequent buses from the Kaohsiung main bus station to Hengchun and/or Kenting.

To/From Taipei There are a few direct buses on the Taipei-Kenting route. If you have the money but not much time, you may consider flying to Kaohsiung airport and catching a bus south to Hengchun or Kenting. Buses go right by the airport entrance and can be flagged down, so it's not necessary to backtrack into Kaohsiung.

Getting Around

Public Transport There is a daytime bus service between Hengchun and Oluanpi about once every 40 minutes, stopping at Kenting along the way. Wild-chicken taxis also regularly patrol the roads. Hitching is another possibility – the Kenting locals might expect payment for this, but Taiwanese from Kaohsiung, Taipei and elsewhere are unlikely to ask hitchhikers for money.

Bikes & Cars Kenting is a great place for two-wheeled transport, both the motorised and pedal-power kind. There are plenty of bikes for hire in Kenting and you'll have no trouble finding a rental shop. A bicycle costs about NT$100 for eight hours. However, Taiwanese bicycles do tend to be on the small side, a handicap for tall Westerners.

You can hire motorcycles and 4WD jeeps all over Kenting. You won't have any trouble finding a rental place – you'll have to climb over the vehicles just to get into some of the restaurants and hotels. Motorcycle prices are NT$100 per hour, NT$300 for four hours, NT$500 for eight hours or NT$600 for 24 hours. Most of the bikes are 125 cc – if you don't have a Taiwanese or international licence, you might have to hire a 50-cc model (which requires no licence).

As for hiring a jeep, I can't see the point. The roads are all surfaced and smooth, so the only purpose of renting a 4WD vehicle is to drive on the beach, which causes significant environmental damage. The Taiwanese seem to find the jeeps irresistible – the reason is that they like to pose for heroic photos sitting behind the steering wheel while parked on the beach.

PINGTUNG

(píngdōng) 屏東

The official administrative seat of Pingtung County, the relatively small city of Pingtung is a nondescript place chiefly used by travellers as a staging post to get to Santimen and Maolin in Kaohsiung County. Many travellers bypass the place entirely, and you shouldn't feel shy about doing the same if Santimen or Maolin aren't on your route.

Getting There & Away

Bus If you're coming from Taitung or Kenting, there are some buses that go directly to Pingtung. However, the majority of buses go to Kaohsiung.

From Kaohsiung, buses depart about every 10 minutes from the terminal on Linsen Rd, one block south of Chienkuo Rd. The bus ride takes about 40 minutes.

Train All trains running between Taitung and Kaohsiung stop in Pingtung. From Taitung, the train journey takes about three hours; from Kaohsiung, about 15 minutes. From either direction, there are only six trains per day, though it may increase in future.

SANTIMEN

(sāndìmén) 三地門

A small town situated where the plains dramatically meet the mountains, Santimen has peaceful surroundings and a white-water river. The population consists mostly of aborigines belonging to the Paiwan tribe.

Santimen consists of three areas – Santimen village, Shuimen and the touristy Taiwan Aboriginal Culture Park. Shuimen is the main market town. Santimen village is on the opposite side of the river from Shuimen, up on a cliff behind trees, and no part of it is visible from Shuimen. Santimen village is great – an authentic and not touristy aboriginal village surrounded by trees and farmland. There is a good temple overlooking the river near the bridge. Many people in Santimen are employed doing embroidery, as aboriginal craft has now become a big business.

As you enter the Santimen area, the road is lined with farms with tall palm trees. These are not coconut palms but betel nut trees.

Taiwan Aboriginal Culture Park

(táiwān shāndì wénhuà yuán qū)
台灣山地文化園區

Three km south of Santimen near the town of Machia *(mǎjiā)* is another aboriginal site geared towards mass tourism. Admission is NT$150 and it's open from 9 am to 5 pm daily. The houses are designed to look like the traditional aboriginal homes, and the park has the requisite aboriginal song and dance shows at 11 am and 3 pm. It's a somewhat scaled-down version of the Formosan Aboriginal Cultural Village near Sun Moon Lake. It might be interesting to visit Taiwan Aboriginal Culture Park first and then Santimen village, as this'll give you a chance to compare fantasy with reality.

Chinese Chewing Gum

One thing you'll undoubtedly find for sale at street stalls everywhere is betel nut, locally referred to as 'Chinese chewing gum'. This is not a food – swallow it and you'll be sorry! The betel nut is in fact the seed of the betel palm (beautiful trees, by the way) and is meant to be chewed. The seed is usually sold with a slit in it, mixed with lime and wrapped in a leaf. Like tobacco, it's strong stuff that you first can barely tolerate but eventually get addicted to. The first time you bite into betel nut, your whole face gets hot – chewers say it gives them a buzz. Like chewing tobacco, betel nut causes excessive salivation – the result is that betel chewers must constantly spit. The disgusting reddish-brown stains you see on footpaths are not blood but betel-saliva juice. Years of constant chewing causes the teeth to become stained progressively browner, eventually becoming nearly black.

If you want to try betel nut you can purchase some for N I \$10 a piece. Like tobacco, betel nut is an important cash crop – many of Taiwan's small farms couldn't survive without it. ■

Getting There & Away

You can get a bus to Santimen from Pingtung (about 35 minutes). From Santimen you can cross the suspension bridge by foot and walk to the park. A faster alternative is to get off the bus at the town of Shuimen, before Santimen, and take a taxi or walk 1.5 km to the Taiwan Aboriginal Culture Park. On weekends and holidays, buses go directly to the tourist park.

From Santimen, a road heads due east into fantastic mountains towards the aboriginal village of Wutai. It would be a lovely place to visit, but a Class A mountain permit is needed. These are difficult to obtain and must be applied for at the Foreign Affairs Police office in Pingtung.

SAI CHIA PARADISE
(sài jiā lèyuán) 賽嘉樂園

This is southern Taiwan's main venue for paragliding (huá xiáng yì) and ultralights (xiǎo fēijī – miniaturised aeroplanes). Even if you'd prefer not to risk your neck soaring above the tree-tops, you might want to be a spectator. Considering how the Taiwanese pile six people on a motorcycle while driving down the wrong side of the road, it's interesting to see what stunts they pull in the air (how many people can you fit on a paraglider?).

Sai Chia Paradise is five km north of Santimen, on the road to Maolin. It's easy enough to find the place on weekends – just look for some aircraft floating around. Outside of hitching, there's no way to get here without your own transport.

LIUCHIU ISLAND
(liúqiú yǔ) 琉球嶼

Also known as Hsiao (little) Liuchiu, the island is visible from Kaohsiung on a clear day. Traditionally, fishing was the main industry, but the locals have mostly graduated from harvesting fish to harvesting tourists. Nonetheless, the island is known for its seafood (mostly purchased from mainland China), secluded coves and coral formations, and at least one good sandy stretch of beach. The island is pretty but not stunningly beautiful. Unfortunately, it's close enough to Kaohsiung for bottles, styrofoam and other detritus from the city to occasionally wash up on the beaches. An effort is now being made to clean it up. The beaches are infinitely cleaner than the those in Kaohsiung, and it's a wonderful, tranquil retreat from the madness of city life.

Liuchiu Island can be visited as a relaxing day trip, but it's more fun to spend the night. Indeed, the island is at its most attractive in the evening when the lights from Kaohsiung glimmer on the tranquil sea. Near the southern end of the island is the Seabed Zoo (hǎidǐ dòngwù yuán), a collection of aquarium-bound marine life which costs you NT$70 to see. There are knowledgeable guides here to explain what you're looking at, but they are strictly Chinese-speaking.

The glass-bottomed boat (hǎidǐ guānguāng chuán) that runs frequently on weekends from Liuchiu harbour is considered one of the big attractions. The boat fare is NT$250. Actually, it's questionable how much you can see since many of the coral formations have been damaged by collectors. You can probably get a better view of the coral at the island's souvenir shops.

Places to Stay

There are currently four places to stay in the Penfu village area. Facing the harbour is the Bailonggong Hotel (☎ 8612536) (báilónggōng dà lùshè). At the time of this writing, it was closed for renovation, but prices are projected at NT$800 for a double.

The Hsiao Liuchiu Hotel (☎ 8611133, 8612558) (xiǎo liúqiú dà fàndiàn) is up the hill, one block from the harbour. This is the top place in town and costs NT$1000 for a double on weekends. There is a 20% discount on weekdays.

The Fuhsing Hotel (☎ 8612617) (fùxīng bīnguǎn) is at 73-1 Minsheng Rd, very close to the Hsiao Liuchiu Hotel. It's nothing fancy, but costs NT$800 on weekends.

The entrance to the Liuchiu Hotel (☎ 8613281) (liúqiú bīnguǎn) faces the Lingshua temple, while the other side looks out over the harbour. Rooms cost NT$800 on weekends.

Getting There & Away

The island has a small, unpaved landing strip. However, it's overgrown with weeds and only used for VIP visits. Unless you have

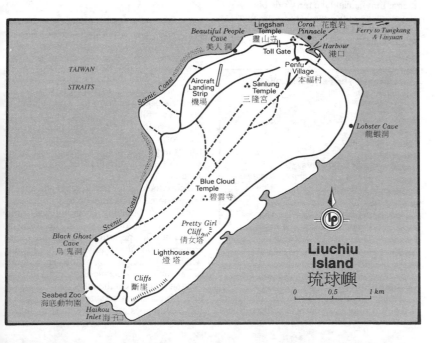

your own ultralight, you'll have to go by boat.

There are two ports which have ferry service to Liuchiu Island. Tungkang (*dōnggǎng*) fishing harbour in Pingtung County is more popular and has cushier boats. The other harbour, in Kaohsiung County, is Linyuan (*línyuán zhōngyún mǎtóu*). Buses to Tungkang leave from the suburban bus terminal in Kaohsiung.

Officially, departures for Liuchiu from Tungkang are at 8.30 am and 3 pm, returning at noon and 4.30 pm. Unofficially, boats go whenever full, which means about once an hour on weekends and holidays. The journey takes 50 minutes one-way and the return fare is NT$210.

For travellers without their own transport, it's most convenient to buy a ticket from the Chan'an Boat Company (☎ 2222123, 2223266) (*zhàn'àn lúnchuán gōngsī*) at 65 Mintsu-2 Rd in Kaohsiung. The ticket costs NT$360 and that includes transport to the pier at Linyuan and the ferry ride both ways. If you make your own way to the pier, the ticket costs NT$280. The bus makes the trip to Linyuan harbour about eight times a day.

Liuchiu Island Ferry Schedule

Weekdays

From Linyuan	From Liuchiu
8 am	9 am
10 am	noon
1.30 pm	3 pm

Weekends & Holidays

From Linyuan	From Liuchiu
8 am	9 am
9 am	noon
10 am	2 pm
11.20 am	3 pm
1.30 pm	4.30 pm

Getting Around

You can walk all the way around the island in a day. Riding a bicycle is more convenient but they don't seem to be available for hire.

You can bring a bicycle on the ferry, though it'll cost you as much as a passenger ticket.

Motorcycles can also be taken on the ferry, but you can rent 50-cc models on the island from a shack facing the Hsiao Liuchiu Hotel. The sign (in Chinese) says 'motorcycle rental' (*jīchē chūzǔ*).

However, there's no need to drive yourself. When you buy your ferry ticket, you can also buy a pass that allows you to ride the blue trucks that drive counter-clockwise around the island. This makes more sense on weekends, when the service is frequent. You can hop off the truck at any time and catch the next one that comes along. However, the trucks are operated by different companies and they don't honour each other's passes. When you buy the pass, you'll be issued a sticker which you should affix to your shirt so the drivers know you indeed have a pass. The passes cost NT$100 for a full day's use.

Kaohsiung County 高雄縣

KAOHSIUNG

(*gāoxióng*) 高雄

Kaohsiung is the second-largest city in Taiwan and the number one seaport. The city has witnessed rapid growth and industrialisation and now has a population of over 1½ million. The home of the China Steel Corporation, China Shipbuilding and the world's fourth-largest container port, Kaohsiung is where one can really see what Taiwan's export-oriented economy is all about.

Those looking for peace, quiet and a view of traditional China may be less impressed. Kaohsiung's booming economy has some unpleasant spin-off effects in the form of crime, traffic, pollution, noise and over-crowding. For many travellers, Kaohsiung will be an overnight stop on the way to some of Taiwan's major scenic attractions, like the Penghu Islands. On the other hand, if you'd like a break from beaches and mountains, Kaohsiung does offer pretty good nightlife. The city has a few worthwhile places to visit,

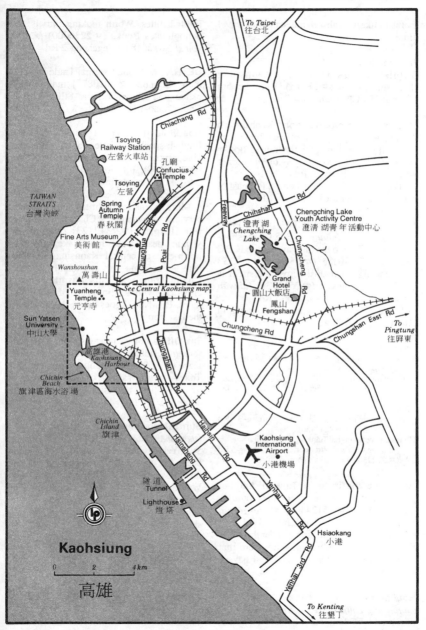

To Taipei
往台北

Chiachang Rd

Tsoying
Railway Station
左營火車站

孔廟
Confucius
Temple

Tsoying
左營

Spring
Autumn Temple
春秋閣

Rd

*TAIWAN
STRAITS*
台灣海峽

Fine Arts Museum
美術館

Chihshan

Chengching Lake
Youth Activity Centre
澄清 湖青 年 活動中心

澄青湖
*Chengching
Lake*

Chungghua

Poai

Rd

Freeway

Chungcheng

Rd

Wanshoushan
萬壽山

See Central Kaohsiung map

Grand
Hotel
圓山大飯店

*Yuanheng
Temple*
元亨寺

鳳山
Fengshan

Sun Yatsen
University
中山大學

Chungshan

Rd

Chungcheng Rd

Chungshan East Rd

*To
Pingtung*
往屏東

高雄港
*Kaohsiung
Harbour*

*Chichin
Beach*
旗津區海水浴場

*Chichin
Island*
旗津

Hsinsheng

Rd

Haihsin

Rd

Kaohsiung
International
Airport
小港機場

Yenhai

Rd

隧道
Tunnel

Lighthouse
燈塔

Hsiaokang
小港

Yenhai 3rd Rd

lp

Kaohsiung

0   2   4 km

高雄

To Kenting
往墾丁

but isn't likely to absorb much of your travel time.

Information

Tourist Offices There is a Kaohsiung Tourism Bureau (☎ 2811513) on the 5th floor at 253 Chungcheng-4 Rd.

Post & Telecommunications Kaohsiung's telephone-company head office offers a rare treat – it's close enough to the train station to walk. The phone company is on the corner of Chihsien and Linsen Rds.

The GPO is on Chungcheng-3 Rd, east of the roundabout on Chungshan Rd.

Money There is an ICBC (☎ 2013001) *(guójì shāngyè yínháng)* at 308 Chungshan-1 Rd, very close to the railway station. ICBC has another office (☎ 2510141) at 253 Chungcheng-5 Rd. Just across the street is the Bank of Taiwan (☎ 2515131) *(táiwān yínháng)* at 264 Chungcheng-5 Rd.

Some foreign banks are represented in Kaohsiung as follows:

American Express Bank
    (měiguó yùntōng yínháng), 5 Chungcheng-3 Rd
    (☎ 2263116, fax 2262368)
Bank Nationale de Paris (BNP)
    10th floor, 2 Chungcheng-3 Rd (☎ 2220401, fax
    2241101)
Citibank
    (huāqí yínháng), 38 Chungcheng-3 Rd
    (☎ 2243433, fax 2243450)
Hongkong & Shanghai Banking Corporation
    (huìfēng yínháng), 3rd floor, 2 Chungcheng-3 Rd
    (☎ 2222500, fax 2233156)

American Institute in Taiwan Another place to look into is the American Institute in Taiwan (AIT) (☎ 2512444) *(měiguó zài tái xiéhuì)*, 3rd floor, 2 Chungcheng-3 Rd. AIT serves as an unofficial embassy for the USA. For travellers, its chief attractions are that they handle visas for the USA and have a notary service.

Bookshops Caves Books (☎ 5615716) *(dūnhuáng shūjú)*, 76-78 Wufu-4 Rd, near the Hotel Kingdom, has a large collection of English titles. Worth looking into is New Schoolmates Books (☎ 2236000) *(xīn xué yǒu shūjú)* at 18 Chungcheng-2 Rd.

CETRA The China External Trade Development Council (☎ 2010877) maintains an office and library on the 8th floor, 456 Chunghsiao-1 Rd.

Hospitals If you need medical attention, English-speaking Western doctors are available at the Kaohsiung Adventist Clinic, (☎ 2010148), suite 503, 5th floor, 101 Wufu-3 Rd. Prices are definitely at the high end of the scale.

More extensive treatment and emergency services are available at Chang Gung Memorial Hospital (☎ 7317123) *(cháng gēng yīyuàn)* near Chengching Lake, seven km north-east of central Kaohsiung. Medical care is good and very reasonably priced at Chang Gung, but this hospital is very crowded, with waiting lists of a week or more. Bus No 60 goes there; the hospital is the last stop.

Tax Office For visa-extension hopefuls and foreign residents wanting to go abroad, the place to go for tax clearance is the National Tax Administration of Kaohsiung, 66 Szuwei-3 Rd, Kaohsiung (☎ 3340111 ext 406-408).

Sun Yatsen University
(zhōngshān dàxué) 中山大學
Sun Yatsen University and the adjacent beach are most easily reached by walking through a tunnel bored straight through Wanshoushan (Long Life Mountain). The campus is pleasant and seems to serve as an unofficial park for locals. Behind a glass showcase you can see Chiang Kaishek's old limousine. At one time this campus was the Generalissimo's personal retreat. It's also worth having a look at the fishing harbour adjacent to the campus.

Chungcheng Cultural Centre
(wénhuà zhōngxīn) 文化中心
The Chungcheng Cultural Centre is similar

Top: Shoreline of Hsiaomen Island, Penghu (RS)
Bottom: Stone walls to protect crops from fierce winds, Penghu (RS)

Top: Two Sisters Pond, Alishan (RS)
Left: Red suspension bridge, Fengshan (MM)
Right: Post Office, Alishan (RS)

to the Sun Yatsen Hall in Taipei. It has art exhibits, operas, exhibitions and classical performances. The program often changes so you'll have to drop by to get the current schedule of events.

The Cultural Centre is at the intersection of Wufu-1 Rd and Hoping-1 Rd.

Temples

Kaohsiung has some interesting temples (*miào*). *The largest is the Yuanheng Temple* (*yuánhēng sì*), built on a big hillside just west of Kushan Rd (*gǔshān lù*). Unfortunately, this is also close to a big cement factory which spews out a lot of dust, but it is still a nice temple. On the 1st floor there are three enormous Buddhas, and if you take the elevator to the 5th floor there are three large statues of the goddess Kuanyin. Bus Nos 19, 31, 43 and 45 stop directly across the street. Just walk up the big hill. The temple is so large that you can't miss it.

In the suburb of Tsoying (*zuǒyíng*) are two magnificent temples within a 10-minute walk of each other. Both are on the shore of a lake. The Spring Autumn Temple (*chūn qiū gé*) has a unique design and includes two pagodas that extend into the lake.

The nearby Confucius Temple (*kǒngzǐ miào*) is a very tranquil place. Just adjacent to the Confucius Temple is another red building which also looks like a temple, but is in fact the temple library. Bus Nos 5 and 19 from Kaohsiung stop near both these temples, and there are trains once an hour.

Kaohsiung Zoo

(*gāoxióng dòngwù yuán*) 高雄動物園
As zoos go, this one isn't exactly a trendsetter, but it makes a welcome break from the din of Kaohsiung's city streets. The zoo is in Wanshoushan Park and admission is NT$10.

Chichin Island

(*qíjīn*) 旗津
I remember when you could only reach this island by boat and it was devoid of cars, but those days are gone – construction of the cross-harbour tunnel has turned most of Chichin into a container port. The north part

of the island is the only area which retains some of its former charm. This area also has a decent beach, and during summer there are lifeguards, ice-cream vendors, and so on.

The main reason to come to Chichin now is to enjoy the seafood restaurants which are also clustered at the north end of the island. One of the best is *Jisheng Seafood Restaurant* (☎ 5719016) (*jíshèng hǎi chǎn*), 186-3 Chungchou-2 Rd. However, prices are definitely not cheap.

You can reach Chichin by taking a short ferry ride from the fishing harbour, which is next to Sun Yatsen University.

Fine Arts Museum

(*měi shù guǎn*) 美術館
Close to Tsoying in the northern area of Kaohsiung is the Fine Arts Museum (☎ 5830651), Taiwan's newest and largest. Displays here are changed regularly. The museum is at 316-1 Chunghua-1 Rd.

Chengching Lake

(*chéngqīng hú*) 澄清湖
Seven km from the centre of town, Chengching Lake is a city reservoir surrounded by a well-landscaped park. It's the only green spot in Kaohsiung besides Sun Yatsen University. The huge Grand Hotel, which resembles a palace, overlooks the lake. Around the lake are some pagodas, pavilions, a golf course and a place to hire rowing boats.

Visit Chengching Lake anytime except Sundays and holidays when it becomes unbelievably crowded. There is a NT$50 entrance fee for the lake area. Bicycles are not permitted on the road around the lake. As I was told by the guard at the gate, 'The bicycles confuse the cars and motorcycles'. Sounds to me like that's not the only thing confused. To reach Chengching Lake, take bus No 60 from the city bus terminal.

Places to Stay – bottom end

The cheapest place in town is the *Kaohsiung Hostel* (3355414) 3rd floor, 39 Tzuchiang-3 Rd, Kaohsiung, on the south-west corner of Tzuchiang and Hsincheng Rd – one block

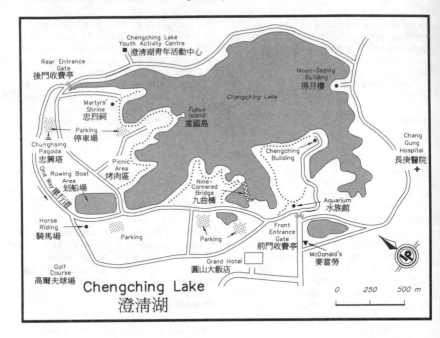

Chengching Lake
澄清湖

Chengching Lake

north of Sanduo Rd. A bed in the dormitory costs NT$160. The best way to get there is bus No 12 to the Far Eastern Department Store on Chungshan Rd and Sanduo Rd, then ring the hostel and someone will come and get you.

A friendly place getting good reviews from travellers is the *IYHF Hostel I* (☎ 2012477, fax 2156322), 120 Wenwu-1 St, one block west of Chunghua Rd and north of Chihsien Rd. Beds are NT$200 to NT$300, and all rooms have air-con. The hostel boasts a TV sitting room, refrigerator, and a place to cook simple meals. Due to popular demand, the owner recently opened *IYHF Hostel II* (☎ 3391533, fax 3361339) at 42 Lingya-2 Rd.

The *Armed Forces Hostel* (☎ 2516411) *(gāoxióng guójūn yīngxióng guǎn)*, 145 Wufu-3 Rd, is open to civilians too, so you needn't enlist in the army to stay there. This enormous place offers rooms from NT$200 to NT$800. Meals are also available.

Towards the south end of town is the *Labourers' Recreation Centre* (☎ 3328110, 3329110) *(láogōng yùlè zhōngxīn)*, 132 Chungshan-3 Rd, near the intersection with Minchuan-2 Rd. It's a huge place occupying a whole block. Singles/triples are NT$200/600. From the railway station, you can get there on bus No 7, 12, 25, 26 or 30.

Close to the Grand Hotel is the *Chengching Lake Youth Activity Centre* (☎ 371 7181, fax 3719183) *(qīngnián huódòng zhōngxīn)*. It's a beautiful place to stay, but it's seven km from the city centre by bus, plus a 1.5-km walk if you don't have your own transport. The dormitory costs NT$180. If it's full, you rent as many blankets as you need and stay in a tent (already set up). They have good meals, which cost NT$50 for breakfast and NT$100 for lunch and dinner, but let the staff know in advance if you want to eat at the hostel. Take bus No 60 to the last stop, which is Chang Gung Memorial Hospital. From there, you must walk past the hospital on the same main road for about 1.5 km. The lake will be to your left. Take the first paved road to your left; this follows the shore of the lake. About 30 minutes of walking on this road brings you to the hostel.

Places to Stay – middle

There's no need to walk very far from the railway station – this area has a thick cluster of mid-range places to stay. On weekends and holidays, it might pack out – in this case, look behind (north of) the railway station.

Front of Station By far the cheapest is the *Hotel Taiwan* (☎ 2216081) *(táiwān dà fàndiàn)* at 285 Chungshan-1 Rd (on the corner of Pate-1 Rd). Doubles start at NT$400.

Just on the other side of Pate Rd is *Hotel Grand China* (☎ 2219941) *(zhōnghuá dà fàndiàn)*, 289 Chungshan-1 Rd. There's no English sign, but it's adjacent to Wendy's, a notable landmark. Doubles are NT$500 to NT$600.

Opposite Kentucky Fried Chicken is the *Jin Dih Hotel* (☎ 2013071) *(Jīndì dà fàndiàn)*, 392 Pate-1 Rd. Comfortable doubles go for NT$760.

The *Himalaya Hotel* (☎ 2516602) *(gāoshān dà fàndiàn)*, 316 Chungshan-1 Rd, has no English sign but is directly north of the sewage canal. This place is noted for its sauna, as the naughty pictures of customers in towels indicates. Doubles start at NT$860.

Directly facing the railway station is *Union Hotel* (☎ 2410101) *(guótǒng dà fàndiàn)*, 295 Chienkuo-2 Rd. This place is fairly up-market with doubles starting at NT$924. Twins are priced NT$1600 to NT$2200 and suites are NT$2600 to NT$4600.

Rear of Station The *Modern Hotel* (☎ 321 8111) *(xiàndài dà fàndiàn)*, 332 Chiuju-2 Rd, is friendly and easy to find. As you exit the rear of the station, cross the road and it's just to your right. Doubles are NT$680 to NT$780.

Just behind the Modern Hotel is *Ming's*

Hotel (☎ 3118477) *(míngshì dà fàndiàn)*, 2 Po'ai-1 Rd. Doubles are NT$820.

If you exit the station and turn immediately to your right without crossing the street, you'll come to the *Dragon Hotel* (☎ 3121151) *(lóngdá dà fàndiàn)*, 339 Chiuju-2 Rd. Doubles here are NT$640 and NT$720.

Exit the station, cross the street, and on your left (right on the corner) is the *Tian'an Hotel* (☎ 3122131) *(tiān'ān dà fàndiàn – no English sign)*, 1 Po'ai-1 Rd. Doubles are NT$700.

Places to Stay – top end

For those who can afford luxury accommodation, the Ambassador Hotel combines luxury with a convenient location. However, the most beautiful hotel in town is the Grand Hotel on the shore of Chengching Lake.

Other top-end hotels include:

Ambassador Hotel
  (guóbīn dà fàndiàn; 500 rooms), 202 Minsheng-2 Rd(☎ 2115211, fax 2811113); doubles NT$3300-4100, twins NT$3900-5600, suites NT$9800-40,000
Buckingham Hotel
  (báijīnhàn dàfàndiàn; 144 rooms), 394 Chihsien-2 Rd (☎ 2822151, fax 2814540); doubles NT$1700 to NT$2000, twins NT$1900 to NT$2400
Chinatrust Hotel
  (zhōngxìn dà fàndiàn; 153 rooms), 43 Tajen Rd (☎ 5217111, fax 5217068); doubles NT$2600 to NT$3200, twins NT$3000 to NT$3500, suites NT$3800 to NT$20,000
Grand Hotel
  (yuánshān dà fàndiàn; 120 rooms), seven km from the centre of town (☎ 3835911, fax 3814889); singles NT$2400 to NT$2600, twins NT$2800 to NT$3000
Hotel Holiday Garden
  (huáyuán dà fàndiàn; 303 rooms), 279 Liuho-2 Rd (☎ 2410121, fax 2512000); doubles NT$3200 to NT$3600, twins NT$3400 to NT$3800
Hotel Kingdom
  (huáwáng dà fàndiàn; 312 rooms), 42 Wufu-4 Rd (☎ 5518211, fax 5210403); doubles NT$3200-4000, twins NT$4000-4200, suites NT$6500-8000

1 Cement Factory
水泥廠

2 Yuanheng Temple
元亨寺

3 Martyrs' Shrine
忠烈祠

4 Sun Yatsen University
中山大學

5 Jisheng Seafood Restaurant
吉勝海產

6 Kingship Hotel
漢王大飯店

7 Doutor Coffee Shop
羅多倫咖啡店

8 Caves Books
敦煌書局

9 Chinatrust & Major hotels
中信大飯店/名人大飯店

10 Hotel Kingdom
華王大飯店

11 Good Time Sporting Goods
好時長運動百貨廣場

12 Ambassador Hotel
國賓大飯店

13 ICBC
中國國際商業銀行

14 Bank of Taiwan
台灣銀行

15 Police (Visa Extensions)
警察局外事課

16 Hotel Holiday Garden
華園大飯店

17 IYHF Hostel I
文武一街120號

18 Hotel Taiwan
台灣大飯店

19 Wendy's & Hotel Grand China
溫蒂漢堡/中華大飯店

20 ICBC & Jin Dih Hotel
國際商業銀行/金帝大飯店

21 Himalaya & Union hotels
高山大飯店/國統大飯店

22 City Bus Terminal
市公車站

23 Highway Buses (Taipei)
台汽客運站(往台北)

24 Country Buses (Taitung)
台汽客運站(往台東)

25 Tian'an Hotel
天安大飯店

26 Ming's & Modern hotels
名仕大飯店/現代大飯店

27 Dragon Hotel
龍達大飯店

28 Highway Buses (Tainan, Pingtung)
台汽客運站(往台南/屏東)

29 Telephone Company
電信局

30 Hsinhsing Market
新興市場

31 GPO
郵政總局

32 Chan'an Boat Company
占岸輪船公司

33 American Institute in Taiwan (AIT)
美國在台協會

34 Chungcheng Cultural Centre
文化中心

35 Norman's Pizza Pub
林德街59號

36 President Department Store
大統百貨

37 Talee Department Store
大立百貨

38 Armed Forces Hostel
高雄國軍英雄館

39 Pig & Whistle Pub
四維四路199號

40 IYHF Hostel II
苓雅二路42號

41 Kaohsiung Hostel
自強三路39號3樓

42 Movie Theatres
三多大戲院

43 Far Eastern Department Store
遠東百貨

44 Labourers' Recreation Centre
勞工休假中心

45 Dollars Megastore
大樂

Hotel Major
   (*míngrén dà fàndiàn*; 216 rooms), 7 Tajen Rd
   (☎ 5212266, fax 5312211); doubles NT$2500 to
   NT$2700, twins NT$2700 to NT$3000, suites
   NT$3800 to NT$10,000
Kingship Hotel
   (*hànwáng dà fàndiàn*), 98 Chihsien-3 Rd
   (☎ 5313131, fax 5313140); doubles NT$2400,
   twins NT$2400 to NT$2400, suites NT$12,000
Summit Hotel
   (*huángtŏng dàfàndiàn*), 426 Chiuju-1 Rd
   (☎ 3845526, fax 3844739); doubles/twins
   NT$2300/2500

Places to Eat

Budget Eats The *Hsinhsing St Market (xīnxīng shìchăng)* is adjacent to the GPO in a long alley running parallel to Chungshan Rd. Besides cheap eats, it's a good place to look for cheapish clothing and shoes. The place packs out at night.

If you're staying at the IYHF Hostel I, just around the corner is *Sihai Doujiang Dian* (☎ 2160222) at 265 Chunghua-3 Rd. This place features low prices, all-night dumplings and early-morning steamed buns with soybean milk. The operating hours are unusual – 9 pm to 10 am.

Liuho-2 Rd *(liùhé èr lù)* has an active night market where the chief form of entertainment is eating. Liuho Rd is a very long street; the night market is only between Chungshan Rd and Tzuli Rd. Plenty of reasonably priced seafood stalls, but the snake soup and anteater are more interesting. During the day, Liuho-2 Rd is known for its steak restaurants. Only at night do the street vendors move in.

The *President Department Store* at the corner of Wufu Rd and Chungshan Rd has something like a traditional Chinese market on the 9th floor. Prices are OK and there is a wide selection of food.

Teng Chef (dèng shīfù) deserves honourable mention – it's a chain store famous for its numerous small Chinese dishes. You can make a whole meal of beef, pork, vegetables and noodles for three people for around NT$100 each. There are three in the city: 82 Chungcheng-3 Rd (near Jenai Rd) (☎ 2821822); 82 Chingnien-2 Rd (near

Wenwu Rd), (☎ 2515622); and 86-1 Chunghua-3 Rd, (☎ 2916722).

The Pie Shop (☎ 5516794) at 124 Wufu-4 Rd gets rave reviews from travellers. It's one place where you can kick back and just forget that you're in Taiwan. Pies are not the only thing on the menu – plenty of Western food is available.

Some of the best pizza in Taiwan can be found at *Melbourne Pizza* (☎ 2821330), 57 Wufu-2 Rd. This place features free home delivery.

Fast Food If you need a break from Chinese food, *Wendy's* and *Kentucky Fried Chicken* have staked out opposite corners of the intersection of Chungshan-1 Rd and Pate Rd, just south of the railway station. Similar cuisine can also be found at *McDonald's* on the corner of Chungshan-2 Rd and Sanduo-3 Rd, next to the Far Eastern Department Store.

Self-Catering For buying various frozen, canned and preserved Western foods, one place to go is the *Box Store* (☎ 2217265) *(jiāhé shāng háng)*, 11 Chungshan Heng Rd. This is a little alley north-west side of the traffic island at the corner of Chungshan-1 and Chungcheng-4 Rds.

Similar fare can be found at *American Eatables* (☎ 2311906), 213 Tatung-1 Rd.

Dollars (☎ 3368667) *(dàlè)* is a megastore at 157 Kuanghua-2 Rd. You need to buy an admission card, after which time you can stock up on cheap goods usually sold in large quantities. It's popular with foreign residents but not much use for the odd traveller passing through.

Upmarket A mid-range place serving primarily Cantonese food is *Xuyuan* (☎ 381 1917), 227 Tatung-1 Rd. Dishes cost around NT$200 and it definitely pays to have a small group to get a wide sampling.

Outstanding Western, Cantonese dim sum, Mandarin Chinese and Japanese teppanyaki dishes can be had at the *Long Life Club* (☎ 3326625) *(chánghè lóu cāntīng)*, 351 Szuwei-2 Rd.

No prizes for guessing the specialty of the

Hong Ping Steak House (☎ 2718156) *(hóngbīn niúpái guǎn)*, 23-4 Chunghua-2 Rd. There is another (☎ 2267851) at 203 Minsheng-1 Rd.

The *New International Western Restaurant* (☎ 2164717) *(xīn guójì xī cāntīng)*, 76 Minsheng-2 Rd, is noted for its fine Western food.

Ka Ra Bour Thai Food (☎ 2246668), 54 Chungcheng-3 Rd, is one of Kaohsiung's few restaurants dishing up spicy Thai food. They have a luncheon special that costs NT$150 per person.

Japanese food fans can get their pickles, seaweed and raw fish at *Daba Riben Liaoli* (☎ 2611840), 53 Minsheng-2 Rd. There is another (☎ 3363750) at 144 Szuwei-2 Rd. Expect to pay Japanese prices.

Hotel food is not to be overlooked. Fine cuisine is to be had at the *Ambassador Hotel* and *Hotel Kingdom* (see Places to Stay for addresses).

Seafood Kaohsiung is famous for seafood, but mostly it isn't cheap. Top of the line in quality (and price) is the *Crab's House* (☎ 2266127) *(xún zhīwū)*, 93 Minsheng-1 Rd. Very similar in price and quality is *Hai Tian Sha* (☎ 2810651), 188 Linsen-2 Rd.

Another classy seafood restaurant (with prices to match) is *Hai Pa Wang* (☎ 333 5168) *(hǎi bà wáng)*, 2 Hsingchung-2 Rd. There is another branch (☎ 2829638) *(dōngqū hǎi bà wáng)* at 160 Kuanghua-1 Rd.

Also in the seafood business is *Sea General Tavern* (☎ 3353379) *(hǎi jiāngjūn)*, 357 Szuwei-2 Rd.

Entertainment

Cinemas There are some movie theatres in town specialising in English-language movies. The best are clustered in a large complex at the intersection of Sanduo-4 Rd and Chengkung-1 Rd known as the *sānduō xìyuàn*.

Coffee Shops Doutor Coffee Shop *(luóduōlún kāfēi diàn)* features something almost unheard of in Taiwan – low prices. A cup of decent coffee served in congenial surroundings costs just NT$35. It's at 51 Wufu-4 Rd, opposite Caves Books.

I Love My Home Coffee Shop (☎ 2319657), 258 Chungshan-1 Rd, is nice but expensive. Don't figure on getting coffee for under NT$200. There is another branch (☎ 2715273) at 104 Liuho-1 Rd.

MTV Kiss is an outstanding MTV place with two locations – both are just down the street from one another. Kiss No 1 (☎ 2729412) is on the 3rd floor, 14 Chungshan-1 Rd. Kiss No 2 (☎ 2819775) is on the 9th floor, 4 Chungshan-1 Rd. All movies are on laser disk and cost is NT$160 per person per film.

One of the largest MTV places that I've ever seen is *jù jiàng* (☎ 2018065), 2nd floor, 40 Minsheng-2 Rd, on the north-west corner of the intersection with Chungshan Rd. It's open 24 hours.

Pubs The Pig & Whistle (☎ 3301006), 199 Szuwei-4 Rd, is a well-known somewhat up-market place. It's open from 11.30 am to 3 am (5 am on Saturdays) and there are live bands upstairs from 9 pm nightly.

Norman's Pizza Pub (☎ 7132402), 59 Linte St, is a popular place with expats. It's behind the Cultural Centre. Prices are mid-range.

The Yenchen district of Kaohsiung (near the Hotel Kingdom) is the place to look for pubs and restaurants catering to foreigners. However, the area is a seaport and sometimes rough – one drunken Korean sailor was stabbed to death recently when he refused to pay his bar bill which he thought was too expensive. It might be wise to ask the price of drinks before ordering.

In the Yenchen district is Stormy Weather (☎ 5514407), 30 Wufu-4 Rd. At Sam's Place (☎ 5211564), 27 Wufu-4 Rd, near the Hotel Kingdom, where you can play darts, eat Western food and drink beer. In the same area is Snow's Pub (☎ 5311886, at 49 Wufu-4 Rd. On the same street is the Brass Rail Tavern (☎ 5315643), 21 Wufu-4 Rd; and Key Largo Pub (☎ 5616901), 88 Wufu-4 Rd.

Amy's, also in Yenchen, has long been

popular. There are two branches, the Beer House (☎ 5318599) at 74 Chihsien-3 Rd, and the Celebrity Room (☎ 5330756) at 115 Wufu-4 Rd. The latter is something like a 'Hard Rock Café'.

Discos The most popular disco in town is Kiss Disco (☎ 3314275), 5th floor, 62 Tzuchiang-3 Rd, not far from the Sanduo Rd and Chengkung Rd intersection.

Things to Buy
Kaohsiung boasts one of the best backpacking and outdoors-oriented stores in Taiwan – the Good Time Sporting Goods Department Store (☎ 5512296) *(hǎo shí cháng yùndòng bǎihuò guǎngchǎng)*, 2 Wufu-4 Rd. As their advertisement says, 'Our store believes in being honesty'.

Good export-quality clothing can be bought from Madame Fashion Company *(zhǔfù shāng chǎng)*, on the north-east corner of the Chungcheng-4 Rd and Chunghua-3 Rd intersection.

Kaohsiung's computer alley is the south side of Chienkuo-2 Rd, between Linsen and Mintsu roads. This area is just east of the main bus stations. There are at least 40 computer shops here, so competition is keen.

One of the biggest department stores in Taiwan is the President Department Store *(dàtǒng bǎihuò gōngsī)*, on the corner of Chungshan Rd and Wufu Rd. The nearby Talee Department Store *(dàlì bǎihuò gōngsī)* is under the same management but is generally more expensive. Both have good restaurants on the top floor and amusement parks on the roof.

The ever-popular Far Eastern Department Store *(yuǎndōng bǎihuò gōngsī)*, at the corner of Chungshan-2 Rd and Sanduo-4 Rd, has a great supermarket in the basement.

Getting There & Away
Air Kaohsiung has domestic air services to Chimei (NT$1305), Hualien (NT$1428), Lanyu (NT$1555), Makung (NT$821), Taipei (NT$1125), Taitung (NT$1130) and Wang'an (NT$1332).

There are direct international flights to Hong Kong, Japan, the Philippines and a few other foreign destinations. There is also a very useful shuttle flight between Kaohsiung and CKS Airport in Taoyuan (NT$1323), but a few rules apply:

• flights will accept only passengers in transit at CKS Airport to connect with same day international flights
• both incoming and outgoing passengers must clear Customs and Immigration at Kaohsiung Airport
• passengers travelling from Kaohsiung to CKS Airport must present themselves for check-in at least 60 minutes before flight departure

Some travel agents which offer reasonably good prices on tickets include:

Southeast Travel Service
(dōngnán lǚxíngshè), 106 Chungcheng-4 Rd (☎ 2312181)
Wing On Travel Service
(yǒng'ān lǚxíngshè), 125-1 Chunghua-3 Rd (☎ 2826760)

There are a number of airlines which have representative offices in Kaohsiung, including:

Cathay Pacific
(guótài hángkōng), 3rd floor, 21 Chunghua-3 Rd (☎ 2013166)
China Airlines
(zhōnghuá hángkōng), 81 Chunghua-3 Rd (☎ 8012674)
Delta Airlines
(dàměi hángkōng) 8th floor, 103 Chungcheng-4 Rd (☎ 2157286)
EVA Airways
(chángróng hángkōng), 177 Szuwei-4 Rd (☎ 3366161)
Hsiaokang Airport (☎ 8061477)
Japan Asia
(rìyǎ hángkōng), 4th floor, 2 Chungcheng-3 Rd (☎ 2231156)
KLM
(hélán hángkōng), Room 8, 11th floor, 206 Kuanghua-1 Rd (☎ 2264210)
Korean Air
(dàhán hángkōng) 13th floor, 2 Chungcheng-3 Rd (☎ 2239340)
Philippine Airlines
(fēilǜbīn hángkōng) Room 6, 15th floor, 235 Chungcheng-1 Rd (☎ 2017181)
Singapore Airlines
(xīnjiāpō hángkōng), c/o Federal Transportation

(fēidá), 5th floor, 282 Chunghua-4 Rd
(☎ 2216001)
Thai Airways
(tàiguó hángkōng) 9th floor, 282 Chunghua-4
Rd, (☎ 2155871)

For domestic flights, you can easily buy tickets at the airport or from travel agents. The airline representative offices are as follows:

Far Eastern Airlines
(yuǎndōng hángkōng), 101 Chunghua-3 Rd
(☎ 2411181)
Formosa Airlines
(yǒngxīng hángkōng), 87 Lunghua St, Hsiokang
district (☎ 8035259)
Great China Airlines
(dàhuá hángkōng), Kaohsiung Airport
(☎ 8017327, 8017608)
Makung Airlines
(mǎgōng hángkōng), Kaohsiung Airport
(☎ 8010869, 8010189)
Taiwan Airlines
(táiwān hángkōng), Kaohsiung Airport
(☎ 8013793)
Trans-Asia Airways
(fùxīng hángkōng), 146 Chungcheng-4 Rd
(☎ 2152868)

Bus There are direct express buses, both Kuokuang (government) and wild chicken, from Taipei and other major cities to the north

Coming from Taitung on the east coast, there are express buses day and night. From Kenting, take a bus to Hengchun, and then another to Kaohsiung.

Train All the major west coast trains pass through Kaohsiung. There is also a train service to Taitung on the east coast.

Sea There are daily ferries to the Penghu Islands (see the Penghu section for details). There are twice-monthly passenger ferries to Okinawa in Japan and a once or twice-weekly ferry to Macau (see the Getting There & Away chapter for details).

Getting Around
To/From the Airport Kaohsiung's Hsiaokang International Airport is south of

the city. Seeing how this is an international airport with frequent flights to Hong Kong, you'd expect airport transport to be good. Unfortunately, there are no express airport buses. Local bus No 12 runs about once every 20 minutes to central Kaohsiung. It doesn't go all the way to the railway station but stops at Chungcheng Rd, a 10-minute walk south of the station. Going the other direction, you can catch bus No 12 at the bus station just in front of the railway station.

The airport taxis have a set fee, usually NT$250 minimum, but ask first. You can save some money by walking outside the airport and hailing a passing cab. They will use the meter and the cost to the railway station is about NT$150.

If you're going to CKS International Airport in Taoyuan (near Taipei), there is an express bus at 6.30 am. Alternatively, take any northbound train to Taoyuan (around four hours) and then take a bus to the airport (30 minutes) or taxi (20 minutes). Alternatively, you can fly directly to CKS Airport from Kaohsiung (see Getting There and Away).

Bus City buses cost NT$10 per ride, or NT$12 for some of the air-con minibuses. You might find it useful to buy a 10-ride bus ticket from the roadside vendors near the major bus stops.

In Kaohsiung, there are three bus terminals adjacent to the railway station. If you're facing the front of the station, the terminal to your left is for local city buses. The terminal to your immediate right is for long-distance (Kuokuang) buses to north Taiwan, and the terminal further to the right is for buses to the surrounding suburban and rural areas, which for some strange reason includes far-off Taitung. There is another bus station on Linsen Rd, one block south of Chienkuo Rd – this terminal has buses to Tainan and Pingtung.

The wild-chicken buses have several small terminals that frequently get moved, but they're always near the main bus station.

Car Cars can be rented from a variety of

sources. One place with English-speaking staff is Elephant Rent-A-Car (☎ 8011133, fax 8013483) at 21 Chungshan-4 Rd (on the road to the airport).

FOKUANGSHAN
(fóguāngshān) 佛光山

Fokuangshan is a large Buddhist monastery about a one-hour ride from Kaohsiung. Besides the temple, pleasant grounds and a Buddhist university, there is a mountain with a huge 32-metre-high golden Buddha surrounded by 480 smaller Buddhas, each one almost two metres tall – a rather impressive sight. There is also a large temple with three huge Buddhas, plus a museum of Buddhist art works (NT$30 admission).

There is an artificial cave with some rather bizarre mechanical statues that move like the ones at Disneyland. Good inexpensive vegetarian meals can be bought in the monastery and it is possible to stay in the dormitory for the night. A donation of around NT$300, which includes food, is customary. Make sure you remove your shoes before entering the big temple with the carpeted floor.

Getting There & Away
To get to Fokuangshan, take a bus from the eastern bus terminal (to the far right of the railway station as you face it). Buses depart about every 20 minutes.

LIUKUEI
(liùguī) 六龜

Liukuei, or 'Six Turtles', is a lovely spot north-east of Kaohsiung. The town occupies a valley walled in by high mountains with a white-water river rushing by. The scenery is even better than in Santimen, but not many people bother to come here. Camping, hiking and rafting along the Laonung River are popular activities.

Getting There & Away
The direct bus service from Kaohsiung is not very frequent; alternatively, you can take a bus to Pingtung and then another to Liukuei. There trip is better by car or motorcycle since

there are many scenic spots by the river to stop and relax along the way.

Just beyond Liukuei, the road continues north until it meets up with the South Cross-Island Highway at Chiahsien. It's a spectacular hike, which you might consider. The hike details are in the South Cross-Island section in this chapter.

If you have your own transport and you visit Liukuei, you should definitely make a stop-off at Maolin as well.

MAOLIN
(mào lín) 茂林

Maolin is a gem – babbling brooks, mountains, hiking trails – all within an hour's drive of Kaohsiung. Tacky commercial development is so far absent. There are a few very makeshift hotels, but most overnight visitors go camping. The road from Maolin into the mountains is about 25 km long and is gradually being extended in the interests of opening new tourist sites. There are many side routes along the way which end at scenic spots. The views are outstanding, and there are many places to stop and walk to the river. You can cross one of the suspension bridges and find waterfalls on the opposite side.

About 15 km from the entrance gate at Maolin is Tona *(duō nà)*. It's a small aboriginal village where the main industry is stonecraft. Flat, smooth slabs of stone of all sizes stand everywhere against walls. Tables, chair seats and small decorative pieces are available for sale. Some of the houses are built from these stones piled like bricks. Some simple food is available in Tona and there is one shoddy hotel. About five km past Tona is Tona Hot Springs *(duō nà wēnquán)*, which is one of the few natural hot outdoor springs in Taiwan that has escaped commercial development (so far).

This place can get busy on weekends as tour buses come up here, though it's hard to imagine how they manoeuvre the twisting, narrow mountain road. On weekdays, you'll have the place to yourself. There is a NT$50 admission charge for the area, plus NT$10 for a mountain permit and NT$5 for a motorcycle.

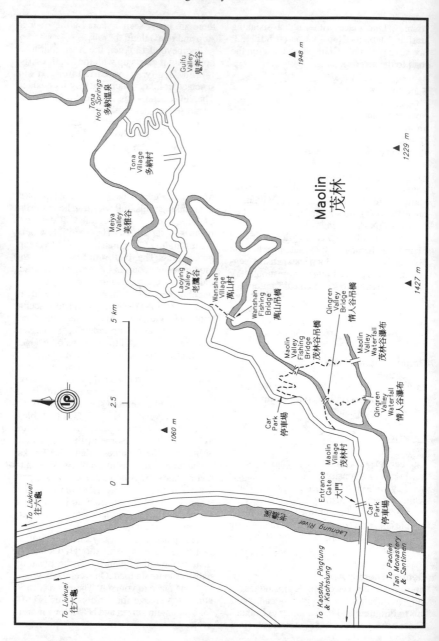

Getting There & Away

Without a tour bus or your own set of wheels, transport is a bit of a problem. During the day, there are buses to Maolin about once every hour or two from either Pingtung or Kaoshu. There are no buses to Tona.

This is one place where having your own vehicle is practically mandatory. A motorcycle is better than a car because the road is narrow, mountainous and winding. It is possible to do it on a 10-speed bicycle, but you'll need to be in good condition because of the hills (my condition proved to be not quite good enough). If you decide to ride, you can first send the bike to Pingtung by train, which will save you the long ride through Kaohsiung's horrendous traffic.

You need a mountain pass to enter this area, but fortunately it is very easy to obtain. You can get it in Maolin, right at the entrance to the area. Just fill out an application (in Chinese) and the pass will be issued immediately. The police will fill it out for you if you can't deal with the language. You should bring your passport or some sort of Chinese ID like a driving licence.

PAOLIEN TAN MONASTERY

(bǎolián dān sì) 寶蓮禪寺

This magnificent monastery is just two km south of Maolin along the road to Santimen. It's one of Taiwan's newest temple complexes, and construction was still continuing during the time of my last visit. There are a large number of nuns in residence here. No buses go to Paolien Tan Monastery, so you need your own transport or else you will have to walk or hitch. If you're not sure of the road, get someone to point you in the right direction.

Islands of Taiwan Straits

THE PENGHU ISLANDS

(pénghú) 澎湖

Consisting of 64 islands about halfway between Taiwan and mainland China, the Penghu archipelago offers a sharp contrast geographically to Taiwan. Penghu is much drier, and covered with brush and grassland rather than dense forests like Taiwan. While Taiwan has towering mountains, Penghu has none – but makes up for it with sandy beaches, quaint fishing villages, blue skies, a turquoise sea, great seafood and no mosquitos. From about May to October, the islands are bathed in brilliant sunshine and take on a special stark beauty that defies description.

Historically, Penghu is significant as it was the route used by European invaders of Taiwan. A large fort still remains on the Penghu Islands. When the Portuguese visited they called these islands the Pescadores. The Dutch occupied the islands for a time, a role emulated by the French and Japanese.

Unlike Taiwan, Penghu is not overpopulated and probably never will be as the locals migrate to Taiwan in search of greater economic opportunities. Tourism is the main industry, followed by fishing and farming, but growing anything is difficult in Penghu's harsh, windswept climate. The islanders have built coral walls to protect the crops (peanuts, sweet potatoes and sorghum) from the fierce winter winds. It's likely that fishing and farming will continue to decline – Penghu's young people have little interest in pursuing such strenuous careers.

Penghu is a great place to visit, but not in winter. From mid-October to March the chilly north wind makes life unpleasant. From May to the end of September, it's fine. The winter winds also cause heavy seas, so a boat trip is doubly unpleasant. If you must visit in winter, it is better to fly.

There are 147 temples in Penghu by official count and, not surprisingly, they are mostly dedicated to Matsu, goddess of the sea. Matsu is believed to protect fishermen from harm on their hazardous journeys. Many of Penghu's temples are old, but they have been restored and are well worth visiting.

The largest island of the 64 is simply called Penghu, and it is almost certainly the one you will see first. There are two other islands attached to Penghu by bridges,

Paisha and Hsiyu. Visiting the other islands requires a boat or small plane.

Makung

(mǎgōng) 馬公

The only city in the islands, Makung has a population of 60,000. It's a picturesque city with its fishing harbour, outdoor fish markets and temples. The place retains a little 'Taiwanese flavour' (chaos, motorcycles), but it's much more sedate and traditional than any other Taiwanese city and there is virtually no air pollution.

I know that I'll eventually have to eat these words, but at present there is not even one 7-Eleven or a McDonald's in the whole place.

There are a few notable temples around. Matsu Temple *(māzǔ gōng)* in Makung is over 400 years old, making it the oldest temple in all Taiwan. Of course, it doesn't look quite that old as it has been fully restored.

Lintou Beach

(líntóu gōngyuán) 林投公園

Near the eastern end of Penghu Island is Lintou beach. There is a NT$50 admission fee, and unfortunately there is a rather heavy military presence around the area. However, it has beautiful white sand and is certainly a relaxing place to stop on your way around the islands. On the west side of the beach is a military cemetery which resembles the Chiang Kaishek Memorial in miniature.

Fengkuei Cave

(fēngguì dòng) 風櫃洞

At the south-western end of Penghu Island is Fengkuei Cave, a big attraction for Chinese tourists who want to see the 'dramatic coastal rock formations'. Personally, I didn't find them very dramatic and there was plenty of rubbish left behind by the tourists. However, the ride out there on a motorcycle is interesting, as there are views of small fishing villages.

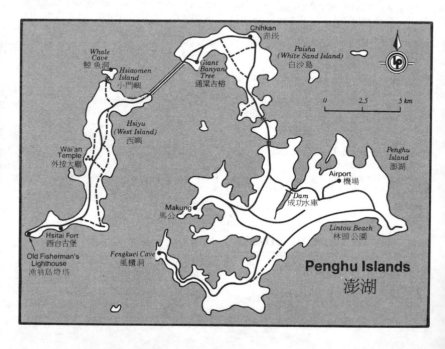

Paisha & Hsiyu Islands
(báishā) (xīyǔ) 白沙島/西嶼

There are two other large islands connected to Penghu by bridges – both are interesting and easy to visit. They're called Paisha (White Sand Island) and Hsiyu (West Island). Paisha's most famous attraction is a large banyan tree *(dà róngshù* or *tōngliáng gǔróng)* over 300 years old. Covering a huge area, the branches are supported by lattice-work, and walking under it is like walking through a cave. Paisha is connected to Hsiyu by the Kuahai Bridge *(kuàhǎi dàqiáo)*, over five km in length and the longest in Taiwan.

Hsiyu is the most beautiful island, with many hidden coves. At the very southern tip of this island is the Hsitai Fort *(xītái gǔbǎo)*, built in 1883 under the Ching (Manchu) Dynasty. It's well preserved and open to the public. It is claimed that on a clear day one can see the mountains of both Taiwan and mainland China from this fort. The air pollution generated on both sides of the Taiwan Straits is decreasing the opportunities to witness this phenomena, though Penghu itself remains perfectly clean.

One of the best seafood restaurants in all the Penghu Islands is not in Makung but on Hsiyu. It's near the bus stop in the village of Hsiyu, which is right in the centre of the island, and is called *qīngxīn yǐnshídiàn* (☎ 9981128).

Connected to Hsiyu by a narrow bridge is the very tiny island of Hsiaomen *(xiǎomén yǔ)*. Despite its small size, it's very scenic. There is a rugged natural stone arch carved by the sea on the north side of this islet.

Places to Stay – bottom end
There are no places to stay on Paisha and Hsiyu islands – everyone stays in Makung unless going to the outlying islands. Accommodation gets a little tight on weekends and holidays during summer, but should be OK at other times. If arriving in peak season during holidays, try to at least get on an early flight – places fill up fast after noon.

The bottom end belongs to the *Teachers' Hostel* (☎ 9273692) *(jiàoshī huìguǎn)*, at 38 Shute Rd, where dormitories that sleep three

people are NT$150 per person, or the *Youth Activity Centre* (☎ 9271124) *(qīngnián huódòng zhōngxīn)*, 11 Chiehshou Rd, where dormitory accommodation starts at NT$200. The Teachers' Hostel is where most budget travellers wind up – the Youth Activity Centre is a beautiful building by the sea but tends to pack out with teenage tour groups.

Places to Stay – middle
There is an abundance of mid-price range hotels all within walking distance of where you get off the Kaohsiung ferry. Most do not have English names, so it really helps if you can recognise the Chinese characters for *lüshè* (see the Facts for the Visitor chapter). Most of these places seem to charge a standard NT$600 for a double during summer, but negotiable to NT$500 in the off-season. Some places which fall into this category include:

Fu Go Hotel
    (fùguó dà lüshè), 31 Sanmin Rd (☎ 9273861)
Hung An Hotel
    (hóng'ān dà lüshè), 16 Sanmin Rd (☎ 9273832)
Donghai Hotel
    (dōnghǎi lüshè), 38 Sanmin Rd (☎ 9272367)
Youzhi Hotel
    (yǒuzhì dà lüshè), 22 Chunghsing Rd (☎ 9272151)

Places to Stay – top end
While there's nothing five-star, there has been a recent sharp increase in cushy accommodation. A small sample follows:

A Seal Grand Hotel
    (èrxīn dà fàndiàn), 10 Minsheng Rd (☎ 9278170, fax 9278179); doubles NT$1100 to NT$2200, twins NT$2420
Four Seas Hotel
    (sìhǎi dà fàndiàn), 3 Chienkuo Rd (☎ 9272960); doubles NT$700
Hotel Chang Chun
    (chángchūn dà fàndiàn), 8 Chungcheng Rd (☎ 9273336, fax 9262112); doubles NT$1200 (breakfast included)
Pao Hua Hotel
    (bǎohuá dà fàndiàn), 2 Chungcheng Rd (☎ 9274881, fax 9274889); doubles/twins NT$1350/2000

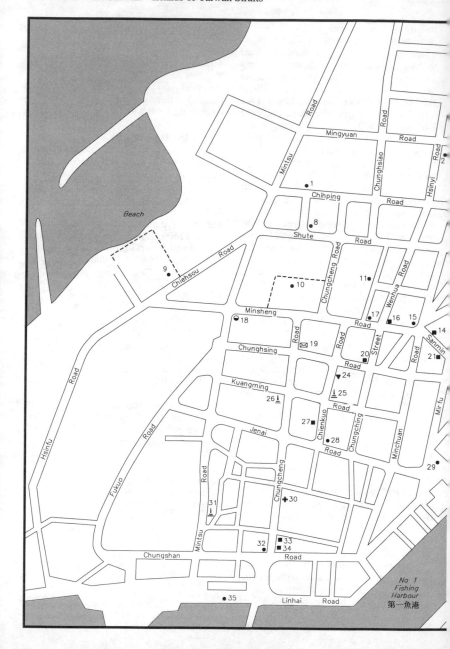

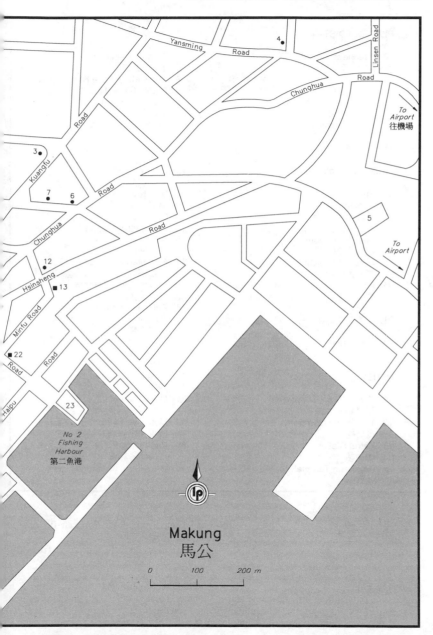

Makung
馬公

PLACES TO STAY

8 Teachers' Hostel
教師會館
9 Penghu Youth Activity Centre
青年活動中心
13 Penghu Royal Hotel
瑞富大飯店
14 Donghai Hotel
東海旅社
16 A Seal Grand Hotel
二信大飯店
20 Youzhi Hotel
有志大旅社
21 Fu Go Hotel
富國大旅社
22 Hung An Hotel
宏安大旅社
27 Four Seas Hotel
四海大飯店
33 Hotel Chang Chun
長春大飯店
34 Pao Hua Hotel
寶華大飯店

PLACES TO EAT

24 Cafeteria
自助餐

OTHER

1 Police (Visa Extensions)
警察局外事課
2 Telephone Company
電信局
3 Petrol Station
加油站
4 Wusheng Temple
武聖廟

5 Martyrs' Shrine
忠烈祠
6 Formosa Airlines
永興航空
7 Car & Motorcycle Hire
飛鴻小客車租費公司
10 Elementary School
中正國民小學
11 Clothing Alley & Market
文康街
12 Trans-Asia Airlines
復興航空
15 Makung Airlines
馬公航空
17 Motorcycle Hire
機車出租
18 Bus Station
公共車船管理處
19 GPO
郵政總局
23 Fish Market
魚市場
25 Chenghuang Temple
城隍廟
26 Peichen Temple
北辰公
28 Bank of Taiwan
台灣銀行
29 Petrol Station
加油站
30 Hospital
醫院
31 Matsu Temple
媽祖宮
32 Motorcycle Hire
機車出租
35 Kaohsiung Ferry
往高雄搭船處

Penghu Royal Hotel
 (*ruìfù dà fàndiàn*), 33 Lane 64, Hsinsheng Rd
 (☎ 9261182, fax 9261128); twins NT$1550 to
 NT$2450

Places to Eat

There is an outstanding little no-name cafeteria one block north of the Chenghuang Temple on the south-east corner of Chienkuo and Chunghsing Rds. You can fill up for NT$50 or so.

Seafood is the local speciality. This stuff is not really cheap, but it's still cheaper than in 'mainland' Taiwan. In Makung, the section of Sanmin Rd right near the fish market is seafood alley. One place in this area that you can try is *Xin Haiwangzi Restaurant* (☎ 9263188) (*xīn hǎiwángzǐ xiǎochībù*), 8

Sanmin Rd. A more classy place is *Four Seas Restaurant* (☎ 9273335) *(sìhǎi cāntīng)*, in the basement of the Four Seas Hotel at 3 Chienkuo Rd.

Things to Buy

Penghu is not an industrial place and therefore offers little that you couldn't buy more cheaply in Taiwan. One exception is the excellent peanut candy. There are many different varieties and they're all good. Since they usually all cost the same, you can mix many different kinds together. A Taiwanese kg (catty) of assorted peanut candy costs about NT$60. The flight back to Taiwan usually reeks of the dried fish, squid and clams that the local tourists take back with them – just be glad it's only a 30 minute flight.

Straw hats are not made locally, but are available everywhere in Penghu and are an essential survival item in the fierce summer sun. There are also some visor caps in tourist colours (zingo-pink or dayglow-orange), in case you feel like dressing up as a clown. A small alley called Wenkang St (see map) is the place to look for clothing.

Getting There & Away

Air Although Penghu is a remote backwater, there are frequent flights to all major cities in Taiwan. These flights are very popular and tend to be booked heavily on weekends and holidays. On weekdays it should be no problem, but arriving at the airport early is advisable if you haven't already bought tickets.

All airlines sell tickets at the airport check-in counters or in Makung at the airline offices. You can book tickets at the following places:

Far Eastern Air Transport
　　(yuǎndōng hángkōng), 4-2 Chihping Rd
　　(☎ 9274891)
Formosa Airlines
　　(yǒngxīng hángkōng), 4 Chihping Rd
　　(☎ 9261089)
Great China Airlines
　　(dàhuá hángkōng), 102 Kuangfu Rd
　　(☎ 9263111)

Makung Airlines
　　(mǎgōng hángkōng), 2 Minsheng Rd
　　(☎ 9276297)
Taiwan Airlines
　　(táiwān hángkōng), Makung Airport
　　(☎ 9211800)
Trans-Asia Airways
　　(fùxīng hángkōng), 2 Shute Rd (☎ 9279800)

Sea During the summer consider going to the islands by boat from Kaohsiung and returning by air. Boats depart from Pier No 1 in Kaohsiung every day at 9 am and arrive in Makung at 12.30 pm. Boats leave Makung at 3.30 pm and arrive back in Kaohsiung at 7 pm. Tickets should be purchased in advance from Southeast Travel Service (☎ 2312181, 2311218), 106 Chungcheng-4 Rd, Kaohsiung. Or you can buy the ticket in Penghu at Southeast Travel (☎ 9261210), 26 Chungshan Rd, Makung, which is right by the pier and adjacent to the Pao Hua Hotel. A one-way ticket in economy class is NT$450.

The boats run daily except for two days a month when they shut down for maintenance.

If you go by boat, you can take a motorcycle or bicycle with you for half the cost of a passenger ticket. This isn't really worth the bother since motorcycle rentals in Penghu are so easy to come by, unless you think you need a bike larger than 50 cc.

Getting Around

To/From the Airport The taxis waiting at the airport were asking NT$160 for the nine-km trip to Makung – not negotiable, since they line up for about an hour. I walked outside the airport and hailed a passing cab; the driver wanted NT$100 but I was able to negotiate it down to NT$50.

Bus Buses go along the main roads at an average rate of one per hour. The airport bus also runs once an hour to Makung. The big buses you see parked near the airport are tour buses.

Taxi It is certainly possible to hire a taxi, but given the large distances between places this could be very expensive. A full-day taxi rental would be at least NT$1500, which should be negotiated in advance.

Bicycle, Motorcycle & Car Getting around Penghu by bus is possible, but given the rural nature of the place the best way to get around is to hire a motorcycle. You can bring one on the boat or rent one upon arrival. A 10-speed bicycle is another possibility, but Penghu is large – Makung to Hsitai Fort is 35 km. There are no big hills, but the sea breezes can be fierce making cycling difficult. I have not seen bicycles for rent anywhere in Penghu. Cars are also available, but are expensive and much less fun than a motorcycle.

There are numerous places renting 50-cc motorcycles. One of the best organised is simply called *Car & Motorcycle Hire* (☎ 9271616) *(fēihóng zhūchē gōngsī)*, 6 Chihping Rd. This rental shop is notable for being the only one in Makung with an English sign. The owner speaks some English.

AROUND PENGHU
Chipei Island
(jíbèi yǔ) 吉貝嶼

To the north of Penghu is Chipei, noted for its excellent beaches made out of a fine coral, not sand. Many say it's the best beach in the Penghu Islands. It's great for swimming, but the lifeguards won't let you use a snorkel.

There are no flights to Chipei, so you have to take a boat. Departures for Chipei are from Chihkan *(chìkǎn)*, a village on the north shore of Paisha Island. From Makung, you can take a bus or taxi to Chihkan and then get the ferry to Chipei.

There are three companies operating boats to Chipei. These are: Hawaii Boat Company (☎ 9932237, 9932049) *(xiàwēiyí chuán gōngsī)*; Paisha Boat Centre (☎ 9931917, 9212609) *(báishā yóulè zhōngxīn)*; and the Aimin Boat Company (☎ 9932232, 9911145) *(aìmín chuán gōngsī)*. They're all in Chihkan.

There is a resort area called *Chipei Sea Paradise (jíbèi hǎishàng lèyuán)* which charges a small admission fee; this is where

most people stay. They have a dormitory for NT$200, while twins are NT$1000. Some people on the island rent out tatami dorms for NT$100 per person. You can camp inside the resort if you bring your own tent. Food is very expensive so bring your own. A wide-brimmed hat is essential, as there are no trees and the sun is powerful. At the resort you can rent sea scooters, windsurfers and other water playthings.

Chimei & Wang'an
(qīměi) (wàng'ān) 七美/望安

For those who really want to get away from civilisation, there are boats and flights to Chimei and Wang'an, two islands to the south of Makung. There isn't much to do on these islands except admire the sea and surf.

Personally, I don't think that either of these two islands is worth the trouble. However, many Taiwanese go there – particularly to Chimei, where they take photographs of themselves standing in front of the Tomb of the Seven Virtuous Beauties. According to local legend, the 'seven virtuous beauties' were seven women who committed suicide when they saw pirate ships approaching because they thought they might be raped. While my sympathies go out to the unfortunate seven women, I've often wondered if the whole story wasn't conjured up by the Chamber of Commerce. It's certainly been a boon to the local tourist industry – you can buy Seven Virtuous Beauties ashtrays, postcards and teacups.

You can fly directly to Chimei or Wang'an from either Kaohsiung or Makung. There is also the odd flight connecting Chimei and Wang'an with each other.

The ferry boat from Makung to Wang'an costs NT$108 for an economy ticket and takes 1½ hours. The ferry from Wang'an to Chimei costs NT$145 and takes three hours.

KINMEN, MATSU & WUCHIU
(jīnmén) (māzǔ) (wūqiū) 金門/馬祖/烏坵

Kinmen – formerly known as Quemoy – and Matsu are two obscure islands just off the coast of the Fujian province in mainland China. Officially, they are not part of Taiwan, but belong to Fujian province even though the ROC controls them. These islands became briefly famous in 1958 when Communist troops started an artillery bombardment of them. The 1955 Formosa Resolution, signed by then President Dwight Eisenhower, had formally granted American protection to Taiwan – for a while it looked as though the USA would reluctantly get dragged into yet another armed conflict with China, only five years after the Korean War had ended.

Between Kinmen and Matsu – and also just a stone's throw from the Chinese mainland – is a third island called Wuchiu. The island is so small and insignificant that the Communists didn't even bother shelling it.

Taiwan's troops are well dug in now, having built huge concrete bunkers which are virtually bombproof. Kinmen even boasts an underground auditorium where live performances and movies are shown to entertain off-duty soldiers.

The lethal artillery duels only lasted a few months, but the propaganda war continued right up to the 1990s. Instead of firing explosives, the opposing sides started firing metal cannisters containing propaganda leaflets at one another. To avoid injuries, this was done according to a regular schedule – Taiwan fired propaganda shells on Monday, Wednesday and Friday while the mainlanders launched theirs on Tuesday, Thursday and Saturday. The cold war was put on hold during Sunday so everyone could enjoy a holiday. Local entrepreneurs took advantage of the opportunity to gather up all the metal shells which were then melted down and forged into meat cleavers. For many years, meat cleavers were a major export of Kinmen. Unfortunately, the cessation of artillery duels has left Kinmen's meat cleaver manufacturers with a shortage of materials, causing the industry to collapse.

Artillery shells were only one of many means by which Taiwan waged psychological warfare against the mainland. Balloons containing pamphlets and various top-secret 'psychological warfare apparatus' were regularly launched from the islands. One balloon drifted all the way to Israel, where it's cannister was opened and the world finally learned what type of 'psychological warfare apparatus' was being used – see-through underwear. During the Tiananmen crisis of 1989, the balloons carried Taiwanese newspapers to inform mainlanders of the events happening in Beijing.

The world's largest neon sign once graced the shores of Kinmen. It proclaimed, in big bright lights visible from Xiamen in mainland China, 'Three Principles of the People, Reunify China!'. The sign became such a major tourist attraction for mainlanders that when the sign was finally turned off, the Xiamen city government formally complained.

In addition to propaganda pamphlets, neon signs and see-through underwear, the Taiwanese army further eroded morale on the mainland by blasting the enemy with gigantic loud-speakers, believed to be the largest in the world. The Communists retaliated with loudspeakers of their own. If you think KTV is horrible enough, just imagine the eardrum-splitting cacophony as the two sides bombarded each other with broadcasts of opposing political viewpoints across the narrow straits.

Kinmen is the largest and most scenic of the islands, and features an amazing collection of mostly reconstructed Ming and Ching dynasty architecture. The unpaid labour of soldiers plus the government's financial largesse has turned Kinmen into a place of very orderly design. Trees and flowers have been planted, potholes have been patched, hedges are regularly trimmed and hardly a scrap of paper or plastic litters the landscape. In other words, Kinmen is considerably cleaner than Taiwan itself. The absence of traffic means the island is almost free of air pollution and noise. In addition, there are 12 tiny islets around Kinmen, but all are occupied by the ROC military and are not open to civilian visitors.

Soldiers outnumber the civilian population on these islands. Matsu is still under martial law, but Kinmen was returned to civilian law in 1993. Evening curfews are observed and lights cannot be used at night unless the windows are shuttered. For 40 years, Kinmen, Matsu and Wuchiu even had their own currency to prevent capital flight, but these days standard NT$ are acceptable.

'Entertaining the military' has brought considerable prosperity to the islands. Entertainment takes various forms – prostitution has been a highly profitable service industry in Kinmen, Matsu and Wuchiu since 1949. The government reported that the military-run *831 Brothel* in Kinmen was closed in 1992 'to protect the health of soldiers' ('831' was the brothel's telephone number). Besides feeding and entertaining the military, Kinmen has one other industry of significance – the production of Kaoliang, Taiwan's strongest brew. Sorghum, from which Kaoliang is distilled, can be seen growing around the island. Hard candy (*gòng táng*) is another Kinmen product and a popular item with Taiwanese tourists. There are many varieties, but the peanut candies are reputed to be the best.

Now for the bad news – all these islands are run by the military and persmission is needed to visit. While a visit to Kinmen can easily be arranged for ROC nationals, the situation is far more restricted for foreigners. Diplomats, dignitaries and a few well-connected journalists can usually get a visitor's permit after some bureaucratic hassles, but most foreigners will not find it possible to make the journey. However, the Tourism Bureau is lobbying for a relaxation of the rules, and it is possible that foreigners will be allowed to visit at least Kinmen sometime during the life span of this book. The Tourism Bureau and travel agents in Taiwan can supply you with the latest information about rules governing foreigners. In the meantime, probably the easiest way for foreigners to get a look at Kinmen is from the other side – from the Chinese port of Xiamen.

When Kinmen is finally opened to foreigners, you can get there on Far Eastern Air Transport (FAT) or Trans-Asia. There are regular civilian flights between Kinmen and Taipei (NT$1544) or Kaohsiung (NT$1376).

As for the possibility of travelling between Kinmen and Xiamen, you'll probably have to wait many more years. Frogmen used to travel back and forth regularly between Kinmen and Xiamen for purposes of spying, and those caught were often shot. Nowadays, Chinese ply this route in one direction only – Taiwan uses Kinmen to expel illegal aliens from the mainland who sneak into Taiwan on fishing boats.

Tainan County 台南縣

TAINAN

(*táinán*) 台南

Tainan is a stronghold of traditional Taiwanese culture – not surprising since this was Taiwan's provincial capital from 1663 to 1885. Today, it's the fourth-largest city in Taiwan – the population is over 700,000 in the city proper, and nearly doubles when you include suburbia. Tainan simply means 'south Taiwan'.

Tainan has a long and colourful history. The Dutch invaded Taiwan in 1624 and set up their capital and military headquarters in Tainan. In 1661, 37 years later, the Dutch were successfully expelled by Cheng Chengkung, known in the West as Koxinga. Koxinga was a Ming Dynasty loyalist who was forced to flee Taiwan from the mainland with 35,000 troops to escape the victorious Ching Dynasty (Manchu) armies. Koxinga died in 1662 at the age of 38, only one year after ousting the Dutch. His supporters managed to maintain a Ming Dynasty stronghold in Taiwan until 1682, when the island was finally captured by the Manchus.

Tainan is the best place in Taiwan for viewing temples. There are over 200 temples in Tainan, though many are increasingly difficult to find because they're tucked away in narrow side-alleys and hidden by the new buildings sprouting up all over the city. While many are small neighbourhood temples, others are huge, including one in the suburb of Luerhmen which is claimed to be the largest temple in East Asia. If you simply stroll around Tainan you'll probably never see the best temples, since only a few are on the main boulevards. The map of Tainan shows where the most interesting temples are.

Being a traditional city, there are frequent Buddhist parades and special ceremonies. At certain times in the lunar calendar, everyone worships and the air is thick with smoke from the burning of 'ghost money' and incense. Tables are set out on the street, well endowed with scrumptious food meant as offerings to the gods. Ironically, Tainan also has the largest Christian population in Taiwan – it's claimed that Christians make up as much as 10% of the city's population.

Temples and monuments are the main attractions in this historical city. With a little effort you can see most of the really interesting ones in a day but you need to start early. Most are within walking distance of each another, but several will require a bus or taxi trip.

Information
Tourist Office The Tourism Bureau (☎ 2265681) has a branch on the 10th floor, 243 Minchuan Rd, Section 1.

Money ICBC (☎ 2231231) *(guójì shāngyè yínháng)* is at 90 Chungshan Rd, one long block from the railway station. The Bank of Taiwan (☎ 2226181) *(táiwān yínháng)* is much further out at 129 Fuchien Rd. Citibank (☎ 2262500) *(huáqí yínháng)* offers cash advances to its card holders from the branch at 83 Yungfu Rd, Section 2.

Post & Telecommunications The GPO is on Chungkung Rd, almost directly opposite the railway station on the big roundabout.

You can buy phonecards from the information counter inside the railway station, and there are direct-dial international phones near the station entrance.

The telephone-company office is inconveniently located on Hsimen Rd.

Film There is one place in Tainan where you can get good quality photoprocessing on B&W film: Tai Chi Photo Supply (☎ 228 6798, 2222234) *(tàijì zhàoxiàng cáiliào háng)*, 11 Kungyuan Rd. It's at the intersection of Kungyuan and Minsheng Rds.

Bookshops The best bookshop in town is Caves Books (☎ 2296347) *(dūnhuáng shūjú)*, 163-169 Chungshan Rd.

Laundry Don't hide your dirty laundry, get it washed cheaply at *bōbō zìzhù xǐyī zhōngxīn* (☎ 2384386), 20-1 Tahsueh Rd. It's next to the 89 restaurant, near Chengkung University.

Hospital Chengkung University Hospital (☎ 2353535) *(chéngdà yīyuàn)* is one of the most modern hospitals in Taiwan. It's on the corner of Hsiaotung Rd and Shengli Rd.

Confucius Temple
(kǒngzǐ miào) 孔子廟
Constructed in 1665 by General Chen Yunghua, a Ming Dynasty supporter, this is the oldest Confucian temple in Taiwan. On 28 September – the birthday of Confucius – a colourful dawn ceremony is held. You may be able to get a ticket from your hotel or a tour agency should you be in Tainan at this time. The temple is at 2 Nanmen Rd, near the main police station.

Directly across the street from the Confucius Temple's main entrance is a small stone archway, which now forms the entrance of a busy alley. No one is certain when the archway was built, but historians estimate it was constructed in 1683 when the Confucius Temple was repaired. There are four stone archways remaining in Tainan and this is the oldest one.

Great South Gate
(dà nánmén) 大南門
Tainan used to be a walled city. The walls were built in 1723 in response to an anti-Manchu rebellion. At one time there were eight gates leading into the city, but only

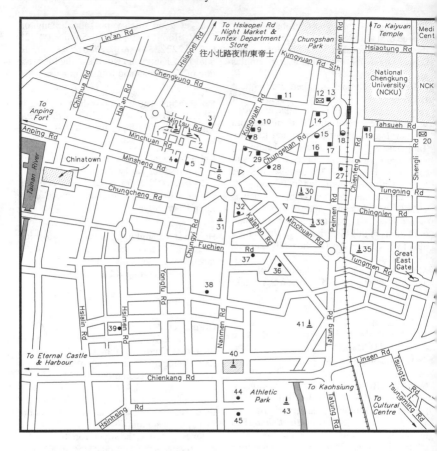

three remain. Of the three gates, the largest and best preserved is the Great South Gate.

The gate is in a small park, half a block south of Fuchien Rd and the Confucius Temple. When you leave the Confucius Temple, turn right and walk south along Nanmen Rd. Pass Fuchien Rd and you'll soon come to a little alley on the right side of the street. A white sign clearly says 'Ta Nan Men' and points into the alley. The fortress-like gate is so large you can't miss it. You're allowed to climb up into the gate and walk around on the top.

The other two gates in Tainan are the Great East Gate on Tungmen Rd and the Little West Gate, which is now relocated on the campus of National Chengkung University, east of Chengkung Lake.

Chihkan Tower
(chìkǎn lóu) 赤崁樓

The Dutch built two forts in Tainan before Koxinga evicted them. One is the Chihkan Tower, also known as Fort Providentia, built in 1653. Very little remains of the original Chihkan Tower, as it was levelled by an earthquake in 1862, rebuilt in 1875 and is currently being restored. Inside there is a

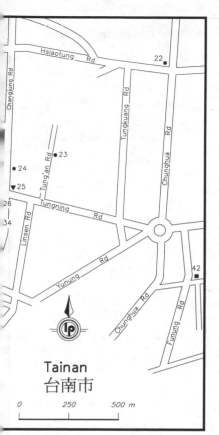

Tainan
台南市

0   250   500 m

is known for his physical strength, while Confucius is revered for his wisdom.

The temple is on Mintsu Rd, directly opposite the Chihkan Tower. It looks unimpressive from the Mintsu Rd side where you first get a glimpse of it, but this is the back entrance to the temple. Walk down the narrow alley next to the temple and you'll soon find the front entrance.

Matsu Temple
(māzǔ miào) 媽祖廟

As you face the Kuankung Temple, you will see an alley on your left. Walk down this alley a short distance and you'll come to the Matsu Temple. In contrast to the Kuankung Temple, which has a very simple, conservative look about it, the Matsu Temple is incredibly colourful. Go around the back and have a look at the temple artwork, all of which is original. Feel free to take photos.

Tien Tan Temple
(tiān tán) 天壇

This temple is one of the most interesting places to visit in Tainan. It is more commonly known by its local name, *tiān gōng*. It is not very large but it is an extremely active Taoist temple, reminiscent of the Lungshan Temple in Taipei. A lot of incense and 'ghost money' is burnt here and plenty of food offerings are made to the ghosts. Occasionally, someone in a trance will be possessed by a ghost.

This temple is often packed with worshippers, but it is best to visit on the first and 16th days of the lunar month if you really want to see some activity. If you visit at the wrong time, it might be very quiet. Try to avoid dinner time, when everyone goes home, unless of course you just want to photograph temple artefacts without being bothered by the crowd.

The temple is hidden away in an obscure alley just off Chungyi Rd *(zhōngyì lù)*, near the intersection with Minchuan Rd.

East Mountain Temple
(dōng yuè diàn) 東嶽殿

This small Taoist temple is one of the liveliest, at least if you hit it at the right time. Many

small museum. Chihkan Tower is at 212 Mintsu Rd, a short walk down the street from the Far Eastern Department Store. The other fort is Fort Anping, also known by its Dutch name of Fort Zeelandia, in Anping, a suburb to the west of Tainan.

Kuankung Temple
(wǔ miào) 武廟

This old temple is dedicated to Kuankung *(guāngōng)*, the saint of martial arts. He stands in contrast to Confucius, who is regarded as the saint of literature. Kuankung

PLACES TO STAY

9 Akira Top Hotel
立人大飯店
11 Redhill Hotel
赤崁大飯店
13 Hotel Yilou & Cake Box Building
一樂大飯店/中華國賓大樓
14 Hotel Tainan
台南大飯店
16 Nanchun Hotel
南春賓館
17 Guang Haw Hotel
光華大飯店
19 Unique & Ailisi hotels
良美大飯店/愛麗思賓館
29 Oriental Hotel
華光大飯店
42 Tainan Student Hostel
台南學苑
44 Labourers' Recreation Centre
勞工休假中心
45 Senior Citizens' Recreation Centre
松柏育樂中心

PLACES TO EAT

8 Hardee Hamburgers
哈帝漢堡
21 Vegetarian Restaurant
& McDonald's
麥當勞
25 Chicken House
香雞城
26 Macanna Beer House
麥崁鈉

OTHER

1 Matsu Temple
媽祖廟
2 Kuankung Temple
武廟
3 Chihkan Tower
赤崁樓
4 Quanmei Theatre
全美戲院
5 New Phase Art Space
新生態藝術環境
6 Tien Tan Temple
天壇

7 Far Eastern Department Store
遠東百貨
10 Shente Hall
慎德堂
12 GPO
郵政總局
15 Hsingnan Bus Company
興南客運
18 Bus Station
(Taipei, Kaohsiung & Chiayi)
台汽客運站
20 Post Office
郵局
22 Liangmei Department Store
良美百貨
23 Mountain & Wilderness
Service Company
堅壘企
24 Xiaomaowu Ice Shop
小茂屋冰園
27 Tuung-Le Supermarket
統麗綜合商場
28 ICBC
中國國際商業銀行
30 Chenghuang Temple
城隍廟
31 Confucius Temple
孔子廟
32 Police (Visa Extensions)
警察局外事課
33 East Mountain Temple
東嶽殿
34 New Life Art Gallery
新心生活藝術館
35 Mito Temple
彌陀寺
36 Koxinga Shrine
延平郡王祠
37 Bank of Taiwan
台灣銀行
38 Great South Gate
大南門
39 Telephone Company
電信局
40 Five Concubines Temple
五妃廟
41 Fahua Temple
法華寺
43 Chuhsi Temple
竹溪寺

of the worshippers come here to communicate with dead relatives or drive evil ghosts out of their homes.

At times, I've seen old women in the temple, with their eyes closed, pounding their fists on the table, talking rapidly and surrounded by a crowd with tape recorders trying to record their words. These women are mediums who communicate with spirits. Exorcism ceremonies also take place here occasionally. The first and 16th days of the lunar month are the busiest times.

The temple has a number of interesting artefacts. The large statues staring down at you are those of General Hsieh and General Fan. General Hsieh is the short, fat one and General Fan is tall and thin. General Fan is often depicted with his tongue hanging out because he committed suicide by hanging himself.

The story goes that General Fan and General Hsieh made an appointment to meet under a bridge by a river. General Hsieh arrived first and was drowned in a flash flood. General Fan arrived later and was so grieved to find his friend dead that he hanged himself. For this reason their statues are placed in many temples as a symbol of sincere loyalty.

The East Mountain Temple is at 110 Minchuan Rd, Section 1. They generally don't mind foreign visitors, but try to maintain a low profile and don't go flashing your camera in people's faces. There is no objection though to photographing the paintings, statues, murals and other temple artefacts.

Chenghuang Temple
(chénghuáng miào) 城隍廟

The Chenghuang Temple is related to the East Mountain Temple, however, it is not nearly so morbid or active but more like the other Taoist temples in Tainan. The figures of General Fan and General Hsieh can also be seen here. Chenghuang is the name of a god worshipped by the Hakka people, who make up some 5% of Taiwan's population. Needless to say, many Hakka people come here. The temple is at 133 Chingnien Rd.

New Phase Art Space
(xīnshēngtài yìshù huánjìng) 新生態藝術環境

There is a trendy art gallery, exhibit hall and auditorium for hip culture. The latter even has performances by foreign bands. There is a good restaurant on the 2nd floor, and an outdoor cafe behind the main building. The cafe has long hours, from 10 am to 11 pm, while the main hall is open from 11 am to 9 pm. The New Phase Art Space (☎ 2267899) is at 138 Yongfu Rd, Section 2.

New Life Art Gallery
(xīnxīn shēnghuó yìshù guǎn) 新心生活藝術館

This small art gallery (☎ 2753957) offers free admission – the art is for sale. It's certainly worth taking a peak if you're in the neighbourhood. It's at 67 Shengli Rd, just south of Chingnien Rd. The gallery is closed on Monday.

Mito Temple
(mítuó sì) 彌陀寺

Constructed in 1718, this colourful temple has recently been restored. It's on Tungmen Rd just east of the railway.

On the 2nd floor of the Mito Temple is one of the most magnificent statues I've seen of the 1000-armed Kuanyin. This image indicates that the goddess is almighty. Eyes have been painted on her hands to demonstrate that she sees all, and she has several smaller heads attached to the top of her head – these many minds indicate her wisdom.

Koxinga's Museum & Shrine
(yánpíng jùnwáng cí) 延平郡王祠

Koxinga is not a god, but a shrine has been built in his honour. He is the national hero who successfully expelled the Dutch from Taiwan. Koxinga and his troops landed in Taiwan in 1661 with the mission of freeing Taiwan from colonial rule and returning it to China. After a six-month siege, the Dutch gave up and were allowed to leave Taiwan without any reprisals, thus ending their 37-year occupation of the island.

All this happened at a time of great upheaval in China. The Ming Dynasty, which was supported by Koxinga, was rapidly losing control of China to the Manchu invaders. Koxinga and his supporters moved to Taiwan with the hope of launching an invasion and destroying the Manchus. Instead, Taiwan fell to the Manchus in 1682. Koxinga never lived to see this. He died in 1663, just one year after his successful mission against the Dutch.

Adjacent to the Koxinga Shrine is an interesting museum containing a large number of paintings, sculptures, a traditional Chinese sedan chair, costumes, and a model of the Dutch Fort Zeelandia. Unfortunately, only a few of the displays have English explanations.

The museum and shrine compound is open from 9 am to 6 pm. Entrance is from Kaishan Rd. You can walk there from the Confucius Temple or take bus No 17.

Fahua Temple

(fǎhuá sì) 法華寺

A short walk from the Koxinga Museum & Shrine, this temple is on Fahua St, an obscure narrow street connecting Kaishan Rd and Chienkang Rd. The Fahua Temple is over 300 years old and well preserved. The temple grounds are peaceful and contain many banyan trees. There are some interesting murals on the walls and they're well worth photographing.

Chuhsi Temple

(zhúxī sì) 竹溪寺

The Chuhsi Temple is one of the largest and most beautiful temples in the city. The temple is in a huge park complex called the Tainan Athletic Park *(tǐyù chǎng)*, just one block south of Chienkang Rd. It's a good area to go jogging, or play tennis and other outdoor sports, so of course the area is busy on weekends and holidays. However, the temple itself is rarely crowded in spite of its impressive size and beauty.

Five Concubines Temple

(wǔfēi miào) 五妃廟

The Five Concubines Temple is more like an altar than a temple. It's very small and is dedicated to honour the five concubines of

Ning Ching, who was a relative of the last Ming emperor. When Ning Ching died, it is said that his five concubines committed suicide. The temple sits in a small park just north of Chienkang Rd. There is no entrance on Chienkang Rd, so you must walk one block further north and enter the park from the back. It is only worth visiting if you are already at the Chuhsi Temple, a five-minute walk away.

Kaiyuan Temple

(kāiyuán sì) 開元寺

One of the oldest and biggest temples in Tainan, the Kaiyuan Temple is a very pleasant classical Buddhist temple with spacious, peaceful grounds, gardens, trees and pagodas. The only problem with going there is that it is really too far to walk from the central area.

To reach the temple take bus No 1, 6 or 17 from the railway station. The bus ride takes about 10 minutes and you get off near the intersection of Kaiyuan Rd and Peiyuan St *(běi yuán jiē)*. Kaiyuan Rd is the big, wide, busy road and Peiyuan St is a small side street. Walk down this street and you'll see the temple on your left. It takes about a minute to walk to from the intersection. A taxi would cost around NT$50 or so from the city centre.

Don't confuse the adjacent hospital with the temple itself. The hospital is a beautiful example of traditional architecture and belongs to the temple.

Anping Fort

(ānpíng gǔbǎo) 安平古堡

This is a place for history buffs. The Anping Fort is also known by its Dutch name, Fort Zeelandia.

The Dutch built the fort in 1653 on what was then the coastline of Taiwan. Since then the coastline has extended several km westward due to siltation, and as a result, the fort no longer commands a sea view. This is one of two forts built in Tainan by the Dutch. The other is Fort Providentia (also called

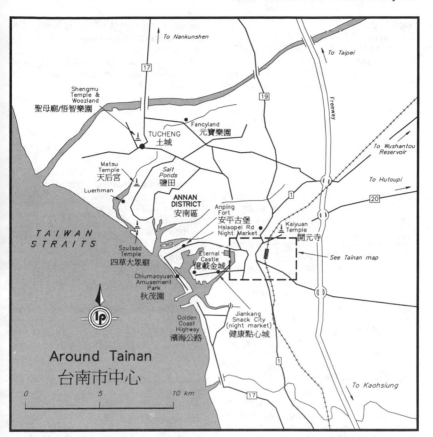

Around Tainan
台南市中心

Chihkan Tower), which is right in the heart of Tainan.

Visiting Anping Fort would be more worthwhile if you could see the original, but unfortunately it was levelled in the 1800s by a powerful typhoon. What you see today is a reconstructed fort and observation tower built in the 1970s.

There is also a temple across the street. However, the site is a pleasant place and you could also take a taxi from there to Anping Beach *(ānpíng hǎishuǐ yùchǎng)*, a short ride away. Bus No 33 goes to the fort. Admission is NT$10.

Eternal Castle
(yìzǎi jīn chéng) 億載金城

The romantically named Eternal Castle was at one time a small fortress with a moat. It was built by French engineers in 1875. Today, one of the original gates still remains in a one-hectare park. Like the Anping Fort, it's mostly of interest to history buffs rather than sightseers.

From Anping Fort, it's a very short taxi ride due south. You could also walk, though you might get lost. The address is 16 Nanwen Rd, Anping District. Bus Nos 15 and 33 go there.

Cultural Centre

(wénhuà zhōngxīn) 文化中心

The Cultural Centre (☎ 2692864), at 375 Chunghua Rd, Section 1, is similar to other cultural centres in Taipei, Taichung and Kaohsiung. Art exhibitions and live performances of opera and classical music are held here. If you'd like to find out the current schedule of events, drop by the centre or call – but it's unlikely that the person answering the phone will speak English.

Luerhmen

(lùěrmén) 鹿耳門

Luerhmen, which literally means 'Deer's Ear Gate', is the name of the site along the river where Koxinga landed in Taiwan on 29 April 1661. However, the main attraction is not the historical site, but the huge temple which has been built nearby.

Actually, there are three temples and they're only a couple of km from each other. There is an interesting story which accompanies the construction of these three temples. Over the years the local people have been involved in a lot of heavy rivalry and three distinct groups have formed. They are in competition with each other as to who will build the largest temple in Taiwan. Thus the temples have never really been finished, as they are in a state of constant expansion.

The only limiting factor is money, and so the temples have a nonstop campaign to raise funds for the never-ending construction. Should you decide that this is a worthy cause, you can donate money and have your name engraved on a marble slab, column or any other temple artefact of your choosing. All the artwork in the temple is engraved with Chinese characters indicating who donated the cash to buy that particular item.

The front runner in the temple-building competition is the Shengmu Temple *(shèngmǔ miào)*. It's adjacent to the community of Tucheng *(tǔchéng)*.

The runner-up in the temple building competition is the Matsu Temple *(tiānhòu gōng)*. Personally, it looks to me like they've got a long way to go if they want to be number one.

Third in line, but coming up fast, is the Szutsao Temple *(sìcǎo dàzhòng miào)*. The appearance is classical Taoist – check out the roof ornaments.

If at all possible, try to visit Luerhmen on the 15th night of the first moon – the Lantern Festival. There are brilliant displays of fireworks. Protective clothing is a must; most people wear motorcycle helmets and faceshields.

Right near the Shengmu Temple and the village of Tucheng is Woozland (☎ 257 3811) *(wùzhì lèyuàn)*, a park known for its fancy waterslides. Popular during the summer, it's a madhouse on weekends but isn't bad during the week. One of Taiwan's well-known TV shows is filmed here. If you're visiting the temple anyway and the weather is hot, the waterslides are a great way to cool off. There are other entertainment machines on offer here – rides, a hologram funhouse, etc. All exhibits and rides cost NT$40 each – you can buy a ticket just for the waterslides if that's all you want. Don't forget to bring a swimsuit and towel.

A few km to the north-east is another amusement park, Fancyland *(yuánbǎo lèyuán)*. However, I give Woozland higher marks as a fun place.

Although technically within the city limits of Tainan, Luerhmen is a long way from the centre. It's in the Annan district, more than 10 km from the city centre. Besides driving yourself, the easiest way to get to Luerhmen is to take bus No 29 from central Tainan. Alternatively, you could take bus No 34 to the Hsimen Rd station *(xīmén lù zhàn)* and then change to bus No 27, 28 or 29. Tainan city bus No 27 goes to the Matsu and Szutsao temples. Along the way, you pass salt-evaporating ponds – this is Taiwan's foremost salt-producing region.

Golden Coast Highway

(bīnhǎi gōnglù) 濱海公路

This is nothing more than an ocean wall crowded with lovers, food stands and fireworks (minor) seven nights a week. It's *the* place to be for Mid-Autumn Festival and, to a lesser extent, Lovers' Festival.

The sea wall is in the south-west corner of

Tainan, right on the beach. You'd have a hard time getting there by public transport at night, which is the best time to go.

Places to Stay – bottom end

There are three hostels in Tainan offering budget accommodation. One good choice is the *Labourers' Recreation Centre* (☎ 263 0174) *(láogōng xiūjià zhōngxīn)*. The address is 261 Nanmen Rd, but the entrance is actually quite a way back from Nanmen Rd on a long driveway. Immediately opposite it is the *Senior Citizens' Recreation Centre* (☎ 2646974) *(sōngbó yùlè zhōngxīn)*. Both hostels charge the same rates: dormitories are NT$180 and double rooms are NT$500. Demand is heavy so call first before trekking out there. From the railway station, you can reach both of these places on bus No 25.

The *Tainan Student Hostel* (☎ 2670526, 2689018) *(táinán xuéyuàn)*, 1 Lane 300, Funung St, Section 1, charges NT$200 for dorm accommodation. This hostel is very clean and usually has empty beds, but for a while they were not accepting foreigners because they had a lot of trouble with Westerners taking drugs. The latest word is that they are now accepting foreigners again, but this could change. The hostel is a fine place to stay, but after 10 pm you can't go in or out – this is to protect the young students from depravity. From the city centre, take bus No 7 or 19.

Places to Stay – middle

The *Nanchun Hotel* (☎ 2221206) *(nánchūn bīnguǎn)*, 60 Mintsu Rd, Section 1, has some of the cheapest private rooms in Tainan. Doubles are NT$500 with polite bargaining, NT$600 otherwise.

Just opposite the railway station on the big roundabout is a 14-storey brown building. There's no English name for this place, but it's shaped something like an ugly cakebox, so foreigners have dubbed it the *Cake Box Building*, though it does have a Chinese name, *zhōnghuá guóbīn dàlóu*. The ground floor is given over to shops and restaurants, but almost every floor upstairs has a hotel,

examples being the Audi, Golf and Galaxy. Best to take the lift to the top floor and walk down, making enquiries as to price. Some of these places specialise in 'short-time' (two hour) rentals.

Peimen Rd, Section 2, is the major road to your right as you exit the railway station. All along the west side of this street are small hotels with Chinese names only. The front doors are usually open and it's easiest enough to spot the lobbies – just drop in and ask the price. The range here is around NT$500 to NT$600.

The *Ailisi Hotel* (☎ 2350807) *(àilìsī bīnguǎn)* is the only cheap hotel behind the railway station – you aren't likely to confuse it with the five-star Hotel Unique next door. As you go out the rear entrance of the station, it's just to your right on Chienfeng Rd. This small place charges NT$550 to NT$600.

The *Guang Haw Hotel* (☎ 2263171) *(guānghuá dà fàndiàn)*, 155 Peimen Rd, Section 1, is certainly one of the best mid-range places. You can identify the hotel by the huge coffee shop on the ground floor. It's less than half a block south of the railway station. Salubrious doubles cost NT$670 and NT$760.

Hotel Yilou (☎ 2269191) *(yīlè dà fàndiàn)* faces the railway station. Doubles range from NT$780 to NT$1200, twins are NT$900 to NT$1300.

The *Oriental Hotel* (☎ 2221131) *(huáguāng dà fàndiàn)*, 143 Mintsu Rd, Section 2, is one of the best bargains in Tainan in this price range. Salubrious doubles are NT$820 to NT$720.

Asia Hotel (☎ 2226171) *(dōngyà lóu dà fàndiàn)*, 100 Chungshan Rd, is at the intersection with Mintsu Rd. Singes/doubles are NT$800/1300, but you can do better elsewhere at this price.

Places to Stay – top end

The *Hotel Unique* (☎ 2366789, fax 2360996) *(liángměi dà fàndiàn*; 430 rooms), 77 Tahsueh Rd W, is just behind the railway station. You can hardly miss it – at 38 stories, it's Tainan's tallest building. A sightseeing attraction in itself, the hotel even boasts

Tainan's only revolving restaurant. Doubles cost NT$3800 to NT$4800, twins NT$4200 to NT$4800, and suites are NT$6000 to NT$60,000.

The *Hotel Tainan* (☎ 2289101, fax 2268502) *(táinán dà fàndiàn)*, 1 Chengkung Rd, has long considered itself to be the leading hotel in town, though it now has 'unique' competition. Doubles go for NT$1800 to NT$2600, twins are NT$2000 to NT$2700.

Redhill Hotel (☎ 2258121, fax 2216711) *(chìkàn dà fàndiàn)*, 46 Chengkung Rd, has doubles for NT$1600 to NT$1800 and twins for NT$2000 to NT$2200.

The *Akira Top Hotel* (☎ 2265261, fax 2210197) *(lìrén dà fàndiàn)*, 88 Kungyuan Rd, is one of the newest up-market places in town. Doubles are NT$1040 to NT$1400, twins are NT$1800 to NT2400.

Places to Eat
Budget Eats Like elsewhere in Taiwan, economically priced noodle shops occupy every street corner, but the area adjacent to National Chengkung University deserves special mention. Not surprisingly, cheap eating establishments catering to the student population surround the campus. Ironically, some of the classiest places in town are also in this area because it's considered a prestigious neighbourhood.

The line-up of eating establishments begins just opposite the main entrance gate of the university and runs down the length of Tahsueh Rd *(dàxué lù)*. Starting near the university post office, there are even more restaurants lining both sides of Shengli Rd.

One of the best bargains in town can be found right inside the campus of National Chengkung University itself. There are several cafeterias on campus, but you'll have to ask a student where they are since they tend to change location. Try to arrive a little early because it gets crowded and the food disappears quickly. University food isn't necessarily the best, but it's cheap. Meal times are normally noon to 1 pm, and 5 to 6.30 pm – the greasy breakfasts aren't worth the trouble.

If it's roast chicken *(shǒupá jī)* you crave, put on the plastic gloves (supplied free) and try the greasy delights at *Chicken House (xiāng jī chéng)* on the corner of Tungning and Changjung Rds. If you want to give yourself indigestion, there's a karaoke on the 3rd floor.

If you have a sweet tooth, one of the best sherbet shops in all Taiwan is *Xiaomaowu Ice Shop (xiǎomàowū bīngyuán)* at 40 Changjung Rd, Section 3. You'll see the sherbet on display, so just point to what you want. Other goodies available if you can order from a Chinese menu is ice-fruit salad *(mìdòu bīng)* or papaya milkshakes *(mùguā niúnǎi)*. There are numerous other ice shops fronting the entrance to Chengkung University on Tahsueh Rd.

Some of the best fruit with ice I've had anywhere in Taiwan is served at the *Chau Nan Fruit Store* (☎ 2242550) *(jiā nán shuǐguǒ diàn)*, 185-4 Nanmen Rd.

Night markets are also a good bet for economy eating, but the ones in Tainan are too far from the centre so the savings are lost in taxi and bus fares. Nevertheless, they're fun – see the Entertainment section.

Fast Food If you want to do something depraved like eating cheeseburgers and French fries in the middle of Chinese food haven, several places can accommodate you. One of the most popular is *89* (☎ 2378838) *(bājiǔ měishí hànbǎo diàn)* at 24 Tahsueh Rd. I don't care much for the hamburgers, but their fried chicken is prime stuff. This place has become something of a hang-out for Tainan's trendies. If it's genuine same-as-home fast food you crave, next door is *McDonald's*.

A good place for Western fast food with a Chinese twist is *Hardee (hādì hànbǎo)* on the corner of Kungyuan and Mintsu Rds, near the Far Eastern Department Store. It's a foreign fast-food chain complete with tacos, but a large part of the menu has been 'Sinicised' for the local market.

Next to Tuntex Department Store *(dōngdìshì)* is where you'll find a *Wendy's* fast-food restaurant.

Top: 'Sea of clouds' as seen from South Cross-Island Highway (RS)
Bottom: Bamboo grove in Chiayi County (RS)

Top: Worship festival in Nankunshen (RS)
Left: Cable car at Tsaoling (RS)
Right: Women in tea plantation, Tsaoling (MM)

Restaurants For a reasonably priced meal in very pleasant surroundings, a good place to try is *wŭkèlā* (☎ 2352867), 115 Shengli Rd, near the university. They have an English-language menu which is available on request.

On Tahsueh Rd next to McDonald's is the *Vegetarian Restaurant (tiānrán sùshí guăn)*. The food is definitely vegetarian; it's a bit oily for my tastes, but 100% natural. They do make very good whole-wheat bread, a rare find in Taiwan.

Lavazza (☎ 2207070), 246 Chungcheng Rd, is on the 3rd floor of a children's department store – a strange venue indeed for Tainan's only Italian restaurant. Great food – I swear by their spaghetti with clams, lasagna and tortellini au salmone. The atmosphere looks formal and wines are served by the bottle, but casual dress (shorts and sandals) are the norm. A filling meal should run around NT$200.

The *Redhill Hotel* (☎ 2258121) *(chìkăn dà fàndiàn)*, 46 Chengkung Rd, has several excellent restaurants on the 1st floor and in the basement, but the Western buffet (available mornings and evenings) is legendary. Check out the breakfast buffet – scrambled eggs, bacon, sausage, Java coffee, French toast, home-fried potatoes, corn flakes with bananas and fresh fruit.

Across the street from the Redhill is a good Sichuan restaurant, *jué sì chuān cài tīng* (☎ 2295133), at 111 Chengkung Rd.

If fancy décor means a lot to you, you can enjoy a meal in air-conditioned comfort at the *Ambassador Restaurant* (☎ 2386666) *(dàshĭ cāntīng)*, 8 Tahsueh Rd. I admire their interior decorating, but personally I find the food overrated.

Good Sichuan-style food is served at *yúyuàn chuān cài cāntīng* (☎ 2285990), 117 Chungyi Rd, near Minchuan Rd. Another good place for Sichuan food is *Today's Restaurant* (☎ 2232881) *(jīnr chuān cài cāntīng)*, 62 Chungcheng Rd. Two doors down is another excellent Sichuan restaurant, *róng xīng chuān cài cāntīng* (☎ 2213134), 56 Chungcheng Rd.

The *Dragon Arch Restaurant* (☎ 224 6332) *(lóngmén xī cāntīng)*, 2nd floor, 215 Fuchien Rd, boasts some of the best Western food in town. It's near the intersection of Fuchien Rd and Chungyi Rd.

The *Diamond Restaurant* (☎ 2253100) *(zhuàn shí lóu cāntīng)* is famous for its dim sum. It's on the 5th floor of the Far Eastern Department Store; take the elevator because the stairs lead to the roof, bypassing the restaurant. The Far Eastern is on the corner of Mintsu and Kungyuan Rds.

Self-Catering Besides the ubiquitous convenience stores and bakeries, there's a supermarket in the basement of the *Far Eastern Department Store* on Mintsu Rd. Tuung-Le Supermarket *(tŏnglì zōnghé shāngcháng)* is also in the centre of town on the south-east corner of Mintsu and Peimen Rds. Wellcome Supermarket *(dīnghăo)* is in north-east Tainan, on Chunghua E Rd, north of Hsiaotung Rd. The other big supermarket is in the basement of the Tuntex Department Store *(dōngdìshì)*.

Entertainment

Tainan's night markets are lively places, especially on Saturday nights during summer. Save your appetite – you'll find plenty to eat. The two largest markets are Jiankang Snack City *(jiànkāng diănxīn chéng)* in the south-west of the city and Hsiaopei Rd Night Market *(xiăobĕi lù yèshì)*. Unfortunately, both are too far from the centre to walk and you'll probably have to take a taxi if you don't have your own wheels – both are a 10-minute ride from the city centre.

Just next to the Hsiaopei Rd night market is a huge shopping mall attached to the Tuntex Department Store *(dōngdìshì)*. In addition to shopping, there is a movie theatre, swimming pool, rides for the kiddies and a fast-food restaurant.

It might seem peculiar, but there is a Chinatown *(zhōngguó chéng)* in Tainan. Chinatown is contained within two large buildings and is a collection of movie theatres, a skating rink, shops and about 100 hole-in-the-wall foodstalls. It's slow during the daytime but hops at night.

Cinemas The cheapest movie theatre in town is *quánměi xìyuàn* (☎ 2224726), 187 Yungfu Rd, Section 2. For only NT$90, you can see two films. Some other movie theatres in Tainan include:

chénggōng xìyuàn
    107 Hai'an Rd (☎ 2223700)
wánghòu xìyuàn
    6th floor, 323 Chungcheng Rd (☎ 2227761)
wángzi xìyuàn
    323 Chungcheng Rd (☎ 2225460)
guóhuā xìyuàn
    3rd floor, 118 Minchuan Rd, Section 2 (☎ 2261213)
zhōngguó cheng xìyuàn
    72 Huanho Rd (☎ 2215110)
yánpíng xìyuàn
    128 Hsimen Rd, Section 2 (☎ 2224282)
dōng'ān xìyuàn
    35 Lane 3, Tungmen Rd, Section 2 (☎ 2375650)
mínzú xìyuàn
    249 Mintsu Rd, Section 2 (☎ 2293528)

Discos Rush (☎ 2218355) is on the 3rd floor, 662 Hsimen Rd, Section 1, opposite the telephone company. This place really gets moving and packs to the rafters on Saturday night. Dancing hours are 8 pm to 4 am, and there's no cover charge after 2 am. There's also no cover charge on Friday night; on Saturday, it's NT$160 (but includes drink coupons); on all other nights it's NT$130.

In the same building on the 6th floor is Penthouse (☎ 2282379). This place is more sedate – there's a dance floor, but the emphasis is halfway between pub and disco. There's a NT$200 cover on Saturday nights (drink coupons included); at other times, it's free but you're expected to drink.

Pubs The No 1 hot spot for foreigners is Dirty Roger (☎ 2747002) at 141 Tungmen Rd, Section 1, very close to Mito Temple. It's run by the venerable Roger, a youngish Chinese who's become an institution in Tainan. Operating hours are 1 pm to 4 am.

Africa (☎ 2412812), 22 Hsinghua St (just off Peimen Rd, Section 1), is a hip, art-deco

coffee shop/pub that has proven very popular with expatriates. Closing time is around midnight depending on what the market will bear.

Terry's Cafe (☎ 2296786) is just above the Nandu movie theatre at 138 You'ai St. This is another art-deco place (California pop motif) with a jazz and folk-music background. It's also a decent place to eat – food is available from noon to 9.30 pm, after which time it's drinks only until 2 am. Check out the big chicken-leg dinner (NT$170) and the coconut iced coffee (same price).

The Pioneer Pub (☎ 2644880), also known as the Band Pub, is a large place notable for its Western (cowboys & Indians) décor and live music. There's no cover charge, but drinks cost about NT$200, or eat a whole meal (dumplings) for NT$150. The pub is at 181 Chinhua Rd, Section 2.

Macanna Beer House *(màikànna)* is geared towards the student crowd at Chengkung University. There are several branches – oldest and still a current favourite is the Shengli branch (☎ 2345882) at 117 Shengli Rd. The Changjung branch (☎ 234 1411) is at 163 Changjung Rd, Section 2.

Another alternative is the Rock Pub *(duòzhú)* on Tungning Rd, just east of Shengli Rd. This place often has live music.

A place that identifies itself as a 'super disco pub' is Royal, in the basement at 20-20 Chungshan S Rd.

Way out in the west part of town, almost to the sea, is Chunghua W Rd. This place has become thick with pubs, nightclubs, karaoke dives and so on – it's geared mostly to a Chinese clientele. One of the more attractive places in this district is Amadeus (☎ 2382408), a loud pub with its own DJ (songs played on request). It's at 249 Chunghua Rd, and is open from 6 pm to 4 am.

Horseback Riding Despite the name, the Yukoteng Race Course (☎ 2280325) *(yù oū dēng xún mǎ yuán)* is not for racing – it's a riding stable where you can ride horses on the beach. Riding lessons are also available. The stables are in the far west of Tainan – continue past Anping Fort (Fort Zeelandia) and you'll find it near a tacky little beachside resort area called Chiumaoyuan Amusement Park *(qiūmào yuán)*. You can get there from the railway station on bus No 15.

MTV Kiss (☎ 2412340), 9th floor, 118 Minchuan Rd, Section 2 (above Kuohua movie theatre) is a cut above any other MTV joint in Tainan. Large-screen, romantic tatami cubicles are only half the attraction – there's also a decent bar and restaurant. All films are on laser disk and cost NT$160 per person per movie.

The 3A MTV (☎ 2212978), 7 Lane 703, Hsimen Rd, Section 1, is just to the north of the telephone-company building. The way it works here is that there's no admission charge, but you must buy drinks or a meal (NT$150 minimum charge) and watch movies for free. The atmosphere is congenial.

Cash Box (☎ 2264621) *(qiánguì)*, 5th floor, 322 Chungcheng Rd, is just down the street from Chinatown. This place offers discreet rooms and a slightly piano-bar appearance.

Mountain Outings Tainan has no mountains, but mountain clubs launch regular weekend expeditions into the surrounding countryside. A good place to enquire about these activities is at a shop selling backpacking gear. One such place with an English-speaking owner, Mr Wu Weichien, is Mountain & Wilderness Service Company (☎ 2373928) *(jiān lěi qǐ)*, 196 Tung'an Rd.

Things to Buy

There are three large department stores in Tainan. Most central is the Far Eastern Department Store *(yuǎndōng bǎihuò gōngsī)*, on the corner of Mintsu and Kungyuan Rds. Newer and larger is the Tuntex Department Store *(dōngdìshì bǎihuò)*, adjacent to the Hsiaopei Rd night market. Liangmei Department Store *(liángměi bǎihuò)* is a high-rise shoppers' haven on the north-west corner of Chunghua E Rd and Hsiaotung Rd.

Tainan has a collection of army-surplus stores on Kungyuan S Rd south of Chungshan Park. All of Taiwan's cities have these stores, but Tainan is unique in having them all clustered together. There are some excellent buys here – I particularly like the running shorts with Chinese military emblems.

There is an excellent English-speaking Twinhead computer dealer called Hi-Tech Information Project Company (☎ 2206156) at 18 Mintsu Rd, Section 2 (don't confuse it with the computer store next door). Service is also good at Sunrise Computer Company (☎ 2344382) *(zǎoyáng)*, 368 Chingnien Rd.

Getting There & Away

Air From Tainan there are flights to Taipei and Makung in the Penghu Islands.

Wing On Travel Service (☎ 2293141) *(yǒng'ān lüxíngshè)*, 91 Minchuan Rd, Section 2, is good for cheap international tickets. Also good is Southeast Travel Service (☎ 2234176), 149 Fuchien Rd, Section 1.

The airlines and their representative offices in Tainan are as follows:

China Airlines
    (zhōnghuá hángkōng), Room B, 2nd floor, 496 Hsimen Rd, Section 1 (☎ 2262181)
EVA Airways
    (chángróng hángkōng), 6th floor, 166-6 Chungshan Rd (☎ 2265292)
Far Eastern Airlines
    (yuǎndōng hángkōng), 116 Yungfu Rd, Section 2 (☎ 2258111)
Great China Airlines
    (dàhuá hángkōng), Tainan Airport (☎ 2602811)
Trans-Asia Airways
    (fùxīng hángkōng), 55 Mintsu Rd, Section 2 (☎ 2227111)

Bus There is no problem in reaching Tainan by public transport from all the other major cities in Taiwan. It's useful to know that there are direct buses to Alishan and Kenting, and once-daily buses heading east along the South Cross-Island Highway.

Train Trains north to Taipei or south to Kaohsiung leave every 30 to 40 minutes from around 6 am to midnight.

Getting Around

To/From the Airport Tainan's airport can be reached by the rather infrequent bus No 36. Failing that, it's a short taxi ride.

Wing On Travel Service (☎ 2293141) operates a bus direct to CKS Airport near Taipei.

NANKUNSHEN

(nánkūnshēn dàitiān fŭ) 南鯤鯓代天府

Along with Peikang, the temple at Nankunshen is considered to be the most active, powerful, colourful and richest temple in Taiwan. Although I repeatedly say throughout this book that you shouldn't visit tourist places on Sunday or holidays, you should make an exception for Nankunshen.

This place is only really interesting on Sunday, especially during holidays. At such times, thousands of enthusiastic worshippers descend on the temple and put on a sensational display of parades, fireworks, chanting, feasting and festivities. Bring lots of film and be prepared to move out of the way quickly when the firecrackers start exploding. However, if you visit on weekdays the place might be nearly deserted.

You may well see some devout worshippers practising a mild form of self-mutilation, running a mace-like instrument across their back, tearing the skin and causing blood to flow. The cuts are not very deep but will usually leave scars. Only men participate in this particular form of worship. Those who do are presumed to be possessed by the gods and therefore immune to pain. The whole purpose of the self-mutilation is to demonstrate the gods' power.

Other worshippers paint their faces and dress up in costumes. They march in a procession, beating on gongs and drums, often carrying a Chinese-style sedan chair for a god to ride in. Meanwhile, firecrackers and skyrockets liven up the atmosphere.

The temple was built in 1662 but has been kept in fine condition. Behind the temple is a garden area. As you approach Nankunshen on the bus, you'll notice that the surrounding countryside resembles pools of mud with nothing growing at all. In fact these are salt-evaporating ponds. This is about the sunniest place on the island and it's adjacent to the sea, so it is naturally Taiwan's major salt-producing region.

Getting There & Away

Getting to Nankunshen is easy. From Tainan, take a bus from the terminal of the Hsingnan Bus Company *(xīngnán kèyùn)*. There are frequent departures and the ride takes about 75 minutes. If you take the bus, get off at the last stop. The terminal is about one block from the temple. To find the temple, just ask anybody for the *nánkūnshēn dàitiān fŭ*. There is also a bus from Kaohsiung.

HUTOUPI

(hŭtóubí) 虎頭埤

About 12 km east of Tainan is Hutoupi, also called Hutoupei *(hŭtóubēi)*. It's basically a small reservoir, park and picnic area. Swimming in the reservoir is not permitted, but it is possible to hire a rowboat and fishing is allowed. The Hsingnan Bus Company goes to Hutoupi from central Tainan. There is a hostel on the far side of the lake, though it's unlikely you'd want to spend the night there.

WUSHANTOU RESERVOIR

(wūshāntóu shuĭkù) 烏山頭水庫

Wushantou Reservoir is also known as Coral Lake *(shānhú tán)*. Like Hutoupi, it attracts picnickers, anglers and boaters. Wushantou is much larger, and high-speed motorboats zip around the lake. A bus to Wushantou departs from the Hsingnan Bus Company *(xīngnán kèyùn)* terminal on Chungshan Rd in Tainan.

It's doubtful you'd want to spend the night there, but if you do the *Wushantou Guest House* (☎ 6983121) *(wūshāntóu guómín lüshè)* offers pricey accommodation. They have doubles for NT$1000 or you can stay in the dorm for NT$300.

KUANTZULING

(guānzĭlíng) 關仔嶺

Kuantzuling is an old hot-springs resort which was popular in the times of the Japanesc occupation. As hot springs go, these are rather unattractive because the water contains some clay, giving it the colour of milk. But it's claimed that the mineral content is good for you, and for this reason real hot-springs enthusiasts still flock to Kuantzuling. During the occupation, the Japanese built their charming wooden inns with tatami mats. These days most of the Japanese inns have disappeared and given way to modern Chinese architecture – 'renaissance concrete box'.

Whether or not you care to soak in the mucky hot springs, this area in the foothills of Taiwan's mountains is pretty. However, the main attraction is the temples. Kuantzuling is one place that is best seen if you have your own vehicle.

The country roads around Kuantzuling are excellent for hiking, except on Sundays or holidays when the tourists in their cars flood into the area. Try to arrive early. When you

get into town you will no doubt be greeted by a mass of wild-chicken taxi drivers who will tell you that it is too far to walk anywhere and that there are snakes and tigers around, but that they will gladly give you a ride for NT$500 or so. It's up to you of course. Hiking will take the whole day, whereas a taxi tour of the area might last for 30 minutes. You can be sure that your driver will do his best to make the tour as short as possible – after all, once he dumps you off he can pick up another passenger. You might want to take a taxi to the Water Fire Cave and then walk from there. You can also reach the Water Fire Cave by bus from Paiho (báihé).

Red Hill Park
(hóngshān gōngyuán) 紅山公園
The first place you should have a look at is Red Hill Park, up the stairs to your immediate left as you walk up the road out of town. It's a 10-minute climb to the park, which is

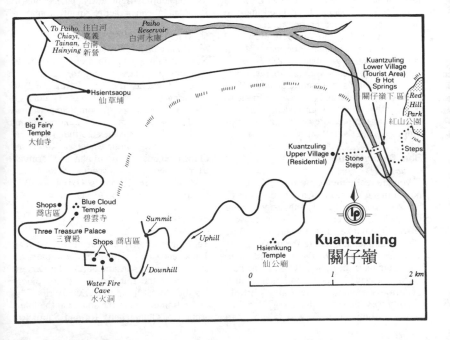

not spectacular but nevertheless worth seeing.

Hsienkung Temple

(xiāngōng miào) 仙公廟

After you've had a look at Red Hill Park, go back down to the road. Follow the road uphill. You can save some time by taking the stone steps (see map). The road loops around while the steps are more direct. Both will bring you to upper Kuantzuling village. Continue along the road out of the village and into the countryside for several km. You'll eventually find a signposted turn-off on your left. This goes to the Hsienkung Temple, a pretty and peaceful temple sitting in the forest.

Water Fire Cave

(shuǐhuǒ dòng) 水火洞

Back on the main road, continue uphill. It gets a bit steep but you'll soon reach the summit of the highway. It drops down and just about 100 metres away you'll find a bunch of tourist shops. It's a good place to have lunch. Just after the first tourist shops, you can walk down to your left and you'll find Water Fire Cave. The hot springs contain so much gas that it bubbles to the surface and ignites, giving the impression of burning water. I saw a picture taken in 1964 of this same place that showed the flame to be over three metres high; today it is much smaller, as the pressure of the gas is dropping.

Blue Cloud Temple

(bìyún sì) 碧雲寺

If you are really tired of walking, there is a bus from the Water Fire Cave to the town of Paiho *(báihé)*, but I really suggest you hang in a little bit longer. Just a 15-minute walk downhill will take you to the attractive Blue Cloud Temple, adjacent to the newer Three Treasure Palace *(sānbǎo diàn)*. From there, you again have the option of taking the bus, but if you walk downhill some more you'll eventually come to Big Fairy Temple *(dàxiān sì)*, which is an interesting place. Just another 10-minute walk will take you to

Hsientsaopu *(xiāncǎopǔ)*. From here you can go by bus to Hsinying or Chiayi, but it may be easier to catch a bus first to Paiho. As it's a much larger town, there are numerous buses to Hsinying and Chiayi, and sometimes there are direct buses to Tainan as well. You could of course go back to Kuantzuling by bus if you want to spend the night there, though few people do that. Other than visiting the hot springs, there isn't much to do in the village of Kuantzuling.

Getting There & Away

You can approach Kuantzuling from either Hsinying or Chiayi. If you are coming from the south, take a train to Hsinying *(xīnyíng)*, then take a bus from the terminal directly across the street from the railway station. Buses go direct to Kuantzuling.

If you're coming from the north, first go to Chiayi and then take a direct bus from the Chiayi Bus Company *(jiāyì kèyùn)* terminal at 501 Chungshan Rd. If you don't get a bus to Kuantzuling right away, take a bus to Paiho and then another to Kuantzuling.

MATOU TEMPLE

(mádòu dàitiān fǔ) 麻豆代天府

North of Tainan is Matou, a small and mostly uninteresting place except for its temple. Also known as the Five King Temple *(wǔwáng miào)*, Matou Temple is a classic Taoist place of worship, complete with firecrackers, gongs and the occasional exorcism. Adding to the festivities are the '18 Levels of Hell' and the 'Four Undersea Kingdoms of the Dragons' – a sort of attached carnival. Come on weekends to see it at its liveliest.

Buses from Tainan's Hsingnan Bus Company can take you to Matou.

YENSHUI

(yánshuǐ) 鹽水

Yenshui is a fairly ordinary town between Tainan and Chiayi. However, the whole town collectively goes insane during the Lantern Festival on the 15th day of the first moon. It's the closest thing to a friendly riot. The real action occurs in the square at the intersection of Chungcheng Rd and Sanfu Rd.

The activities start at 7 pm and continue past midnight.

It's the world's most spectacular display of fireworks. One after another, people ignite giant cardboard honeycombs stuffed with rockets; each one costs over NT$100,000. It's open warfare – the honeycombs are often aimed right into the crowd. There are similar fireworks displays in Luerhmen and Peikang, but nothing quite matches the grandeur of Yenshui. People from all over Taiwan converge on this town – the crowd is estimated at several hundred thousand.

As a veteran of Yenshui, I can say that the fireworks will be the least of the hazards you face. Much more dangerous are the spectators. With thousands of people standing shoulder to shoulder, the wild pushing and shoving becomes deadly. The sedan chairs charging through the crowd cause many injuries. The chance of being trampled should not be taken lightly. If you get up front, the safest thing to do is actually to run into the firecrackers, not away from them – this way you temporarily leave the crowd behind. There are always a few fistfights, usually resulting from arguments about whose firecracker hit whose girlfriend. Even though motor vehicles are supposedly banned during the festival, there are at least a few drunken birdbrains who enthusiastically drive their motorcycles right into the crowd at high speed. The ambulances do good business. So do the pickpockets.

Wear old clothing, since the sparks can burn little holes in cloth. A motorcycle helmet with faceshield is essential survival gear. An amazing number of people don't wear any protection at all – as any eye surgeon in the local hospitals can tell you. It is possible to carry a camera, but a large one dangling from your neck is certain to get broken. Much safer would be a small camera that fits in your pocket.

Down in the crowds it gets very hot, but you can expect the weather to be cold at this time of year. It's best to carry a couple of sweaters or jumpers and tie them securely around your waist when you get ready to plunge into the crowds. Wearing a small backpack or daypack would be very inconvenient. The little packs that attach to your belt are much more secure in these crowds. Don't carry anything that you can't stuff into your pockets or beltpack, because you need both hands free to manoeuvre through the crowd and keep your balance.

The best location is on somebody's rooftop or terrace overlooking the square. This is where the TV cameras are set up. To get these choice spots, you either have to know somebody or arrive early and expect to pay for the privilege. There are a few awnings that you might be able to climb onto (at your own risk), but it's not easy. Expect every square cm of space to be fully occupied.

Everything you need can be purchased in Yenshui. Street vendors capitalise on the situation and sell motorcycle helmets and face shields. Safety glasses are not widely available in Taiwan. There is no shortage of food and drink.

A motorcycle or bicycle is the most practical way to get into and out of Yenshui during this festival. You can take the train to Hsinying and then walk seven km or take a taxi to Yenshui, but start out early if you're going to depend on public transport.

Perhaps the best plan is to avoid Yenshui and instead visit the fireworks displays in Luerhmen and Peikang; your chances of injury are less in those places and you can watch the Yenshui display on TV. It's usually broadcast several weeks later.

SOUTH CROSS-ISLAND HIGHWAY
(nánbù héngguàn gōnglù) 南部橫貫公路
Running between Tainan on the west coast and Taitung on the east coast, the South Cross-Island Highway climbs into the wilderness of Taiwan's mountains. Unlike the heavily used Central Cross-Island Highway, the South Cross-Island Highway has much less traffic. The area is blessed with spectacular scenery every km of the way. This route is occasionally closed because of landslides, especially during the rainy season from late May to early September, but despite this, it

is well worth making this trip if you want to see rural Taiwan at its best.

Most people do this trip from west to east. This makes sense if you want to hike the middle section (highly recommended) as the west side is a gentle slope and the east side drops down steeply. The hike is popular with students, so there can be a large number of hiking groups during school holidays.

The trip can be made by car, bus or on foot. It can be done in a day if you simply want to rush through on a bus, but if you want to hike the central section, you should allow two to three days.

From both Tainan (west side) and Taitung (east side) there is a bus, but neither make the trip all the way across the highway. Rather, the two buses meet midpoint on the highway at Tienchih (*tiānchí*), just after noon. Passengers from one bus transfer to the other to complete the trip over the mountains. The buses depart about 2 pm. Hikers coming from Tainan can get off the bus, have lunch and then start walking. Both buses cost NT$177.

Hiking from West to East

About four hours of walking from Tienchih takes you to the top of the highway at Yakou (*yǎkǒu*), at an elevation 2728 metres. There is a large tunnel, about 500 metres in length, and you have to walk through it. A torch (flashlight) is absolutely necessary as the tunnel is not lit and is totally dark in the centre – it's rather spooky in there.

Once you are out of the tunnel, walk downhill for a short distance and there are some buildings off to the right. This is the Yakou Mountain Hostel, where you can spend the night. It's best to have reserved a room in advance. They used to always permit travellers to sleep on the dining room floor for a small fee, but recently the management has become more obstinate – you might have to beg. Alternatively, camp next to the hostel. It is *cold* at 2500 metres, so a sleeping bag and warm clothes are called for.

The hostel is the only place that has food and it is very poor food at that, so bring your own. If you want to eat at the hostel you have

to reserve meals in advance, though they have a little kiosk selling cookies and other junk food.

If you get up early the next morning you can admire the extraordinary sunrise. As one traveller wrote:

Walk to the top of the pass at daybreak for lovely mountain vistas and, if conditions are good, for a beautiful display of the sea of clouds...I stayed there over an hour in extreme wind, some rain, some sun, and saw the most spectacular cloud show I have ever seen. The ever-changing patterns and colours raced over the summit at a speed I couldn't believe.

Ruthli F Kemmerer

Walk down the road past the beautiful waterfall. It's a full day's walk downhill to Litao (*lìdào*), about 30 km or seven hours by foot. Litao is an aboriginal village at 1070 metres elevation and there is a youth hostel. Good food is available in Litao from the little shop by the bus station.

Buses departs Litao at 8 am and 2.30 pm, heading down to Kuanshan on the east coast. If you still have the energy, you can get up early and walk for two hours from Litao to Wulu (*wùlù*); the nine km walk takes you through a gorge that rivals Taroko Gorge in its beauty. The first bus stops in Wulu at 8.20 am, but unless you start out from Litao at 6 am you won't catch it. Of course, you can get the second bus in the afternoon.

Side Trips

If you want a real challenge, you can climb Kuanshan (*guānshān*), not to be confused with the small city of Kuanshan near Taitung. Kuanshan is a peak just to the south-west of the Yakou Youth Hostel. It's 3666 metres in elevation. You begin the climb from Yakou. A class A mountain pass is supposedly needed, but there is nobody up there to check. Not that I advocate you knowingly do anything illegal, of course.

You can spend an extra night along this highway in Meishan on the west side. Meishan is a large aboriginal village and there's a youth hostel. There's nothing to do but relax and go for walks. There is a river nearby but the scenery is more exciting in Yakou, at the top of the highway.

Places to Stay

You don't really have much choice, as there are only three youth hostels along this route. Camping is another possibility; although there aren't any real camping grounds. You are allowed to pitch a tent next to a youth hostel. If you desire luxury accommodation, you'd better stay in Tainan or Taitung.

Meishan Mountain Hostel
(*méishān shān zhuāng*) (☎ 07-7470134); dormitory NT$150
Yakou Mountain Hostel
(*yăkŏu shān zhuāng*) (☎ 089-329891); dormitory NT$150
Litao Mountain Hostel
(*lìdào shān zhuāng*) (☎ 089-329891); dormitory NT$150

Places to Eat

Bring extra food along or you'll be sorry. All three youth hostels have meals, but only if they are booked in advance. The meals also leave a lot to be desired – 'gastronomic purgatory' might be a fair description. This particularly applies to Yakou, where for NT$80 they serve up some sort of paste that's supposed to be breakfast.

Some food is available from noodle stands near the bus terminals in Meishan and Litao, but nothing is available in Yakou (besides the paste) except for some biscuits.

Getting There & Away

There is only one bus a day in either direction over this highway. From Tainan, buses depart at 7.30 am from the Hsingnan Bus Company (*xīngnán kèyùn*) terminal on Chungshan Rd. If you're travelling in the other direction, the bus departs from Taitung at 8 am and makes a 30-minute stop in Kuanshan (*guānshān*) from 9 to 9.30 am before continuing.

West-Central Taiwan 台灣中西部

If you have travelled down the east coast you would have already seen some of Taiwan's spectacular mountains, but the really big peaks are in this part of the country. It's here that you find Yushan, which at 3952 metres is the highest peak on the island. In just a few hours you can ascend by train or bus from coconut and banana groves to alpine forests.

This is where Taiwan's urban residents escape to when they have a holiday. The mountain resorts of Alishan, Tsaoling, Tungpu and Hsitou draw larger and larger crowds every year. In the foothills is Sun Moon Lake, a honeymoon resort which rivals Tienhsiang on the east coast.

The narrow coastal strip of west-central Taiwan is pancake-flat, agricultural land. A highly productive rice-growing region, this area is also rich in culture. It's here that you can see the enormous worship festivals at Peikang, and nearby Lukang is one of the most historical cities in Taiwan.

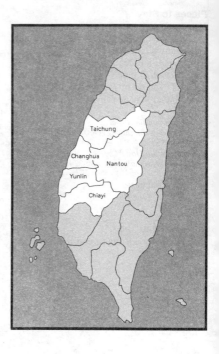

Chiayi County 嘉義縣

CHIAYI
(jiāyì) 嘉義

A small city in the centre of Taiwan, Chiayi is the departure point for numerous journeys into Taiwan's high mountains. Travellers will probably be most interested in the trip to Alishan, Taiwan's leading mountain resort. It isn't likely you'll want to go out of your way to tour Chiayi itself, but you may elect to spend a night there on your way to or from the mountains. A nice side trip from Chiayi is to the temple city of Peikang.

Chiayi is one city in Taiwan where it's still possible to rent a motorcycle – you might consider doing so to explore the mountains.

Information
Money ICBC (☎ 2241166) is at 259 Wenhua Rd near the Far Eastern Department Store.

There is a Bank of Taiwan (☎ 2224471) at 306 Chungshan Rd.

Bookshops Kingstone Bookstore (☎ 22 22670) is at 494 Chungshan Rd, half a block from the railway station. Although the selection of English books is very limited, the magazine collection will help preserve your sanity.

Travel Agents A good travel agent for international tickets is Wing On Travel Service (☎ 2277001) *(yǒng'ān lǚxíngshè)*, 240 Linsen W Rd. Also recommended is Southeast Travel Service (☎ 2277025), 490 Chungshan Rd.

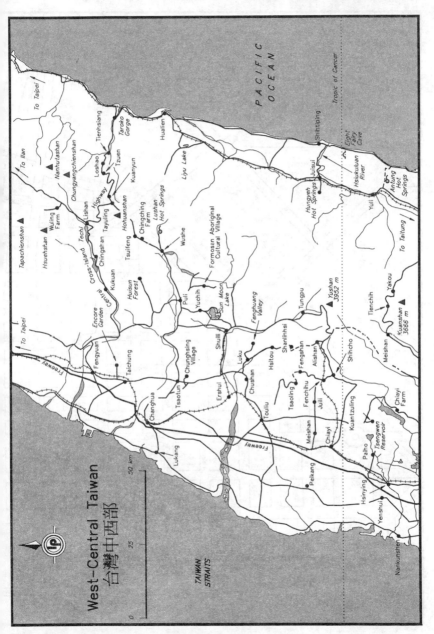

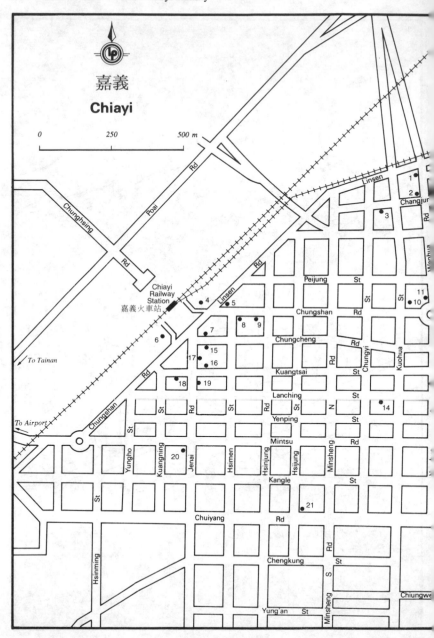

嘉義

Chiayi

0   250   500 m

Chunghsing Rd

Poai Rd

Linsen

Changjur Rd

Wenhua

1
2
3

Chiayi
Railway
Station
嘉義火車站

To Tainan

Linsen Rd

Peijung St

Chungshan Rd

Chungcheng

Kuangtsai St

Lanching St

Yenping St

Mintsu Rd

Kangle St

Chungyi St

Kuohua

11
10
14

4
5
8 9
7
6
15
17 16
18 19

St Rd St Rd N St

To Airport

Chungshan Rd

Yungho St

Kuangning St

Jenai

Hsimen St

Hsinjung

Hsijung

Minsheng Rd

20

21

Chuiyang Rd

Chengkung St

Minsheng S Rd

Yung'an St

Hsinming St

Chiungwe

1 ICBC
國際商業銀行

2 Gallant Hotel
嘉南大飯店

3 Jiazhou Hotel
嘉洲大飯店

4 Taiwan Bus Company
(West Coast Cities)
台汽客運

5 Laotang Noodle Shop
老唐牛肉麵

6 Chiayi County Bus Company
(Alishan & Juili)
嘉義縣公車站

7 Tongyi & Yongxing hotels
統一大飯店/永興大旅社

8 Police (Visa Extensions)
警察局外事課

9 Chiayi Bus Company (Peikang)
嘉義客運

10 Bank of Taiwan
台灣銀行

11 Night Market
夜市

12 Telephone Company
電信局

13 GPO
郵政總局

14 Chaotian Temple
朝天宮

15 Jiaxin Hotel
嘉新大飯店

16 Hotel Country
國園大飯店

17 Motorcycle Hire
& Chetou Noodle Shop
機車出租/車頭牛肉麵

18 Kowloon Hotel
九龍大飯店

19 Penglai Hotel
蓬萊旅社

20 Park 'N Shop (supermarket)
百佳超市

21 Wantai Hotel
萬太大飯店

Wufeng Temple

(*wúfèng miào*) 吳鳳廟

Wufeng temple is 12 km east of Chiayi, and was built in honour of a man named Wufeng.

The circumstances of his death have become one of the most popular folk stories in Taiwan.

Wufeng was born in 1699 and lived in the Chiayi area. He worked as a liaison between the government and the aborigines. He became a good friend of the aborigines and learnt to speak their language.

At that time, the aborigines engaged in head-hunting. Wufeng was unable to dissuade them from continuing this grisly practice. One day, Wufeng summoned the aborigines to his office and told them that the next morning, a man on horseback, wearing a red robe and hat, would pass by his office. He told the aborigines that they could decapitate this man, but that it would be the last head they would ever take.

Just as he said, a man in red robes did appear the next morning. The aborigines duly ambushed him and quickly cut off his head, only to discover shortly afterwards that it was Wufeng himself. Horrified at what they had done, the aborigines gave up the practice of head-hunting.

Although this story is frequently told in Taiwan and is believed by the Chinese, many aborigines dispute it. It's been the source of bitter argument for years, but there is really no way to know the truth about Wufeng since he's not available for comment. Perhaps he never even existed.

Adjacent to Wufeng temple is the Alishan Fantasy World (*ālǐshān yóulè shìjiè*). Basically, it's a kiddie amusement park.

You can get to the temple by taking a bus from the Chiayi County Bus Terminal, which is in front of the railway station; there's a bus about every 70 minutes. There is a small museum in the temple that charges an outrageous NT$100 for admission.

Places to Stay

The cheapest place in town is the *Penglai Hotel* (☎ 2272366) (*pénglái lüshè*), 534 Jenai Rd, where dumpy but pleasant rooms cost NT$150/300.

Yongxing Hotel (☎ 2278246) (*yǒngxīng dà lüshè*), 710 Chungcheng Rd, is second cheapest at NT$400, but try bargaining. I had the distinct impression that there was much discussion going on in Taiwanese about how much they should charge the foreign devil.

Jiaxin Hotel (☎ 2222280) *(jiā xīn dà fàndiàn)*, 687 Chungcheng Rd, is very nice and has doubles for NT$500 and NT$600. On the other side of the street is *Tongyi Hotel* (☎ 2252685) *(tǒng yī dàfàndiàn)*, 720 Chungcheng Rd, where doubles are NT$550 to NT$650.

The *Kowloon Hotel* (☎ 2254300) *(jiǔlóng dà fàndiàn)*, 595 Kuangtsai St, is excellent value at NT$580/900 for doubles/twins.

Over near the International Commercial Bank of China is *Jiazhou Hotel* (☎ 2232077) *(jiāzhōu dà fàndiàn)* at 283 Changjung St. It seems a good deal at NT$600 for a double.

Hotel Country (☎ 2236336) *(guóyuán dà fàndiàn)*, 678 Kuangtsai St, is an up-market establishment with doubles from NT$900 to NT$1100, twins NT$1200 and suites for NT$3100.

The *Wantai Hotel* (☎ 2275031, fax 2275030) *(wàntài dà fàndiàn)*, 46 Hsinjung Rd, is one km south of the railway station. It's a top-notch place with doubles for NT$880.

The most expensive place is the *Gallant Hotel* (☎ 2235366, fax 2239522) *(jiānán dà fàndiàn)*, 257 Wenhua Rd, with doubles for NT$1300 to NT$1900, twins for NT$2200 to NT$2500 and suites for NT$3200 to NT$4200.

Places to Eat

As in most Chinese cities eating places are ubiquitous, but an area that deserves special mention is the night market on Wenhua Rd, near the Chungshan Rd roundabout. The area is active in the daytime too, but at night it really comes to life.

Chetou Noodle Shop at 542 Jenai Rd is adjacent to several shops renting motorcycles. Prices are low, with beef noodles *(niúròu miàn)* selling for NT$50 for a small bowl, or NT$70 for the large size. This place is conveniently located if you're staying at the Penglai Hotel.

Chungshan Rd is lined with restaurants on both sides, and various noodle and rice shops

spill out into the side alleys. The little nameless hole-in-the-wall places are cheapest, but for nicer surroundings try *Laotang Beef Noodles* (☎ 2232662) *(lǎotáng niúròu miàn)* at 504 Chungshan Rd. Beef noodles *(niúròu miàn)* are the obvious specialty, but also try the dumplings *(shuǐjiǎo)*.

Chiayi's best bakery is *New Taiwan* (☎ 2222154) *(xīn táiwān bǐngpù)*, 294 Chungshan Rd, near the intersection with Wenhua Rd. Right across the street is *Chicken Rice (jī ròu fàn)*, 325 Chungshan Rd, legendary in Chiayi for its fried chicken.

If you prefer self-catering, one of Chiayi's best supermarkets is *Park 'N Shop (bǎijiā chāoshì)* on the south-west corner of Mintsu Rd and Jenai Rd.

Getting There & Away

Air Great China Airlines has flights from Chiayi to Makung (Penghu Islands) and Taipei. China Airlines does not fly to Chiayi but maintains a booking office. The airline booking offices are as follows:

China Airlines
    (zhōnghuá hángkōng), Room 3, Building 6, 316 Chuiyang Rd (☎ 2230116)
Great China Airlines
    (dàhuá hángkōng), Shuishang Airport (☎ 2361959, 2361960)

Bus The north-south freeway passes through Chiayi, and there are frequent transport services from all the major points to the north and south.

In Chiayi, there are three bus terminals near the railway station. The terminal to your right as you face the railway station belongs to the Taiwan Bus Company *(táiqì kèyùn)*. They run buses to major cities in Taiwan such as Taipei, Taichung, Tainan and Kaohsiung. The terminal to your left as you face the railway station is the Chiayi County Bus Company (☎ 2238372) *(jiāyì xiàn gōngchē zhàn)*, which serves mountain areas like Alishan and Juili. The Chiayi Bus Company (☎ 2222308) *(jiāyì kèyùn)* is on Chungshan Rd and serves Peikang and other coastal areas of Chiayi County.

Train As it sits right on the north-south railway, Chiayi has express train service to Taipei and Kaohsiung about once every 30 minutes.

Getting Around

Bus Chiayi has a skeletal bus network – buses are tolerably frequent on big streets like Chungshan Rd but scarce elsewhere.

Taxi There are no meters and taxi drivers want a flat NT$70 for any destination within the city limits. Fares beyond the city have to be negotiated.

Motorcycle Perhaps renting a motorcycle is the real reason to come to Chiayi. If you want to explore the backwaters, doing it by motorcycle makes sense, especially since the bus service continues to decline. There are three shops in a row with motorcycles for hire at 544, 546 and 548 Jenai Rd. The cost is NT$200 per day for a 50-cc bike, but escalates to NT$1000 for the fancy models with racing stripes.

PEIKANG

(běigǎng) 北港

Only about 30 minutes by bus from Chiayi, the town of Peikang is the home of the beautiful Chaotien Temple *(cháotian gong)*, the oldest and largest Matsu temple in Taiwan. True, you can get tired of temple viewing, but with the possible exception of Nankunshen, this temple is the most important in Taiwan. Chaotien Temple has the most activity, which includes parades and ceremonies, and the most money. If you find yourself in Chiayi with a few extra hours on your hands, it's certainly worth the trip to Peikang.

Almost any time you visit this temple there is likely to be something going on, but the best time to visit is on Sundays or holidays, when things are really jumping. The bus will be crowded on those days, but it's worth it.

If you want to see a super-worship festival, which may have over 100,000 partici-pants, then try to visit on the birthday of Matsu, the Goddess of the Sea, which falls on the 23rd day of the 3rd moon in the lunar calendar. In the Western solar (Gregorian) calendar, that would fall sometime between the middle of April and the middle of May.

I should warn you that attending a super-worship festival poses some tactical problems, especially getting there and back again. Every bus, taxi, car, motorcycle, bicycle, skateboard and ox-cart will be heading into Peikang at the same time. I don't know if anyone has done a count of the number of pilgrims who go there on Matsu's birthday, but it would be in the hundreds of thousands – 'people mountain people sea'. If you can't handle such crowds, you'd better visit Peikang at some other time.

Another huge celebration takes place in Peikang during the Lantern Festival, on the 15th day of the 1st moon, which is two weeks after the Lunar New Year – it's similar to the display at Yenshui.

Places to Eat

As you face the temple entrance, just to your right is a meat and fish market. It's very much in the traditional style and worth exploring – good things to eat, and if you're not hungry this place is still an attraction in itself.

Getting There & Away

You can take a bus to Peikang from Chiayi. Buses operated by the Chiayi Bus Company *(jiāyì kèyùn)* at 501 Chungshan Rd depart every 10 minutes. The bus stops at the temple dormitory in Hsinkang *(xīngǎng)* first (the dorm looks like a temple, so don't get confused), then continues on to Peikang. The bus terminal in Peikang is several blocks from the temple. Just ask someone how to get to the Chaotien Temple *(cháotiān gōng)* and they'll point you in the right direction.

TSENGWEN DAM & RESERVOIR

(zēngwén shuǐkù) 曾文水庫

Tsengwen Dam & Reservoir are in the foothills of the Central Mountains, straddling the border between Tainan and Chiayi counties. The reservoir is now the largest lake in Taiwan, though I feel that Sun Moon Lake is far more beautiful. Nevertheless, Tsengwen Reservoir is a nice trip if you have the time. Swimming is not allowed, but boating is OK. If you want to, you can swim in the river just below the dam.

Although the view from the dam is scenic, a more interesting place to visit on the shore of the reservoir is Chiayi Farm (*jiāyì nóngchǎng*). It isn't so much a farm as a resort with fancy European houses. Entrance to the 'farm' costs NT$60.

The Tsengwen Dam area has a number of hiking trails – unfortunately, most of them are not marked. If you can find a Chinese person to guide you, try to do the hike from Tsengwen Reservoir to Little Switzerland (*xiǎo ruìshì*). It doesn't really look like Switzerland, but it's a good walk nonetheless.

Try not to visit Tsengwen Reservoir during the dry season, when the lake is low and has a 'bathtub ring' around it. The dry season is generally from October to April. When the lake is full it's very attractive and the water pouring from the dam's floodgates is impressive.

Places to Stay

A couple of km below the dam is the *Tsengwen Youth Activity Centre* (☎ 575 3431, fax 5753455) (*qīngnián huódòng zhōngxīn*), run by the China Youth Corps. They have dormitory accommodation for NT$150 and double rooms from NT$500 to NT$1000. There is also a camping area where you can rent out tents and quilts. You can swim in the nearby creek, just across the highway.

The *Chiayi Farm Guest House* (☎ 252 1710) (*jiāyì nóngchǎng guómín bīnguǎn*) is up-market accommodation on the lakeside. Doubles cost NT$1200. There is also a camping ground at Chiayi Farm.

Getting There & Away

Tsengwen Dam can be approached from two routes – one from Chiayi and one from Tainan. The Chiayi route is more scenic, but it's possible to do a loop trip.

The Chiayi County Bus Company (*jiāyì xiàn gōngchē*) has three buses daily to Chiayi Farm at 8 am, 1 and 4.40 pm. Perhaps a more fun way to do this trip would be to rent a motorcycle in Chiayi and ride – the highway to look for is Route 3.

In Tainan, buses depart for Tsengwen Dam from the Hsingnan Bus Company (*xīngnán kèyùn*) terminal on Chungshan Rd. The trip takes about 1½ hours and the bus packs out on Sunday.

ALISHAN
(*ālǐshān*) 阿里山

This is Taiwan's top-rated mountain resort and well worth a visit. After the busy cities and the subtropical heat, Alishan is literally a breath of fresh air. At 2200 metres in elevation, the climate is cool and bracing. Climbing the mountains and breathing the cool air does wonders for your health – a trip to Alishan could restore a mummy to its former strength and vitality.

The views are impressive in any direction you'd care to look. In the morning, you can look out over the 'sea of clouds' with jagged peaks sticking out like islands. In the afternoon, when the fog usually rolls in and envelops Alishan, the forest has an eerie, timeless beauty of its own. There are plenty of magnificent old cedar trees and pines, a sharp contrast to the palms and banana plants on the plains below. Alishan attracts many tourists in the spring when the cherry trees are blossoming. Finally, there is Yushan (Jade Mountain), which at 3952 metres is Taiwan's highest mountain and one of the highest peaks in East Asia. Climbing Yushan is just one of the many interesting hikes in the Alishan area. A class A mountain permit is required to climb Yushan.

If you come to Alishan, come prepared for the cold. Even in summer, it's certainly chilly at night. Many people don't seem to realise this and come unprepared. Fortunately, there is a way to survive. Several hotels rent out jackets for NT$100 a day. The jackets are

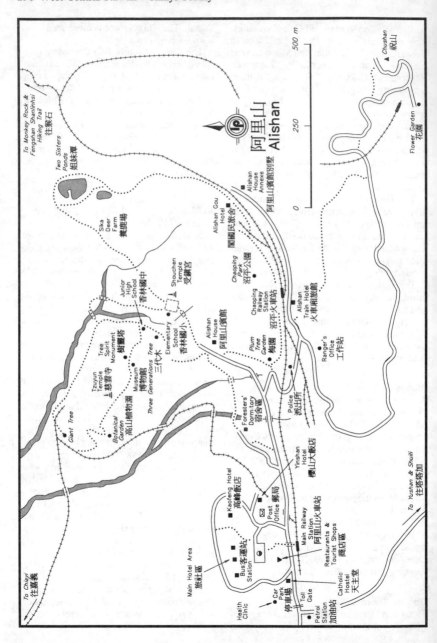

To Monkey Rock & Fengshan Shanlinhsi Hiking Trail 往獨石

Two Sisters Ponds 姐妹潭

Sika Deer Farm 養鹿場

Junior High School 香林國中

Tree Spirit Monument 樹靈塔

Tzuyun Temple 慈雲寺

Museum 博物館

Botanical Garden 高山植物園

Giant Tree 神木

Three Generations Tree 三代木

Elementary School 香林國小

Shouchen Temple 受鎮宮

Alishan House 阿里山賓館

Plum Tree Garden 梅園

Chaoping Park 沼平公園

Chaoping Railway Station 沼平火車站

Alishan Gou Hotel 閣國民旅舍

Alishan House Annexe 阿里山賓館別墅

阿里山 Alishan

Chushan 祝山

Flower Garden 花園

Alishan Train Hotel 火車廂旅館

Ranger's Office 工作站

Foresters' Dormitory 宿舍區

Police 派出所

Yinshan Hotel 櫻山大飯店

Kaofeng Hotel 高峰飯店

Post Office 郵局

Main Railway Station 阿里山火車站

Main Hotel Area 旅社區

Bus Coach Station 客運站

Restaurants & Tourist Shops 商店區

Catholic Hostel 天主堂

Health Clinic

Car Park 停車場

Toll Gate

Petrol Station 加油站

To Chiayi 往嘉義

To Yushan & Shuili 往塔塔加

500 m
250
0

usually coloured fire-engine red, with the hotel's name in big letters on the back.

The frequent afternoon thunderstorms, especially in the spring and summer, can also be a problem. If you get soaked you can freeze to death, so don't attempt any hiking in the area without proper waterproof clothing. Finally, one thing which must be organised in advance is money because there is no bank which changes travellers' cheques in Alishan.

Given all its charms, it's no wonder that Alishan is popular. Unfortunately, it's a little too popular – definitely avoid the weekends and holidays if you can. The transformation that takes place on weekends is truly amazing. On Saturday morning, it's so calm and peaceful you could hear a pin drop. Around 2 pm the first tourists start to arrive. By evening it resembles downtown Taipei. Even the trees seem to wilt under the stress. Sunday is also busy, but around 3 or 4 pm the crowds vanish like magic. It's as if a tidal wave rolled in and rolled out again. Serenity returns and Alishan is just a sleepy mountain village once more, at least until the following weekend.

Alishan lies within the borders of Yushan National Park. There is an NT$90 admission charge. They charge half-price for people shorter than 145 cm (I'm not making this up).

Information

Tourist Office There is a Tourist Service Centre (☎ 2679917) *(lükè fúwù zhōngxīn)* just opposite the bus station. Staff changes are frequent – sometimes they have someone on duty who can speak English and sometimes not. This place can give you maps and general advice about hotels, hikes and weather conditions. If you arrive on a busy day and all the hotels are full, talk to them – they might be able to help you out.

Emergency There is a Public Health Clinic *(wèishēng suǒ)* near the Catholic Hostel. Given the Taiwanese propensity for reckless driving, they do pretty good business on weekends.

Alishan Loop Hike

The easiest hike is a four-km walk going in a loop past the Two Sisters Ponds, an elementary school, a few temples and a museum. There is also the Sacred Tree, said to be 3000 years old. Although the tree is only 1.5 km from Alishan village, there is a tourist train that goes there twice a day, taking five minutes each way to complete the journey. Departure times from Alishan station are 7.45 am and 4.15 pm; the train returns at 7.55 am and 4.25 pm, so you get a big five minutes to see the tree. The one-way train fare is NT$10.

You can stroll up to the summit of Chushan, which is very peaceful and beautiful at any time other than the dawn rush hour.

You can also walk along the road leading to Yushan, but you cannot go further than the checkpoint without a mountain permit. The checkpoint is about a two-hour hike from Alishan.

Highly recommended is the hike to Fengshan, a fantastic 10 hour or longer trek. Or you can walk to the resort area of Shanlinhsi. More details are provided further on.

Sunrise at Chushan

The dawn trek to Celebration Mountain or Chushan *(zhùshān)* is religiously performed by virtually everybody who comes to Alishan. In fact, it's almost mandatory. Hotels typically wake up all their guests around 3 to 4 am (depending on what time the sun rises) so that they can stumble out of bed and begin the hour-long pilgrimage up the mountain. It's cold at this hour, so dress accordingly and bring a torch if you have one. There are minibuses and a train for those who can't handle the hike.

I personally feel that the walk is well worth the effort. You even see old ladies doing it barefoot because they soon discover their high-heeled shoes are a handicap. Finding your way is not difficult, and if it's a weekend or holiday you'll be swept along by the crowd.

If you're walking, you have the choice of two routes: the road or the stone steps. I prefer the steps as you avoid the obnoxious smoke-spewing minibuses with their blaring horns. When you reach the summit, you can enjoy a cheap breakfast from any of the numerous vendors with their pushcarts. Or you can have a more expensive breakfast in heated comfort at Sunrise House on the summit.

Minibuses depart from the main parking area in Alishan and also from Alishan House, which is near the youth hostel further up the mountain. The buses are frequent and don't run to any particular schedule, but they'll probably start at around 4 am during summer and a little later in winter (to coordinate with the sunrise). At NT$150 for the round-trip, the minibuses are more expensive than the train.

The train departs from the main Alishan station and also makes a stop at Chaoping Station. The departure time is about 45 minutes before sunrise – in summer, I took the train at 4.10 am. Inquire the day before to be sure about the time. The one-way fare is NT$50 and the trip takes 30 minutes. Total distance by train is six km.

If you go on a weekend you'll really understand what the Chinese mean by the saying 'people mountain people sea'. By the time the sun makes its debut, there will be 5000 or more people vying for space on the summit. It seems to get more crowded all the time, and if this continues, they'll have to schedule *two* sunrises every morning. Just as the sun pops over the horizon, you'll hear the gentle roar of 5000-plus camera shutters going off simultaneously.

A mad stampede then begins as everyone races to be the first one back to the minibus. My suggestion is to let them fight it out. The riot ends fairly quickly and in 45 minutes every last soul will have vacated the mountain, as if they had never been there. It's nice to linger on the summit for a while, to see the sun hanging over Yushan – Taiwan's highest peak – and to look down on the fog-filled valley below. You can then take a leisurely walk down to Alishan and you won't see anybody along the way if you wait long enough.

Monkey Rock

(shíhóu) 石猴

After the sunrise, many of those racing back to Alishan want to get there in time for the morning train out to the sacred tree (which you can easily walk to), and after that, to Monkey Rock.

Monkey Rock itself is just a rock – it's the nine-km train ride out there on a steam locomotive that interests the tourists, and the views of the valleys below are impressive. The price is rather high for the short distance – NT$100 one way, NT$160 for the round trip but a slight discount for students.

Monkey Rock Train Schedule		
Alishan to Monkey Rock		
Train No	*Depart*	*Arrive*
61	9 am	9.40 am
67	1.30 pm	2.10 pm
Monkey Rock to Alishan		
Train No	*Depart*	*Arrive*
62	10.40 am	11.10 am
68	3.10 pm	3.40 pm

You can also walk this route, but it's an 18-km round-trip and somewhat dangerous. The major problem is the tunnels. You should bring a torch as the tunnels are totally black inside and dangerously narrow. Don't linger inside – getting hit by a train could ruin your whole day. Another danger is the railway bridges – you have to step from one sleeper to the next, and if your foot misses the target it could be a rough landing.

Along the way you will pass a sign in English saying that you need a mountain pass. Ignore it, everyone else does. After the first bridge, but before the tunnel, you'll find a signposted trail on the right side of the tracks leading off to an aboriginal village.

At Monkey Rock railway station, there is a trail that drops down steeply. This goes to Fengshan and Shanlinhsi, two resort areas covered in detail further on in this book. This is a fantastic hike and can be done in one (very long) day. Start early.

The trail is signposted clearly enough, but all in Chinese characters. You might want to do this with some Chinese hiking companions. During school holidays, if you catch the morning train to Monkey Rock with your gear, you will undoubtedly meet some student hikers heading out to Fengshan or Shanlinhsi.

Places to Stay

There seems to be no middle ground – either you camp out, stay in a tatami closet or pay through the nose for luxury. There is no official camping area – if you roll out a sleeping bag in the forest where it's not conspicuous, no one is likely to hassle you. Remember that it often rains at night. On weekends when the hotels fill up, I've even seen people sleeping on the floor of the railway station – you can probably get away with that if you do it late at night and get up early (about 4 am) when the station opens. It's not real comfy – the station's concrete floor feels like a block of ice.

Many travellers like the *Catholic Hostel* (☎ 2679602) *(tiānzhǔ jiào táng)*, which has dorm beds for NT$250 and doubles for NT$1200. It's at the lower end of the village, just past the entrance gate on the north side of the road.

The area just to the north of the bus station is Alishan's main cluster of hotels. *Kaofeng Hotel* (☎ 2679739) *(gāofēng dà fàndiàn)* is one of the more popular ones with travellers. Tatami dormitories are NT$300 per person. The tatami rooms come in closet size for two persons or larger four-person style. Double rooms with shared bath cost from NT$800, or NT$1200 with private bath. Luxury twins go for NT$1800 to NT$2400. You can also eat at the hotel for NT$150. A sign in the lobby says 'Jocker for Rent' – could they mean 'Jacket'?

Near the Kaofeng Hotel is the *Shenmu Hotel* (☎ 2679666) *(shénmù bīnguǎn)*. This place is very secretive about their prices and you have to bargain. The lowest-priced tatami with shared bath can be had for NT$300, but it's like pulling teeth. The better rooms are the same as elsewhere in Alishan – NT$1200 and up.

The *Gau Shan Ching Hotel* (☎ 2679716) *(gāo shān qīng bīnguǎn)* is in the same neighbourhood. Doubles/twins start at NT$1200/1800. Next door is the even pricier *Meiliya Villa* (☎ 2679745) *(měilì yǎ shān zhuāng)* where doubles/twins begin at NT$1600/2800.

When you're facing the post office shown on the Alishan map, off to the left you'll see a small road going uphill. Follow that and you'll come to the *Yingshan Hotel* (☎ 267 9919, 2679979) *(yīngshān dà fàndiàn)*. On weekdays, doubles/twins cost NT$1200/1800, but on weekends it's NT$1800/2500.

Pricewise, you can do better than this. Beyond Chaoping Station is the *Alishan Gou Hotel* (☎ 2679611, 2679911) *(gé guómín lǚshè)*. Doubles/twins start at NT$700/980, with the fanciest rooms rising to NT$2100. It's a long walk from the bus station, but the hotel runs a shuttle bus.

Also in this relatively isolated neighbourhood is *Alishan House* (☎ 267 9811, fax 2679596) *(ālǐshān bīnguǎn*; 60 rooms). Long considered the top place, it now looks like a bargain compared to the ridiculous prices charged elsewhere. Doubles/twins cost NT$1500/1800 and suites are NT$3500. Alishan House also operates the *Alishan Train Hotel* (☎ 267 9621) *(huǒchē xiāng lǚguǎn)* which, as the name implies, is a hotel built inside restored railroad cars; doubles cost NT$1500. Both Alishan House and the Train Hotel are near the Chaoping Station, and neither offers a discount on weekdays. Book for Alishan House at the Alishan House annexe.

The *Foresters' Dormitory (sùshè qū)* is not really a dormitory but rather a collection of houses mostly occupied by government workers and some local people. When Alishan books out on weekends (a frequent occurrence), you can sometimes rent rooms in the homes of local people. This is known as *mínfáng*, which means 'people's house'. The standard of accommodation varies but is generally mediocre – it's usually a tatami attic and you'll have to share with several other people. Don't expect bargains – NT$800 and up for a double is typical. To get into the Foresters' Dormitory, it's best to inquire first at the tourist information office near the bus station. If your Chinese is good, just ask around for *mínfáng*.

There is also a cheap dormitory-style hostel called the *Alishan Youth Activity Centre* (☎ 2679561) (*qīngnián huódòng zhōngxīn*). Unfortunately, it suffers from one fatal problem – it's not really in Alishan. It's in Erwanping, six km down the hill in the direction of Chiayi. Unless you have your own transport, it seems like a very impractical place to stay, plus you'll have to buy another admission ticket every time you return to Alishan from the hostel. You can camp here (but why bother?), or stay in an eight-bed dormitory for NT$300. Doubles cost a heart-stopping NT$1800.

Places to Eat

The general consensus of opinion is that Alishan has the worst food in Taiwan. Almost every restaurant in Alishan is in the plaza near the bus terminal – all are expensive and a few are dishonest. In particular, be careful of the restaurants serving 'fire pot' (*huǒguō*) – a stew where you throw everything into a pot of boiling water sitting on a burner in the centre of the table. What they often do is throw a lot of things into the stew that you didn't order, and then charge you for them. How can you argue after you've eaten it? And not only is it all expensive, but generally poor quality.

Most hotels have restaurants for their guests. None are cheap, but the food is edible (except maybe for breakfast which is generally horrible). The cheapest way to eat in Alishan is to buy food from the two grocery stores on the east side of the plaza (near the post office). You can buy instant noodles and just add hot water. Most hotels have hot-water drinking fountains – hot enough to make soup or really burn yourself. You'll also need chopsticks and a spoon – many hotels will give you free disposable chopsticks from the hotel restaurant. The grocery stores also sell bread, fruit and other goodies, all reasonably priced.

Besides the restaurants in the plaza, you will see some occasional roadside vendors selling food from pushcarts during tourist rush hours.

Things to Buy

There is plenty of the usual tourist junk for sale, but one thing worth buying is an Alishan bathrobe. Actually, I've seen identical bathrobes in other mountain resorts in Taiwan, so maybe I should call it a 'mountain bathrobe'. Whatever you want to call it, they are very warm, comfortable and durable – I've had one for years. A full-length bathrobe costs around NT$400, but you may get it cheaper depending on your bargaining abilities.

Getting There & Away

Bus It's not as exciting as the train, but the bus is significantly cheaper at NT$139 from Chiayi. The travelling time is 2½ hours going uphill, two hours coming down. Chiayi to Alishan by road is 79 km. The bus stops for a 10-minute break at the halfway point at Shihcho (*shízhūo*). As the bus approaches Shihcho, you can see many tea plantations. This is also the point where the weather starts getting noticeably cooler.

Like elsewhere in rural Taiwan, the public bus service is declining rapidly as cars and tourist coaches take over the market. On weekdays, buses leave Chiayi at 7 and 10 am, and 1 pm; on weekends, there are additional departures at 8.30 am and 3 pm. Buses depart Alishan for Chiayi at 10 am, 2 and 4 pm on weekdays; weekends have additional buses at 8.30 am and noon.

From Taipei, there is an express bus to Alishan that departs at 8.30 am. Going the other way, the bus leaves Alishan at 9.30 am. The fare is NT$372 and the trip takes at least six hours. On weekends there are at least two buses on this route with different departure times, so you need to check.

From Kaohsiung there is a daily bus that stops in Tainan along the way. It departs Kaohsiung at 7.20 am. From Alishan, the daily bus to Kaohsiung and Tainan leaves at

1.45 pm. An additional bus runs on weekends. The fare to Kaohsiung is NT$238, or NT$205 to Tainan. Travel time from Kaohsiung to Alishan is about five hours.

From Taichung, daily departures are at 8 am. An additional bus departs at 11 am on holidays. From Alishan to Taichung, daily departures are at 1 pm, with an additional bus at 9.30 am on weekends. The bus makes a stop in Changhua. The Taichung to Alishan fare is NT$244; Changhua to Alishan costs NT$209. Taichung to Alishan travel time is just under four hours.

Train Getting to Alishan can be half the fun. Until fairly recently there was no road at all, but one of the world's most beautiful railroads instead. This narrow-gauge railway was built by the Japanese during their occupation of Taiwan and came into use around 1912. It was built mainly to exploit the timber resources of the mountains, not to develop Alishan into a tourist resort.

Many forests were badly depleted during the Japanese occupation, but reforestation has almost fully restored the area to its former beauty. Logging is still carried on in this area at a sustained rate, but it is only a minor industry nowadays.

Building the railroad was certainly a major engineering feat. The train passes through 50 tunnels, crosses 80 bridges, and climbs from the subtropics to the pine forests in just 72 km. It's a very scenic train ride if you have clear weather, but many travellers have been disappointed because fog in Taiwan's mountains is so common. Your best defence is to get the earliest train, as the mornings are usually clear.

If you arrive in Chiayi by train, you can get on the Alishan train and buy your ticket on board. You don't have to go into the station to buy a ticket, but doing so has an advantage – there is a better chance that you'll get a reserved seat and not have to stand. A 15% discount is offered on round-trip tickets, though it would be far cheaper to take the bus for the return trip. If you do buy a round-trip ticket, you book the return journey in Alishan.

The one-way fare is NT$367 for 1st class, NT$346 for 2nd class and NT$289 for the local train. Despite high prices and pretty heavy bookings, the train has been a consistent money loser for many years. When leaving the railway station in Alishan you will be charged the NT$90 national-park admission fee – there's no way to escape.

Apparently, the majority of visitors prefer to take the train in the uphill direction. Consequently, there are three trains daily going uphill but only two going down. The extra carriages from the third uphill train are attached to the two returning trains. The 1st-class train *does not* stop at Chiayi station – you have to catch it at Peimen, a few km to the north (take a taxi). The 3rd-class train is a local – it stops in every station along the route.

Alishan Train Schedule

Uphill

	Chiayi	Peimen	Fenchihu	Alishan
1st class		9.30 am	11.21 am	12.35 pm
2nd class	12.30 pm	12.37 pm	2.28 pm	3.42 pm
3rd class	1.30 pm	1.37 pm	3.37 pm	4.55 pm

Downhill

	Alishan	Fenchihu	Peimen	Chiayi
1st class	9.25 am	10.41 am	12.30 pm	
3rd class	1.10 pm	2.30 pm	4.30 pm	4.35 pm

Wild-Chicken Taxi Wild-chicken taxi drivers hang around the Chiayi railway and bus station area and will approach any foreigner and yell, 'Alishan! Alishan!'. There is no reason to deal with them because the bus service is fine, unless of course you come in the evening after the last bus has departed. Expect to pay at least NT$1800 for a taxi. They are only legally permitted to carry a maximum of four passengers per taxi, so the trip would cost NT$450 each.

Bicycle Yes, it can be done, but you'll need to be in outstanding physical condition. One traveller wrote:

I rode to Alishan from Chiayi. It's a good seven-hour ride and I don't recommend it to anyone who's not in shape, but it's a spectacular trip. There is a small, barely travelled back road to Shihcho which is beautiful. Then the last 20 km straight up to Alishan are on the main highway. The ride down was unforgettable!

Karl Krueger

HIKES AROUND ALISHAN
Yushan

(yùshān) 玉山

Yushan, which translates as 'Jade Mountain', is Taiwan's highest peak. At an elevation of 3952 metres, it's higher than Japan's Mt Fuji and is one of the highest peaks in East Asia. Climbing it is certainly a beautiful trip and the only thing keeping most travellers from doing so is that a class A mountain pass is needed. You must get the pass through a licensed mountain club.

The club should make some arrangements for equipment – if not, you must prepare your own. Either way, expect to carry a sleeping bag, wet-weather gear and lots of warm clothing. Don't forget food – the summit of Yushan is one place in Taiwan where you won't find a noodle shop.

The approach to Yushan is via Taiwan's 'New Central Highway' *(xīn zhōng gōnglù)*, which runs between Alishan and the town of Shuili. The highest point of the highway is at Tatachia *(tătǎjiā)* where it reaches 2610 metres. Now that bus service has collapsed, the only way you can get there is to drive, hitch, walk or go by tour bus with at least 50 others. At Tatachia, you'll find *Tungpu Lodge (dōngpǔ shāng zhuāng)*, where you can spend the night. At least you can try – it tends to fill up fast with climbing parties, so if you don't get there early to claim your bed, you'll have to stake out a piece of real estate in the nearby forest. Nearby is Lulin Lodge *(lùlín shān zhuāng)*, but that one is reserved for government officials and other VIPs.

The usual goal of first day climbing parties is to reach *Paiyun Hostel (páiyún shān zhuāng)*, where you can spend the night for NT$150. Again, don't be surprised if you have to spend the night in your tent, or sleeping in the open if you don't have one. Standard Chinese climbing procedure is to depart Paiyun Hut in the middle of the night to reach the peak in time for the sunrise. During the busy season (school holidays) you may have to line up to stand on the summit. After the requisite photo session, most climbers head straight back to Tatachia and manage to return to Taipei by the evening.

There is an alternative route for the descent that leads to Tungpu *(dōngpǔ)* (see Tungpu section for more details). If you want to come down by way of Tungpu, be sure to get your mountain pass endorsed for it. If you take this route don't leave any luggage in Alishan as you won't be going back that way. My own opinion is that the Tungpu route is better – it's longer with a bigger elevation change, but far less crowded. You can also ascend this way, though it will be more work.

Hike to Fengshan or Shanlinhsi

There are two routes, one from Monkey Rock via Thousand People Cave and one from Tashan (Pagoda Mountain) via Shihmengku. The first route is more difficult, requiring 10 hours or more, while the second is easier (about six hours) but the trail is likely to be more crowded.

There is also a third option. If you take the trail from Monkey Rock, you come to a fork – one branch leads to Shanlinhsi. If you go this way, you bypass Fengshan entirely. All three options are good, so it's your choice. Having done all three, I personally prefer the

Alishan Hiking Region
阿里山健行區

Monkey Rock to Fengshan route even though it's not the easiest. No matter which route you pursue, the walk is almost entirely downhill – Alishan is 2190 metres, Shanlinhsi is 1600 metres, and Fengshan is 750 metres in elevation.

Monkey Rock Route You can start by either taking the train to the end of the line at Monkey Rock or walking. If you walk, start out early because it's at least a 10-hour walk from Monkey Rock to Fengshan, plus an additional two hours if you walk from

Alishan. Monkey Rock to Shanlinhsi is about eight hours.

Coming from Alishan, just off to the left of the tracks at Monkey Rock is a trail which drops steeply. If someone is around, ask them if this is the trail to Fengshan and Shanlinhsi since it's the same trail for the first few km. You go down, down and down. When you reach the bottom, turn right and walk along the dirt road. You eventually come to a signposted junction in the trail. The right fork goes to Shanlinhsi and Hsitou, the left fork goes to Fengshan. If you take the left fork you go downhill some more, eventually coming to Thousand People Cave (*qiān rén dòng*). This is a magnificent overhanging cave: it's so large that it can supposedly hold 1000 people, though I think they'd have to be rather thin to fit in there. The cave is frequently used by hikers as shelter from the rain.

Continuing along, the trail makes another steep descent, eventually leading to Tzuyueh Waterfall (*cíyùe pùbù*). When you reach the bottom of the falls, the path levels out and eventually becomes a dirt road. The obnoxious whine of motorcycles in the distance reminds you that civilisation is not far off. After crossing the bridge over the river, you come to some farm houses and several hostels where you can spend the night.

The only bad thing about this hike is the possibility of getting lost. The trail is quite well marked in Chinese characters, but that isn't much use if you can't read them. If you hang around Monkey Rock in the morning, especially on the weekends, it's likely that you'll meet some university students doing either the hike to Fengshan or the hike to Shanlinhsi. They will often be happy to have you join their group. However, you should be able to manage it yourself – just don't get off the main trail.

Tashan Route This is the more popular route, often crowded on weekends. Tashan is along the railroad tracks on the way to Monkey Rock. Again, you can take the train or walk on the tracks. You descend steeply from the tracks. The first major site you hit is Shihmengku (*shímènggǔ*, or Stone Dream Valley). Further down the trail is Hsienmengyuan (*xianmèngyuán*, or Fairy Dream Garden). The trail meets up with the route from Monkey Rock just before reaching Fengshan.

FENGSHAN

(*fēngshān*) 豐山

The scenery around Fengshan is superb and hiking is the main activity. In fact, you may have no other choice than to walk – there is currently no public bus service to Fengshan. The road is treacherous, but that has never

stopped the Taiwanese – tour buses do come up here on holidays and the quiet little village becomes a weekend carnival. The town is blissfully tranquil during the week and hasn't yet been ruined by commercialisation.

Hikes

To/from Alishan Most people walk from Alishan to Fengshan (downhill) rather than the other way. There are two routes – the shorter one is via Tashan, the longer is by way of Monkey Rock. See the Alishan section for details.

Around Fengshan About an hour east of town on the trail leading towards Alishan is Tzuyu Waterfall (*cíyù pùbù*). About two hours east of town on another trail (further south) is *shímènggǔ*, an area known for its interesting slick-rock formations. A one-hour walk north of town takes you to Shihpan Valley Waterfall (*shípángǔ pùbù*), a series of six small waterfalls.

You can easily hike five km to the Taiho Hostel and from there do several other walks (see Taiho Hostel Area).

To Tsaoling The bustling tourist resort of Tsaoling is perched on a neighbouring mountainside – it would be visible from Fengshan were it not for one hill blocking the view. I highly recommend doing this hike, and indeed you may have no other option given the lack of bus service to Fengshan. However, there is one major obstacle. Hiking to Tsaoling requires crossing the Alishan River, which is only feasible during the dry season from October to about March or April. It is very dangerous during the wet season, which begins around April and continues until September. The river becomes a raging torrent at times. Even during the dry season, the fast-moving water can sometimes be thigh deep if it has rained recently. A rope or bamboo pole can be useful. Never attempt it during or after a thunderstorm. The walk only takes about 2½ hours in good conditions, but longer if the water is deep.

I did it in October with no equipment

except for a bamboo pole. The fast-moving water was almost crotch deep and it was scary. I returned a month later and did the same walk – the water was only ankle deep. If you want to do it after a typhoon, bring an inflatable raft, a pair of oars, a life jacket, some prayer beads and incense. As the river meanders through a canyon, you have to cross it about five times. Start out early in the morning – if the river is impassable you can always just return to Fengshan. The locals usually know the condition of the river and can advise you if the walk is feasible.

The first two km of the hike involves walking down a footpath. When you reach a tea plantation, you have to drop down to the riverbed (see the Alishan Hiking Area map). As in many farming areas, there are some unfriendly dogs around the tea plantation – carrying a stick is advisable. The stick will come in handy anyway for fording the river. If you're a dedicated dog hater, you can avoid them completely by walking in the riverbed and bypassing the plantation. Walking in the riverbed is interesting, but slower and more difficult.

In Taiwan, nothing stays the same for long. Progress, if it can be called that, is about to come to Fengshan. A new bridge and highway is under construction which will connect Fengshan to Tsaoling. When this is completed, it will be possible to drive between the two resorts. No one could tell me just when this is scheduled to happen, but 1995 is more or less the target year. However, even when the bridge is opened, I still suggest walking the river route if it's not in flood stage. Not only is the scenery better on the river, but the road will climb, turn and zigzag through the hills, making it a more lengthy and difficult walk.

To Fenchihu or Juili If the route to Tsaoling is impassable due to flooding, you could walk from Fengshan to Fenchihu (*fēnqíhú*), about 30 km uphill on a narrow but paved road. Most would prefer walking the other direction (downhill). From Fenchihu you can catch the Alishan to Chiayi train. Hitching is possible but traffic is usually very light.

In the village of Taiho, the road forks and you can walk to Juili. This route is even further than a direct Fengshan-Fenchihu walk. See the Alishan Hiking Region map for details.

Places to Stay

There are five hotels in Fengshan with little to choose between them. However, the one I liked best was *Fengji Hotel* (☎ 2661363) (*fēngjí shān zhuāng*), where beautiful dorms go for NT\$150. Doubles/twins are NT\$800/1000 with private bath. The food is great – they grow it themselves.

Just down the road is *Fengye Hotel* (☎ 2661197, 2661606) (*fēngyè shān zhuāng*), which charges the same prices and is also friendly and comfortable.

There is also a small grocery store in town where you can buy instant noodles and other packaged sustenance.

Getting There & Away

After years of tottering on the brink of bankruptcy, the public bus service to Fengshan has collapsed. If you don't have your own vehicle, walking, hitching, signing up for a tour or renting a motorcycle in Chiayi are your options.

Things are about to change. Construction of the Fengshan-Tsaoling bridge should provide year-round access and might revive the bus service. Unfortunately, I can't tell you exactly when this is going to happen.

TAIHO HOSTEL AREA
(*tàihé shān zhuāng*) 太和山莊

Just five km from Fengshan, the small lodge called Taiho Mountain Hostel can easily be reached on foot from Fengshan in less than two hours. Don't confuse the Taiho Mountain Hostel with the village of Taiho, which is several km further up the road. There are some nice hikes near the hostel, in particular the climb up Big Buddha Mountain (*dàfóshān*). Anyone can point you towards the peak, which takes about three hours to climb.

Places to Stay

If you come here, you'll probably stay at the *Taiho Mountain Hostel* (☎ 2661222) *(tàihé shān zhuāng)*. It costs NT$150 for a tatami, NT$800 a double and NT$1200 a twin.

Unfortunately, there might be a problem – according to the neighbours, the hostel may be closing. I was told various stories about a death in the family, the owner being away and so on. If you want to be sure that a bed will be available when you arrive, it would be prudent to ring up the hostel first. Don't expect any English to be spoken.

FENCHIHU
(fènqǐhú) 奮起湖

Fenchihu is a small town between Alishan and Chiayi, in a scenic, heavily forested area 1400 metres above sea level. If you took the train to Alishan, you would have passed right through it. Although most tourists head directly to Alishan, Fenchihu has begun to attract some of the overflow crowds, especially on weekends when Alishan's hotels book out solid. Nevertheless, Fenchihu has got a long way to go before it becomes an international resort.

Actually, I don't think Fenchihu will ever challenge Alishan because it doesn't have any really special scenery. There are some nice hikes in the area and Fenchihu is pleasant, cool, forested and refreshing, but that's all. The brisk climate is a relief from the steamy plains below. City-weary residents from Taipei like to go there to relax and it's certainly a good place for that. However, those looking for spectacular vistas and steep hiking challenges should head directly for Tsaoling or Tungpu.

Apart from tourism, the other big industry in Fenchihu is horticulture. Greenhouses are everywhere and the owners won't object if you come in and have a look. Of course, they would be happier if you bought something.

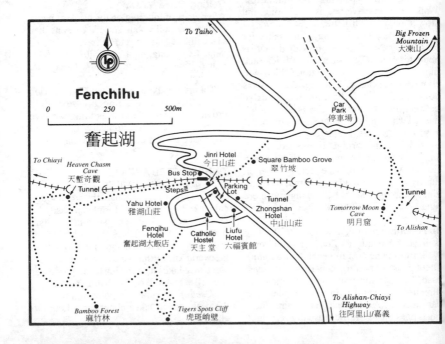

Prices are very reasonable, but unless you'll be living in Taiwan for a while, I can only recommend that you browse. Travelling around Asia with a potted bamboo tree may be aesthetically pleasing but isn't exactly convenient.

Big Frozen Mountain
(dàdòng shān) 大凍山

The Chinese certainly seem to like getting up at 4 am to climb a mountain and view the sunrise. If you are in Fenchihu on a weekend or holiday, you might as well get up with everyone else. The best view is from the summit of Big Frozen Mountain *(dàdòng shān)*, where everyone goes to greet the morning sun. It's a 500 metre increase in elevation from Fenchihu and about a two-hour walk one way from the hotel area. When there are lots of people some hotels run a minibus halfway up the mountain, so you only have a one-hour walk.

On a clear morning you can see Chiayi. Of course, some people (I won't mention any names) are satisfied with getting up later and admiring the sunrise from the window of their hotel room.

Other Hikes

If you want an easy hike, it's a short walk uphill from the railway station area to the bamboo grove *(cuì zhúpō)*. Here you can see some very rare 'square bamboo'. Look closely – the stems are almost perfectly square.

Among the locals, the hike that's most popular is to Heaven Sky Cave *(tiānqiàn qíguān)*, which is to the west (downhill) of Fenchihu. The hike takes about three hours for the round trip. The caves are small and they are definitely not suitable for claustrophobics. You've got to crawl through on your hands and knees and a torch is mandatory. But the walk leading down to the caves is nice, even if you decide not to crawl in.

The hike I like best is to Tomorrow Moon Cave *(míng yuè kū)* – not a true cave, but an overhanging rock formation. It's steep in parts but be very interesting to walk through. Other hiking destinations include the

Bamboo Forest *(màzhú lín)* and Tiger Spots Cliff *(hǔbān qiàobì)*.

Some hotels offer free, guided hiking tours of the area to all guests, but they require a group of at least 30 people. Most travellers will probably not be in Taiwan with 29 friends, but if you arrive on a weekend or holiday you can join any group of Chinese tourists. Of course, on weekends and holidays there is always the risk that all the hotels will be full.

Places to Stay

Prices are rising, but still haven't reached the ridiculous levels of Alishan. Fortunately, most places have tatami dormitories. Except on weekends, you can get into a dormitory by yourself without having to organise a big group.

Because there is usually someone around who can speak at least broken English, many foreigners prefer the *Catholic Hostel* *(tiānzhǔ jiào táng)* (☎ 2561035). Dormitories cost NT$150 and doubles are NT$800 on weekends.

The *Jinri Hotel* (☎ 2561034) *(jīnrì shān zhuāng)* is right next to the railway station and operates a good restaurant. Dormitories are NT$150, doubles/twins cost NT$800/ 1200. The same prices are charged at the very friendly *Yahu Hotel* (☎ 2561097) *(yǎhú shān zhuāng)*, but they offer a 20% discount on weekdays.

The *Zhongshan Hotel* (☎ 2561052) *(zhōngshān shān zhuāng)* is a clean-looking hotel with very friendly management. Doubles/twins are NT$800/1200. The nearby *Liufu Hotel* (☎ 2561776) *(liùfú bīnguǎn)* looks a bit shoddy on the outside but is OK inside. Doubles/twins are priced from NT$800/1200.

The most expensive place in town is the *Fenqihu Hotel* (☎ 2561888, fax 2561899) *(fènqǐhú dà fàndiàn)*. Doubles/triples are NT$1500/1800, twins are NT$2200.

Getting There & Away

Bus There are only two buses a day between Fenchihu and Chiayi. The 55-km trip takes at least one hour and costs NT$70 one way.

Buses depart Chiayi at 6.30 am and 3 pm. Buses depart Fenchihu for Chiayi at 8.30 am and 5.15 pm.

The Alishan to Chiayi bus does not pass through Fenchihu. If coming from Alishan by bus, you could get off at the rest stop at Shihcho *(shízhūo)* and then walk or hitch five km to Fenchihu.

Train If you're coming by train from Alishan, it's convenient to stop off in Fenchihu. All trains make this stop, even the 1st-class express. The fare between Alishan and Fenchihu is NT$148 in 1st class and NT$138 in 2nd class. From Chiayi to Fenchihu, the 1st-class fare is NT$225 and 2nd class is NT$209. See the train schedule in the Alishan section for arrival and departure times.

Motorcycle If you've rented a bike in Chiayi, Fenchihu makes a good staging area for trips to Fengshan and Juili.

JUILI
(ruìlǐ) 瑞里

Juili is a sleepy village consisting of just a few houses, an elementary school and some scattered hotels. Although the scenery isn't quite as spectacular as around Alishan, Juili is worth visiting as it has been barely touched by commercialism. There are pleasant hikes through bamboo forests, some nice waterfalls and a long, narrow cave to crawl through. Basically, it's a fine place for hiking and relaxing, so if you need a few days of pleasant, peaceful surroundings, come to Juili. It is possible to hike from Juili to Taiho, Fengshan, Tsaoling or Fenchihu.

Hikes

Among the things to see around Juili are the Cloud Pool Falls *(yúntán pùbù)* and Twin River Falls *(shuāngxī pùbù)*.

The Chinese say that a journey of 1000 miles begins with a single step. There are 1600 stone steps between Swallows Cliff *(yànzǐyái)* and the Juili Elementary School, as you'll clearly remember if you decide to walk this route. Not recommended for cardiac patients. The Swallows Cliff is an interesting overhanging rock formation – rather like a cave with one side missing.

Chinese hikers also like to visit the Magic Cave *(míhún gōng)*, but I didn't find it very interesting. It's a long narrow hole you can crawl through, with no stalactites or other formations inside – not really worth the trouble. However, the walk through the bamboo forest to get there is very pleasant.

As in Alishan, crowds of people get up before dawn to hike up a mountain in order to view the sunrise. Juili's sunrise viewing spot is Changshan. From there it's possible to hike to Fenchihu.

You can hike from Juili to Taiho along a paved road, and from there to Fengshan. It is possible to hitch but traffic is very light (on weekdays), mostly farmers on motorcycles. On weekends you won't be able to see the trees from the exhaust pipes. Hiking from Juili to Tsaoling is possible via Fengshan, but involves a dangerous river crossing. See the Fengshan section for details. In two days of heavy walking, you could reach Juili from Alishan.

Places to Stay

I especially enjoyed my stay at the *Ruolan Hotel* (☎ 2501210) (ruòlán shān zhuāng). The management is very friendly, the rooms are clean and the food is great. On weekends, dorm prices are NT$250 and doubles/twins are NT$600/1000. There is a 20% discount on weekdays. Breakfast costs NT$50, lunch and dinner NT$120. The Ruolan Hotel is not right on the main road, but you can get off the bus at the Chingye Hotel, from where you have to walk about 20 metres down a footpath. The hotel is perched on the steep side of a mountain.

Another place to consider is the *Chingye Hotel* (☎ 2501031) (qīngyè shān zhuāng), with dorm/doubles at NT$250/600.

Right near the Juili Elementary School is the *Meihua Hotel* (☎ 2501522, 2501222) *(méihuā shān zhuāng)*, where the dormitory costs NT$250 and doubles/twins are NT$1000/1200.

One of the newest hotels in the area is

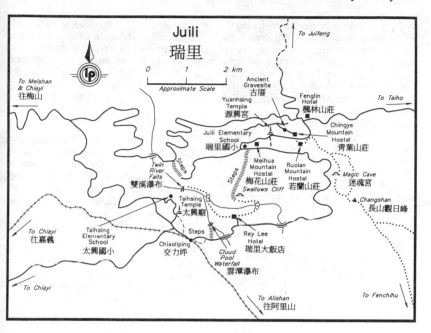

Juili
瑞里

To Juifeng

0   1   2 km
Approximate Scale

To Meishan
& Chiayi
往梅山

Ancient
Gravesite
古厝

Yuanhsing
Temple
源興宮

Fenglin
Hotel
楓林山莊

To Taiho

Juili Elementary
School
瑞里國小

Chingye
Mountain
Hostel
青葉山莊

Twin
River
Falls
雙溪瀑布

Steps

Meihua
Mountain
Hostel
梅花山莊

Ruolan
Mountain
Hostel
若蘭山莊

Magic Cave
迷魂宮

Steps
Swallows Cliff

Tahsing
Temple
太興廟

Changshan
長山觀日峰

To Chiayi
往嘉義

Tahsing
Elementary
School
太興國小

Steps

Chiaoliping
交力坪

Cloud
Pool
Waterfall
雲潭瀑布

Rey Lee
Hotel
瑞里大飯店

To Chiayi

To Alishan
往阿里山

To Fenchihu

Fenglin Hotel (☎ 2501095) *(fēnglín shān zhuāng)*. Doubles start at NT$1000.

The *Rey Lee Hotel* (☎ 2501310, fax 2501314) *(ruìlǐ dà fàndiàn)* is the largest, fanciest and most expensive hotel in town. It can be busy even on weekdays, and on weekends it's a real circus. The only real advantage over the competition is that it's much closer to the railway station, a factor to consider when you're carrying a heavy backpack. That makes no difference if you're talking the bus. Dormitories are NT$350, while doubles are NT$1200 and twins cost from NT$1600 to NT$2200.

Getting There & Away

You can get to Juili by bus, train or wild-chicken taxi. If you take the train you'll have to do some walking to reach any of the hotels – but walking is what Juili is all about. The buses can drop you off right next to your hotel.

Bus The Chiayi County Bus Company *(jiāyì xiàn gōngchē)*, which is right next to the railway station, runs a bus to Juili twice a day. The first is at 10.30 am, but this one only goes as far as the Rey Lee Hotel – if you want to stay elsewhere, you have to walk a few more km. The second bus departs Chiayi at 3.40 pm – it terminates at the tiny outpost of Juifeng but you can get off at any hotel in Juili. Since Juili is spread out over the mountainsides, it's wise to tell the driver which hotel you want to get off at. If you're not sure where you want to stay, get off at the Juili Elementary School *(ruìlǐ guóxiǎo)* and walk from there.

Going the other way, the bus collects passengers from the hotels at 6.30 am. There is also an afternoon bus at 1.30 pm from the Rey Lee Hotel only. The bus journey takes two hours and price depends on where you get off, but is under NT$100.

Train Juili is about halfway between Alishan

and Chiayi and can be reached by taking the Alishan train. You can get off the train in the tiny town of Chiaoliping *(jiāolìpíng)*. However, only one train a day (the local train) stops in Chiaoliping. The 1.30 pm train from Chiayi arrives in Chiaoliping at 3.04 pm. The 1.10 pm train from Alishan stops in Chiaoliping at 3.03 pm.

From Chiaoliping, get someone to point you in the right direction and walk on the paved trail that parallels the railway tracks. The path quickly cuts off to the left and drops downhill into the forest. A five-minute walk along the trail leads you to a road and after another 40 minutes of hiking you come to the first hotel, the Rey Lee Hotel *(ruìlǐ dà fàndiàn)*.

From this hotel, it takes over an hour to walk to the Juili Elementary School, which is the centre of central Juili. The fastest route is to take the trail that drops steeply down to the river and the Swallows Cliff, then uphill again. You have to climb 1600 stone steps if you take this route; exhausting but much shorter than the road.

Taxi From Chiayi, the wild chickens want NT$1500 and can carry up to four people for this price.

Walking It is possible to walk from Juili to Taiho, a distance of 18 km. Hitching is a possibility but traffic on this road is very light. From Taiho you can reach Fengshan, Tsaoling or Fenchihu.

Yunlin County 雲林縣

TOULIU
(dǒuliù) 斗六
Touliu is a small city north of Chiayi. Although the town itself is hardly a tourist attraction, it is an important transit point for travellers heading to Tsaoling, one of Taiwan's premier mountain resorts.

If you have an hour or two to spare in Touliu, there is a very interesting temple called Shanhsiu Temple *(shàn xiū gōng)*.

Locals also call it the Confucius Temple *(kǒngzǐ miào)*, though it's really not a true Confucian temple. Very few tourists go to this temple, but it's interesting architecturally. You can walk to the temple from the Touliu railway station.

Places to Stay
It's quite possible that you'll have to spend a night in Touliu, which is fortunate since it's cheap. The bottom of the market belongs to the *guìbīn dà lüshè* (☎ 5324188), 1 Chenpei Rd, where singles/doubles with private bath are NT$300/400. Despite the low price, rooms aren't bad at all.

Another good place with friendly management is the nearby *Shin Dou Hotel* (☎ 5323923) *(xīndū dà lüshè)*, 1 Chungshan Rd, where singles/doubles are NT$400/450.

Right at the corner of Chungshan Rd and Taiping Rd is the *Jincheng Hotel* (☎ 532 3954) *jīnchéng lüshè*, where singles/doubles cost NT$400/500.

Moving up in price, there is the *Hua Shih Hotel* (☎ 5324178) *(huáshì dà fàndiàn)* at 112 Tatung Rd. This place is very convenient for the bus terminal to Tsaoling. Doubles/twins cost NT$600/700.

The *Huacheng Hotel* (☎ 5324123) *(huáchéng dà fàndiàn)* at 160 Minsheng Rd is the most convenient for the railway station. Doubles/twins are NT$700/800.

For those who want to go luxury class, there is the *Fortune Hotel* (☎ 5341666) *(fúshén dà fàndiàn)*, where doubles/twins cost NT$1000/1600.

Places to Eat
Besides the usual collection of unnamed noodle and rice shops surrounding the railway station, there's *Chicken House*, Taiwan's answer to Kentucky Fried Chicken. It's on the circle near the Fortune Hotel.

If you can't tolerate imitations, there's a real *Kentucky Fried Chicken* at the intersection of Chungshan and Tatung Rds.

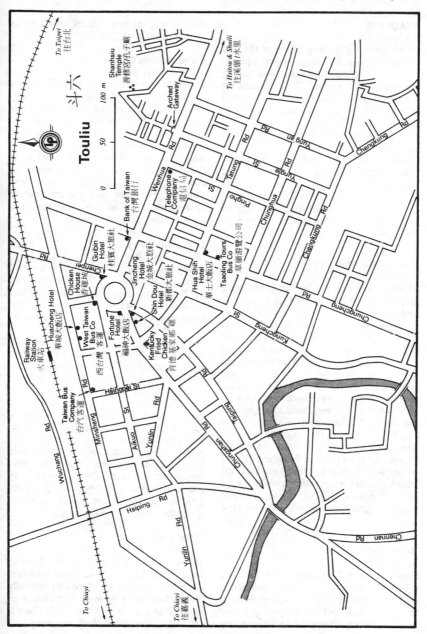

Touliu

100 m
50
0

To Taipei 往台北

To Hsitou & Shuili 往溪頭/水里

Shanhsiu Temple 善修宮孔子廟

Arched Gateway

Wenhua

Bank of Taiwan 台灣銀行

Telephone Company 電信局

Chenpei

Rd

Rd

Rd

Tatung St

Pingho

Chunghua

Yung an Rd

Chengkung Rd

Chenglung Rd

Chungcheng Rd

Guibin Hotel 佳賓大旅社

Jincheng Hotel 金城大旅社

Chicken House 香雞城

Shin Dou Hotel 新都大旅社

Hua Shih Hotel 華士大飯店

Tsaoling Tours Bus Co 草嶺遊覽公司

Fortune Hotel 福神大飯店

Kentucky Fried Chicken 肯德基炸雞

West Taiwan Bus Co 西台灣客運

Huacheng Hotel 華城大飯店

Railway Station 火車站

Taiwan Bus Company 台汽客運

Wuchang Rd

Minsheng St

Aikuo St

Yunlin Rd

Hsingpei St

Changshan Rd

Bunho Rd

Kungcheng St

Chungcheng Rd

Hsiping Rd

Yunlin Rd

Chennan Rd

To Chiayi 往嘉義

To Chiayi 往嘉義

TSAOLING

(cǎolǐng) 草嶺

In my opinion, Tsaoling is one of the best mountain resorts in Taiwan, at least equal to Alishan. Tsaoling offers as many hiking opportunities as Alishan. The mountains are not terribly high; Tsaoling is only about 800 metres above sea level, making it a good place to hike in winter while places like Alishan shiver. Nor is Tsaoling shrouded in the notorious 'Alishan fog'.

One of the nice things about Tsaoling is that it caters to both the windshield tourist who likes an organised bus tour as well as the rugged individualist who prefers to scramble up and down the mountains on foot. If you want a bus tour, it can be most easily arranged through the hotels.

Penglai Waterfall

(pénglái pùbù) 蓬萊瀑布

The road that runs by the Green Mountain Hotel leads to this waterfall. Ask anybody and they'll point you in the right direction. Walk several km down the road and you will eventually reach a cable car. The operator will certainly try to persuade you to take the cable car, which costs NT$50 one way and NT$100 for the round trip. However, there is a trail just to the left of the cable car; the hike isn't difficult and it costs nothing.

Either way, you will come to the base of the waterfall, where there is another cable car, this one goes to the top of the waterfall and is operated by a different owner. He charges the same prices as the other cable car owner. Again, there is a trail just to the left which goes to the top of the waterfall – it's a steep, 15-minute walk, so it's your choice. It is definitely worth going up there as the view is great.

Stone Wall

(shíbì) 石壁

From the top of Penglai Waterfall there is a hiking trail that goes several km upstream to the Stone Wall. It's not actually a wall, but a riverbed of slick-rock – as slippery as greasy noodles but very interesting. I walked on this

thing during the rain – thank goodness for my lug-soled boots.

Water Curtain Cave

(shuǐlián dòng) 水簾洞

To get to this cave from Tsaoling village, find the Rainbow Vacation Hotel *(cǎihóng dà fàndiàn)*, which is just below the main village area. Face the entrance of the hotel and just off to the left you'll see some stone steps which descend steeply. Follow these steps and you will soon reach a bee farm. Continue down and you will eventually come to a waterfall and cave called Water Curtain Cave. From there you can descend to the river. There are some huts there and people selling food and drinks.

Lost Soul Valley

(duàn hún gǔ) 斷魂谷

From Water Curtain Cave, there are two places you can go. The first place is called the Lost Soul Valley. As the name implies, it's a little hard to find. To reach it, cross the small stream and head downstream along the river. On your right you'll find a road heading uphill. You walk uphill some way until the road forks. The left (lower) fork leads to Lost Soul Valley. A bunch of food vendors have set up stalls near the base of the Spring-Autumn Cliffs. Besides the cliffs, there are some small waterfalls and hiking trails. There is some quicksand near one of the waterfalls, so watch out for it. The quicksand swallowed one of my friend's shoes – perhaps they should call this Lost Sole Valley. Avoid this area during the rainy season (summer) as the cliffs are unstable. In one tragic incident in 1986, over 20 hikers were buried alive by a mudslide. However, it's perfectly safe in the dry season.

Great Steep Wall

(chào bì xióng fēng) 峭壁雄風

The second place is easy to find. Starting from Water Curtain Cave, head upstream along the river. On your left you'll eventually find a place where there are some ropes set up to climb the big rock face. This place is called the Great Steep Wall. It's pretty safe

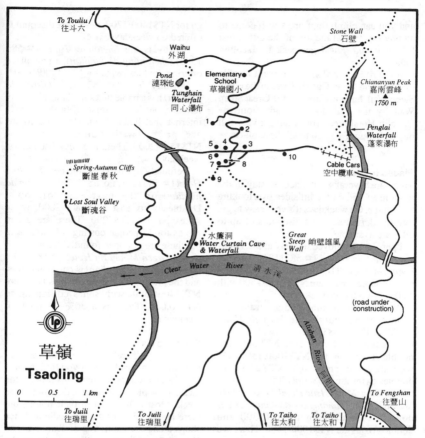

1 Venus Motel
愛之旅飯店

2 Tsaoling Mountain Hostel
草嶺山莊

3 Green Mountain Hotel
高山青大飯店

4 Holiday Inn
假期大飯店

5 Sing Ming Hsiu Hotel
新明修大飯店

6 Tsaoling Hotel
草嶺大飯店

7 Rainbow Vacation Hotel
踩虹大飯店

8 Yunglih & Shennung hotels
永利賓館/神農賓館

9 Bee Farm
蜂房

10 Shiuling Hotel
秀嶺大飯店

and you can climb right up. You'll come to an obvious trail at the top of the cliffs; just follow it and you'll get back to Tsaoling village.

If the river is in flood, you won't be able to walk from Water Curtain Cave to the Great Steep Wall, but you can reach the Great Steep Wall by the trail that descends from the Yunglih Hotel area. You'll have a very full day of hiking if you go to all these places.

Places to Stay

There are several good places to stay in the town itself and on the hillsides overlooking the village. On weekdays it's very easy to get into the dormitories and discounts of up to 30% are available.

I personally enjoyed my stay at the *Tsaoling Mountain Hostel* (☎ 5831121) (*cǎolǐng shān zhuāng*). The dorms cost NT$200, while doubles/twins are NT$1000/1500 with a 20% discount on weekdays.

Another place that budget travellers should check out is the *Yunglih Hotel* (☎ 5831012, fax 5831438) (*yǒnglì bīnguǎn*). On weekends, dorms cost NT$300 and doubles/twins go for NT$1000/1500. On weekdays, dorms cost NT$200 and doubles/twins are NT$800/1200.

The *Sing Ming Hsiu Hotel* (☎ 5831116, fax 5831322) (*xīnmíngxiū dà fàndiàn*) has dorm accommodation for NT$300 and doubles/twins are NT$1000/1500. There is a 30% discount on weekdays.

The *Venus Motel* (☎ 5831153, fax 5831306) (*aìzǐlü fàndiàn*) costs NT$1000 for a double. The location way up on a hill means it's quiet, but it's a long walk to anywhere unless you have your own set of wheels.

The *Tsaoling Hotel* (☎ 5831228) (*cǎolǐng dà fàndiàn*) costs NT$1000/1500 for doubles/twins. Suites cost NT$2000 to NT$3000. The dorms are not normally open to individuals, but you may talk your way in. It's NT$200 per person for eight persons.

The *Rainbow Vacation Hotel* (☎ 583 1218) (*cǎihóng dà fàndiàn*) is relatively expensive for what you get. Doubles/twins go for NT$1400/1700, but a 30% discount is offered on weekdays.

Nearby is the *Shennung Hotel* (☎ 583 1385) (*shén nóng dà fàndiàn*), a new place offering doubles/twins for NT$1200/1600.

Holiday Inn (☎ 5831389) (*jiàqí dà fàndiàn*) has a name that sounds suspiciously familiar, but it's no relation to the famous international hotel chain. However, rooms are pricey with doubles/twins for NT$1500/2000. There is a 50% discount on weekdays.

Definitely up-market is the new *Shiuling Hotel* (☎ 5831211, fax 5831226) (*xiùlǐng dà fàndiàn*) on the east edge of town. Doubles/twins cost NT$1800/2800, while suites go for NT$3200. There are group rooms for 15 people costing NT$300 each, but these are not open to individuals.

The *Green Mountain Hotel* (☎ 5831201) (*gāoshānqīng dà fàndiàn*) is rated four stars, and the prices reflect this. Doubles/twins are NT$1400/1500, with suites costing up to NT$10,000. There is a 30% discount on weekdays.

Places to Eat

Surprisingly, there's not the assortment of restaurants in Tsaoling that you find in most of Taiwan's resorts. Perhaps this reflects the fact that the place is dead five days out of the week. Most tourists eat in their hotels, but there are a couple of small noodle and rice shops along the main drag of Tsaoling. The *Yunglih Hotel* has a small restaurant on the 1st floor that's open to anyone who walks in, and the food is good. A few small grocery stores scattered around town can supply you with snacks.

Getting There & Away

The easiest and most direct way to get to Tsaoling is from the small city of Touliu (*dǒuliù*), which is just north of Chiayi. There are plenty of buses and trains operating between Touliu and Chiayi.

There is only one small private bus company that makes the journey to Tsaoling. It serves as a good example of how Taiwan's car revolution has crippled bus service – a few years ago there were six buses daily to Tsaoling but now there are only two. The one-way fare is NT$120. The buses are run by Tsaoling Tours Bus Company (☎ 532 2388, 5326788) (*cǎolǐng yóulǎn gōngsī*), 47 Chungcheng Rd. Buses leave Touliu for Tsaoling at 8.30 am and 4 pm; they leave Tsaoling for Touliu at 6.30 am and 2 pm. An extra bus is put on during weekends and holidays.

As already mentioned, you can hike from Alishan to Fengshan and then to Tsaoling. The last leg of the journey follows the Alishan River, and is beautiful but impossible during most of the wet season. When the new bridge to Fengshan is finished, this will no longer be an issue.

Nantou County 南投縣

HSITOU
(xītóu) 溪頭

Hsitou – commonly misspelled 'Chitou' or 'Shitou' – is a beautiful mountain park and forest reserve south of the Sun Moon Lake area. At an elevation of 1150 metres, the climate is perfect most of the year.

Like Sun Moon Lake, it's a prime spot for honeymooners. In Taiwan, couples on their honeymoon often dress very formally: the groom in a dark suit and tie, and the bride in a *qípáo*, a Chinese slit dress. Where else in the world can you see hikers dressed in a tuxedo, or in a slit dress, high heels and make-up? Of course you will also see plenty of young people in less formal attire. It's a zoo on weekends or holidays – seems like half the population of Taipei suddenly descends on Hsitou like vultures on a carcass.

The forest reserve was originally established by the Japanese during their occupation of Taiwan. It is now run by the Forestry Department of National Taiwan University, in Taipei. Reforestation has been a major project, and a highly successful one at that. Unfortunately, the Forestry Department has been less successful at dissuading the central government from continuing with massive road building and hotel development projects in the mountains.

For tourists, the main attraction of the forest reserve is the opportunity to stroll through the thick groves of fir trees and bamboo. One of the great things about Hsitou is that it has a gate across the entrance which keeps most (but not all) cars and motorcycles out. However, you won't be disturbed by vehicles once you get onto the numerous hiking paths. Admission to the forest reserve costs NT$80.

From Hsitou, you can hike up to Fenghuangshan, a mountain two km to the north-east. At 1697 metres it's not extremely high, but the view is good.

On the way up to Hsitou the bus passes through Luku *(lùgǔ)*, Taiwan's prime tea-growing region. If you have a window seat you'll get good views of the tea plantations. Just above the plantations are fantastic bamboo forests.

Whatever you do, bring toilet paper. The tourist shops sell wind-up panda bears, plastic BB guns and firecrackers but mundane items like toilet paper are nowhere to be found. As I discovered in a moment of desperate need, it's the little things in life that are most important. In an emergency, I suppose you could use leaves, but watch out for the stinging nettles.

Places to Stay

The main advantage of staying in the park is that there are fewer vehicles. This is also where you can find cheap dormitory accommodation. Just remember that if you go outside of the park, you'll have to pay another admission fee to get back in.

Camping is the cheapest option, and indeed, might be your only option during a weekend or holiday. You have to bring your own tent, and the camping fee is a pretty ridiculous NT$250. The camping area is outside the park and you will have to pay the NT$80 admission fee each time you go in.

There are only two hotels outside the park gate. One is the *Mingshan Hotel* (☎ 612121) *(míngshān biéguǎn)*. The 12-person dorm

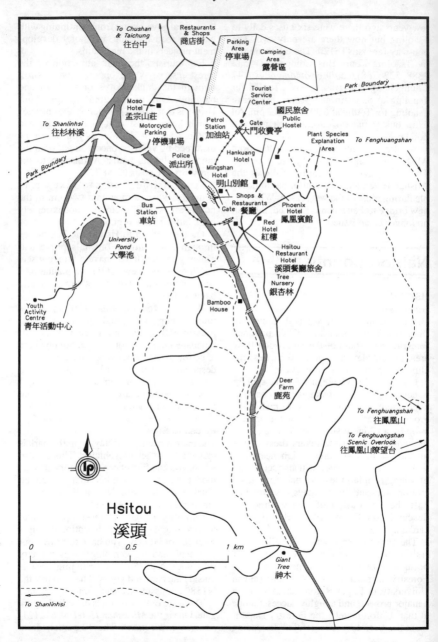

To Chushan & Taichung 往台中

Restaurants & Shops 商店街

Parking Area 停車場

Camping Area 露營區

Park Boundary

Tourist Service Center 國民旅舍

Moso Hotel 孟宗山莊

To Shanlinhsi 往杉林溪

Motorcycle Parking 停機車場

Petrol Station 加油站

Gate 大門收費亭

Public Hostel

Plant Species Explanation Area

To Fenghuangshan

Park Boundary

Police 派出所

Hankuang Hotel

Mingshan Hotel 明山別館

Bus Station 車站

Shops & Restaurants Gate 餐廳

Phoenix Hotel 鳳凰賓館

University Pond 大學池

Red Hotel 紅樓

Hsitou Restaurant Hotel 溪頭餐廳旅舍

Tree Nursery 銀杏林

Youth Activity Centre 青年活動中心

Bamboo House

Deer Farm 鹿苑

To Fenghuangshan 往鳳凰山

To Fenghuangshan Scenic Overlook 往鳳凰山瞭望台

Hsitou
溪頭

0   0.5   1 km

Giant Tree 神木

To Shanlinhsi

costs only NT$150 per person, but individual travellers *cannot* get in. Double rooms start at NT$600, but during summer accommodation is tight and you'll probably be forced up-market into a room costing NT$1100 or more.

Also outside the gate, near the petrol station, is the *Moso Hotel* (☎ 612131, fax 612130) *(mèngzōng shān zhuāng)*. This is a classy place with twins starting at NT$1500.

Budget travellers should aim for the *Youth Activity Centre* (☎ 049-612161, fax 612322) *(huódòng zhōngxīn)*, where it costs NT$180 to stay in the dormitory. Getting in without reservations is close to impossible except in the dead of winter (excluding Chinese New Year). This place is inside the park gate and you'll have to walk about one km to reach it.

Everything else inside the park gate falls under the administration of the National Taiwan University Forestry Department. The *Hsitou Restaurant Hotel* (☎ 612111, fax 612106) *(xītóu cāntīng lüshè)* is where you should stop to find out about everything inside the forest reserve – they book the rooms. Coming from the bus stop, it's immediately to your left as you go through the gate. Their line-up of hotels includes the following:

Red Hotel
    (hóng lóu) three to five persons, NT$2500
Phoenix Hotel
    (fènghuáng bīnguǎn) twins NT$900 to NT$1300
Hankuang Hotel
    (hànguāng lóu) twins NT$1300
Public Hostel
    (guómín lüshè) twins NT$1500 to NT$1800
The Villas
    (biéshù), two to eight persons NT$1300 to NT$4500

The *Taiwan University Forestry Dormitory (táidà shíyànlín xuéshēng sùshè)* is meant primarily for the use of the forestry students from National Taiwan University. It's attached to the Red Hotel. However, they have been known to allow travellers to stay there, provided you can ingratiate yourself with the staff and they want to practise their English. Dormitory accommodation costs

NT$250. Once again, inquire at the Hsitou Restaurant Hotel and be on your best behaviour – they don't have to accept you, and probably won't.

Places to Eat

Unless you're eating in the hotel you're staying at, the only choice is a row of shops just outside the entrance gate near the bus station. The prices are a little high because you're paying for the pine trees and fresh air.

Getting There & Away

The most frequent, direct buses are from Taichung, departing from the southbound-bus terminal behind the railway station. The trip takes two hours and the fare is NT$127. The bus is actually marked Shanlinhsi in Chinese, but it stops in Hsitou first before continuing up the mountain.

If you are coming from south Taiwan, you can get a bus directly from Chiayi (NT$137) or Touliu (NT$78) to Hsitou. No matter where you're coming from, you can always get a bus to Chushan *(zhúshān)* at the base of the mountain, and then a bus from Chushan up to Hsitou. Chushan to Hsitou costs NT$45.

From Sun Moon Lake, it's a little more complicated. You have to take a bus to Shuili, then a bus to Chushan *(zhúshān)* and then another bus to Hsitou. You can easily get a bus from Sun Moon Lake to Shuili, but it terminates at the bus terminal of the Taiwan Bus Company *(táiqì kèyùn)*. To reach Chushan, you have to get a bus from the terminal of the Yuanlin Bus Company *(yuánlín kèyùn)*. See the Shuili map for details.

SHANLINHSI
(shānlínxī) 杉林溪

Hsitou actually has two sections: the forest reserve area, which is called Hsitou, and the Shanlinhsi area, some 20 km away and considerably higher at 1600 metres elevation. If you go to Hsitou also try to make it to Shanlinhsi, as it offers different scenery, some beautiful waterfalls and a cooler climate. There are plenty of hiking trails in Shanlinhsi and you can even hike to Alishan.

Brochures and advertisements for Shanlinhsi call it 'Sun Link Sea', a silly attempt to substitute an English rhyme for the Chinese words. If you ask anybody how to get to 'Sun Link Sea' they won't have the faintest idea of what you're talking about, so use the Chinese.

Entrance to Shanlinhsi costs NT$150. This high price hasn't kept down the crowds – it looks like a tourist convention on summer weekends, but in winter you may have the opposite problem, as everything closes down and food is scarce.

Hike to Alishan

People often hike from Shanlinhsi to Alishan or from Alishan to Shanlinhsi. From Shanlinhsi to Alishan it's uphill, so of course it's easier to begin the hike from Alishan. It's a long, 27-km walk that takes a full day, so start at dawn.

The beginning of the trail at Shanlinhsi is not very obvious, so ask people and check the map of Shanlinhsi in this book. You have to walk up an unpaved forestry road first, then climb a steep embankment and you will find yourself on the trail. The trail is marked with a sign in Chinese pointing to Alishan. After eight hours of walking you reach the railway tracks at Monkey Rock and then it's another eight km on foot along these tracks through many tunnels and over numerous bridges to Alishan. A torch is needed for the tunnels. (Also refer to the Train Ride to Monkey Rock entry in the Alishan section earlier in this chapter.)

Places to Stay

Considering how much they are raking in from the admission fee, accommodation ought to be free. Unfortunately, that isn't the case. The *Sun Link Sea Hotel* (☎ 612211, fax 612216) *(shānlínxī dà fàndiàn)* is really a complex of hotels (over 600 rooms in total!) spread around the Shanlinhsi area. All are near the bus terminal. If you can get into the dormitories, they cost NT$150 for a 10 person room, but you'll probably have to bring nine friends along or round up some Chinese students on the bus. Doubles are NT$1100 to NT$1600, twins NT$1500 to NT$1600.

The best deal in Shanlinhsi is the camping ground *(lùyíng qū)*, where you can set up your tent free of charge. How much longer it remains free is subject to speculation.

Getting There & Away

The transport details are the same as for Hsitou. All buses going to Hsitou continue on to Shanlinhsi. There are buses connecting

To Hsitou
往溪頭

Toll Gate
大門收費亭

Green Dragon
Waterfall
青龍瀑布

Tourist
Village
聚英村

Bus
Station
車站

To Forest
Park
往森林公園

Shanlinhsi
Hotel
杉林溪大飯店

Villas
別墅區

Camping
Area 露營區

Yen An
Waterfall
燕庵瀑布

杉林溪
Shanlinhsi

0   0.5   1 km

Beginning
of trail

To Alishan
往阿里山

Sunglungyen
Waterfall
松瀧岩瀑布

Hsitou and Shanlinhsi every 30 minutes. The last bus down is at 4.30 pm. Wild-chicken taxis are also readily available.

FENGHUANG VALLEY BIRD PARK
(fènghuáng gǔ niǎoyuán) 鳳凰谷鳥園

Fenghuang Valley has an aviary (☎ 753100) which you can enter and watch some 280 species of birds fly around. It's nice, but touristy – not so great that you'll want to go out of your way to go there unless you're a dedicated bird-watcher.

Admission to the bird park is NT$100 and it's open from 7 am to 5 pm daily.

If you want to see Fenghuang Valley, you can get a bus from Chushan *(zhúshān)*, a large town at the base of the mountain below Hsitou. If you're already in Hsitou, you have to go back down to Chushan and then get a bus back up to Fenghuang. There are a few buses direct from Taichung.

Finding your way is easy if you're driving your own car or motorcycle, because there are many English signs pointing the way – apparently the Tourism Bureau is heavily promoting the place. Don't confuse Fenghuang Valley with Fenghuangshan. Fenghuangshan is a mountain next to Hsitou and is approached by a slightly different route.

SHUILI
(shuǐlǐ) 水里

Shuili is not a tourist attraction – it's an essential transit point at the south end of Sun Moon Lake. If you are travelling between Sun Moon Lake and Tungpu or Hsitou, you must go through Shuili. Cheap accommodation options make it a good place to spend the night.

You can obtain a map of nearby Yushan National Park from the park headquarters at 112 Minsheng Rd (☎ 773121).

Places to Stay
There are many hotels clustered around the railway station, though most have signs only in Chinese. Cheapest in town is the *Huantai Hotel* (☎ 772137) *(huántài dà lüshe)*, 83 Minchuan Rd. Doubles with electric fan are

NT$300, while air-con pushes the tariff to NT$500. Rooms are comfortable and clean, and all have attached bath.

An economical and reasonably clean hotel is *Yazhou Hotel* (☎ 772151) *(yǎzhōu dà lüshè)*, 266 Minchuan Rd. A double room is NT$500. For the same price, you can stay at the *Apollo Hotel* (☎ 772110) *(hóngbīn dà lüshe)*, 140 Minsheng Rd.

Getting There & Away
Bus Some confusion is caused by the fact that there are two bus terminals in Shuili. The

Yuanlin Bus Company (☎ 770041) *(yuánlín kèyùn)* faces the railway station, and this is the one offering buses to Tungpu, Chushan and Ershui. The other bus terminal belongs to the Taiwan Bus Company (770054) *(táiqì kèyùn)*, and this is where you catch buses to Sun Moon Lake. Buses from Taichung to Shuili cost NT$110.

To reach Shuili from major cities in south Taiwan (like Chiayi), first take a train to either Touliu *(dǒuliù)* or Ershui *(èrshuǐ)*. Ershui is closer and I recommend doing it that way. From both Ershui and Touliu there are buses to Shuili.

Train There is a very interesting small train that runs between Ershui and Shuili. The bus is sometimes faster, but the train is definitely more fun.

It's important to know that Shuili is not the last stop, but trains continue for another four minutes to a railway depot called Chechung – be sure you get off in Shuili. Going the other way, most trains from Shuili terminate in Ershui but a few continue on to Taichung.

TUNGPU
(dōngpǔ) 東埔

For me, Tungpu is it – the best mountain resort in Taiwan, even better than Alishan and Tsaoling. At 1120 metres above sea level the climate is just perfect. The area is mountainous, with abundant waterfalls and hot springs.

If you love hiking, Tungpu is a treat: the scenery could hardly be more spectacular. Tungpu even has a 'back door' route for climbing Yushan, Taiwan's highest peak. There is little else to do in Tungpu but hike all day and soak those tired muscles at night in the hot springs. If this appeals to you, then visit Tungpu. If you're not a hiker, you might as well skip Tungpu because there is no place for riding around in a car or tour bus. All the scenic attractions are outside the village and must be reached by walking on some fairly steep trails. My great fear is that this will change – let us only hope that no evil genius at the Chamber of Commerce decides to build a 'scenic freeway' to the summit of Yushan.

Tungpu is also not a place for people who fear heights, as many of the trails offer breathtaking, panoramic views from the edges of sheer cliffs. That said, try not to miss Tungpu. It's one of the most challenging hiking spots in Taiwan.

Rainbow Waterfall
(cǎihóng pùbù) 彩虹瀑布

If you want to take a short walk on your first day, you can hike up to Rainbow Waterfall. The path is easy to find. Just walk up the main street of Tungpu, going uphill, and when you reach the Shenghua Hotel take the trail to the left. The way is obvious – rubbish left by hikers marks the route. The walk up to the falls takes about 30 minutes; 20 minutes to come back down.

Take a nice soak in the hot springs and get

Train Schedule Ershui/Shuili *

Ershui to Shuili

Depart	Arrive
5.31 am	6.10 am
7.45 am	8.24 am
10.04 am	10.43 am
12.04 pm	12.43 pm
1.33 pm	2.12 pm
3.49 pm	4.28 pm
5.33 pm	6.12 pm
7.36 pm	8.15 pm
9.37 pm	10.16 pm

Shuili to Ershui

Depart	Arrive
6.21 am	7.23 am
8.52 am	9.30 am
10.54 am	11.34 am
12.54 pm	1.31 pm
2.23 pm	3.01 pm
4.40 pm	5.20 pm
6.23 pm	7.01 pm
8.26 pm	9.03 pm
10.27 pm	11.05 pm

* Schedule subject to change

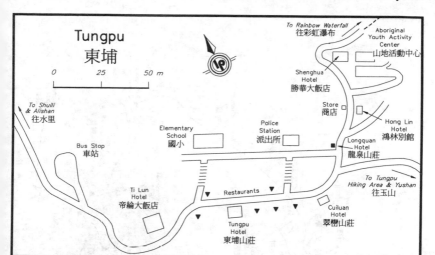

a good rest for the next day's hike, because it's a long, uphill trail.

The Route to Yushan

You can't get to Yushan in one day, and indeed, you would need a special permit if you want to (legally) reach the summit. However, you can hike along the Yushan trail as far as Patungkuan without a permit and even camp out along the way (see the Yushan Hiking Region map in the Around Alishan section).

Starting from Tungpu, take the dirt road that drops slightly downhill and winds around the mountain. Before long you will come to a path on the left that goes steeply uphill. The path is well marked and has a sign in Chinese characters. If you miss the path, you'll soon come to a village, in which case you have come too far. Following the path uphill, you'll reach Father & Son Cliff *(fùzǐ duànyaí)*. The path looks unstable and is not for the chicken-hearted. I predict that at some point in the future, this part of the trail will collapse and it will be necessary to carve a new route. Don't linger here too long, in case it decides to collapse while you're standing on it.

Continuing past Father & Son Cliff, you'll eventually reach a fork in the trail. The right trail drops steeply downhill to the river below and is well marked with a large sign in Chinese, which is an advertisement. This track leads to Happy Happy Hot Springs *(lè lè wēnquán)*. Although it's a beautiful place, I can't recommend that you go there – it has been commercialised in rather poor taste. If you do go, you will find a small cable car operated by an electric winch for crossing the river. There is a sign telling you to help yourself. You get in the cable car, push a button and before long you're on the other side of the river. Just as you step out, somebody jumps out of the bushes and demands NT$100 per person for crossing the river.

If that doesn't make you Happy Happy, continue down the trail and you'll find a restaurant. The food is OK but the prices are double those in Tungpu. There is also a hotel charging NT$600 per person for a basic tatami. Just across the river, via another cable car, are the hot springs. They are beautiful, with many natural rock formations. To help you enjoy the scenery, the management has spray-painted cute names in Chinese characters right next to each formation. Some of the

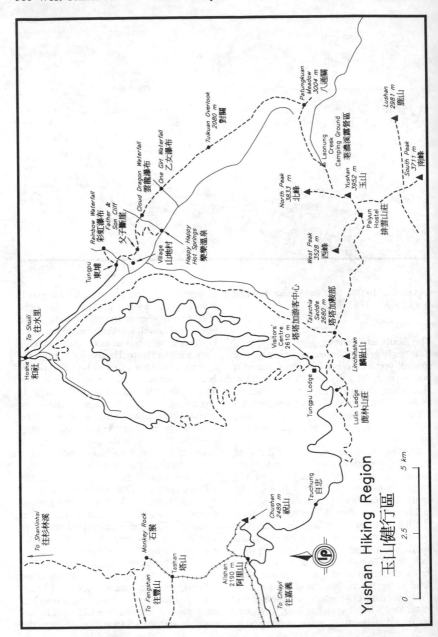

Yushan Hiking Region 玉山健行區

rock formations look like they've been modified to make them more exotic.

If you decide to bypass Happy Happy, take the left fork of the trail going uphill and you'll reach Cloud Dragon Waterfall *(yúnlóng pùbù)*. Further on is One Girl Waterfall *(yī nü pùbù)*.

You can continue up the trail as far as Twin Pass *(duì guān)* at 2080 metres elevation. It's unlikely that you'll be able to go much further in one day and still have time to return to Tungpu. The return is along the same route and when you reach Tungpu you can soak those tired muscles in the hot springs before falling into an exhausted and satisfied sleep. Happy Happy.

If you want to continue along the trail it leads to High View Picnic Area, and then on to Patungkuan *(bātōngguān)*, a lush, green alpine meadow at 3000 metres altitude. There is a mountain hut here, but it's dirty and basic and has no water – fill up your water bottle at a stream 15-minutes walk before you reach the hut. You'll need a sleeping bag, and if the hut is filled by other climbing parties you may wish you had a tent too.

From Patungkuan, you could reach the summit of Yushan, Taiwan's tallest peak. However, if you plan to go higher than Patungkuan you need a class A mountain pass. It is possible to sneak in, and some people try it because this back route is not so heavily patrolled as the main route from Alishan. However, if you run into the Yushan National Park Police, don't say I sent you. There's a steep fine if you get caught without a pass.

Alternatively, you could take the easier route and climb Yushan from Alishan, then descend through Patungkuan and wind up in Tungpu. It's an exciting trip, but any such expedition is for experienced hikers only, with a mountain pass and the necessary equipment such as a heavy-duty wet weather gear and sleeping bag.

Climbing Yushan by way of Tungpu would take three days. Climbing from Alishan and back the same way could be done in two days.

Places to Stay

The *Aboriginal Youth Activity Centre* (☎ 701515) *(shāndì huódòng zhōngxīn)* has dormitory accommodation for NT$100 and doubles for NT$700 to NT$900. It's at the high end of town, a short but steep uphill walk. The baths use hot-spring water, a real treat.

The *Hong Lin Hotel* (☎ 701569, 791326) *(hónglín biéguǎn)* is excellent value (on weekdays at least). Doubles are NT$500 in a beautiful wooden room, a pleasant break from the usual concrete-box architecture of youth hostels. The management is friendly.

A reasonable deal for budget accommodation is *Cuiluan Hotel* (☎ 701818) *(cuìluán shān zhuāng)*, with doubles at NT$500 without bath. Actually, if you don't mind sharing your bed, you can squeeze four people in here for the same price, making it the cheapest place in town. Doubles with private bath cost NT$800.

Longquan Hotel (☎ 701061, 701587) *(lóngquán shān zhuāng)*, is clean and pleasant. Doubles cost NT$700 on weekdays and NT$1000 on weekends.

Tungpu Hotel (☎ 701090) *(dōngpǔ shān zhuāng)* gets a lot of praise from travellers, but at NT$1000/1320 for doubles on weekdays/weekends, it's not a budget hotel.

Right next to the Aboriginal Youth Activity Centre is the *Shenghua Hotel* (☎ 701511) *(shènghuá dà fàndiàn)*, where doubles cost NT$1300 to NT$1400.

The fanciest place in town is at the lower end of the village near the bus stop, the *Ti Lun Hotel* (☎ 701616) *(dìlún dà fàndiàn)*, where doubles are NT$1400 on weekdays and NT$1800 on weekends.

Places to Eat

A lot of people eat in their hotels, which is fine except that you usually have to order the meal at least a few hours in advance and be there when it is served. If you'd rather just eat when you feel like it, there are several little restaurants at the lower end of town near the Ti Lun Hotel.

The cheapest way to eat dinner is to buy instant noodles (styrofoam bowl included) from one of the grocery stores in town. You'll need chopsticks and a spoon. Most hotels have drinking fountains that supply boiling water as well as cold.

Getting There & Away

You can take a bus directly from the town of Shuili (south of Sun Moon Lake) to Tungpu. There are two bus companies with separate terminals in Shuili, so make sure you get the right one. The bus terminal you want is operated by the Yuanlin Bus Company (☎ 77 0041) (yuánlín kèyùn). There are seven buses a day on weekdays and 10 a day on weekends and holidays.

The first bus departs Shuili at 7 am and the last bus at 5 pm. I won't give the schedule, as it changes often. The trip takes about 1½ hours going uphill, and one hour coming down.

Before you get to Tungpu, you must first get to Shuili. If you are coming from Sun Moon Lake, that's easy enough: just take a bus directly to Shuili, which takes about 30 minutes. The bus will drop you off at the Taiwan Bus Company terminal – walk over to the Yuanlin Bus Company terminal. If you're coming from Hsitou, first go to the bottom of the mountain by taking a bus to Chushan (zhúshān), and then a bus to Shuili. If you're coming from either north or south Taiwan, take the train to (èrshuǐ), then the bus or shuttle train to Shuili.

For a while, there was a bus service between Alishan and Shuili, via Tungpu. Now it appears that this service has been withdrawn, yet another victim of the car revolution. According to the old schedule, buses departed Alishan at 2.30 pm for Shuili and Tungpu. Perhaps it will be come back into existence some day (wishful thinking).

SUN MOON LAKE

(rì yuè tán) 日月潭

Sun Moon Lake is one of Taiwan's busiest resort areas, attracting a large number of honeymooners and domestic tourists. It's popular for a good reason. It's easily Taiwan's most beautiful lake – the clear, sparkling blue waters set against the magnif-icent mountain backdrop is a wonderful sight to behold. The elevation is 760 metres, giving the area a pleasant climate most of the year. Naturally, it's best to visit during weekdays to avoid the large crowds that regularly descend on the place. Even on weekdays expect to see many tour buses, often carrying groups of visiting dignitaries, overseas Chinese and tourists from Japan and elsewhere. There are many things to see around the lake and it takes at least a full day to have a good look at this place.

Sun Moon Lake is a natural lake, but during the Japanese occupation a dam was built to raise the lake's level and generate hydroelectric power. At that time, the electric power generated was sufficient to supply all of Taiwan's needs. This dam still generates power, but with the island's heavily industrialised economy and rising standard of living, hydroelectricity can now supply only a fraction of the total demand. Today Taiwan depends on nuclear power and coal-fired plants for most of the island's electricity.

Water Sports

The locals say the lake has piranhas! I have my doubts, though I concede it's possible. I haven't heard of anyone being eaten lately, so you can probably relax.

There isn't any real swimming beach – indeed, swimming is officially prohibited except for one day of the year, when thousands flock to Sun Moon Lake to participate in a mass swim. There are numerous places where you can rent a rowing boat or canoe and no one is likely to stop you from diving overboard, especially if you do it at night. Some of the Taiwanese tourists have even taken to skinny dipping at night – a cultural (not to mention legal) taboo. I guess it's just another sign of Taiwan's modernisation.

You can row out to Kuanghua Island (guānghuá dǎo) in the middle of the lake. If rowing is too much exercise for you, there are motorised boats for rents, and the latest innovation is yachts. There are also opportunities for water-skiing at the Asia Country Club.

Most of the boat trips originate on the south shore of the lake. Two likely places to find boats for rent are at the pier near Tehuashe and the Hsuankuang Temple.

Fishing in the lake is permitted and is very popular with the locals.

Peacock Garden
(kǒngquè yuán) 孔雀園
This is the most touristy thing to see at the lake. If you want to pursue your fine-feathered friends with a camera lens, the Peacock Garden is on the north-east shore of the lake.

Temples & Pagoda
Wenwu Temple *(wénwǔ miào)* is a large and beautiful structure very close to the Chinatrust Hotel. Be sure to check out the temple shop for scroll paintings and other arts & crafts.

Hsuanchuang Temple *(xuánzhuàng sì)* is at the far end of the lake. It's up on a hill and

surrounded by a collection of souvenir shops, but it's still less touristy than the Wenwu Temple.

Within walking distance of Wenwu Temple is the Tzuen Pagoda *(cīēn tǎ)*. This relatively peaceful place (on weekdays at least) is well worth your time. Climb the pagoda for a magnificent view of the lake.

Tehuashe Aboriginal Village
(déhuàshè) 德化社
This a half-hearted attempt to give tourists an idea of what a traditional aboriginal village used to look like. The nearby Formosan Aboriginal Cultural Village is a much more sincere effort, but that one costs NT$250 while the one at Tehuashe is free.

Places to Stay
Sun Moon Lake Village The main tourist area just near the bus station is a cornucopia of accommodation. Compared to most of the

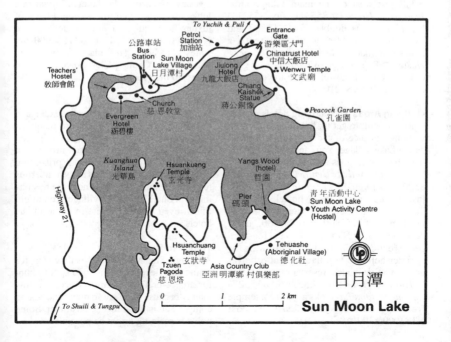

hotels scattered around the lake, the village is also the cheapest area.

Cheapest of the lot seems to be the *Sun Ho-Yung Hotel* (☎ 855364) *(sōnghè yuán dà fàndiàn)*. Doubles on weekdays cost NT$500.

Just opposite the bus station is the friendly *Min Ren Hotel* (☎ 855338) *(míngrén dà fàndiàn)* with doubles/twins costing NT$600/800.

The *Skyline Inn* (☎ 855321, fax 855325) *(tiānlú dà fàndiàn)* is perhaps so-named because it literally dominates the skyline of Sun Moon Lake Village. This enormous hotel isn't especially cheap – doubles are NT$1500 to NT$1900, twins NT$1600 to NT$2300, and suites for NT$2800 to NT$8000.

The *Ming Shin Hotel* (☎ 855357) *(míngshèng dà fàndiàn)*, has doubles with a shared bath for NT$500, or NT$850 with private bath.

Two big (and pricey) hotels are located on a hill just west of the main village area. *Evergreen Hotel* (☎ 855311, fax 855314) *(hánbì lóu)* has doubles for NT$800 and twins from NT$1100 to NT$1200. It's a better deal than the neighbouring *Teachers' Hostel* (☎ 855991) *(jiàoshī huìguǎn)*, a government-owned 'hostel' where the cheapest doubles cost NT$1210.

Outlying Areas The outlying hotels are not really difficult to get to, but none are within walking distance of the bus station in Sun Moon Lake Village. You can get there on the local bus which goes around the lake.

The *Youth Activity Centre* (☎ 850070, fax 850037) *(qīngnián huódòng zhōngxīn)* is just a fancy name for a hostel. It's near Tehuashe on the southern shore of the lake. Doubles cost NT$800 to NT$3000, and a dormitory bed is NT$250. Demand for dorm beds is extremely heavy here, and during the summer holidays you haven't got a prayer unless you've made a reservation.

Jiulong Hotel (☎ 855206, 855327) *(jiǔlóng dà fàndiàn)* looks a bit like a temple from the outside. Doubles/twins cost NT$1000/1200.

Chinatrust Hotel (☎ 855911, fax 716 4755) *(zhōngxìn dà fàndiàn)*, 23 Chungcheng Rd, has doubles/twins for NT$2700/2900 and suites for NT$4800 to NT$6000. It's not in the village, but near the Wenwu Temple.

Asia Country Club (☎ 850001, fax 85 0173) *(yǎzhōu míng tán xiāng jùlèbù)* on the south shore is Sun Moon Lake's super-deluxe accommodation. Ironically, it can be cheap (by country-club standards) if you are willing to stay in a tent – camping costs NT$700 with tents and sleeping bags provided. A complete 'camping package' is available for NT$2500, which includes access to yacht cruises, water-skiing, meals, the whole lot. There are a number of other accommodation possibilities – enquire if interested.

Yangs Wood (☎ 850000, fax 850080) *(zhéyuán)* is unique in Taiwan – the all-wooden exterior is more reminiscent of a Canadian mountain lodge than east Asia. I've never seen any other hotel in Taiwan that looks this good from the outside. Plenty of luxury here, but at a price – doubles are NT$3500, twins NT$4500 to NT$6900 and suites NT$8900. This place is associated with the Asia Country Club, so you can gain access to their facilities.

Places to Eat

Sun Moon Lake is one of the most expensive resort areas in Taiwan. There are plenty of places to eat, but the emphasis is on pricey seafood restaurants (real mountain seafood?). For double the usual price, you can get noodle or rice dishes in the numerous restaurants lining the street near the bus terminal in Sun Moon Lake village. You might find it even cheaper to eat in some of the hotels.

Things to Buy

Although Sun Moon Lake isn't cheap for eating and sleeping, it's a good spot to hunt for arts & crafts souvenirs. Prices are low mainly because there are so many shops, and competition is good for the customer. Some polite bargaining might be possible.

Getting There & Away

There are several directions you can approach from, but it's easiest to get to Sun Moon Lake from Taichung.

To/From Taichung In Taichung, catch buses from the Gancheng bus terminal. There are plenty of wild-chicken taxi drivers hanging around this place who will grab any Westerner by the arm and yell in his/her face, 'Sun Moon Lake'. Ignore them and buy a bus ticket for NT$129. The buses go directly to the lake in two hours. If you've just missed the bus and don't want to wait for the next one, first take a bus to Puli, then get another bus to Sun Moon Lake.

To/From Taipei There is a direct bus departing from the north bus terminal. The travelling time is slightly more than four hours. An alternative would be to take a bus or train to Taichung or Puli first, and then transfer to the Sun Moon Lake bus.

Getting Around

If you are a hiker, you could walk from Sun Moon Lake village to Tzuen Pagoda at the opposite side of the lake, but it's a long way and will take most of the day. Fortunately, there are buses plying this route at the rate of about one an hour between 8 am and 5 pm. If you miss the last bus back you can take a taxi or hitch.

Sun Moon Lake looks like an excellent place to ride a bicycle. As yet, I haven't seen any bicycle rental shops that aren't attached to the hotels. Yangs Wood offers bicycle rentals to their guests, and I expect that other hotels will take note and start offering the same service.

Taking a tour by taxi is not unreasonable if you can organise a group to share the cost. The easiest way to do this is to form a group while on the bus going to the lake and include some Chinese tourists. Let them do the bargaining and don't pay until the tour is finished.

ABORIGINAL CULTURAL VILLAGE

(*jiǔ zú wénhuà cūn*) 九族文化村

A very short distance north-east of Sun Moon Lake is the Formosan Aboriginal Cultural Village. For those with an interest in Taiwan's aboriginal culture, this is a worthwhile trip. Although commercialised, the reproductions of aboriginal dwellings, arts and crafts are realistic and quite tastefully done.

There is a NT$250 entrance fee to this area, but it's not too unreasonable since you can easily spend half a day there. The 'tribal villages' are spread out over a large area, so you need to do a lot of walking or take the tourist minibus. On weekends and holidays there are continuous aboriginal song and dance shows, all free of charge.

When you first enter the grounds, you come into a large European-style garden and château – about as appropriate as an igloo in the Sahara Desert. They seem to have been thrown in as an added tourist attraction for locals, who don't get many opportunities to see the palaces of Europe. On the other hand, the gardens are very beautiful and save you the cost of a trip to France in case you haven't been there.

Just up the hill from the gardens, there is a small plaza where the aboriginal song and dance shows are performed. Just adjacent to the plaza is a museum housing aboriginal artefacts, both original and reproductions.

You can follow either the footpath or the road up the mountainside. There are nine villages in all. Each one represents a separate tribe, except for the Tsou-Shao village which represents two tribes. There are a total of 10 aboriginal tribes in Taiwan: the Ami, Atayal, Bunun, Paiwan, Puyuma, Rukai, Shao, Saisiat, Tsou and Yami.

For additional information about the Formosan Aboriginal Cultural Village, you can phone their office on ☎ 49-895361. It's open daily from 7 am to 5.30 pm.

Getting There & Away

Although it's very close to Sun Moon Lake, there are no direct buses to the village. You have to take a bus from Sun Moon Lake

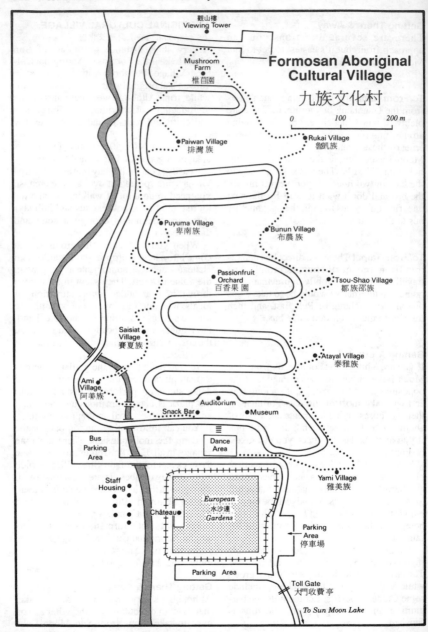

観山樓
Viewing Tower

Mushroom
Farm
椎茸園

**Formosan Aboriginal
Cultural Village**

九族文化村

0   100   200 m

● Rukai Village
魯凱族

● Paiwan Village
排灣族

● Puyuma Village
卑南族

● Bunun Village
布農族

● Passionfruit
Orchard
百香果園

● Tsou-Shao Village
鄒族邵族

Saisiat
Village
賽夏族

● Atayal Village
泰雅族

Ami ●
Village
阿美族

Snack Bar ●   ● Auditorium   ● Museum

Bus
Parking
Area

Dance
Area

Yami Village
雅美族

Staff
Housing

Château ●

European
水沙連
Gardens

Parking
Area
停車場

Parking   Area

Toll Gate
大門收費亭

To Sun Moon Lake

village to Yuchih *(yúchí)*, and then another bus to the Formosan Aboriginal Cultural Village. The buses depart Yuchih at 7.30, 9.20 and 11.05 am, and 1, 2.35, 3.30 and 5 pm.

There are direct buses from the town of Puli *(pǔlǐ)*. They leave at 7, 8.40 and 10.30 am, and 12.20, 2, 3 and 4.30 pm.

PULI
(pǔlǐ) 埔里

Dead in the centre of Taiwan, just north of Sun Moon Lake, is the town of Puli. It's definitely not a tourist attraction, but it is an important transit point for many scenic areas. Many travellers wind up staying here because of the convenient location.

One hazard – Puli's narrow streets, lack of footpaths and lack of traffic lights make it a bit dicey walking around. It was here that a speeding car broke its mirror against my backpack.

Probably the best site in town is the Chenghuang Temple *(chénghuáng miào)*. Puli does have an active and interesting night market – if you're spending the evening, check it out.

Places to Stay

It is possible you may have to spend a night in Puli if you arrive late and need to catch a bus the next morning. One advantage of staying in Puli is that it is easy to find cheap accommodation and food, even on holidays when nearby expensive resorts like Sun Moon Lake are packed out.

In the west part of town near the night market is the *Hohuan Hotel* (☎ 984036) *(héhuān dà fàndiàn)*, 67 Chungcheng Rd, Section 2. At NT$500 for a comfortable double, it's one of the cheapest deals in Puli.

Nearby is the *Yongfeng Hotel* (☎ 982304) *(yǒngfēng lǔshè)*, 280 Nanchang St, where singles/doubles cost NT$500/550 with private bath.

If you want to be closer to the centre, the *Jinshan Hotel* (☎ 982311, 984317) *(jīnshān dà fàndiàn)*, 127 Tungjung St, has comfortable doubles with private bath for NT$600. Just next door at the *Xindongjing Hotel*

(☎ 982556, 983256) *(xīndōngjǐng bīnguǎn)*, 113 Tungjung Rd, the same prices are charged but the rooms are a little bit tattered. On the same street at No 103 is the *Dongfeng Hotel* (☎ 982287)*(dōngfēng dà lǔshè)* which also charges NT$600 for a double.

The *Tianyi Hotel* (☎ 998100, fax 982017) *(tiānyī dà fàndiàn)* at 89 Hsi'an Rd, Section 1, offers fine rooms for NT$1200.

Also in the up-market league is the flashy *Sun Wang Hotel* (☎ 900111, fax 900200) *(shānwáng dà fàndiàn)*, 399 Chungshan Rd Section 2. Doubles cost NT$1200.

Places to Eat

In the evening, there are plenty of cheap places to eat in the market at Tunghua Rd and Nanchang St. There's a cluster of low-priced restaurants around the Taiwan Bus Company terminal.

Encor Home Kitchen (☎ 996141) *(yǎgē)*, 146 Peitse St, deserves honourable mention as one of the trendiest places in town. This is where Puli's young crowd hangs out in the evening to eat, sip coffee or Coke, to see others and to be seen. Prices are mid-range.

Getting There & Away

There are two important bus terminals in Puli. The large bus terminal belongs to the Taiwan Bus Company *(táiwān qìchē kèyùn)*. Down the street, about half a block away, is the Nantou Bus Company *(nántóu kèyùn)* East Station. There is also a Nantou Bus Company station on the other side of town. Buses to Wushe stop at both stations.

From Taichung, direct buses to Puli leave from the Gancheng bus station and cost NT$105. For details of how to get from Puli to places of interest in the area, refer to the Getting There & Away sections for Huisun Forest, Wushe, the Formosan Aboriginal Cultural Village and Chingching Farm.

HUISUN FOREST
(huìsūn lín chǎng) 惠蓀林場

To the north of Puli in a mountain valley, the Huisun Forest was originally intended as a

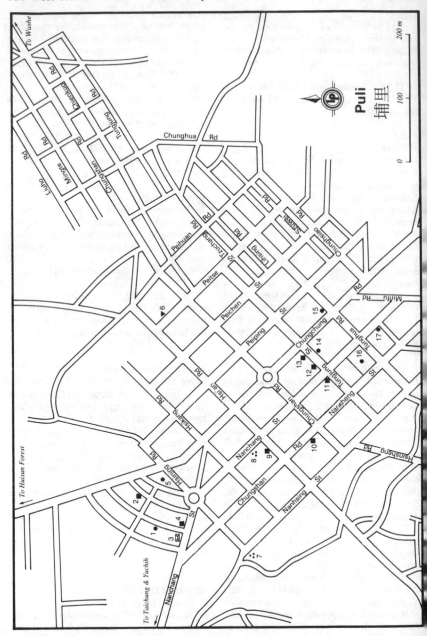

Puli
埔里

1 Nantou Bus Company (Puli Station)
南投客運東站
2 Hohuan Hotel
合歡大飯店
3 Post Office
郵局
4 Yongfeng Hotel
永豐旅社
5 Night Market
夜市
6 Encor Home Kitchen
雅哥
7 Matsu Temple
媽祖廟
8 Chenghuang Temple
城隍廟
9 Tianyi Hotel
天一大飯店
10 Sun Wang Hotel
山王大飯店
11 Dongfeng Hotel
東峰大旅社
12 Xindongjing Hotel
新東京大旅社
13 Jinshan Hotel
金山大飯店
14 Bank of Taiwan
台灣銀行
15 Taiwan Bus Company
台灣客運
16 Market
市場
17 Nantou Bus Company (East Station)
南投客運埔里站

is a white-water river rushing through a canyon and you can camp nearby. There is also a lodge with economically priced rooms.

All things considered, if you are on a hurried trip through Taiwan, you could bypass Huisun without feeling you've missed something big. On the other hand, if you have the time and desire to spend a couple of days in a beautiful, pine-scented valley with nice hiking trails, it's worth the trip. I feel it is too hot in summer, but pleasant during autumn, winter and spring.

Hiking is the main activity in Huisun. Refer to the Huisun Forest map for the main trails. The hike to Frog Rock *(qīngwā shí)* is steep but one of the best in the valley. During the week, walking along the main road through the valley is pleasant, but on weekends and holidays the traffic can be too heavy. Admission to Huisun Forest costs NT$90.

Places to Stay

There are several places to stay and everything is under the same management. Reservations are a good idea on weekends and holidays; call the *Service Centre* (☎ 941041, fax 941245) *(fúwù zhōngxīn)*. If you arrive without a reservation, go to the Service Centre to book a place for the night.

There is a wide range of accommodation available. Dormitories cost NT$200 per person while doubles go for NT$1200.

nature reserve project for the Forestry Department of Chunghsing University in Taichung. However, it's been transformed into a picnic, camping and hiking spot. Although not as spectacular as Alishan, Tungpu, Hohuanshan and other mountain resorts in Taiwan, some consider Huisun a better place to go in the winter because it is warmer. At 1000 metres above sea level, the climate is milder than the higher mountains. Furthermore, Huisun has not been ruined by commercialisation, at least not yet.

The valley is heavily forested with pines and there are a number of hiking trails. There

Getting There & Away

Buses to Huisun are not frequent. There are only two buses daily from Puli and the trip takes about 1½ hours. Buses leave Puli at 8.50 am and 2.15 pm; going the other way, they leave Huisun at 10.40 am and 3.55 pm. On weekends and holidays only, there are two buses from Tsaotun *(cǎotún)*, a town 17 km south of Taichung. Buses leave Tsaotun at 8 am and 2.45 pm; they leave Huisun for Tsaotun at 10 am and 4.40 pm. The buses are operated by the Nantou Bus Company *(nántóu kèyùn)*.

WUSHE

(wùshè) 霧社

At 1148 metres above sea level, Wushe offers a cool mountain retreat with magnificent scenery. The town sits on a mountain ridge, and in the valley just below there is a large reservoir. Although many tour buses come through on the weekends, you can easily escape them by walking down to the reservoir. To get there, just walk down the road through the village by the school. The reservoir, named Green Lake *(bì hú)*, is most beautiful during the spring and summer wet season. In the dry season the water level drops and a great deal of mud is revealed. Even then, the surrounding countryside is still magnificent, the peaceful surroundings are invigorating and the air is fresh and cool.

If you prefer a less strenuous activity to hiking down to the lake, walk down the street leading out of town. On the left side of the road there is a 'moon gate'. Walk through it, heading uphill, and you will soon come to a peaceful temple, surrounded by trees. A perfect place to sit and contemplate the meaning of life, the universe and other such things worthy of contemplation.

In 1930, Wushe was the scene of a violent uprising of the local aboriginal population against the Japanese occupation forces. The Japanese, with their usual efficiency, quickly crushed the rebellion and left over 1000 dead. There is a mural in the youth hostel depicting this battle and there is a plaque by the temple to honour those who died.

Places to Stay

Unless you have a tent and do some back-country camping, there is no cheap place to stay. The main street of town is lined with several mid-range hotels. Perhaps the best deal is the *Wuying Hotel* (☎ 802360) *(wùyīng dà lüshè)*, 59 Jenho Rd (the main street of town), which charges NT$900 for a double. Push for a discount on weekdays, especially during the off-season.

The *Wushe Mountain Hostel* (☎ 802611) *(wùshè shān zhuāng)*, operated by the China Youth Corps, has evolved from a budget youth hostel into a slick up-market government-owned cash cow. It's right at the end of the main street on the hill. Double rooms cost a cool NT$1800. You can no doubt arrange lower prices here if you arrive with 10 travelling companions.

Getting There & Away

Getting to Wushe is easy. There are a few direct buses a day from Taichung – if you catch one, fine, but if not just take a bus to Puli. If you are coming from Sun Moon Lake, also take a bus to Puli. The bus will drop you off by the large bus terminal in Puli, which belongs to the Taiwan Bus Company *(táiwān qìchē kèyùn)*. From there walk down the street about two blocks to a hole-in-the-wall bus terminal operated by the Nantou Bus Company *(nántóu kèyùn)* to buy a ticket to Wushe. Puli to Wushe is 24 km up a steep highway through a scenic gorge.

LUSHAN HOT SPRINGS

(lúshān wēnquán) 蘆山溫泉

At 1200 metres elevation and nine km east of Wushe, Lushan offers hot springs and delightful mountain scenery. Actually, most of the hot springs aren't particularly natural because they have been taken over by hotels and are simply indoor bathtubs. You don't have to stay in the hotel to use the hot baths, but then you have to pay an entrance fee if you want to 'take a rest' *(xiūxí)* – not always cheap either. After you've had a nice soak in the hot water, go outside and admire the view.

Lushan is a village perched precariously on both sides of a steep gorge with a river rushing through the centre of town. The two sides of the town are connected by a foot suspension bridge. This feature gives the town a unique advantage as no cars can cross the bridge, therefore making one side of town almost traffic-free. I do say 'almost' because there is always some moral cretin who doesn't want to walk and instead takes a motorcycle across the footbridge. The peace and quiet is also marred by the 'walking tractors' – small cargo vehicles powered by lawn-mower engines and used to haul food and other goods to the hotels. Still, if you get a room away from the narrow streets, you can easily escape the whining sound of the infernal combustion engine.

There is a pleasant short hike from the village along the gorge. Going upstream, you will soon find a little restaurant perched on the cliffs. There is a man there selling eggs which you can cook in the hot springs. He also sells oolong tea by the pot, so you can sit and drink tea and watch the river rush by. If you need some more exercise, I found a path that seems to go on forever – where it ends I do not know. To find it, go up the hill just behind the police station, passing a small hotel. You will see the powerline towers. Follow them for a while and the service road narrows into a path going up, up and up.

Places to Stay

There are so many hotels in this town that you begin to wonder if anyone in Lushan lives in a real house. The *Police Hostel* (☎ 802529) *(jǐngguāng shān zhuāng)* is marginally cheaper than other places. As the name implies, it's a government-owned place and the police get priority, but they allow others to stay there if they have space. Usually you can get in on weekdays during the off-season. Of course, if you're planning to break the law, you'd best do it in another hotel. Double rooms with shared bath are NT$800 in high season, or half that in low season. The hostel has hot-spring baths.

Moving up-market, there is the *Skyline Inn* (☎ 802675, 802288) *(tiānlú dà fàndiàn)*, where twins cost NT$1000 to NT$1800. Considering the very glitzy atmosphere, it appears to be good value.

The *Honeymoon Hotel* (☎ 802355) *(mìyuè guǎn dà fàndiàn)* is not known for being cheap – doubles/twins cost a breathtaking NT$1800/2600 for the 'economy' rooms, NT$3600 for cushier accommodation.

Getting There & Away

Buses to the hot springs run about once an hour from nearby Wushe. There are occasional direct buses from Taichung and nine buses daily from Puli. Just before reaching Lushan, the bus crosses one of the highest bridges in Taiwan – this has recently become a popular venue for bungy jumping.

CHINGCHING FARM

(qīngjìng nóngchǎng) 清境農場

Perched 1750 metres above sea level, Chingching (quiet) Farm is undergoing a transformation from an agricultural region into a tourist resort. And as one old farmer told me, it's not so quiet any more, at least not on weekends when the tour buses, cars and motorcycles roll in carrying camera-clicking tourists. During the week it's still very quiet and that's the time to visit if you wish to see this famous orchard area. However, nearby Hohuanshan is more scenic and offers better hiking opportunities.

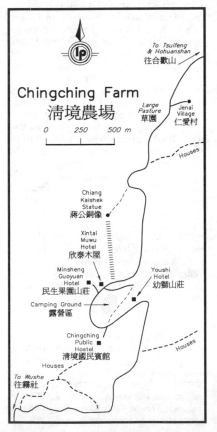

Chingching Farm is not actually one farm, but a group of farms strewn along the highway that runs from Wushe to the top of Hohuanshan. In addition to the orchards, where you can pick your own fruit for a fee (based on weight), they also raise cows. There aren't many places in Taiwan where you can see cows and this is one of the main reasons why Chingching Farm is such a big attraction for the city folk. Also, the Chinese have a real affection for grass – not the kind you can smoke, but the kind that cows munch on. Chingching Farm has one very large pasture, and Chinese tourists flock there to take endless photos of each other standing in the grass and cow manure.

I've seen some impressive motor vehicle accidents in Taiwan, but none come close to what I witnessed at Chingching Farm in August, 1993. A huge truck overloaded with marble ploughed into five cars, leaving 11 dead (including the truck driver) and 20 injured. Imagine that. The truck literally landed on the front steps of a major tourist hotel. This was the first time I'd seen the locals gather round and burn ghost money right amongst the dead bodies – it was explained to me that after a particularly violent accident, this was necessary to keep the spirits from haunting the place.

Places to Stay

Hotels fill up fast on weekends. There are several camping grounds in Chingching Farm. In the past, they used to rent out equipment but these days they expect you to supply your own. The camping fee is NT$40.

The *Youshi Hotel* (☎ 802533) *(yòushī shān zhuāng)* is a government-owned hotel. Talk to the manager here if you want to stay in the adjacent camping ground. Double rooms in the hotel cost NT$770.

The *Minsheng Guoyuan Hotel* (☎ 802364, 802639) *(mínshēng guǒyuán shān zhuāng)* has doubles for NT$800. Dormitories are aimed towards groups – NT$2000 for 10 people, but solo travellers might have a chance of getting in during the off-season.

The *Xintai Muwu Hotel* (☎ 993392)

(xīntài mùwū) has doubles/twins for NT$800/1200. The owners should have consulted a geomancer before construction – this is where the previously mentioned marble truck came to rest. Perhaps you'll sleep better by asking for a room that doesn't face the highway.

The *Chingching Public Hostel* (☎ 80 2748, fax 802203) *(qīngjìng guómín bīnguǎn*; 128 rooms) is another government-owned place. Doubles are NT$1320 to NT$1650, and twins/suites cost NT$1870/2750.

Restaurants as such are practically non-existent, but most of the hotels do meals. Cheaper – and in my opinion, better – food is available from stalls in the main market area next to the Xintai Muwu Hotel. In season, this is also the place to find fruit for which Chingching Farm is famous.

Getting There & Away

To reach Chingching Farm, take a bus from Puli or Wushe. It's an eight-km ride from Wushe. When going up the mountain, sit on the right side of the bus for the best view.

The same bus goes higher up the mountain to the tiny village of Tsuifeng, where you begin the six-hour hike to Hohuanshan. You could stay at Chingching Farm and get this bus to Tsuifeng the next morning if you wish to do the Hohuanshan hike, or stay in Wushe.

HOHUANSHAN

(héhuānshān) 合歡山

No doubt many visitors to Taiwan will be surprised to learn that in this subtropical island there is a ski resort. Hohuanshan (Harmonious Happiness Mountain) reaches an elevation of 3416 metres and the summit is above the tree line. At this height it is cool even in summer, but in winter the night temperatures can dip well below freezing and in some years there is sufficient snowfall in January and February to permit skiing. However, the skiing isn't very good – the ski lift broke down years ago and hasn't been repaired. So 'skiing' consists of walking up the hill yourself and sliding back down.

During the rest of the year it is certainly worth visiting Hohuanshan for the magnificent views. In the morning, you can usually witness that beautiful Taiwanese phenomenon, the 'sea of clouds'. In the afternoon, the clouds rise and often envelop the summit. When this happens, it's like being inside a ping-pong ball.

Hohuanshan is reached by a paved highway that connects Tayuling to Wushe. It's the highest road in Taiwan, reaching an elevation of 3275 metres at Wuling Pass. This is the westernmost part of Taroko National Park.

Hohuanshan is peaceful during the off season, but when it snows everybody converges on the mountain. People in Taiwan have few opportunities to see snow, so when it falls on Hohuanshan everyone who can makes the pilgrimage there to see the white stuff. On winter weekends, it looks like a car park in Taipei.

If you survive the cold night, the next morning you may encounter hikers heading off to climb Chilaishan *(qíláishān)*. This is the large, jagged-faced mountain immediately to the east of Hohuanshan and easily visible on a clear day. If you are invited to go climbing Chilaishan, you should be aware that it's notorious in Taiwan as the site of many fatal accidents. The high body count stems from severe weather changes and a vertical, crumbly, rocky face. The mountain is dominated by a tremendous jagged, sawtooth ridge. The 'trail' follows this ridge line and offers numerous opportunities for hang-gliding and skydiving. During the frequently foggy and windy weather, hikers have been known to be blown right over the edge.

Places to Stay

There is a youth hostel near where the bus drops you off in Tayuling. See the section on Hualien County in the East Coast chapter for details.

At Hohuanshan there is only one place to stay, *Pine Snow Hostel* (☎ 802732) *(sōng xuě lóu)*. The dormitory costs NT$200 per bed, and twins are NT$1200 to NT$2200. There are no stores in or near the hostel, so bring food, film, toilet paper, a torch and plenty of warm clothes. If you don't have a reservation, bring a sleeping bag because there is only one quilt for every guest and there probably will be no extras. If all the beds are taken, you might be allowed to roll out a sleeping bag on the dining room floor when it's time for lights out, but don't count on it.

In any event, be prepared for a cold night. At 3400 metres you are no longer in the tropics, so be sure to bring your winter woollies. No matter how nice the weather might be, it can change in minutes during the day, and at night the temperature absolutely plummets.

Places to Eat
The *Pine Snow Hostel* is the only place that has food or anything else. Prepared meals are available but only if you made a reservation in advance. Otherwise, they probably won't even have enough leftovers for you. You are therefore strongly advised to bring extra food unless you want to forage for nuts and berries.

Getting There & Away
One major tactical problem with visiting Hohuanshan is that there is no bus service along the road that leads to the top of the mountain and the lodge. You have two options, walk or hitch. There is plenty of traffic during the summer peak season. During the cold months, few come here except when the TV stations report snow at Hohuanshan – then there's a sudden full-fledged rush hour. There are two routes, and ideally you should go up one way and down the other. Either route may be closed occasionally due to landslides, and during snowstorms tyre chains are required.

North Side The north side is shorter and steeper. If you walk from Tayuling, it's a steep but breathtakingly beautiful walk of nine km – four hours uphill or three hours downhill. Certainly the best way to appreciate the scenery is on foot.

South Side From Puli, you can get a bus to Tsuifeng *(cuìfēng)* (elevation 2310 metres) and from there it's 15 km, or about 6½ hours of walking. The bus departs Puli from the Nantou Bus Company Station *(nántóu kèyùn zhàn)*. There are no taxis in Tsuifeng, nor is there a regular place to stay. If you talk to some of the local aborigines, they can arrange a *mínfáng* (stay in somebody's home) for low cost, but don't expect a word of English to be spoken. Otherwise, you'll have to camp out. The nearest place that has regular hotels is Chingching Farm. The bus from Puli passes through Wushe and Chingching Farm, and terminates in Tsuifeng. Start early because the weather is usually clearest in the morning.

Changhua County 彰化縣

CHANGHUA
(zhānghuà) 彰化
There is little reason to make a special trip to Changhua. The town has a notable temple, but for most travellers Changhua will be a stopover on the way to or from Lukang. If you do get off the bus or train in Changhua, the main attraction is Pakuashan *(bāguà-shān)*, a small mountain park in the city topped with a very large Buddha, 22 metres tall. You can go inside and look out of various windows which have been made where his eyes, ears, etc are. Adjacent to the Buddha are some colourful pagodas and a temple. It's certainly touristy on weekends but tranquil enough at other times.

Changhua also boasts a Confucius Temple *(kǒng miào)*, one of the oldest in Taiwan. It's dead quiet most of the time, but comes to life on Teachers' Day (28 September) when there is a dawn ceremony.

Information
Tourist Office There is an obscure branch of the Tourism Bureau (☎ 7232111) on the 3rd floor, 39 Kuangfu Rd.

Money ICBC (☎ 7232111) *(guójì shāngyè yínháng)* has a branch at 39 Kuangfu Rd.

1 Lees Hotel
雲河賓館
2 Changhua Bus Company
彰化客運站
3 Jongye & Jincheng hotels
紅葉大旅社/金城旅社
4 Taiwan Hotel
台灣大飯店
5 Diyi Hotel
第一旅社
6 Sanhuo Hotel
三和大旅社
7 Rich Royal Hotel
富皇大飯店

8 Ing Shan Hotel
櫻山大飯店
9 Post Office
郵局
10 Police (Visa Extensions)
警察局外事課
11 ICBC
中國國際商業銀行
12 Lungshan Temple
龍山廟
13 Confucius Temple
孔子廟
14 Yongda Hotel
永大大飯店

Places to Stay

Taichung is a more interesting city to spend the night in, but if you decide to stay in Changhua, consider the following places. All of them are near the railway station.

Directly across the street from the railway station is the *Diyi Hotel (dìyī lǚshè)*, where grotty-looking doubles cost NT$350 to NT$550.

The *Hongye Hotel* (☎ 7222667) *(hóngyè dà lǚshè)*, 5 Lane 100, Chang'an St, has doubles with shared bath for NT$300. Next door is the *Jincheng Hotel* (☎ 7225379) *(jīnchéng lǚshè)*, which charges NT$350 a single. The *Sanhuo Hotel* (☎ 7224646) *(sānhé dà lǚshè)*, 31 Lane 96, Yunghsing St, looks like a dump but charges NT$600 a double.

The *Ing Shan Hotel* (☎ 7229211) *(yīngshān dà fàndiàn)*, 129 Chang'an St, is excellent value with singles/doubles for NT$550/650. This is the one I'd go for in Changhua.

Rich Royal Hotel (☎ 7236615) *(fùhuáng dà fàndiàn)* is the best place to stay if you're driving your own vehicle. It's the first hotel I've ever seen with a car park in the lobby! Rooms cost NT$880, NT$1030 and NT$1180. The address is 97 Chang'an St.

Lees Hotel (☎ 7236164) *(yúnhé bīnguǎn)*, 566 Chungcheng 1st Rd, is a plush and friendly place where doubles/twins are NT$780/980.

Yongda Hotel (☎ 7224666, fax 7227249) *(yǒngdà dà fàndiàn)* has very nice-looking doubles for NT$750. It's at 120 Chungcheng Rd, Section 2 – the lower floor is a restaurant, you have to go up the stairs to find reception.

The *Taiwan Hotel* (☎ 7224681, fax 7246474) *(táiwān dà fàndiàn; 70 rooms)*, 48 Chungcheng Rd, Section 2, is Changhua's deluxe accommodation. Doubles are NT$945, twins are priced between NT$1155 and NT$1470 and suites cost NT$2730 to NT$2940.

CHANGHUA TAIWANESE CULTURAL VILLAGE

(zhānghuà táiwān mínsú cūn) 彰化台灣民俗村
This is one of Taiwan's newest theme parks. In fact, it's so new that I haven't been there yet because it wasn't quite open as we went to press with this book. The emphasis here is supposed to be on Taiwanese culture, a refreshing change from the rapidly multiplying 'aboriginal cultural villages'. The Changhua Taiwanese Cultural Village (☎ 7870088, fax 7870521) is at 30 Yachun Sanfen Rd, Huatan Wan, Changhua County.

LUKANG

(lùgǎng) 鹿港
Lukang (Deer Harbour) is mainly of interest to historians. The town was a thriving port in the 1600s and remained so until it was closed in 1895 by the Japanese. For a glance at the past, wander through the narrow alleys. There are many original buildings still standing, but modernisation has had a big impact – don't expect to find a perfectly preserved ancient Chinese village. The Taiwanese reckon Lukang is a major tourist attraction – I reckon you'd have to be a real history buff to get excited about it. Arts and crafts may be a better reason for a visit – Lukang is filled with shops making traditional Chinese furniture and religious artefacts.

Lukang Folk Arts Museum

(lùgǎng mínsú wénwù guǎn) 鹿港民俗文物館
Probably the best sight in Lukang is the Lukang Folk Arts Museum (☎ 7772019), at 152 Chungshan Rd. The museum contains a large collection of porcelain, furniture, lacquerware, musical instruments, a bridal sedan chair and other interesting artefacts. The entrance fee is a rather steep NT$100, or NT$50 for students. The entrance to the museum is not obvious from Chungshan Rd. A notable landmark is the police station, just to the left of which is a narrow alley. Follow the alley to the end, then turn left and you'll see the museum about 100 metres in front of you.

Temples

Lukang has two major temples and several minor ones. The largest is Lungshan Temple

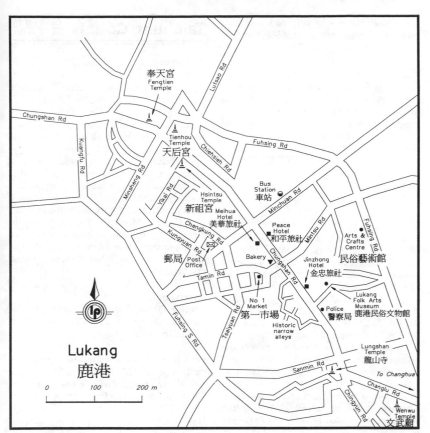

Lukang
鹿港

0   100   200 m

(lóngshān sì), dedicated to Kuanyin, the goddess of mercy. The runner-up is the Tienhou Temple (tiānhòu miào), dedicated to Matsu, goddess of the sea. Both were close to falling apart by the 1970s, but have now been restored.

Smaller but interesting temples include Fengtien Temple (fèngtiān gōng), Hsintsu Temple (xīnzǔ gōng) and Wenwu Temple (wénwǔ miào).

Places to Stay

Although many tourists visit Lukang, very few spend the night there. As a result there are only a few old hotels in town, some of which double as brothels. Many people stay in nearby Changhua where there is a wider selection of hotels.

The *Peace Hotel* (☎ 7772600) *(hépíng lüshè)*, 230 Chungshan Rd, has singles/doubles for NT$600/1000 with private bath. It looks rather tattered around the edges, but I suppose it would do for the night. Nearby is the *Meihua Hotel* (☎ 777 2027) *(měihuá lüshè)*, 253 Chungshan Rd, where doubles are NT$500 but rooms are often full.

Jinzhong Hotel (jīnzhōng lüshè) at 104

Chungshan Rd is relatively new and nice looking. Doubles start at NT$600.

Places to Eat

Lukang is famous for its good food. A local speciality is 'cow's tongue cake' *(niú shí bǐng)*. It's not really made out of a cow's tongue, but it resembles one in shape and size. It's best eaten hot. It's available from street vendors or from the numerous bakeries that line the streets. In front of the Tienhou Temple are about five stores all selling delicious oyster omelettes and oyster soup.

Things to Buy

Lukang is famous for its handicrafts. Those wanting to purchase such things will be in ecstasy. In the factories, which are easy enough to find along Chungshan Rd in Lukang, you can buy statues, monuments, wood carvings, tables, paintings, embroidery and pottery. Also worth checking out is the Arts & Crafts Centre *(mínsú yìshù guǎn)* on Fuhsing Rd near Mintsu Rd.

In many cases, you can negotiate with the artisan who made the goods, which theoretically means you should get them cheaper. Lukang may well be one of the best places in the world to buy such things. If you're planning on buying something heavy, like furniture, you'll need the services of a freight forwarder such as YTT (☎ 02-8313123) in Taipei.

Getting There & Away

Lukang is 21 km south-west of Taichung. If you come by train, get off at Changhua and take a bus from the Changhua Bus Company terminal (across the street from the railway station). The trip only takes 15 minutes.

From Taichung, the Changhua Bus Company *(zhānghuà kèyùn)* has a hole-in-the-wall station behind the railway station. You can catch a bus there, which will stop briefly in Changhua before continuing on to Lukang; the journey takes about an hour.

Taichung County 台中縣

TAICHUNG

(táizhōng) 台中

Taichung, which means 'central Taiwan', is the third-largest city on the island and is known as an educational and cultural centre rather than an industrial area. However, it's increasingly becoming a big city, with all the urban headaches of crime, traffic and pollution. There are many universities and it's a good place to study Chinese if you'd rather not be in Taipei. For tourists, the city itself is not a big attraction, but Taichung is a major jumping-off point for trips into the spectacular Central Mountain Range. If you're touring Taiwan's mountains you are almost certain to stop off in Taichung, and it's also quite likely that you'll have to spend at least one night there.

Information

Tourist Office There is a branch of the Tourism Bureau (☎ 2270421) on the 4th floor, 216 Minchuan Rd.

Post & Telecommunications The GPO is on the corner of Minchuan and Shihfu Rds. The phone company is one block away at Shihfu and Minsheng Rds.

Money ICBC (☎ 2281171) *(guójì shāngyè yínháng)* is at 216 Minchuan Rd. The Bank of Taiwan (☎ 2224001) *(táiwān yínháng)* is at 140 Tzuyu Rd, Section 1. Citibank (☎ 3233223) *(huāqí yínháng)* has cash-advance service to its card holders from the branch at 154 Taichung Kang 1st Rd.

Bookshops Caves Books (☎ 3265559) *(dūnhuáng shūjú)* has a shop at 302 Taichung Kang Rd, Section 1, next to McDonald's. There is another branch of Caves (☎ 227 3339) at 22-3 Taiping Rd.

There are numerous branches of the chain store *New Schoolmates Books (xīn xué yǒu shūjú)*. Closest to the railway station is a branch (☎ 2250169) in the basement at 32

Luchuan E St. Not far from the Lai Lai Department Store is another (☎ 2257999) at 28-3 Taiping Rd. In the north part of the city is a branch (☎ 2960123) on the 3rd floor, 192-1 Wenhsin Rd, Section 4.

Central Bookshop (zhōngyāng shūjú) at 125 Chungcheng Rd has a small collection of English books upstairs and English magazines on the ground floor.

Hospital Taichung Hospital (☎ 2222506) *(táizhōng yīyuàn)* is at 199 Sanmin Rd, Section 1, at the corner of Minchuan Rd.

Natural Science Museum
(zìrán kēxué bówùguǎn) 自然科學博物館
This museum (☎ 3226940) is one of Taichung's biggest attractions. Adjoining the museum is the Space Theatre *(tàikōng jùchǎng)*. The whole complex is constructed in an ultra-modern style, but is very tastefully done and worth a visit. The address is 1 Kuanchien Rd, which is near the Hotel National in Taichung's most prestigious neighbourhood. It's only 10 minutes by bus from the centre. To get there take green bus No 22, 48, 103, 106, 107 or 135, or red bus No 22, 37, 38, 45, 46, or 48. The museum is open daily except Monday and the day after national holidays.

Taichung Park
(táizhōng gōngyuán) 台中公園
This is a pleasant park with a lake where boating is permitted. It's just off Kungyuan Rd.

Confucius Temple
(kǒngzǐ miào) 孔子廟
Though not as old and rustic-looking as the one in Tainan, this temple is larger and more colourful. Like other Confucius temples, it has a dawn ceremony on 28 September, the birthday of Confucius. The temple is on Shuangshih Rd, about a 20 minute walk from the railway station, or you can take red bus No 10, 11, 40 or 46. It's closed on Monday.

Martyrs' Shrine
(zhōngliè cí) 忠烈祠
If you visit the Confucius Temple, it's very convenient to visit the Martyrs' Shrine, as the two are adjacent to each other. The shrine is in honour of those who died fighting for their country. On 29 March (Youth Day) a ceremony is held there.

Paochueh Temple
(bǎojué sì) 寶覺寺
A few blocks beyond the Confucius Temple is the Paochueh Temple at 140 Chienhsing Rd. This temple features a huge Buddha, 31 metres tall. The Chinese call him Milefo, a derivation of the original Indian name Maitreya. Services are held at 5 am and 7 pm and they can last for several hours. You can take green bus No 6, 14, 16 or 17 to get there.

Universities
(dàxué) 大學
Taichung has four well-known universities. As a tourist you may not have a big interest in universities, but one worth seeing is Tunghai University *(dōnghǎi dàxué)*, a private co-ed school with a beautiful campus and innovative architecture. This seems to be the unofficial city park – it's certainly larger and more attractive than the real parks in Taichung. The campus is a long way from the centre so you must take a bus or taxi. You can get there by taking either red bus No 38 or green bus No 22 to the last stop, which is inside the campus.

The largest university in Taichung is Chunghsing *(zhōngxīng dàxué)*, a public coeducational institution. Fengchia University *(féngjiǎ dàxué)* is a private co-ed school. Chingyi University *(jìngyí xuéyuàn)* is a private women's college in Shalu, eight km north-west of Taichung.

Cultural Centre
(wénhuà zhōngxīn) 文化中心
The Cultural Centre (☎ 2257311) is similar to the ones in Kaohsiung and Tainan. Featuring opera, art exhibits and concerts, the Cultural Centre will probably be of more interest to residents than travellers. To get the current schedule of events, drop by the centre or call. The address is 600 Yingtsai Rd,

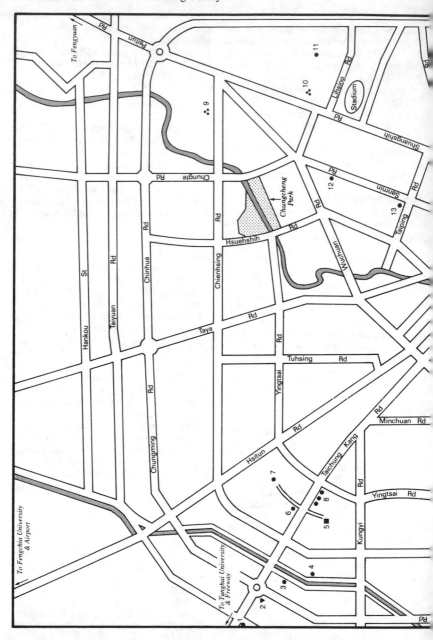

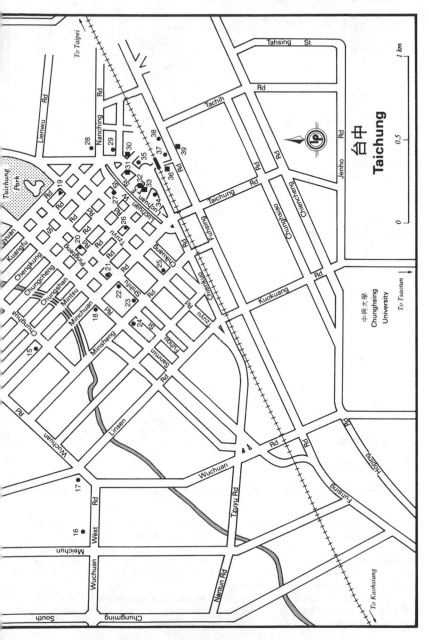

1	Crazy Pub 精誠路16號	21	GPO 郵政總局
2	McDonald's 麥當勞	22	City Hall 市政府
3	Frog Pub 華美西街一段105號	23	Telephone Company 電信局
4	Luigi's Pub 華美街392號	24	Police (Visa Extensions) 警察局外事課
5	Hotel National 全國大飯店	25	Bank of Taiwan 台灣銀行
6	Caves Books 敦煌書局	26	First Hotel & Chaku Chugui Teashop 第一旅社/茶窟出軌
7	Natural Science Museum 自然科學博物館	27	Shopping Mall 第一廣場
8	Pubs 啤酒屋	28	Gancheng Bus Station 干城車站
9	Paochueh Temple 寶覺寺	29	Chienkuo Tool Market 建國市場
10	Confucius Temple 孔廟	30	Plaza Hotel 達欣大飯店
11	Martyrs' Shrine 忠烈祠	31	Crown & Chance hotels 王冠大飯店/巧合大飯店
12	Zhongyou Department Store 中友百貨	32	Jiancheng & Zhongzhou hotels 建城旅社/中洲旅社
13	Lai Lai Department Store 來來百貨	33	Dongcheng & Palace hotels 東城旅社/華宮大飯店
14	Swimming Pool 游泳池	34	Fengyuan Bus Company 豐原客運站
15	ICBC 國際商業銀行	35	Northbound Buses 台汽台中站
16	Museum of Art 美術館	36	Yeong Du Hotel 永都大飯店
17	Cultural Centre 文化中心	37	Southbound Buses 台汽南站
18	Taichung Hospital 台中醫院	38	Changhua Bus Company 彰化客運站
19	McDonald's 麥當勞	39	Twinstar Hotel 雙星大飯店
20	Central Bookstore 中央書局		

near Wǔchuan Rd. Take red bus No 3 or green bus No 20.

Taiwan Museum of Art

(měi shù guǎn) 美術館

This is one of Taiwan's best art museums. The exhibits are rotated, so you'll need to call or pick up a schedule of events if you want to find out what's on.

The museum (☎ 3723740) is at 2 Wuchuan W Rd, right next to the Cultural Centre. It's open Tuesday to Saturday from 9 am to 5 pm, Sunday from 9 am to 8 pm and is closed on Monday. Admission is NT$20.

Places to Stay – bottom end

Taichung has no youth hostels, so if low price is paramount you'll have to stay at a run-down old hotel. Best in the budget class is the *First Hotel* (☎ 2222205) *(dìyī lüshè)*, 51 Chikuang St *(jìguāng jiē)*, where singles start at NT$300 with private bath. The hotel is just a few blocks from the railway station.

If you're willing to stay in a closet-sized room and use a shared bath, one of the cheapest places in town is *Zhongzhou Hotel* (☎ 2222711) *(zhōngzhōu lüshè)*, 2nd floor, 129 Chienkuo Rd – singles/doubles cost NT$200/250. It's on the roundabout behind the bus stop just opposite the railway station, between Chungcheng Rd and Chungshan Rd. Just to the left of this place is a narrow alley called Lane 125 – here you'll find *Jiancheng Hotel* (☎ 2222497) *(jiànchéng lüshè)*, 10 Lane 125, Chienkuo Rd. Singles/doubles are NT$200/250 with shared bath, or NT$350 with private bath. The *Dongcheng Hotel* (☎ 2225001) *dōngchéng dàlüshè*, 14 Chungshan Rd, has doubles starting at NT$250 with shared bath, NT$350 with private bath.

Places to Stay – middle

The *Fuh Chun Hotel* (☎ 2283181, fax 2283187) *(fùchūn dà fàndiàn)*, 1 Chungshan Rd, is one of the best deals in town with doubles from NT$530 to NT$980, twins from NT$880 to NT$1200. The lower-priced rooms are perfectly clean, have private bath and are air-conditioned. The hotel's restaurant is also a good, cheap place to eat. It's on the roundabout opposite the railway station.

Just next door is the *Fuhsing Hotel* (☎ 2225005) *(fùxīng dà fàndiàn)*, 3-1 Chungshan Rd, doubles with private bath are NT$530 to NT$780, twins from NT$780 to NT$1050.

As you emerge from the underpass stairs at the rear of the railway station, just you find yourself in an alley. Immediately ahead (still in the alley) is the *Yeong Du Hotel* (☎ 222 8350) *(yŏngdū dà fàndiàn)*, No 10, Alley 5, Lane 149, Fuhsing Rd, Section 4. Singles are NT$450 and NT$550; doubles cost NT$600.

Also behind the railway station is the impressive *Twinstar Hotel* (☎ 2261811, fax 2248346) *(shuāngxīng dà fàndiàn)*, 158

Fuhsing Rd, Section 4. It's a fancy place – doubles/twins cost NT$1200/1500.

Immediately to your right as you exit the front of the railway station is the *Plaza Hotel* (☎ 2293191, fax 2293197) *(dáxīn dà fàndiàn)*, 180 Chienkuo Rd. Doubles cost NT$770 and NT$880.

Hotel Chance (☎ 2297161, fax 2251845) *(qiǎohé dà fàndiàn)*, 163 Chienkuo Rd, has doubles for NT$840. It's to the right and across the street when exiting the railway station.

Almost next door is the *Crown Hotel* (☎ 2292175, 2292180) *(wángguān dà fàndiàn)* at 184 Chienkuo Rd. Excellent singles are NT$500, doubles/twins cost NT$700/900.

The *Palace Hotel* (☎ 2224081), *(huágōng dà fàndiàn)*, 6 Chungshan Rd, is a comfortable place near the front of the railway station. Doubles are NT$600 to NT$880.

Ming King Hotel (☎ 2245577, fax 2207327) *(míngjūn dà fàndiàn)*, 11 Chungcheng Rd, has doubles for NT$1180. The management seems willing to bargain except when full, but don't expect to be able to knock off more than 20%.

Places to Stay – top end

Evergreen Laurel Hotel
(*chángyíng guìguān jiǔdiàn; 354 rooms*), 6 Taichung Kang Rd (☎ 3289988, fax 3288642), Section 2; doubles NT$3600 to NT$4000, twins NT$3800 to NT$4200, suites NT$7000

Hotel National
(*quánguó dà fàndiàn; 450 rooms*), 257 Taichung Kang Rd, Section 1 (☎ 3213111, fax 3213124); doubles NT$2680 to NT$2940, twins NT$2880 to NT$3360, suites NT$4000 to NT$15,000

Park Hotel
(*jìnghuá dà fàndiàn; 150 rooms*), 17 Kungyuan Rd (☎ 2205181, fax 2225757); doubles NT$1600 to NT$1900, twins from NT$2100 to NT$2300, suites NT$2800 to NT$3800

Plaza International Hotel
(*tōngháo dà fàndiàn; 305 rooms*), 431 Taya Rd (☎ 2956789, fax 2930099); doubles/twins are NT$3200/3400, suites NT$5500 to NT$6000

Taichung Hotel
(*táizhōng dà fàndiàn; 180 rooms*), 152 Tzuyu Rd, Section 1 (☎ 2242121, fax 2249946; doubles NT$1500 to NT$2300, twins NT$2500, suites NT$3000 to NT$4000

Places to Eat

The best night market stretches along the length of Chunghua Rd. The local speciality is seafood but you can buy just about anything.

Big roasted chickens can be had at *míngzhì hànbǎo zhàjī* (☎ 2206726), opposite the Far Eastern Department Store, on the corner of Tzuyu and Chungcheng Rd.

If pizza is on your mind, check out *Boston Pizza* (☎ 2206285), 2nd floor, 131 Tzuyu Rd, Section 2. It's near the Park Hotel.

Denver Restaurant (☎ 3272287), 4 Kuanchien Rd, is near the Natural Science Museum. This place features fine Western food, including a good range of sandwiches and booze to go with it. It's open 11 am until midnight.

Entertainment

Pubs & Discos Most pubs are either closed or empty during the day, but things start moving around 7 pm and the action continues until at least until 1 am.

Frog Pub (☎ 3211197, 3215752) *(qīngwā)*, 105 Huamei W St, Section 1, serves decent spaghetti, submarine sandwiches and one-litre beers (so heavy you can barely hold the glass!). This is also one of two places that caters almost exclusively to foreigners, and there is a great noticeboard here with information about apartments for rent, furniture for sale, teaching jobs, etc. The pub is open from 9 am until 2 am.

The other place heavily geared towards the expatriate market is nearby Luigi's (☎ 3212582), 392 Huamei St. It's a combination Italian restaurant, music hall and pub.

Crazy Pub (☎ 3203002), 16 Chingcheng Rd, is perhaps more disco than pub – the loud music seems to make the whole street vibrate. The clientele is mostly Chinese, though all with money and strong eardrums are welcome.

If pub-crawling interests you, there are few other places near the Hotel National. Foremost amongst these is the Pig & Whistle (☎ 3226555), 394 Yingtsai Rd, which boasts British-style décor and caters to a mixed Chinese/foreign crowd. Check out the

Mexican food, including the tequila sunrises. Minimum charge here is NT$300, which includes two drinks. The Pig is open daily from 11.30 am to 3 am.

Some other choices near the Hotel National include the Amigo (☎ 3210080), 225 Taichung Kang Rd, Section 1; Wagon Wheel (☎ 3211339), 229 Taichung Kang Rd, Section 1; and Blue Bay (☎ 3259488), Basement, 247 Taichung Kang Rd , Section 1 – this last one is definitely an up-market place.

Teahouse A popular place in the centre for foreigners and locals alike is Chaku Chugui (☎ 2235481), 51-53 Chikuang St, almost adjacent to the First Hotel. Look for the set of railroad tracks running through the shop (it's fake though, no trains). The teahouse's name cards are designed to look like Taiwanese train tickets. Besides tea, this place also serves beer and snacks and is a good place to meet young people.

Beer Houses Wenhsin Rd in the north part of the city is Taichung's kinky neighbourhood, filled with 'love motels' and the biggest 'barbershops' I've ever seen. Nevertheless, it's also the location of gigantic beer gardens, most of which are respectable places. They cater to a mostly upper-class Chinese clientele, serve good food and are not exactly cheap. About the largest is Beer City (☎ 2917788) *(qīngmài dàcāntīng)*, 199 Wenhsin 4th Rd.

Activities

Bungy Jumping Bungee International is based in Taipei, but there is a contact in Taichung (☎ 2525523).

Swimming There is a public swimming pool on the north-east corner of Shuangshih Rd and Chingwu Rd, opposite the rear entrance of Taichung Park. It's only open in summer.

Bowling If you like bowling and billiards, visit the New Taichung Bowling Centre (☎ 2228041) *(xīn táizhōng bǎolíng qiúguǎn)*, 14 Shihfu Rd. Another place to try is Amber Lanes (☎ 2321177) (húpò bǎolíng qiúguǎn), 111 Taya Rd.

Things to Buy

The cheapest large store in Taichung is Da Da Department Store, at 32 Luchuan E St. Better quality at higher prices can be found at the Far Eastern Department Store, 48 Tzuyu Rd, Section 2. Just around the corner is the Evergreen Department Store, at 63 Tzuyu Rd, Section 2; this is probably the most expensive store in Taichung.

Zhongyou Department Store (zhōngyǒu bǎihuò) on Sanmin Rd is a complex of three enormous buildings. When taken together, it's Taiwan's largest shopping mall. Don't confuse it with the nearby Lai Lai Department Store (lái lái bǎihuò gōngsī) at 125 Sanmin Rd.

Taichung's second largest shopping mall, (dìyī guǎngchǎng), is more centrally located at the corner of Chungcheng Rd and Luchuan W Rd.

See's at 113 Wenhua Rd in the Hsitun district is a good place for quality, inexpensive clothing.

Lane 49, Chungshan Rd, is also known as 'computer alley' – over a dozen computer and electronics stores are here.

The Taichung Tool Market (jiànguó shìcháng) is a fascinating place to wander around, even if you don't buy anything. There are some good buys, though if you want to keep your backpack light you'd better avoid buying a jackhammer, air compressor or hydraulic press. Less bulky but useful items on sale here include key chains and pocket knives.

Getting There & Away

Air A good travel agent for international tickets is Wing On Travel Service (☎ 225 1191) (yǒng'ān lüxíngshè), 91 Chienkuo Rd, not far from the railway station. Also good is Southeast Travel Service (☎ 2261171) (dōngnán lüxíngshè), 218 Chienkuo Rd

Taichung's airport has an interesting history – it was a prime US military base during the Vietnam War. It's still one of Taiwan's major Air Force bases, and one of the places where Taiwan is testing its home-grown Indigenous Defence Fighter (IDF).

As for civilian aircraft, you can fly to Makung, Hualien, Taipei and Taitung.

Three international airlines have booking offices in Taichung even though they don't fly there. The international airlines are:

Cathay Pacific
    (guótài hángkōng), Room A, 8th floor, 239 Minchuan Rd (☎ 3212999)
China Airlines
    (zhōnghuá hángkōng), Room 1, 2nd floor, 44 Sanmin Rd, Section 2 (☎ 2293961)
Delta Airlines
    (dàměi hángkōng) 10th floor, 185 Minchuan Rd, Taichung (☎ 2250371)
EVA Airways
    (chángróng hángkōng), Room 4, 9th floor, 20 Talung Rd (☎ 3240190)
Japan Asia
    (rìyà hángkōng), 393 Taichungkang Rd, Section 1 (☎ 3217700)

Domestic carriers are also represented. Their booking offices are as follows:

Formosa Airlines
    (yǒngxīng hángkōng), 100 Minhang Rd (☎ 2914236)
Great China Airlines
    (dàhuá hángkōng), 100 Minhang Rd (☎ 2967630, 2967635)
Taiwan Airlines
    (táiwān hángkōng), 3rd floor, No 4-2, Lane 9-11, Taichung Kang Rd, Section 2 (☎ 3232901)

Bus Located just 105 km south of Taipei on the major north-south freeway and railway line, you won't have trouble getting to Taichung. In addition to the north-south freeway buses, there are also buses coming over the mountains from Hualien on the east coast, via the scenic Central Cross-Island Highway. There are direct buses to many scenic areas in central Taiwan, such as Sun Moon Lake, Hsitou, Alishan, and Wushe (via Puli).

From Taipei the bus fare to Taichung is NT$194. There are three major bus terminals in Taichung and at least two important minor ones. The big one in front of the railway station (táiqì táizhōng zhàn) is for northbound buses, including those to Taipei. The bus terminal behind the railway station (*táiqì nán zhàn*) is for southbound buses (Kaohsiung, Hsitou, Chiayi, etc). For country buses (Sun Moon Lake, Puli, Nantou, Wushe, Lishan, Hualien, but not Hsitou), you need to go to the Gancheng bus terminal (*gānchéng chēzhàn*), two blocks north-east of the railway station.

As for minor stations, a useful one is the station operated by Changhua Bus Company (*zhānghuà kèyùn*); here you can catch a bus to Lukang and Changhua. This bus station is also behind the railway station.

Perhaps a more useful hole-in-the-wall station is for the Fengyuan Bus Company (*fēngyuán kèyùn*). It's on the roundabout, opposite the railway station and directly adjacent to the Fuh Chun Hotel. This bus company serves Taichung County, including Fengyuan, Kukuan, Encore Gardens and Kuanyin Temple (but not Lishan).

Tonglien Bus Company, the best-established of Taiwan's wild chickens, has a bus terminal at the intersection of Taichung Kang Rd and the freeway. You can get buses here to Taipei and Kaohsiung.

Train Trains from Taipei or Kaohsiung run every 30 to 40 minutes.

Getting Around
To/From the Airport The airport is in the Hsitun district in the north-west of the city. Green bus No 36 goes to the airport.

Bus If you have a day to spend in Taichung, there are a few interesting things to see and do. If you decide to get around on the city bus, a special note is in order. Taichung has two bus companies. The Taichung Bus Company (*táizhōng kèyùn*) operates green buses, and the Renyou Bus Company (*rényǒu kèyùn*) operates red buses. This can create a bit of confusion for the uninitiated. For example, a green bus No 22 goes to different places from a red bus No 22.

The fare is NT$12 on ordinary buses and NT$15 for air-conditioned buses – the exact fare is required.

Car Car rentals are available from the English-speaking staff at Central Auto Rental (☎ 2927000, fax 2962913), 112-100 Chungching Rd.

ENCORE GARDENS
(*yǎgē huāyuán*) 亞哥花園
This large private garden in the foothills 10 km north-east of Taichung is decorated with European architecture. In terms of raking in the cash, this is one of Taiwan's 'big three' theme parks (the other two are Window on China and the Formosan Aboriginal Cultural Village). Most travellers should give it a miss – it's a good escape from the city for Taichung residents rather than an international tourist attraction. There is far better natural scenery in the magnificent mountains in the eastern part of Taichung County. In the evenings, the big attraction is supposed to be the 'water dance' (*shuǐwǔ*), a fountain with coloured lights and music.

The Encore Gardens are heavily touted in glossy tourist pamphlets, so if you have time and can afford the admission fee, you might want to have a look. It costs NT$180 during the daytime and NT$250 at night.

Fengyuan Bus Company has buses from the roundabout in front of Taichung railway station which go to Encore Gardens. Departing from almost the same spot is red bus No 2, which also goes to the gardens.

KUANYINSHAN
(*guānyīnshān*) 觀音山
About 1½ km south-west of Encore Gardens is Kuanyinshan, a mountain topped by a statue of the Goddess of Mercy. It's actually a very nice climb, though steep with plenty of stone steps. The views from the top are rewarding.

The directions for getting to Kuanyinshan are the same as for Encore Gardens.

CHUNGHSING VILLAGE
(*zhōngxīng xīn cūn*) 中興新村
I wouldn't call this a tourist attraction. However, many of the English-language tourist maps published in Taiwan mark Chunghsing Village with a star, circle or

something else to show that it's a special place, but then offer no explanation why it is so. I finally went there to find out what makes it so notable.

Chunghsing Village is in fact the capital of Taiwan. That is, Taiwan province – remember, Taiwan is not officially a country but a province of China. Taipei is not Taiwan's capital – rather, it's the provisional capital of the Republic of China until the KMT retakes the mainland and re-establishes its former capital at Nanjing. Just what will become of Chunghsing Village if maverick legislators succeed in their bid to do away with the Taiwan provincial government remains a big question mark.

Chunghsing Village strives to be a model city, relatively easy to do thanks to government subsidies. Since all the buildings are owned by the government, development is strictly controlled. Constructing elaborate and expensive buildings is no problem thanks to the national treasury cash cow. Given all the high-level Taiwanese officials whose children live in southern California, perhaps it's no surprise that Chunghsing Village looks so much like an American suburb.

Most travellers probably wouldn't want to spend their time there, but some may want to have a look as it is only a short distance away from Taichung. Frequent highway buses heading south of Taichung stop there, including the Sun Moon Lake bus.

KUKUAN
(gǔguān) 谷關

Kukuan is a small town and hot-spring resort about two hours by bus from Taichung. Being rather close to the city, it gets very crowded on weekends, but it's OK at other times. The scenery is certainly good, though not as spectacular as higher up in the mountains. Kukuan has an elevation of 750 metres.

The hot springs are piped into hotel baths; unfortunately there are no outdoor pools. In addition to the hot springs, another attraction is the hike up to Dragon Valley Waterfall *(lónggǔ pùbù)*. It's an easy hike – only 3.3

km for the round trip. However, it's in a park and they charge a steep NT$100 admission. Within the park is a zoo, botanical garden and souvenir vendors. To find the park, cross the footbridge near the Dragon Valley Hotel and just follow the trail. Junk food to feed the monkeys is on sale everywhere.

In summer, swimming in the river is a big attraction. There is at least one spot under the big footbridge where the pools are deep enough to dive off the rocks, a popular activity with the local kids.

Orientation
The town is divided into two – one half is next to the highway and the other on the north bank of the river. You get to the north side by crossing a footbridge, or larger bridge (for vehicles) on the eastern (uphill) part of the village. The north side is definitely the nicer part of town, since it has little traffic because the few roads are dead ends.

Places to Stay
Kukuan is overrun with tourists on weekends and holidays and virtually every hotel is full. On weekdays business is very slow and most hotels offer 20% off the rates quoted here; some even offer 50% discounts.

Across the footbridge on the north bank is the *Kukuan Hot Springs Hotel* (☎ 5951126) *(gǔguān wēnquán shān zhuāng)*, the only place with cheapish tatami rooms. On weekends, doubles cost an eye-popping NT$700, but there is a 50% discount on weekdays.

Just up the hill is the quiet and secluded *Wenshan Hotel* (☎ 5951265) *(wènshān dà lüshè)*, where twins start at NT$800. The pleasant park-like surroundings make this one well worth considering.

Also on the north bank is the *Dongguan Hot Springs Hotel* (☎ 5951235) *(dōngguān wēnquán lüshè)*, where doubles/twins cost NT$1000/1100. Directly across the lane is the slightly more up-market *Mingzhi Hotel* (☎ 5951111) *(míngzhì dà fàndiàn)*, where twins cost NT$1300 to NT$1600.

Utopia Holiday Hotel (☎ 5951511, fax 5951518) *(jiàqí dà fàndiàn)* is also on the north bank, with a good view overlooking the river. It's a great place to stay, but it's not budget class – doubles/twins cost NT$1100/3100.

On the south (busy) side of town is the *Kukuan Hotel* (☎ 5951355, fax 5951359) *(gǔguān dà fàndiàn)*. All rooms are twins and cost NT$1600. The rear patio is relatively quiet and has a good view of the river, so try to get a room on this side of the building. This hotel has the most convenient transport – the bus station for the Fengyuan Bus Company is almost directly opposite.

The *Dragon Valley Hotel* (☎ 5951325, fax 5951226) *(lónggǔ dà fàndiàn)* is the huge high-rise right in the congested middle of town. It seems very out of place with the natural surroundings, but that certainly hasn't hurt business. Doubles/twins go for NT$2000/2200.

Getting There & Away
Buses from Taichung are frequent, starting at 6 am. Most of the buses to Kukuan are operated by the Fengyuan Bus Company. The fare is NT$121.

The Taiwan Bus Company operates long-distance buses between Taichung and Lishan, which all stop in Kukuan along the way. To catch these buses in Taichung, go to the Gancheng bus station (see Taichung map).

You can also catch buses in Fengyuan, which is further north than Taichung. If you're coming from Taipei by train, this will save you about two hours.

In Kukuan the bus stop is at the east (uphill) end of town, right in front of the Kukuan Hotel. The buses don't stop in the centre of town and it's useless trying to flag them down there.

CENTRAL CROSS-ISLAND HIGHWAY
(zhōngbù héngguàn gōnglù) 中部橫貫公路
This spectacular highway connects Taroko Gorge on the east side of Taiwan (Hualien County) with the city of Taichung on the west, a distance of 195 km. Virtually every km of this highway offers a stunning view of lush forests and towering mountain peaks, and should not be missed if you have the

time. The road is occasionally closed due to landslides, especially after a typhoon – which is not surprising considering that in many places the road is carved out of sheer cliffs.

Places to Stay
Assuming you travel from west to east, you will come across youth hostels in the following order. Unfortunately, you can't rely on these – they can be packed out to overflowing during summer holidays, and closed during winter, but it never hurts to ask. The wisest thing to do is bring a tent and camp out by the hostels. Refer to the Youth Hostels map in the Facts for the Visitor chapter for locations.

Chingshan Mountain Hostel
  (qīngshān shān zhuāng) (☎ 04-5244103); dormitory NT$200, triples NT$1000
Techi Mountain Hostel
  (déjī shān zhuāng) (☎ 04-5981592; reservations 5244103); dormitory/doubles NT$200/800
Tayuling Mountain Hostel
  (dàyǔlǐng shān zhuāng) (☎ 04-5991009; reservations 038-691111); dormitory NT$200
Kuanyun Mountain Hostel
  (guānyún shān zhuāng) (☎ 04-5991173; reservations 038-691111); dormitory NT$200
Tzuen Mountain Hostel
  (cíēn shān zhuāng) (☎ 038-691111); dormitory NT$200
Loshao Mountain Hostel
  (luòshào shān zhuāng) (☎ 038-691111); dormitory/double NT$200/800
Tienhsiang Youth Activity Centre
  (tiānxiáng huódòng zhōngxīn) (☎ 038-691111); dormitory/double NT$200/800

Getting Around
It takes slightly more than eight hours by bus to travel non-stop across the island on this highway. From Hualien, buses depart for Taichung at 7.35, 9.35 and 11.05 am. Going in the other direction, buses depart Taichung for Hualien at 7, 8 and 9.30 am. The fare is NT$459. You can also catch the bus in Tienhsiang. Although the trip can be done in one day, I recommend taking at least three days because there is plenty to see along the way. The side trips to Wuling Farm and Hohuanshan are particularly outstanding.

For those with even more time, energy and ambition, it is possible to do this journey by foot or bicycle if you're really fit. I know it sounds crazy, but there are actually quite a few hikers who walk nearly the entire length of the Central Cross-Island Highway. It's best to do it on weekdays, when traffic is minimal. To do the journey by foot takes at least five days and life is made easier by the fact that you can always change your mind and catch a bus. The highest point is Tayuling, just across the county line in Hualien County. From Tayuling, you can walk to Hohuanshan, one of Taiwan's most beautiful mountains.

If you prefer to walk down rather than up, you can take a bus to the summit of the highway at Tayuling and then walk downhill all the way, either towards Hualien (east) or Taichung (west). During the cold months (November to May), I suggest you walk from Tayuling towards Taichung (west) because the east side of the island gets locked in by cold rain and fog. The west side is usually sunny – in fact, winter is the dry season.

If you're not heading to south Taiwan, then Fengyuan is an important transit point at the western end of the highway. It's about an hour north of Taichung. You can get a train from Taipei to Fengyuan and bypass Taichung completely. This saves nearly two hours on a trip from Taipei to the Central Cross-Island Highway.

LISHAN

(líshān) 梨山

Lishan, or 'Pear Mountain', is a small farming community along the Central Cross-Island Highway. Some 1900 metres above sea level, the area is famous for growing cold-weather fruits like apples, peaches and pears, which cannot grow in the subtropical lowlands. It is a retreat for city-bound tourists seeking refuge from the summer heat. Hiking opportunities are limited in Lishan because most of the land is occupied by orchards. However, the nearby area is spectacular. It's also a useful transit point for the trip to Wuling Farm and Snow Mountain.

Fruit Market

(shuǐguǒ shìcháng) 水果市場

This is what the Chinese come for. You'll hardly have to look for the fruit market –

during the summer months, that's just about all Lishan is. The area near the bus station has the thickest cluster of stalls.

For all the fame and fuss, the prices really aren't a bargain. The locals know about the outrageous price of fruit in Taipei and they gear their prices accordingly. However, in Lishan there's at least no doubt about the freshness – it's likely the fruit was picked the same morning. Some orchards even charge an admission fee and let you pick your own, then weigh the contents and charge you as you depart.

The dried fruits are a much better deal and they make good lightweight snacks for travelling.

Lishan Culture Museum

(líshān wénwù guǎn) 梨山文化博物館
On the east side of Lishan is a church, and across the highway is an intersection with another road. Follow it uphill, past the elementary school and you'll come to the museum. From the centre of Lishan, the hike is only about 1.5 km. The museum is small but interesting.

Lucky Life Mountain Farm

(fúshòushān nóngchǎng) 福壽山農場
Continuing uphill on the same road (five km from Lishan), you'll come to the Lucky Life Mountain Farm. You'll easily recognise the area by the statue in front of the small farmhouse. The area is surrounded by orchards, and the view from the back porch of the surrounding mountains is fantastic.

Heaven's Pool

(tiānchí) 天池
Follow the same road all the way to the summit of the mountain – 12 km from Lishan with an elevation of 2590 metres. Morning is the best time to visit, when the weather is likely to be clear but cold. As long as the clouds cooperate, the view is spectacular. The pool, the house next to it and the surrounding grounds are maintained as a sort of sacred shrine – this was Chiang Kaishek's summer mountain retreat.

You might note – with a certain bit of irony – that Chiang's habit of seeking out quiet mountain retreats and pools got him into big trouble once. In China's Shaanxi Province in 1936, Chiang was kidnapped by his own generals while resting at Huaqing Pool. Coincidentally, the pool was on the slopes of a mountain also called Lishan.

Except for the odd tour bus, there are no buses going to Heaven's Pool. Hitching is a distinct possibility though.

Places to Stay

So many tour buses arrive in Lishan on weekends and holidays that it's a wonder the mountain doesn't collapse. Accommodation is very tight at these times, so you're definitely better off arriving on a weekday. The following rates are for weekdays during summer. During winter, hotels are empty and you can often bargain a 50% discount.

The cheapest place in town is the *Guocheng Hotel* (☎ 5989279) *(guóchéng dà lüshe)* at 54 Chungcheng Rd. Doubles without/with private bath are NT$500/700, but you can bargain that down at least NT$100 on weekdays, even during summer.

Just opposite the bus station is the *Lishan Guest House* (☎ 5989501, fax 5989505) *(líshān bīnguǎn; 100 rooms). It's one of the most beautiful luxury hotels in Taiwan and not outrageously expensive for the level of accommodation provided. Doubles are NT$800, twins NT$1300 to NT$1600 and suites cost NT$3600 to NT$4800. It's often full and difficult to get in over the weekend.

Chungcheng Rd, the main road in town, is actually part of the Cross-Island Highway. It's mostly lined with restaurants, but there are a few hotels including the tattered-looking *Lishan Hotel* (☎ 5989261) *(líshān lüshè)*, which charges NT$500/800 for a doubles without/with attached bath. The more up-market *Fu Chung Hotel* (☎ 598 9506, fax 5981991) *(fúzhōng dà fàndiàn)*, 61 Chungcheng Rd, has doubles for NT$1200.

One block south of Chungcheng Rd and running parallel to it is Mintsu Rd, which is where most of the hotels are. The cheapest of this lot is *Guangda Hotel* (☎ 5989216) *(guǎngdá dà lüshè)*, 21 Mintsu Rd (next to the fire station), which has doubles with private bath for NT$800. The *Yanhualou Hotel* (☎ 5989615, 5989511) *(yànhuá lóu dà lüshè)* at 22 Mintsu Rd has doubles for NT$700. The *Shengxin Hotel* (☎ 5989577, fax 5981203) *(shèngxīn dà fàndiàn)* has doubles for NT$800. The *Li Tu Hotel* (☎ 598 9256, 5989512) *(lìdū dà lüshè)* charges NT$1000 for a double. *Haowangjiao Hotel* (☎ 5989512) *(hǎowàngjiǎo dà fàndiàn)*, 52 Mintsu Rd, charges NT$1000 to NT$1200 for doubles.

The ill-fated *Lishan Public Hostel* *(guómín lüshè)* is a fancy place built on a steep slope just below the bus station area. The slope has proved unstable and the hotel's car park has just about collapsed. The hostel is closed and looks unlikely to reopen.

Getting There & Away

Lishan is easily reached by any bus going along the Cross-Island Highway between Hualien and Taichung.

From Taichung there are 13 buses daily, the first departing at 6 am and the last leaving at 2.30 pm. Most of the buses from Taichung terminate in Lishan but a few continue to Hualien. The trip takes 3½ hours and costs NT$214. From Hualien, the buses cost NT$246 and leave at 7.35, 9.35, 11.05 and 11.50 am, taking 4½ hours to reach Lishan. You pay just NT$186 and save an hour if you board the bus at Fengyuan rather than Taichung.

There are three buses daily going to Lishan from the north-east coast cities of Ilan (NT$212) and Lotung (NT$213).

WULING FARM

(wǔlíng nóngchǎng) 武陵農場

Wuling Farm was originally conceived as a government-sponsored agricultural project to grow fruit and to resettle retired servicemen who fought for the Republic of China on the mainland. Increasingly the area is attracting tourists, especially young hikers who want to challenge Taiwan's second highest peak, Hsuehshan *(xuěshān)*, or 'Snow Mountain', which is 3884 metres in

elevation. The area is now part of Hsuehpa National Park.

Wuling Farm is beautiful and mostly non-commercialised, though there is now a NT$90 admission fee to the area.

Hikes

A mountain permit is required for Hsuehshan, but there is no one around to check it. It's a 10 to 12 hour climb to the summit. There are two huts along the way where you can spend the night. The first one, Chika Hut *(qīkǎ shān zhuāng)*, is a two-hour

hike from the trailhead and has water. The second one, Three Six Nine Hut *(sān liù jiǔ shān zhuāng)*, is an additional six-hour climb and has no water. There are no facilities at the huts, so you'll need a sleeping bag, food, stove and other backpacking paraphernalia.

A much easier hike is to Yensheng Waterfall *(yānshēng pùbù)*. It's at the top end of the valley past the Youth Activity Centre. From there you can also climb Peach Mountain *(táoshān)*, which has an elevation of 3324 metres.

Places to Stay

There are three places to stay in Wuling. The *Wuling Guest House* (☎ 5901183, fax 590 1085; 54 rooms) *(wǔlíng guómín bīnguǎn)* is the classiest, with twins/triples at NT$1600/1800.

The *Wuling Farm Travel Service Centre* (☎ 5901259) *(wǔlíng nóngchǎng lüyóu fúwù zhōngxīn)* is notably cheaper and is right near the bus stop. Rooms cost NT$750 to NT$1000.

Enquire at the Service Centre if you want to stay in the camping ground. No equipment is supplied so you need to bring your own.

Aside from camping, the cheapest place is the *Wuling Mountain Hostel* (☎ 5901020) *(wǔlíng shān zhuāng)*, but it's a five-km hike up the valley road from the last bus stop. The dormitory costs NT$195 and doubles are NT$1350.

All hotels can be full, even on weekdays, during summer. On weekdays when the kids are back in school, you shouldn't have any trouble. Weekends and holidays are always problematic unless a convenient typhoon blows the tour buses away.

Places to Eat

While the *Wuling Guest House* can dish up pricey meals, the best bet for budget travellers are the instant noodles (hot water supplied) from the shop inside the *Wuling Farm Travel Service Centre*.

Getting There & Away

Wuling Farm is 25 km north-east of Lishan, just off the branch highway leading down to the coast at Ilan. It's most easily reached by bus from Lishan. There are six buses daily, departing from Lishan at 8.30 and 9 am, noon, and 1, 2 and 4.50 pm. This schedule includes the buses going from Lishan to Ilan and Lotung, all of which also stop at Wuling Farm. Buses between Lishan and Wuling Farm cost NT$47.

Index

Thanks

Thanks to the following travellers who wrote to us with information on Taiwan:

Susanne Bauder (D), Bruno Bertuccioli (USA), Rachel Braslow (USA), Linda Brennan (USA), K Mark Brown, Pascal Bruyere (F), Daniel Bryant (C), Reynaldo Bustamante (Tai), Andreas Martin Butz (D), Peter Byron (Aus), Charly Caupe (F), Davina Te-min Chen (USA), Lilly Chen (Tai), Paul Cheng, Tim Clarke, William Combs, Serena Crawford, Taffy H Crockett, Sean Curtin, Hans Damon (NL), Melanie Davenport (USA), Claes de Kresse (Dk), Rick Drain (USA), Christian Drexler, Billy Fenster, Lothar Finger, John W Fitzgerald (USA), Richard Ford (USA), Richard Foster, Monika Fry (NZ), Craig Fukushima (USA), Linda Grasselier (NL), Captain W V Gray (Aus), Michael Gropszorf, Kerry Haigh (C), David & Greeba Hughes (UK), Y H Hwang (Tai), Lisa Jackson (UK), Al Jaffee (USA), Jerry Kagen, Lothar M Kirsch (D), Karl Krueger, Eric Lai (USA), Nadine Nigel Leavitt (USA), Joe Leavy, Darlene Lee, Simon Lee (HK), Ralf Leutz (D), Konrad Leutz (D), Greg Liano (USA), Hubert Maass, Andrew Malone (HK), Dr Manfred Malzahn, Michael McGregor, Frank & Ann McSweeny (USA), Sabine Mecking (D), Tamara Mikinski (USA), Dennis Mogerman (USA), Kay & Chris Nellins (UK), Chris Nelson (USA), Mrs Laura O'Connor (UK), Jerry Olsen, Amy Palmer, Tracy Parsons (UK), Brandt Pascoe (USA), Sandi Polizoydis, Kika Rahner (RSA), Gerald Rau (USA), John Roxburgh (USA), Robert Rubin (USA), Zdenek Slanina, Peter Stepanek, Mike Sullivan, Mark Swain (USA), Mark & Vivian Szubo (C), Mike Tagin, Joy Tang, Andrzej Urbanik (PL), Angelo Verna, Kenneth Viking, Keith Vincent (Aus), Jeff Douglas Wilkerson, Jody Wong (C), George Yang (Tai)

Aus – Australia, C – Canada, D – Germany, Dk – Denmark, F – France, HK – Hong Kong, NL – Netherlands, NZ – New Zealand, PL – Poland, RSA – Republic of South Africa, Tai – Taiwan, UK – United Kingdom, USA – United States of America

PLANET TALK
Lonely Planet's FREE quarterly newsletter

We love hearing from you and think you'd like to hear from us.

When...*is the right time to see reindeer in Finland?*
Where...*can you hear the best palm-wine music in Ghana?*
How...*do you get from Asunción to Areguá by steam train?*
What...*is the best way to see India?*

For the answer to these and many other questions read PLANET TALK.

Every issue is packed with up-to-date travel news and advice including:

- *a letter from Lonely Planet founders Tony and Maureen Wheeler*
- *travel diary from a Lonely Planet author - find out what it's really like out on the road*
- *feature article on an important and topical travel issue*
- *a selection of recent letters from our readers*
- *the latest travel news from all over the world*
- *details on Lonely Planet's new and forthcoming releases*

To join our mailing list contact any Lonely Planet office (address below).

LONELY PLANET PUBLICATIONS
Australia: PO Box 617, Hawthorn 3122, Victoria (tel: 03-819 1877)
USA: Embarcadero West, 155 Filbert St, Suite 251, Oakland, CA 94607 (tel: 510-893 8555)
TOLL FREE: (800) 275-8555
UK: 10 Barley Mow Passage, Chiswick, London W4 4PH (tel: 081-742 3161)
France: 71 bis rue du Cardinal Lemoine – 75005 Paris (tel: 1-46 34 00 58)

Also available: Lonely Planet T-shirts. 100% heavyweight cotton (S, M, L, XL)

Guides to North-East Asia

Beijing - city guide
Beijing is the hub of a vast nation. This guide will help travellers to find the best this ancient and fascinating city has to offer.

North-East Asia on a shoestring
Concise information for independent low-budget travel in China, Hong Kong, Japan, Macau, North Korea, South Korea, Taiwan and Mongolia.

China - a travel survival kit
This book is the recognised authority for independent travellers in the People's Republic. With essential tips for avoiding pitfalls, and comprehensive practical information, it will help you to discover the real China.

Hong Kong, Macau & Canton - a travel survival kit
This practical guide has all the travel facts on these three close but diverse cities, linked by history, culture and geography.

Japan - a travel survival kit
Japan combines modern cities and remote wilderness areas, sophisticated technology and ancient tradition. This guide tells you how to find the Japan that many visitors never see.

Korea - a travel survival kit
South Korea is one of the great undiscovered destinations, with its mountains, ancient temples and lively modern cities. This guide also includes a chapter on reclusive North Korea.

Mongolia - a travel survival kit
Mongolia is truly a destination for the adventurous. This guide gives visitors the first real opportunity to explore this remote but newly accessible country.

Seoul - city guide
It is easy to explore Seoul's ancient royal palaces and bustling market places with this comprehensive guide packed with vital information for leisure and business travellers alike.

Tibet - a travel survival kit
The fabled mountain-land of Tibet is slowly becoming accessible to travellers. This guide has full details on this remote and fascinating region, including the border crossing to Nepal.

Tokyo - city guide
Tokyo is a dynamic metropolis and one of the world's leading arbiters of taste and style. This guide will help you to explore the many sides of Tokyo, the modern Japanese miracle rolled into a single fascinating, sometimes startling package.

Also available:
Cantonese phrasebook, **Mandarin Chinese** phrasebook, **Korean** phrasebook, **Tibet** phrasebook, and **Japanese** phrasebook.

Lonely Planet Guidebooks

Lonely Planet guidebooks cover every accessible part of Asia as well as Australia, the Pacific, South America, Africa, the Middle East, Europe and parts of North America. There are five series: *travel survival kits*, covering a country for a range of budgets; *shoestring guides* with compact information for low-budget travel in a major region; *walking guides*; *city guides* and *phrasebooks*.

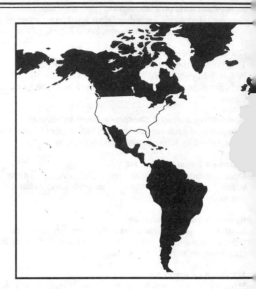

Mail Order

Lonely Planet guidebooks are distributed worldwide. They are also available by mail order from Lonely Planet, so if you have difficulty finding a title please write to us. US and Canadian residents should write to Embarcadero West, 155 Filbert St, Suite 251, Oakland CA 94607, USA ; European residents should write to 10 Barley Mow Passage, Chiswick, London W4 4PH; and residents of other countries to PO Box 617, Hawthorn, Victoria 3122, Australia.

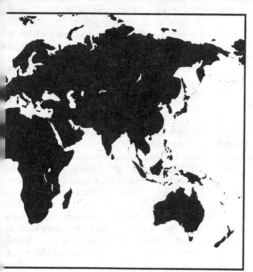

Indian Subcontinent
Bangladesh
India
Hindi/Urdu phrasebook
Trekking in the Indian Himalaya
Karakoram Highway
Kashmir, Ladakh & Zanskar
Nepal
Trekking in the Nepal Himalaya
Nepali phrasebook
Pakistan
Sri Lanka
Sri Lanka phrasebook

Africa
Africa on a shoestring
Central Africa
East Africa
Trekking in East Africa
Kenya
Swahili phrasebook
Morocco, Algeria & Tunisia
Arabic (Moroccan) phrasebook
South Africa, Lesotho & Swaziland
Zimbabwe, Botswana & Namibia
West Africa

Central America & the Caribbean
Baja California
Central America on a shoestring
Costa Rica
Eastern Caribbean
Guatemala, Belize & Yucatán: La Ruta Maya
Mexico

North America
Alaska
Canada
Hawaii

South America
Argentina, Uruguay & Paraguay
Bolivia
Brazil
Brazilian phrasebook
Chile & Easter Island
Colombia
Ecuador & the Galápagos Islands
Latin American Spanish phrasebook
Peru
Quechua phrasebook
South America on a shoestring
Trekking in the Patagonian Andes
Venezuela

Europe
Baltic States & Kaliningrad
Central Europe on a shoestring
Central Europe phrasebook
Dublin city guide
Eastern Europe on a shoestring
Eastern Europe phrasebook
Finland
France
Greece
Hungary
Iceland, Greenland & the Faroe Islands
Ireland
Italy
Mediterranean Europe on a shoestring
Mediterranean Europe phrasebook
Poland
Scandinavian & Baltic Europe on a shoestring
Scandinavian Europe phrasebook
Switzerland
Trekking in Spain
Trekking in Greece
USSR
Russian phrasebook
Western Europe on a shoestring
Western Europe phrasebook

The Lonely Planet Story

Lonely Planet published its first book in 1973 in response to the numerous 'How did you do it?' questions Maureen and Tony Wheeler were asked after driving, bussing, hitching, sailing and railing their way from England to Australia.

Written at a kitchen table and hand collated, trimmed and stapled, *Across Asia on the Cheap* became an instant local bestseller, inspiring thoughts of another book.

Eighteen months in South-East Asia resulted in their second guide, *South-East Asia on a shoestring*, which they put together in a backstreet Chinese hotel in Singapore in 1975. The 'yellow bible' as it quickly became known to backpackers around the world, soon became *the* guide to the region. It has sold well over half a million copies and is now in its 8th edition, still retaining its familiar yellow cover.

Today there are over 140 Lonely Planet titles in print – books that have that same adventurous approach to travel as those early guides; books that 'assume you know how to get your luggage off the carousel' as one reviewer put it.

Although Lonely Planet initially specialised in guides to Asia, they now cover most regions of the world, including the Pacific, South America, Africa, the Middle East and Europe. The list of *walking guides* and *phrasebooks* (for 'unusual' languages such as Quechua, Swahili, Nepali and Egyptian Arabic) is also growing rapidly.

The emphasis continues to be on travel for independent travellers. Tony and Maureen still travel for several months of each year and play an active part in the writing, updating and quality control of Lonely Planet's guides.

They have been joined by over 50 authors, 90 staff – mainly editors, cartographers & designers – at our office in Melbourne, Australia, at our US office in Oakland, California and at our European office in Paris; another five at our office in London handle sales for Britain, Europe and Africa. Travellers themselves also make a valuable contribution to the guides through the feedback we receive in thousands of letters each year.

The people at Lonely Planet strongly believe that travellers can make a positive contribution to the countries they visit, both through their appreciation of the countries' culture, wildlife and natural features, and through the money they spend. In addition, the company makes a direct contribution to the countries and regions it covers. Since 1986 a percentage of the income from each book has been donated to ventures such as famine relief in Africa; aid projects in India; agricultural projects in Central America; Greenpeace's efforts to halt French nuclear testing in the Pacific and Amnesty International. In 1993 $100,000 was donated to such causes.

Lonely Planet's basic travel philosophy is summed up in Tony Wheeler's comment, 'Don't worry about whether your trip will work out. Just go!'.